The Best of the Achaeans

9/4/81

The Best of the Achaeans

Concepts of the Hero
in Archaic Greek
Poetry

Gregory Nagy

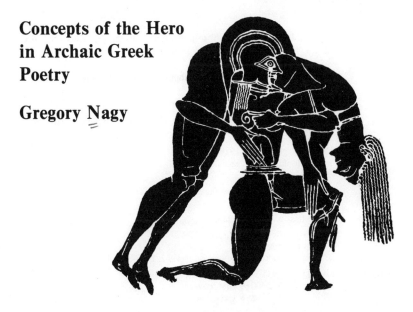

The Johns Hopkins University Press / Baltimore and London

This book has been brought to publication with the generous assistance
of the David M. Robinson Publication Fund.

The Johns Hopkins University Press, Baltimore, Maryland 21218
The Johns Hopkins Press Ltd., London

Originally published, 1979
Johns Hopkins Paperbacks edition, 1981

Library of Congress Cataloging in Publication Data

Nagy, Gregory
　　The best of the Achaeans.

　　Bibliography: pp. 355–73
　　Includes index.
　　1. Greek poetry—Themes, motives. 2. Heroes in literature. I. Title
PA3015.H47N34　　　881′.01′09351　　　79–9907
ISBN 0-8018-2200-9 (hardcover)
ISBN 0-8018-2388-9 (paperback)

Cover and title page design: Ajax carrying the corpse of Achilles,
adapted from the handle of the François Vase.

Contents

Foreword

The Best of the Achaeans is in part a book about ambiguity; it is therefore perhaps proper that this foreword begin with a promise and a warning. The promise is of a work of extraordinary originality and interest; the warning is that the argument presented here is both complex and incomplete.

An ambiguity is not two contrasting facts, but the double meaning of a single fact. So in this case, a book original and interesting in this way could not be either simple or complete. Gregory Nagy has explored the implicit ideas of early Greek epic, a labyrinth in which every turning leads somewhere. The trail of implication is pursued, first this way, then that; often it is necessary to double back and pick up a previous point, only to start off again in a new direction. Wherever a trail is abandoned it would have been possible, in principle, to follow it further. The result is not a definitive account but rather a report on some things one reader has seen; it is a challenge to us to read again and think further.

Nagy presents an outline or preliminary sketch of what one might call the "epic world view." His concern is not with particular works per se but with the underlying system of meanings common to the epic tradition and inherited by Greek poets down to Pindar. This is a system, not as geometry is a system, but as a culture is a system; there is a high degree of redundancy, of alternative ways of expressing the same or similar ideas, of making similar distinctions. Terms are not connected by relations of identity but of analogy; themes are displayed through their variations. Nagy's method is, of necessity, free-associative; he proceeds as the cultural ethnographer does—by taking one point and looking about for connections. Since he is working with texts, Nagy explores these connections first through word study; he maps out co-occurrences in epic diction, then asks what is behind the patterns he observes. This in turn leads to an inquiry into patterns on

vii

the thematic level; similar incidents and relationships are seen to recur. As the patterns multiply and replicate, they tend to validate one another; the whole analysis is stronger than any of its parts.

But those who expect overwhelming evidence and irrefutable arguments will not be happy with this book. In spite of its deep learning, this is not a work of *Wissenschaft* but of vision. The patterns seen are in the eye of the beholder, like a visual *Gestalt*; the critic can only describe what he sees, and if we then fail to see it, too, the fault may well be with us. Or it may not, for the pattern may not be there to be seen. It is impossible to believe that in a book of such complexity every point is right; our challenge is again to look for ourselves and describe what we see.

The Best of the Achaeans, then, will provoke thought, solve some problems, and create others. It will mean different things to different readers. It here falls to me, as one who has had the privilege of debating the book with its author, to say something of what I have found in it.

First, this is a book about the special place of the *Iliad* in the epic tradition—the special place, that is, of our *Iliad*, which centers on Achilles. For Nagy, the *Iliad* is the realization of one perspective within a tradition that also permitted others—in effect, other "Iliads." Nagy finds traces of these other perspectives within the *Iliad* itself. There could, for instance, have been a telling of the Troy story centering on Aeneas (Ch.15§3) or one that joined the stories of Troy and Thebes and contrasted two generations of heroes (Ch.9§§19–22). Most important, Nagy finds in the *Odyssey* traces of a version of the Troy story centering on the contrast between Achilles and Odysseus (Ch.1§8, Ch.2§§10–17).

Of these two heroes, Achilles seems the less complete. He is forced to choose between **nóstos**, a return to his home, and **kléos**, immortal fame. Odysseus, however, achieves both. Achilles is the great hero of **bíē**, force; Odysseus, who is not lacking in **bíē**, also has the complementary quality of **mêtis**, craft—and Troy finally falls not to the **bíē** of Achilles but to the **mêtis** of Odysseus. Thus, the problem of the *Iliad* can be stated this way: from what perspective does the less complete hero become the greater figure, so that in the *Iliad* we know Odysseus is reduced to near insignificance?

This question seems, on examination, to address the issue of heroism itself. Achilles, for all his being different from other heroes—precisely because of his one-sidedness, in fact—turns out to be the hero *par excellence*. The hero, after all, is not a model for imitation but rather a figure who cannot be ignored; his special excellence is not integration but potency. Therefore, while **mêtis** is not unheroic, **bíē** is the primary heroic quality (Ch.20§§1–3). The **bíē** of Achilles is at a level that associates him with the elemental powers of wind and fire, in contrast to the organic potencies of lesser figures. Nagy finds Achilles to be the heir of an Indo-European tradition according to which the hero embodies certain elementary forces (Ch.20§§5–12).

It is the elemental character of heroic force that gives it its characteristic ambiguity—an ambiguity schematically set out in Hesiod's Myth of the Five Ages (Ch.9§§1–17) and also in the contrast between the first and second expeditions against Thebes (Ch.9§§18–22). The hero is preeminently the warrior, one capable of inflicting harm. This capacity is positively evaluated when it is acculturated, that is, when it is employed on behalf of the hero's **phíloi**, those to whose honor and welfare he is unreservedly committed. This is **bíē** in the service of **díkē**, justice. Always latent, however, is **bíē** in its raw natural state; while the hero becomes godlike in his capacity to ward off destruction (Ch.5§§10–11), he is also latently the savage beast.

The ambiguity of the epic hero is recurrently enacted in stories turning on the **daís**, feast. As its Greek name implies, the **daís** is an occasion of sharing; in this key social institution, relations between the **phíloi** are enacted and reinforced by the distribution of proper shares of meat, and relations with the gods are enacted through sacrifice (Ch.7§14). The **daís**, however, also has a negative aspect; it is often the scene of **éris** and **neîkos**, strife and conflict, quarrels about precedence and privilege. The key example in the Troy story is the **daís** at the wedding of Peleus and Thetis, where the **éris** that led to the Trojan war arose (Ch.7§16). The institution of sacrifice also originated, we must remember, in a **daís** with a negative aspect: Prometheus tricked the gods into accepting the bones as their portion of the feast (Ch.11§§4–5). Thus, while sacrifice enacts the relation of mortals to the gods, it also reenacts the occasion of their separation from the gods.

When the latent aspect of the **daís** surfaces, sharing gives way to snatching—which can also be ritualized, as at Delphi (Ch.7§§9–12). The heroes tear food from one another like predators tearing their prey; indeed, as they fall to open warfare, they become potentially each other's meat and threaten to devour one another's bodies (Ch.7§22).

The ambiguity of the hero is also enacted in the plot of the *Iliad*, through the shifting effects of Achilles' **bíē**. Initially, the hero's greatness consists in his ability to inflict harm upon the enemy. When, however, he quarrels with his own people and withdraws, he leaves them exposed to those enemies and thus becomes a source of harm to his own people. And since he is unable, finally, to separate from his **phíloi**, he finally inflicts harm upon himself. Achilles' **mênis**, wrath, turns against him when it causes the death of Patroklos, his other self (Ch.17§4).

The *Iliad* is therefore a story about the death of its hero, even though Achilles does not actually die in the story. It is as though the death of Achilles is too painful a theme to be treated directly in the *Iliad*; it can be told only in the *Odyssey*, where Achilles appears as one among the other heroes (Ch.6§24). The ultimate harm inflicted by the hero on his **phíloi** is the **ákhos** or **pénthos**, grief, evoked by his own death; the *Iliad*, which treats this theme (although indirectly), may be considered a dramatic lament or narrative mourning for the defeated hero. Such a narrative must involve the recognition of yet another ambiguity: even the positive aspect of heroic **bíē**, that which wards off destruction, has its own negative aspect, since the hero dies and leaves his **phíloi**.

The hero is between god and man. Men die, while the gods live forever; the hero, however, does both. After death he is immortal in two different senses: immortal in cult and immortal in song. He receives **tīmế**, cultic observance, and **kléos**, the fame of those whose stories are told by the bards.

Nagy sees these two kinds of immortality as being in competition: heroic cult is essentially local, since it asserts that the hero benefits specifically the place where he is buried, while epic is a Panhellenic enterprise; it tells stories that belong to all Greeks. Therefore, heroic cult has been deleted from epic, except for certain almost accidental evidences. Similarly, heroic cult, which celebrated the potency of the hero (his essence, as it were), could speak of his continued happy existence in the Isles of the Blessed, while epic, which told of the past existence of heroes, sees that story as concluded within the epic of Homer, allowing only the negative survival of the shadowy **psūkhế**, psyche, in Hades. Further, in cult, the hero can be associated with a god; in epic (at least in the cases of Achilles and Hector), the same god will appear as the hero's adversary. Heroic cult, in other words, celebrates the transformation of the hero from mortal to immortal, his reception into the company of the gods, and thus promises a connection between man and god. Heroic epic, by contrast, immortalizes the dead hero, but only in the memory of man; it immortalizes the death of the hero at the hand of god and thus reminds us of the separation of god and man.

I would like to see this comparison as suggestive of a continuing contrast within early Greek culture, that between the prophets and the poets. The prophets elaborated mysteries and eschatological cults; special developments of this tradition can be found in the Pythagoreans, in Empedocles, and in the myths of Plato and some of his successors. The prophets look to another world. The poets tell stories of this world—its mythical history, cosmic origins, and ordering. They bring us not a revelation but a pseudo-empiricism; their successors include historians and natural philosophers.

No doubt this is overly schematic, but I find it helpful to see in early epic the foundation of that secular, empirical, and humanistic way of thinking that is so strikingly specific to the Greeks—and at the same time to be reminded that for Greeks of all periods there were other ways of thinking. The Homeric gods differ from the gods of cult—the Demeter of Eleusis, the Persephone of Locris—just as the Homeric heroes differ from those of cult; they represent internally differentiated aspects of a synchronically cohesive system.

About the prophets Nagy has little to say, except insofar as they are echoed by the poets. About the poets he says a great deal, much of which is new. Here his book goes beyond the epic voices of Homer and Hesiod and illuminates Archilochus, Aesop, and Pindar. The poet, like the hero, is seen as an ambiguous figure, capable of praise and also of blame, of elevated discourse and also of low mockery. In praising man, the poet raises him to the level of the gods, makes of him a demigod; in blaming man, he lowers him to the level of a beast, calling him dog, or deer, or crow. Praise and blame, furthermore, correspond to sharing and snatching; the ambiguity of song mirrors the ambiguity of the feast, the proper occasion of song within the poetic tradition. Like the feast, song can express man's aspiration to that primeval time before strife came into the world, when men and gods feasted together and were one. Song can also express the latent, bestial aspect of the feast or the unity of man and beast through another view of primeval time, that of the animal fable, when beasts shared in the speech of men (Ch.19§6).

The poet is himself a kind of hero, since he has an ambiguous relation to his proper god (Ch.18§§6–10) and can at death become the object of cult (Ch.16§§3–8, Ch.18§1). He has, however, a privileged position among heroes and is a privileged guest at the feast; he can both partake and observe. He can praise and thus repay the hospitality he receives; he can also discuss the institution of praise, its dangers and limits (we are familiar with both from Pindar). He can blame and thus take part in strife; he can also discuss the nature of strife and blame his fellows for giving way to it (Ch.16§10). In poetry, early Greek culture becomes self-reflective.

All this provokes further thought about, for instance, the later generic contrast between tragedy and comedy and, more broadly, about the character of a culture where the poets, rather than kings, priests, or sages, were the dominant, culture-shaping figures. As we move down in time from the base Nagy has established in early epic, we naturally find changes, but we also find remarkable continuities. The categories established in *The Best of the Achaeans* are unexpectedly relevant to classical Greece. Thus, what began as a book about the special status of the *Iliad* has become, in the course of its development, a book about what it meant to the Greeks to be Greek.

From the rich detail of Nagy's complex account, I draw a few themes that begin to define this continuing "Greekness." First, this was a culture that saw itself in terms of tense oppositions, one that defined the human condition as a pervasively uncertain set of relations to nonhuman realms. This gives us a new sense of Greek humanism: mankind is placed at the center of the universe because humanness is a synthesis of the cosmic categories. But, by the same token, mankind is the battleground of those warring categories. Thus, Greek balance and moderation are the counterparts of the Greek passion for the extremes; in these terms, we can better understand an art that combined an aspiration to formal purity with a content filled with pity and terror, the grotesque and the monstrous.

Second, the Greeks often saw their cultural condition as the result of an irremediable error. As Nagy shows, this is the familiar form of **aítion**: the ritual is explained as the enactment and recurrent redress of an ancient wrong. This Greek version of the Fall, further, is not from innocence into sin but from primeval harmony into conflict. Nagy identifies at least three such falls: Prometheus's deception of Zeus, the Judgment of Paris, and the quarrel between Agamemnon and Achilles. Each is followed by a tense settlement that does not so much resolve the conflict as acculturate it and thus make it permanent. Prometheus's deception of Zeus brings about the separation of man and god, enacted through the institution of sacrifice (and in Hesiod's *Works and Days* through the necessity of sexuality and labor). The Judgment of Paris results in the Trojan War and its attendant catastrophes—results, that is, in the disappearance of the heroic world, which is enacted through heroic cult. The quarrel of Achilles and Agamemnon results in the death of Achilles and thus in his establishment as the figure through whose story, more than any other, the Greeks confronted the meaning of death—a confrontation embodied in the *Iliad*.

The *Iliad* is thus seen as a kind of cultural institution, parallel to institutions of social interaction or of cult. Like Diotima in the *Symposium*, Nagy places Homer with the law givers and religious teachers, with Lycurgus and Pythagoras. Since the Homeric epics, not Holy Scripture, served the Greeks throughout their history as the basis of education and the texts of first and last resort, Nagy's placement of Homer is surely right. But we should notice that for us, with our partially Semitic heritage, the concept of Homer makes an odd sort of scripture. The epic does not preach; it is a narrative almost without commentary (which is one reason it is still so fresh and accessible). For classical Greece, the meaning of the world was best stated, not in a creed or a sacred history, but in a story. The story does not demand our belief but (as in the case of any fiction) the suspension of our disbelief and a response to the story's meaning. Achilles and the other heroes are as real for us as they were for the Greeks; they were always, in some sense, the creation of the poetic tradition that celebrates them. That tradition created figures who died, and it mourned their death; this recurrent mourning—the source of the tragic vision—gives a perennially valid definition of man's place in the world. "The Best of the Achaeans" is still for us the prototypical hero; the *Iliad* is his *monumentum* (literally, tomb) *aere perennius*. As Théophile Gautier wrote:

> Les dieux eux-mêmes meurent
> Mais les vers souverains
>   Demeurent
> Plus forts que les airains.

University of Chicago   James M. Redfield

Acknowledgments

It took a long time to write this book, and I now have anxieties about whether I can recall the names of all those who have given advice along the way. The list that I offer here may be incomplete, and I hope that anyone accidentally left out will not think me an ingrate. Let me start with those who have endured the final version of the manuscript: D. Gerber, M. Griffith, A. Henrichs, L. Muellner, M. Nagler, J. Nagy, D. Petegorsky, and C. Watkins. Those who have been exposed to parts or all of earlier versions, written or oral, include A. Bergren, V. Bers, D. Boedeker-Raaflaub, W. Burkert, J. S. Clay, C. Dadian, O. M. Davidson, A. L. and S. Edmunds, H. Foley, J. Fontenrose, D. Frame, J.D.B. Hamilton, R. Ingber, N. Lain, C. Montgomery, B. Nagy, L. Nagy, A. Nussbaum, P. Pucci, T. G. Rosenmeyer, J. Schindler, D. Sinos, L. Slatkin, D. Stewart, E.D.T. Vermeule, T. Walsh, C. H. Whitman. Also M. Lefkowitz and F. Zeitlin. It goes without saying that none of these friendly critics is responsible for any of the mistakes or omissions that doubtless remain.

Some of the writing was done at Princeton, and I had the pleasant experience of working there in the autumn of 1977 as a member of the Institute for Advanced Study. I am especially grateful to C. Habicht, J. F. Gilliam, and H. A. Thompson of the Institute, and to W. R. Connor of Princeton University's Classics Department, for their help in providing the most ideal conditions for research.

My material has been much improved by contact with M. Detienne and J.-P. Vernant, who kindly arranged to have me give a presentation before an audience of their colleagues and students in the spring of 1978. I thank the entire *équipe* in Paris for all their intellectual stimulation and warm hospitality.

Parts of the work were also presented as the John U. Nef Lectures of 1978, sponsored by the Committee on Social Thought in conjunction with the Departments of Classics and Linguistics at the University of Chicago. I am very grateful for having had the opportunity to test my material on such a discerning audience. J. M. Redfield was in that audience, and he has been my work's indispensable psychopomp ever since. I am most indebted to him for all his patient and helpful criticism.

The second chapter, which is for me the core of the whole enterprise, was originally conceived as a contribution to a projected Festschrift in honor of J. H. Finley. The project did not succeed, and the contributors were left to their own devices. When Mr. Finley reads my piece "The Best of the Achaeans," I hope that he will accept it as an attempt on my part to honor an extraordinarily creative teacher.

Finally, I dedicate the whole work to the light-hearted Holly, who has been for my life the essence of εὐφροσύνη.

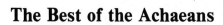

The Best of the Achaeans

Introduction | A Word on Assumptions, Methods, Results

§1. My approach to archaic Greek poetry is based on two major working assumptions. One, the mechanics and artistry of a given poem are traditional not only on the level of form—let us call it *diction*—but also on the level of content—let us call it *theme*. Two, the diction is a most accurate expression of the theme.

§2. The basis for my understanding of Greek poetic diction is the work of Milman Parry on Homeric phraseology, which can be summed up in his concise definition of the formula: "a group of words which is regularly employed under the same metrical conditions to express a given essential idea."[1] The mechanical nature of the formula is reflected by what Parry called the principle of economy.[2] Denys Page restates the principle: "Generally speaking, for a given idea within a given place in the line, there will be found in the vast treasury of phrases one formula and one only."[3] Page goes on to offer an illustration by examining all the Homeric expressions for the concept of "sea":[4]

For this one idea, "the sea," and for its expression in noun + epithet phrases only, he [the poet] relied upon his memory to provide him with a ready-made formula for almost every requirement; and the traditional vocabulary was now so highly developed, so refined and reduced, that for each requirement he found never, or hardly ever, more than one single formula. He has no freedom to select his adjectives: he must adopt whatever combination of words is supplied by tradition for a given part of the verse; and that traditional combination brings with it an adjective which may or may not be suitable to the context.

§2n1. Parry 1971 [= 1930] 272.
§2n2. Parry, pp. 276, 279.
§2n3. Page 1959.224.
§2n4. Page, pp. 225–226.

1

There is, however, something troublesome here about the insistence on the poet's lack of freedom to say accurately whatever he means. It seems as if the factor of metrics were in control of what can or cannot be said. In this particular case of adjectives describing the sea, for instance, we are being told that the poet had no choice but to accept the various epithets that tradition had thrust upon him to fill out the various metrical positions of the Greek hexameter.

§3. In short, Parry's work on the mechanics of Homeric diction has caused a serious problem of esthetics for generations of Hellenists reared on the classical approaches to the *Iliad* and *Odyssey*: how can compositions that have always seemed so deliberate and integral in their artistry result from a system of diction that is so mechanical—one might almost say automatic? For various Homeric experts the solution lies in objecting to various aspects of Parry's findings: the genius of Homer must somehow be rescued from the workings of a formulaic system.[n] For me, however, it is easier to accept Parry's work and to proceed from there by looking for a solution in the factor of tradition itself.

§4. Let us take another glance at the Homeric deployment of epithets. Granted, Parry's descriptive approach shows us that the choice of epithets is regulated by metrical factors. On the other hand, the historical approach of comparative reconstruction reveals much more.[1] From my own previous studies using this approach, I have learned that certain fixed noun + epithet combinations in Homeric diction go back to a time that predates the very existence of the Greek hexameter;[2] further, that the choice of epithet is ultimately determined by themes that can be reconstructed all the way to a period when Greek was not yet differentiated from its sister languages in the Indo-European family.[3] With the help of such findings, I have developed the theory that Greek meter itself is a long-range result of regularizations in the formal patterns of traditional poetic

§3n. There seem to be two favorite modes of objection. One is to scoff at the primary typological parallel adduced by Parry and his successor Albert Lord, to wit, the living epic traditions preserved by the South Slavic peoples (on which see Lord 1960). The second is to worry about whether Homer was literate or illiterate. I will not stun the reader at this point with massive doses of bibliography documenting these objections.

§4n1. In the field of linguistics, this approach is designated simply as the "comparative method": Meillet 1925.

§4n2. Nagy 1974.229–261.

§4n3. Ibid.

diction.[4] Granted, diction is indeed regulated by meter from the descriptive point of view, but this regulation is from the historical point of view only the result of a more basic principle, namely, that diction is ultimately regulated by theme.[5]

§5. My theory, then, has it that theme is the overarching principle in the creation of traditional poetry like the *Iliad* and the *Odyssey*; also, that the formulaic heritage of these compositions is an accurate expression of their thematic heritage. Such a theory helps account for the problems raised by Parry's theory of the formula. Did the poet really *mean* this or that? Did he really *intend* such-and-such an artistic effect? My general answer would be that the artistic intent is indeed present—but that this intent must be assigned not simply to one poet but also to countless generations of previous poets steeped in the same traditions. In other words, I think that the artistry of the Homeric poems is traditional both in diction and in theme. For me the key is not so much the genius of Homer but the genius of the overall poetic tradition that culminated in our *Iliad* and *Odyssey*.

§6. To my mind there is no question, then, about the poet's freedom to say accurately what he means. What he means, however, is strictly regulated by tradition. The poet has no intention of saying anything untraditional. In fact, the poet's inherited conceit is that he has it in his power to recover the exact words that tell what men did and said in the Heroic Age.[n]

§4n4. Nagy, pp. 140–149. Even from a descriptive point of view, I will consistently argue that Homeric epithets are indeed appropriate to the themes associated with the words that they describe.

§4n5. Nagy 1976b.

§6n. More at Ch.15§§7–8, where the factor of regional variation also is taken into account. It stands to reason that different poets on different occasions will draw their material from different local traditions and that the poetic versions of what exactly happened in the past will differ from tradition to tradition. The important thing to keep in mind, however, is that variant traditions function as multiforms (cf. Ch. 3§2). Regional variations are themselves an aspect of what we call traditional oral poetry (cf. Lord 1960 *passim*). What the poet tells is true or false, depending on where he tells it: the local traditions on which the poet's immediate audience has been reared constitute the ultimate criterion of "truth." Such an ideology is clearly documented in Radloff's study of Kirghiz poetry (1885) and is still visible in Homeric passages that allude to the poet's tailoring the contents of his song to the predilections of his audience; see Svenbro's illuminating discussion (1976.5–73). I should stress that such poetic tailoring need not be interpreted as untraditional: it could just as easily be a matter of adjusting to local traditions. In the case of Homeric Epos, however, the tendency is to avoid localized idiosyncrasies: see the suggestive remarks of Svenbro, pp. 42–43, who correlates this tendency with what he sees as an ongoing process of text fixation. Unlike Svenbro, however, I would emphasize the factor of the **pólis** 'city-state' less

§7. These theoretical underpinnings have fostered a general attitude of literal mindedness in my approach to the concept of the hero
in archaic Greek poetry. In the pages that follow, I will as a policy
assume that the application of an epithet—whether it be fixed or
particularized—is thematically appropriate as well as traditional.[1]
Moreover, my working assumption extends from the usage of
epithets in particular to the usage of words in general: the entire
formula, to repeat, is an accurate response to the requirements of
traditional theme.[2] I stress this point now in order to prepare the
reader for the oncoming plethora of transliterated Greek words that I
will be continually citing in my discussion of central poetic themes.
My reliance on key words in context cannot be dismissed as a
reductive and oversimplified method of delving into the thematic
complexities of archaic Greek poetry, if indeed the words themselves
are functioning elements of an integral formulaic system inherited
precisely for the purpose of actively expressing these complexities.
The words should not be viewed merely as random vocabulary that
passively reflects the themes sought by the poet. The semantic range
of a key word in context can be expected to be as subtle and complex
as the poetry in which it is encased.

§8. In the course of confronting the diverse problems entailed by
my overall inquiry, I have found that the most striking confirmation
of my literal readings has been the remarkable pattern of correspondences between the deployment of key words on the one hand and,
on the other, the artistic unity of the *Iliad* and the *Odyssey* as
compositions. I should emphasize that the positing of a unitary *Iliad*
and a unitary *Odyssey* has been for me not an end in itself, one that
is continually threatened by contextual inconsistencies in this Homeric passage or that. Rather, it has been a means for solving the
problems presented by these inconsistencies. Whatever Homeric
passages seem at first to be inconsistent in the short range may in the
long range be the key to various central themes of the overall *Iliad* or

---

than the factor of Panhellenism (see §§14–15 below); within the context of the **pólis**,
there seems to be ample opportunity for regional variations (§14n4).

§7n1. On the distinction between fixed and particularized epithets, see Parry 1971
[= 1930] 153–165. In a critique of Parry's formulation (Nagy 1976b.243–244), I made
the strategic error of applying the term particularized also to fixed epithets that are
restricted to describing one entity.

§7n2. For examples of thematic accuracy in the deployment of epithets in particular
and words in general, see Ch.2 and Ch.5 respectively. Consider also my comments on
the epithet **korunḗtēs** 'club wielder' at Ch.20§11n1.

Odyssey—central messages that are hidden away from those of us, such as we are, who have not been raised by Hellenic society as the appreciative audience of Epos.

§9. Unlike most Homerists who perceive an artistic unity in the *Iliad* and the *Odyssey*, however, I would still prefer to reconcile what I see with what Parry has discovered about formulaic composition, with all that his discoveries imply about the traditional predetermination of diction. In this respect I find myself in the congenial company of Michael Nagler,[1] although my work lays less emphasis on the poet's thought processes and more on the poet's tradition. From my point of view, the way to reconcile the factor of formulaic composition with the factor of artistic unity is to infer that both are a matter of tradition. The unity of a masterpiece like the *Iliad* may itself be the product of a lengthy evolution in the artistic streamlining of form and content.[2]

§10. If indeed tradition is a principal factor in the artistic integrity of an archaic Greek poem, it follows that we need not simply attempt to ascribe an *Iliad* or an *Odyssey* to the creativity of one genius, the poet Homer. I prefer to follow the same line of reasoning in the case of Hesiodic poetry. Whatever unity we may discover in the *Theogony* and in the *Works and Days* need not lead us to the certainty that we have just found the "author" called Hesiod. Nor can we with any certainty recover an "author" by the name of Homer (or by any other name) on the basis of the Homeric *Hymns*. Granted, the *Theogony* itself names Hesiod as its composer (verse 22);[1] or again, the Homeric *Hymn to Apollo* actually presents itself as a poem composed by a blind poet from Chios whose songs are heard throughout the city-states of the Hellenes—surely the figure of Homer himself (verses 166–176).[2] Nevertheless, we will have a chance to see that the references made by an archaic poem to its composer, or "author," are not so much a personal attempt by the poet to identify himself but rather a formal reflection of the poetry upon its own importance: the archaic poem presents itself retrospec-

§9n1. Nagler 1974; see also Austin 1975 and Frame 1978.
§9n2. Cf. Pagliaro 1970.39–40 on the theories of Giambattista Vico; also Nagy 1974.11. I have developed the theory more fully at Ch.2§18 and Ch.5§§18–19. In fact, I was tempted to have those paragraphs here, but I finally decided to place them in specific contexts where the point could perhaps be made more strongly.
§10n1. Cf. Ch.17§9.
§10n2. Cf. §15 below.

tively as something transmitted by the ultimate poet.[3] Even the poems of a historical figure like Pindar tend to present their composer as a mere function or instrument of the poetry itself. In short, an archaic poem establishes its authority primarily by asserting the traditions upon which it is built.

§11. My criteria, then, for determining the integrity of poetic composition do not directly involve questions of authorship. In the case of something like Hesiod *fragment* 204MW, for example, it does not matter for my purposes whether this piece of archaic poetry was or was not composed by a person who may be identified as Hesiod: all that matters to me is whether I have comparative evidence to show that the given poetry is traditional in theme and diction and that its traditions are cognate with the ones we find in the *Theogony* or *Works and Days*.[n]

§12. I should add that any single composition may well be built from multiple traditions. In fact, the Homeric poems are prodigiously versatile in integrating a plethora of various different traditions in epic narrative.[1] Moreover, they even adapt and then integrate a variety of traditions in poetic genres other than epic.[2] My point remains, however, simply that the unity achieved by the *Iliad* and the *Odyssey* in their integration of various different traditions is itself an overall tradition.

§13. In archaic Greek poetry, the principle of unity in composition may be the result of social as well as artistic factors. In the Homeric *Hymn to Apollo*, for example, the integrity of the poem results from the fusion of two traditions about Apollo, the Delian and the Pythian, but the artistic fusion of the two distinct traditions implies a corresponding social fusion of two distinct audiences. The worship of Delian Apollo is the founding principle uniting the city-states on the Aegean Islands and on the coast of Asia Minor—precisely those Hellenic areas that are not included in the vast affiliation of city-states united in the worship of Pythian Apollo at Delphi.[n] Since the

§10n3. Ch.17§§8–9.

§11n. More on Hesiod *fr.* 204MW at Ch.11§§13–15.

§12n1. Cf. Ch.3§§1–2, 19.

§12n2. Cf. Ch.6 on lamentation, Ch.11–Ch.15 on praise- and blame-poetry. To go one step further: Homeric Epos even adapts and integrates the formal conventions of actual prayers. See Muellner 1976.

§13n. See Giovannini 1969.67, who also points out that the areas not included in the world of the Pythian Apollo correspond to the areas not included in the Homeric *Catalogue of Ships* in *Iliad* II.

Homeric *Hymn to Apollo* is appropriate to the city-states under the sway of the Delian as well as the Pythian Apollo, its range of audience is truly Panhellenic in scope.

§14. Mention of the Panhellenic orientation that we find in the Homeric *Hymn to Apollo* brings us now to a vital contribution to our understanding of Homeric composition—from the field of archaeology. A recent archaeological synthesis by Anthony Snodgrass has made it clear that the eighth century B.C., the very era in which the *Iliad* and the *Odyssey* approached their ultimate form, was a watershed in the evolution of Hellenic civilization; alongside the emergence of the **pólis** 'city-state' as a general institution with a strong trend of localized traditions (cult, law, etc.), there emerged a commensurately strong trend of intercommunication among the elite of the city-states—the trend of Panhellenism.[1] Some specific manifestations of the latter trend are:

- establishment of the Olympic Games
- establishment of the Pythian Apollo's Sanctuary and Oracle at Delphi
- organized colonizations
- proliferation of the alphabet.

Such institutions as the Olympic Games and the Delphic Oracle, both stemming from the eighth century, are of course monumental feats of intersocial organization and also of intercultural synthesis.[2] Significantly, the same can be said of Homeric Epos itself. From the internal evidence of its contents, we see that this poetic tradition synthesizes the diverse local traditions of each major city-state into a unified Panhellenic model that suits most city-states but corresponds exactly to none; the best example is the Homeric concept of the Olympian gods, which incorporates, yet goes beyond, the localized religious traditions of each city-state.[3] We also know that the *Iliad* and the *Odyssey* had proliferated throughout the city-states at the time that they reached their present form; it may be, then, that the Panhellenic nature of Homeric Epos is due not only to its composition but also to its proliferation.[4]

§14n1. Snodgrass 1971.421, 435; cf. West 1973.182.
§14n2. Snodgrass, pp. 352, 376, 416–417, 421, 431; cf. West ibid.
§14n3. Cf. Rohde I 25–27.
§14n4. In this connection, it is vital to point out that the Homeric *Iliad* and *Odyssey* are radically different in scope and artistry from the epics of the so-called Cycle— namely, the *Cypria*, *Aithiopis*, *Little Iliad*, *Iliou Persis*, *Nostoi*, and *Telegonia* (the fragments of which will be cited consistently from Allen 1912). I rely on the definitive

§15. Moreover, composition and proliferation need not necessarily be related as an *event* followed by a *process*: the evolution of the fixed texts that we know as the *Iliad* and *Odyssey* may be envisaged as a cumulative process, entailing countless instances of composition/performance in a tradition that is becoming streamlined into an increasingly rigid form as a result of ever-increasing proliferation.[1] Again we come to the image of that blind singer from Chios, the poet in the Homeric *Hymn to Apollo* (166–176).[2] If indeed such a figure amounts to an idealized retrojection based on the poetic tradition's sense of its own glory,[3] then we may also see the actual factor of proliferation reflected in the poet's boast that his songs are heard throughout the city-states of mankind:

ἡμεῖς δ' ὑμέτερον κλέος οἴσομεν ὅσσον ἐπ' αἶαν
ἀνθρώπων στρεφόμεσθα πόλεις εὖ ναιεταώσας

And we [the poet] will carry on your glory [kléos][4] wherever on earth we go, throughout the well-inhabited city-states [pólis plural] of men.

H.Apollo 174–175

In this connection, we cannot afford to ignore the actual existence of poetic organizations like the **Homērídai** of Chios and the **Kreōphu-**

---

article by Griffin 1977, who demonstrates convincingly the uniqueness of the *Iliad* and the *Odyssey* in relation to the Cyclic poems. Griffin implicitly ascribes this uniqueness to "Homer." Instead, I prefer to stress the factor of Panhellenism: the *Iliad* and the *Odyssey* seem to be the only epics that ultimately achieved a truly Panhellenic status. To put it another way: I suggest that the Cyclic epics are so different from the two Homeric epics not because they are either more recent or more primitive but rather because they are more local in orientation and diffusion. For example, consider the myth in *Vita Herodotea* 15 (Allen, pp. 202–203) that tells how Homer was commissioned to dictate not only the *Little Iliad* but also a composition called the *Phokais*—when he traveled to Phokaia! On the relationship of the Cycle with the local ktísis ('colonization') poetry of various city-states, see Ch.7§§27–29 (esp. §28n3; cf. also Ch.8§12n2). On the relationship of the Cycle with the *Iliad* and the *Odyssey*, cf. Ch.3§§1–2.

§15n1. It is significant that the proliferation of the alphabet and of the Homeric poems seems to be contemporaneous. As for the context of performance, I cite the international format of the institution known as the **panéguris** 'gathering, festival', on which see Wade-Gery 1952.2-6; one example is the Delian festival as reflected in lines 146-150 of the Homeric *Hymn to Apollo* and as discussed by Thucydides 3.104. I agree with Wade-Gery's argument that there is also internal evidence for the existence of such institutions within the *Iliad* and the *Odyssey* (ibid.), although I cannot agree with other aspects of his presentation.

§15n2. Cf. §§13–14 above.

§15n3. Cf. Ch.17§§8–9; cf. also Ch.18§4.

§15n4. On **kléos** in the sense of "glory" *as conferred by poetry*, see Ch.1§§2–4. The poet is referring to the **kléos** that he will make for the Deliades (named in *H.Apollo* 157); note that their **kléos** is destined never to perish (verse 156).

leîoi of Samos—both of which had a heritage of strong Panhellenic affiliations.[5] The very concept of **Hómēros** may be reflected by the inherited function of the **Homērídai**.[6] In sum, I think of Homeric poetry as a masterpiece of organization not only in an artistic but also in a social dimension.[7]

§16. The Panhellenic character of the *Iliad* and the *Odyssey* is actually reflected—albeit indirectly—by the two Panhellenic institutions that we have considered, the Sanctuary of Apollo at Delphi and the Olympics. As we shall see later in detail, the death of Achilles is a theme officially celebrated in the **paiā́n** 'paean', a form of song performed in worship of Apollo at Delphi (Pindar *Paean* 6).[1] Also, Achilles was traditionally mourned by the women of Elis in a ceremony that inaugurated the holding of the Olympics every four years (Pausanias 6.23.3).[2] As we shall also see, these traditional practices concerning Achilles reflect a latent dimension of the prime figure of Panhellenic Epos: even in classical times and beyond, he was also a figure in cult.

§17. We will have ample opportunity to examine the religious dimension of the Hellenic hero in cult. For now I wish only to insist on the most fundamental aspect: that the hero must experience death. The hero's death is the theme that gives him his power—not only in cult but also in poetry. We as readers of Hellenic poetry can still sense it. When a hero enters combat in the Homeric Epos, we are fully aware of the intense seriousness of it all: he will confront death. Not even the lofty Olympians can match that, since they cannot die; when the pro-Achaean gods enter combat with their pro-Trojan counterparts in *Iliad* XXI, the results cannot be fatal—and they cannot be serious either. For the Achilles of Homeric Epos, on the

§15n5. On the subject of the **Homērídae/Kreōphuleîoi** in particular and **rhapsōidoí** in general: Burkert 1972b. Further details at Ch.9§25. On the expression used by **rhapsōidoí** to designate their inherited function, "to recite Homer," see Ch.6§6n4. On the meaning of **rhapsōidós** 'rhapsode', see Ch.17§10n5.

§15n6. More at Ch.17§§9–13.

§15n7. Even the root *ar- in **Hómēros** and **Homērídai** (on which see Ch.17§9 and n2) is thematically appropriate for designating both social and artistic cohesion: Ch.17§12, esp. n5. Here as elsewhere, questions of etymology will enter the discussion. I should note at the outset that I intend to avoid building my arguments on the meanings of names; still, they frequently serve as convenient points of departure for any overall examination of traditional themes associated with the names of mythical figures (cf. Ch.5§1, Ch.8§9, etc.).

§16n1. Ch.4 (esp. §§4–6); also Ch.5§9, Ch.7 (esp §§4, 24–30).

§16n2. Ch.6§§26 and 30.

other hand, I will argue that the reality of death has a religious dimension that corresponds to the traditional ideology of hero cults.

§18. In this connection, it would be apt for me to quote a particularly intuitive observation linking the factor of hero cults with the factor of artistic unity in Homeric composition:[1]

> It was only natural that the zeal of our specialists, be they philologians, historians, or archaeologists, should have led them far too frequently to proceed as if the Homeric poems were a *rudis indigestaque moles*. But in so doing they have tried, quite unconsciously and with the best intentions, to break the spiritual law which decrees that no human speech or communication, in prose or in verse, shall have any real meaning for those who fail to pay attention to the whole, or for those who are bored and inattentive whenever an author says something which is foreign to their personal and private interests. The poems respond to such students by promptly falling into fragments; they decay into masses of unrelated symbols. It is therefore the duty of the historian and of the archaeologist to expand their definitions of history to include the history of Greek religion and of Greek poetry; it will then become clear that Homer's transformation of history is founded upon hero worship, and that the Homeric poems deliberately and on the whole successfully suppress the post-Mycenaean aspect of Greece, and magnify the glory of the heroes in a most unhistorical but most poetical manner.

So much for intuition; what about evidence? Here again we get a vital contribution to our understanding of Homeric poetry from the field of archaeology. The Greek religious institution of hero cults, in much the same form that we see even in the classical era, can be traced back all the way to the eighth century B.C.—the same archaic era in which the *Iliad* and the *Odyssey* were attaining their ultimate form.[2]

§19. Accordingly, I have set as my main goal the answer to this vital question about the Achilles of our *Iliad*: does this Panhellenic figure possess the religious dimension of a cult hero even within Epos? There are other questions that are related: how is myth stylized in epic, and how does poetry in general express the connections between myth and ritual? In the course of my lengthy inquiry into the problem of heroes in cult, heroes in epic, I will be presenting a wealth of evidence in the form of passages from archaic Greek poetry in general and from Homeric Epos in particular.[1] From

§18n1. Hack 1940.481.
§18n2. Snodgrass 1971.191–193, 398–399. Further discussion at Ch.6§28.
§19n1. The important testimony of Athenian drama has been as a rule left out of

a careful reading of these passages, we will, I hope, enhance our overall understanding of the many-sided heroes who appear in them. In some cases, we will even discover a heroic dimension in the figures who are said to be the actual makers of Greek poetry—including Homer.[2] But the focus is not on Homer but on Achilles and Odysseus. My prime concern is that each of us may arrive at his own understanding of whoever is "best of the Achaeans."

consideration in this phase of my research; I hope to undertake a separate treatment of this vast area in a future project.
§19n2. Ch.17§§10–13.

Part I
Demodokos, *Odyssey, Iliad*

1 | The First Song of Demodokos

§1. Homeric Epos has the power not only to define the hero but to articulate this very power. In my search for evidence in support of such a claim—and this search will extend throughout my presentation—I will of course have to struggle with the overwhelming dimensions of the *Iliad* and the *Odyssey*. It is especially difficult to find an appropriate place to begin. How to approach two such monumental compositions, representing as they do the culmination of perhaps over a thousand years of performer-audience interaction? Already at this point, I stress these important factors of performer and audience, in light of the discoveries made by Milman Parry and Albert Lord about the traditional nature of Homeric composition.[1] We see at work here an inherited medium where the composition can be simultaneous with performance—or at least, where composition becomes a reality only in performance.[2] In fact, I find this factor of performance an ultimately suitable point of departure. We are about to examine *Odyssey* viii 72–82, the description of a poet's performance as actually narrated by Homeric Epos. In this description we may discover a vantage point from which we are allowed an instant glimpse into the artistic unity of the *Iliad* and the *Odyssey* combined.

§2. Unlike Indic epic, where narrative is enclosed within the overall framework of dialogue or dialogue-within-dialogue, oftentimes in accretions of seemingly never-ending inner circles,[1] Greek epic de-

§1n1. See especially Lord 1960, *The Singer of Tales*. The papers of Milman Parry have been collected by Adam Parry, 1971.

§1n2. In her far-reaching survey of traditional "oral" poetry as attested among the various peoples of the world, Finnegan 1977.52–87 adduces instances where composition seems to precede performance and where composer and performer are distinct (cf. Old Provençal *trobador* 'composer' compared to *joglar* 'performer'). I must say that Finnegan's synthesis (1977), much as I admire it for its breadth, cannot replace Lord's synthesis (1960), which remains the definitive study of "oral" poetry in depth.

§2n1. Part I of Dumézil's *Mythe et épopée* I (1968) can serve as a convenient introduction to the nature of Indic epic.

livers the narrative directly in the persona of the poet. The invoking of the Muses at the start of a Greek epic is the tag of the poet's own performance. The immediacy of performance, however, is counter-balanced by an attitude of remoteness from composition. The performer feels himself distant enough to intimate that the message of his composition comes not from him but from tradition. As the poet tells the Muses before he launches into the *Catalogue of Ships*:

ὑμεῖς γὰρ θεαί ἐστε, πάρεστέ τε, ἴστε τε πάντα,
ἡμεῖς δὲ κλέος οἶον ἀκούομεν οὐδέ τι ἴδμεν

You are goddesses; you are always present, and you know everything; but we [poets] only hear the **kléos** and know nothing.

II 485–486[2]

Accordingly, the poet invokes the Muses to tell him how it all happened (II 484). He behaves as an instrument, as it were, in the hands of the Muse, whose message is equated with that of creative tradition. He passes on the **kléos**, let us call it the "glory," of heroes. And yet, the word **kléos** itself betrays the pride of the Hellenic poet through the ages. Etymologically, **kléos** should have meant simply "that which is heard" (from **klúō** 'hear'), and indeed the poet hears **kléos** recited to him by the Muses (again, II 486). But then it is actually he who recites it to his audience. Here the artist's inherited message about himself is implicit but unmistakable. In a word, the Hellenic poet is the master of **kléos**. "That which is heard," **kléos**, comes to mean "glory" because it is the poet himself who uses the word to designate what he hears from the Muses and what he tells the audience. Poetry confers glory.[3] The conceit of Homeric poetry is

§2n2. I will consistently refer to the books of the *Iliad/Odyssey* in upper-/lower-case roman numerals. My translations are based on those of Lattimore 1951/1965, with adjustments.

§2n3. For an extensive discussion of Greek **kléos** and its Indic cognate *śrávas* as "glory" conferred by the "hearing" of poetry (Indo-European root *kleu̯- 'hear'), I cite my earlier work on the subject, hidden within a comparative study of Greek and Indic meter (Nagy 1974.231–255). See also Schmitt 1967.61–102. For a parallel semantic development in yet another Indo-European language group besides Greek and Indic, we may adduce the evidence of Slavic, where *slava* means "glory" while *slovo* means both "word" and "epic tale." As Puhvel (1976.263) observes, both *slava* and *slovo* are independently derived from the same root *kleu̯- 'hear' as in Greek **kléos**. It does not follow, however, that *slava* came to mean "glory" without the intermediacy of poetic tradition: compare the discussion of Slavic names with second element *-slav* in Schmitt, p. 89. Moreover, there is good reason to believe that the Indo-European root *kleu̯- itself had been a traditional word not only for "hear" in general but also "hear poetry" in particular (cf. Schmitt, pp. 90–93, 202, etc.).

that even a Trojan warrior will fight and die in pursuit of κλέος ...
'Αχαιῶν "the **kléos** of the Achaeans" (XI 227).[4] If you perform
heroic deeds, you have a chance of getting into Achaean epic. The
Achaean singer of tales is in control of the glory that may be yours.

§3. As Marcel Detienne has shown in detail,[1] the verb **mi-mnḗ-
skō**, designating the function of the Muses at II 492 (μνησαίατ') and
elsewhere, means not so much that the Muses "remind" the poet of
what to tell but, rather, that they have the power to put his mind or
consciousness in touch with places and times other than his own in
order to witness the deeds of heroes (and the doings of gods).[2] He is
independent of seeing the here and now; he need only *hear* the
kléos. For him, a thing like blindness cannot help but serve as a
proof, a veritable emblem, of his artistic independence.

§4. Enter Demodokos, the blind poet of the Phaeacians in *Odyssey*
viii. This figure **Dēmódokos** 'received by the **dêmos**'[1] is an appropriate idealization of an artist by the art form of epic. Through the
persona of Demodokos, the epic of the *Odyssey* can express many

§2n4. I find it significant that this mention of **kléos** comes shortly after an invocation
of the Muses (XI 218). The goddesses are being asked a question: who was the first
hero on the Trojan side to be killed by Agamemnon at this point in the narrative (XI
219–220)? The answer follows as the narrative resumes: it was Iphidamas (XI
221–231). And the hero's motive for fighting on the Trojan side is indicated with these
words: μετὰ κλέος ἵκετ' 'Αχαιῶν 'he came in pursuit of the **kléos** of the Achaeans' (XI
227).

§3n1. Detienne 1973.9–16, 20; also Vernant 1959.

§3n2. When Hektor says that there should be a **mnēmosúnē** 'reminder, memory' of
his setting fire to the ships of the Achaeans (VIII 181), he is in effect saying that this
moment should be recorded by epic. This is precisely what happens at XVI 112–113,
where the Muses are specially invoked to tell "how it was that the fire first fell upon
the ships of the Achaeans." On **Mnēmosúnē** personified, who is mother of the Muses,
see Hesiod *Th.* 98–103 and the discussion at Ch.6§5. The word **Moûsa** itself (from
*mont-i̯a) may well stem from the same root *men- that we find in **mi-mnḗ-skō** and
mnē-mosúnē: Nagy 1974.249–250, 253n24.

§4n1. The meaning is made explicit at xiii 27–28, where Demodokos is described as
lāoîsi tetīménos 'honored by the people'. On the function of the **dêmos** 'district' as the
social setting for the poet's activity, see xvii 381–387, as discussed at Ch.12§13. The
poet **Phémios** also has an expressive name, derived from **phémē** 'prophetic utterance'
(as at ii 35). The meaning of **Phémios** is likewise made explicit, at xxii 376: he is
described as **polúphēmos** 'having many prophetic utterances' (for the semantics,
compare the discussion of **polúainos** at Ch.12§19n1). Note too his expressive
patronymic **Terpiádēs** (xxii 330), derived from **térpō** 'give pleasure'. This verb
conventionally designates *in poetry* the effects *of poetry* (as at i 347, where Phemios is
said to **térpein** 'give pleasure' to his audience). Compare also the patronymics
Polutherseídēs (Ch.14§11) and **Harmonídēs** (Ch.17§11). For more on Demodokos and
Phemios, see Rüter 1969.233–234.

things about itself as a composition—far beyond what the medium of performance could let the poet say in his own persona when he invoked his own Muse. As Samuel Bassett has remarked in another connection, "Homer has carefully groomed the Phaeacian bard for his part."[2] After the Phaeacians have had their fill of food and drink, the time for an evening's entertainment is at hand. The Muse, or perhaps we should say "a Muse," impels the poet Demodokos to sing the "**kléos** [plural] of men" (κλέα ἀνδρῶν: viii 72–73), from a story that had a **kléos** of great impact "at that time":

οἴμης τῆς τότ' ἄρα κλέος οὐρανὸν εὐρὺν ἵκανε . . .

from a story-thread[3] that had at that time a **kléos** reaching up to the vast heavens . . .

viii 74

§5. I have not yet reached the point where I can examine what Demodokos then sang. Suffice it now to observe that he performs not just one but three separate compositions in *Odyssey* viii, all of them pertinent to the themes of the overall *Odyssey*. What is more important for now, the performances of the idealized poet seem to be themselves idealized within the narrative. Outside the narrative, on the other hand, the composition of the *Odyssey* itself is idealized in such a way that it has become unperformable. Not only for the *Odyssey* but for the *Iliad* as well, an important aspect of idealization is amplitude and comprehensiveness. In size and in arrangement, they are truly monumental structures. Between the two of them, the *Iliad* and the *Odyssey* manage to incorporate and orchestrate something of practically everything that was once thought worth preserving from the Heroic Age. Their monumental scale, however, has far outgrown the earlier and ideal context of performance, namely, an evening's dinner-hour entertainment as described by Odysseus himself before he begins his own narration:

ἦ τοι μὲν τόδε καλὸν ἀκουέμεν ἐστὶν ἀοιδοῦ
τοιοῦδ' οἷος ὅδ' ἐστί, θεοῖς ἐναλίγκιος αὐδήν.
οὐ γὰρ ἐγώ γέ τί φημι τέλος χαριέστερον εἶναι
ἢ ὅτ' ἐϋφροσύνη μὲν ἔχῃ κατὰ δῆμον ἅπαντα,
δαιτυμόνες δ' ἀνὰ δώματ' ἀκουάζωνται ἀοιδοῦ

§4n2. Bassett 1938.118.
§4n3. The prehistory of the word **oímē** 'story' reveals that it had conveyed the imagery of weaving (hence "story thread"): Durante 1976.176–179 (*pace* Chantraine III 783–784).

ἥμενοι ἐξείης, παρὰ δὲ πλήθωσι τράπεζαι
σίτου καὶ κρειῶν, μέθυ δ' ἐκ κρητῆρος ἀφύσσων
οἰνοχόος φορέῃσι καὶ ἐγχείῃ δεπάεσσι·
τοῦτο τί μοι κάλλιστον ἐνὶ φρεσὶν εἴδεται εἶναι.

It is indeed a good thing to listen to a poet
such as this one before us, who is like the gods in speech.
For I think there is no occasion accomplished that is <u>more pleasing</u>[1]
than when <u>mirth</u>[2] holds sway among all the **dêmos**,[3]
and the feasters up and down the house are sitting in order and listening to
    the singer,
and beside them the tables are loaded
with bread and meats, and from the mixing bowl the wine-steward
draws the wine and carries it about and fills the cups.
This seems to my own mind to be the best of occasions.

                                                                        ix 3–11

The dinner-hour performer described here is none other than
Demodokos himself. By contrast, the *Odyssey* acknowledges its own
monumental scale with the narrative that Odysseus is about to
perform, starting at Book ix. As the inner narrative of his own
adventures by Odysseus begins to exceed—by way of its actual
length—the span of an evening's entertainment, the outer narrative
has Alkinoos urge the inner narrator to continue with the following
words:

νὺξ δ' ἥδε μάλα μακρὴ ἀθέσφατος· οὐδέ πω ὥρη
εὕδειν ἐν μεγάρῳ· σὺ δέ μοι λέγε θέσκελα ἔργα.
καί κεν ἐς ἠῶ δῖαν ἀνασχοίμην, ὅτε μοι σὺ
τλαίης ἐν μεγάρῳ τὰ σὰ κήδεα μυθήσασθαι.

This night is very long—immeasurably so. It is not yet time
to sleep in the palace. But go on telling me about your wondrous deeds.
And I myself could hold out until the bright dawn, if only
you could bear to tell me, here in the palace, of your sufferings.[4]

                                                                        xi 373–376

What goes for the adventures of Odysseus in the inner narrative goes
also for the entire composition: the *Odyssey* itself is here in effect jus-

----

§5n1. On the implications of χαριέστερον 'more pleasing [having more **kháris**]', see
Ch.2§13n2; also Ch.5§39.
§5n2. On the theme of **eüphrosúnē** 'mirth' in the community: Ch.5§39.
§5n3. On the **dêmos** as the community/audience of **Dēmódokos**: §4n1.
§5n4. For other passages where the audience stays awake far into the night for the
sake of listening to tales, see xv 390–401, xvii 513–521, xxiii 308–309. Cf. Maehler
1963.28–29.

tifying the evolution of its own dimensions. The idealized performances of Demodokos, on the other hand, have retained and thus in a sense compensated for this element of dinner-hour entertainment that had been lost in the idealized compositions of the *Odyssey* and the *Iliad.* Of course, it cannot be emphasized enough that both the *Iliad* and the *Odyssey* must have evolved within the medium of composition during performance, performance during composition. The paradox is that the compositions were developed to the point where they came to defy the traditional format of their performance.[5]

§6. Earlier, I had referred to the "artistic unity of the *Iliad* and the *Odyssey* combined." The wording was meant to convey what I consider the ultimate token of self-reflexiveness in Homeric poetry. The *Odyssey,* in the words of David Monro, "never repeats or refers to any incident related in the *Iliad.*"[1] Denys Page amplifies:[2]

It is as if the Odyssean poet were wholly ignorant of that particular story which is told in the *Iliad.* Nowhere is there any allusion to the wrath of Achilles or to the death of Hector, or indeed to any other incident, large or small, described in the *Iliad.* Yet the *Odyssey* often pauses to narrate some part of the Trojan story and refers freely to a variety of older and contemporary Epic poems—*always excluding the Iliad.* There is Helen's tale of Odysseus' entry into the city of Troy in disguise (4.235ff.); there is Menelaus' story of the wooden horse (4.266ff.); we hear of Odysseus' valour in battle over Achilles' corpse (5.309ff.), and of the rivalry between Odysseus and Ajax (11.543ff.); Nestor tells at some length of a quarrel between Agamemnon and Menelaus (3.103ff.); Demodocus sings of a quarrel between Odysseus and Achilles (8.74ff.). Are we seriously asked to believe that a poet (or poets) who knew the *Iliad* might compose a poem of 12,000 lines concerning one of the *Iliad*'s greatest heroes without ever showing the slightest awareness of that poem?

Page argues that the *Iliad* and the *Odyssey* are thus unconnected. And yet, it is precisely the size of the *Iliad* and the *Odyssey* that forces me to believe the opposite.[3] Both the *Iliad* and the *Odyssey* are so ambitiously comprehensive that their sheer size would make it seem inevitable for them to overlap in their treatment of at least

§5n5. Kirk (1962.281) compares the size of the Homeric compositions with the "leap from the largeish pot to the perfectly colossal one" in the evolution of monumental amphoras/craters during the Geometric Period. What interests me in this comparison is that the colossal size of a utensil defies its own utility.

§6n1. Monro 1901.325.

§6n2. Page 1955.158.

§6n3. Cf. the arguments of Kirk 1962.299–300.

some events related to Troy—unless there was a deliberate avoidance of such overlapping. If the avoidance was indeed deliberate, it would mean that the *Odyssey* displays an awareness of the *Iliad* by steering clear of it. Or rather, it may be a matter of evolution. Perhaps it was part of the Odyssean tradition to veer away from the Iliadic. Be that as it may, the traditions of the *Iliad* and the *Odyssey* constitute a totality with the complementary distribution of their narratives and, to me, there seems to be something traditionally self-conscious about all this. It is as if there were a traditional suppression of anything overtly Iliadic in the *Odyssey*.

§7. What I have offered so far, of course, is just an intuition. Perhaps I can be more convincing if I find positive rather than negative evidence. What I need is a specific instance where the *Odyssey* unmistakably alludes to an Iliadic scene without duplicating it. Monro's Law would be violated only by duplication, not by allusion. For example, the passing reference in *Odyssey* xxiv 77 to mixing the ashes of Achilles and Patroklos is not a duplication of two other references to the same mixing in *Iliad* XXIII 91–92 and 243–244. Even if we were to accept the argument that Patroklos had been perhaps an exclusively Iliadic figure,[1] the parallelism of references fails to overturn Monro's Law. Inside our *Iliad*, the references to the mixing of ashes are themselves allusions to future events that are projected as occurring outside the *Iliad*. One of the artistic triumphs of our *Iliad*, as Cedric Whitman has shown, is that it makes the painful death of Achilles ever present by allusion inside the *Iliad*, even though the actual death scene lies in the future, outside the *Iliad*.[2] The future for the *Iliad* is a suitable past for the *Odyssey*.

§8. There is, however, someone who could bridge the gap between past and future. The poet has such powers, granted by the Muses. The poet of the *Theogony*, for example, says that they breathed into him a wondrous voice:

. . . ἵνα <u>κλείοιμι</u> τά τ' ἐσσόμενα πρό τ' ἐόντα

. . . so that I may <u>give **kléos**</u> to the future and the past

Hesiod Th. 32

It is at this point that I am at last ready to consider the first performance of Demodokos, poet of the Phaeacians. He is singing the κλέα ἀνδρῶν '**kléos** [plural] of men' (viii 73), and the **kléos** of

---

§7n1. Cf. Dihle 1970.159, with bibliography.
§7n2. Whitman 1958 chapter IX.

his song reached all the way up to the heavens (viii 74). Perhaps this **kléos** also bridges the gap between *Iliad* and *Odyssey*:

αὐτὰρ ἐπεὶ πόσιος καὶ ἐδητύος ἐξ ἔρον ἕντο,
Μοῦσ' ἄρ' ἀοιδὸν ἀνῆκεν ἀειδέμεναι κλέα ἀνδρῶν,
οἴμης τῆς τότ' ἄρα κλέος οὐρανὸν εὐρὺν ἵκανε,
νεῖκος 'Οδυσσῆος καὶ Πηλείδεω 'Αχιλῆος,
ὥς ποτε δηρίσαντο θεῶν ἐν δαιτὶ θαλείῃ
ἐκπάγλοις ἐπέεσσιν, ἄναξ δ' ἀνδρῶν 'Αγαμέμνων
χαῖρε νόῳ, ὅ τ' ἄριστοι 'Αχαιῶν δηριόωντο.
ὣς γάρ οἱ χρείων μυθήσατο Φοῖβος 'Απόλλων
Πυθοῖ ἐν ἠγαθέῃ, ὅθ' ὑπέρβη λάϊνον οὐδὸν
χρησόμενος· τότε γάρ ῥα κυλίνδετο πήματος ἀρχὴ
Τρωσί τε καὶ Δαναοῖσι Διὸς μεγάλου διὰ βουλάς.

But when they had their fill of drinking and eating,
the Muse impelled the singer to sing the glories [**kléos** plural] of men,
from a story-thread which had at that time a glory [**kléos**] reaching the vast
   heavens:
the quarrel of Odysseus and Achilles son of Peleus,
how they once fought at a sumptuous feast of the gods,
with terrible words, and the king of men, Agamemnon,
rejoiced in his mind that the best of the Achaeans were fighting.
Thus had oracular Phoebus Apollo prophesied to him,
at holy Delphi, when he had crossed the stone threshold
to ask the oracle. For then it was that the beginning of pain started rolling
upon both Trojans and Danaans, on account of the plans of great Zeus.

viii 72–82

§9. These verses have been a puzzle for ancient as well as modern exegetes. The passage was already a landmark of literary controversy, a **zétēma**, at the time of Aristarchus.[1] Nowhere else in attested Greek epic do we find a tradition reporting an overt **neîkos** 'quarrel' between Odysseus and Achilles, which is described here in words appropriate to the baneful **neîkos** between Agamemnon and Achilles in *Iliad* I. The only direct trace of any altercation between Odysseus and Achilles appears in surviving fragments of the *Syndeipnoi* "Banqueters" by Sophocles (*frr.* 562–571 Pearson).[2] The playwright, in the opinion of such analysts as Peter Von der Mühll and Wolfgang Kullmann, must have derived the theme of the altercation from a

---

§9n1. See Lehrs 1882.174.
§9n2. For an introduction: Pearson 1917 II 198–201 (cf. Radt 1977.425–430).

scene in the epic Cycle, somewhere in the middle of the *Cypria*.[3] The theory goes further; the **neîkos** in *Odyssey* viii is supposed to have been based on the same purported scene in the *Cypria*. In the middle of the Proclus summary of the *Cypria* (p. 104.23–24 Allen), however, we find only that Achilles had a quarrel with Agamemnon over not being invited to a feast of the Achaeans at Tenedos. Accordingly, Von der Mühll and Kullmann adjust their theory; Odysseus must have been featured in the *Cypria* as taking the side of Agamemnon and goading a recalcitrant Achilles to rejoin the Achaean expedition (cf. Sophocles *fr.* 566).

§10. It would require separate argumentation to refute the notion that our *Odyssey* postdated the *Cypria* and even derived material from it.[1] What is more important for now, the theory that the **neîkos** 'quarrel' scene of *Odyssey* viii was modeled on a **neîkos** scene in the *Cypria* fails to account for the precise manner in which the theme is treated by Demodokos. The form and content of *Odyssey* viii 75–81 are noticeably tailored to suit the beginning of an epic poem.[2] The unitarians Walter Marg and Klaus Rüter go even further, in pointing out that these verses in *Odyssey* viii are eerily reminiscent of the way in which the *Iliad* itself begins.[3] There too we find a programmatic correlation of the following themes: Achilles, son of Peleus (I 1 ~ viii 75); Agamemnon, king of men (I 7 ~ viii 77); the beginning of grief for Trojans and Achaeans alike (I 2–5 ~ viii 81–82); the involvement of Apollo (I 8–9 ~ viii 79–82); the Will of Zeus (I 5 ~ viii 82). If indeed verses 75–82 of *Odyssey* viii are based on a scene in another epic, then an incident which is supposed to occur in the middle of the *Cypria* does not seem a likely traditional model. At best, we can rescue the relevance of the *Cypria* here by imagining some lost epic tradition that began with a dispute between Achilles and Odysseus and to which both *Cypria* and *Odyssey* had alluded.

§11. Marg and Rüter would argue that the **neîkos** 'quarrel' between Achilles and Odysseus in *Odyssey* viii is a pastiche actually based on the opening of our *Iliad*, where Achilles and Agamemnon

§9n3. Von der Mühll 1954.1–5, Kullmann 1960.100, 272, etc. Despite my disagreements, I should note my special admiration for Kullmann's important work.

§10n1. See further at Ch.3§1.

§10n2. Cf. Notopoulos 1964.33.

§10n3. Marg 1956.16–29, Rüter 1969.247–254. For a guide to the recent controversies between unitarians and analysts, see Fenik 1964, esp. pp. 8–15, 30–35.

have their unforgettable **neîkos**.[1] To support this interpretation, they adopt George M. Calhoun's theory of the misunderstood oracle. Agamemnon was happy, the reasoning goes, because Apollo had told him that Troy would be taken only after the "best of the Achaeans" had a quarrel; at the time, he supposedly did not realize that the oracle had meant Achilles and himself, rather than Achilles and Odysseus.[2] I agree that Agamemnon must have misunderstood Apollo's oracle, but I disagree with Calhoun's theory about the actual misunderstanding. I find this theory hard to reconcile with Rüter's own reconstruction of the traditional cause for such a quarrel. As Rüter argues,[3] the thematic conventions of Epos pitted the **aristeíā** 'prestige'[4] of Achilles against that of Odysseus in the form of a quarrel over whether Troy would be captured by might or artifice respectively. The scholia to viii 75 and 77 suggest an epic tradition that has Achilles advocating might and Odysseus, artifice as the means that will prove successful in capturing Troy.[5] We can also infer from the scholia (A) to *Iliad* IX 347 that Aristarchus apparently considered this Iliadic verse to be an allusion to just such a tradition. The context of IX 347 is this: Achilles is rejecting the pleas of Odysseus that he rescue the hard-pressed Achaeans; Odysseus and the other Achaean leaders, Achilles tells him, should devise a way to keep the enemy's fire from reaching the Achaean ships. Achilles seems to be saying: "you come to me now that you need my might; well, just leave me alone and go see how far your artifice will get you!"[6] If might is more important than artifice, then Achilles is more important than Odysseus. The quarrel between Odysseus and Achilles would have centered on who is the "best of the Achaeans," just like the quarrel between Agamemnon and Achilles.[7]

§12. The disadvantages to Calhoun's theory of the misunderstood oracle become more apparent: (1) Agamemnon would be ignoring his

§11n1. Marg ibid., Rüter ibid.

§11n2. Calhoun 1937.11.

§11n3. Rüter 1969.249–251.

§11n4. For an introduction to the complex subject of **aristeíā**, the prestige that a hero gets from his grandest moments in epic narrative, see Schroeter 1950 and Müller 1966.

§11n5. See further at Ch.3§§5–8. Of course, the *Iliad* itself acknowledges that Troy was to be captured by way of artifice, as inspired by Athena (XV 70–71).

§11n6. See Rüter, p. 250. I postpone a detailed look at the passages concerned until Ch.3§§5, 7.

§11n7. See further at Ch.3§8.

own heroic worth if he understood Odysseus and Achilles to be the "best of the Achaeans," and (2) such a misunderstanding would result in slighting the heroic worth of Odysseus within the *Odyssey* itself.[n] It would then be an absurdity for Odysseus to praise the compositions of Demodokos, as he does at viii 487–488 and 496–498.

§13. My suspicion is that the oracle was not misunderstood in its prophecy of a quarrel between Achilles and Odysseus specifically. The reference to Achilles and Odysseus as the "best of the Achaeans" at viii 78 may have served to reveal that the poetic repertory of Demodokos is in control of two distinct themes that permeate the *Iliad* and the *Odyssey*—themes that define the central hero of each epic.

§12n.   I offer my own interpretation of Agamemnon's misunderstanding at Ch.4§7.

2 | The Best of the Achaeans

§1. It is an overall Iliadic theme that Achilles is "best of the Achaeans," as I will now try to show.[1] The title is hotly contested. The central grievance of Achilles in the *Iliad* is that Agamemnon has dishonored him, and in this context the hero of the *Iliad* is regularly called **áristos Akhaiôn** 'best of the Achaeans' (I 244, 412; XVI 271, 274).[2] During his quarrel with Achilles, Agamemnon, too, is specifically described as one who lays claim to the title **áristos Akhaiôn**:

ὃς νῦν πολλὸν ἄριστος 'Αχαιῶν εὔχεται εἶναι

who boasts that he is now by far the best of the Achaeans

I 91

ὃς μέγ' ἄριστος 'Αχαιῶν εὔχεται εἶναι

who boasts that he is by far the best of the Achaeans

II 82

The first of these verses is spoken by Achilles himself, whose very actions in *Iliad* I had challenged Agamemnon's claim.

§2. When the great *Catalogue* of *Iliad* II, recounting the resources of each major Achaean hero, reaches Agamemnon, the men who followed him to Troy are described as πολὺ πλεῖστοι καὶ ἄριστοι 'by far the most numerous and the best [**áristos** plural]' (II 577). Later, Agamemnon himself is said to excel:

οὕνεκ' ἄριστος ἔην, πολὺ δὲ πλείστους ἆγε λαούς

§1n1. In my discussion of the epithets designating the "best," the reader will notice that I proceed without assuming that the placement of epithets is conditioned simply by metrical factors. Such an assumption would have failed to account for the fact that Homeric diction is traditional not only in form but also in content. For the theoretical underpinnings of my procedure, I cite Nagy 1974.140–149 and 229–261. See also Intro.§7.

§1n2. Cf. also IX 110, where Agamemnon is said to have dishonored ἄνδρα φέριστον 'the best [**phéristos**] man'.

because he was the <u>best [**áristos**]</u>, and he led the most numerous host

II 580

The tradition here grudgingly assigns him the title of "best" by virtue of his being the leader of the "best." But the *Catalogue* comes to a close with the words:

οὗτοι ἄρ᾽ ἡγεμόνες Δαναῶν

So now, these were the leaders of the Danaans.

II 760

The poet then follows up with a question:

τίς τ᾽ ἄρ τῶν ὄχ᾽ ἄριστος ἔην, σύ μοι ἔννεπε Μοῦσα

Who, then, was by far the <u>best [**áristos**]</u>? Tell me, Muse!

II 761

The simple question is then expanded into a compound question: who was the best among the Achaeans *and among their horses* (II 762)? The Muse's answer is an elaborate exercise in ring composition. First, let us look at the horses: those of Eumelos were best (II 763–767). Then the men: well, Ajax was best [**áristos**] (II 768)—that is, so long as Achilles persisted in his anger and refrained from fighting:

ὄφρ᾽ Ἀχιλεὺς μήνιεν· ὁ γὰρ πολὺ <u>φέρτατος</u> ἦεν

so long as Achilles was angry; for he was by far the <u>best [**phértatos**]</u>.[1]

II 769

Which brings us back to the horses: those of Achilles were actually the best after all (II 770). But since Achilles was out of sight when the first superlative came around, his horses were out of mind. Achilles, however, is never out of mind in the *Iliad* when it comes to asking who is best of the Achaeans.[2] The great Ajax, then, is here being demoted from the best to the second best of the Achaeans by what seems to be premeditated afterthought. He also gets the same sort of treatment from the epic tradition in *Iliad* VII, in a passage that deserves detailed attention.

§2n1. The word for "best" here is **phértatos**, synonymous with **áristos** at lines 761 and 768. Although the first form has a separate heritage of social connotations (cf. Palmer 1955.11–12), it is clearly a synonym of the second form in the diction of Homeric poetry. Achilles (and he only) is twice in the *Iliad* addressed as φέρτατ᾽ Ἀχαιῶν 'best [**phértatos**] of the Achaeans' (XVI 21, XIX 216).

§2n2. My general thinking on the **aristeíā** of Achilles has been much stimulated by the perceptive observations of Segal 1971b.

§3. Hektor is about to challenge 'Αχαιῶν ὅς τις ἄριστος 'whoever is best [**áristos**] of the Achaeans' to a duel (VII 50).¹ He boasts that this unnamed Achaean will be killed and thus become part of an epic story glorifying the deeds of Hektor. The hapless unknown Achaean, by performing an **aristeíā**,² would become part of a **kléos**, but the **kléos** would belong to the winner, Hektor. Here is how Hektor says it:

καί ποτέ τις εἴπῃσι καὶ ὀψιγόνων ἀνθρώπων,
νηὶ πολυκληῗδι πλέων ἐπὶ οἴνοπα πόντον·
"ἀνδρὸς μὲν τόδε σῆμα πάλαι κατατεθνηῶτος,
ὅν ποτ' ἀριστεύοντα κατέκτανε φαίδιμος Ἕκτωρ."
ὥς ποτέ τις ἐρέει· τὸ δ' ἐμὸν κλέος οὔ ποτ' ὀλεῖται.

And some day, someone from a future generation will say,
as he is sailing on a many-benched ship over the wine-dark sea:
"This is the tomb of a man who died a long time ago,
who was performing his **aristeíā** when illustrious Hektor killed him."
That is what someone will say, and my **kléos** will never perish.

VII 87–91

The tomb of this unknown Achaean challenger would be at the Hellespont (VII 86), clearly visible to those who sail by. And it so happens that epic tradition assigns such a tomb to Achilles himself:

ἀκτῇ ἔπι προὐχούσῃ, ἐπὶ πλατεῖ Ἑλλησπόντῳ,
ὥς κεν τηλεφανὴς ἐκ ποντόφιν ἀνδράσιν εἴη
τοῖς οἳ νῦν γεγάασι καὶ οἳ μετόπισθεν ἔσονται.

on a jutting headland, by the broad Hellespont,
so that it may be bright from afar for men coming from the sea,
those who are now and those who will be in the future.³

xxiv 82–84

It is Achilles who should have answered Hektor's challenge to the one who is best of the Achaeans. This is the hero whose father had taught him "to be best [**áristos**] always" (αἰὲν ἀριστεύειν: XI 784). Achilles will die, yes, and his ashes will indeed be enshrined at the Hellespont. But, ironically, it is Hektor who will be killed by

---

§3n1. Hektor's challenge was formulated for him by the seer Helenos (VII 47–53), who himself thinks that Diomedes is κάρτιστον 'Αχαιῶν 'best [**kártistos**] of the Achaeans' (VI 98).

§3n2. At Ch.1§11n4, I approximated this complex word with the notion of "grand heroic moments."

§3n3. For further discussion of this passage: Ch.20§22.

Achilles.[4] It is Hektor who will become part of an epic story glorifying the deeds of Achilles. By performing his fatal **aristeíā**, Hektor will become part of a **kléos**, as he says it at VII 91, but the **kléos** will belong to the winner, Achilles[5] The *Iliad* belongs to Achilles. It is to Achilles that the Iliadic tradition assigns the **kléos** that will never perish. Achilles himself says it:

ὤλετο μέν μοι νόστος, ἀτὰρ κλέος ἄφθιτον ἔσται

I have lost a safe return home [**nóstos**], but I will have unfailing glory [**kléos**].[6]

IX 413

We may have lost countless other epic compositions, but the *Iliad* has survived and endured. The confidence of the *Iliad* in its eternal survival is the confidence of the master singer. For Achilles, the **kléos** of the *Iliad* tradition should be an eternal consolation for losing a safe return home, a **nóstos**. There is also irony here for Achilles. Hektor's insulting boast hits the mark in that Achilles will be killed and will be buried where Hektor's words predict. But the greatest irony is reserved for Ajax, the second best of the Achaeans. Before we can get to him, however, other things have yet to happen in *Iliad* VII.

§4. After Hektor issues his challenge, no one dares to respond but Menelaos. If no one takes up the challenge, he says in the form of a public reproach,[1] it will be a subject of future public reproach as well for the Achaeans (VII 96–97),[2] and that will be a "thing without **kléos**" (ἀκλεές: VII 100).[3] The Achaeans had better behave as

§3n4. For other instances of Homeric irony where a hero's speech is partially validated but also partially invalidated by the events of the traditional narrative, see XVI 241–248 as discussed at Ch.17§4 (the valid and nonvalid aspects are made explicit at XVI 249–252). See also XX 179–183, as discussed at Ch.15§3.

§3n5. When the moment of his death at the hands of Achilles approaches, Hektor expresses his wish to die ἐϋκλεῶς 'with good **kléos**' (XXII 110) and not ἀκλειῶς 'with no **kléos**' (XXII 304). Cf. Ch.10§13n2.

§3n6. On the semantics of **áphthito-** 'unfailing' as a mark of immortality, see Ch.10§§3,5–19.

§4n1. As Menelaos begins to speak, he νείκει ὀνειδίζων 'made **neîkos**, making **óneidos**' (VII 95). Both **neîkos** and **óneidos** mean 'blame, reproach' and indicate the language of blame poetry; the whole subject will be discussed at length in Ch.12.

§4n2. The potential reproach that is in store for the Achaeans is called **lōbē** by Menelaos (VII 97). Again, **lōbē** means 'blame, reproach' and indicates the language of blame poetry: Ch.14§§5(n1),6.

§4n3. On the antithesis between the **kléos** of epic poetry and the shame of blame poetry: Ch.14§10.

heroes, for Epos is keeping them under observation. As Menelaos prepares to fight Hektor, the poet of the *Iliad* turns away from the audience of his performance and addresses directly the persona in his composition:

ἔνθα κέ τοι, Μενέλαε, φάνη βιότοιο τελευτὴ
"Εκτορος ἐν παλάμῃσιν, ἐπεὶ πολὺ φέρτερος ἦεν

At that point, Menelaos, the end of your life would have appeared,
in the clutches of Hektor, <u>since he was better by far</u>.

VII 104–105

What prevented the death of Menelaos from appearing here in the narrative was the intervention of his fellow Achaeans. In particular, his brother Agamemnon is holding Menelaos back, urging him not to fight "a better man" (ἀμείνονι φωτί: VII 111). Menelaos is told that even Achilles would not fight, "and he is far better than you" (ὅ περ σέο πολλὸν ἀμείνων: VII 114).

§5. At this point, Nestor too reproaches the Achaeans (VII 123–161).[1] His words are in fact so compelling that all nine of the "pan-Achaean champions" (ἀριστῆες Παναχαιῶν: VII 159) volunteer straightway to face Hektor. They are Agamemnon, Diomedes, the Ajaxes, Idomeneus, Meriones, Eurypylos, Thoas, and finally, Odysseus (VII 162–168). Lots are drawn to narrow the list down to one. The Achaeans are meanwhile praying that the winner of the lottery should be Ajax or Diomedes or Agamemnon (VII 177–180). The effect of the prayer on the narrative is that our attention is narrowed down to three out of nine. Of these three, we have already seen Agamemnon claiming the title "best of the Achaeans." Diomedes, too, gets this title, but only in Book V of the *Iliad.* Book V is his finest hour, his **aristeíā**, and this is where he is twice called **áristos Akhaiôn** 'best of the Achaeans.' Both times, however, the specific moment is sinister. In one passage, the archer Pandaros has just shot Diomedes with an arrow, and he is boasting that he has wounded the "best of the Achaeans" (ἄριστος 'Αχαιῶν: V 103).[2] For an audience

§5n1. VII 161: ὣς νείκεσσ' 'thus he made **neîkos** [reproach]'.
§5n2. It is precisely this kind of boasting that a hero seeks to avoid hearing from his opponent, in order to protect his epic prestige. Thus when Glaukos is wounded by the arrow of Teukros, an archer on the Achaean side (XII 387–389), the Trojan ally tries to hide "lest one of the Achaeans see him wounded and boast [verb **eukhetáomai**] with words [**épos** plural]" (XII 390–391). The use of **épos** [plural] is of special interest here: this word can refer not only to the words of a figure in epic but also to the poetic form of the given words (see Ch.15§7 and n1).

brought up on the tradition that Achilles himself was killed by the arrow of another archer,[3] the superlative of this boast has an ominous ring in the *Iliad*. In the other passage, the goddess Dione is consoling her daughter Aphrodite, who has just been wounded by Diomedes (V 406–415). He should beware, she says, lest a man stronger than her daughter should fight him (V 411); then Diomedes would be killed and his wife would have to mourn him, the "best of the Achaeans" (ἄριστον 'Αχαιῶν: V 414). Elsewhere in his **aristeíā**, Diomedes is described only one other time as "best" (ἄριστον: V 839), but not specifically as the best of the Achaeans. So much for Diomedes, whose heroic momentum is finally thwarted by Zeus himself at VIII 130–171.[4] As for Agamemnon, he, too, gets the general epithet "best" one other time besides the instances already discussed. This time, the setting is Book XI, the setting for his own **aristeíā**. And here, too, the specific moment is sinister. Hektor has just wounded Agamemnon, and he is exulting that his enemy, "the best man," has withdrawn from the fighting (ὥριστος: XI 288).[5] So much, then, for Agamemnon.

§6. We can finally turn to Ajax, second best to Achilles among all the Achaeans. Here is a man destined by epic tradition to lose the most important contest of his heroic existence, a contest of **aristeíā** with Odysseus.[1] But the *Iliad* allows him to win a lottery this time. His winning changes nothing in the course of oncoming events, since Ajax and Hektor then proceed to fight to a draw. At the end of their inconclusive duel, Hektor even compliments Ajax by calling him "best of the Achaeans" ('Αχαιῶν φέρτατος: VII 289), on the grounds that he excels in both might and artifice (VII 288–289). Ajax himself had boasted of his excellence in these very qualities (VII 197–198).[2] Since the audience has already been made aware that Ajax is second best, Hektor's words and the outcome of a draw have the effect of

§5n3. On the killing of Achilles by Paris: Ch.4§4.

§5n4. Diomedes himself admits defeat at XI 317–319 (on which see Ch.5§25). See also Whitman 1958.134.

§5n5. Even the diction of Homeric poetry affirms that the wounding of a hero thwarts his **aristeíā**. For example, when Paris wounded Makhaon, he παῦσεν ἀριστεύοντα 'stopped him from performing his **aristeíā**' (XI 506).

§6n1. Cf. *Little Iliad*/Proclus p. 106.20–23 Allen. For a review of the details, see Kullmann 1960.79–85.

§6n2. The excellence of Ajax in both might and artifice is thus implicitly bested by the excellence of Achilles in might. It will also be bested by the excellence of Odysseus in artifice (n1).

presaging the outcome of a fatal defeat for Hektor when he comes to confront Achilles himself. As for Ajax, he will fight on, even as the situation of the Achaeans keeps getting worse and worse in the face of Hektor's onslaught. But finally even Ajax is turned back by Zeus himself (XI 544; XVI 102, 119–121).[3] The stage is now set for Hektor's confrontation with Achilles—or with whoever must stand in for Achilles.[4]

§7. Besides Diomedes, Agamemnon, Ajax, and Achilles, no other Achaean in the *Iliad* gets the epithet "best of the Achaeans."[n] Others also may be best, but only in categories that are restricted as subdivisions of the Achaeans. Thus Periphas may be "best of the Aetolians" (V 843), Kalkhas may be "best of the bird-watching seers" (I 69), and Teukros may be "best of the Achaeans in archery" (XIII 313–314). Similarly, in the Games of Book XXIII, different Achaeans turn out to be best in different athletic events. Thus Diomedes is best at driving the chariot (XXIII 357), Epeios is best at boxing (XXIII 669), and Agamemnon is best at spear throwing, as Achilles himself acknowledges (XXIII 891). Such a restricted acknowledgment, however, is all that Agamemnon will ever get from Achilles in the *Iliad*.

§8. There are two isolated instances that at first seem like exceptions to the proposition that only four Achaean heroes vie for the epithet "best of the Achaeans" in the *Iliad*. In one passage, Menelaos is telling Antilokhos the ghastly news of Patroklos' death:

ἤδη μέν σε καὶ αὐτὸν ὀίομαι εἰσορόωντα
γιγνώσκειν ὅτι πῆμα θεὸς Δαναοῖσι κυλίνδει,
νίκη δὲ Τρώων· πέφαται δ' ὥριστος Ἀχαιῶν,
Πάτροκλος, μεγάλη δὲ ποθὴ Δαναοῖσι τέτυκται.

I think that you already see, and that you realize,
that a god is letting roll a pain upon the Danaans,

§6n3. The words of Ajax himself set the significance of his eventual withdrawal. Those who flee, he says, get no **kléos** (XV 564). All the same, the heroic status of Ajax as second best after Achilles is reaffirmed at XVII 279–280.

§6n4. It is said more than once in Book XI that by now all the heroes who are **áristoi** 'best' have been incapacitated: lines 658–659, 825–826 (cf. also XVI 23–24). Achilles himself observes in particular that Diomedes and Agamemnon have been put out of commission (XVI 74–77). His words contrast the inability of Diomedes with the ability of Patroklos "to ward off the devastation" at the Battle of the Ships (λοιγὸν ἀμῦναι/ἀμύνων at XVI 75/80). See Ch.5§12 and n1.

§7n. I do not count the sporadic instances of **áristos** in the plural, as at V 541 (Krethon and Orsilokhos are called Δαναῶν ἄνδρας ἀρίστους 'men who are best [**áristoi**] among the Danaans').

and that victory belongs to the Trojans: the best [áristos] of the Achaeans
has been killed,
Patroklos, that is; and a great loss has been inflicted on the Danaans.

XVII 687–690

Patroklos, however, had not vied overtly with Achilles for the title
"best of the Achaeans." Rather, he became the actual surrogate of
Achilles, his alter ego.[1] The death of Patroklos is a function of his
being the **therápōn** of Achilles: this word **therápōn** is a prehistoric
Greek borrowing from the Anatolian languages (most likely some-
time in the second millennium B.C.), where it had meant "ritual
substitute."[2] In death, the role of Patroklos becomes identified with
that of Achilles, as Cedric Whitman has eloquently reasoned.[3] The
death of Patroklos inside the *Iliad* foreshadows the death of Achilles
outside the *Iliad*.[4] At the very beginning of his fatal involvement, the
Patroklos figure had immediately attracted an epithet otherwise
appropriate to the prime antagonists of the *Iliad*. It is Achilles and
Hektor who are appropriately ἶσος Ἄρηϊ 'equal to Ares' in the *Iliad*,[5]
except for the one time when Patroklos leaves the tent of Achilles
and comes out of seclusion:

ἔκμολεν ἶσος Ἄρηϊ, κακοῦ δ᾽ ἄρα οἱ πέλεν ἀρχή

He [Patroklos] came out, equal to Ares, and that was the beginning of his
doom.[6]

XI 604

When Achilles recalls the prophecy that the "best [áristos] of the
Myrmidons" will die while he is still alive (XVIII 9–11), he is under
the spell of a premonition that Patroklos has just been killed. Within
the *Iliad*, however, the "best of the Achaeans" is surely also the
"best of the Myrmidons," in that the Myrmidons of Achilles are a

§8n1. See Ch. 17§4.
§8n2. See Van Brock 1959; cf. Householder/Nagy 1972.774–776 and Lowenstam
1975.
§8n3. Whitman 1958.136–137, 200–202. Note that Achilles is acknowledged as
áristos 'best' by Glaukos at XVII 164–165 on the basis of the feats performed by
Patroklos, who is called the **therápōn** of Achilles in this very context.
§8n4. See Pestalozzi 1945.
§8n5. For a listing of attestations: Ch.17§5.
§8n6. Cf. Nagy 1974.230–231; further discussion at Ch.17§5. Other than Hektor and
Achilles/Patroklos, the only other Iliadic figure who is called **îsos Árēï** 'equal to Ares'
is the hero Leonteus (XII 130). The evidence of Homeric diction indicates that the
epic traditions about Leonteus were parallel to those about Patroklos, in that both
figures are connected with the theme that the hero in death is a **therápōn** of Ares:
Ch.17§5n8.

subcategory in relation to the Achaeans. By dying, Patroklos gets the titles "best of the Myrmidons" and "best of the Achaeans" because he has taken upon himself not only the armor but also the heroic identity of Achilles.[7] The death of Achilles is postponed beyond the *Iliad* by the death of Patroklos.

§9. The other isolated instance that seems at first to be out of step with the rest of the *Iliad* occurs in Book X, the *Doloneia*. The Achaeans are deliberating about who should accompany Diomedes on a special expedition against the Trojans; both Ajaxes volunteer, as well as Meriones, Antilokhos, Menelaos, and, finally, Odysseus (X 228–232). Agamemnon at this point tells Diomedes to choose the "best" hero out of the group (ἄριστον: X 236) and not to pick someone inferior for reasons of etiquette, not even if the inferior one should be "more kinglike" (βασιλεύτερος: X 239). Agamemnon's motive is made clear by the narrative: "he feared for blond Menelaos" (X 240). For the second time now, we see Menelaos being spared from death. Without hesitation, Diomedes then names Odysseus, with whom he is sure to return in safety and who "excels at thinking" (περίοιδε νοῆσαι: X 247).[1] If that were all that there was to it, Odysseus might seem to be eligible for the title "best of the Achaeans." But at this point the words of Odysseus himself break in:

Τυδεΐδη, μήτ᾽ ἄρ με μάλ᾽ αἴνεε μήτε τι νείκει·
εἰδόσι γάρ τοι ταῦτα μετ᾽ ᾽Αργείοις ἀγορεύεις

Son of Tydeus! Give me neither too much praise nor too much blame;[2]
you are saying these things in the presence of Argives who know.

X 249–250

It is as if he were saying: "the Achaeans are aware of the tradition, so please do not exaggerate."[3] With the words of Odysseus himself, the epic tradition of the *Iliad* has pointedly taken Odysseus out of contention.[4] And the contention is here expressed by **neikéō** (νείκει:

§8n7. For more on the wearing of Achilles' armor by Patroklos: Ch.9§33n2.

§9n1. On the semantics of noun **nóos** 'thinking' and verb **noéō** 'think' in Homeric poetry: Frame 1978. On the use of **noéō** to express the notion of taking the initiative: Ch.3§13n.

§9n2. The verbs **ainéō** 'praise' and **neikéō** 'blame' indicate the poetry of praise and blame: Ch.12§3.

§9n3. It is an established theme of praise and blame poetry that the audience is well aware of the traditions with which it is presented: Ch.12§§18–19.

§9n4. The figure of Diomedes himself is here directly pertinent to the epic reputation of Odysseus, since there are numerous epic traditions featuring these two heroes on joint expeditions (for a list: Fenik 1964.12–13). Significantly, different epic

X 249), a verb derived from the same noun **neîkos** that was used to designate the quarrel of Achilles and Odysseus in the first song of Demodokos (νεῖκος: viii 75).[5]

§10. In contrast to the *Iliad*, it is an overall theme of the *Odyssey* that Odysseus is indeed **áristos Akhaiôn** 'best of the Achaeans'. In its elaboration of this theme, as I will try to show, the *Odyssey* deploys subtle references not only to a *Doloneia* tradition in particular[n] but also to an Iliadic tradition in general.

§11. In the *First Nekuia* of *Odyssey* xi, when Odysseus meets the shade of Achilles, he addresses Achilles as "best of the Achaeans" (φέρτατ' 'Αχαιῶν: xi 478). But the *Odyssey* then has Achilles saying that he would rather be alive and the lowliest of serfs than to be dead and the kingliest of shades (xi 489–491). As Klaus Rüter sees it,[1] Achilles seems ready to trade places with Odysseus, whose safe homecoming will be marked by a painful transitional phase at the very lowest levels of the social order. The words of Achilles in the *First Nekuia* are ironically conjuring up the glorious days of the *Iliad* when he had said:

ὤλετο μέν μοι νόστος, ἀτὰρ κλέος ἄφθιτον ἔσται

I have lost a safe return home [**nóstos**], but I will have unfailing glory [**kléos**].

IX 413

The destiny of the *Odyssey* is that Odysseus shall have a **nóstos** 'safe return home'.[2] From the retrospective vantage point of the *Odyssey*, Achilles would trade his **kléos** for a **nóstos**. It is as if he were now ready to trade an *Iliad* for an *Odyssey*. By contrast, at a moment when Odysseus is sure that he will perish in the stormy sea, he wishes that he had died at Troy (v 308–311):

... καί μευ κλέος ἦγον 'Αχαιοί

... and then the Achaeans would have carried on my **kléos**.

v 311

---

traditions give more or less credit to one or the other figure. In the *Little Iliad*, for example, it is Diomedes and not Odysseus who brings back Philoktetes (Proclus p.106.24–25 Allen); see Fenik, p. 13n2 and Severyns 1938.365–369.

§9n5. Besides meaning 'quarrel, fight, contention', the word **neîkos** also designates the poetry of blame: Ch.12§3.

§10n. Cf. Muellner 1976.96n43.

§11n1. Rüter 1969.252–253.

§11n2. On the semantics of **nóstos** in Homeric poetry: Frame 1978. On **nóstos** as not only 'homecoming' but also 'song about a homecoming': Ch.6§6n2.

§12. If Achilles has no **nóstos** in the *Iliad,* does it follow that Odysseus has no **kléos** in the *Odyssey?* How can someone have the **kléos** of the Achaeans if he calls someone else the "best of the Achaeans"? As in the *Doloneia,* Odysseus again seems to be taking himself out of contention—this time by giving the title to Achilles, at xi 478. Also at xi 550–551, he calls Ajax the most heroic Achaean "next to Achilles" (μετ' ἀμύμονα Πηλείωνα: xi 551). But Odysseus can afford to be generous in spirit to the two most heroic Achaeans of the *Iliad* tradition; the *Odyssey* will make him the most heroic Achaean in the *Odyssey.*

§13. In the *Second Nekuia* of *Odyssey* xxiv (15–202), the narrative again looks back to an *Iliad* tradition and beyond. We find here the shades of Achilles, Patroklos, Antilokhos, Ajax, and Agamemnon. Achilles himself concedes that Agamemnon too has left behind a **kléos** for the future (xxiv 33). Agamemnon in turn says that Achilles will have **kléos** for all time (xxiv 93–94); he adds that his own **nóstos** was sinister, that it resulted in an unheroic death (xxiv 95–97). At this point, the retrospective preoccupation switches from *Iliad* to *Odyssey.* The shades of Amphimedon and the other suitors arrive in the underworld, and Amphimedon retells the Revenge of Odysseus (xxiv 121–190). The story covers the heroic deeds of Odysseus, what amounts to his **kléos,** in the second half of the *Odyssey.* When the retrospective tale is done, the Agamemnon figure speaks again, and his effusive words function as a song of praise not only for Odysseus, to whom they are addressed, but also for Penelope:[1]

ὄλβιε Λαέρταο πάϊ, πολυμήχαν' Ὀδυσσεῦ,
ἦ ἄρα σὺν μεγάλῃ ἀρετῇ ἐκτήσω ἄκοιτιν·
ὡς ἀγαθαὶ φρένες ἦσαν ἀμύμονι Πηνελοπείῃ,
κούρῃ Ἰκαρίου· ὡς εὖ μέμνητ' Ὀδυσῆος,
ἀνδρὸς κουριδίου. τῷ οἱ κλέος οὔ ποτ' ὀλεῖται
ἧς ἀρετῆς, τεύξουσι δ' ἐπιχθονίοισιν ἀοιδὴν
ἀθάνατοι χαρίεσσαν ἐχέφρονι Πηνελοπείῃ,
οὐχ ὡς Τυνδαρέου κούρη κακὰ μήσατο ἔργα,
κουρίδιον κτείνασα πόσιν, στυγερὴ δέ τ' ἀοιδὴ
ἔσσετ' ἐπ' ἀνθρώπους, χαλεπὴν δέ τε φῆμιν ὀπάσσει
θηλυτέρῃσι γυναιξί, καὶ ἥ κ' εὐεργὸς ἔῃσιν.

§13n1. In Ch.14§5n1 and n3, I propose that this passage reflects a formal tradition of praise poetry centering on the theme of Penelope, as distinguished by the contrasting blame poetry about Clytemnestra.

O fortunate son of Laertes, Odysseus of many wiles!
It is truly with great merit [aretē] that you got a wife.
For the mind of blameless Penelope, daughter of Ikarios, was sound.
She kept her lawful husband, Odysseus, well in mind.
Thus the <u>kléos</u> of his **aretē** shall never perish,
and the immortals shall fashion for humans a song that is pleasing[2]   for
   sensible Penelope,
unlike the daughter of Tyndareos, who devised evil deeds,[3]
killing her lawful husband; and among humans,[4]
she will be a hateful song.[5] She will make for women an evil reputation,
females that they are—even for the kind of woman who does noble things.

xxiv 192-202

§13n2. The adjective χαρίεσσαν that describes **aoidé** 'song' here at line 198 is derived from **kháris**, a noun that conveys simultaneously the social aspect of *reciprocity* as well as the personal aspect of *pleasure*. Cf χαρίεσσαν ἀμοιβήν 'compensation that has **kháris**' at iii 58; on the reciprocity between poet and patron, see Ch.12§21n3. In the Homeric *Hymn to Hestia* (*Hymn* 24), the poet prays that his **aoidé** 'song' have **kháris** (line 5); by implication, the pleasure that it gives is linked with the reward he will receive. See further at Ch.5§39.

§13n3. These themes correspond to the actual name **Klutaiméstrē**, a form indicating that the wife of Agamemnon is "famed" (**Klutai-**, from the same root **kleu̯-* as in **kléos**) on account of what she "devised" (**-méstrē**, from verb **médomai**). The element -**méstrē**, from **médomai** 'devise', corresponds to the theme of κακὰ μήσατο ἔργα 'she devised [**médomai**] evil deeds' at line 199. As for the element **Klutai-** 'famed', it corresponds to the theme of στυγερή ... ἀοιδή 'hateful song' at line 200. This hateful song will be not simply *about* the wife of Agamemnon. Rather, the song is being presented as the very essence of **Klutaiméstrē**. (On the formal variant **Klutai-mnéstrē** as in the latinized *Clytemnestra*, see Nagy 1974.260; for more on the semantics of **médomai**, see Nagy, pp. 258–261.)

§13n4. To my knowledge, instances of **epì** + accusative in the sense of "among" are restricted in Homeric diction to **anthrópous** 'humans' as the object of the preposition. This syntactical idiosyncrasy can be correlated with an interesting thematic association: the expression **ep' anthrópous** 'among humans' is conventionally linked with **kléos** (X 213, i 299, xix 334, xxiv 94) and its derivatives (XXIV 202, xiv 403). It is also linked with **aoidé** 'song' at xxiv 201. Because of this parallelism between **kléos** and **aoidé**, and because **kléos** designates the glory conferred by poetry (Ch.1§2), I infer that **ep' anthrópous** 'among humans' in these contexts indicates an audience in general listening to poetry in general. Calvert Watkins suggests to me that the original force of **epí** in this collocation may indeed be directional.

§13n5. To continue with the inference that the collocation of **aoidé** 'song' at line 200 with **ep' anthrópous** 'among humans' at line 201 implies a sort of universal *audience* listening to the song about Clytemnestra: what men will *hear* about **Klutai-méstrē** is of course not the positive **kléos** of praise poetry (on which see Ch.12§3). Rather, it is blame poetry (see Ch.14§5n1). Ironically, when he had set out for Troy, Agamemnon had left behind an **aoidós** 'singer, poet' to guard Clytemnestra (iii 267–268). When Aigisthos persuaded her to betray Agamemnon by way of adultery, he took the **aoidós** to a deserted island (iii 270–271). In this way, the **aoidós** could not have *seen* the

As my translation shows, I find myself interpreting this passage to mean that Penelope is the key not only to the **nóstos** but also to the **kléos** of Odysseus. I understand **kléos** at verse 196 as belonging primarily to Odysseus himself and that it is his **areté** 'merit' to have won a Penelope (rather than a Clytemnestra).[6] If this interpretation is correct, then we see in the *Second Nekuia* a triadic assignment of **kléos** to Agamemnon, Achilles, and Odysseus. Odysseus gets the best **kléos**, through his wife. Through Penelope, he has a genuine **nóstos**, while Agamemnon gets a false one and Achilles, none at all.

§14. Such an interpretation is not ad hoc; rather, it takes into account the overall structure of the *Odyssey*. The Revenge of Odysseus is treated throughout the *Odyssey* as a genuinely heroic theme, worthy of **kléos**. And the prime stimulus for revenge is Penelope herself. Already in the *First Nekuia*, Odysseus is asking his mother in the underworld whatever happened to Penelope: is she steadfast . . .

ἢ ἤδη μιν ἔγημεν ᾿Αχαιῶν ὅς τις ἄριστος

or has whoever is the best [**áristos**] of the Achaeans already married her?

xi 179

The *Odyssey* can afford to let Odysseus put the question in this form, if indeed the narrative is confident of his heroic destiny in the *Odyssey*. Since his prime heroic act in the *Odyssey* is the killing of Achaeans who are pursuing his wife, Penelope is truly the key to his **kléos**. Penelope defines the heroic identity of Odysseus. Significantly, the expression ᾿Αχαιῶν ὅς τις ἄριστος 'whoever is best [**áristos**] of the

---

adultery, but the shameful behavior is nevertheless *heard* by the audience, which listens to the hateful **aoidé** 'song' about Clytemnestra. We see here a striking Homeric attestation of two traditional themes concerning the generic poet. One, he does not need to be an eyewitness and thus actually to *see* deeds in order to tell about them, since he can *hear* about them from the Muses (Ch.1§3). Two, he can regulate social behavior with his power to blame evil deeds (cf. Ch.14§12n4, Ch.15§8n8, Ch.16§10n6). On iii 267–268, see also Svenbro 1976.31 and n88.

§13n6. Compare the maxim told by Penelope to the disguised Odysseus at xix 329–334 (on which see further at Ch.14§6), where the good host gets the **kléos** of praise while the bad host gets the ridicule of blame. In being hospitable to the would-be beggar, Penelope is striving to match the former hospitality of Odysseus himself, who is described as the ultimate good host (xix 309–316). By implication, the **kléos** of being a good host belongs primarily to Odysseus. But Penelope herself is part of this **kléos**: at xix 325–328, she says that her own excellence will be recognized only if she is a good host to the would-be beggar. So also at xxiv 197–198: the **aoidé** 'song' about her is part of the overall **kléos** of Odysseus. A similar interpretation is possible at xix 107–114.

Achaeans' is restricted in the *Odyssey* to the single question: "who will marry Penelope?" (xvi 76, xviii 289, xix 528; cf. xx 335). The Homeric audience is being conditioned for the **aristeíā** of Odysseus.

§15. In particular, there are two passages that accentuate the inevitable outcome, the incontrovertible conclusion, that Odysseus is the "best of the Achaeans." At xv 521, Telemachus is telling the seer Theoklymenos that the suitor Eurymakhos, "by far the best man" (πολλὸν ἄριστος ἀνήρ), wants to marry Penelope. At this point in the narrative, a hawk appears, with a dove in its talons. The seer is quick to interpret: the omen is good, for it shows that no family in Ithaca is "more kingly," βασιλεύτερον, than that of Odysseus (xv 525–534). The omen has corrected the misuse, the misapplication, of the epithet "by far the best man."[1] There is an even more drastic correction in the case of the obnoxious Antinoos, another prominent suitor. The stage is set when Odysseus, in the guise of a beggar, is asking for alms from Antinoos:

δός, φίλος· οὐ μέν μοι δοκέεις ὁ κάκιστος Ἀχαιῶν
ἔμμεναι, ἀλλ᾽ ὤριστος, ἐπεὶ βασιλῆϊ ἔοικας

Give, friend! For you seem to be not the <u>worst</u> of the Achaeans,
but the <u>best</u> [**áristos**], since you seem like a king.

xvii 415–416

Noblesse oblige, but Antinoos crudely refuses. Later on in the *Odyssey*, he is the very first suitor to be shot dead by the arrows of an angry Odysseus (xxii 8–21). At this point, the other suitors are not yet aware that the archer is Odysseus himself; thinking that the shooting was accidental, they rail at Odysseus, exclaiming that he has just killed "the very best" of the Ithacan fighting men (ὃς μέγ᾽ ἄριστος / κούρων εἰν Ἰθάκῃ: xxii 29–30). In view of the previous action, the characterization "best" seems ironically misapplied. Antinoos may have looked like a king, but he did not behave like one.[2]

§16. To sum up: unlike Achilles, who won **kléos** but lost **nóstos** (IX 413), Odysseus is a double winner. He has won both **kléos** and **nóstos**. Accordingly, in his quest for his own heroic identity, Telemachus is confronted with a double frame of reference in the figure of his father:

§15n1. Cf. Whitman 1958.341n13 on the traditional device of misstating for the purpose of soliciting an omen to correct the misstatement.

§15n2. There is more irony when the **psūkhaí** of the suitors reach Hades. Agamemnon wonders whether they had all been "chosen" as the **áristoi** 'best men' in a community (xxiv 107–108).

νόστον πευσόμενος πατρὸς φίλου, ἤν που ἀκούσω

I am going to find out about the **nóstos** of my father, if I should hear.

ii 360

πατρὸς ἐμοῦ κλέος εὐρὺ μετέρχομαι, ἤν που ἀκούσω

I am going after the widespread **kléos** of my father, if I should hear.

iii 83

§17. Curiously, in all these instances where Odysseus is the "best of the Achaeans," he earns the title not for doing what he did at Troy but for doing what he did within the *Odyssey* itself. This restriction is all the more remarkable in view of the tradition, displayed prominently within the *Odyssey* itself, that Odysseus, not Achilles, can take credit for the destruction of Troy; Demodokos himself tells how it all happened in his third performance, a composition about the Trojan Horse (viii 499–520).[1] We too have already heard of it in verse 2 of Book i. Moreover, in the first song of Demodokos, "the **kléos** of which at that time reached the vast heavens" (viii 74), Odysseus was characterized along with Achilles as "best of the Achaeans" because one of these two heroes was destined to be the destroyer of Troy. In the epic composition of Demodokos, Odysseus is implicitly "best of the Achaeans" because tradition upholds his claim to have destroyed Troy. The poet Demodokos lives up to the challenge of Odysseus that he recite the story of the Trojan Horse κατὰ μοῖραν 'according to destiny' (viii 496). Within the conventions of epic composition, an incident that is untraditional would be ὑπὲρ μοῖραν 'beyond destiny'. For example, it would violate tradition to let Achilles kill Aeneas in *Iliad* XX, although the immediate situation in the narrative seems to make it inevitable; accordingly, Poseidon intervenes and saves Aeneas, telling him that his death at this point would be "beyond destiny" (ὑπὲρ μοῖραν: XX 336).[2] Demodokos, then, is hewing to tradition in giving

§17n1. More on this composition at Ch.6§9.

§17n2. For a stimulating discussion, see Pestalozzi 1945.40. On destiny and epic plot, see Kullmann 1956; cf. also Fränkel 1962.62–64. For a recent synthesis, I cite Mathews 1976. My translation of **moîra** as 'destiny' in the contexts of XX 336 and viii 496 does not reveal the full semantic range of the word, which will be discussed further at Ch.7§21. The context of viii 496 is pertinent to that discussion, in that Odysseus rewards Demodokos for his songs by giving him a choice cut of meat (viii 474–483). The poet receives this award at a feast, where the portions of food are actually designated as **moîrai** (viii 470). To repeat, Odysseus challenges Demodokos to recite the story of the Trojan Horse κατὰ μοῖραν 'according to **moîra**' (viii 496).

Odysseus the credit that is his due for having destroyed Troy. The triumph of the *Iliad*, however, is that Achilles becomes explicitly the "best of the Achaeans" without having destroyed Troy. Because of the *Iliad* tradition, it seems that the **kléos** of Odysseus at Troy was preempted by the **kléos** of Achilles. Such a triumph, however, could have been achieved only through sustained artistic reaction to the predilections of audiences who listened generation after generation to the **kléos** of the Achaeans.

§18. In this connection, it seems appropriate to reaffirm my general opinion about the *Iliad* and the *Odyssey*: the structural unity of such epics results, I think, not so much from the creative genius of whoever achieved a fixed composition but from the lengthy evolution of myriad previous compositions, era to era, into a final composition.[n] In other words, I think that the **kléos** of Achilles and the **kléos** of Odysseus, through generations of both shifting and abiding preferences in performer-audience interaction, have culminated in our *Iliad* and *Odyssey*. These epics are Panhellenic in the dimension of time as well as space. If, then, our *Iliad* and *Odyssey* are parallel products of parallel evolution, it becomes easier to imagine how the extraordinarily renowned **kléos** of Achilles could preempt the **kléos** of Odysseus at Troy. The audience will have to hear about the destruction of Troy by Odysseus not in the *Iliad* but in the *Odyssey*. This feat of Odysseus at Troy, which entitles him to be ranked with Achilles as "best of the Achaeans" in the first song of Demodokos, has been sidetracked in the *Iliad*—but not entirely.

§18n. Cf. Intro.§9.

3 | A Conflict between Odysseus and Achilles in the *Iliad*

§1. As we have already seen, some experts argue that the quarrel of Achilles and Odysseus in *Odyssey* viii is a pastiche actually based on the opening of our *Iliad*, where Achilles and Agamemnon have their memorable quarrel.[1] But in this line of reasoning there is a flaw that we have yet to single out: it presupposes that one text (the *Odyssey*) is here referring to another text (the *Iliad*). The same sort of flaw afflicts the argument of other experts who seek to show that the Odyssean passage in question refers to some lost passage in the Homeric Cycle (specifically, the *Cypria*).[2] Even if we were to accept for the moment the dubious notion that parts of the Homeric Cycle are drawn from some text that predates our *Iliad* and *Odyssey*, the fundamental objection remains the same: when we are dealing with the traditional poetry of the Homeric (and Hesiodic) compositions, it is not justifiable to claim that a passage in any text can refer to another passage in another text. Such a restriction of approaches in Homeric (and Hesiodic) criticism is one of the most important lessons to be learned from the findings of Milman Parry and Albert Lord on the nature of traditional "oral" poetry.[3]

§1n1. See Ch.1§§10–11.

§1n2. Ch.1§10.

§1n3. The lesson has not yet been learned, I fear, by what still seems to be a majority of Homerists. To list some prominent examples would be unproductive. Instead, I send the reader to the collection of Parry's writings (1971) and to Lord's synthesis (1960), which remain indispensable. For a useful formulation rejecting the methodology of positing *exemplum* and *imitatio* on a textual level, see Edwards 1971.189: "Given two poems A and B, now in a written text, however well a word or phrase fits its context in A, it is impossible to prove that it was invented for that place *at the moment when the text of A became fixed*. We can never rule out the existence of an older place X, which provided a common source for both A and B at the lines in question, so making their chronological relationship impossible to determine. This remains true even if X was only an older version of A." Instead of the wording "older

§2. I will confine myself, then, to examining whether a poem that is composed in a given *tradition* may refer to other *traditions* of composition. Thus, for example, our *Odyssey* may theoretically refer to traditional themes that are central to the stories of the *Cypria*—or even to the stories of the *Iliad*, for that matter. But even in that case, such traditional themes would have varied from composition to composition. There may theoretically be as many variations on a theme as there are compositions. Any theme is but a multiform, and not one of the multiforms may be considered a functional "Urform." Only by hindsight can we consider the themes of our *Iliad* to be the best of possible themes.

§3. In the specific case of *Odyssey* viii 72–82, we do indeed see what amounts to an Iliadic overture in the thematic combination of Achilles, Agamemnon, grief for Trojans and Achaeans, involvement of Apollo, and the Will of Zeus. Nevertheless, we may not infer that these themes were based specifically on the opening of our *Iliad*.[n] There are traditional elements in the epic opening reported by *Odyssey* viii 72–82 that go beyond the scope of the opening in *Iliad* I. These elements may still be considered "Iliadic" only in the sense that clear traces of them are indeed to be found in our *Iliad*. But they are not within the actual opening of *Iliad* I; instead, they surface here and there in the rest of the composition.

§4. For a striking illustration, I begin with the reference in *Odyssey* viii 78 to the quarreling Achilles and Odysseus as "the best of the Achaeans" (**áristoi Akhaiôn**), where the context of their quarrel is a **daís** 'feast' (viii 76). Let us compare a scene in *Iliad* VIII, where Agamemnon seeks to revive the fighting spirit of the demoralized Achaeans. He stands on the ship of Odysseus (VIII 222), which is exactly halfway between the ships of Ajax on one extreme and

---

place," however, I would prefer to substitute a phrase that does not connote the existence of an older *text*.

§3n. Marg 1956 takes the position that the **neîkos** 'quarrel' of viii 72–82 must be an "invention" based on the opening of the *Iliad*, since such a **neîkos** between Achilles and Odysseus is not directly attested anywhere else. This position is challenged by Maehler 1963.27n1, who points out that this argument from silence fails to take into account the traditional nature of such quarrel scenes between prominent Achaeans. On the topic of traditional quarrel scenes in epic, I find the discussion by Girard 1902.249 particularly suggestive. I would add that narratives about quarrels allow the genre of epic to accommodate the diction of other genres that are otherwise unsuitable to it, such as the diction of blame poetry—a genre that functions as the converse of praise poetry. Discussion at Ch.12§6.

Achilles on the other (VIII 223–226),[1] and begins his speech with these words:

αἰδώς, ᾿Αργεῖοι, κάκ᾿ ἐλέγχεα, εἶδος ἀγητοί·
πῇ ἔβαν εὐχωλαί, ὅτε δὴ φάμεν εἶναι ἄριστοι,
ἃς ὁπότ᾿ ἐν Λήμνῳ κενεαυχέες ἠγοράασθε,
ἔσθοντες κρέα πολλὰ βοῶν ὀρθοκραιράων,
πίνοντες κρητῆρας ἐπιστεφέας οἴνοιο,
Τρώων ἄνθ᾿ ἑκατόν τε διηκοσίων τε ἕκαστος
στήσεσθ᾿ ἐν πολέμῳ· νῦν δ᾿ οὐδ᾿ ἑνὸς ἄξιοί εἰμεν
῝Εκτορος, ὃς τάχα νῆας ἐνιπρήσει πυρὶ κηλέῳ.

Shame, Argives! Though splendid in appearance, you are base objects of blame.[2]
Where have the boasts gone, when we said that we are the best [áristoi]?[3]
These boasts you uttered, saying empty words, at Lemnos,
when you were eating the abundant meat of straight-horned oxen
and drinking from great bowls filled to the brim with wine,
how any one of you could each stand up against a hundred or even two
    hundred Trojans
in battle. But now we cannot even match one of them,
Hektor, who is about to set fire to our ships with burning fire.

VIII 228–235

In verses 231–232, we note that the setting for this scene of boasting is equivalent to a **daís**, which in viii 76 had served as the setting for the scene of quarreling between Odysseus and Achilles. In the present passage, the key words for understanding its affinity with viii 72–82 are at VIII 229: **áristoi** 'best', in collocation with the plural noun **eukhōlaí** 'boasts', derived from the verb **eúkhomai** 'boast'. Agamemnon's own claim to be "best of the Achaeans" is in fact formulated with this same verb:

ὃς νῦν πολλὸν ἄριστος ᾿Αχαιῶν εὔχεται εἶναι

who now boasts to be by far the best of the Achaeans

I 91

---

§4n1. I feel tempted to compare this arrangement with the relative ranking of Achaean heroes in the *Iliad* and the *Odyssey* traditions: Achilles and Ajax are best and second-best in the former, while Odysseus is best in the latter. See again Ch.2, esp. §6n2.

§4n2. Cf. Ch.14§14, esp. n3.

§4n3. On the use here of **phēmí** 'say' (φάμεν) as a substitute for **eúkhomai** 'boast': Muellner 1976.83.

ὃς μέγ᾽ ἄριστος ᾽Αχαιῶν εὔχεται εἶναι
who <u>boasts</u> to be by far the <u>best of the Achaeans</u>

II 82

From the intensive studies of Leonard Muellner on the behavior of **eúkhomai** 'boast' and its substitute **phēmí** 'say' in Homeric diction, we know that these words are used by or of a hero to express his superiority in a given area of heroic endeavor.[4] Take, for example, V 171–173, where we hear that no one in Lycia can boast (**eúkhetai:** 173) to be better than Pandaros in archery (171), and that the hero thus gets **kléos** in this area of endeavor (172).[5] We may compare **kléos** at *Odyssey* viii 74, correlated with **neîkos** 'quarrel' between the **áristoi Akhaiôn** 'best of the Achaeans', Odysseus and Achilles himself (viii 78). Granted, the scene of **eukhōlaí** 'boasts' at Lemnos is presented at VIII 228–235 not as a quarrel among various Achaeans with various areas of heroic superiority but rather as a collective affirmation of the Achaeans' superiority over the Trojans. Such a perspective of collectivity stays in effect, however, only so long as the narrative remains general by not quoting any individual hero. Once the Homeric narrative quotes a hero as he actually **eúkhetai** 'boasts', the factor of comparison and even rivalry with other heroes becomes overt.[6] Ironically, the boasts of all the other Achaeans during their onetime feast at Lemnos now sound empty because the hero who is "best" *when all heroic endeavors are taken into account* is not at hand to stop the overwhelming might of Hektor.

§5. Among the areas of heroic endeavor that serve as conventional points of comparison when a hero boasts, we actually find **bíē** 'might' (e.g., XV 165) and the equivalent of **mêtis** 'artifice, stratagem' (e.g., XVII 171).[1] In this connection, we may note again that the reference in *Odyssey* viii 78 to the quarreling Achilles and Odysseus as the "best of the Achaeans" seems to be based on an epic tradition that contrasted the heroic worth of Odysseus with that of Achilles in terms of a contrast between **mêtis** and **bíē**. The contrast apparently took the form of a quarrel between the two heroes over whether Troy would be taken by might or by artifice. The scholia to *Odyssey*

§4n4. Muellner, pp. 81–83.
§4n5. Discussion by Muellner, p. 82.
§4n6. See again Muellner, pp. 79–83.
§5n1. See Muellner, p. 83; for **phrénes** 'thinking' as an attribute of **mêtis**, consider the epithet **epíphrōn** 'having **phrénes**' as applied to **mêtis** at xix 326.

viii 75 and 77 point to such an epic tradition, where Achilles is advocating might and Odysseus, artifice, as the means that will prove successful in destroying Troy.[2] We have also considered the testimony of the scholia (A) to *Iliad* IX 347, from which we learn that Aristarchus apparently thought this particular Iliadic passage (IX 346–352) to be an allusion to precisely the same tradition that we are now considering, namely, the rivalry of Achilles and Odysseus as indicated in *Odyssey* viii 72–82.[3] In *Iliad* IX 346–352, we find Achilles in the act of rejecting the request of Odysseus that he rescue the hard-pressed Achaeans:

ἀλλ᾽, Ὀδυσεῦ, σὺν σοί τε καὶ ἄλλοισιν βασιλεῦσι
φραζέσθω νήεσσιν ἀλεξέμεναι δήϊον πῦρ.
ἦ μὲν δὴ μάλα πολλὰ πονήσατο νόσφιν ἐμεῖο,
καὶ δὴ τεῖχος ἔδειμε, καὶ ἤλασε τάφρον ἐπ᾽ αὐτῷ
εὐρεῖαν μεγάλην, ἐν δὲ σκόλοπας κατέπηξεν·
ἀλλ᾽ οὐδ᾽ ὣς δύναται σθένος Ἕκτορος ἀνδροφόνοιο
ἴσχειν

Let him [Agamemnon], Odysseus, along with you and the other kings
devise a way[4] to ward off the destructive fire from the ships.
He has indeed labored greatly in my absence,
and he has even built a wall and driven a ditch around it
—wide and big it is—and he has fastened stakes inside.
Even so he cannot hold back the strength of Hektor the man-killer.

IX 346–352

In effect, the words of Achilles defiantly and ironically challenge Odysseus, Agamemnon, "and the other kings" (IX 346) to rely on *artifice* at the very moment when they are desperately in need of his *might.*

§5n2. See Ch.1§11. Cf. Rüter 1969.249–251, Marg 1956.22, Girard 1902.253. These discussions do not raise the possibility, as I do here, that there was indeed an epic tradition—independent of our *Iliad* and *Odyssey*—about a quarrel between Achilles and Odysseus. Marg in fact explicitly rejects the possibility (p. 20). As I am about to argue, however, the internal evidence of *Iliad* IX contains clear traces of such an independent epic tradition. The information of the scholia, on the other hand, is admittedly garbled except for the clear delineation of "might" compared to "artifice": ἀνδρεία/σύνεσις, βιάζεσθαι/δόλῳ μετελθεῖν (scholia *ad* viii 75), σωματικά/ψυχικά, ἀνδρεία/μηχανὴ καὶ φρόνησις (scholia *ad* viii 77).

§5n3. See Ch.1§11. Cf. Lehrs 1882.174. Scholia (A) *ad* IX 347: πρὸς τὸ ἐν Ὀδυσσείᾳ ζητούμενον "νεῖκος Ὀδυσσῆος καὶ Πηλείδεω Ἀχιλῆος," ὅτι ἐμφαίνει καὶ νῦν ἀναιρῶν τὴν ἐπιχείρησιν τῶν περὶ Ὀδυσσέα, λεγόντων βουλῇ καὶ λόγῳ αἱρεθήσεσθαι τὴν πόλιν· νῦν γὰρ οἷον ἐπισαρκάζων λέγει.

§5n4. On *phrázomai* as a verb that denotes the activity of *mêtis*: Detienne/Vernant 1974.25n32 (in connection with Hesiod *W&D* 85–86). Cf. §7n2 below.

§6. There are still further allusions to the theme of a dispute over might against artifice. Our *Iliad* preserves, in evocative contexts, the very words which must have signaled the rival means to a common end. The word **bíē** 'might', on the one hand, is a conventional Iliadic measure of Achilles' superiority, as in the following juxtaposition:

πρεσβύτερος δὲ σύ ἐσσι· βίῃ δ' ὅ γε πολλὸν ἀμείνων

You [Patroklos] are older; but he [Achilles] is much better in **bíē**

XI 787

The word **mêtis** 'artifice, stratagem', on the other hand, characterizes Odysseus in particular: in the *Iliad* and the *Odyssey*, only he is described with the epithets **polúmētis** 'of many artifices' and **poikiló-mētis** 'of manifold artifices'. He is frequently called **Diï mêtin atálantos** 'equal to Zeus in artifice'. The polarity of **bíē** 'might' and **mêtis** 'artifice' is clearly visible in old Nestor's advice to his son about the art of chariot racing:

ἀλλ' ἄγε δὴ σύ, φίλος, μῆτιν ἐμβάλλεο θυμῷ
παντοίην, ἵνα μή σε παρεκπροφύγῃσιν ἄεθλα.
μήτι τοι δρυτόμος μέγ' ἀμείνων ἠὲ βίηφι·
μήτι δ' αὖτε κυβερνήτης ἐνὶ οἴνοπι πόντῳ
νῆα θοὴν ἰθύνει ἐρεχθομένην ἀνέμοισι·
μήτι δ' ἡνίοχος περιγίγνεται ἡνιόχοιο.

Come, my **phílos**, put in your **thūmós** every sort of **mêtis**,
so that prizes may not elude you.
It is with **mêtis** rather than **bíē** that a woodcutter is better.
It is with **mêtis** that a helmsman over the wine-dark sea
steers his swift ship buffeted by winds.
It is with **mêtis** that charioteer is better than charioteer.

XXIII 313–318

In such a traditional celebration of **mêtis** 'artifice' at the expense of **bíē** 'might', we see that superiority is actually being determined in terms of an opposition between these qualities.

§7. With these passages serving as background, we now move back to the evidence of IX 346–352,[1] where Achilles is defiantly challenging Odysseus and the other Achaean chieftains to survive the Trojan onslaught without the benefit of his own might. As his speech draws to a close, the final words of Achilles to Odysseus can be understood as conveying an underlying awareness and even bitterness. Let the

§7n1. §5.

Achaeans, Achilles tells Odysseus, devise "a better **mêtis**" to ward off the fire of the Trojans and thus save the Greek ships:

ὄφρ' ἄλλην φράζωνται ἐνὶ φρεσὶ μῆτιν ἀμείνω,
ἥ κέ σφιν νῆάς τε σαῷ καὶ λαὸν 'Αχαιῶν
νηυσὶν ἔπι γλαφυρῆς, ἐπεὶ οὔ σφισιν ἥδε γ' ἑτοίμη,
ἥν νῦν ἐφράσσαντο ἐμεῦ ἀπομηνίσαντος.

that they should devise² in their thoughts another **mêtis** that is better
and that will rescue their ships and the host of the Achaeans
who are at the hollow ships. For this one [this **mêtis**],
which they now devised² during the time of my anger, does not suffice.

IX 423–426

The reference is to Nestor's original stratagem to build the Achaean Wall, and this stratagem actually is designated in that context as **mêtis** (VII 324). Ironically, Nestor's later stratagem, to send the Embassy to Achilles, is also designated in the narrative as **mêtis** (IX 93). Ironically too, Odysseus is the one who is pleading for what the Achaeans most sorely need at this point, the might of Achilles. For the moment, the **mêtis** 'artifice' of Odysseus (and Nestor) is at a loss, and the **bíē** 'might' of Achilles is implicitly vindicated.

§8. Of course, the primary and central grievance of Achilles in our *Iliad* is against Agamemnon; any grievance of his against Odysseus that may have surfaced in Book IX must be secondary and marginal, as we can see clearly in IX 346–352.¹ Furthermore, even when we accept as traditional the theme of a quarrel between Achilles and Odysseus, we must keep in mind that the quarrel between Achilles and Agamemnon in *Iliad* I is in all likelihood an equally traditional theme.² It would be useless to argue that one theme or the other was older. All we can say is that the quarrel of Achilles and Odysseus is an alternative traditional theme that would have been suitable for testing the heroic worth of Achilles in a different dimension. Whereas the conflict of Achilles and Agamemnon contrasts martial with social superiority,³ the conflict between Achilles and Odysseus is on a

§7n2. Compare the use of **phrázomai** 'devise' here at IX 423 and 426 with its use at IX 347. At §5n4, we have noted that this word functions as a verb of **mêtis**.
§8n1. §5.
§8n2. For a discussion of epic precedents: Davidson 1980.
§8n3. On the traditional nature of this contrast, see again Davidson, pp. 26–28 on the Indo-European epic theme of an opposition between *dux* and *rēx*; cf. also Muellner 1976.83n27.

different axis of opposition: **biē** 'might' against **mētis** 'artifice'. I submit that the epic theme of such a conflict is maintained as an undertone in *Iliad* IX, by means of including Odysseus in the Embassy to Achilles.

§9. In fact, this theme may help account for a notorious problem involving the Embassy Scene of *Iliad* IX. The problem is, simply put, that this passage features some dual constructions in places where we might have expected the plural.[1] Instead of plunging into the vast bibliography on the subject,[2] I propose simply to examine the passage anew, attempting to correlate how the dual constructions are deployed in the story with how the story itself applies to the tradition of a conflict between Odysseus and Achilles. I should note at the outset, however, that the evidence for this conflict has already been established in the preceding discussion and stands by itself. It does not depend on the discussion that follows. As for what I am about to argue, there is considerable room for disagreement. But I hope to show, at the very least, that the Embassy Scene as we have it is not a clumsy patchwork of mutually irreconcilable texts but rather an artistic orchestration of variant narrative traditions.

§10. We take up the story at a point where King Agamemnon and the Achaeans finally despair of resisting the onslaught of Hektor and the Trojans without the aid of Achilles, who has withdrawn from the fighting. At a meeting of the elders, Nestor suggests that an embassy be sent to Achilles, bringing to him an offer of settlement from Agamemnon (IX 93–113). Agamemnon agrees and makes a lavish offer (IX 114–161), whereupon Nestor suggests that there be three emissaries: Phoinix, Ajax, and Odysseus (IX 162–172). Nestor's original plan calls for Phoinix to go first, followed by Ajax and Odysseus, followed by the heralds Odios and Eurybates:

§9n1. Besides the various interpretations of Book IX based on the premise that the dual constructions designate an actual pair, we also come upon the argument that these dual *forms* may have a plural *function*. There is, however, no grammatical justification for such a claim, and the sporadic instances in Homeric poetry where duals may seem to function as plurals cannot be cited as parallels to the situation in Book IX. In each instance, there is an ad hoc explanation available, so that the theory of dual-for-plural remains unproved. See Page 1959.324–325 for discussion and bibliography.

§9n2. For a conscientious survey, I cite Lesky 1967.103–105. Segal's (1968) comparison of the compressed Embassy Scene of *Iliad* I (320–348) with the expanded scene of *Iliad* IX helps us understand better the traditional narrative themes that are deployed (see especially his p. 104), but his discussion leaves room for disagreement on the question of the dual constructions in IX.

εἰ δ' ἄγε, τοὺς ἂν ἐγὼ ἐπιόψομαι, οἱ δὲ πιθέσθων.
Φοῖνιξ μὲν πρώτιστα Διὶ φίλος ἡγησάσθω,
αὐτὰρ ἔπειτ' Αἴας τε μέγας καὶ δῖος Ὀδυσσεύς·
κηρύκων δ' Ὀδίος τε καὶ Εὐρυβάτης ἅμ' ἑπέσθων.

But come, let those upon whom I am looking take on the task.
First of all, let Phoinix, dear to Zeus, take the lead;
and after him the great Ajax and brilliant Odysseus,
and of the heralds let Odios and Eurybates accompany them.

IX 167–170

The crucial expression is Φοῖνιξ . . . ἡγησάσθω at verse 168: "let Phoinix . . . take the lead." As the emissaries proceed on their way to Achilles, the one who actually takes the lead is not Phoinix but Odysseus:

τὼ δὲ βάτην προτέρω, ἡγεῖτο δὲ δῖος Ὀδυσσεύς.

And the two were moving along, and brilliant Odysseus led the way.

IX 192

The word ἡγεῖτο here at IX 192 is in direct contrast with the corresponding ἡγησάσθω of IX 168 ("he led the way" compared to "let him lead the way" respectively). In contradiction of the original plan, Odysseus is now leading the way instead of Phoinix.

§11. As we consider the dual construction τὼ δὲ βάτην προτέρω 'and the two were moving along' here in the second passage (IX 192), let us not immediately assume that we are dealing with the emergence of an earlier version involving two emissaries as opposed to the first passage (IX 167–170), which is supposed to present a later version involving three emissaries. Instead, at least for the moment, let us take the thematic progression from the first passage to the second passage as a given of the narrative at hand. In that case, the dual in the second passage must refer to Ajax and Phoinix, not to Ajax and Odysseus. The plan of the first passage had called for Ajax and Odysseus to be led by Phoinix. Instead, we now see Ajax and Phoinix being led by Odysseus.

§12. Rather than assume that Phoinix, in Denys Page's words, "mislaid himself"[n] in the forgetful mind of the composer, let us suppose that Odysseus simply asserted himself in the actual narrative of the composition. Old Nestor, as the originator of the plan to send an embassy, had after all made a point of stressing the role of Odysseus when the emissaries were sent off:

§12n. Page 1959.298.

τοῖσι δὲ πόλλ᾽ ἐπέτελλε Γερήνιος ἱππότα Νέστωρ,
δενδίλλων ἐς ἕκαστον, ᾽Οδυσσῆϊ δὲ μάλιστα,
πειρᾶν ὡς πεπίθοιεν ἀμύμονα Πηλείωνα.

And the Gerenian horseman Nestor gave them many instructions,
making signs with his eyes at each, <u>especially at Odysseus</u>,
that they try to persuade the blameless son of Peleus.

IX 179–181

§13. The self-assertion of Odysseus goes beyond taking the lead in the procession to the tent of Achilles. When the emissaries are about to deliver their message to Achilles, Ajax gives Phoinix the signal to begin, but it is Odysseus who takes the initiative:

νεῦσ᾽ Αἴας Φοίνικι· *νόησε δὲ δῖος ᾽Οδυσσεύς*

Ajax nodded to Phoinix; <u>and brilliant Odysseus took note</u> . . . [n]

IX 223

Instead of Phoinix, it is Odysseus who now gives the first speech (IX 225–306); only then does Phoinix speak (IX 434–605), then Ajax (IX 624–642). In the end, Phoinix stays behind with Achilles, and it is Odysseus who leads the Embassy back to the tent of Agamemnon:

. . . οἱ δὲ ἕκαστος ἑλὼν δέπας ἀμφικύπελλον
σπείσαντες παρὰ νῆας ἴσαν πάλιν· *ἦρχε δ᾽ ᾽Οδυσσεύς.*

. . . and they each took a double-handled cup
and made a libation; then they went back to the ships, <u>and Odysseus led the way</u>.

IX 656–657

As the leader of the Embassy, it is he who reports to Agamemnon the reply of Achilles (IX 673 ff.).

§14. This pattern of self-assertion on the part of Odysseus reflects in particular on one of his many traditional roles, that of the trickster. By taking the lead among the emissaries, he puts himself in the position of being the one who actually delivers the terms of compensation proposed by Agamemnon for settlement with Achilles (IX 260–299, reporting IX 120–158). In doing so, Odysseus makes a

---

§13n. For the use of **noéō** 'take note, think' in contexts of "taking the initiative," see especially X 224–226, 247; V 669 (with reference to Odysseus); also IX 104–108 (with reference to Nestor). For the traditional combination of **neúō** 'nod' and **noéō** 'take note' in situations where signals are sent and received respectively, see *Odyssey* xvi 164–165 (Athena nods to Odysseus, who gets the message and then takes the initiative); also xvi 283. Cf. Köhnken 1975.32. For an important study of Homeric **nóos** and related words, I cite again Frame 1978.

significant adjustment to Agamemnon's original message by failing to repeat Agamemnon's reaffirmation of social superiority over Achilles (IX 160–161). As Cedric Whitman argues, the acceptance of such compromised terms by Achilles would thus have aborted his heroic stature in the *Iliad*.[n] The success of Odysseus in the Embassy would have entailed the failure of Achilles in his own epic. Accordingly, the suspicion of Achilles upon hearing the speech of Odysseus seems justified:

ἐχθρὸς γάρ μοι κεῖνος ὁμῶς ᾿Αἴδαο πύλῃσιν
ὅς χ᾿ ἕτερον μὲν κεύθῃ ἐνὶ φρεσίν, ἄλλο δὲ εἴπῃ

For he is as hateful [ekhthrós] to me as the gates of Hades,
whoever hides one thing in his thoughts and says another.

IX 312–313

§15. These strong words are framed by Achilles' outright rejection of the speech by Odysseus (IX 308–311, 314–429). Moreover, even before he heard the offer that he rejects so forcefully, Achilles may have already considered Odysseus to be the sort of **ekhthrós** 'hateful one, enemy' that is described in IX 312–313. We come back to the moment when Achilles sees the Embassy approaching:

στὰν δὲ πρόσθ᾿ αὐτοῖο· ταφὼν δ᾿ ἀνόρουσεν ᾿Αχιλλεὺς
αὐτῇ σὺν φόρμιγγι, λιπὼν ἕδος ἔνθα θάασσεν.
ὡς δ᾿ αὔτως Πάτροκλος, ἐπεὶ ἴδε φῶτας, ἀνέστη.
τὼ καὶ δεικνύμενος προσέφη πόδας ὠκὺς ᾿Αχιλλεύς·
"χαίρετον· ἦ φίλοι ἄνδρες ἱκάνετον· ἦ τι μάλα χρεώ.
οἵ μοι σκυζομένῳ περ ᾿Αχαιῶν φίλτατοί ἐστον."

And they stood in front of him, and Achilles jumped up, amazed,
still holding the lyre, leaving the place where he was sitting.
Likewise Patroklos, when he saw the men, stood up.
Greeting the two of them, swift-footed Achilles said:
"Hail to the two of you: you have come as friends. I need you very much—
you two who are the dearest to me among the Achaeans, even now when I am angry."

IX 193–198

The last three verses of this passage all contain dual constructions, as if there were only two emissaries rather than three. Furthermore, the two are addressed by Achilles as "most dear [**philos**]" to him among all the Achaeans, ᾿Αχαιῶν φίλτατοι (IX 198).[1] If indeed Achilles later

---

§14n. Whitman 1958.191–192; cf. Rosner 1976.320.
§15n1. For the function of the untranslatable word **philos** 'dear, friend' and its

implies that Odysseus may be an "enemy" (**ekhthrós**) to him, is Odysseus being excluded from his greeting? Certainly the definition that we find for **ekhthrós** 'enemy' in IX 312–313[2]—a definition framed by the words of Achilles himself—applies to the epic behavior of Odysseus. As we see most clearly in his own epic, the *Odyssey*, he continually says one thing and means another.[3]

§16. Let us pursue the hypothesis that the duals in IX 196–198[1] refer to Ajax and Phoinix, and that Odysseus is being excluded by Achilles in his reference to the Achaeans who are "most dear [**philos**]" to him (φίλτατοι: IX 198). On the level of form, we can say that the dual pronoun τώ of IX 196 recapitulates the τώ of IX 192,[2] which immediately precedes in the narrative. In IX 192, the dual τώ sets off Ajax and Phoinix from Odysseus; as I have already argued, it is here that Odysseus first seizes the initiative and takes the lead in the Embassy, with his fellow emissaries being relegated to the dual τώ.[3] Now the dual τώ in IX 196 takes up where the last dual left off in IX 192, and we may continue with the understanding that it refers to Ajax and Phoinix.

§17. On the level of content, this interpretation is viable if an "Embassy of Ajax and Phoinix to Achilles" had been a stock theme of Greek epic tradition and if the story of an enmity between Odysseus and Achilles had likewise been traditional. If we find evidence to support these two propositions, then we could also claim that the Embassy episode of *Iliad* IX has, from the standpoint of, say, an audience in the eighth century B.C., much higher artistic

derivatives in Homeric narrative, see Ch.6§13; see also Sinos 1975.65–81 on the ethical principle of **philótēs** that informs our *Iliad*.

§15n2. §14.

§15n3. See again §14; this trait of Odysseus corresponds to his epithet **polúainos** (Ch.12§19n1).

§16n1. §15.

§16n2. §10.

§16n3. Granted, the subject + verb construction of 'Οδυσσεὺς + ἡγεῖτο 'Odysseus led the way' at IX 192 does not by itself rule out the possibility that Odysseus is *included in* rather than *excluded from* the dual construction that immediately precedes. Köhnken (1975.35) argues for inclusion, citing XXIV 95–96: there Iris is the leader (ἡγεῖτο) of two, Thetis *and herself*. But I must point out that this situation is not directly analogous, since the actions of the other member of the pair, Thetis, are designated in the singular, not the dual. Thus I am still bound to understand the dual constructions of IX 192 as referring to Ajax and Phoinix. On the other hand, Köhnken's citing of ἡγεῖτ(ο) 'led the way' at XXIV 96 is useful for our understanding of IX 657, where Odysseus leads (ἦρχε) the Embassy back to the tent of Agamemnon. Besides himself and the heralds, only Ajax is left.

merit than what we can see in a text without attested precedents. Then we could confidently reject any superficial impression of ours that the Embassy is an imperfect story, marred by a clumsy deployment of misplaced duals.

§18. If the stock theme of an "Embassy of Ajax and Odysseus to Achilles" had been original to the Iliadic tradition for this particular period in the course of the Trojan War narrative—as Page and other analysts infer—then the final Iliadic treatment that we see attested in Book IX, with the "Embassy of Ajax, Odysseus, and Phoinix to Achilles," should have required the conversion of all duals into plurals, especially at the moment when Achilles greets the emissaries (IX 193–198). Instead, Achilles greets them in the dual! The purported grafting of Phoinix into this scene is thus only partially successful, in that the role of Phoinix fails to get its proper due. As Page exclaims, "Unhappy Phoenix, Achilles' oldest friend, not a single word of you!"[n] We are left with the impression that the story has faults beyond remedy.

§19. If, on the other hand, the stock theme of an "Embassy of Ajax and Phoinix to Achilles" had been traditional, then we see in *Iliad* IX the insertion of Odysseus on the level of form and the self-assertion of Odysseus on the level of content. Of course, we may in the meantime reject the assumption of some analysts that any such insertion is a *textual* phenomenon: all we need say is that the composition integrates another traditional element. If, in turn, the insertion of Odysseus into the Embassy story carries with it the traditional theme of an enmity between him and Achilles, then the narrative of *Iliad* IX may allow the retention of duals referring to the pair of Ajax and Phoinix when the time comes for Achilles to greet the Embassy. For an audience familiar with another version of the story where Achilles had only two emissaries to greet, the retention of the dual greeting when Odysseus is included in the Embassy surely amounts to an artistic masterstroke in the narrative. The exclusion of Odysseus in the dual greeting would serve to remind the audience of the enmity between him and Achilles.

§20. We should consider whether there are any formal traces of material for a traditional story where only Ajax and Phoinix are emissaries to Achilles. For this purpose, let us contrast the way in which the narrative in Book IX handles the pair of Ajax and Phoinix

§18n. Page 1959.300.

with the way in which it handles the pair of Ajax and Odysseus. When Odysseus is set off from Ajax and Phoinix, the latter pair is designated in the dual. This is what I propose to be the case in IX 192[1] and 196–198.[2] Conversely, when the narrative overtly sets off Phoinix from Ajax and Odysseus, it designates this pair consistently in the plural. Besides IX 656–657,[3] I can also cite the following:

ἀλλ' ὑμεῖς μὲν ἰόντες ἀριστήεσσιν 'Αχαιῶν
ἀγγελίην ἀπόφασθε—τὸ γὰρ γέρας ἐστὶ γερόντων—

But you must go back to the chieftains of the Achaeans
and give them this message—for that is the privilege of the Elders—[4]

IX 421–422

The ὑμεῖς μὲν ... here is immediately contrasted with Φοῖνιξ δ(ὲ) ..., which follows at IX 427. Achilles is asking Phoinix to stay with him, while the other emissaries are to go back carrying the message of his refusal. Elsewhere too, Achilles distinguishes Phoinix from the others, to whom he refers not in the dual but in the plural:

οὗτοι δ' ἀγγελέουσι, σὺ δ' αὐτόθι λέξεο μίμνων
εὐνῇ ἔνι μαλακῇ

These men will take the message; but you must stay here
and lie down on the soft bed.

IX 617–618

In sum, dual constructions fail to appear in every triadic situation where Ajax and Odysseus are *explicitly* set off from Phoinix. This evidence, then, goes against the possible counterclaim that the dual constructions of IX 192 and 196–198[5] might refer *implicitly* to Ajax and Odysseus. It therefore remains tenable to claim that they refer instead to Ajax and Phoinix. Furthermore, these references may be *explicit* in the narrative of Book IX, if indeed there existed a traditional epic story that told of Achilles being angry at Odysseus. Then the dual constructions of IX 196–198 express a pointed exclusion of Odysseus from those who are "most dear [**phílos**]" to Achilles (φίλτατοι: IX 198).[6]

§20n1. §10.
§20n2. §15.
§20n3. §13.
§20n4. We may note with interest the collocation of **gérōn** 'elder' with **géras** 'privilege, honorific portion' at IX 422.
§20n5. §§10 and 15 respectively.
§20n6. There is an ad hoc explanation for the duals in the Homeric *Hymn to Apollo* (verses 456, 487, 501) that may be pertinent to the problem of the duals in *Iliad* IX.

§21. This much said, I leave the problem of the dual constructions in *Iliad* IX and return to the broader problem of establishing the relationship between the expanded passage of the Embassy Scene and the compressed passage of *Odyssey* viii 72–82. So far we have been dealing with only one specific theme that seems to be shared by these two passages, namely, a conflict between Achilles and Odysseus. Besides this theme, however, there are a number of accessory themes that also seem to be shared by these two passages. Let us examine these comparable themes by using as our frame of reference the compressed narrative of *Odyssey* viii 72–82.

1) The dispute of Achilles and Odysseus took place at a sacrificial feast or **daís** (θεῶν ἐν δαιτὶ θαλείῃ: viii 76). Compare this setting of a **daís** 'feast, portion' with the first words of Odysseus to Achilles in the Embassy Scene:

χαῖρ', Ἀχιλεῦ· δαιτὸς μὲν ἐΐσης οὐκ ἐπιδευεῖς
ἠμὲν ἐνὶ κλισίῃ Ἀγαμέμνονος Ἀτρεΐδαο
ἠδὲ καὶ ἐνθάδε νῦν· πάρα γὰρ μενοεικέα πολλὰ
δαίνυσθ'· ἀλλ' οὐ δαιτὸς ἐπηράτου ἔργα μέμηλεν,
ἀλλὰ λίην μέγα πῆμα, διοτρεφές, εἰσορόωντες
δείδιμεν

Hail, Achilles! You will not be without a fair **daís**
either in the tent of Agamemnon son of Atreus
or here and now. There is at hand much that would suit you,
for you to have as **daís**. But the concern is not about a pleasant **daís**.
Rather, we are facing a great **pêma** [pain], O **diotrephḗs**,
and we are in doubt.

IX 225–230

The sacrificial nature of the **daís** 'feast' in the tent of Achilles is implicit (IX 219–220),[1] and the triple reference to the procedure of a

---

These dual constructions in the *Hymn to Apollo* occur in the quoted words spoken by the god to the Cretans. The narrative is presenting a dialogue between Apollo and the "leader of the Cretans" (Κρητῶν ἀγός: 463), who is speaking on behalf of the other Cretans. Accordingly, Apollo's random dual references to them may be elliptic: the leader (A) plus the others (B). Elliptic duals (A+B instead of A+A) and elliptic plurals (A+B+C ... instead of A+A+A ...) are an Indo-European heritage in the Greek language; see Schwyzer/Debrunner 1950.50–52. Conceivably, Achilles may be "grammatically correct" when he gives a dual greeting to the leader of the Embassy (A) plus the others (B) at IX 196–198. Cf. Thornton 1978. But the ambiguities remain: maybe someone is still being excluded. Cf. also Köhnken 1978, replying to Thornton's article.

§21n1. See further at Ch.7§19.

daís within the first four verses of the speech by Odysseus to Achilles may suggest an echo of a well-established theme.[2]

2) the dispute of Achilles and Odysseus was an omen that Troy would be destroyed—but not before enormous grief, **pêma**, afflicted not only the Trojans but also the Achaeans (πήματος ἀρχή: viii 81). Compare the **pêma** that afflicts the Achaeans at IX 229.[3]

3) The omen that Troy would be destroyed was predicted for Agamemnon by Phoebus Apollo "at holy Delphi, when he [Agamemnon] had crossed the stone threshold to ask the oracle" (viii 79–81). Compare the incidental reference of Achilles to Delphi in his answer to Odysseus:

οὐδ' ὅσα λάϊνος οὐδὸς ἀφήτορος ἐντὸς ἐέργει,
Φοίβου Ἀπόλλωνος, Πυθοῖ ἔνι πετρηέσσῃ

nor all the things contained within the stone threshold of the Archer,
Phoebus Apollo, in rocky Delphi.

IX 404–405

This passage contains the only reference to Delphi in our *Iliad* (except for the purely geographical reference in the Great Catalogue, II 519).

4) The quarreling Achilles and Odysseus are called "best of the Achaeans" (ἄριστοι Ἀχαιῶν: viii 78). Compare the speech of Phoinix, where he calls the emissaries the "best" (ἀρίστους: IX 520) as well as the "most dear [**philos**]" to Achilles among all the Argives (φίλτατοι Ἀργείων: IX 522). These two superlatives, however, both seem to be only partially applicable to the three emissaries. The title "best" may suit Ajax and Odysseus but not necessarily Phoinix.[4] The title "most dear," on the other hand, may well apply to Ajax and

§21n2. Again, Ch.7§19.

§21n3. Quoted at item (1) above.

§21n4. One of the main points made by Köhnken (1975) is that the reference by Phoinix to the "best" (ἀρίστους: IX 520) applies more to Ajax and Odysseus than to himself. But we also have to reckon with the reference, again made by Phoinix, to the "most dear" (φίλτατοι: IX 522), which in turn seems to apply more to Ajax and himself than to Odysseus. Thus the problem of the dual greeting by Achilles remains (IX 197–198), since the emissaries are called "most dear of the Achaeans" here (Ἀχαιῶν φίλτατοι: IX 198). Even if the greeting by Achilles were casual, it would be hard to justify the exclusion of his beloved mentor. Besides, Köhnken's own catalogue of other Iliadic passages where Phoinix is mentioned (p. 28) shortens the gap between the heroic stature of Ajax and Odysseus on the one hand and that of Phoinix on the other.

Phoinix only, with the exclusion of Odysseus. On this basis alone, the ethical stance of the Embassy may well be undermined—from the heroic perspective of Achilles.

§22. Taken separately, any one of these four convergences in detail between the compressed narrative of *Odyssey* viii 72–82 and the expanded narrative of the Embassy Scene in *Iliad* IX is not enough to make a case for the existence of a common epic heritage. Taken together, however, all four of them serve to corroborate the argument that both the compressed and the expanded narratives draw from a stock epic theme—details and all—about an enmity between Achilles and Odysseus. Even without these four convergences, we have strong evidence for this theme in a fifth convergence. As we have already observed in the Embassy Scene, Achilles replies to Odysseus with an ad hoc definition of **ekhthrós** 'enemy' that actually fits the epic role of Odysseus, the consummate dissembler (IX 312–313).[n] The words of Achilles and the corresponding epic actions of Odysseus combine to make the message of *Iliad* IX explicit. As in *Odyssey* viii 72–82, the first song of Demodokos, a traditional enmity exists between these two preeminent heroes of Greek epic.

§22n. §14.

4 | The Death of Achilles and a Festival at Delphi

§1. The quarrel between Achilles and Odysseus in the first song of Demodokos, viii 72–82, dramatizes the antithesis of two inherited central themes built into the *Iliad* and the *Odyssey*, namely, the qualifications of Achilles and Odysseus respectively for the title "best of the Achaeans." Their epic actions are striving to attain what is perhaps the most distinctive heroic epithet that the **kléos** of the Achaeans can confer upon a mortal. In the first song of Demodokos, the poet—or let us say Demodokos—comments not only on the *Odyssey* but also on the *Iliad* itself. Or better, I should say, "an Iliadic tradition" instead of "the *Iliad*." Moreover, Monro's Law is not overturned, in that this quarrel between Odysseus and Achilles in *Odyssey* viii is no playback of the quarrel between Agamemnon and Achilles in *Iliad* I. There are basic differences in roles as well as in characters.

§2. As we have seen, there are elements of diction and theme in the first song of Demodokos that must stem from an independent and idiosyncratic tradition and simply cannot be based on the opening of *Iliad* I. One of the most divergent and interesting aspects of the quarrel between Achilles and Odysseus is that it took place "at a sumptuous feast of the gods" (θεῶν ἐν δαιτὶ θαλείῃ: viii 76). Besides the intrinsic meaning here, the other Homeric contexts where feasts of the gods are mentioned make it clear that this expression denotes a sacrifice.[n]

§3. By good fortune, we have indirect evidence about the nature of such a sacrifice, especially from Pindar's *Paean* 6. This piece was composed for performance at a Delphic festival called the **theoxénia**. Within the framework of this ancient festival, the gods were treated

§2n. See especially iii 336 and 420; also xiv 251. Cf. Ch.3§21.

59

as actual participants at the sacral banquet of their worshippers.[1] The institution of **theoxénia** 'having a host-and-guest relationship with the gods' survives elsewhere too in the Hellenic world of the classical period,[2] and there is reason to suppose that its ritual traditions—if not the ritual itself in its attested form—were already attested at the time that our *Odyssey* took on its present shape.[3] Since the first song of Demodokos in *Odyssey* viii makes a thematic connection between Apollo's Delphi and a 'feast of the gods' attended by Achaean heroes, the preeminence of Apollo at the Delphic **theoxénia**[4] leads me to suspect that we are witnessing a Homeric reflex of the ritual traditions surrounding this festival.[5] Furthermore, there are ominous implications for Achilles in the lore connected with the **theoxénia**. It seems as if the death of Achilles were a traditional theme that is appropriate for a paean performed at the **theoxénia**.

§4. Pindar's fragmentary *Paean* 6 was evidently composed for an **agón** 'contest' at the Panhellenic festival of the Delphic **theoxénia**; the poet describes himself as:

ἀγῶνα Λοξία καταβάντ' εὐρὺν
ἐν θεῶν ξενίᾳ

entering the broad contest place of Loxias [Apollo]
at the **theoxénia**

Pindar Paean 6.60–61SM

By the very fact that it is a paean, the poem is a glorification of Apollo.[1] In particular, it commemorates a tradition concerning a quarrel of the gods:

καὶ πόθεν ἀθαν[άτων ἔρις ἄ]ρξατο.[2]

§3n1. For a suggestive discussion, adducing the comparative evidence of other festivals parallel to the **theoxénia**: Gernet 1968 [=1928] 32–33.

§3n2. For a survey: Nilsson 1906.160–162.

§3n3. This supposition is developed further at Ch.7§§8–13, 17–20, 25–30.

§3n4. Apollo is preeminent at the Delphic **theoxénia** not necessarily because of any special affinity with the practice of **theoxénia** but rather simply because of his preeminence at Delphi itself.

§3n5. The citations at n3 apply here as well.

§4n1. On this function of the paean, cf. also Ch.5§9. On the Panhellenic nature of the Delphic **theoxénia**, consider the lines that immediately follow those just quoted, at *Paean* 6.62–63: θύεται γὰρ ἀγλαᾶς ὑπὲρ Πανελλάδος 'sacrifice is being made on behalf of splendid All-Hellas' (cf. Radt 1958.131–134). The poem goes on to say that the festival had been instituted as a result of a promise contained in a prayer offered by the community at a time long ago when it had been afflicted by a famine (lines 63 ff.); the food of the **theoxénia**, then, is a factor of compensation.

§4n2. For the editors' restoration of ἔρις here at line 50, cf. ἔριξε at line 87, referring to the same quarrel.

ταῦτα θεοῖσι [μ]ὲν
πιθεῖν σοφοὺ[ς] δυνατόν,
βροτοῖσιν δ' ἀμάχανο[ν εὑ]ρέμεν·

and from what causes the quarrel of the immortals began,
these things the skilled can ascertain from the gods,
but otherwise it is impossible for mortals to discover

Pindar Paean 6.50–53

Then the Muses are invoked to inspire a retelling (54–58). Mention
of a sacrifice (62–64) is followed by a considerable lacuna, and when
the text resumes we hear that Apollo in the guise of Paris has killed
Achilles on the battlefield (78–80).[3] An elaboration follows concerning the consequences of Apollo's action:

'Ιλίου δὲ θῆκεν ἄφαρ
ὀψιτέραν ἅλωσιν

and he straightway caused
the capture of Troy to happen later

Pindar Paean 6.81–82

There is further elaboration at 87–89, where we learn specifically that
Apollo "had a quarrel" (ἔριξε: 87) with Hera and Athena.[4] Since this
elaboration is bracketed, before and after, by a description of how
and why Achilles died, the inference is that the death of Achilles had
something to do with the quarrel between Apollo on one side, Hera
and Athena on the other. Since the gods' quarrel involves the
capture of Troy, is it parallel with the quarrel of Achilles and
Odysseus over whether Troy would be captured by **bíē** 'might' or by
mêtis 'artifice'? Since the battles of heroes are matched by the
battles of their divine patrons in the Homeric theme of **theomakhíā**,
we may expect a thematic match between heroic and divine quarrels
as well. There is also a formal match that may be cited in this regard:
the Muses are asked to explain the cause of the **éris** 'quarrel'
between Achilles and Agamemnon at *Iliad* I 8 in much the same way
that they are asked to explain the **éris** among the gods at *Paean*
6.50–61.

§5. The evidence may seem meager at this point, but there must
have been something about Achilles that was particularly offensive to
Apollo. Conversely, we know that Paris, the antagonist and future
killer of Achilles, offended the same gods whom we now see

§4n3. The *Iliad* itself refers to the interaction of Apollo and Paris in the killing of
Achilles: see XIX 416–417, XXII 358–360.
§4n4. Cf. n2.

quarreling with Apollo in *Paean* 6, namely, Hera and Athena. The offense of Paris was the outgrowth of a quarrel that took place at a banquet given by the gods to celebrate the wedding of Peleus and Thetis, the parents of Achilles himself. This quarrel of the gods served as the epic theme for the opening of the *Cypria* (Proclus summary p. 102.14–16 Allen), and there are clear references to the same epic tradition in *Iliad* XXIV 25–30. Moreover, the *Cypria* presents this quarrel as a fitting epic theme for the opening of the entire Trojan War! The grievance of Hera and Athena against Paris was that he made a choice favoring Aphrodite instead of them (*Cypria*/Proclus p. 102.16–19). The Iliadic allusion to this tradition, however, also alludes to a grievance of Apollo against Achilles. It seems as if the polarization of Hera and Athena on one side and Apollo on the other corresponds not only to the hostility of the first two divinities against Paris but also to the hostility of the third against Achilles.[1] The three divinities are continuing their quarrel in *Iliad* XXIV 25–63. In the course of their quarrel, Apollo describes Achilles as a brute who is like a ravenous lion, without any control over his **bíē** 'might' (XXIV 42).[2] In Pindar's *Paean* 6, at the very moment that Apollo destroys Achilles, the hero is described as βιατάν 'endowed with **bíā** [epic **bíē**]' (line 84). One of the reasons, then, for Apollo's enmity may well have been the championing of **bíē** by Achilles. A more general reason, however, is yet to emerge from our ongoing scrutiny of the characteristics common to the god and the hero. It is too early at this point to attempt a precise formulation, and I offer here only the essentials: *the hostility of Apollo and Achilles has a religious dimension, in which god and hero function as ritual antagonists.*[3]

§6. Even though the actual concept of ritual antagonism between Apollo and Achilles remains to be articulated, we can already see the stark consequences of this antagonism in the dimension of myth. In Pindar's words:

πρὸ πόνων
δέ κε μεγάλων Δαρδανίαν
ἔπραθεν, εἰ μὴ φύλασσεν 'Από[λ]λ[ω]ν·

before the great suffering,
he [Achilles] would have destroyed Troy,

§5n1. For more on god-hero antagonism as a factor in determining the alignments of various gods in the Trojan War, see Ch.8§12.

§5n2. Further discussion at Ch.7§22.

§5n3. See Ch.7 (esp. §4) and Ch.8 (esp. §§1–5).

if Apollo had not been protecting it

Pindar *Paean* 6.89–91SM

By killing Achilles, the god Apollo postponed the destruction of Troy and thus brought about a great deal of suffering that otherwise would not have happened. In the *Iliad* too, there is allusion to the tradition that great suffering was caused by the death of Achilles. The death of Patroklos in the *Iliad*, which duplicates the death of Achilles beyond the *Iliad*, is announced with the following words:

ὄφρα πύθηαι
λυγρῆς ἀγγελίης, ἣ μὴ ὤφελλε γενέσθαι.
ἤδη μέν σε καὶ αὐτὸν ὀίομαι εἰσορόωντα
γιγνώσκειν ὅτι πῆμα θεὸς Δαναοῖσι κυλίνδει,
νίκη δὲ Τρώων· πέφαται δ' ὤριστος Ἀχαιῶν,
Πάτροκλος, μεγάλη δὲ ποθὴ Δαναοῖσι τέτυκται.

that you may learn
of the ghastly news, which should never have happened.
I think that you already see, and that you realize,
that a god is letting roll a pain [**pêma**] upon the Danaans,
and that victory belongs to the Trojans; the best of the Achaeans has been
      killed,
Patroklos, that is; and a great loss has been inflicted on the Danaans.

XVII 685–690

Only here in the *Iliad* does Patroklos get the epithet that elsewhere distinguishes Achilles, "best of the Achaeans"; the death of Patroklos is being presented as a prefiguration of the death of Achilles.[1] By dying, the "best of the Achaeans" is the source of great **pêma** 'pain' for the Achaeans. For the Trojans too, Achilles is the greatest **pêma**—in the words of Hektor and Priam themselves (XXII 288 and 421 respectively). That is, Achilles is a **pêma** for the Trojans *so long as he is fighting against them.* When he withdraws from the fighting, however, there is **pêma** for the Achaeans and **kûdos** 'glory of

§6n1. See Ch.2§8. In this connection, the wording πῆμα θεὸς Δαναοῖσι κυλίνδει 'a god is letting roll a **pêma** upon the Danaans' here at XVII 688 is directly comparable to τάχα οἱ μέγα πῆμα κυλίσθη 'surely a great **pêma** rolls down upon him' at XVII 99—words applied by Agamemnon to any mortal who dares to fight Hektor *and thus undertake a confrontation with Apollo himself* (XVII 98–99). Patroklos had done so, but Agamemnon dares not do likewise (XVII 100–101). The stance of Patroklos in his confrontation with Apollo is described as πρὸς δαίμονα 'facing the **daímōn** [divinity]' (XVII 98), which conveys the theme of ritual antagonism between god and hero (see Ch.8§§3–4 and Ch.17§5). On the collocation of **pêma** 'pain' and **kulíndō** 'roll' [as a rock], note also the parallel at viii 81–82 as quoted in §7 below.

victory' for the Trojans (VIII 176),[2] a situation that is recognized as the Will of Zeus by Hektor (VIII 175, XII 235–236) and by the narrative itself (XII 255, XV 592–599).[3] In short, Achilles is a **pêma** for the Trojans when he is at war and a **pêma** for the Achaeans both when he withdraws from war and when he dies.

§7. With the background of these patterns in traditional diction, the words of Demodokos assume an ominous tone:

τότε γάρ ῥα κυλίνδετο πήματος ἀρχὴ
Τρωσί τε καὶ Δαναοῖσι Διὸς μεγάλου διὰ βουλάς

for then it was that the beginning of <u>pain [pêma]</u> started rolling
upon both Trojans and Danaans, on account of the <u>plans</u> of great Zeus[1]

viii 81–82

When Agamemnon rejoiced at the quarrel between Achilles and Odysseus, who were "the best of the Achaeans" (viii 78), he rejoiced at a sign that presaged the destruction of Troy. In his joy he was unaware of the intervening pain yet to be inflicted on the Achaeans by the withdrawal and then by the death of Achilles. His joy was justified in the distant future but unjustified in the events at hand. In Pindar's words, the destruction was not to happen πρὸ πόνων 'before suffering' (*Paean* 6.89). Our *Iliad* presents a highly sophisticated variation on this theme, in the episode of Agamemnon's False Dream. As in the first song of Demodokos, the impetus is the **boulé** 'plan, will' of Zeus (II 5). As in the song of Demodokos, the promise is that Troy will be destroyed (II 12–15, 29–32). As in the song of Demodokos, Agamemnon arrives at a premature conclusion:[2]

τὰ φρονέοντ' ἀνὰ θυμὸν ἅ ῥ' οὐ τελέεσθαι ἔμελλον·
φῆ γὰρ ὅ γ' αἱρήσειν Πριάμου πόλιν ἤματι κείνῳ,
νήπιος, οὐδὲ τὰ ἤδη ἅ ῥα Ζεὺς μήδετο ἔργα·
θήσειν γὰρ ἔτ' ἔμελλεν ἐπ' ἄλγεά τε στοναχάς τε
Τρωσί τε καὶ Δαναοῖσι διὰ κρατερὰς ὑσμίνας

---

§6n2. On the function of **kûdos** 'glory of victory' in Homeric narrative: Benveniste 1969 II 57–69.

§6n3. Further discussion of **pêma/kûdos** and the Will of Zeus at Ch.20§§15–17.

§7n1. The double-edged πήματος ἀρχή 'the beginning of the **pêma** [pain]' is a thematic germ of the Achilles figure: even his name may be explained as taking its form from the concept "grief for the people": *Akhí-lāu̯os. See Ch.5. Cf. also the expression νείκεος ἀρχή 'the beginning of the strife' (XXII 116), as discussed at Ch. 11§12 and n.

§7n2. Cf. Ch.7§25n1.

thinking in his **thūmós** about things that were not to be:
for he thought that he would capture Priam's city on that very day,
the fool; he did not know <u>what things Zeus was planning to do.</u>
For he [Zeus] was yet to inflict <u>pains [**álgea**]</u> and groaning
on both Trojans and Danaans in battles of **krátos**.[3]

II 36–40

From the standpoint of our *Iliad*, the story to be told concerns some
of those "pains" [**álgea**] that are yet to intervene before the capture
of Troy. In fact, the same word **álgea** is deployed at the very
beginning of our *Iliad* to designate the countless "pains" of the
Achaeans (I 2), caused by the **mênis** 'anger' of Achilles (I 1) and
motivated by the Will of Zeus (Διὸς δ' ἐτελείετο βουλή: I 5).

§8. Demodokos, then, is alluding to an *Iliad*, but not to our *Iliad*.
Like our *Iliad*, the *Iliad* that Demodokos could have sung would
feature the **mênis** 'anger' of Achilles and Apollo. Unlike our *Iliad*,
however, this Iliadic tradition would feature Odysseus, not Agamemnon, as the prime offender of Achilles. Unlike our *Iliad*, this *Iliad*
would have the chief resentment of Achilles center on the slighting
of his **bíē** 'might'. An *Iliad* composed by Demodokos would have
been a poem with a structure more simple and more broad, with an
Achilles who is even perhaps more crude than the ultimately refined
hero that we see emerging at the end of our *Iliad*. I have little doubt
that such an *Iliad* was indeed in the process of evolving when it was
heard in the *Odyssey* tradition which evolved into our *Odyssey*.
Demodokos had heard the **kléos** and passed it on in song.

§7n3. On the word **krátos**: Ch.5§25.

Part II
Hero of Epic, Hero of Cult

5 | The Name of Achilles

§1. The theme of **pêma** 'pain, grief' as we find it in the first song of Demodokos (viii 81) seems to be recapitulated in the very name of Achilles. As we consult Pierre Chantraine's etymological dictionary of Greek under the entry **Akhilleús**, we find listed a number of different explanations that have been offered over the years to account for the name of Greek epic's preeminent hero.[1] My discussion will center on one of these, namely, Leonard Palmer's suggestion that **Akhil(l)eús** is a shortened form of *Akhí-lāu̯os,[2] meaning "whose **lāós** [host of fighting men] has **ákhos** [grief]."[3] By examining this reconstruction in detail, I hope to add further evidence to my thesis that the thematic germ of the Achilles figure entails **pêma** for the Trojans when the hero is at war and a **pêma** for the Achaeans both when he withdraws from war and when he dies. I should emphasize, of course, that this thesis is already supported by the textual evidence presented in the last chapter—and that it does not depend on the etymology of the name **Akhil(l)eús**. Whether or not we are to accept Palmer's proposed etymology, however, we stand to gain additional perspectives on Achilles in the course of examining the constituent themes associated with his name. Two key words will be involved: **ákhos** and **pénthos**, both meaning "grief."

§2. We begin by taking note of the numerous morphological details in support of the proposition that **Akhil(l)eús** is derived from *Akhí-

§1n1. Chantraine I 150.

§1n2. Palmer 1963.79. Here in Ch.5 and in Ch.6, I am offering a revised version of an article that I wrote for Palmer's Festschrift (Nagy 1974c).

§1n3. Technically, this posited *bahuvrīhi* compound should be translated "he who has the **lāós** grieving" or "he whose **lāós** has **ákhos**." (The Sanskrit grammatical term *bahuvrīhi* literally means "he who has much rice.") For the interpretation of **lāós** as "host of fighting men" in the context of epic, see Jeanmaire 1939.11–111 and Vian 1968.59. For the connection of Greek **lāós** with Hittite *laḫḫa-* 'military campaign' and *laḫḫiyala-* 'warrior', see Heubeck 1969 and Watkins 1976b.122.

lāu̯os 'whose lāós has ákhos'.[1] Plausible as it is, however, this reconstruction will not carry conviction unless we can be satisfied that the posited meaning 'whose lāós has ákhos' is intrinsic to the function of Achilles in myth and epic.[2] We will have to examine how the notion of an Achilles figure relates to the notions of ákhos 'grief' and lāós 'host of fighting men'.

§3. Such an examination can be valid, of course, only if the Achilles figure itself is intrinsic to the traditions of Greek myth and epic.[1] Further, we must be ready to assume that the mythopoeic

§2n1. Palmer (1963.79) compares what appears to be another shortened form, Pénthi-los, to be derived from *Penthí-lāu̯os 'whose lāós has pénthos [grief]', where the first component penthi- follows the inherited Caland pattern: penthi- compared to pénthos 'grief', parallel to akhi- compared to ákhos 'grief'. (On such patterns see the original formulation by Caland 1893.592; see also Nussbaum 1976.) Palmer (ibid.) adduces such other examples as Kūdi-áneira 'whose men have glory [kûdos]', and Oidi-pódēs 'whose feet have swelling [oîdos]', etc. As a parallel to the hypothetical truncation of *-lāu̯os in Akhil(l)eús (from *Akhí-lāu̯os), we may cite the coexistence of the forms Sthénelos (V 111, etc.) and Sthenélāos (XVI 586). To explain the optional doubling of the -l- in the epic forms of Akhil(l)eús, Palmer (ibid.) points out that expressive gemination seems to be a characteristic of shortened forms, adducing Khárillos/Kharíllēs compared to Kharí-lāos (from *-lāu̯os); for the forms, see Bechtel 1917.285. (On Kharila, see further at §39 below; also compare the formal pair Kharila and Kharí-lāos with Iólē and Ió-lāos respectively.) We may add Périllos, apparently a by-form of Perí-lāos (see Jeffery 1976.139); cf. also Philleús and Phileús, as discussed by Perpillou 1973.172 and 241n8. There remains the problem of the suffix -eús in Akhil(l)eús: here too Palmer can point to formal parallelisms, showing from the evidence of both Linear B and later Greek that this suffix is especially characteristic of shortened names (Palmer, p. 78; cf. also Perpillou, pp. 167–299). As another possible instance where compounded *-lāu̯os is ultimately truncated to -leús, Palmer (p. 80) adduces epic Nēleús and Attic Neíleōs (from *Neeleōs from *Nehé-lāu̯os, apparently attested as the name ne-e-ra-wo in a Linear B tablet from Pylos, Fn 79.5); see Ruijgh 1967.369–370. In addition, I cite the by-form of Iólē, namely Ióleia (Hesiod fr. 26.31MW), and the masculine Ió-lāos; the feminine type Ióleia implies a corresponding *Ioleús. Finally, we may compare the formal types Iólāos and Ióleia with Prōtesílāos and Penthesíleia.

§2n2. As precedent, I cite Frame 1978.82–83, 86, 96–99, 112 on the mythology underlying the form *Nehé-lāu̯os (n1), which means something like "bringing the lāós back home to safety"; Frame connects the root *nes- of *Nehé-lāu̯os not only with Nēleús and Neíleōs but also with Nés-tōr, the name of the son of Neleus. Compare the root *ag- in Agéleōs (xxii 131, 247), from *Agé-lāu̯os 'bringing/leading the lāós', and also in Ák-tōr (II 513, etc.). The contraction of *Nehe- to Nē- in Nēleús implies that the replacement of *Nehé-lāu̯os by *Nehe-leús had already taken place during a pre-Ionic phase in the development of Homeric diction (see Wackernagel 1953 [= 1914] 1156–1157 and n2).

§3n1. The single most convincing piece of writing on the subject of Achilles' inherited central role in the Iliadic tradition remains that of Whitman 1958 (Ch.IX). His book and Lord's (1960, esp. Ch.IX on the Iliad) have been invaluable for my present efforts.

theme of **Akhil(l)eús** inspired the naming of historical figures called **Akhil(l)eús**—if there be any—rather than the other way around.[2] Lastly, we must be sure that the traditions of Greek myth and epic are old enough to be dated back, at the very least, to a time when a formation like *Akhí-lāuos could have existed.

§4. For the moment, let us consider only the traditions of epic. In both form and content, the heritage of Homeric diction can be traced back all the way to Indo-European prototypes.[1] Even the internal evidence points to centuries of development. From Milman Parry's detailed studies on the formulaic nature of Homeric diction,[2] we can absorb a sense for appreciating the immense stretches of time that must have been required for an evolving poetic medium to refine its diction to such degrees of economy and artistic effectiveness.[3] What applies to the Homeric compositions must apply commensurately to the Hesiodic, as we learn from the studies of Edwards and others.[4]

§5. Not only for Homeric tradition in particular but also for myth in general, we have the warranty of deep archaism wherever we find mythical themes encased in such preservative media as the poetic traditions inherited by Pindar.[1] Combining internal analysis with the comparative method, we can establish not only that the traditional poetic forms of Pindar and other masters of lyric sometimes predate even Homeric counterparts,[2] but also that their traditional poetic

§3n2. I raise this issue to allow for the possibility that the name spelled *a-ki-re-u* in Linear B (Knossos tablet Vc 106; cf. Pylos tablet Fn 79) stands for *Akhil(l)eús. For an articulate comparison of the historical Pylos and a possibly historical Nestor with the mythopoeic Pylos and the mythopoeic Nestor, I cite Frame 1978. For a useful general discussion of the relationship between the mythopoeic requirements of epic and the realia of history: Lord 1970.29–30.

§4n1. I cite primarily my own monograph on the subject (Nagy 1974), certainly not because I think of it as authoritative but because it reflects a stage of work that has led to my present interests. Instead of listing here the parallel work of my associates in Indo-European poetics (such as Muellner 1976, Watkins 1977, Frame 1978), I prefer to pay them tribute with citations wherever they are in order. For a general introduction to the language of Indo-European poetry: Schmitt 1967 and Durante 1971/1976.

§4n2. I cite again his collected papers, Parry 1971; cf. also Lord 1960/1968.

§4n3. Cf. Nagy 1974.49–102; also Fenik 1968.229 and Lord 1974.193-199.

§4n4. Edwards 1971, with further bibliography.

§5n1. This observation about Pindar (which applies also to Bacchylides) will be developed as my argument proceeds, especially in Chs.7, 12, 14, 20. We have already had occasion to observe the archaism of Pindaric traditions in the case of *Paean* 6, as discussed at Ch.4.

§5n2. Cf. Gentili 1972, esp. p. 73; also Pavese 1967, 1972.

themes can sometimes be traced back all the way to Indo-European prototypes.[3]

§6. In short, the testimony of the early Greek poetic traditions about **Akhil(l)eús**, by virtue of their formal and thematic archaism, can justifiably be applied as a test for Palmer's reconstruction *Akhí-lāu̯os. We must therefore examine whether the notion framed by *Akhí-lāu̯os (and *Penthí-lāu̯os, for that matter) corresponds to the functions of **ákhos (pénthos)** and **lāós** in the poetic traditions. In addition, we must examine whether such a correspondence extends to the Achilles figure itself. Since the primary poetic tradition about Achilles is the *Iliad*, a brief examination of its central themes, and of the diction expressing these themes, will have to be the first task.

§7. The artistic unity of our *Iliad*, and the controlling function of the Achilles figure therein, can perhaps best be seen in the deployment of its central themes. Complex as it is in its ramifications, the plot is simple in its essence. The **tīmḗ** 'honor' of Achilles has been slighted (I 505–510, 559, etc.). He becomes angry and withdraws from the war, leaving our narrative with an opportunity to test the worth of the other prominent Achaean warriors of epic against the onslaught of Hektor and his Trojans. The Achaeans fall short and are forced to make appeals for the help of Achilles. Although Achilles refuses to come to the rescue, his comrade Patroklos becomes his surrogate.[1] Patroklos rescues the Achaeans but is killed by Hektor through the intervention of the god Apollo.[2] Achilles now enters the war to kill Hektor, thereby finally establishing his own place in epic by the positive action of fighting in battle. His negative action of withdrawing from battle had set the stage for showing that only he could have rescued the Achaeans. By functioning as his surrogate, however, Patroklos anticipates the epic destiny of Achilles, which is to rescue the Achaeans and to be killed in the process through the intervention of Apollo. It is Patroklos who rescues the Achaeans in our *Iliad*; for the moment, at least, the Trojans have been repelled by the time Achilles enters the battle and establishes his own place in the epic, by killing Hektor.

§8. The *Iliad* does more than simply orchestrate these central themes into an artistic unity: it also names them. Either the narrative

§5n3. For a particularly striking example from Pindaric poetry, see Benveniste 1945 on *Pythian* 3.45–53.
§7n1. Ch.2§8.
§7n2. Ch.4§6.

or the characters within the narrative can actually refer to the central themes inside the *Iliad*, with special designations. For example, the invocation at the beginning of the *Iliad* announces the content of the narrative simply by naming the **mênis** 'anger' of Achilles:[1]

μῆνιν ἄειδε θεὰ Πηληϊάδεω 'Αχιλῆος

Sing, goddess, the **mênis** of Achilles son of Peleus.

I 1

Through the preeminent placement of the word **mênis**, the theme of Achilles' anger is singled out by the composition as the most central and hence most pervasive in the Iliadic tradition. Furthermore, the subsequent application of **mênis** is restricted by the composition specifically to the anger that Achilles felt over the slighting of his **tīmế** at the very beginning of the action. The anger that Achilles felt later over the killing of Patroklos is nowhere denoted by **mênis**. In fact, the only instance where **mênis** applies to heroes rather than gods in the *Iliad* is the mutual anger between Achilles and Agamemnon.[2] We see in these restrictions on the application of **mênis** a

§8n1. It is traditional for an archaic poem to begin with a word that names the main subject of the narrative in the manner of a title (in this case, **mênis** at I 1), followed by an epithet and a relative clause setting forth the relationship of the title word to the main subject (in this case, how the **mênis** of Achilles was baneful and caused devastation for the Achaeans, at I 2–5). Consider also the openings of the *Odyssey*, *Theogony*, *Works and Days*, *Little Iliad*, and nearly all the Homeric *Hymns*.

§8n2. The only exception is the **mênis** of Aeneas against King Priam (ἐπεμήνιε: XIII 460), which must have been the central theme of another epic tradition—this one featuring Aeneas as its prime hero. See Ch.15§2. On the restriction of **mênis** to Achilles among the heroes of the *Iliad*, compare also the use of **mémonen** 'he is in a rage' at XXI 315 (Ch.20§5n4). For the significance of this restriction from the religious standpoint of god-hero antagonism, see Ch.8§3. On the semantics of **mênis**: Considine 1966 and Watkins 1977. Adducing the evidence of Homeric diction, Watkins argues that **mênis** must have resulted from a deformation of *mnā-nis, containing the root *mnā- (*mneə₂-) as in **mé-mnē-mai** 'to have in mind'. This enlarged root *mnā- is built from *men- as in Greek **ménos**, an abstract noun indicating a "state of mind" as manifested in such phenomena as "power" (on the semantics: Nagy 1974.266–269) or, as it turns out, "anger." Watkins has found three Iliadic passages (I 207, 282; XXI 340) where **ménos** is used not only in the sense of "anger" *but also as a functional equivalent of mênis*. I would add the evidence of **meneaínō** 'be angry, furious, in a rage', a verb formally derived from this noun **ménos** (cf. Chantraine III 685). In view of Watkins' convincing argument that **mênis** is a *reciprocal* notion, I cite *Iliad* XIX 58, where Agamemnon tells Achilles: **éridi meneḗnamen** 'we were angry [at each other] in **éris**'. The word **éris** 'strife' here refers to their quarrel at the beginning of the *Iliad* (see further at Ch.7§17 and Ch.12§6). Note that Achilles himself predicts at XIX 63–64 that the Achaeans "will long remember," **mnḗsesthai**, the mutual **éris** between him and Agamemnon (see Ch.19§3). Accordingly, I see no reason to dismiss as adventitious the designation of Agamemnon's anger against Achilles as **mênis** at I 247:

distinctive Iliadic association of this word with all the epic events that resulted from Achilles' anger against Agamemnon, the most central of which is the devastation suffered by the Achaeans. Again, the wording at the very beginning of the *Iliad* announces the theme of devastation by referring to the countless **álgea** 'pains' of the Achaeans caused by the **mênis** of Achilles:

ἢ μυρί᾽ Ἀχαιοῖς ἄλγε᾽ ἔθηκεν

which [the **mênis**] made countless **álgea** for the Achaeans.

I 2

§9. Like the word **mênis**, **álgea** 'pains' too serves as a key to the plot of the *Iliad*.[1] Just as Apollo chronologically has **mênis** over the abduction of Chryseis (I 75) before Achilles has **mênis** over the abduction of Briseis, so also the Achaeans have **álgea** from Apollo before they get **álgea** from Achilles:

τοὔνεκ᾽ ἄρ᾽ ἄλγε᾽ ἔδωκεν ἑκηβόλος ἠδ᾽ ἔτι δώσει
οὐδ᾽ ὅ γε πρὶν Δαναοῖσιν <u>ἀεικέα λοιγὸν ἀπώσει</u>
πρὶν . . .

For that reason the far-shooter gave—and will give—**álgea**,
and he will not <u>remove the disgraceful devastation **[loigós]**</u> from the Danaans
    until . . .

I 96–98 (cf. also 110)

And the remedial action, as we see from I 97 here, is denoted by λοιγὸν ἀπώσει 'will remove the devastation **[loigós]**'. When this **loigós** 'devastation' is removed with the appeasement of Apollo's anger, the Achaeans sing a **paiéōn** 'paean' to him (I 473), where the name of the song is also the epithet denoting the healing powers of the god.[2] Since the **álgea** that Apollo had visited upon the Achaeans was a **loimós** 'plague' (I 61, 97), the use of **paiéōn** at I 473 is all the more apt.[3]

Ἀτρείδης δ᾽ ἑτέρωθεν ἐμήνιε 'the son of Atreus, on the other side, had **mênis**'. The expression ἑτέρωθεν 'on the other side' even underscores the reciprocity of the **mênis** between the heroes. Achilles, however, as the prime hero of the *Iliad* and as the determinant of its action, is also the determinant of this anger that serves as the epic's central theme.

§9n1. Since the word **álgea** 'pains' is announced by the relative clause that expands on the "title" **mênis** (§8n1), it is a formal as well as functional key.

§9n2. Cf. Nagy 1974.135–137; also Burkert 1977.228.

§9n3. On the relationship of the **paiéōn/paiā́n** 'paean' to the death of Achilles himself, see Intro.§16; also Ch.4 (esp. §§4–6), and Ch.7 (esp. §§4, 24–30).

§10. To repeat, **álgea** in the diction of the *Iliad* may denote two kinds of grief for the Achaeans: (1) the plague resulting from the **mênis** of Apollo and (2) the dire military situation resulting from the **mênis** of Achilles. In the case of the plague, the remedial action was denoted by λοιγὸν ἀπώσει 'will remove the devastation [**loigós**]' (I 97); in fact, the narrative quotes directly the actual prayer to Apollo by Apollo's priest:[n]

ἤδη νῦν Δαναοῖσιν ἀεικέα λοιγὸν ἄμυνον

Ward off now from the Danaans the disgraceful devastation [**loigós**]!

I 456

Elsewhere in the *Iliad*, as we examine the word **loigós** beyond I 97 and 456, we find that its accusative λοιγόν occurs exclusively in combination with the same verb ἀμυν- 'ward off' that we find here in I 456. And from the contexts of these combinations, the fact emerges that the dire military situation resulting from the **mênis** of Achilles calls for the same remedial action, from the standpoint of the diction, as did the plague resulting from the **mênis** of Apollo:

... λοιγὸν ἀμύνῃς   XVI 32
... λοιγὸν ἀμῦναι   I 341, XVI 75, XVIII 450
... λοιγὸν ἀμύνων   XVI 80.

§11. In fact, the diction of the *Iliad* can designate the plight of the Achaeans during the Battle of the Ships as simply λοιγὸν Ἀχαιῶν 'the devastation [**loigós**] of the Achaeans' at XXI 134, where the Achaeans are then immediately described, in Achilles' own words, with the following narrative gloss:

οὓς ἐπὶ νηυσὶ θοῇσιν ἐπέφνετε νόσφιν ἐμεῖο

whom you killed at the swift ships in my absence.

XXI 135

The **loigós** of the Achaeans during the Battle of the Ships happened because they were "apart from Achilles," who had **mênis**. Already in Book I, the words of Achilles had alluded to their future predicament:

ὅππως οἱ παρὰ νηυσὶ σόοι μαχέοιντο Ἀχαιοί

that the Achaeans be safe as they fight at the ships

I 344

§10n. On the strictly regulated subgenre of prayers as quoted within Homeric narrative: Muellner 1976.17–67.

It was in this future context, in what amounts to the title of a future episode in the narrative ("Battle of the Ships"), that the words of Achilles first raised the possibility that he would be needed then for the role of warding off the **loigós** of the Achaeans:

> ... εἴ ποτε δὴ αὖτε
> χρειὼ ἐμεῖο γένηται ἀεικέα λοιγὸν ἀμῦναι

> ... if ever there will be
> a need for me to ward off the disgraceful devastation [**loigós**]

I 340–341

§12. As the narrative approaches this epic destiny of Achilles with the ever-worsening plight of the Achaeans during the Battle of the Ships, the hypothetical subject of λοιγὸν ἀμύνειν 'ward off the devastation' remains Achilles only up to a certain point:

> αἴ κε μὴ 'Αργείοισιν ἀεικέα λοιγὸν ἀμύνῃς

> if you do not ward off the disgraceful devastation [**loigós**] from the Argives

XVI 32

Already here the speaker is Patroklos, who becomes soon hereafter the actual subject of the expression on the level of form and the surrogate of the action on the level of content. And it is Achilles who sends him off to battle with these words:

> ἀλλὰ καὶ ὣς Πάτροκλε νεῶν ἀπὸ λοιγὸν ἀμύνων
> ἔμπεσ' ἐπικρατέως

> Even so, Patroklos, ward off the devastation [**loigós**][1] from the ships
> and attack with **krátos**.[2]

XVI 80–81

The outcome will bring more grief.

§13. As we hear from the retrospective narrative of XVIII 444–456, where Thetis retells briefly the entire *Iliad* up to the moment at hand, Achilles "had refused to ward off the devastation [**loigós**]" (ἠναίνετο λοιγὸν ἀμῦναι: XVIII 450) and Patroklos had taken his place—only to be killed by Hektor through the intervention of Apollo (XVIII 451–456). The god had thus given the emblem of victory, the **kûdos**, to Hektor (XVIII 456).[1] When Achilles finally wins back the

---

§12n1. By contrast, even Diomedes cannot "ward off the devastation [**loigós**]" from the ships (λοιγὸν ἀμῦναι), as Achilles observes with satisfaction at XVI 74–75.

§12n2. On **krátos**, see §25.

§13n1. On **kûdos**, see the reference at Ch.4§6n2.

kûdos by killing Hektor, he calls on the Achaeans to sing a **paiéōn** (XXII 391), and the song is to begin as follows:

ἠράμεθα μέγα κῦδος· ἐπέφνομεν Ἕκτορα δῖον

We won a big **kûdos**; we killed brilliant Hektor!

XXII 393

The **paiéōn** here is to be contrasted with the only other one in the *Iliad*, at I 473, where it had celebrated the remedy for the **álgea** 'pains' of the Achaeans. True, the killing of Hektor has reversed the situation for the opposing sides: now it is the Achaeans who have the **kûdos** (XXII 393) and the Trojans who have **álgea** (XXII 422) because of Achilles, who is a **pêma** 'pain' for the Trojans (XXII 421–422). In fact, he is for them the **pêma mégiston** 'greatest pain' (XXII 288), in Hektor's own words. Previously, it had been Hektor who was called a **pêma** by the Achaeans (XI 347, cf. VIII 176), and in fact their plight during the onslaught of Hektor was also a **pêma** (IX 229).[2]

§14. It remains to ask whether the Achaeans will be rid of grief after Hektor is killed. Clearly they will not, since the death of Achilles will itself be an ultimate **pêma** for them—as is presaged by the words announcing the death of Patroklos (XVII 688–689).[n]

§15. Moreover, the death of Patroklos is visualized as a **pêma** not only for the Achaeans but for himself as well. Contemplating how the hero died, Agamemnon offers this generalization: any mortal who dares to fight Hektor *and thereby undertake a confrontation with Apollo* will get a **pêma** (XVII 98–99).[1] This generalization surely applies also to Achilles: the death of the hero will be a **pêma** both for the Achaeans and for himself.[2]

§16. In short, the figure of Achilles is pervasively associated with the theme of grief. The program of the *Iliad*, which is equated with the Will of Zeus (I 5/II 38), decrees countless **álgea** 'pains' for Trojans and Achaeans alike (I 2/II 39)—all because Achilles became angry in a quarrel.[1] Beyond the *Iliad*, in the first song of Demodokos, we find Achilles again in a quarrel, and grief is again decreed (**pêma** 'pain': viii 81) by the Will of Zeus (viii 82).[2] Moreover, the Iliadic

§13n2. See Ch.4§6.
§14n. See Ch.4§6.
§15n1. See Ch.4§6n1.
§15n2. Cf. Ch.17§5.
§16n1. Ch.4§7.
§16n2. Ibid.

identification of a depersonalized force called **pêma mégiston** 'great-est pain' with the epic persona of Achilles, as at XXII 288, makes the hero seem like the very essence of grief.

§17. So far, we have been examining the relationship of the Achilles figure with the central theme of grief in the *Iliad* without actually considering the word **ákhos** and its deployment within the composition. The evidence that we have already seen, however, leads us to expect that any Iliadic diction involving **ákhos** should also directly involve the Achilles figure, if indeed the name **Akhil(l)eús** had once designated the epic function of the hero in its being derived from *Akhí-lāu̯os 'whose **lāós** has **ákhos**' = 'he who has the host of fighting men grieving'.[n]

§18. Before we proceed, however, a few precautions may be taken about the nature of our evidence. We may by now have satisfied ourselves, on the basis of the Iliadic diction, that there is a thematic association between the Achilles figure and the notion of grief. The diction seems orchestrated to fit the main themes, or better, to express these themes by way of the placement of certain key words. For example, the deployment of the expression λοιγὸν ἀμυν- 'ward off devastation [**loigós**]' had indirectly told its own story about how Achilles' **mênis** caused grief for the Achaeans. The associations of key words keep retelling the main themes of the *Iliad* on a formal level, beyond the more fundamental level of the actual narrative. But it is essential to keep in mind that such orchestration of the forms in such a way as to fit the main themes is a *result*, not a *cause*. In Greek epic, as also elsewhere in traditional poetry, inherited themes are expressed by inherited forms which are highly regulated by the formulaic system of the genre.

§19. To put it another way: from the intensive studies of Parry and Lord on the nature of formulaic language, we expect to see in Homeric poetry the automatic distribution of set phraseology appro-priate to set themes. Conversely, our knowledge of formulaic behavior tells us that we cannot expect any given composition within the tradition to require any alterations or modifications in the inherited phraseology of its hexameters for the purpose of accommo-dating the composition's sense of its own unity. If we do indeed discern the reality of an artistically unified *Iliad*, then we must also be ready to say that the unity of our *Iliad* is itself traditional. This is not

§17n. §2n1.

to detract from a work of genius. Nor is it the same thing as claiming that the *Iliad* is the work of some committee of composers. Rather, I would say simply that the genius behind our *Iliad*'s artistic unity is in large part the Greek epic tradition itself. In order to accept this proposition, we may have to force ourselves to imagine the immensely creative process of this tradition, with all the many centuries of what must have been the most refined sort of elite performer/audience interaction that went into the evolution of the *Iliad* and *Odyssey* as we know them.[n]

§20. With these thoughts in mind, I return to the evidence of Iliadic diction, on **ákhos** and **Akhil(l)eús**. If we are now about to discover a pervasive nexus between these two elements in the *Iliad*, I would then infer that such a nexus is integrated in the inherited formulaic system and hence deeply rooted in the epic tradition. Accordingly, the internal evidence of epic may well corroborate the proposed derivation of **Akhil(l)eús** from **ákhos**.

§21. As we turn now to the deployment of **ákhos** in the *Iliad*, we immediately come upon an overt equation of this word with the expression **páthon álgea** 'suffered pains', involving the same word **álgea** that we have already seen in the context of designating the grief that the Achaeans suffered from the **mênis** of Achilles (ἄλγεα: I 2) and from the **mênis** of Apollo (ἄλγεα: I 96, 110). This equation of **ákhos** with **páthon álgea** is to be found in the words of Achilles himself:

αἰνὸν ἄχος τό μοί ἐστιν, ἐπεὶ πάθον ἄλγεα θυμῷ

the terrible **ákhos** that I have, since I suffered pains [**álgea**] in my **thūmós**

XVI 55

In the present case, however, **álgea** designates the grief of Achilles over his loss of **tīmḗ** 'honor' (XVI 59), not the grief of the Achaeans. For Achilles to suffer his own **álgea** qualifies here as **ákhos** (XVI 55), yet we find only thirty-three hexameters earlier that the grief of the Achaeans during the Battle of the Ships also qualifies as **ákhos**:

μὴ νεμέσα· τοῖον γὰρ ἄχος βεβίηκεν Ἀχαιούς

Do not be angry: for such an **ákhos** has beset the Achaeans.

XVI 22

§19n. Cf. Intro.§9.

The word **ákhos** signals *le transfert du mal*:
the **ákhos** of Achilles leads to
the **mênis** of Achilles leads to
the **ákhos** of the Achaeans.

§22. Such a transfer has a religious dimension, as we can see from the traditions of the Homeric *Hymn to Demeter*. The **ákhos** of Demeter is instantaneous with the abduction of the Kore (*H.Dem.* 40, 90–91). Her resulting **mênis** (*H.Dem.* 350) causes devastation in the form of cosmic infertility (351 ff.). The **tīmaí** 'honors' of the Olympians are thus threatened (353–354), and it is only with the restoration of Kore that Demeter's **mênis** ceases (410), as her **ákhos** abates (ἀχέων: 436). Demeter thereupon gets her appropriate **tīmaí** (461), and her anger (468) is replaced with fertility (469, 471 ff.).

§23. Besides all the obvious convergences here, we must also note an important divergence from the pattern of Achilles: once Demeter's **mênis** ceases, so too does her **ákhos**. This theme is also found directly in the cult traditions, as we see, for example, in the report about the Demeter of Arcadian Phigalia: the **Moîrai** 'Fates' persuaded her both "to lay aside her anger and to cease in her grief" (ἀποθέσθαι μὲν τὴν ὀργήν, ὑφεῖναι δὲ καὶ τῆς λύπης: Pausanias 8.42.3).[n] The pattern is different with the grief of Achilles. The abduction of Briseis brings instantaneous **ákhos** for Achilles (I 188), but this grief is not removed by the restoration of the girl, the vindication of his **tīmḗ**, and the cessation of his terrible **mênis**. Before these three events take place, the **ákhos** of Achilles is made permanent by the death of his surrogate Patroklos. When Achilles hears the news that Patroklos has been killed, his **ákhos** is instantaneous in the narrative (XVIII 22), and for this **ákhos** there is to be no remedy, as the earlier words of Odysseus had already predicted for Achilles:

αὐτῷ τοι μετόπισθ᾽ ἄχος ἔσσεται, οὐδέ τι μῆχος
ῥεχθέντος κακοῦ ἔστ᾽ ἄκος εὑρεῖν

You yourself will have an **ákhos** in the future,
and there will be no way to find a remedy for the bad thing once it is done.

IX 249–250

§23n. For the function of the **Moîrai** here, compare the etymology of Modern Greek μοιρολόγι/*mirolòyi* 'lamentation', as discussed by Alexiou 1974.110–128. For her argument that the word is derived from **moîra**, we may add the evidence from the latter-day Greek dialects in Southern Italy, where the form *ta morolòya* 'funeral lamentations' seems to be derived from the equivalent of classical **móros**, synonym of **moîra**. See Rohlfs 1964.334.

As Thetis predicts, Achilles will have grief for the rest of his life (ἄχνυται: XVIII 442–443). Earlier, he was grieving for Briseis (ἀχέων: XVIII 446); now he can grieve for Patroklos (ἀχεύων: XVIII 461), and after this **ákhos** there can be no other:

> ... ἐπεὶ οὔ μ' ἔτι δεύτερον ὧδε
> ἵξετ' ἄχος κραδίην, ὄφρα ζωοῖσι μετείω

... for never again will an **ákhos** like this enter my heart while I am among the living

XXIII 46–47

§24. Whereas Achilles is the man of constant sorrow, the Achaeans have **ákhos** intermittently. And each time that they get a remission of **ákhos** in the *Iliad*, Achilles figures as the key factor. Initially, Apollo's **mênis** had given them grief because of the abduction of Chryseis; their grief was relieved when Chryseis was restored, whereas the consequent abduction of Briseis gave grief to Achilles. Later, Achilles' own **mênis** gave the Achaeans grief, which was then relieved when Patroklos beat back the onslaught of the Trojans at the Battle of the Ships. The consequent death of Patroklos then left Achilles without respite from grief.

§25. During the intermittent period of **ákhos** for the Achaeans, the Trojans are described as having **krátos** 'superior power', and the complementary distribution of these two Homeric themes of **ákhos**/ **krátos** is controlled by the Will of Zeus, the self-proclaimed "plot" of our *Iliad*. The key passage is I 509–510, where we find an overt correlation of the grief that is about to beset the Achaeans with the temporary awarding of **krátos** to the Trojans, and the correlation is under the control of Zeus. It is up to Zeus both to give **krátos**, as here (I 509), as well as to take it away, and the Achaeans in their plight fully realize the absence of **krátos**.[1] Diomedes speaks for them all when he says:

> ... ἐπεὶ νεφεληγερέτα Ζεὺς
> Τρωσὶν δὴ βόλεται δοῦναι κράτος ἠέ περ ἡμῖν

... since Zeus the cloud-gatherer
wills to give the **krátos** to the Trojans instead of us.[2]

XI 318–319

§25n1. See Benveniste 1969 II 76–77.

§25n2. Ajax too comes to realize this: XVI 119–121. Moreover, Homeric diction itself confirms that the presence or absence of **krátos** on the one or the other military side depends on the Will of Zeus. When the Achaeans briefly and unexpectedly regain

That is, Diomedes speaks for all except for Achilles, who stands outside the common good of the Achaean host. For Achilles, the transfer of **krátos** from the Achaeans to the Trojans leads to his own **tīmḗ** (I 505–510), and the restoration of his **tīmḗ** is equivalent to the Will of Zeus (cf. also II 3–5), which in turn comes to pass with the grief of the Achaeans at the Battle of the Ships (I 2–5, 559; IX 608–609). When he is praying to Zeus, Achilles says it himself:

τίμησας μὲν ἐμέ, μέγα δ' ἴψαο λαὸν 'Αχαιῶν

You have given **tīmḗ** to me and great harm to the **lāós** of the Achaeans

XVI 237

With exactly these same words, the priest Chryses had prayed to Apollo (I 454); there too the **lāós** of the Achaeans was having grief, but that time it was still the **mênis** of Apollo that was causing it, not the **mênis** of Achilles.

§26. Who, then, is this warrior, whose **tīmḗ** is instrumental in taking **krátos** from the **lāós** of the Achaeans and bringing them **ákhos** instead? Surely it is *Akhí-lāu̯os, the one who has grief for and of the **lāós**. The individual **ákhos** of the Achilles figure leads to the collective **ákhos** of the Achaean host during the Battle of the Ships, but it was their own earlier **ákhos** during the plague that had led to Achilles' **ákhos**. If there had been no abduction of Chryseis, leading to the **ákhos** of the Achaeans, there would have been no abduction of Briseis, leading to the **ákhos** of Achilles. Achilles was as instrumental in ridding the Achaeans of their first **ákhos** as he was in bringing upon them the second; in fact, he had even prayed to Zeus for the grief that would come upon them (XVIII 74–77; cf. I 408–412).

§27. The Homeric theme of **ákhos** reflects not only on the individual nature of the Achilles figure but also on the collective

---

the upper hand and *almost* capture Troy at XVII 319–322, they almost do so κάρτεϊ καὶ σθένεϊ σφετέρῳ 'with their own **krátos** and strength' (XVII 322). But this would-be event is designated as ὑπὲρ Διὸς αἶσαν 'beyond the **aîsa** [allotment, fate] of Zeus' (XVII 321). In other words, it is *untraditional*, since whatever runs counter to the traditional plot of the narrative is conventionally designated as "beyond destiny": Ch.2§17, Ch.7§21n2, Ch.15§3n9. On the Διὸς βουλή 'Will of Zeus' as the traditional plot, see also Ch.7§17 and the comments on viii 577–580 at Ch.6§8; cf. Ch.6§24n3 and Ch.10§17. In the present episode, the would-be event of Troy's capture is not only untraditional; it is also *almost* accomplished by an untraditional application of **krátos**, in that the word is here described as being at the disposal of the Achaeans rather than Zeus. For more on the correlation of destiny and **krátos**, see the discussion of the expression **Moîra krataiḗ** at §30.

nature of the Achaean **lāós**. As for the word **lāós**, its traditional use in Homeric diction also reinforces the proposed reconstruction ***Akhí-lāu̯os**, inasmuch as **lāós** serves to designate the Achaeans specifically in a *social* sense: the Homeric **lāós** is a warrior society, a *Männerbund*.[1] As such, the function of the **lāós** corresponds ideologically to the Indo-European "second function," in terms of Georges Dumézil's formulation.[2] This warrior society of the **lāós**, as my former student Dale Sinos has shown in detail, sets the ethical standards of our *Iliad* in terms of the bonds that unite the **phíloi** 'friends', who are the members of the **lāós**.[3] The epic stance of the individual Achilles toward the collective **lāós** thus presents an ethical problem that we will have to examine presently; for the moment, however, the pertinence of **ákhos** is the major issue. Here too, we will see that the theme of **ákhos** is central. When Achilles has his first **ákhos**, over Briseis, it separates him from the **lāós**. When he has his second **ákhos**, over Patroklos, it reintegrates him with the **lāós**.

Supplement: The Name of the Achaeans

§28. When the first **ákhos** of Achilles separated him from the **lāós**, the **lāós** then got **ákhos** too. This theme of transference from the individual to the collective introduces yet another factor relevant to the etymology of **Akhil(l)eús**, namely the etymology of the word "Achaeans," **Akhaioí**. In Homeric diction, this name **Akhaioí** functions as the synonym of **Danaoí** and **Argeîoi**, but its association with other words is idiosyncratic. In particular, I draw attention to the extremely common Homeric collocation of **lāós/lāôn** with **Akhaiôn**

§27n1. For a detailed exposition: Jeanmaire 1939.11–111; see also Vian 1968.59 and Palmer 1955. These references are also important for appreciating the function the *ra-wa-ke-ta* = ***lāu̯āgétās** in the Linear B tablets. For detailed studies on Indo-European Männerbund: Wikander 1938 (after Höfler 1934) and Przyluski 1940. On Pindaric **lāgétās**, see Suárez de la Torre 1977 (and cf. Ch.6§26n1 below).

§27n2. See Yoshida 1964.6 and Vian 1968 passim; cf. Lejeune 1960.139 and 1968.31–32; also Palmer 1955 passim. From the prodigious work of Georges Dumézil on the Indo-European three functions, I cite the one bibliographical entry that is by far the most important collection of comparative source material for students of Greek epic: Dumézil's *Mythe et épopée* I (1968). It bears stressing, however, that the value of the evidence presented in this work is strictly comparative in nature. Almost all the evidence is taken from non-Greek epic traditions, and the significance of this comparative material for the study of Greek epic is always implicit and hardly ever made explicit.

§27n3. Sinos 1975.65–81. On the function of the word **phílos** and its derivatives in Homeric narrative: Benveniste 1969 I 338–353.

(and **Akhaïkón**). Since **lāós** is a *social* designation, we are encouraged to see here a parallel semantic function in the name that serves as its defining genitive, **Akhaiôn** (construction of the type *urbs Romae)*.[1] Accordingly, we have an answer to the possible objection that **Akhaioí** cannot be derived from **ákhos**—on the grounds that the name may refer to a genuine people as well as an epic collective. The answer is this: the process of ethnic naming may itself be a social function, and the designation of a people may involve a mythopoeic or even ritualistic level. Surely such levels are present in the Homeric synonyms of **Akhaioí**, namely, **Danaoí** and **Argeîoi**.[2]

§29. In fact, such mythopoeic and ritualistic levels are also present in the cult designation of Demeter as **Akhaiá** precisely in the context of her **ákhos** over the abduction of Kore. In Plutarch's *De Iside* 378d, we read reports of mourning rites (πενθίμοις θυσίαις) practiced by various peoples during the period of sowing (October/November) to lament the abduction of the Kore. After citing the Thesmophoria of the Athenians, where he describes the second day of the festival (12 Pyanopsion) as a period of lamentation, Plutarch's survey turns to a corresponding ritual period in Boeotia:

καὶ Βοιωτοὶ τὰ τῆς Ἀχαιᾶς μέγαρα κινοῦσιν, ἐπαχθῆ τὴν ἑορτὴν ἐκείνην ὀνομάζοντες ὡς διὰ τὴν τῆς Κόρης κάθοδον ἐν ἄχει τῆς Δήμητρος οὔσης.

And the Boeotians activate the chambers [**mégara**] of the **Akhaiá**, giving their festival a name of grief because of Demeter's **ákhos** over the Descent [**káthodos**] of the Kore.

Plutarch De Iside 378e

There is an overt correlation here between Demeter's cult title **Akhaiá** and her **ákhos** 'grief' over the Descent of the Kore;[1] furthermore, her individual grief is correlated with the collective grief of the community that worships her. These correlations of the name **Akhaiá** are presented as a fact of cult; they are independent of the surface resemblance of the forms **ákhos** and **Akhaiá**. I propose that we are dealing here with something more than a mere lexicographical association, as we might have thought if we had access only to such information as the following gloss:

§28n1. See Jeanmaire 1939.26–43, esp. p. 27.

§28n2. On **Danaós/Danaaí**, see especially Hesiod *fr.* 128MW, in conjunction with my discussion (Nagy 1973.161) of the element **dan-** in **Ēri-danós**. On **Argeîoi/Argeíē**, see Clader 1976 Ch.III sec.3, following Frame 1971.

§29n1. See Festugière 1959 for a discussion of the expression μέγαρα κινοῦσιν and of the calendar dating of the **káthodos**. Cf. also Quinn 1971.146.

'Αχαία [sic]· ἐπίθετον Δήμητρος. ἀπὸ τοῦ περὶ τὴν Κόρην ἄχους, ὅπερ ἐποιεῖτο ἀναζητοῦσα αὐτήν

Akhaia: epithet of Demeter. From the **ákhos** that she had over the Kore when she was looking for her.

Hesychius s.v.

As we have already seen, the word **ákhos** is the *traditional* designation of Demeter's grief over the abduction of the Kore (*H.Dem.* 40, 90, 436), just as **Akhaiá** serves as a *traditional* epithet of the grieving Demeter during a ritual period of lamentation. Even if we were to assume that the association of **ákhos** with **Akhaiá** results from a contrived etymology, we would still have to concede on the basis of Plutarch's report that the contrivance itself must be traditional and deeply archaic, not some random figment of a lexicographer's imagination.[2]

§30. Besides the traditional association of **ákhos** with **Akhaiá** in cult, we have also seen the association of **ákhos** with **Akhaioí** in the central themes of the *Iliad*. This convergence of evidence leads us to suspect a lexical relationship between **ákhos** and **Akhaio/ā-**, and there are interesting morphological parallels that may serve as corroboration. Let us first compare the es-stem **ákhos** and adjectival **Akhaió-** with the es-stem **krátos** (/**kártos**) and adjectival **krataió-**.[1] This match is interesting from the thematic as well as formal point of view, since we have already seen that the word **krátos** (/**kártos**) is used in Homeric diction to designate the converse of **ákhos**, where the back-and-forth struggle of the Achaeans and Trojans is being described.[2] When the Achaeans are hard pressed with **ákhos** 'grief', it is the Trojans who have the **krátos** 'superior power' (I 509–510, etc.); conversely, when the Trojans are hard pressed, it is the Achaeans who have the **krátos** (VI 386–387, etc.).[3] It also seems pertinent to the back-and-forth theme of the Achaean/Trojan struggle that a noun for

§29n2. See again Festugière 1959.
§30n1. I postpone until appendix §8 the problem of the Latin borrowing *Achīuī*, on the basis of which **Akhaió-** is conventionally reconstructed as *Akhaiu̯ó-.
§30n2. §§25–26.
§30n3. Cf. §§25–26 above. Note too the frequent application of the adjective **krateró-** to nouns designating "battle," notably **husmī́nē** and **phúlopis.** Conversely, **pólemos** 'war' is conventionally designated in Homeric diction as **dusēkhḗs** 'having bad **ákhos**' (on which see Chantraine I 302). At XVIII 242, **phúlopis** is designated as **krateré** and its synonym **pólemos** as **homoíios.** Whatever the etymology of **homoíios** (see Chantraine III 799), it seems to convey the theme that the evil of war afflicts all (cf. XVIII 309).

which the adjective **krataió-** serves as fixed epithet is the word for "fate": verse-final **Moîra krataié̄**, as at V 83, XVI 334, etc.[4]

§31. The adjective **krataió-** seems to be formed from the element **kratai-/kartai-**, as attested in compound adjectives like **krataí-pedon** 'whose ground is firm [has **krátos**]' (xxiii 46: applying to **oûdas** 'floor').[1] In parallel onomastic formations, we find **krati-** as well as **kratai-**: thus **Kratí-dēmos** 'whose **dêmos** has **krátos**' as well as **Kratai-ménēs** 'whose **ménos** [might] has **krátos**'.[2] On the basis, then, of its compounding patterns as well as its variant **krati-**, we may consider the element **kratai-** as part of a so-called Caland System.[3] Such a system would include the abstract noun with stem in **-es-** (**krátos/kártos**; Aeolic **krétos** even shows the expected e-grade of the root) and the adjectives with stems in **-u-** (**kratú-**) and **-ro-** (**krateró-**) compared to **-i-** in the first part of compounds (**kratai-**).[4] The vowels immediately before **-ro-** and **-i-** in **krateró-** and **kratai-** respectively are problematical,[5] but the overall system of **krátos** is

§30n4. On the correlation of fate and **krátos**: §25n2.

§31n1. Cf. **kratai-gúaloi** 'whose plates are firm = have **krátos**' (XIX 361), applying to **thórēkes** 'breastplates', and **kartaí-poda** 'whose feet are firm = have **krátos**' (Gortynian Code IV 36), applying to larger cattle rather than **próbata** = sheep and goats; cf. Pindar *O*.13.81, where **kartaí-pod'** designates a bull. The translation "firm" for **kratai-** in **krataí-pod-** and **krataí-pedo-** is perhaps overly specific. More simply, the notion of **krátos** mediates between the foot and its footing. In the case of **krataí-pedo-** even a floor has **krátos** by way of giving a firm footing. As for **krataí-pod-**, compare **khalkó-pod-** 'whose hooves are of bronze' (VIII 41), applying to horses. Here too, the emphasis seems to be on firmness as a mark of superiority; cf. **krater-ónukh-** 'whose hooves/claws have **krátos**', applying to horses (V 329, etc.), asses (vi 253), and wolves (x 218).

§31n2. See Bechtel 1917.256.

§31n3. For the term, see Nussbaum 1976.

§31n4. On the basis of the Greek evidence, I see no need to posit, as does Benveniste (1969 II 77–83), the conflation of two separate roots in this system. The notion of "firm, hard" (cf. n1) is not necessarily at odds with **krátos** in the sense of "superiority in a trial of strength" (Benveniste's working definition: 1969 II 77 = 1973.362). Even **kratúnō**, which Benveniste translates as "harden," can be interpreted further as "prepare for superiority = **krátos**"; hence such direct objects as **phálangas** 'phalanxes' in the *Iliad* (XI 215).

§31n5. Schmitt (1967.112n685) has noticed an interesting detail: as an epithet, **krateró-** is a variant of **hieró-** in combinations with the noun **ís** + genitive of the hero's name (as periphrasis for the plain name). Thus we find **kraterè̄ ... ìs Oduseôs** at XXIII 720 besides **hierè̄ ìs Tēlemákhoio** at ii 409, xviii 405, etc. Note also **krateròn ménos** + genitive of the hero's name at XVI 189 and XXIII 837 besides **hieròn ménos** + genitive of the hero's name at vii 167, viii 2, etc. (At *H.Apollo* 371 **hieròn ménos** combines with the genitive of **Éélios** 'Sun'.) In the case of **hieró-**, we may confidently reconstruct *isə-ro-, so that the vowel **e** seems to be a reflex of *ə (see Schmitt, pp. 111–114). The construction of **hieró-** + noun meaning "power" + genitive of name is not only a periphrasis of the simple name but also an obviation of a Caland System compound formation with *isə-i- as the first member; see Schmitt, p.111n678. Schmitt

clear enough to allow comparison with what seems to be the system
of **ákhos**:

krátos	kratú-	krati-	kratai-	krataió-
ákhos	akhu-	*akhi-	*akhai-	Akhaió-

§32. The **u**-stem **akhu-** is visible in the **n**-infix verb **ákh-n-u-tai**
(ἄχνυται, as at XVIII 443) corresponding to the noun **ákhos**, and
also in **akheúōn** (ἀχεύων, as at XVIII 461), verse-final variant of
verse-medial **akhéōn** (ἀχέων, as at XVIII 446); we have in fact
already examined all three of these forms in the specific context of
Achilles' grief.[n] The type **akhéōn** must in turn be compared with
kratéōn (κρατέων, as at XVI 172).

§33. An **i**-stem *akhi- has already been posited as the first member
in the reconstructed compound *Akhí-lāu̯os 'whose **lāós** has **ákhos**'.
As for the hypothetical variant *akhai- (cf. **kratai-** and **krati-**), it may
well be visible in the name **Akhai-ménēs**, the Greek formal reinter-
pretation of Old Persian *Haxā-maniš*. The morphological integrity of
Akhai-ménēs (compared to **ákhos**) as a Greek formation is validated
by such parallel formations as attested in the names **Kratai-ménēs**
(compared to **krátos**) and **Althai-ménēs** (compared to **álthos**).[n] Note
also the form **akhai-menís**, the name of a plant (pseudo-Dioscorides
3.110).

§34. The **es**-stem noun corresponding to the name **Althai-ménēs**
'whose **ménos** [might] has **álthos**' requires special attention.[1] In

---

accordingly posits (ibid.) a *bahuvrīhi* epithet *isəi-ménes- as the basis for the
periphrasis **hieròn ménos** (+ genitive of the name described by this epithet). In view
of the parallelism **hieròn/krateròn** + **ménos** in Homeric diction, we may perhaps also
posit *kr̥tai-ménes-. The attested name **Kratai-ménēs** would be only an indirect reflex,
however; *kr̥təi- should yield **krati-**. The compound element **kratai-/kartai-** seems to
be a conflation of *kr̥ti- (from *kr̥təi-) and *kr̥ta- (from *kr̥tə-, without -i-), and the
latter seems to be attested as the adverb **kárta** 'very'. As Alan Nussbaum points out to
me, it is possible for elements of the Caland System, when they appear as the first
member of compounds, to bear the suffix *-ə2- in place of the more usual *-i-: consider
alkă- as in **Alkă-thoos** (Homeric: XII 93, etc.) and **Alkă-ménēs** (Bechtel 1917.35)
besides **alkĭ-** as in **alkĭ-phrōn, Alkĭ-ménēs**, etc. For an example of a compound
without either connecting vowels *-i- or *-ə2-, consider Homeric **aîth-ops** as compared
to **Aithí-ops**.

§32n. See §23.

§33n. The name **Akhai-ménēs** may be attested in Linear B as *a-ka-me-ne* (Knossos
tablet X 82 + 8136), although other readings of this spelling are also possible. See
Chadwick/Baumbach 1963.178. Compare also **krataiós** and **kratai-** with **araiós** and
arai-. The latter is attested in the Homeric place name **Arai-thurée** (II 571), the
meaning of which is something like "whose entrance is narrow"; cf. **araiḕ** ... **eísodos**
'narrow entrance' at x 90. For **thúrai** in the sense of "entrance," see ix 243, etc.

§34n1. On the cult of the hero **Althai-ménēs** at Rhodes: Rohde I 116 and n1.

Hesychius, the entry **álthos** is glossed as **phármakon** 'cure, drug'; the derivative **an-althḗs** 'incurable' is actually attested in the epic tradition (*Iliou Persis fr.* 5.6 Allen). This noun **álthos** corresponds to **althaíā**, the name of a plant that cures wounds (Theophrastus *Historia Plantarum* 9.15.5), and to **Althaíē**, the name of Meleager's mother (IX 555);[2] we must also compare **krataiá**, likewise the name of a plant (pseudo-Dioscorides 2.180).[3] The semantics of these forms suggest the possibility, however remote, that **álthos** (/**Althaíē**) may have been a thematic converse of **ákhos** (/**Akhaiá**). Compare the function of **ákos** 'cure' as the converse of **ákhos** 'grief':

αὐτῷ τοι μετόπισθ' ἄχος ἔσσεται, οὐδέ τι μῆχος
ῥεχθέντος κακοῦ ἔστ' ἄκος εὑρεῖν

You yourself [Achilles] will have an **ákhos** in the future, and there will be no way
to find an **ákos** for the bad thing once it is done.[4]

IX 249–250

§35. In view of such formal correspondences as

| krátos | Kratai-ménēs | krataió- |
| álthos | Althai-ménēs | althaíā- |

it would be tempting to consider

| ákhos | Akhai-ménēs | Akhaió- |

as a set of related forms. One formal problem that stands in the way is the Latin borrowing *Achīuī*, on the basis of which **Akhaió-** is conventionally reconstructed as *Akhaiu̯ó-.[1] Also, the form *a-ka-wi-ja-de* in the Linear B texts (KN C 914) has been tentatively interpreted as *Akhaiu̯iān-de 'to Achaea'.[2] Yet I can find no morphological precedent for reconstructing a suffix *-u̯ó- as in *kratai-u̯ó- or *Akhai-u̯ó-. On the other hand, it may be possible to reconstruct **krataió-** and **Akhaió-** as original compounds containing the root *ui̯- 'force' as second element. The key is the verse-final form **krataiís/Krátaiin** in the *Odyssey* (xi 597/xii 124).

§36. At xi 597, **krataiís** (nominative) designates the supernatural force that sends the rock of Sisyphus rolling back again and again to

§34n2. For a discussion of these forms: Chantraine 1968.60.

§34n3. Cf. Strömberg 1940.82.

§34n4. The **kakón** 'bad thing' here at IX 250 turns out to be the death of Patroklos, which is again predicted as a **kakón** at XI 604.

§35n1. For more on *Achīuī*, see appendix §8. As for the Hittite form *Aḫḫii̯au̯a-*, there is no convincing evidence to prove any connection with the Greek word for "Achaean": Steiner 1964.

§35n2. Chadwick/Baumbach 1963.178.

its starting point. At xii 124, **Kratâiin** (accusative) designates the mother of the man-eating immortal monster Scylla; according to the instructions of Circe, Odysseus and his men must call on **Kratâiis** to restrain Scylla from attacking them again (xii 124–126). Among other interpretations of the name **Kratâiis**, the scholia (*ad* xii 597) offer **krataià ís** 'force that has **krátos**', with the immediate context cited as justification. In the appendix, I argue on morphological grounds that **krataiis** is in fact the personification of an adjective originally shaped **kratai-u̯ĭ-* 'whose **ís** [force] has **krátos**'.[1] For a semantic parallel, I adduce the compound **Kratai-ménēs**, which can be translated "whose **ménos** [might] has **krátos**." Also, I adduce the expression **kraterè . . . ìs Odusêos** (XXIII 720), which amounts to a periphrasis of an epithet + name combination such as **kratai-ménēs Oduseús*.[2] In arguing for the parallelism of **ménos** and **ís** in **Kratai-ménēs** and **kratai-uĭs*, I can cite such epic combinations as **hieròn ménos** + genitive (vii 167, viii 2, etc.) and **hierè ís** + genitive (ii 409, xviii 405, etc.).[3]

§37. In the appendix, I also present arguments in favor of interpreting the adjectives **krataió-/Akhaió-** as derived from compounds shaped **kratai-u̯ĭ-/*akhai-u̯ĭ-* 'whose **ís** has **krátos/ákhos**'.[1] In the case of **kratai-u̯ĭ-*, we have just considered the semantic parallel of **Kratai-ménēs** 'whose **ménos** [might] has **krátos**', where the element **ménos** has the inherited function of being a synonym of **ís**. There is also another semantic parallel, one that is even closer to the posited compound **krataió-** on a formal level. Since the word **bíē** 'might' also functions as a synonym of **ís** (e.g., **ís** at XI 668 is equated with **bíē** at XI 670), we may now in addition cite the adjective/name **krataí-bios/Krataí-bios** 'whose **bíē** has **krátos**'.[2] So much for the reconstruction **kratai-u̯ĭ-*. As for **akhai-u̯ĭ-*, I should note simply that its posited meaning "whose **ís** had **ákhos**" corresponds to the primary martial function of the **Akhaioí** 'Achaeans' in epic action: their prowess entails **ákhos** for the enemy and, simultaneously, **krátos** for themselves.[3] Moreover, the Iliadic tradition features an interesting variation on this theme: because Achilles

§36n1. Appendix §§1–2.
§36n2. See §31n5.
§36n3. Ibid.
§37n1. Appendix §§3–7.
§37n2. For the adjective, see *Anecdota Graeca* (ed. J. A. Cramer) 318.5 and Eustathius 1938.1; for the name, see Bechtel 1917.256.
§37n3. §§25–26, 30.

withdraws from battle, the Achaeans temporarily lose **krátos** to the Trojans and they themselves are overwhelmed by **ákhos**. Epic diction actually conveys this reversed position of the Achaeans in terms of **ákhos** and **bíē**, synonym of **ís**:

τοῖον γὰρ ἄχος βεβίηκεν ’Αχαιούς

For such an **ákhos** has brought **bíē** upon the Achaeans.[4]

XVI 22

These words are spoken by Patroklos to Achilles, and they introduce a concrete description of the Achaeans’ plight now that all the major heroes save Achilles have been knocked out of action by Hektor’s onslaught (XVI 23–29). The perfect formation **bebíēken** ‘has brought **bíē** upon’ at XVI 22 reverses the martial function of the Achaeans from active to passive: they “whose **ís** has **ákhos**” are no longer inflicting **ís** but are themselves afflicted by it, so that they, rather than the enemy, get the resulting **ákhos**.[5] To sum up, the warrior needs **bíē** to win in battle, but **bíē** is not enough. One can have **bíē** and still lose without the **krátos** that only Zeus can grant.[6] Even the cosmic régime of the Olympians is actually maintained by the combination of **Krátos** and **Bíē** personified (Hesiod *Th.* 385–401). Thus he who is **krataí-bios** ‘whose **bíē** has **krátos**’ is one who not only has **bíē** but also wins because he has been granted **krátos** by the gods. The same goes for the **kraterè** . . . **ís** of Odysseus at XXIII 720. But winning is an ambiguous prospect for the **Akhaioí**: their **ís** may fail to have **krátos** from the gods, and so the **ákhos** may be destined for them rather than the enemy.

§38. So much, then, for the argument that **Akhaiá/Akhaioí** is treated by epic diction as a derivative of **ákhos** ‘grief’. When we add the evidence of the strong thematic links between these words, we gain an important perspective on the *social* function of **ákhos**. On the level of cult, the title **Akhaiá** shows that the community becomes involved in the **ákhos** of Demeter by performing rites of lamentation. On the level of epic, the title **Akhaioí** shows that **ákhos** can afflict an entire aggregate of warriors. We had started our discussion of **Akhaiá/Akhaioí** by stressing the social implications in the compo-

§37n4. See also X 145, likewise referring to the plight of the Achaeans (cf. X 172).

§37n5. For the notion that a victim can be afflicted by the **bíē** of the enemy, cf. XI 467: Menelaos fears that the Trojans are overcoming Odysseus with **bíē** (**bióiato**), since he is alone. Consider also expressions like **è thanátōi biētheìs è noúsōi** ‘overcome by the **bíē** of either death or disease’ (Herodotus 7.83).

§37n6. So also with athletics: in order to win, the athlete needs both **bíē** and **krátos** (Hesiod *Th.* 437); cf. Pindar *I.*8.5.

nent **lāós** of the reconstructed *Akhí-lāu̯os.[n] Now we see that the social implications extend to the component **ákhos** as well.

§39. In this light, we may compare *Akhí-lāu̯os 'whose **lāós** has grief' with the name **Kharílāos** (from *Kharí-lāu̯os) 'whose **lāós** has mirth', as used in Archilochus *fr.* 168W. The poem addresses Kharilaos and then promises to give him pleasure by making him laugh:

᾽Ερασμονίδη Χαρίλαε,
  χρῆμά τοι γελοῖον
ἐρέω, πολὺ φίλταθ᾽ ἑταίρων,
  τέρψεαι δ᾽ ἀκούων

Kharílāos, son of Erásmōn!
I will tell you something to be laughed at,
you most **phílos** [dear] of **hetaîroi** [companions]!
and you will get pleasure hearing it.

Archilochus fr. 168W

There are implications not only in the name **Kharílāos** but also in the patronymic **Erasmonídēs** 'son of **Erásmōn**', which is related to **erásmios** 'lovely'; this adjective elsewhere describes the bloom of youth that inspires poetry (Anacreon *fr.* 375P).[1] Moreover, the verb **térpō/térpomai** 'give/get pleasure' conventionally designates the effect of poetry (e.g., i 347).[2] We may also note the combination of **erásmios** 'lovely' and **terpnós** 'pleasurable' in Semonides 7.52W and compare the collocation of **Erasmonídēs** (᾽Ερασμονίδη) and **térpomai** 'get pleasure' (τέρψεαι) in this poem of Archilochus. My point is that the pleasure and laughter promised by the poem are actually embodied in the element **khari-** of **Kharí-lāos**.[3] This element, as found in the noun **kháris**,[4] conveys the notion of "pleasure, mirth" in conventional descriptions of poetry and its effects;[5] moreover, the context of such pleasure is *social*.[6] As the narrating Odysseus says in

---

§38n. Above, §28.

§39n1. The poem itself is a *response* to **hḗbē** 'bloom of youth'. Its words say that whoever turns his thoughts to **hḗbē**, which is **erasmíē** 'lovely', will dance to the sound of the flute. For a parallel correlation of song and dance, cf. *Odyssey* i 421–423.

§39n2. Ch.1§4n1. Again, cf. also *Odyssey* i 421–423.

§39n3. There are also other instances in Archilochean poetry where the function of a character seems to be conveyed by his name: see especially Ch.12§21 on **Lukámbēs**. Cf. also the poetic function of the patronymic **Terpiádēs**: Ch.1§4n1.

§39n4. For an introduction to the relationship of noun **kháris** and verb **khaírō** 'be well, be glad, be happy', see Latacz 1966.125–127.

§39n5. Ch.1§5(n1), Ch.2§13(n2).

§39n6. Ibid. On the notion of reciprocity conveyed by **kháris**, see Benveniste 1969 I 199–202.

ix 3–11, there is no accomplishment "having more **kháris**" (χαριέστερον: line 5) than the **eüphrosúnē** 'mirth' that everyone in the
dêmos 'district' experiences from the dinner hour performance of a
poet.[7] So too with **Kharí-lãos**: he will get pleasure and laugh as "the
most **phílos** [dear] of the **hetaîroi** [companions]" (φίλταθ' ἐταίρων:
line 3). In other words, the audience of the poem is a *community*
(comprised of **phíloi** 'friends').[8] And the notion of community is also
embodied in the element **lãós** of **Kharí-lãos**.[9]

§40. If indeed the semantics of **Kharí-lã(u̯)os** and ***Akhí-lãu̯os** are
comparable, we may note with interest the reaction of the **lãós** when
Achilles suspends his **mênis** 'anger':

ὣς ἔφαθ', οἱ δ' ἐχάρησαν ἐϋκνήμιδες Ἀχαιοὶ
μῆνιν ἀπειπόντος μεγαθύμου Πηλεΐωνος

Thus he [Achilles] spoke. And the fair-greaved Achaeans were happy
that the great-hearted son of Peleus unsaid his **mênis**.

XIX 74–75

Since the **mênis** 'anger' of Achilles had caused **ákhos** 'grief' for the
Achaeans during the Battle of the Ships,[n] it is significant that the
suspension of this same **mênis** now causes them "mirth"—as
conveyed by the root **khar-** in ἐχάρησαν 'were happy' at XIX 74.
This same root constitutes the first element of the compound **Kharí-
lãos** 'whose **lãós** has mirth.'

§41. As we have seen, another traditional word for the dire
military situation of the Achaeans during the Battle of the Ships is
loigós 'devastation'.[1] Since the grief caused by the **mênis** of Achilles
is thus a devastation as well, we may suppose that a name like
Kharílãos could convey the notion that the **lãós** has mirth *because
some devastation is suspended*. In view of this possibility, let us
consider the social function of the name **Kharila** in Delphic myth and
ritual. From the report of Plutarch *Quaestiones Graecae* 293e, we
learn that **Kharila** designates not only a Delphic festival but also the
figure commemorated in that festival. The corresponding myth tells
that **Kharila** was a starving girl who begged for a share of food that

§39n7. For the text, see Ch.1§5. On the theme of **eüphrosúnē** 'mirth' in the
community, see also Ch.12§15n5. On the **dêmos** as the community/audience of
Dēmódokos, see Ch.1§4n1.
§39n8. See further at Ch.13§2.
§39n9. On **lãós**: §27 above.
§40n. §21.
§41n1. §§9–11.

was being distributed in the community by the king; when the king knocked her away with his shoe, she hanged herself. During the enneateric festival of **Kharila**, a ritual dummy that is also called **Kharila** is knocked away by the king of the festival, whereupon it is hanged by its neck and then buried. As is generally agreed, the theme of the festival is fertility by way of banishing hunger.[2] Both the myth and the ritual of **Kharila** reveal an archaic social foundation in general and an archaic judicial system in particular.[3] On the basis of the social function inherited by the name **Kharila**, I suggest that the form may be a truncated variant of *Kharílāụos. We have in fact already seen other such variants: **Khárillos** and **Kharíllēs**.[4]

§41n2. Nilsson 1906.466–467, with further references; also Usener 1912/1913 [= 1875] 116–119 on the parallel Italic ritual of *saecula condere*.

§41n3. Glotz 1904.ix,64; Gernet 1968 [= 1928] 58, [1948–1949] 231–232.

§41n4. §2n1. I leave the accent of **Kharila** unmarked because I cannot verify the quantity of the last syllable. We are impeded here by the fact that this name is attested only in the text of Plutarch.

6 | Lamentation and the Hero

§1. The social dimensions of the actual word **ákhos** 'grief' have so far been explored mainly in terms of its thematic relationship with the concept of **lāós** 'host of fighting men' in epic diction. The time has now come to explore the meaning of **ákhos** on its own terms.

§2. In Homeric diction, **ákhos** 'grief' functions as a formulaic variant of another es-stem, **pénthos**. Both words designate the grief of Achilles over his loss of **tīmé** (ἄχος: I 188, XVI 52, 55; πένθος: I 362); also, both words designate the grief of Achilles over his loss of Patroklos (ἄχος: XVIII 22, XXIII 47; πένθος: XVIII 73). Finally, not only **ákhos**, as at XVI 22, but also **pénthos** designates the collective grief of the Achaeans, as at IX 3; in this passage, there is special emphasis on the grief of their king Agamemnon, which is called **ákhos** as well, at IX 9. Outside the poetic diction, we find expressions like πένθος ποιήσασθαι 'have public mourning [**pénthos**]' (Herodotus 2.1.1; cf. 2.46.3, 6.21.1).[1] Even inside the poetic diction, the collective aspect of **pénthos** is apparent in its application to the public mourning for Hektor (XXIV 708).[2]

§3. This collective aspect is also apparent in the opposition of **pénthos** to **kléos**. When the healer Makhaon is summoned to heal the wound of Menelaos, the Trojan who had wounded him is said to have **kléos** as opposed to the collective **pénthos** of the Achaeans:

> ... τῷ μὲν κλέος, ἄμμι δὲ πένθος

... for him **kléos**, for us **pénthos**

IV 197–207

---

§2n1. Cf. also the parallel use of **pénthos** in inscriptions (e.g., Sokolowski 1955 no. 16.11–13).

§2n2. Cf. also XVI 548–553: it is **pénthos** that makes the Trojans want to recover the body of Sarpedon.

Whereas the word **kléos** is used in traditional poetic diction to designate the public prestige of Epos or praise-poetry,[n] the word **pénthos** can indicate the public ritual of mourning, formally enacted with songs of lamentation (as at XXIV 708-781, especially 720-722).

§4. The traditional relationship of **pénthos** with **kléos** is reflected by its fixed epithet **álaston** 'unforgettable', which is morphologically parallel to **áphthiton** 'unfailing', the fixed epithet of **kléos** (IX 413).[1] There is also an important thematic connection with **kléos** in the application of **álaston** to both **pénthos** (XXIV 105, xxiv 423) and **ákhos** (iv 108), since the meaning of **álaston** is coordinate with the inherited theme of **mnēmosúnē** 'memory'. The conceit of Homeric poetry is that the sacred mnemonic power of the Muses is the key to the **kléos** of epic. The **aoidós** 'singer' sings what he sings because the **Moûsai** put his mind in touch with the realities of the past (μνησαίατ’ II 492, κλέος II 486, Μοῦσαι II 484).[2]

§5. This is not the place for a detailed survey of the word **kléos** in its function of expressing the very notion of epic poetry within epic poetry—a task that I have attempted elsewhere.[1] I confine myself here to the differences between the traditional genres of poetry, as expressed by the contrast of **kléos** with **pénthos/ákhos**. Not only does the epithet **álaston** 'unforgettable' of **pénthos/ákhos** conjure up the traditional theme of **mnēmosúnē** 'memory', which is inherent in the poetic concept of **kléos**, but also the word **pénthos** itself is used by the poetry of the Homeric and Hesiodic traditions as a foil for **kléos**.[2] For a striking example, consider this Hesiodic passage:

εἰ γάρ τις καὶ πένθος ἔχων νεοκηδέϊ θυμῷ
ἄζηται κραδίην ἀκαχήμενος, αὐτὰρ ἀοιδὸς
Μουσάων θεράπων κλέεα προτέρων ἀνθρώπων
ὑμνήσῃ μάκαράς τε θεούς, οἳ Ὄλυμπον ἔχουσιν,
αἶψ’ ὅ γε δυσφροσυνέων ἐπιλήθεται οὐδέ τι κηδέων
μέμνηται

And if someone has **pénthos** and is distressed having **ákhos**
in a **thūmós** beset with new cares, yet, when a singer,
therápōn of the Muses,[3] sings the **kléos** [plural] of men of old

§3n. Ch.1§2, Ch.12§3; cf. Nagy 1974.229-261.
§4n1. Nagy 1974.256.
§4n2. Ch.1§3.
§5n1. Nagy 1974.244-255; see also Koller 1972.
§5n2. Nagy, pp. 255-261.
§5n3. On the notion "**therápōn** of the Muses": Ch.17§§3-9, Ch.18§§1-6.

and also the blessed gods that inhabit Olympus,
at once he <u>forgets</u> his sorrows, and his cares
he no longer <u>remembers</u>.

Hesiod Th. 98–103

When the singer sings "the **kléos** [plural] of men of old," the song is
in the tradition of an *Iliad* or an *Odyssey*; when he sings "the blessed
gods," the song is in the general tradition of a *Theogony*.[4] (I avoid
saying "*the* Iliad" or "*the* Theogony" in order to suggest that the
diction refers simply to established poetic traditions rather than fixed
texts.) The conceptual association of Theogonic poetry with the word
kléos is made overt a few hexameters earlier in the Hesiodic
Theogony, where the Muses are designated as the ones who <u>make</u>
<u>into</u> **kléos** (κλείουσιν) the **génos** 'genesis' of the gods:[5]

θεῶν γένος αἰδοῖον πρῶτον <u>κλείουσιν</u> ἀοιδῇ

With song they first <u>make into **kléos**</u> the genesis of the gods, thing of
reverence that it is.

Hesiod Th. 44

A few hexameters later, after the contrast of **kléos** with **pénthos** (*Th.*
98–103), the Muses are finally invoked to sing the contents of our
Theogony, with the following words:[6]

χαίρετε τέκνα Διός, δότε δ᾽ ἱμερόεσσαν ἀοιδήν·
<u>κλείετε</u> δ᾽ ἀθανάτων ἱερὸν <u>γένος</u> αἰὲν ἐόντων

Hail, children of Zeus! Grant an entrancing song.
<u>Make into **kléos**</u> the sacred **génos** [genesis] of the immortals,[7] who always
are.

Hesiod Th. 104–105

The inherited function of our *Theogony*, then, is to give **kléos** to the
genesis of the gods. The hearing of such **kléos** is a remedy for
pénthos, as we learn from the passage that inaugurated this discussion, the artistic manifesto of *Th.* 98–103. In Theogonic language,
Mnēmosúnē 'mnemonic power' gave birth to the **Moûsai** 'Muses',
who were to be the **lēsmosúnē** 'forgetting' of ills:[8]

§5n4. Cf. Kullmann 1956, esp. pp. 11, 20.
§5n5. Cf. also line 33: ὑμνεῖν ... γένος.
§5n6. Cf. West 1966.189.
§5n7. The connection of **génos** here with the notion of "theo*gony*" is made even
more explicit at *Th.* 114–115. On the traditional nature of theogonic poetry: Duban
1975.
§5n8. On the etymology of **Moûsai**: Ch.1§3n2.

τὰς ἐν Πιερίῃ Κρονίδῃ τέκε πατρὶ μιγεῖσα
Μνημοσύνη, γουνοῖσιν Ἐλευθῆρος μεδέουσα,
λησμοσύνην τε κακῶν ἄμπαυμά τε μερμηράων

They were born in Pieria to the one who mated with the son of Kronos,
to **Mnēmosúnē**, who rules over the ridges of Eleuther—
born to be a **lēsmosúnē** of ills and a cessation of anxieties.[9]

Hesiod *Th.* 53–55

§6. Let us now turn from the **kléos** of the Theogonic tradition to
"the **kléos** [plural] of previous men," as our *Theogony* calls it (κλέεα
προτέρων ἀνθρώπων: verse 100). To repeat, **kléos** is used in epic
diction to designate the epic tradition itself.[1] Presently, however, we
are concerned only with the specific use of this word as an antithesis
of **pénthos/ákhos**. We begin with the song of Phemios in *Odyssey* i;
his subject is the **nóstos** 'homecoming' of the Achaeans (i 326–327),[2]
and his song brings grief rather than entertainment to one of his
listeners, who happens to be the wife of Odysseus. Penelope asks the
singer to stop his song, because it brings her **pénthos álaston**
'unforgettable grief' (i 342). Just before, her words had described the
aoidoí 'singers' generically as those who give **kléos** to the deeds of
heroes and gods:

ἔργ᾽ ἀνδρῶν τε θεῶν τε, τά τε κλείουσιν ἀοιδοί

the deeds of men and gods, which the singers make into **kléos**

i 338

Just after, she says that *she always has her husband on her mind*
(μεμνημένη αἰεί: i 343), and then we hear the following description
of Odysseus:

τοῦ κλέος εὐρὺ καθ᾽ Ἑλλάδα καὶ μέσον Ἄργος

who has **kléos** far and wide throughout Hellas and midmost Argos

i 344

From the standpoint of an audience listening to the medium of epic,

§5n9. Cf. also *Th.* 61.
§6n1. Nagy 1974.244–255.
§6n2. Even this narrative obeys the convention of beginning with a
word that serves as title (in this case, **nóstos** at i 326), followed by an epithet and then
a relative clause that sets forth the relationship of the title word to the main subject (in
this case, how Athena caused the **nóstos** of the Achaeans from Troy to be a baneful
one indeed: i 327). See Ch.5§8n1. Thus the word **nóstos** here designates not only the
homecoming of the Achaeans but also the epic tradition that told about their
homecoming.

the word **kléos** can apply to the epic of Odysseus, to the narrative tradition of the *Odyssey*. From the standpoint of Penelope as a character within the epic, however, the **kléos** of Odysseus, with all its hardships, entails personal involvement: it brings to mind a grief that cannot be swept away from the mind (cf. μεμνημένη αἰεί 'remembering always': i 343). Telemachus does not yet realize the extent of his own involvement in the unfolding action when he rebukes his mother and urges the singer to continue his song, on the grounds that it is fitting entertainment for an audience (i 346–347). The story of the poet's song is the Will of Zeus, he says (i 347–350),[3] and the song is popular with its audience:

τὴν γὰρ ἀοιδὴν μᾶλλον ἐπικλείουσ' ἄνθρωποι
ἥ τις ἀκουόντεσσι νεωτάτη ἀμφιπέληται

For men would rather <u>continue to make into **kléos**</u>[4] the song
that is the newest to make its rounds with the listeners.

i 351–352

On one level, the song is νεωτάτη 'newest' for an audience of epic, in that it tells of actions that will lead to the **nóstos** 'homecoming' of Odysseus, the last Achaean to come home from Troy. On another level, the song is "newest" specifically for Telemachus, in that he is about to become involved in the actions of this **nóstos**.[5]

§7. The factor of personal involvement or noninvolvement decides whether an epic situation calls for **pénthos** or **kléos**. The figure of Menelaos sets the tone for the involvement of Telemachus. As a warrior who had shared in the hardships of the Achaeans at Troy, Menelaos tells Telemachus that Odysseus is the warrior whose absence he misses and mourns the most of all (iv 100–105; see especially ἀχεύων 'having **ákhos**' at 100). There is a reason for this:

... ἐπεὶ οὔ τις 'Αχαιῶν τόσσ' ἐμόγησεν
ὅσσ' 'Οδυσεὺς ἐμόγησε καὶ ἤρατο. τῷ δ' ἄρ' ἔμελλεν
αὐτῷ κήδε' ἔσεσθαι, ἐμοὶ δ' ἄχος αἰὲν ἄλαστον

§6n3. On the Will of Zeus as the plot of the narrative, see the comments on viii 577–580 at §8; also Ch.5§25n2 and Ch.7§17.

§6n4. For the semantics of **kleíō/epikleíō**, compare **ainéō/epainéō**, the technical and programmatic words for "praise" in praise poetry (e.g., Pindar *O*.4.14/*P*.2.67; see Detienne 1973.18–22). Cf. also the technical word used by **rhapsōidoí** for the notion of "recite Homer": **Hómēron epaineîn** (Plato *Ion* 536d, 541e).

§6n5. See also n2 above. For further discussion of the two-level application of **kléos** to characters within the narrative and to the audience outside the narrative: Nagy 1974.11–13.

... since none of the Achaeans struggled so much
as Odysseus struggled and achieved. For him there would be
cares in the future, whereas I would have an **ákhos álaston** [unforgettable
grief] always.

iv 106–108

This unforgettable **ákhos** now finally involves Telemachus, as he
hears from Menelaos how Odysseus is probably being mourned, at
this very minute, by his father, wife, and son (iv 110–112).
Telemachus indeed begins to weep (iv 113–116), and from here on
we find communal weeping at the table of Menelaos when the story
of Odysseus comes up (see especially iv 183–185), since he is
presently the only Achaean left who is still without a **nóstos**:

... κεῖνον δύστηνον ἀνόστιμον οἶον ...

... that wretched one, the only one who has not come home ...

iv 182

Later on, Helen tells Menelaos and his guests—Telemachus included—a story of Troy as an entertainment during dinner:

ἦ τοι νῦν δαίνυσθε καθήμενοι ἐν μεγάροισι
καὶ μύθοις τέρπεσθε· ἐοικότα γὰρ καταλέξω

Sit now and dine in the palace, and be entertained
by the stories. For the things that I will say in proper order are appropriate.

iv 238–239

Her entertaining story, however, begins on a note of grief:

πάντα μὲν οὐκ ἂν ἐγὼ μυθήσομαι οὐδ᾽ ὀνομήνω,
ὅσσοι Ὀδυσσῆος ταλασίφρονός εἰσιν ἄεθλοι·
ἀλλ᾽ οἶον τόδ᾽ ἔρεξε καὶ ἔτλη καρτερὸς ἀνὴρ
δήμῳ ἔνι Τρώων, ὅθι πάσχετε πήματ᾽ Ἀχαιοί

I could not possibly tell of or name
all the struggles that are the share of the enduring Odysseus.
but I will tell of this one thing that he did and endured—
—that man of **krátos**—in the district of Troy, where you Achaeans suffered
pains [**pêma** plural].

iv 240–243

All the characters listening to the story are personally involved, and
we would expect its words to arouse instant grief on their part, were
it not for what Helen did before telling her tale. She put a
phármakon 'drug' in their wine (iv 220), described as:

νηπενθές τ᾽ ἄχολόν τε, κακῶν ἐπίληθον ἁπάντων

without **pénthos**, without anger, making one forget all ills

iv 221

One who drinks it would not even mourn the death of his mother, father, brother, or son (iv 222–226). What would otherwise be a **pénthos** for Helen's audience can thus remain a **kléos**, since there is no personal involvement.

§8. Such a distinction between **kléos** and **pénthos** is even more vivid when Odysseus himself becomes personally involved. He is an unidentified member of the audience as the poet Demodokos starts singing the κλέα ἀνδρῶν 'kléos [plural] of men':

Μοῦσ' ἄρ' ἀοιδὸν ἀνῆκεν ἀειδέμεναι κλέα ἀνδρῶν
οἴμης τῆς τότ' ἄρα κλέος οὐρανὸν εὐρὺν ἵκανε

The Muse impelled the singer to sing the **kléos** [plural] of men
from a story thread that had at that time a **kléos** reaching up to the vast heavens.

viii 73–74

The story of the singer concerns "the beginning of pain [**pêma**]" (πήματος ἀρχή: viii 81) that befell Achaeans and Trojans alike, "on account of the plans of great Zeus" (Διὸς μεγάλου διὰ βουλάς: viii 82). Odysseus immediately begins to weep, though he hides his grief (viii 83–95). Later on, the still-unidentified Odysseus compliments the Trojan story of the poet as "correct":

λίην γὰρ κατὰ κόσμον 'Αχαιῶν οἶτον ἀείδεις,
ὅσσ' ἔρξαν τ' ἔπαθόν τε καὶ ὅσσ' ἐμόγησαν 'Αχαιοί

You sing in very correct fashion the fate of the Achaeans,
all the things that they did and suffered and struggled for.

viii 489–490

He then asks Demodokos to shift ahead in subject matter (μετάβηθι: viii 492) and sing about the Trojan Horse (viii 492–495). The poet obliges, beginning within a traditional framework (ἔνθεν ἑλὼν ὡς ... 'taking it from the place in the story where ...': viii 500), and the cumulative effect of his Trojan story is that Odysseus again bursts into tears (viii 521–534). This time the host Alkinoos draws attention to the still-unidentified guest's grief (**ákhos**: viii 541), and he calls on Odysseus to explain what amounts to an internalized lamentation:

εἰπὲ δ' ὅ τι κλαίεις καὶ ὀδύρεαι ἔνδοθι θυμῷ
'Αργείων Δαναῶν ἰδὲ 'Ιλίου οἶτον ἀκούων.
τὸν δὲ θεοὶ μὲν τεῦξαν, ἐπεκλώσαντο δ' ὄλεθρον
ἀνθρώποις, ἵνα ᾖσι καὶ ἐσσομένοισιν ἀοιδή

Tell why you weep and lament within your thūmós
upon hearing the fate of the Argive Danaans and of Ilion.
The gods fashioned it, and they were the ones who ordained
destruction for men, so that it might be a song for men yet to be.

viii 577–580

What is an **ákhos** for Odysseus is for future audiences simply a
"song" like the *Iliad*, with its plot enacted by the Will of Zeus and
his gods.

§9. The plot in this third song of Demodokos is strikingly parallel
to the plot of the Cyclic *Iliou Persis* as we find it in the Proclus
summary (pp. 107–108 Allen). But there is an interesting variation.
On the one hand, the narrative in the *Iliou Persis* draws to a close
with the destruction of Troy and such specific scenes as the killing of
Astyanax by Odysseus and the enslavement of Andromache by
Pyrrhos (p. 108.8–9).[n] On the other hand, the narrative of Demodokos is interrupted, before it draws to a close, by the weeping of
Odysseus. The action stops just when various Achaean heroes are
performing their various grisly feats during the destruction of Troy,
such as the killing of Deiphobos (viii 516–520). At this point, the
weeping of Odysseus is compared *by way of a simile* to the weeping of
a widow who is taken as captive by a ruthless enemy after the
destruction of her city and the killing of her husband (viii 523–531).
The husband is described as a hero who fell in front of his city,
where he was defending both the community and his children (viii
524–525). The resemblance with Hektor is unmistakable. The generic
situation in the simile is thus strikingly parallel to the specific
situation of Andromache at the end of the *Iliou Persis*. In this sense,
the simile that pictures the weeping of Odysseus completes the
narrative that his weeping had interrupted. And the captive widow
also has **ákhos** (viii 530), so that the **ákhos** of Odysseus is
universalized: he now feels the grief of his own victims in war, and
his involvement is thus complete.

§10. In sum, we see from the evidence of epic itself that the **kléos**
heard by its audiences may be **ákhos/pénthos** for those involved in
the actions that it describes. Alkinoos perceives the **ákhos** of
Odysseus when he sees his guest's reaction to the **kléos** sung about
the Trojan War. As a considerate host, he even asks Odysseus

---

§9n. See Friis Johansen 1967.28 on the corresponding theme in archaic iconog-
raphy: warriors killing children in the presence of women. In fact, the iconographical
evidence indicates "a coherent *Iliou Persis* narrative as source" (Friis Johansen, p. 36).

whether he had a male relative or **hetaîros** 'comrade' who died at Troy (viii 581–586). This theme brings us back to the *Iliad*, where Achilles has **ákhos/pénthos** (XVIII 22/73) over the death of Patroklos, his **hetaîros** (XVIII 80, etc.). It is this grief that impels him to go forth finally and fight, and here is how Achilles says it:

> ... νῦν δὲ <u>κλέος</u> ἐσθλὸν ἀροίμην
>
> ... but now let me win worthy <u>kléos</u>

XVIII 121

After the death of Patroklos, the Achilles figure uses the expression νῦν δέ 'but now' (as also here) no fewer than fifteen times in our *Iliad*.[1] With his **ákhos/pénthos** over Patroklos, "Achilles enters the realm of **kléos**."[2]

§11. By entering his war, Achilles knowingly approaches certain death (XVIII 95–99), which in turn will bring **pénthos** to his mother (XVIII 88).[1] The choice for him had been clear all along: either a **nóstos** without **kléos** (IX 414–415) or **kléos** without **nóstos** (IX 412–413). If he gives up a safe homecoming—that is, if he chooses not to be the hero of a story about homecoming—Achilles will die at Troy but will have a **kléos** that is **áphthiton** 'unfailing' (IX 413). In other words, he will be the central figure of an epic tradition that will never die out.[2] And the key to the **kléos** of Achilles' epic is the **ákhos/pénthos** over Patroklos.

§12. We are now ready to consider the semantics of the name **Pátroklos** (cf. I 345, etc.)/**Patrokléēs** (cf. I 337, etc.),[1] a compound formation referring to the **kléos** 'glory' of the **patéres** 'ancestors' (on the latter meaning of the word **patéres**, see VI 209, etc.). These two notions of "glory" and "ancestors" within the compound **Patrokléēs**(/**Pátro-klos**) should be compared with the two notions in the combination κλέεα = **kléos** [plural] and προτέρων ἀνθρώπων = "previous men" in Hesiod *Th.* 100 (where **kléos** [plural] is antithetical to **pénthos** at verse 98). The semantics of κλέεα προτέρων ἀνθρώπων 'the **kléos** [plural] of previous men', an expression that had provided the starting point for this discussion of **ákhos/pénthos** and **kléos**, has a parallel in epic, where the specific application is to

§10n1. Bassett 1933.58.
§10n2. Sinos 1975.104.
§11n1. At XXIV 105, her **pénthos** is described as **álaston** 'unforgettable'.
§11n2. Ch.2§11; cf. also Nagy 1974.250–255.
§12n1. Cf. **Etéoklos** in Hesiod *fr.* 70.34MW, a by-form of **Eteokléēs**; also **Díoklos** (*H.Dem.* 153), a by-form of **Diokléēs/Dioklês** (*H.Dem.* 474, 477).

Achilles himself. Here is the Iliadic parallel to the combination in
Hesiod *Th.* 100:

οὕτω καὶ τῶν πρόσθεν ἐπευθόμεθα κλέα ἀνδρῶν
ἡρώων . . .

We learn this also from the **kléos** [plural] of men of the past,
who were the heroes . . . [2]

IX 524-525

These words introduce the story that Phoinix tells Achilles, taken
from the epic tradition of Meleager. As Dale Sinos has shown in
detail, this story is intended to illustrate the ethical principle of
philótēs 'being a **phílos**' in warrior society.[3] It is an epic *exemplum*, or
κλέα ἀνδρῶν '**kléos** [plural] of men', set before Achilles so that he
may be persuaded to lay aside his anger and to rejoin his **hetaîroi**
'comrades-in-arms', who are his **phíloi**.[4]

§13. As we proceed to consider the story of Meleager, we must
keep in mind the *institutional* and *sentimental* connotations of this
word **phílos/phíloi**, conventionally translated as "friend" when it is a
noun and as "dear" or "one's own" when it is an adjective. For a
suggestive discussion, I refer to Benveniste's acute reading of **phílos**
in its Homeric contexts.[1] For now, however, I merely cite what he
sees as the results of his findings:[2]

It would take many chapters to list and analyze with the necessary care all
the examples of *phílos* where it is said to be "possessive." We believe,
however, that we have interpreted the most important. This re-examination
was necessary to expose a long-standing error, which is probably as old as
Homeric exegesis, and has been handed down from generation to generation
of scholars. The whole problem of *phílos* deserves a full examination. We
must start from uses and contexts which reveal in this term *a complex net-
work of associations, some with the institutions of hospitality, others with usages of
the home, still others with emotional behavior* [italics mine]; we must do this in
order to understand plainly the metaphorical applications to which the term
lent itself. All this wealth of concepts was smothered and lost to view once
phílos was reduced to a vague notion of friendship or wrongly interpreted as a
possessive adjective. It is high time we learned again how to read Homer.

§12n2. To justify my interpretation of this passage, I cite Schmitt 1967.93–95.
§12n3. Sinos 1975.67–70. For further observations about the intent of this story:
Rosner 1976.
§12n4. Sinos 1975.70–79.
§13n1. Benveniste 1969 I 338–353.
§13n2. Benveniste 1969 I 352–353 = 1973.288.

§14. The story of Meleager, like the story of Achilles, tells of the hero's withdrawal from battle. Like Achilles, Meleager is angry:

... χόλον θυμαλγέα πέσσων

... mulling his anger, which caused pain for his **thūmós**

IX 565

The same words apply to the anger of Achilles:

... χόλον θυμαλγέα πέσσει

IV 513

Compare also these words addressed to Achilles:

παύε᾽, ἔα δὲ χόλον θυμαλγέα

Stop! Abandon your anger, which causes pain for your **thūmós**.[1]

IX 260

The parallels are even deeper: while the anger of Achilles was preceded by the anger of Apollo, the anger of Meleager (IX 525, 553) was preceded by the anger of Apollo's sister, Artemis (IX 533–535).[2] Just as Achilles is destined by tradition to die at the hands of Apollo himself (XXI 275–278; cf. Pindar *Paean* 6.78–80), so also Meleager (Hesiod *fr.* 25.9–13MW).[3]

§15. I save the most important point of comparison for last: the comrades of Meleager, his **hetaîroi**, rate as next-to-highest in the narrative sequence that catalogues those who have ties to the hero and who are now entreating him to rejoin his comrades-in-arms. The ranking of the hero's social affinities at IX 574–591 implicitly presents Meleager as one who loves the *elders* not so much as the *priests* not so much as his *father* not so much as his *sisters* not so much as his *mother* not so much as his **hetaîroi** not so much as his *wife*. As the studies of J. T. Kakridis have shown, variations in the listing of a hero's affinities represent a relative ranking of these affinities in Homeric narrative and constitute a poetic convention in itself.[1] In comparison with other attested occurrences of this convention, which Kakridis calls "the ascending scale of affection," the position of the **hetaîroi** in the Meleager story is noticeably high.[2] This preeminence can be seen not only on the level of theme but also on the level of

§14n1. For additional parallelisms on the level of diction between the stories of Meleager and Achilles, see Rosner 1976.323.

§14n2. Cf. Lord 1967.243.

§14n3. At XXI 275–278, Apollo alone is pictured as killing Achilles; at XIX 416–417 and XXII 358–360, on the other hand, Achilles is killed by Apollo *and* Paris.

§15n1. Kakridis 1949.21–24.

§15n2. Kakridis, p. 21.

form. Here is how the **hetaîroi** of Meleager, his comrades-in-arms, are described:

> ... ἑταῖροι,
> οἵ οἱ κεδνότατοι καὶ φίλτατοι ἦσαν ἁπάντων

> ... the **hetaîroi**,
> who were for him the most cherished and most **phíloi** of all

IX 585–586

On the level of theme, the one relation in the listing that outranks even the **hetaîroi** is the wife of Meleager, Kleopatre. This name **Kleo-pátrē** (IX 556) combines the same notions **kléos** 'glory' and **patéres** 'ancestors' as that of **Pátroklos ~ Patro-kléēs**. By their very etymologies, these compound names **Kleo-pátrē** and **Patro-kléēs** convey with their mutually inverted members a parallel epic theme.[3] For Achilles, then, the story of Meleager has a distinct message: in his own ascending scale of affection as dramatized by the entire composition of the *Iliad*, the highest place must belong to Patroklos, whose name has the same meaning as the name of Kleopatre. In fact, Patroklos is for Achilles the πολὺ φίλτατος ... ἑταῖρος—the '**hetaîros** who is the most **phílos** by far' (XVII 411, 655). The words of Achilles himself put it this way, as we find him in a later scene grieving for his fallen comrade:

> ἀλλὰ τί μοι τῶν ἧδος, ἐπεὶ φίλος ὤλεθ' ἑταῖρος,
> Πάτροκλος, τὸν ἐγὼ περὶ πάντων τῖον ἑταίρων

> But what pleasure is there for me in these things? For my **phílos hetaîros**
> has perished,
> Patroklos, to whom I gave more **tīmé** than to all the other **hetaîroi**.

XVIII 80–81

§16. For Phoinix, however, the code of the Meleager story, as he introduces it, has a different message.[1] In his words, the Achaeans who are "most **phíloi**" to Achilles (φίλτατοι: IX 522) are now entreating him to rejoin them in their desperate battle. As Achilles refuses to relent, another of the three delegates describes the hero with these words of reproach:

> ... οὐδὲ μετατρέπεται φιλότητος ἑταίρων

> ... and he is not swayed by being **phílos** of his **hetaîroi**

IX 630

§15n3. Cf. Howald 1946.132.
§16n1. On the terms *code* and *message* (as used by Jakobson 1960), see further at Ch.12§§18–19.

The speaker here is Ajax, and he is speaking for all his fellow delegates as he affirms that they all want to be, among all the Achaeans, "the most **phíloi**" to Achilles (φίλτατοι: IX 642). Achilles himself, who had been brought up by his father to choose "being **phílos**" over strife (φιλοφροσύνη: IX 256), actually addresses the delegates as "the most **phíloi** of the Achaeans" ('Αχαιῶν φίλτατοι: IX 198; cf. 204). Nevertheless, the delegates fail in their attempt to persuade Achilles to rejoin the **phíloi**. The κλέα ἀνδρῶν = 'kléos [plural] of men', the story about Meleager as told by Phoinix "in the midst of all the **phíloi**" (ἐν ... πάντεσσι φίλοισι: IX 528), points Achilles first towards the individual **phílos**, Patroklos, and only the death of this comrade will finally lead the central hero of the *Iliad* back to the collective **phíloi**. As Sinos has argued in detail, Patroklos is the link of Achilles to the **phíloi**.[2] When Patroklos enters the war as the surrogate of Achilles, the Trojans are terrified, thinking that Achilles has cast aside his **mênis** so that he may rescue his **phíloi**:

μηνιθμὸν μὲν ἀπορρῖψαι, φιλότητα δ' ἑλέσθαι

that he has cast aside his state of **mênis** and has chosen being **phílos** instead.

XVI 282

But it is really Patroklos who restores the **philótēs** 'state of being **phíloi**' between Achilles and the Achaeans. As Sinos points out, Patroklos will have to sacrifice himself and die so that Achilles may recognize his social obligation to his **phíloi**:[3]

οὐδέ τι Πατρόκλῳ γενόμην φάος οὐδ' ἑτάροισι
τοῖς ἄλλοις, οἳ δὴ πολέες δάμεν "Εκτορι δίῳ

I did not become the Light[4] for Patroklos or for the other **hetaîroi**
who fell in great numbers at the hands of brilliant Hektor.

XVIII 102–103

§17. The delegates to Achilles fail where the death of Patroklos succeeds. Despite their claim to be the most **phíloi** to Achilles, he rejects their offer of compensation to him because—from the standpoint of the *Iliad*—Patroklos is even more **phílos** than they. This ultimate motivation, however, is not yet manifest in Book IX, as Ajax is expressing his outrage at the rejection:

§16n2. Sinos 1975.
§16n3. Sinos 1975.74.
§16n4. The same notion of "becoming the Light" for men by virtue of being their savior is more fully expressed by way of simile: see Ch.20§20.

αὐτὰρ ᾿Αχιλλεὺς
ἄγριον ἐν στήθεσσι θέτο μεγαλήτορα θυμόν,
σχέτλιος, οὐδὲ μετατρέπεται φιλότητος ἑταίρων
τῆς ᾗ μιν παρὰ νηυσὶν ἐτίομεν ἔξοχον ἄλλων,
νηλής· καὶ μέν τίς τε κασιγνήτοιο φονῆος
ποινὴν ἢ οὗ παιδὸς ἐδέξατο τεθνηῶτος.
καί ῥ᾿ ὁ μὲν ἐν δήμῳ μένει αὐτοῦ πόλλ᾿ ἀποτείσας,
τοῦ δέ τ᾿ ἐρητύεται κραδίη καὶ θυμὸς ἀγήνωρ
ποινὴν δεξαμένῳ· σοὶ δ᾿ ἄλληκτόν τε κακόν τε
θυμὸν ἐνὶ στήθεσσι θεοὶ θέσαν εἵνεκα κούρης
οἵης.

But Achilles
has made savage the great-hearted **thūmós** within his breast,
the wretch. And he has no care for being **phílos** with his **hetaîroi**,
the way we honored him by the ships far beyond the others,
the pitiless one. And yet it can happen that a man takes compensation from
    the murderer of his own brother or of his own son who is killed.
And the offending party pays much and stays there in the district,
while the injured party's heart is curbed, and so too his proud **thūmós**,
once he accepts the compensation. But the gods have placed in you
a **thūmós** that is unyielding and bad,
all on account of one girl.

IX 628–638

Achilles may be the most **phílos** to his comrades-in-arms, but they
are not the most **phíloi** to him. Ajax thinks that the girl taken away
from Achilles by Agamemnon, with the passive acquiescence of the
Achaeans, is even more **phílē** than they. This theme again conjures
up Kleopatre, who was indeed by implication the most **phílē** to
Meleager—especially in view of what Achilles himself had said of the
girl Briseis, who was taken from him:

ἐπεὶ ὅς τις ἀνὴρ ἀγαθὸς καὶ ἐχέφρων
τὴν αὐτοῦ φιλέει καὶ κήδεται, ὡς καὶ ἐγὼ τὴν
ἐκ θυμοῦ φίλεον, δουρικτητήν περ ἐοῦσαν

    Since whatever man is good and sensible
loves his own wife [has a wife who is **phílē** to him] and cares for her. So also
    I loved her [she was **phílē** to me]
with all my **thūmós**, even though she was only a prisoner.

IX 341–343

There is another connection in what Achilles says just before this
profession that Briseis is **phílē** to him:

ἢ μοῦνοι φιλέουσ' ἀλόχους μερόπων ἀνθρώπων
'Ατρεῖδαι;

Or is it that the Atreidai are the only men
who <u>love</u> their wives [whose wives are **phílai** to them]?

IX 340–341

The wife in question here is distinctly not **phílē**: she is Helen, cause
of the entire Trojan War.

§18. To continue: Ajax thinks that Briseis ranks highest in the
ascending scale of affection that determines the behavior of Achilles.
In the passage already quoted, the protest of Ajax is founded on the
surface inequity: whereas another man would accept compensation
from the killer of his own brother or son, Achilles persists in refusing
compensation from Agamemnon and the Achaeans—who had merely
taken away from him a girl-prisoner (IX 628–638). And yet, as we
have seen, the theme of Briseis as **phílē** to Achilles conjures up the
theme of Kleopatre as **phílē** to Meleager. The words of Ajax are a
code with one message for Ajax himself but with quite another
message for the audience of our *Iliad*. Meshing with the theme of
Kleopatre, the words of Ajax indirectly point toward Patroklos as the
ultimate **phílos**. But now we will also see that the theme serving as a
foil for that of the girl, namely the readiness of a man to accept
compensation from the killer of his own brother or son, also points
to Patroklos.

§19. From the retrospective vantage point of Book XXIV, Apollo is
telling why the hero Achilles is so repellent to him:

μέλλει μέν πού τις καὶ φίλτερον ἄλλον ὀλέσσαι,
ἠὲ κασίγνητον ὁμογάστριον ἠὲ καὶ υἱόν

For a man could easily lose someone else who is <u>more</u> **phílos**,
either a brother from the same womb or even a son.

XXIV 46–47

More **phílos** than whom? Patroklos, of course! Here the issue is no
longer whether or not Achilles is to accept compensation from
Agamemnon and the Achaeans for the taking of a girl, but rather,
whether or not he is to accept compensation first from Hektor and
later from his family and the Trojans in general for the killing of
Patroklos. Apollo is repelled by the refusal of Achilles to show pity
and cease taking vengeance on Hektor's corpse. The theme of a
brother's or son's death is already at work in the words of Ajax at IX
628–638, but there it serves as a foil for the taking of a girl, not yet

directly for the actual killing of Patroklos. In both passages, IX 628–638 and XXIV 46–47, the constant is the pitiless temperament that refuses compensation.

§20. The same temperament we find frozen in the artistic microcosm of the Shield of Achilles, *Iliad* XVIII. This panorama of universal situations applying to the central themes of the *Iliad* features as one of its main scenes the image of a litigation between two parties:

> ὁ μὲν εὔχετο πάντ᾽ ἀποδοῦναι
> δήμῳ πιφαύσκων, ὁ δ᾽ ἀναίνετο μηδὲν ἑλέσθαι

One man, in his declaration to the **dêmos**, was saying that he paid [the compensation for murder] in full,
while the other [the man with ties to the victim] was refusing to take anything.

XVIII 499–500

For the translation and exegesis, I am guided by the brilliant work of Leonard Muellner,[1] who has also shown that the archetypal quarrel pictured here concerned whether the man with affinities to the victim is or is not bound to accept the compensation offered him—the word for which is **poiné** (XVIII 498), precisely the same term that was applied to the compensation offered for the hypothetical death of one's brother or son in the speech of Ajax (IX 633, 636). In addition, Muellner points out that the syntax of μηδέν at XVIII 500 must mean that the little man in the picture on the shield will absolutely never accept any compensation.[2] This utter inflexibility of an aggrieved party who is permanently frozen into the picture reflects the same temperament that is so repellent to Apollo in the heroic figure of Achilles. Apollo says of him:

> ᾧ οὔτ᾽ ἄρ φρένες εἰσὶν ἐναίσιμοι οὔτε <u>νόημα</u>
> <u>γναμπτὸν</u> ἐνὶ στήθεσσι, λέων δ᾽ ὣς ἄγρια οἶδεν

His thinking is not right and his <u>sense of **nóos**</u>
is not <u>flexible</u> within his breast, but like a lion he knows savage ways.

XXIV 40–41

Old Phoinix had already entreated him with these words:

> ἀλλ᾽, Ἀχιλεῦ, πόρε καὶ σὺ Διὸς κούρῃσιν ἕπεσθαι
> τιμήν, ἥ τ᾽ ἄλλων περ <u>ἐπιγνάμπτει νόον</u> ἐσθλῶν

§20n1. Muellner 1976.105–106.
§20n2. Ibid.

So, Achilles, you too must grant that the Daughters of Zeus [**Litaí** 'Prayers', personified] be given their honor,
which <u>makes flexible</u> the <u>**nóos**</u> of others, good as they are.

IX 513–514

What Ajax had said against Achilles still applies when Apollo says it again:

ἄγριον ἐν στήθεσσι θέτο μεγαλήτορα θυμόν

He made savage the great-hearted **thūmós** within his breast.

IX 629—Ajax

... ἄγρια οἶδεν

... he knows savage ways

XXIV 41—Apollo

νηλής...

pitiless one ...

IX 632—Ajax

... ἔλεον μὲν ἀπώλεσεν

... he lost pity

XXIV 44—Apollo

§21. The savage and inflexible temperament of Achilles is a constant extending all the way to *Iliad* XXIV, which marks the point where pity begins to set in and the ultimate heroic refinement of the Iliadic hero is about to be achieved.[n] The remarkable thing is that the ethical dilemma of the *Iliad* is already set in the Embassy Scene of Book IX, where the words of the Achaean delegates—without their being aware of it—are a code that carries the message of Patroklos for Achilles.

§22. Just as Patroklos led Achilles to rejoin his comrades-in-arms, it was Kleopatre who had impelled Meleager to reenter his war. The words of Kleopatre had conjured up the grief that happens when a city is destroyed:

... καί οἱ κατέλεξεν ἅπαντα
κήδε' ὅσ' ἀνθρώποισι πέλει τῶν ἄστυ ἁλώῃ·
ἄνδρας μὲν κτείνουσι, πόλιν δέ τε πῦρ ἀμαθύνει,
τέκνα δέ τ' ἄλλοι ἄγουσι βαθυζώνους τε γυναῖκας

... and she told him in their proper order
all the cares that befall men whose city is captured:

§21n. See Rosner 1976.321–322, supplementing Whitman 1958.203–207 and Segal 1971.18 ff.

they kill the men, fire reduces the city to ashes,
and strangers lead away the children and deep-girdled wives

IX 591–594

Within this highly compressed presentation, we see the same themes as in the formal lamentation of Andromache (XXIV 725–745) during the public **pénthos** for Hektor. In Andromache's lament, the thematic setting for her personal grief is the portended collective grief surrounding the portended destruction of the city.[1] In fact, Kleopatre herself has the stance of lamentation (ὀδυρομένη 'mourning', IX 591), just as those who "mourn" Hektor (ὀδύρονται: XXIV 740). Furthermore, Kleopatre even has a by-name that connotes the very essence of **pénthos**:

τὴν δὲ τότ᾽ ἐν μεγάροισι πατὴρ καὶ πότνια μήτηρ
᾽Αλκυόνην καλέεσκον ἐπώνυμον, οὕνεκ᾽ ἄρ᾽ αὐτῆς
μήτηρ ἀλκυόνος πολυπενθέος οἶτον ἔχουσα
κλαῖεν ὅ μιν ἑκάεργος ἀνήρπασε Φοῖβος ᾽Απόλλων

And her father and mother in the palace called her **Alkuónē**,
because her mother had the fate of an **alkúōn**, a bird of much **pénthos**,
and wept because far-reaching Apollo snatched her away.[2]

IX 561–564

In sum, it was the grief conjured up by **Kleo-pátrē** that impelled Meleager to enter the war and thus undertake the epic deeds that resulted in "the **kléos** [plural] of men who lived before, heroes" (τῶν πρόσθεν ... κλέα ἀνδρῶν ἡρώων: IX 524–525). Similarly, the grief caused by the actual death of **Patro-kléēs** leads to the "unfailing **kléos**" of Achilles in the epic tradition of the *Iliad* (κλέος ἄφθιτον: IX 413).[3]

§23. Because of **Patro-kléēs**, Achilles gets **kléos**. Conversely, because of *****Akhí**-lāu̯os, Patroklos gets **ákhos/pénthos** from the

§22n1. For the tradition of lamentation over the destruction of cities: Alexiou 1974.83–101. Compare the **ákhos** of the captive woman in viii 530, corresponding to the **ákhos** experienced by Odysseus when he is about to hear Demodokos narrate the destruction of Troy. Discussion at §9.

§22n2. Cf. *Anthologia Palatina* 9.151.8, where only the Nereids remain after the destruction of Corinth: σῶν ἀχέων μίμνομεν ἀλκύονες. For the traditional connection of (h)alkúones and Nereids, see Theocritus 7.59–60. See also Alexiou 1974.97: "Like the folk songs for the fall of Constantinople, many of these ballads open with the theme of weeping birds—nightingales, swallows and cuckoos—which, as sole survivors of the disaster, bring the news to others and are called upon to join in the general lamentation."

§22n3. For a possible allusion to this theme in the *Odyssey*: §10. Note the last words of Andromache's first lament for Hektor: κλέος εἶναι 'that there be **kléos**' (XXII 514).

Achaeans. In general, the **ákhos** that Patroklos gets from Achilles at XXIII 47 is formalized in a public dimension as the Funeral Games throughout *Iliad* XXIII.[1] In particular, this **ákhos** is formalized when Achilles leads the Achaeans in lamentation for Patroklos:

> ... οἱ δ᾽ ᾤμωξαν ἀολλέες, ἦρχε δ᾽ Ἀχιλλεύς

... and they all wailed together, and Achilles led them

XXIII 12

> τοῖσι δὲ Πηλεΐδης ἁδινοῦ ἐξῆρχε γόοιο

The son of Peleus led them in frequent **góos** [lamentation].

XXIII 17

Similarly, in the public **pénthos** over Hektor (XXIV 708), Andromache leads the Trojan women in songs of lamentation for her husband:

> παρὰ δ᾽ εἷσαν ἀοιδοὺς
> θρήνων ἐξάρχους, οἵ τε στονόεσσαν ἀοιδὴν
> οἱ μὲν ἄρ᾽ ἐθρήνεον, ἐπὶ δὲ στενάχοντο γυναῖκες.
> τῇσιν δ᾽ Ἀνδρομάχη λευκώλενος ἦρχε γόοιο

And they seated next to him [Hektor's corpse] **aoidoí** [singers, poets] who were to lead in the **thrênoi** [lamentations].
They sang a wailing song, singing **thrênoi**. And the women wailed in response,
and white-armed Andromache led them in the **góos** [lamentation].

XXIV 720-723

The dimension of singing lamentations, which is only implicit in the epic use of the words **ákhos/pénthos** by way of contrast with **kléos**, is here made explicit. As Margaret Alexiou has shown in detail, the traditional genre of lamentation is an integral element in funerary ritual, requiring an interplay of two subgenres: the kin sing **góoi** while poets sing **thrênoi**, as described in the Iliadic passage we have just considered.[2] The genre of epic, however, imposes numerous restrictions on its own thematic treatment of lamentations. Nowhere, for instance, can we see epic overtly telling the contents of the **thrênoi**, even though they are suitable for singing by **aoidoí** 'singers, poets', as at 720-721 above; only **góoi** are "quoted," as at XXIV 725-745 (Andromache), 748-759 (Hekabe), and 762-775 (Helen).[3]

§23n1. More details at §30.
§23n2. Alexiou 1974.10-14. I should note that the semantic distinction between **góoi** and **thrênoi** is generally not maintained in the diction of Athenian tragedy.
§23n3. See Alexiou, p. 13, with more details about the social prestige of the **thrênos**.

§24. There is an even more important restriction evident in epic: the *Iliad* itself does not treat the tradition of lamentations for Achilles within the actual context of a real funerary ritual. True, Thetis and her sister Nereids have a stylized wake for Achilles as if he were a corpse being laid out for the **próthesis** 'wake' (cf. especially XVIII 71),[1] and the stylized mourning for Achilles commences immediately after he gets his permanent **ákhos**, from hearing the news that Patroklos is dead (XVIII 22–73). But the Iliadic tradition requires Achilles to prefigure his dead self by staying alive, and the real ritual of a real funeral is reserved by the narrative for his surrogate Patroklos. Only outside our *Iliad*, in the retrospective format of the *Odyssey*, can we witness the actual wake of Achilles, with the Muses and his own kin, the Nereids, singing lamentations over his corpse (xxiv 58–61).[2] As we have already seen from its other retrospective glimpses of the Trojan War story, our *Odyssey* treats Iliadic traditions as if it were referring to other poetic traditions, such as that of lamentation itself.[3]

§25. The point remains, then, that the epic tradition of the *Iliad* assigns the overtly ritual dimension of **ákhos/pénthos** to Patroklos. Conversely, the **kléos** that Achilles gets from the *Iliad* is distinctly nonritual on the level of epic. As we have seen from the internal evidence of epic itself, the κλέα ἀνδρῶν 'kléos [plural] of men' are intended as an elevated form of *entertainment*, and they bring **ákhos/pénthos** only to those who are involved in the **ákhos/pénthos** that the **kléos** may happen to describe. For the uninvolved audience of epic, the death of Patroklos is a subject for **kléos**. For the involved Achilles, it is **ákhos/pénthos**. It follows, then, that the death of Achilles himself would be **ákhos/pénthos** for those involved and thus unsuitable for the **kléos** of epic. From the fact that our *Iliad* substitutes the death of **Patro-kléēs**, we may infer that the death of Achilles may have been unsuitable for the **kléos** of the Iliadic tradition partly *because the audience itself was involved* in his death. There is a religious dimension here. Communal involvement in

§24n1. See Kakridis 1949.67–68.

§24n2. Cf. Alexiou 1974.10–14. Here too (as at XXIV 721), **thrênoi** are being sung (xxiv 61); however, now the singers are not **aoidoí** (as at XXIV 720) but the Muses themselves (xxiv 60). Cf. also Pindar *P.*3.100–103: the death of Achilles causes **góos** for the Danaans.

§24n3. For example, the narrative convention of the **Diòs boulé** 'Will of Zeus' as at *Iliad* I 5 is treated as a foil by *Odyssey* i 7 (see Maehler 1963.23) as well as by viii 577–580.

ákhos/pénthos requires the rituals of cult, as we have already seen from the evidence on the cult of Demeter **Akhaiá**. By performing ritual lamentations, the community involves itself with the **ákhos** of Demeter over the **káthodos** of Kore.

§26. The death of Achilles would be an **ákhos** not only to the **lāós**, in epic, but also to the community at large, in cult.[1] There are clear traces that we can cite from the hero cults of Achilles in the classical and even postclassical periods. For just one example, let us consider a custom in Elis that Pausanias mentions in connection with various local athletic traditions—among them the restricted use of a site with the epichoric name of **hieròs drómos** 'sacred run' (6.23.2). On an appointed day at the beginning of the Olympic Games, as the sun is sinking in the west, the women of Elis perform various rituals to worship Achilles (τοῦ Ἀχιλλέως δρῶσιν ἐς τιμήν), and the ritual that is singled out specifically is that of mourning (κόπτεσθαι: Pausanias 6.23.3).[2] Whereas Achilles gets **kléos** from epic, he gets **ákhos/pénthos** from cult.[3]

§27. This is not the place, of course, to attempt a detailed exposition of how the cult of heroes in Greek religion is decidedly not some relatively late phenomenon, motivated somehow by the stories of heroes in Greek epic.[1] The monumental work of Erwin

§26n1. For the traditional use of the word **lāós** outside the context of epic to designate the community at large, see Benveniste 1969 II 91–95, esp. on **léïton**, **leitourgíā**. Note that **léïton** is described in Herodotus 7.197 as a word proper to the **Akhaioí**.

§26n2. For this and other examples of cult practices in honor of Achilles, see Nilsson 1906.457. In the case of Pausanias 6.23.2, I am unsure about any direct connection between the **hieròs drómos** 'sacred run' and the lore surrounding Achilles, but it may be worth pointing out this hero's specific affinity with the theme of running; see esp. Ch.20§9 (cf. also XVIII 56 as discussed at Ch.10§11 and n4).

§26n3. Cf. Herodotus 5.67.5, where the earliest known stages of the local cult of Adrastos at Sikyon are being described: τά τε δὴ ἄλλα οἱ Σικυώνιοι ἐτίμων τὸν Ἄδρηστον καὶ δὴ πρὸς τὰ πάθεα αὐτοῦ τραγικοῖσι χοροῖσι ἐγέραιρον 'the people of Sikyon gave tīmḗ to Adrastos in various ways; in particular, they honored him [gave him géras] with tragic songs/dances corresponding to the things that he suffered [páthos plural]'. On **páthos** 'thing suffered' as related to **pénthos** 'grief', see Nagy 1974.258–260. Both nouns are derived from the root *kʷenth- as in the verb **páskhō** 'experience, suffer', which also functions as the passive of **poiéō** and **dráō** 'do' (in this sense, **páthos** is the passive of **drâma**). The epic combination **pénthos álaston** 'unforgettable grief' must be compared with ἄλαστα δὲ / ϝέργα πάθον κακὰ μησα- μένοι in Alcman 1.34–35P: "they suffered [verb **páskhō**] unforgettable things [álaston plural] for having devised evil."

§27n1. See especially Rohde I 146–199. For a strong critique of the opposing view as represented by L. R. Farnell, see Brelich 1958.99n81, who comments also on the irony

Rohde remains one of the most eloquent sources for our understanding the **hḗrōs** 'hero' as a very old and distinct concept of traditional Greek religion, requiring cult practices that were also distinct from those of the gods. The cult of heroes was a highly evolved transformation of the worship of ancestors, within the social context of the city-state or **pólis**.[2] As a parallel, I would propose that the κλέα ἀνδρῶν / ἡρώων '**kléos** [plural] of men who were heroes' of *Iliad* IX 524–525 represents the evolution of Greek epic from earlier "stories about the ancestors," as still represented by the names **Kleo-pátrē/Patro-kléēs**, and, vestigially, by the function of the traditional figures assigned to these names.

§28. In order to understand the Homeric perspective on **hḗroes**, the emergence of Homeric Epos must be seen in its social context, dated to the eighth century B.C. This same era is marked by the emergence of (1) the **pólis** and (2) intensive intercommunication among the elite of the various **póleis**, a phenomenon which we have defined as Panhellenism.[1] I will leave the details and documentation to Anthony Snodgrass and others,[2] confining myself here to the problem of contrasting the cult of heroes, which is restricted to the local level of the **pólis**, with the Homeric **kléos** of heroes, which is Panhellenic and thus free from such restrictions. The point is, essentially, that the eighth century B.C. is the setting not only for the emergence of Homeric Epos but also for the upsurge of hero cults,[3] an institution that reflects not the beginnings but rather the strong revival of a continuous heritage.[4] Following Rohde, we may properly

---

that Farnell is a noted commentator on the poetry of Pindar. See also the criticism of Farnell by Pötscher 1961.336n91.

§27n2. Cf. Rohde I 108–110; also Brelich 1958.144n202, Nilsson I 186, Schnaufer 1970.34, Alexiou 1974.19.

§28n1. See Intro.§14.

§28n2. See Intro.§14nn1–2.

§28n3. On which see Snodgrass 1971.191–193. Cf. Intro.§18.

§28n4. Snodgrass, pp. 398–399. I cannot agree with the argument of Coldstream 1976 that the upsurge of hero cults in the eighth century is a mere *result* of Homeric poetry. Snodgrass himself has offered a refutation of this view in a paper presented at the Convegno internazionale sulla ideologia funeraria nel mondo antico, Naples/Ischia 6–10 December 1977 (sponsored by the Istituto Universitario Orientale [Naples] and the Centre de Recherches Comparées sur les sociétés anciennes [Paris]). The title of the paper read by A. Snodgrass was: "The Origins of the Greek Hero-Cults"; other papers include: J.-P. Vernant's "L'idéologie de la mort héroïque," A. Schnapp-Gourbeillon's "Les funérailles de Patrocle," and N. Loraux's "Mort civique et idéologie de la cité." In developing my present argument, I draw considerable encouragement from the views of Vernant and his colleagues.

refer to such a heritage in terms of ancestor worship, which later became hero cult.[5] It is in the context of the **pólis** that the worship of ancestors evolved into the cult of heroes.[6] Moreover, the epic tradition was also evolving within the same context. The internal evidence of the *Iliad* and the *Odyssey* reflects the ideology of the **pólis** in general[7]—but without being restricted to the ideology of any one **pólis** in particular.[8] Here, then, is the central issue: the Panhellenic Epos is the product of the same era that produced an upsurge in local hero cults.

§29. The hero of cult must be local because it is a fundamental principle in Greek religion that his power is local.[1] On the other hand, the *Iliad* and the *Odyssey* are Panhellenic. What results is that the central heroes of this epic tradition cannot have an overtly religious dimension in the narrative. Such a restriction on the self-expression of epic led Rohde to misunderstand the Homeric evidence on heroes. In general, his thesis was that the overall Homeric silence on the subject of hero cults implies an absence of even the ideological background.[2] In specifics, however, Rohde himself noticed sporadic instances in the *Iliad* and the *Odyssey* where some sort of reference is indeed being made to hero cults, but he did not integrate this evidence, which went against his thesis. Each of these instances would require a detailed exposition, but I restrict the discussion here to just one instance that reflects on the status of Patroklos/Achilles in the *Iliad*.

§30. As Rohde himself had noticed, the Funeral of Patroklos at *Iliad* XXIII has several features that connote the rituals of hero cults.[1] For example, the wine libation (XXIII 218–221) and the offering of honey with oil (XXIII 170; cf. xxiv 67–68) "can hardly be regarded as anything but sacrificial."[2] Such marginal details of cult, as also the integral element of singing lamentations at XXIII 12 and 17,

---

§28n5. Rohde I 108–110, 228–245, esp. 235n1.

§28n6. Cf. Rohde I 167–171. This evolution can be correlated with the obsolescence of the **thrênos** as a genre, and with the history of vigorous legislation against it; see Alexiou 1974, esp. pp. 13, 18–19, 104, 108.

§28n7. Snodgrass 1971.435; see also Luce 1978.

§28n8. Cf. Intro.§14.

§29n1. Rohde I 184–189: once a hero ceases to be epichoric, he may become a god. Cf. also Rohde's discussion on pp. (I) 59–65, 141–145, 159–166, etc.

§29n2. For a sensible critique: Hack 1929; also Sinos 1975.91–94.

§30n1. Rohde I 14–22.

§30n2. Rohde I 16n1 = 1925.45n13.

give ritual *form* to the **ákhos** of Achilles for Patroklos at XXIII 47.[3] Even the central epic action of Book XXIII, the Funeral Games of Patroklos, has ritual form.[4] In Homeric narrative, the funeral of a hero is the only occasion for athletic contests (XXIII 630–631: Amarynkeus; xxiv 85–86: Achilles himself).[5] In classical times, local athletic contests were still motivated as funeral games for the epichoric hero (cf., e.g., Pausanias 8.4.5). As a general principle, the **agón** was connected with the cult of heroes, and even the Great Panhellenic Games were originally conceived as funeral games for heroes.[6] The custom of mourning for Achilles at the beginning of the Olympics (Pausanias 6.23.3) is a striking instance of this heritage.[7] As a parallel, epic offers a corresponding single event in the mourning for Patroklos that inaugurates the Funeral Games in Book XXIII. Even though there are hints within the *Iliad* that the Funeral of Patroklos is presented as a grand beginning of cult (XXIV 592–595),[8] the overt singularity of the event forced Rohde to rule it out as a parallel to the cult of heroes, which is recurrent.[9] And yet, the *Iliad* itself is a singularity. What is recurrent in ritual is timeless in the epic tradition, just like the **kléos áphthiton** of Achilles.

§30n3. Besides the element of song, we also find that of dance. In Aristotle *fr.* 519 Rose (on which see the correction made by Meuli 1968 [= 1926] 70n3; also West 1978.372n1), there is a report of a tradition that Achilles danced the **purrhíkhē** at the pyre of Patroklos. From the same source (ibid., *ap.* scholia to XXIII 130), we hear of a funerary custom in Cyprus: τῶν βασιλέων κηδευομένων προηγεῖτο πυρριχίζων ὁ στρατός 'at the funerals of kings, the procession was led by the army, who danced the **purrhíkhē**'. Compare the proceedings at the Funeral of Patroklos, XXIII 131–137 (and the commentary of Rohde I 165–166n1).

§30n4. See Sinos 1975.83–88 on the significance of the **sêma** at XXIII 331.

§30n5. Rohde I 14–22. Kirk (1968.115) refers to the chariot contest at the Funeral Games of Amarynkeus as "an apparent predecessor of the Olympic Games."

§30n6. Rohde I 151–152 and Nilsson 1951 [=1911] 99–100.

§30n7. It should be noted, however, that the primary hero of the Olympics is Pelops (Pausanias 5.13.1); see Burkert 1972.108–119.

§30n8. Rohde I 55–59, esp. p. 59n1; Sinos 1975.92–94.

§30n9. Rohde I 148–152.

7 | The Death
of Pyrrhos

§1. As we contemplate the ritual aspects of the Iliadic hero, we are faced with a conflict between a trend and a constant: while Achilles is becoming Panhellenic by way of Epos, the powers of the hero in hero cult remain strictly local.[1] By evolving into the hero of the epic tradition that culminated in our *Iliad*, the Achilles figure stands to lose his overtly ritual aspects. For illustration, let us consider the inherited poetic diction describing the prestige of a typically local hero in cult, and compare the words that our *Iliad* chooses to describe the destiny of its own prime hero. By losing his chance to be exempt from mortality and by being awarded as compensation a hero cult at Eleusis that will last for all time to come, the youthful Demophon is described in the Homeric *Hymn to Demeter* as getting a **tīmḗ** that is **áphthitos** 'unfailing' (*H.Dem.* 261, 263).[2] The epithet here is crucial, because heroes are generically distinguished from gods by virtue of *not* having a **bíos** 'lifespan' that is **áphthitos** (Simonides 523.3P).[3]

§1n1. For a brief survey of cult practices in honor of Achilles, see Nilsson 1906.457; cf. also Ch.6§§26/30 above and Ch. 20§24n3 below.

§1n2. The word **tīmḗ** can specify the "honor" that a god or hero receives in cult. (The article s.v. τιμή in Liddell and Scott does not allow for such a distinct semantic category.) The diction of Herodotus about matters of ritual provides adequate illustration for this particular usage of **tīmḗ**, as at 1.118.2 (cult of a god) and 1.168 (cult of a hero). As for the verb **tīmáō** in the sense of "worship," see Herodotus 1.90.2, 2.50.3, 2.75.4, 5.67.5 (in the last passage, the cult of the god Dionysos is designated in the same terms as the cult of the hero Adrastos, on whom see also the verb **tīmáō** at Herodotus 5.67.4). For a clear discussion of **tīmḗ** as "cult," see Rudhardt 1970.6–7; also Rohde I 99n1. Besides, see Richardson 1974.260–261 on the Homeric *Hymn to Demeter* 311–312, where the theme of the gods' getting **tīmaí** is explicitly correlated with the observance of their respective cults by mortals (see also *H.Dem.* 353, 366–369). Note that the cult figure gets **tīmḗ** from two directions: the "honor" is performed by mortals but determined by immortals. On the status of Demophon as a **daímōn** of cult: Ch.10§10.

§1n3. On the semantics of **áphthito-**: Ch.10§§3–19. The word for "heroes" in this passage from Simonides is **hēmítheoi**, which is appropriate in the dimension of cult. See Ch.9 in general and §§15–17, 31 in particular.

Achilles, on the other hand, names as compensation for his impending death not **tīmḗ** but a **kléos** that is **áphthiton** 'unfailing' (IX 413). Whereas **tīmḗ** 'honor' is conferred by cult,[4] the prestige that **kléos** brings is the undying glory of Epos.[5] Within the timelessness of epic, the Funeral of Patroklos will have to serve as indirect compensation to Achilles for the absence of the ritual **tīmḗ** that is his due. Outside of epic, however, there evolved another form of indirect compensation that befits the Panhellenic hero in the dimension of cult.

§2. The historical setting is unique: it is Delphi, the Panhellenic Sanctuary for the Oracle of Apollo, where the presiding Hero is none other than the son of Achilles, Pyrrhos/Neoptolemos.[1] In Pindar's words, the Hero of Delphi is destined to be one of the Aeacids (Aiakos → Peleus → Achilles → Pyrrhos → ...), and the Aeacid to be chosen is the son of Achilles:

> ... ἐχρῆν δέ
> τιν' ἔνδον ἄλσει παλαιτάτῳ
> Αἰακιδᾶν κρεόντων τὸ λοιπὸν ἔμμεναι
> θεοῦ παρ' εὐτειχέα δόμον, ἡροΐαις δὲ πομπαῖς
> θεμισκόπον οἰκεῖν ἐόντα πολυθύτοις

... but it had to be that
one of the royal Aeacids be inside the most ancient grove
for all time to come, by the well-built abode of the god,
and that he should have his home as the one which presides
over the Heroes' Processions, which are distinguished by
many sacrifices[2]

Pindar N.7.44–47

§1n4. See n2. For the interpretation of **tīmā́** at Pindar *N*.7.31 as applying to Pyrrhos, see Köhnken 1971.46. For the possibility that "the **tīmā́** of the Hero" in the Amphictionic law *SIG*[3] 145.32 (380 B.C.) refers to Pyrrhos: Burkert 1966b.437. In this case, the word **tīmā́** specifies the sacrifice of a bull to the Hero.

§1n5. Ch.1§2. We must also contrast Achilles and Demophon in this regard with Anchises in the Homeric *Hymn to Aphrodite*: in compensation for his mortality, Anchises wins immortality neither for his **kléos** nor for his **tīmḗ**, but rather for the continuation of his progeny, the Aeneadae (*H.Aphr.* 196–197, 239–end).

§2n1. For the tradition of the double name, see *Cypria fr.* 14 Allen. The names **Púrrhos/Neoptólemos** are more appropriate to cult/epic respectively; see especially Usener 1912/1913 [= 1904] 460–461. For the sake of convenience, I will refer to the hero as Pyrrhos. Consider also the interesting variant verse for *Iliad* XIX 327, where we find **Purês** instead of **Neoptólemos** (for a discussion: Delcourt 1965.31–32).

§2n2. On the validity of this Pindaric testimony about the cult of Pyrrhos, see Fontenrose 1960.191–198, with polemics and bibliography. On *Nemean 7* itself, see especially Köhnken 1971.37–86 and Lloyd-Jones 1973.

By Pindar's time, the institutions of Delphi reflect no longer simply a **pólis** that happens to have a sanctuary of Panhellenic importance, but rather, the reverse: the entire community of Delphi now functions as a sacral extension of the Sanctuary.[3] Accordingly, the status of Pyrrhos at Delphi transcends that of the typical hero: whereas the hero of a **pólis** is by nature local, the son of Achilles is more of a Panhellenic figure by virtue of being Hero of Delphi.

§3. There would be no gain in our trying to retroject the figure of Pyrrhos as the Hero of Delphi all the way to, say, the eighth century B.C.[1] It is enough to say that the inherited epic themes associated with this figure are so close to the inherited ritual themes of the Hero at Delphi that an identification was in effect by the time the Sanctuary evolved into the form known to Pindar. In the poet's own words (*N.*7.44–47), other Aeacids would have been equally appropriate as Hero of Delphi—Achilles included. But the bones of Achilles—and bones are the basis for establishing the locale of hero cults—anchor him in the *Iliad* as the Hero of the Hellespont.[2] The Panhellenic stature of the *Iliad* has thus precluded Achilles as Hero of Delphi, and the Delphic sanctuary of Apollo has in turn developed a Panhellenic ideology that complements the *Iliad*. In short, the identification of Pyrrhos with the Hero enshrined at Delphi is another in a series of interrelated Panhellenic phenomena that go far beyond the local constraints of Hellenic religion.[3]

§4. The reality of the cult, however, is based on localization: Pyrrhos was Hero of Delphi because of the local belief that he was buried there (Pindar *N.*7.34–35). In fact, his grave and the cult that goes with it were officially recognized to be part of the precinct of Apollo himself, as we learn not only from the words of Pindar

§2n3. For a key factor in this transformation, the First Sacred War of ca. 590 B.C., see Wiechers 1961, esp. p. 24.

§3n1. I refer to the discussion of the problem by Fontenrose 1960.198–205.

§3n2. On the burial of Achilles at the Hellespont: Ch.20§§22–24. On the function of bones in hero cults, see Rohde I 159–166; cf. also Ch6§29.

§3n3. The Homeric tradition itself, I submit, is informed by many such interrelated Panhellenic phenomena. Following the reasoning of Pfister 1948.151, I would even suggest that the Homeric *Catalogue of Ships* in *Iliad* II amounts to a Panhellenic survey of the Homeric heroes from the diverse local standpoints of their primary cults, the locations of which are represented as their respective homelands. On the possibility that the systematization of the *Catalogue* is derived from Delphic traditions, I cite Giovannini 1969.51–71.

(above, *N*.7.44–47)[1] and the detailed reports of Pausanias (10.24.6; cf. 1.4.4) but also from the archaeological evidence.[2] This institutional symbiosis of the Hero's cult with that of Panhellenic Apollo must be correlated with the numerous myths which, although they vary in detail, converge on the theme that Apollo killed Pyrrhos, just as he had killed the father Achilles.[3] A sampling of the documentation can wait until we finish confronting a vital detail: the death of the father and the death of the son are both celebrated as parallel events in Pindar's *Paean* 6 to Apollo (lines 78–80: Achilles; lines 117–120: Pyrrhos). Even the traditional exultation **iè ié** of the paean bursts forth immediately following the words retelling the death of Pyrrhos (*Paean* 6.121–122). Since *Paean* 6 was composed specifically for a Delphic setting and in honor of Apollo, we should be especially mindful of the central role of its hero as the ritual antagonist of the god. For we see here a striking illustration of a fundamental principle in Hellenic religion: antagonism between hero and god in myth corresponds to the ritual requirements of symbiosis between hero and god in cult.[4]

§5. Now we are ready to examine some of the variant myths about how Pyrrhos actually met his death, and we begin with those that have a bearing on the Achilles figure as well. One version has Pyrrhos attempting to plunder the riches of Delphi; Apollo thwarts him and brings about his death.[1] There is an important parallel in the figure of the impious **Phlegúās** and/or the band of plundering warriors called **Phlegúai**,[2] who similarly attacked or even burned down the Delphic shrine and were, in some versions of the myth,

§4n1. See also Pherecydes *FGrH* 3.63, 64a–b; Asclepiades *FGrH* 12.15. Note the interesting additional detail that Pyrrhos was first buried under the threshold of Apollo's temple, only to be transferred later into the area of the god's **témenos** 'precinct' (for discussion, see Delcourt 1965.44; cf. also Rohde I 197).

§4n2. See Burkert 1972.136n12 for the basic bibliography; also Fontenrose 1960.191–198 and Burkert 1966b.440n2.

§4n3. For a collection of references to the testimonia: Fontenrose, p. 212.

§4n4. See Burkert 1972.17n41, 68; also Burkert 1966.102–104 and 1975.19. Cf. Delcourt 1965.38.

§5n1. Pausanias 10.7.1 (cf. also 2.5.5); scholia to Pindar *N*.7.58, 150a; Strabo 421. For parallelisms with the traditional lore about King Pyrrhos of Epeiros, see Delcourt 1965.42–43. I should note, however, my disagreement with the notion that the lore about the historical figure is the source for the theme of plundering associated with the mythical figure (cf. also Burkert 1966b.437).

§5n2. The parallelism with Pyrrhos is pointed out by Burkert 1966b.437. On **Phlegúās** as the eponym of the **Phlegúai**: Strabo 442c.

destroyed by Apollo.[3] Even the name **Phlegúās** 'fiery' (from **phlégō** 'burn') is semantically comparable to **Púrrhos** 'fiery red'.[4]

§6. The theme of plundering Delphi, common to Pyrrhos and Phlegyas, also applies to Achilles himself in the *Iliad*—albeit indirectly. In the only Iliadic mention of Delphi (aside from the reference in the Great Catalogue, II 519),[n] Achilles is renouncing the prospect of plundering the riches of Apollo's sanctuary there, which have just been juxtaposed with the riches contained in the citadel of Troy (at IX 401–403):

οὐδ' ὅσα λάϊνος οὐδὸς ἀφήτορος ἐντὸς ἐέργει,
Φοίβου Ἀπόλλωνος, Πυθοῖ ἔνι πετρηέσσῃ.
ληϊστοὶ μὲν γάρ τε βόες καὶ ἴφια μῆλα,
κτητοὶ δὲ τρίποδές τε καὶ ἵππων ξανθὰ κάρηνα.

nor all the things contained within the stone threshold of the Archer,
Phoebus Apollo, in rocky Delphi.
For cattle and fat sheep can be plundered
and tripods can be won, as well as tawny heads of horses.

IX 404–407

It is remarkable that a theme so appropriate to the Hero of Delphi on the level of cult should apply in particular to the Achilles figure in the single instance where the *Iliad* conjures up directly the traditions of Delphi.

§7. This Homeric focusing of theme is all the more remarkable when we consider the additional evidence of the *Odyssey*, which likewise has only two overt references to Delphi. One of them is out of focus for our immediate purposes (xi 581), but the other brings us back to the first song of Demodokos (viii 72–82), which in turn will lead us back to the death of Pyrrhos. Demodokos is singing about the

§5n3. Pausanias 10.7.1; Ephorus *FGrH* 70.93; Servius *ad* Virgil *Aeneid* 6.618; scholia *ad* Statius *Thebaid* 1.713; Eustathius *ad* XIII 301; etc. For an extensive discussion of the myths associated with the name **Phlegúās/Phlegúai**: Vian 1960.219–222. We may note in particular the claim, in the scholia (T) to *Iliad* XIII 302, that the verb **phleguân** in the dialect of Phokis means **hubrízein** 'commit **húbris**'. For the connotations of **húbris**, see Ch.9§§9–10.

§5n4. See Vian 1960.221. For the mythological connection of the Pyrrhos and Achilles figures with the themes of fire, see, in general, Delcourt 1965. One of the most interesting points of formal convergence is the epithet **Purrhaiē** of Thetis (Hesychius s.v.), who dips the infant Achilles into fire much as Demeter had done to Demophon; see Delcourt, pp. 36–37, Detienne/Vernant 1974.136, and Richardson 1974.237–238.

§6n. On the theory that the *Catalogue* is organized on the basis of Delphic traditions: Giovannini 1969.51–71.

Oracle of Apollo at Delphi, and how it has revealed to Agamemnon a prophecy that applies in a particular setting, to wit, at a **daís** 'feast' of the gods (θεῶν ἐν δαιτὶ θαλείῃ: viii 76), where Achilles and Odysseus are having a quarrel. This quarrel is described as the "beginning of grief [**pêma**]" (πήματος ἀρχή: viii 82) for Achaeans and Trojans alike, and we have seen that the death of Achilles is a major theme implied by the notion of **pêma** as it applies to the Achaeans.[n] Such a thematic correlation of the death of Achilles with Delphi/sacrifice/quarrel presents us with a mythological ensemble that is parallel, however indirectly, to another variant myth about the death of Pyrrhos.

§8. The myth that we are about to consider is the same one that is celebrated by Pindar in his *Paean 6* to Apollo, composed for the occasion of the **theoxénia** at Delphi.[1] From the words of this composition, we see that Pyrrhos met his death at Delphi as the direct result of a quarrel over slices of meat that were being distributed at a sacrifice:

> ἀμφιπόλοις δὲ
> κ]υρ[ιᾶν]² περὶ τιμᾶν
> δηρι]αζόμενον κτάνεν³
> ἐν τεμέ]νεϊ φίλῳ γᾶς παρ' ὀμφαλὸν εὐρύν

When he [Pyrrhos] quarreled with the attendants
over his rightful **tīmaí**,
he [Apollo] killed him
in his own precinct, right by the broad center of the Earth.

Pindar Paean 6.117–120

In another variation on this myth, the killer is not Apollo himself but one of his temple attendants:[4]

> ᾤχετο δὲ πρὸς θεὸν
> κτέατ' ἄγων Τροίαθεν ἀκροθινίων·
> ἵνα κρεῶν νιν ὕπερ μάχας
> ἔλασεν ἀντιτυχόντ' ἀνὴρ μαχαίρᾳ.
> βάρυνθεν δὲ περισσὰ Δελφοὶ ξεναγέται

§7n. Ch.4§6.

§8n1. For the relationship of Pindar's *Paean* 6 to *Nemean* 7, see especially Köhnken 1971.71–72, with bibliography. For a pioneering study: Finley 1951.

§8n2. On the basis of μυρίαν in the scholia to *Nemean* 7.94, Boeckh had suggested μοιριᾶν instead of κυριᾶν. For the morphology, I would compare **moírios/moirídios** with **koúrios/kourídios**. (For **koúrios**, see *Iliad* XIII 433c.)

§8n3. For the argument in favor of this reading, see Lloyd-Jones 1973.131, *pace* Fontenrose 1960.223n14.

§8n4. In Greek ritual, the priest or attendant may preside as a stand-in for the god himself: cf., e.g., Pausanias 6.20.9.

And he went to the god
bringing the riches of first-fruit offerings from Troy.
And there a man with a <u>mákhaira</u> smote him
as he got into a quarrel over slices of meat.
And the Delphians, <u>conductors of xénoi</u>, were greatly vexed.

Pindar N.7.40–43

The thematic ingredients of (1) the attendant with the **mákhaira** 'sacrificial knife' and (2) the Delphians as **xenāgétai** 'conductors of **xénoi**' have interesting variants in still other versions of the myth, where the killer is named as (1) **Makhaireús**, son of **Daítās**,[5] or (2) **Philoxenídēs**.[6]

§9. Taken on the level of myth, these themes are all pertinent to the ritual of the Delphic **theoxénia**, which actually involved the awarding of slices of meat from the sacrificial table.[1] Consider the following testimonium, which seems to have survived for us only because of a quaint detail in the ritual proceedings:

διατέτακται παρὰ Δελφοῖς τῇ θυσίᾳ τῶν Θεοξενίων, ὃς ἂν κομίσῃ γηθυλλίδα μεγίστην τῇ Λητοῖ, λαμβάνειν μοῖραν ἀπὸ τῆς τραπέζης.

There is an arrangement among the Delphians, at their festival of the **Theoxénia**, that whoever brings the biggest **gēthullís** [a vegetable] to Leto is to get a slice of meat from the sacrificial table.

Polemon ap. Athenaeus 372a

We should note in particular the sacrificial motif of exchanging a vegetal offering for a slice of the sacrificial victim's meat—called a

---

§8n5. Asclepiades *FGrH* 12.15; Callimachus *fr.* 229.7 Pfeiffer; Strabo 421. From these sources, we also learn of the tradition that one of the descendants of Makhaireus was Brankhos, founder of Apollo's Oracle at Didyma near Miletos.

§8n6. Scholia to Euripides *Andromache* 53. On the semantics of the word **xénos**: Ch.12§§12–16.

§9n1. On the reciprocity of the **theoxénia**, in that the roles of host and guest are interchangeable for gods and men, see Gernet 1968 [= 1928] 32–33. The figure of Pindar himself, by virtue of his poetry on the subject, becomes incorporated into the myths surrounding the Delphic **theoxénia**—and eventually even into the ritual itself; for a collection of testimonia, see Deneken 1881.9–10. Here again, the most pervasive theme is that a choice cut of meat from the sacrificial table is to be awarded to Pindar, to Pindar's ghost, or to his descendants. There is a particularly interesting ritual detail in *Life of Pindar* p. 92.50–53 Westermann [1845] (see also Drachmann I, p. 216): every day, as the **neōkóros** 'temple attendant' is about to close the entrance to Apollo's temple, he calls out to Pindar that the poet should have his meal with the god. Note too the tradition that **Theóxenos** (praised in Pindar *fr.* 123SM) was the poet's lover (*Life of Pindar* p. 102.11 Westermann). On the connection between the myths in the traditional *Lives* of poets and the rituals surrounding the hero cults of poets, see Ch.18.

moîra. In Pindar's *Nemean* 7, we have seen Pyrrhos himself being featured as one who acts in the ritual manner of the Delphic **theoxénia**, in that he is making a grand offering from the rich spoils of Troy in return for a slice of meat from the sacrificial table (above, line 42). In fact, even his offerings are called **akrothínia** 'first fruits [of war]' (line 41)—a word with vegetal connotations in that it is primarily appropriate for designating "first fruits [of Earth]" (e.g., Aeschylus *Eumenides* 834; etc.).[2] Pyrrhos gets involved in a quarrel over not receiving his due **moîra** of meat, and *Paean* 6 describes the issue in dispute as **kūriân** [or **moiriân**!] **perì tīmân** 'concerning his rightful **tīmaí**' (line 118).[3] Moreover, the theme of being deprived of one's **moîra** of meat at the sacrificial table is actually attested in the ritual lore of Delphi.

§10. In a fragment from the *Life of Aesop* tradition, we see the following ritual scenario about a particular sacrificial custom at Delphi:[1]

... ἐπὰν [εἰσέ]λθῃ τ[ις] τῷ θεῷ θυσιάσ[ων ο]ἱ Δελφ[ο]ὶ περ[ι]εστήκασι τὸν βωμ[ὸ]ν ὑφ᾽ ἑαυτοῖς μαχαίρας κ[ο]μίζοντες. σφαγιασαμένου δὲ τοῦ ἱερείου [emended to ἱερέως] καὶ δείραντος τὸ ἱερεῖον καὶ τὰ σπλάγχνα περιεξελομένου οἱ περιεστῶτες ἕκαστος ἦν ἂν ἰσχύσῃ μοῖραν ἀποτεμνόμενος ἄπεισιν, ὡς πολλάκις τὸν θυσιάσαντα αὐτὸν ἄμοιρ[ο]ν ἀπι[έ]ναι. ...

When someone goes in for the purpose of initiating sacrifice to the god, the Delphians stand around the altar carrying concealed **mákhairai**. And after the priest has slaughtered and flayed the sacrificial victim and after he has apportioned the innards, those who have been standing around cut off whatever **moîra** of meat each of them is able to cut off and then depart, with the result that the one who initiated the sacrifice oftentimes departs without having a **moîra** himself.

*Pap.Oxy.*1800 *fr.* 2 ii 32–46
= Aesop *Testimonia* 25 Perry

The internal motivation for this interesting description has to do with a story about Aesop and how he ridiculed this ritual at Delphi.[2]

---

§9n2. For a particularly interesting Delphic attestation, see the regulations of the Labyadai, *DGE* 323 D.47; the semantics of **akro-thin-** 'top of the heap' are of course readily transferable from agricultural to military contexts (cf. Pindar *O*.2.4 and *O*.10.57 besides *N*.7.41).

§9n3. For **moiriân**, see again §8n2.

§10n1. The pertinence of this text was noticed by Burkert 1966b.439.

§10n2. For the rest of the text, also connected with this particular story, see Ch.16§7; also Wiechers 1961.15–16.

Elsewhere too, we find what seem to be mostly jesting allusions to the same ritual practice, as in the following proverb:[3]

Δελφοῖσι θύσας αὐτὸς οὐ φαγῇ κρέας

If you sacrifice at Delphi, you will not eat any meat yourself.

> *Corpus Paroemiographorum*
> *Graecorum* I 393 (*Appendix*
> *Proverbiorum* I 95)

§11. Such allusions, if we did not have an actual description of the ritual, would have impressed us as nothing more than anticlerical jokes at the expense of the Sanctuary and its proverbially greedy attendants. But the description in the *Life of Aesop* fragment presents the scenario of a free-for-all over slices of meat *as a genuine ritual practice*—and not simply as a matter of greedy behavior on the part of the attendants.[1] As we will have a chance to observe later, the *jest* may present the ritual practice as if it really were greedy behavior, but even the jesting itself may have had a formalized ritual basis.[2] The point remains that there is indeed a ritual basis to the customary free-for-all over the slices of sacrificial meat, as we can also see from such parallels as the festival of ritualized greed at Lykosoura in Arcadia (Pausanias 8.37.8).[3] There is apparently even an element of ritualized stealth in the Delphic proceedings: consider the expression κ[ρύ]φα 'stealthily', applied again to the attendants in another fragment describing how Aesop ridiculed the Delphians' ritual custom.[4]

§12. Even more important for now, the program of the ritual as described in the *Life of Aesop* tradition converges closely with the program of the myth about the death of Pyrrhos as described in Pindar's *Paean* 6 and *Nemean* 7. Both myth and ritual feature the themes of (1) a wrangle over slices of meat that takes place between the sacrificer and the attendants who perform the sacrifice and (2) the sacrificer's being deprived of his share. In fact, the convergence of themes is so close that we may see in the death of Pyrrhos the official Delphic myth that integrates the ideology of the ritual.

§10n3. For further allusions, in comedy and elsewhere, see Wiechers 1961.16–18; cf. Delcourt 1965.39.

§11n1. Cf. also the scholia to Pindar *N.*7.62, describing the attendants' behavior towards Pyrrhos in these words: ὡς ἔθος αὐτοῖς 'as was their custom'.

§11n2. See Ch.16§10, esp. n7.

§11n3. For this and other parallels, see Burkert 1966b.440n1. Cf. *H.Apollo* 535–536; cf. also the expression κρέα διαρπάζοντας 'snatching away the cuts of meat' describing the Delphians in Pherecydes *FGrH* 3.64a.

§11n4. Scholia Florentina (=*Pap.Soc.Ital.* 1094), line 23, to Callimachus *fr.* 191 Pfeiffer; see also Burkert 1966b.439n2.

However, the myth has the sacrificer himself, Pyrrhos, becoming the ultimate victim of the sacrifice—butchered at the table of the god by the very knives that sliced the meat to be shared in the ritual.[n]

§13. We come back to the first song of Demodokos in the *Odyssey* (viii 72–82), where the implicit theme of a future death for Achilles is correlated with the three other themes of Delphi/sacrifice/quarrel. We have now witnessed a myth about the death of Pyrrhos that—on an altogether different level—has a parallel correlation of these three other themes. The parallelism can be observed in the dimension of form as well: the verb describing the quarrel of Pyrrhos in the Pindaric narrative, **[dēri]azómenon** (*Paean* 6.119), corresponds to the one that twice describes the quarrel of Achilles in the Homeric, **dērísanto/dērióōnto** (viii 76/78). Some aspects of the parallelism, however, are still problematical. Whereas Pyrrhos is killed during a quarrel at a sacrifice in Delphi, the death of Achilles is merely presaged in Delphi—and indirectly at that: Agamemnon apparently thinks that the quarrel of Achilles at a sacrifice is only a sign that Troy will be taken, not realizing that it is also a sign of future **pêma** for the Achaeans when Achilles withdraws and again later when he dies. The relationship of Achilles to the themes of Delphi/sacrifice/quarrel obviously requires still further scrutiny. Let us begin by going beyond the **daís** 'feast' of the gods at viii 76, in an attempt to understand the overall testimony of hexameter diction about the hero's relationship to sacrifices in particular and to feasts in general.

§14. Not just for Achilles but for any Homeric character, the eating of meat at feasts is by nature a sacrificial occasion: in the words of George M. Calhoun, "every meal was a sacrifice and an act of worship, and every sacrifice a meal."[1] By treating the Homeric hero simply as an idealized man taken out of the second millennium B.C., this statement may be overly one-dimensional in its view of epic action,[2] but it remains a valid observation about the contents of

---

§12n. On the connection of the Aeacids, especially Achilles and Pyrrhos, with the mythology of rituals featuring the **pharmakoí** 'scapegoats' of Apollo, see Wiechers 1961.43–49, with bibliography; cf. also Toepffer 1888.144. For the basic text on **pharmakós**, see Harpocration s.v., based on Istros *FGrH* 344.50 (on which there is more at Ch.16§2). For a **pharmakós**, our attested material indicates stoning or being thrown off a cliff as the primary modes of death; in the case of stoning, we see a specific application of this theme to Pyrrhos in Euripides *Andromache* 1085–1165.

§14n1. Calhoun 1962.446; cf. Motto and Clark 1969.124n21.

§14n2. For an alternative view, where we see the Homeric hero's actions not as something modeled on how we ordinary mortals behave but as the epic dimension of heroes who also have a ritual dimension, see Ch.9.

Homeric narrative: feasts where meat is consumed are indeed regularly occasioned by sacrifice. The Homeric word for such occasions is **daís/daíte** (e.g., iii 33/44, etc.),[3] and both nouns are etymologically derived from the verb **daíomai** 'divide, apportion, allot'. Consider the following Homeric collocation of verb and noun:

μοίρας δασσάμενοι δαίνυντ' ἐρικυδέα δαῖτα

Apportioning **moîrai** [portions], they feasted a very glorious **daís** [feast].

iii 66

We will have more to observe about **moîrai** later. For now it will suffice to add that the notion of "division" latent in **daís** becomes overt in expressions involving δαιτὸς ἐίσης 'of an equal **daís**' (as at I 468, 602; II 431; VII 320; XXIII 56)—denoting situations where everyone has his proper share at the sacrificial feast.[4]

§15. Is there, then, a special relationship of Achilles to the **daís**? Certainly this seems to be so not only in the case of Achilles but also in the case of all his heroic lineage, according to the Hesiodic passage that describes the Aeacids as follows:

... πολέμῳ κεχαρηότας ἠΰτε δαιτί

... delighting in war as well as in the **daís**

Hesiod *fr.* 206MW

The key, I submit, to such a close relationship of the Aeacids to the **daís** is the etymological connection of the word with the notion inherent in **daíomai** 'divide, apportion, allot'. This notion constitutes a mythological theme that runs through the whole line of Aeacids, starting with the prime ancestor himself. The hero Aiakos, in the words of Pindar, was so fair and just as to be worthy of settling matters pertaining to the gods themselves:

Αἰακὸν ... κεδνό-
τατον ἐπιχθονίων. ὃ καὶ
δαιμόνεσσι δίκας ἐπείραινε

Aiakos ... the most cherished of mortals,
who rendered **díkai** [judgments, justice] even for the gods[1]

Pindar *I.*8.22–24

§14n3. At iii 420, there is a more specific reference to the very same occasion: θεοῦ ἐς δαῖτα θάλειαν 'to the sumptuous **daís** of the god [Poseidon]'.

§14n4. Cf. Motto and Clark 1969.118–119. Of course, everyone gets an *equal* share not in the sense of the *same* amount but in the sense of varying amounts equal to the varying worth of each hero. For example, Ajax at VII 321–322 gets a choice cut of meat in a distribution (**daís**) that is described as **eísē** 'equal' at VII 320.

§15n1. The use here of **daimones** to designate "gods" makes the reverse theme of a

The correlation here of the word **díkē** with the concept of making fair allotments reminds us of the wording used to describe how the honor of Achilles himself is to be formally vindicated in the *Iliad*. As the actual setting for Agamemnon's finally giving acceptable compensation to Achilles in return for having at the outset deprived him of his fair share, Odysseus proposes the holding of a special **daís**:

αὐτὰρ ἔπειτά σε δαιτὶ ἐνὶ κλισίης ἀρεσάσθω
πιείρῃ, ἵνα μή τι δίκης ἐπιδευὲς ἔχῃσθα

But let him [Agamemnon] make amends to you [Achilles] with a rich **daís** in the tents,
so that you may have no lack in **díkē**.

XIX 179-180

It is at this **daís** that Achilles finally accepts the compensation offered by Agamemnon (XIX 268-281), even bidding his fellow Achaeans to go and feast (XIX 275)—though only after considerable hesitation.[2]

§16. As we now follow the line of Aiakos down to his son Peleus, the association of the Aeacids with the themes of the **daís** becomes more involved. In the words of Pindar, the hero Peleus actually feasted with the gods:

καὶ θεοὶ δαίσαντο παρ' ἀμφοτέροις
καὶ Κρόνου παῖδας βασιλῆας ἴδον χρυ-
σέαις ἐν ἕδραις, ἕδνα τε
δέξαντο

And the gods had a **daís** with each of them [Peleus and Kadmos],
and they [Peleus and Kadmos] saw the royal children of Kronos sitting on their golden seats, and they received wedding-gifts from them.

Pindar *P*.3.93-95

The singular occasion for the **daís** of Peleus, where the Olympian gods themselves attended, was the feast of his wedding with

---

mortal's deciding allotments for the gods even more striking, since the word **daímōn** is derived from the same root as found in **daíomai** 'divide, apportion, allot'. For the etymology, see Chantraine I 246-247. For the Homeric theme of **daímōn** as "he who apportions," see Kullmann 1956.51-56 (cf. also Borecký 1965.75 on Pindar *P*.3.81-82); also Richardson 1974.257 on the expression **daímonos aísēi** (further discussion at §21n1).

§15n2. After Odysseus proposes the **daís**, Agamemnon approves the proposal and calls it **en moírēi** '[said] in proper measure [moîra]' (XIX 186). Achilles, however, wishes not to eat while his comrade lies unburied and unavenged (XIX 199-214), but Odysseus argues for the necessity of having a feast before fighting (XIX 216-237). In this context, Zeus is called the **tamíēs polémoio** 'apportioner of war' (XIX 224); in nonmetaphorical contexts, the **tamíēs/tamíē** is a male/female functionary who allots food (e.g., XIX 44).

Thetis—a traditional theme celebrated by the *Cypria* as an appropriate setting for the onset of the entire Trojan Cycle (Proclus p. 102.14–15 Allen). There is an evocative reference to the theme of this **daís** even in the *Iliad*, where Hera reminds Apollo that he too had attended:

πάντες δ' ἀντιάασθε, θεοί, γάμου· ἐν δὲ σὺ τοῖσι
δαίνυ' ἔχων φόρμιγγα

And all you gods attended the wedding.[1] And you too were feasting among them, and you had your lyre with you.

XXIV 62–63

At this **daís** celebrating a marriage that led to the conception of Achilles himself, Zeus willed that **Éris** 'Strife' would bring about a **neîkos** 'quarrel' among the gods; these specific themes of **éris/neîkos** at a **daís** constitute the opening scene of the *Cypria* in particular and of the Trojan Cycle in general (Proclus p. 102.13–19: **Éris/neîkos** at 14/15).[2] Short range, these themes are appropriate to the motivation of the Trojan War; long range, the very same themes also provide a setting for the evolution of Achilles as a heroic figure.[3]

§17. We come back again to the first song of Demodokos in the *Odyssey* (viii 72–82), where the theme of a future death for Achilles is implicitly signaled by a quarrel at a sacrifice. The sacrifice is described as a **daís** of the gods (viii 76), and the quarrel is a **neîkos** (viii 75). The **neîkos** and all else that happened thereupon are described as the Will of Zeus (viii 82), which is the same traditional

§16n1. The verb **antiáō/antiáomai** 'come forth [to get]' used at XXIV 62 is appropriate for describing the coming of a god in order to receive the sacrifice that is being offered to him (cf., e.g., I 67, i 25, etc.).

§16n2. The **éris/neîkos** then extends to the figure of Paris, who has to choose from among Hera, Athena, and Aphrodite (*Cypria*/Proclus p. 102.14–19 Allen; also *Iliad* XXIV 25–30). In the Judgment of Paris, he brings about **neîkos** for Hera and Athena (νείκεσσε: XXIV 29) but **aînos** for Aphrodite (ἤνησ': XXIV 30). For the social and poetic significance of **aînos/neîkos** in the sense of praise/blame, see Ch.11§16 and the following Ch.12.

§16n3. The *Thebais* tradition (*fr.* 3 Allen) also concerns a quarrel, specifically over portions of meat. Oedipus curses his sons because they once gave him the wrong **moîra** of meat (the **iskhíon** 'haunch, ham' rather than the **ômos** 'shoulder'). The theme of the fatal strife that ensues between the brothers **Eteo-kléēs** and **Polu-neíkēs** is even reflected in their names; for the implication of poetic genre in the contrast of **kléos**/praise and **neîkos**/blame, see Ch.14§12n3 (cf. also Ch.12§7n3). The theme of the **moîrai** of Oedipus is probably reflected in the expression μήλων ἕνεκ' Οἰδιπόδαο 'on account of the sheep of Oedipus' (Hesiod *W&D* 163). For the correlation of **mêla** 'sheep' and the theme of **moîrai**, see §22n1 below.

device that motivates the **neîkos** at the beginning of the *Cypria* (Proclus p. 102.13–14; *Cypria fr.* 1 Allen).[1] Likewise at the beginning of our *Iliad*, the Will of Zeus (I 5) leads to **éris** 'strife' between Achilles and Agamemnon (ἐρίσαντε: I 6; ἔριδι: I 8),[2] and this strife takes the form of a **neîkos** 'quarrel' (ἔριδας καὶ νείκεα: II 376).[3] In the words of Agamemnon, **éris** 'strife' is a theme that defines the very character of Achilles:

αἰεὶ γάρ τοι ἔρις τε φίλη πόλεμοί τε μάχαι τε

<u>éris</u> is always dear to you, as well as wars and battles[4]

I 177

§18. In the beginning of the *Iliad*, we can now see a marked divergence in theme. The setting for the strife and quarreling between Achilles and Agamemnon is *not* a feast—let alone a sacrifice.[1] In fact, it is just the opposite. During the time that Achilles and Agamemnon were having their quarrel, Zeus and all the Olympians were away at a **dais** (κατὰ δαῖτα: I 424) in the far-off land of the Aithiopes (I 423–424), situated at the extremities of the universe.[2] Whenever the gods are away at such a **dais** with the remote Aithiopes, the efficacy of a sacrifice by the heroes in the here-

§17n1. Zeus wants to alleviate the Earth by depopulating the many heroes who weigh upon it (*Cypria fr.* 1 Allen). For more on the Will of Zeus, see n3 and Ch.5§25n2.

§17n2. See also I 177, 210, 277, 319.

§17n3. At XIX 270–274, Achilles says that his quarrel with Agamemnon was the Will of Zeus, so that many Achaeans may die; at the very next verse, XIX 275, he bids the Achaeans to go and eat at Agamemnon's feast.

§17n4. Compare this characterization ("strife and war") with Hesiod *fr.* 206MW about the Aeacids in general ("feasts and war"), as discussed at §15. Note too that the same words that characterize Achilles at I 177 recur at V 891 to characterize none other than the god of war himself, Ares! The symmetry is more extensive: whereas Achilles is reproached by the socially superior Agamemnon, Ares is reproached by Zeus himself!

§18n1. In the attested evidence, the closest thing to a quarrel between Achilles and Agamemnon in the context of a **dais** is the incident at Tenedos as told in the *Cypria* (Proclus p. 104.21–24 Allen). Here the **mênis** 'anger' of Achilles seems to center on his not being invited in time to a banquet, on account of which he loses **tīmḗ** (see the brief summary in Aristotle *Rhetoric* 1401b1γ; note too the wording: **mênis** and **atīmazómenos**).

§18n2. For the geographical symbolism of the Aithiopes and their realm, see Ch.10§§25–45. As for the chronology of *Iliad* I, there are of course many details that remain unclear. This much is for sure, however: at the time Thetis is speaking to Achilles, his quarrel with Agamemnon has just happened, and it is here that she tells how Zeus and the other Olympians had left for the Aithiopes *on the day before* (I 423–425).

and-now of the epic narrative is in question.[3] Yet the notion of "divide, apportion, allot" inherent in the institution of the **daís** is very much present in the Strife Scene that begins the *Iliad*, even if the **daís** itself is notably absent as a setting. The word **daíomai** 'divide, apportion, allot' is actually used in *Iliad* I to describe the grievance of Achilles over his being deprived of his fair allotment in the spoils of war (δάσσαντο: I 368, to be read in the overall context of I 365–392, especially 392).

§19. In the beginning of the *Iliad*, the more pervasive mode of describing the loss by Achilles of his fair share is by way of the noun **tīmḗ** 'honor' and the verbs formally related to it (see especially I 505–510, 558–559; II 3–4).[1] The word **tīmḗ**, as we have seen, is also appropriate for designating what it was that Pyrrhos had pursued by quarreling over slices of meat: the hero's wrangle was "on account of his rightful **tīmaí**" (**kūriân** [or **moiriân**!] **perì tīmân**: Pindar *Paean* 6.118).[2] As for Achilles, he loses his **tīmḗ** 'honor' specifically because Agamemnon has taken away his **géras** 'honorific portion':[3]

> ... ἀτάρ μιν νῦν γε ἄναξ ἀνδρῶν Ἀγαμέμνων
> ἠτίμησεν· ἑλὼν γὰρ ἔχει γέρας, αὐτὸς ἀπούρας

But Agamemnon, king of men, has taken away his **tīmḗ**;
for he got and keeps his **géras**, having himself taken it away.

I 506–507

In this particular case, of course, the **géras** is a captive girl. Elsewhere in the *Iliad*, however, the same word refers to a choice cut of meat, *le morceau du héros*, awarded to the foremost warrior of the moment:

§18n3. See Lowenstam 1975.132–133, esp. on XXIII 205–209.

§19n1. On the use of **tīmḗ** to specify "cult", see §1n2 above. Motto and Clark (1969.119) draw a parallel between the loss of **tīmḗ** by Achilles and the incident in the story of Meleager (IX 533–537) where Artemis is deprived of her share in a sacrifice—which, we may note, qualifies as a **daís** (δαίνυνθ': IX 535).

§19n2. See §8. Consider also the periodic sacrifice of a bull as "the **tīmā́** of the Hero" in a Delphic inscription (§1n4), where the unnamed hero may be Pyrrhos.

§19n3. For more on **géras** in the sense of "honorific portion" (and **tīmḗ** 'honor'), see Benveniste 1969 II 43–50. Beyond the material discussed by Benveniste, I cite the evidence of inscriptions dealing with sacral regulations, where the same word **géras** (especially in the plural: **gérē**) specifies a cut of sacrificial meat that is destined for the god who presides over the sacrifice or, less directly, for the priest who performs the sacrifice. For documentation, see Stengel 1910.169–171, Puttkammer 1912.2, and Gill 1974.127–128. Note that the vocabulary of sacral regulations frequently fails to distinguish the god's portion from the priest's (Puttkammer, pp. 16–18 and Gill, pp. 128–131). In poetry too, we find the use of **géras** and **tīmḗ** in contexts that overtly specify cult—e.g., Hesiod *Th.* 392–396. On *H.Hermes* 112–141, see Kahn 1978.41–73.

αὐτὰρ ἐπεὶ παύσαντο πόνου τετύκοντό τε <u>δαῖτα</u>,
<u>δαίνυντ᾽</u>, οὐδέ τι θυμὸς ἐδεύετο <u>δαιτὸς</u> ἐΐσης·
νώτοισιν δ᾽ Αἴαντα διηνεκέεσσι <u>γέραιρεν</u>
ἥρως ᾽Ατρεΐδης, εὐρὺ κρείων ᾽Αγαμέμνων

But when they finished with their efforts and prepared the **daís** [feast],
<u>they had the **daís** [feasted]</u>, and there was no **thūmós** lacking in a fair **daís**
[allotment].
And wide-ruling Agamemnon the hero, son of Atreus, <u>gave as **géras**</u> to Ajax
the whole back [of beef].[4]

VII 319–322

Let us contrast again the concern over the **tīmḗ** of Achilles in *Iliad* I:
The situation is unlike that of Ajax in *Iliad* VII, in that *Iliad* I lacks
the setting of a **daís**. Even later on in the *Iliad*, there seems to be a
set of insistent allusions to this initial Iliadic divergence from the
theme of the **daís**, as when Odysseus says to Achilles:

χαῖρ᾽, ᾽Αχιλεῦ· <u>δαιτὸς</u> μὲν ἐΐσης οὐκ ἐπιδευεῖς
ἠμὲν ἐνὶ κλισίῃ ᾽Αγαμέμνονος ᾽Ατρεΐδαο
ἠδὲ καὶ ἐνθάδε νῦν· πάρα γὰρ μενοεικέα πολλὰ
<u>δαίνυσθ᾽</u>· ἀλλ᾽ οὐ <u>δαιτὸς</u> ἐπηράτου ἔργα μέμηλεν ...

Hail, Achilles! You are not without a fair **daís**
either in the tent of Agamemnon son of Atreus
or here and now. There is at hand much that would suit your **ménos**, for you
to have as **daís**. But the concern is not
about a pleasant **daís** ...

IX 225–228

The detailed side-stepping here of the theme of a **daís** draws all the
more attention to it. The wording of this passage, so strikingly
parallel in detail to the one we have considered immediately before
(VII 319–322), again conjures up for us the theme of awarding, in
the context of a **daís**, the choice cut of meat—this time to the
foremost warrior of the *Iliad* in its entirety. And the speaker is

---

§19n4. The translation "whole" for **diēnekéessi** at VII 321 is based on the evidence
of the inscriptions: in the language of sacral regulations, **diānekés** marks a portion of
meat that is not subdivided, like a whole leg or a whole back (see Puttkammer, p. 11).
Ajax gets the choice cut of meat for having fought with Hektor, who had challenged
whoever is the "best of the Achaeans" to fight him (VII 50–51, 73–75); see Ch.2§3.
The theme of "the champion's portion," *le morceau du héros*, has important Celtic
parallels, discussed by Arbois de Jubainville 1899.45–47, 52, 62–63; cf. also Girard
1902.262, 268–271. In Old Irish saga, the two most relevant narratives are the *Tale of
MacDathó's Pig* and *Bricriu's Feast*; translations are conveniently available in Cross and
Slover 1936.199–207/254–280.

Odysseus, who had quarreled in another traditional scene with Achilles himself at a **daís** where the preeminence of the epic heroes was somehow at stake (viii 72–82). Later on in the *Iliad*, again it will be Odysseus who proposes a **daís** as the setting for Agamemnon's making amends to Achilles (XIX 179–180), and it will be at this **daís** that Achilles finally accepts compensation for his loss of **tīmế** (XIX 268–281).[5]

§20. The time has come to underscore an interesting contrast that has been emerging between the figures of Achilles and Pyrrhos. For the Achilles of our *Iliad*, the restoration of **tīmế** happens at a **daís**—but the same does not hold for the Strife Scene where he had originally lost that **tīmế**. Pyrrhos, on the other hand, has his Strife Scene on account of his **tīmaí** at an overt sacrifice; furthermore, his actions mirror closely on the level of myth the proceedings of the sacrifice on the level of ritual. To put it another way, our story of Pyrrhos is much closer to a ritual quarrel over cuts of sacrificial meat than our story of Achilles, where the narrative elements have been considerably stylized—especially in *Iliad* I.

§21. The epic stylization that affects the theme of a choice cut of meat for Achilles, *le morceau du héros*, actually runs very deep. In certain instances of Homeric diction, even the comparative approach secures the notion of "allotment, portion" for words that designate the epic destiny of Achilles. Such is the case with **aîsa**, designating the Iliadic destiny of Achilles in contexts stressing his excessively brief lifespan (e.g., I 416, 418); when we turn to the comparative method, we find such related forms as Oscan *aiteis*, functionally equivalent to Latin *partis* (genitive of *pars* 'share, allotment').[1] More overtly, the word **moîra** not only functions as a synonym of **aîsa** in some Homeric contexts where it carries the sense of "fate".[2] It also designates specifically "cut of meat" in other contexts (e.g., iii 66).[3]

§19n5. §15.

§21n1. For a discussion of the etymology and semantics of **aîsa**: Chantraine I 38–39. For the interesting collocation **daímonos aísēi** at *H.Dem.* 300, see Richardson 1974.257. We may add that there are in fact sporadic attestations, in the corpus of surviving sacral regulations, of **aîsa** designating "portion of meat" (see Puttkammer 1912.40n8).

§21n2. See Lee 1961.196–197. Consider especially the use of **aîsa/moîra** in expressions for "according to destiny" ~ "contrary to destiny": **kat' aîsan** (XVII 716, etc.) and **katà moîran** (I 286, etc.) ~ **hupèr aîsan** (III 59, etc.) and **hupèr moîran** (XX 336). For more on the convention itself: Ch.2§17, Ch.5§25n2, Ch.15§3n9.

§21n3. For **moîra** as "cut of meat" in sacral inscriptions, cf. Gill 1974.124n6. The epic convention of correlating the plot at hand with the Will of Zeus (on which see

Finally, for yet another example of stylized imagery that is traditionally connected with the theme of a champion's portion for Achilles, I cite the complex word **kḗr**.[4] In the plural, **kêres** at IX 411 specifically designates the two possible courses of epic action between which Achilles must choose[5]—a **nóstos** 'safe homecoming' with a long life on the one hand or, on the other, a brief life with a **kléos** 'glory' that is everlasting (IX 410–416).[6]

§22. Such highly elaborated formal imagery surrounding the Achilles figure in the *Iliad* distances him considerably from Pyrrhos, that stark figure of a savage warrior who is lunging after a choice cut of meat to which he lays claim. And yet, the same *Iliad* that stylizes the actions of Achilles to their ultimate epic refinement can also bridge the vast distance of heroic evolution and suddenly picture Achilles on the most fundamental level of savage behavior. The god Apollo, who brought about the death of both father and son, says these words to mark the hero of the *Iliad*, Achilles himself:

> λέων δ' ὣς ἄγρια οἶδεν
> ὅς τ' ἐπεὶ ἄρ μεγάλῃ τε βίῃ καὶ ἀγήνορι θυμῷ
> εἴξας εἶσ' ἐπὶ μῆλα βροτῶν, ἵνα <u>δαῖτα</u> λάβῃσιν

But, like a lion, he [Achilles] knows savage ways
—a lion that yields to its great **bíē** and overweening **thūmós**,
and goes after the sheep of men, in order to get a **daís**.[1]

XXIV 41–43

The use of the word **daís** in this image of stark savagery is particularly striking as it applies to the Achilles figure. Actually, this

---

again Ch.5§25n2) seems to be the basis for the imagery inherent in **tamíēs polémoio** 'apportioner of war' as epithet of Zeus (XIX 224, etc.); see §15n2.

§21n4. Note the correlation of **Moîrai** and **Kêres** in Hesiod *Th.* 217 (see West 1966.229). For the difficulties of the etymology and semantics, see Chantraine II 526. For an attempt at deriving the word **kḗr** from the same root *ker- 'cut' as in Latin *carō, carnis* 'meat, flesh', see Lee 1961; his most important contribution, in any case, is at pp. 196–197, where he lists the parallel combinations of **kḗr** and **moîra** in Homeric diction.

§21n5. For an interesting local-oriented variation on this theme, see XIII 663–672; for parallel applications of **kḗr** and its themes to Achilles/Herakles, see XVIII 115/117.

§21n6. The **kléos** is **áphthiton** 'unfailing' in that it is a glory conferred by poetry; for the poetic connotations of **kléos**, see Nagy 1974.244–255. On the contrast in genre between **kléos** and **nóstos**: Nagy, pp. 11–13; also Ch.2§§3 and 11, to be read in conjunction with Ch.6§6nn2 and 5.

§22n1. Note that the **daís** of the lion is the meat of sheep, the prime sacrificial animals at Apollo's Delphi, and that the god's attendants are conventionally described as slaughtering them eagerly with **mákhairai** 'knives' (*H.Apollo* 535–537).

characterization of the Iliadic hero is quite in tune with a latent dimension that keeps surfacing at moments of intense heroic anguish, as when Achilles is grieving over his dead **hetaîros**:

οὐδέ τι θυμῷ
τέρπετο, πρὶν πολέμου στόμα δύμεναι αἱματόεντος

nor was he gladdened in his **thūmós**
until he entered the jaws of bloody war

XIX 312–313

The verb **térpomai** 'be gladdened' can conventionally designate gratification by way of eating (e.g., XI 780), and it is precisely this theme of eating that functions as the immediate context for the passage under consideration. The elders of the Achaeans are imploring Achilles to eat (XIX 303–304), but he refuses and insists on keeping a fast (XIX 304–308, 319–321); while he is fasting, he actually reminisces about the meals that Patroklos used to serve up to him (XIX 314–318, especially 316). This grim juxtaposition of two images, the bloody jaws of war and the hero who goes without meals while Patroklos lies unavenged, is only part of a ghastly Iliadic theme that finally comes to a head at the moment when a victorious Achilles is standing triumphant over the sprawled figure of a dying Hektor and says:

αἲ γάρ πως αὐτόν με μένος καὶ θυμὸς ἀνείη
ὤμ' ἀποταμνόμενον κρέα ἔδμεναι, οἷα ἔοργας

I wish that somehow my **ménos** and **thūmós** impelled me
to slice you up and eat your meat raw, for the things you did.

XXII 346–347

We recall the simile, uttered by Apollo himself, comparing Achilles to a carnivorous lion whose **thūmós** impels it to its **daís** 'feast' of sheep (XXIV 41–43).[2] So also here, the **ménos** and **thūmós** of Achilles are bringing our hero to the verge of a bestial deed. In another simile comparing Achilles with a raging lion (XX 164–175), the beast is described as impelling itself to fight:

... ἑὲ δ' αὐτὸν ἐποτρύνει μαχέσασθαι

... and it is impelling itself to fight

XX 171

§22n2. The expression "yielding to the **thūmós**" at XXIV 42–43 (θυμῷ / εἴξας) is a reflexive equivalent of the active expression "[the **ménos** and] the **thūmós** impel," as at XXII 346 (μένος καὶ θυμὸς ἀνείη). See n3.

The stance of the beast is then directly compared to the manner in which the **ménos** and **thūmós** of Achilles impel him to fight:

ὣς ᾿Αχιλῆ᾽ ὄτρυνε μένος καὶ θυμὸς ἀγήνωρ

so also the **ménos** and overweening **thūmós** of Achilles impelled him onwards[3]

XX 174

In effect, then, the simile is saying that Achilles has the **thūmós** of a lion, in that the beast's intrinsic behavior is set in the same way as Achilles is driven by his **thūmós**. Little wonder, then, that Achilles qualifies as **thūmoléōn** 'he who has the **thūmós** of a lion' (as at VII 228).[4] Little wonder, moreover, that the mother of Hektor reviles Achilles as **ōmēstḗs** 'eater of raw meat' (XXIV 207).[5]

§23. By the end of the *Iliad*, however, these hideous dimensions of the heroic temperament are a thing of the past, as compassion finally takes hold of Achilles and he restores the body of Hektor to the grieving father. What is more, the setting for this ultimate scene of heroic compassion and refinement is again a feast—this time initiated by Achilles himself (XXIV 599–601). No sooner said than done, the feast is held, and we get our last Iliadic glimpse of Achilles as he presides over the affair—and actually apportions the sacrificial meat:

... ἀτὰρ κρέα νεῖμεν ᾿Αχιλλεύς

... and Achilles distributed the meat

XXIV 626

§24. To sum up our survey: the Aeacids, we now see, have a special affinity to the theme of the **daís**, but for Achilles the Homeric tradition expresses this affinity in a manner that downplays the ritual aspects of the **daís**. For the Achilles figure, the most overt—or the least downplayed—Homeric manifestation of the ritual element is the first song of Demodokos at viii 72–82, where the hero's future death

§22n3. Note that the active construction here ("the **ménos** and the **thūmós** impelled") is drawn into a parallel, by way of the simile, with a reflexive construction at XX 171 ("the lion is impelling itself"). For the relationship of **ménos** and **thūmós**, see XXII 312–313, where Achilles fills his **thūmós** with savage **ménos** (μένεος δ᾽ ἐμπλήσατο θυμὸν / ἀγρίου); this passage is in the immediate vicinity of the threat to eat Hektor raw (XXII 346–347). On the savagery of Achilles, see esp. Redfield 1975.

§22n4. In the *Iliad*, Herakles is the only other hero who also qualifies (V 639).

§22n5. Achilles is the only Homeric hero to be described with this epithet, otherwise restricted to beasts (e.g., dogs at XXII 67). See also Robertson 1940.177–180 on Pindar *N*.3.48: the phrasing here concerns animals not yet dead, whose marrow will be sucked by the savage young hunter Achilles (see also Apollodorus 3.13.6).

is implicitly linked with the themes of Delphi/sacrifice/quarrel—and these are the same themes that frame the death of Pyrrhos as it is presented in Pindar's *Paean* 6 and *Nemean* 7.

§25. The narrative of viii 72–82, however, is so compressed that we are still left with a number of mysteries surrounding the **neîkos** 'quarrel' of Achilles and Odysseus. Perhaps the most intriguing question is this: we know that the **neîkos** happened at a **daís** of the gods (viii 76), but why is this **daís** connected with a prophecy that emanates specifically from Delphi (viii 79–81)? From what we have seen of the close parallelism between the story of how Pyrrhos died at Delphi and the themes of viii 72–82, we are led to speculate whether the **daís** where Achilles and Odysseus quarreled is a theme that actually incorporates Delphic lore. If this were the case, then the epic scene that opens the first song of Demodokos would be even more ritual in orientation than we had imagined, what with the sacral ideology of Delphi as an informing principle. The contrast with the opening of the *Iliad*, where the **neîkos** of Achilles and Agamemnon lacks even the setting of a feast—let alone a sacrifice—would then be all the more remarkable.[1] We may add that the opening of the first song of Demodokos is in any case a treatment with more ritual undertones than even the opening of the *Cypria*, where the **daís** that serves as the setting for the **neîkos** of the gods is presented from a narrative vantage that stresses not so much a sacrifice by heroes to gods but rather a feast attended by heroes and gods together.[2]

§26. What kind of epic composition can we imagine that commences not only with an overt sacrifice as the opening scene but also with links to the sacral lore of Delphi? To confront the first part of the question, let us look at the evidence of allusions in actual Homeric diction and theme. The most suggestive passage for our purposes is the lengthy Cretan narrative in *Odyssey* xiv (192–359),

§25n1. The *Iliad* not only veers away from the themes of Delphi: it also presents the word **óssa** 'voice' in a negative light, which may be significant in view of this word's association with the oracular voice of Apollo (see Pindar *O.*6.61–62). In the *Iliad*, the False Dream that almost aborts the Trojan Expedition (and by extension the *Iliad* itself) is equated with **Diòs ángelos** 'messenger of Zeus' (II 26, 63, 94), which in turn is equated with **óssa** personified (II 93). Compare Agamemnon's false expectations upon hearing the False Dream (II 36–40) with his false expectations upon hearing the Oracle of Apollo (viii 77–82).

§25n2. Even though the **daís** at the Wedding of Peleus and Thetis is presented more as a banquet than as a sacrifice, the diction at XXIV 62–63 describes the attendance of Apollo and the other gods in a manner appropriate to gods who come to receive sacrifice. See §16n1.

told by Odysseus in the guise of a Cretan princeling. The main adventure, an expedition led by our Cretan adventurer to plunder the wealth of Egypt (xiv 245–286), is twice directly correlated in the narrative with the great Achaean expedition to Troy (xiv 229–231, 235–242). In fact, the hero of the narrative claims that he not only fought in the Trojan War but also was actually the leader of the Cretan contingent, along with the mighty Iliadic hero, Idomeneus himself (xiv 237–238). Since the narrative endeavors to enhance the scale of the Egyptian expedition so as to match the epic proportions of the Trojan expedition, it is important to observe precisely how the launching of the enterprise is described. Significantly, the Cretan leader of the expedition to Egypt holds an overtly sacrificial **daís** lasting for six days (xiv 249–251), and only thereafter can his ships sail off. From this passage, then, we infer that a **daís** might be an appropriate setting to open a narrative about a Trojan expedition.

§27. We come now to the second part of our question: why should Delphi be connected with the theme of the **daís** at which Achilles and Odysseus quarreled? Here the historical evidence about Delphi itself may be pertinent. From the eighth and seventh centuries B.C. onward, by virtue of its becoming a centralized Panhellenic repository of myriad local religious traditions, the Delphic Oracle was evolving into the ideological and political center that coordinated the launching of expeditions for the purpose of founding new cities and for other such monumental enterprises.[1] From the standpoint of a local epic that relates the founding of one city or the destruction and plundering of another, the setting of a **daís**—especially in the context of Delphi—could provide for an appropriate opening scene.[2]

§28. The *Iliad* as we have it, on the other hand, is of course a composition that goes far beyond the dimensions and interests of any local epic tradition. Our *Iliad* is clearly Panhellenic in scope, and an opening like the one in the first song of Demodokos may have fallen far too short of the thematic range that Homeric Epos requires. But whether or not the specific themes in the first song of Demodokos are worthy of Iliadic standards, it is more important for us now to stress two facts about our *Iliad* that pertain directly. First, the isolated

§27n1. See Vian 1963.83 and Parke/Wormell I 78–79; cf. also Snodgrass 1971.416–417. For a useful bibliography on the Panhellenic importance of Delphi: Giovannini 1969.66n2.

§27n2. For a survey of attested epic traditions about colonizations and the prominent role played in such poetry by the Delphic Oracle of Apollo, see Schmid 1947.148–153.

Iliadic reference to Delphi actually concerns Achilles: aside from the *Catalogue* reference (II 519),[1] all that remains is the one mention of Delphi which, as we have seen, apparently confronts Achilles with the remote thematic alternative of plundering Delphi instead of Troy (IX 404–405).[2] Second, we are about to see that there are Iliadic references to local epic traditions concerning Achilles, although they are as a rule merely marginal. In the *Iliad*, such references could not be allowed to interfere with the Panhellenic central theme of the expedition to Troy—an expedition that goes far beyond local epic interests.[3]

§29. The Trojan expedition, as it is presented in its ultimate form by our *Iliad*, is a grand theme which, by converging on the one main goal of Troy, unites on the level of content the heroic and material resources of the various cultural centers that may each once have had their own epic traditions about conquering various territories.[1] Aside from its centralized thematic concern about the expedition to Troy, however, the *Iliad* also manages some marginal references to epic traditions about various other expeditions to other places, notably Lesbos (IX 129, 271, 664), Skyros (IX 668), Tenedos (XI 625), and Lyrnessos and Pedasos (XIX 60; XX 90–92, 188–194; cf. XI 104–112).[2] These expeditions all involve territories that would have been Aeolic at the time that our *Iliad* took its present shape,[3] and the

§28n1. On the Delphic orientation of the *Catalogue*: Giovannini 1969.51–71.

§28n2. See §6.

§28n3. For an interesting introduction to the traditional genre of **ktísis** ('colonization') poetry, see in general Schmid 1947. One of the most important lessons to be learned from Schmid's book is that **ktísis** poetry is fundamentally local rather than Panhellenic in orientation, and that its contents are therefore continually subject to shifts each time the colony itself undergoes shifts in population or politics. Another is that the hero in a **ktísis** poem may be presented overtly as a cult figure (see esp. Schmid, p. 138).

§29n1. See Schmid 1947, esp. pp. 4–8, 83–87, 141–148; also Norden 1922.16 on *Iliad* II 653–670, the earliest attested passage that refers overtly to the genre of **ktísis** poetry. In this particular instance, the **ktísis** of Rhodes, we already see the conventional themes of (1) a formal **arkhaiologíā** and (2) a description of tribal divisions (Norden, ibid.). As I have done with other Iliadic passages, I reject any assumption that II 653–670 involves the interpolation of a distinct *text* that is later in date than the main body of the *Iliad*. Instead, I would again argue that we see in this passage the incorporation of a distinct poetic *tradition*.

§29n2. There are further references in the *Cypria* (Proclus p. 101.4–11; p. 102.10–12 Allen). See Bethe 1927 III 66–75 for an interesting discussion; I disagree, however, with the relative chronologies offered, as well as with the ad hoc theories of textual interpolation (notably in regard to the passages in *Odyssey* xxiv about the funeral mound of Achilles).

§29n3. On the archaeological evidence for the Aeolic settlement of the Troad by the end of the eighth century B.C.: Cook 1973.360–363.

Iliadic references to them consistently stress the heroic preeminence of Achilles.[4] This emphasis on Achilles is particularly striking in the case of Lesbos: the *Iliad* says that Achilles himself captured all Lesbos (IX 129, 271), and the significance of such a heroic deed seems to have less to do with the epic fate of nearby Troy and far more with the here-and-now of a Homeric audience in the eighth or seventh century B.C.[5] The *Iliad* is here verifying something that applies from the standpoint of this era: that the affinity of the Achilles figure with this particular Aeolic island is a matter of acknowledged tradition, incorporated even by Panhellenic Epos.[6]

§30. From the standpoint of such localized epic traditions, the first song of Demodokos would have been appropriate as the opening of an epic composition about an expedition undertaken by Achilles. Such a composition would have acknowledged the Oracle of Delphi as the authority that inspired the epic expedition, and the setting of a sacrifice would provide an appropriate opening Strife Scene for motivating the eventual death of the main hero who undertook the enterprise. This much I can now say with somewhat more confidence, having found a distant parallel in the form of a Strife Scene at a Delphic sacrifice, leading to the death of Pyrrhos, son of Achilles.

§29n4. For a discussion of these expeditions in terms of **ktísis** poetry, see Schmid 1947.83–87, esp. p. 86.

§29n5. Similarly with the Hellespont, its navigational importance as the passage to the Black Sea concerns not the second millennium B.C. but rather the period of politically organized colonizations—that is, from the eighth and seventh centuries onwards. See Ch.20§24. For the importance of the thematic affinity between the Achilles figure and the Hellespont, see Ch.20 in general.

§29n6. If we try to reconstruct the situation backward as well as foward in time, we observe that there are stories connecting Achilles with the conquest of Lesbos that are attested in the classical period as well. A particularly interesting example is the story of Achilles and Peisidike (Parthenius *Erotica* 21), which tells how the hero captured the Lesbian city of Methymna. A variant of this story is localized at Pedasos and seems to be attested already in the Hesiodic tradition (*fr.* 214MW). See again Schmid, pp. 83–87, 141–148.

8 | The Death of Hektor

§1. By comparing the death of Achilles with the death of Pyrrhos, we have come to see more clearly the factor of ritual antagonism between god and hero. If, of course, we had only the *Iliad* as evidence, this factor would be much more difficult to discern in the case of Achilles, whose own antagonism with the god Apollo is so poetically stylized and elaborated as to suit the artistic framework of Panhellenic Epos. Even within such a monumental structure, however, the basic outlines emerge clearly enough. Although the death of Achilles himself at the hands of Apollo is deferred beyond the *Iliad*, the death of his surrogate Patroklos is presented in a manner that makes the experience apply directly to the hero of the *Iliad*.[n]

§2. Aside from this basic observation on the level of theme, we can also adduce detailed evidence on the level of diction. We have seen that the *Iliad* applies **mênis** 'anger' as a word appropriate specifically to Achilles among heroes, and that his **mênis** over his loss of **tīmḗ** 'honor' results from the earlier anger of Apollo, likewise specified as **mênis**, over his respective loss of **tīmḗ**. The first **mênis**, of Apollo, had caused what is called a **loigós** 'devastation' for the Achaeans in the form of a plague; the second **mênis**, of Achilles, then causes them devastation in the form of a dire military situation inflicted by Hektor at the Battle of the Ships. This second devastation is also specifically called a **loigós**. Moreover, both the first and the second **loigós** are described as bringing **álgea** 'pains' to the Achaeans. The first **loigós** is removed when the plague is lifted, whereupon the Achaeans sing a **paiḗōn** 'paean' to Apollo; the second is removed when Hektor is killed, and this time Achilles bids them to sing,

§1n. See again Ch.2§8 on the function of Patroklos as **therápōn** of Achilles and Ch.6§§23–26 on the mourning over Patroklos as a substitute for the mourning over Achilles.

142

again, a **paiéōn**.[1] We could go on multiplying examples of thematic and formal convergences between Apollo and Achilles. For instance, Walter Burkert is so struck by the physical resemblance in the traditional representations of the god and the hero—especially by the common feature of their both being unshorn in the manner of a **koûros**[2]—that he is moved to describe Achilles as a *Doppelgänger* of Apollo.[3] For now, however, let us simply adhere to this main point: that god and hero mirror each other, both formally and thematically, in the dimension of ritual.

§3. In order to observe how the formal and thematic matchings between Apollo and Achilles are actually enacted in an epic scene of ritual antagonism, let us contrast the Iliadic stance of Achilles with that of the intrepid Diomedes, who in his own right actually dares to wound the Olympian gods Aphrodite and Ares in *Iliad* V. After three consecutive attempts, even Diomedes shrinks from a fourth and final confrontation with Apollo (V 432–444), and in doing so he is specifically described as avoiding the god's **mênis** (**mênin aleuá-menos**: V 444). At the moment that he is making this fourth attempt, Diomedes qualifies as **daímoni îsos** 'equal to a **daímōn**' (V 438, which is then reported at V 459), and the deployment of this epithet coincides with the climax of ritual antagonism between the god and the hero.[n]

§4. When Patroklos, the surrogate of Achilles, confronts Apollo four consecutive times in two separate but closely related scenes, he too qualifies during his fourth attempt in both scenes as **daímoni îsos** 'equal to a **daímōn**' (XVI 705, 786). In the first scene, Patroklos shrinks from a fourth and final confrontation with the god—and he lives (XVI 705–711). In the second scene that follows shortly thereafter, Patroklos fails to avoid the fourth and final confronta-

§2n1. For citations and further discussion of how all these words function in the *Iliad*, see Ch.5§§8–16.

§2n2. Compare Apollo's epithet **akersekómēs** 'unshorn' (as at XX 39) with the hair-shearing scene of Achilles at XXIII 140–153. Burkert (1975.19) stresses the association of this theme with vestigial aspects of what anthropologists would call initiation. Cf. also Brelich 1958.361.

§2n3. Burkert 1975.19. Cf. Chirassi Colombo 1977. In this connection, we may note that Achilles even swears by Apollo (I 86), and that the significance of this theme emerges from a careful study of the word **apeiléō** 'predict, threaten' and its deployment in the *Iliad*. I refer to a forthcoming work by Leonard Muellner, who also explores the thematic and formal links between **apeiléō** and **Apéllōn/Apóllōn**.

§3n. For more on the word **daímōn**: Ch.9§§5–6 (cf. Lowenstam 1975). Cf. also Muellner 1976.82–83 on XX 102.

tion—and he is killed (XVI 786–789). In the first scene, Patroklos, like Diomedes, is specifically described as avoiding the god's **mênis** (**mênin aleuámenos**: XVI 711); in the second scene, he has intrinsically incurred it.[1] So also with Achilles himself: when the time comes for his own final confrontation with Apollo, the hero of the *Iliad* will die by failing to avoid the god's **mênis,** and the diction of the *Iliad* itself predicts this. Consider the "rehearsal" at XX 447–454, where the action would have proceeded as it had in the second confrontation scene of Patroklos at XVI 786–789, if only Apollo had not made the action void (XX 441–446).[2] But even if the epic action of Achilles is here ineffectual, his stance of antagonism towards Apollo is ominously clear: as he is making his fourth attempt, he too is **daímoni îsos** 'equal to a **daímōn**' (XX 447).

§5. With the perspective of ritual at our disposal, and with the evidence of the traditional epic diction that keeps formally matching the figures of Achilles and Apollo, we may now even ask whether the antipathy of the god toward the Achaeans in the *Iliad* has less to do—at least in origin—with his sympathy toward the Trojans and more with the theme of his antagonism toward the hero of the *Iliad*. In order to assure ourselves that the factor of ritual antagonism between god and hero can actually determine the antipathies of various gods in the epic tradition of the Trojan War, let us now turn to the figure of Hektor, the prime enemy of Achilles in the *Iliad*.

§6. The question is, which Olympian god would qualify as Hektor's ritual antagonist? Let us suppose that the heroic pattern of Hektor is inverse to that of his prime epic opponent. In that case, the Olympian who should bring about his death is Athena. And indeed, just as Paris *and* Apollo are named by the *Iliad* as the killers of Achilles (XIX 416–417, XXII 359–360), so also the death of Hektor is described as being actually caused by Athena, albeit with Achilles and his spear serving as her instrument (XXII 270–271, 445–446). Athena not only intervenes overtly in the final duel of Hektor and Achilles (see especially XXII 222–223, 275–277, 298–299); she even says that Achilles *and* she are to be the ones who vanquish Hektor (XXII 216–218).

§7. The mutual function of Athena and Apollo as the ritual antagonists of the two prime heroes who will fight each other in the *Iliad*,

---

§4n1. More on this crucial scene at Ch.17§5.
§4n2. Cf. also XXII 7–20.

Hektor and Achilles respectively, becomes overt in *Iliad* VII 17–61.
There the two Olympians, championing the Achaeans and Trojans
respectively, decide to call a halt to the general battle between the
two warring sides and to bring about instead a one-to-one conflict
that pits Hektor against "whoever is best of the Achaeans" (VII 50).[1]
At VII 58–61, as the preparations take place for a duel that should
have matched Hektor against Achilles himself,[2] we get a singularly
uncanny picture of the two main Olympian antagonists of Hektor and
Achilles, Athena and Apollo, in the shape of two birds perched on
the Tree of Zeus, observing the events that unfold—and all along
"delighting in the heroes" (ἀνδράσι τερπόμενοι: VII 61).

§8. If indeed we may call Athena the ritual antagonist of Hektor,
what is there in the hero that mirrors the goddess? To put it another
way, how do the figures of Hektor and this divinity converge in
theme and form? Let us first consider Hektor's heroic attributes and
then his aspirations. Among his attributes, we note that Hektor is the
only Trojan in the *Iliad* who is described as "equal to Zeus in **mêtis**"
(Διὶ μῆτιν ἀτάλαντε: VII 47, XI 200).[1] In the words of Agamemnon
himself (X 47–52), no other Trojan had performed more deeds of
mêtis (μητίσασθαι: X 48) against the Achaeans than Hektor.[2] In this
respect, then, the function of the hero has a close affinity to Athena,
the goddess of **mêtis** incarnate.[3] Here is a divine figure who not only
boasts that her **mêtis** confers upon her the **kléos** that is hers from
poetry (μῆτι ... κλέομαι: xiii 299): the poetic tradition actually
establishes her as daughter of Zeus and **Mêtis** personified (Hesiod
Th. 886–900).

§9. Another of Hektor's traditional attributes is his reputation for
protecting the city and its people. At VI 402–403 and XXIV 729–730,
this basic function of the hero is heralded in what can almost be
described as programmatic fashion. In fact, **Astúanax**, his son's

§7n1. The essence of the gods' will is understood by Helenos, who imparts it to
Hektor (VII 44–53). See Ch.2§3.

§7n2. See again Ch.2§3.

§8n1. On **mêtis**, see Ch.3§§5–8.

§8n2. The Achaeans' loss, which is in proportion to Hektor's gains in **mêtis** (X
43–52), is also equated with lack of **boulè kerdaléē** 'crafty planning' (βουλῆς ... /
κερδαλέης: X 43–44). Compare this use of **boulé** 'plan, planning' in the context of
mêtis with the uncanny image of Hektor as he "plans his plans," **boulàs bouleúei** (X
415), at the **sêma** 'tomb' of Ilos, local hero of Troy. For the semantics of **sêma**,
cognate of Indic *dhyáma* 'thought', see Sinos 1975.83–90.

§8n3. See Detienne/Vernant 1974, esp. pp. 167–175, 176–200.

name, comes directly from the father's function of protecting the **ástu** 'city':[1]

τόν ῥ' Ἕκτωρ καλέεσκε Σκαμάνδριον, αὐτὰρ οἱ ἄλλοι
'Αστυάνακτ'· οἶος γὰρ ἐρύετο Ἴλιον Ἕκτωρ

Hektor used to call him [his son] Skamandrios, but the others
called him **Astúanax**; for Hektor alone protected Ilion.[2]

VI 402–403

What is more, the name of **Héktōr** himself is an agent noun derived
from the verb **ékhō** in the sense of "protect," as is attested precisely
in the context of Hektor's protecting the city of Troy and its
inhabitants:

ὅς τέ μιν αὐτὴν
ῥύσκευ, ἔχες δ' ἀλόχους κεδνὰς καὶ νήπια τέκνα

... you [Hektor] who guarded it [the city],[3]
and you protected the cherished wives and helpless children[4]

XXIV 729–730

φῆς που ἄτερ λαῶν πόλιν ἑξέμεν ἠδ' ἐπικούρων
οἶος·

Perhaps you [Hektor] think that you will protect
the city [**pólis**] all alone, without the fighting men and the allies.[5]

V 473–474

§9n1. For a correlation of the word **ástu** itself with the theme of a protecting Hektor,
see XXIV 499.

§9n2. This passage is the clearest example of a traditional convention in the naming
of heroes: the son is named after one of the father's primary heroic characteristics. See
Clader 1976.30–31 on **Megapénthēs** 'he who has great **pénthos**', the son of Menelaos
(iv 11); the father's **ákhos/pénthos** 'grief' is a traditional epic theme (e.g., iv
108–110). Cf. also the son of Nestor, **Peisí-stratos** 'he who persuades the army'. As
for the son of Odysseus himself, **Tēlé-makhos**, his name may mean either "he who
fights far away [at Troy]" or perhaps "he who fights from far away [with arrows]"; both
characterizations are appropriate to the father. Finally, see van der Valk 1958.147n164
on the names of two of Herakles' three children by Megara: **Thērímakhos** 'he who
fights beasts' and **Dēïkóōn** 'vigilant in battle' (*vel sim.*; cf. Chantraine II 551). These
names correspond respectively to five of the hero's labors involving beasts and to five
involving treacherous enemies. (The themes of Hades/death and Hesperides/life round
out the number of labors to twelve.)

§9n3. The pronoun is referring to the **pólis** 'city' of Troy, at XXIV 728.

§9n4. On the semantics of **népios** 'helpless': Edmunds 1976.

§9n5. Chantraine (II 330) considers the derivation of **Héktōr** from **ékhō** without
discussing the semantics of the verb. The article by Meier 1976 helps fill the gap,
although I think that his definition of the semantic sphere of **ékhō** is overrestrictive.
The notion of "domination" need not always imply "domination by conquest."
Consider the semantics of **ktízō**, etc.

In this respect, too, the function of the hero has a close affinity to Athena, who is worshiped by the Trojans as the official guardian of their city. She is the goddess whose idol is enshrined in their citadel, and it is to her that they as a community pray in their hour of need (see especially VI 286–311). In fact, when they specifically pray to Athena that she ward off the onslaught of Diomedes, the verb that designates the action is a derivative of **ékhō** (ἀπόσχῃ: VI 277). What is more, she is invoked in their prayers as **(e)rusíptolis** 'protector of the city' (ῥυσίπτολι: VI 305), which is a generic cult epithet of Athena that we find applied exclusively to her in both of the two attested Homeric *Hymn(s) to Athena* (11.1, 28.3).[6]

§10. Both of these attributes showing an overlap between the figures of Hektor and Athena—as paragon of **mêtis** and as guardian of the city—are significantly involved in the actual death of the hero. The scene of Hektor's demise (at *Iliad* XXII) is motivated by an earlier scene of deliberation in the Council of the Trojans (XVIII 243–314), where Hektor goes against the pattern of action that is marked out even by his name. He advocates an *offensive* strategy in response to the impending onslaught of Achilles, whereas his counterpart Poulydamas is advocating a *defensive* strategy. The immediate stance of Poulydamas as a counterpart of and alternative to Hektor is highlighted in the narrative by the manner in which this hero is described: he was born on the same night as Hektor (XVIII 251), and he had the reputation of excelling with words whereas Hektor excelled "with the spear" (XVIII 252).[n] Significantly, the scene of deliberation ends with the stratagem that wins approval, that of Hektor, being described as bad in contrast with that of Poulydamas (XVIII 310–313); moreover, the narrative specifies that Athena had here taken away Hektor's senses (XVIII 311), and that the hero's **mêtis** had gone bad (κακὰ μητιόωντι: XVIII 312). For good measure, when the time comes for Hektor's final confrontation with Achilles, Athena again takes away Hektor's senses—this time by actively deluding him (XXII 222–247, 296–299).

§9n6. For more on the generic cult function of Athena as protector of the city: Nilsson I 346–349. For another distinctive epithet that apparently emphasizes the protective and defensive aspects of Athena, consider **alalkomenēís** as at IV 8 and V 908. On the derivation from **alalkeîn** 'ward off', see Chantraine I 57. For a survey of traditional themes featuring Athena on the defensive and offensive, see Vian 1968.58.

§10n. On the spear as an emblem of **bíē** (as opposed to **mêtis**), see the use of **bíē** at Hesiod *W&D* 148, in the context of *W&D* 143–155 as discussed at Ch.9§9; see also §12. Compare the image of Achilles as a boy, armed with nothing but a spear (Ch.20§8).

§11. We come now to the question of Hektor's aspirations in the *Iliad*. The hero himself says that he wishes he were immortal and "honored"—specifically like Athena and Apollo:

εἰ γὰρ ἐγὼν ὣς
εἴην ἀθάνατος καὶ ἀγήρως ἤματα πάντα,
τιοίμην δ' ὡς τίετ' Ἀθηναίη καὶ Ἀπόλλων,
ὡς νῦν ἡμέρη ἥδε κακὸν φέρει Ἀργείοισιν

If only I were
immortal and unaging for all days to come,[1]
and if only I got **tīmḗ** [were honored] just as Athena and Apollo get **tīmḗ**
[are honored]
—as surely as this day brings misfortune to the Argives.

VIII 538–541

What is more, he is accused by Poseidon (in the form of Kalkhas) of boasting that he is the child of Zeus:

Ἕκτωρ, ὃς Διὸς εὔχετ' ἐρισθενέος πάϊς εἶναι

Hektor, who boasts to be the child of mighty Zeus.[2]

XIII 54

In fact, Hektor himself wishes that he were the child of Zeus:

εἰ γὰρ ἐγὼν οὕτω γε Διὸς πάϊς αἰγιόχοιο
εἴην ἤματα πάντα, τέκοι δέ με πότνια Ἥρη,
τιοίμην δ' ὡς τίετ' Ἀθηναίη καὶ Ἀπόλλων,
ὡς νῦν ἡμέρη ἥδε κακὸν φέρει Ἀργείοισι

If only I were the child of aegis-bearing Zeus
for all days to come, and the Lady Hera were my mother,
and if only I got **tīmḗ** just as Athena and Apollo get **tīmḗ**
—as surely as this day brings misfortune to the Argives.

XIII 825–828

For the second time, we see an overt comparison of the hero with the gods Athena and Apollo. And the epithet **Diòs páïs** 'child of Zeus' is equally unmistakable: when they had met at the Tree of Zeus in the context of planning the duel that pits Hektor against whoever is the best of the Achaeans, both Apollo and Athena were

---

§11n1. On the function of this wording in the process of immortalization: Ch.10 §30n2.

§11n2. Having studied the inherited phraseology of **eúkhetai/eúkheto** 'boast', Muellner observes (1976.78): "This, the ultimate genealogy, is being put forward not as pretentious or boastful but true." For amplification, see the important discussion by Muellner at pp. 50–52, 80(n23).

specifically designated as son/daughter of Zeus (VII 23/24).[3] After Hektor is dead, his own father says of him:

Ἕκτορά θ᾽, ὃς θεὸς ἔσκε μετ᾽ ἀνδράσιν, οὐδὲ ἐῴκει
ἀνδρός γε θνητοῦ παῖς ἔμμεναι, ἀλλὰ θεοῖο

Hektor, who was a god among men; and he seemed
to be the child not of a mortal but of a god.[4]

XXIV 258–259

The wording here conveys a striking variation on the conventional theme of a hero's getting **tīmḗ** from the community:

... θεὸς δ᾽ ὣς τίετο δήμῳ

... and he got **tīmḗ** from the **dēmos**, like a god

V 78, X 33, XI 58, XIII 218, XVI 605[5]

On the level of epic, of course, the hero gets **tīmḗ** by virtue of his reputation as a warrior; on the level of ritual, on the other hand, the hero gets **tīmḗ** in the form of cult—which is what the word **tīmḗ** itself can actually designate.[6] In the specific case of Hektor, the **tīmḗ** to which he aspires is that of Apollo and Athena themselves, and it is hard to imagine a more direct way for epic to convey the ritual aspect of a hero.

§12. The epic tradition of the *Iliad* has neither the vocabulary nor really the thematic need to distinguish the cult of heroes from the

---

§11n3. The specific wording **Diòs páïs** 'child of Zeus', as applied to Hektor (XIII 54), is also appropriate for female divinities (e.g., viii 488).

§11n4. Note too Muellner 1976.50 on VII 298, where the women of Troy are described as **eukhómenai** 'praying' to Hektor (dative): "This is the only place in all the Homeric corpus (including **eúkhomai** in secular contexts) where a dative noun after **eúkhomai** is *not* a god or a collection of gods."

§11n5. In the *Iliad*, this expression is applied respectively to Dolopion, priest of Skamandros; Agamemnon; Aeneas; Thoas; and Onetor, priest of Zeus Idaios. Its significance can best be appreciated by considering more closely what is represented by the **dēmos**, described here as the source of **tīmḗ** for the hero. See n6.

§11n6. On **tīmḗ** in the sense of "cult": Ch.7§1n2. Moreover, we have observed *en passant* in Ch.6§29 that cult practices were a strictly localized phenomenon in archaic Greek religion. Accordingly, the Homeric association of **tīmḗ** with **dēmos** (n5) is of utmost significance, in view of the connotations this word inherits. Derived from the root *dā- 'divide, allot, apportion' (Chantraine I 274), **dēmos** had originally meant something like "district," and this intrinsic local connotation is still overt in numerous Homeric contexts (e.g., V 710; XVI 437, 514; etc.); see especially Detienne 1968.131 on **dēmos** in *Odyssey* ii 32, 44 and Herodotus 1.62. It is even possible that the element **dēmo-** in compound names like **Dēmophóōn** (*H.Dem.* 234: "shining for the **dēmos**") and **Dēmódokos** (viii 44, etc.: "approved by the **dēmos**") emphasized the localized functions of such figures. For more on the name **Dēmophóōn**: Ch.10§10n4.

cult of gods. The hero's ritual antagonism with a divinity can find its epic expression in his aspiration to get the same **tīmḗ** as his divine counterpart, and the narrative leaves it at that. More directly, the plot of epic represents the ritual antagonism in a format where the god actually contrives the hero's death. What epic will not represent, however, is the symbiosis of god and hero in cult. On the level of epic, the Trojans cannot worship Hektor as the main protector of their city, in a manner that complements their worship of Athena.[1] For the *Iliad*, even the worship of Athena by the Trojans is a difficult theme to elaborate, because of the fundamental antagonism that exists between her and Hektor, the prime hero who protects the Trojans. For the *Iliad*, the narrative focus on the antipathy that Athena has for Hektor blurs whatever sympathy she would have had for the Trojans. The scene where the Trojans pray to her is but a vestige of her relation to them.[2] And aside from this one scene with its strong ritual orientation, the *Iliad*, with its overall epic orientation, highlights instead the sympathy of Athena toward Achaean champions like Achilles, parallel with the sympathy of Apollo toward Hektor.

§12n1. For a latent reference to the worship of Hektor: §11n4.

§12n2. Thus I disagree with the notion (cf. Bethe 1927 III 19–20) that the scene in *Iliad* VI where the Trojans worship Athena necessarily represents a "new" tradition—let alone that the passage itself is an interpolation. As for the observation that Athena's being guardian of Troy seems to be a more central theme in the *Iliou Persis* (Proclus pp. 107–108 Allen), it does not necessarily follow that such a divergent thematic treatment is less archaic than that of the *Iliad*. Newer compositions like the *Iliou Persis* may in fact use older themes than what we find in the *Iliad*. The theme of Athena's being guardian of Troy may well suit the political realities of the eighth or seventh centuries B.C. in the Troad, but the theme itself may be much more archaic.

9 | Poetic Categories for the Hero

§1. In the *Iliad*, Hektor's aspiration to get the same **tīmé** that is accorded to Athena (and Apollo) not only formalizes the antagonism between hero and god; it also implies a slighting of the superior god's **tīmé** by the inferior hero. On the level of Homeric discourse, the dimension of cult that is conveyed by the word **tīmé** is latent in such situations, so that the hero's stance amounts to what seems to be—on the surface of the narrative—simply a slighting of the god's honor. On the level of Hesiodic discourse, by contrast, the **tīmé** of the gods in an analogous situation is overtly expressed in terms of cult.[n]

§2. The passage in question comes from the Myth of the Five Generations, in the *Works and Days*. Let us join the narrative midstream, at the description of the Second, or "Silver," Generation of Mankind, and how it came to grief after having enjoyed only the briefest span of adolescence (*W&D* 132–134). We are now about to be told the reason for this sudden demise:

ὕβριν γὰρ ἀτάσθαλον οὐκ ἐδύναντο
ἀλλήλων ἀπέχειν, οὐδ᾽ ἀθανάτους θεραπεύειν
ἤθελον οὐδ᾽ ἔρδειν μακάρων ἱεροῖς ἐπὶ βωμοῖς,
ἣ θέμις ἀνθρώποισι κατ᾽ ἤθεα. τοὺς μὲν ἔπειτα
Ζεὺς Κρονίδης ἔκρυψε χολούμενος, οὕνεκα τιμὰς
οὐκ ἔδιδον μακάρεσσι θεοῖς οἳ Ὄλυμπον ἔχουσιν

For they could not keep wanton **húbris** from each other,
and they were unwilling either to be ministers to the immortals
or to sacrifice on the sacred altars of the blessed ones,
which is the socially right thing for men, in accordance with their local customs.

---

§1n.   For **tīmé** as "cult," see Ch.7§1n2.

151

And Zeus the son of Kronos was angry and made them disappear,
because they did not give **tīmaí** to the blessed gods who control Olympus.

Hesiod W&D 134–139

§3. In this passage, remarkable as it is for both its explicitness and
its precision, we see the institutional observance of cult being overtly
expressed in terms of giving the gods **tīmaí**.[1] This point is essential
as we read further in the *Works and Days*. For, despite the fact that
the men of the Silver Generation did not give **tīmaí** to the gods, *they
still receive what they had failed to give*:

δεύτεροι, ἀλλ᾽ ἔμπης τιμὴ καὶ τοῖσιν ὀπηδεῖ

They are second in rank, but nevertheless they too get **tīmḗ**.

Hesiod W&D 142

The Silver Generation is "second," of course, to the First, or
"Golden," Generation (*W&D* 109–126); by implication, it is to the
Golden rather than Silver Generation that **tīmḗ** is primarily due—
next to the gods themselves.[2] Also by implication, the **tīmḗ** received
by the Golden and Silver Generations comes from sacrifice, as
performed by the mankind of the here-and-now.

§4. It is not immediately clear from these Hesiodic verses, however, if the Silver Generation actually represents a classification of
heroes, in their ritual dimension as antagonists of gods. The
specifically heroic nature of the Silver Generation becomes explicit
only when we see how it complements the nature of the Golden
Generation, with which it is formally and thematically coordinated.
This coordination was observed in the irreplaceable *Psyche* of Erwin
Rohde, and it is his reading that I will attempt to reformulate here.[1]
The narrative of the *Works and Days* makes it clear that the lifespan
of the Silver Generation would have been but a copy of the Golden,
had it not been for the former's committing **húbris** 'outrage' (*W&D*
134–135).[2] The **húbris** of the Silver Generation is a consequence of
its nature, which is to be contrasted with that of the Golden (*W&D*
129). In the case of the Golden Generation, the Hesiodic description
of its nature is explicitly appropriate to heroes *as they are worshiped in
cult*:

§3n1. Cf. Rohde I 99n1.
§3n2. Rohde I 99.
§4n1. See Rohde I 91–110.
§4n2. For the significance of the opposition between **húbris** and **díkē** in the *Works
and Days*, I will rely on the study of Vernant 1966 [= 1960].

τοὶ μὲν δαίμονές εἰσι Διὸς μεγάλου διὰ βουλὰς
ἐσθλοί, ἐπιχθόνιοι, φύλακες θνητῶν ἀνθρώπων
οἵ ῥα φυλάσσουσίν τε δίκας καὶ σχέτλια ἔργα,
ἠέρα ἑσσάμενοι πάντη φοιτῶντες ἐπ᾽ αἶαν,
πλουτοδόται· καὶ τοῦτο γέρας βασιλήϊον ἔσχον

And they are the **daímones**, by the Will of Zeus.
They are the good,[3] the **epikhthónioi**, the guardians of mortal men.
They guard the **díkai** and against bad deeds.
Invisible, they roam all over the Earth,[4]
givers of wealth. And they had this too as a **géras**, befitting kings.[5]

Hesiod *W&D* 122–126

Whereas the Silver Generation commits **húbris**, the Golden is here described as upholding **díkai** (*W&D* 124). We will have more to say presently about this contrast in **húbris/díkē**, as also about the explicitly heroic characteristics of the Golden Generation; for now, the most important thing to observe is the description of this class of mankind as **epikhthónioi** (*W&D* 123).[6]

§5. As Rohde points out,[1] the epithet **epi-khthónioi** marks the earthbound condition of mankind (besides *W&D* 123, see *Th.* 416, *Iliad* IV 45, etc.; **khthōn** = 'earth'), as compared to the celestial existence of the Olympian gods, who are **ep-ouránioi** (see *Iliad* VI 129, etc.; **ouranós** = 'sky'). We must keep in mind that the function of **epi-** 'on, at' in these two formations is simply to associate figures with places. That much said, we now come to the description of the Silver Generation as the **hupo-khthónioi** 'those who abide under the earth':

τοὶ μὲν ὑποχθόνιοι μάκαρες θνητοὶ καλέονται

And they are called the **hupokhthónioi**, blessed mortals.

Hesiod *W&D* 141

§4n3. On the connotations of **esthlós** 'worthy, good': Ch.10§1n2, §3n2.

§4n4. For the interpretation of ἠέρα ἑσσάμενοι 'wrapped in mist' at *W&D* 125 as "invisible," see Rohde I 96n3.

§4n5. On **géras** 'honorific portion', see Ch.7§19n3; on the connotations of βασιλήϊον 'befitting **basilêes** [kings]', see §31.

§4n6. For cogent arguments against the bracketing of *W&D* 124–125, see Rohde I 96n1; also Vernant 1966 [= 1960] 29. Albert Henrichs calls my attention to a remarkable parallelism between *W&D* 122–126 and the parabasis of Aristophanes *Heroes* = *fr.* 58 Austin. See Merkelbach 1967 and Gelzer 1969 (esp. pp. 123 ff.).

§5n1. Rohde I 97n1; so also the Proclus commentary. Cf. also Goldschmidt 1950.37, Vernant 1966 [= 1960] 25 and 1966b.274, and West 1978.182.

Let us juxtapose the corresponding description of the Golden Generation:[2]

ἐσθλοί, ἐπιχθόνιοι, φύλακες θνητῶν ἀνθρώπων

They are the good, the **epikhthónioi**, the guardians of mortal men.

Hesiod *W&D* 123

True, the Silver Generation abides <u>beneath</u> the earth by virtue of being **hupo-khthónioi**, but this formation does not imply that the Golden Generation abides <u>above</u> the earth by virtue of being **epikhthónioi**. As Rohde surveys the association of institutional hero cults with figures like Amphiaraos, Trophonios, Althaimenes, Teiresias, Erekhtheus, Phaethon, and others, he finds that the characteristics of these heroes match closely those of the Golden Generation, *and yet their abodes in cult are all under the earth.*[3] Even the diction of Hesiodic poetry bears out this feature. A figure like Phaethon is specifically called a **daímōn** in his function as **neopólos múkhios** 'underground temple-attendant' of the goddess Aphrodite (*Th.* 991).[4] As we have already seen, those in the Golden Generation are also specifically called **daímones** (*W&D* 122).

§6. The essence, then, of the Golden and Silver Generations is that together they form a complete picture of the hero in cult. The evidence of Hesiodic diction even corroborates that both generations—not just the Golden—qualify as **daímones**.[1] In this respect, they are both like the Olympian gods, who also qualify as **daímones** (e.g., *Iliad* I 222, etc.).[2]

§7. If indeed the First and Second Generations of Mankind are designed as complementary categories, it remains to ask why a distinction was made in the first place. The answer is available in a study by Jean-Pierre Vernant, who has observed that the entire Myth

§5n2. For the textual problems at *W&D* 122–123, see West, pp. 181–182.

§5n3. Rohde I 111–145.

§5n4. See Rohde I 135n1, as well as Ch.10§§22–36 below; also Sinos 1975.17–37.

§6n1. The etymology of **daímōn** as 'he who apportions' (see Ch.7§15n1) is paralleled by the epithet **ploutodótai** 'givers of wealth' at *W&D* 126, correlated with **daímones** at *W&D* 122. For a warning against equating the **daímones** of Hesiodic diction with the **daímones** of Plato's usage, see Rohde I 96n2. Cf. also Detienne 1963, esp. the preface by J.-P. Vernant. Finally, consider the comment on the word by Nock 1972 [= 1944] 580n21: "It is a word of reflection and analysis."

§6n2. The Olympian gods in turn have some cult functions that properly belong beneath the Earth, in which contexts they qualify as **khthónioi** (e.g., *W&D* 465, *Th.* 767) or **múkhioi** (see Rohde I 135n1 for a survey of attestations in cult; cf. also Hesiod *Th.* 119).

of the Five Generations is permeated with the central theme of contrasting **díkē** with **húbris**.[1] The composition of the *Works and Days* elaborates this theme even further in the lengthy moral (*W&D* 213-285) that follows the Myth of the Five Generations (*W&D* 106-201).[2] We have, in fact, already seen that the concept of **díkē** characterizes the First Generation, as compared to the **húbris** of the Second. We must now add that the Third Generation is again characterized by **húbris** (ὔβριες: *W&D* 146);[3] furthermore, it is then set off from the Fourth Generation for the specific reason that the Fourth has **díkē**, as compared to the Third (δικαιότερον: *W&D* 158).[4] By virtue of **díkē**, the Fourth is also superior to the Third (δικαιότερον καὶ ἄρειον: *W&D* 158), whereas the Second had been inferior to the First (πολὺ χειρότερον: *W&D* 127). In other words, Generation I, which is marked by **díkē**, serves as a positive foil for Generation II, marked by **húbris**; correspondingly, Generation III, which is marked by **húbris**, serves as a negative foil for Generation IV, again marked by **díkē**. As for Generation V, which describes the realities of the Hesiodic world, the good is to be mixed in with the bad (*W&D* 179). In this world of the here-and-now, **húbris** is engaged in an ongoing struggle with **díkē** (*W&D* 213-218 and beyond). I could put it another way: Generation V is the quintessence of the four opposing types of human condition, Generations I versus II, and III versus IV. The here-and-now incorporates all the oppositions of the past and the hereafter.

§8. It remains to ask what kind of human condition is represented by Generations III and IV. My answer will be based on the proposition that Generations I and II together form an integral picture of the hero in cult. Correspondingly, I propose that Generations III and IV together form a complete picture of the hero in epic. Furthermore, just as Generation I had represented the positive side

§7n1. Vernant 1966 [= 1960] 20, 24-26.

§7n2. Within this passage (*W&D* 213-285), the words **díkē/húbris** occur no fewer than 27/4 times (derivatives included). On the intervening **aînos** of the hawk and the nightingale (*W&D* 202-212), see Puelma 1972; also Ch.12§18 below.

§7n3. Whether we read the textual variant ὔβριες or ὔβριος, the present argument remains unaffected.

§7n4. The inherited meaning of a comparative like **dikaióteros** is not "X has more **díkē** [than Y]" but "X has **díkē** [as compared to Y, who does not]." Similarly, Homeric **skaióteros** [compared to **dexiós**] is not "X is more left [than Y]" but "X is left [as compared to Y, which is right]"; also, **dexíteros** [compared to **skaiós**] is not "X is more right [than Y]" but "X is right [as compared to Y, which is left]"; see Benveniste 1948.115-125.

of Generation II, so also Generation III represents the negative side of Generation IV.

§9. As in our discussion of the first two generations, let us approach the next two by beginning with the negative side of the picture. The Third or "Bronze" Generation is depicted as bent on nothing but **húbris** and war:

Ζεὺς δὲ πατὴρ τρίτον ἄλλο γένος μερόπων ἀνθρώπων
χάλκειον ποίησ', οὐκ ἀργυρέῳ οὐδὲν ὁμοῖον,
ἐκ μελιᾶν, δεινόν τε καὶ ὄβριμον· οἷσιν Ἄρηος
ἔργ' ἔμελε στονόεντα καὶ ὕβριες

And Zeus made another Generation of **méropes** men, the Third.
And he made it <u>Bronze</u>, not at all like the Silver.
A Generation born <u>from ash trees</u>, violent and terrible.
Their minds were set on the woeful deeds of Ares and <u>acts of **húbris**</u>.[1]

Hesiod W&D 143–146

Their very birth and essence, ash trees and bronze respectively, add up to a prime emblem of war: the generic spear of epic diction has a staff made of ash wood and a tip made of bronze, so that a Homeric word for "spear" like **énkhos** can bear either the epithet **meílinon** 'of ash' (e.g., V 655) or **khálkeon** 'of bronze' (e.g., V 620).[2] The description of the Bronze Generation continues, with more details about their savage ways:

οὐδέ τι σῖτον
ἤσθιον, ἀλλ' ἀδάμαντος ἔχον κρατερόφρονα θυμόν,
ἄπλαστοι· μεγάλη δὲ βίη καὶ χεῖρες ἄαπτοι
ἐξ ὤμων ἐπέφυκον ἐπὶ στιβαροῖσι μέλεσσιν.
τῶν δ' ἦν χάλκεα μὲν τεύχεα, χάλκεοι δέ τε οἶκοι,
χαλκῷ δ' εἰργάζοντο· μέλας δ' οὐκ ἔσκε σίδηρος.
καὶ τοὶ μὲν χείρεσσιν ὑπὸ σφετέρῃσι δαμέντες
βῆσαν ἐς εὐρώεντα δόμον κρυεροῦ Ἀίδαο,
νώνυμνοι· θάνατος δὲ καὶ ἐκπάγλους περ ἐόντας
εἷλε μέλας, λαμπρὸν δ' ἔλιπον φάος ἠελίοιο.

And they did not eat grain,
but their hard-dispositioned **thūmós** was made of hard rock.

§9n1. We may take special note here of the close association between the Bronze Generation and Ares, on which see Vian 1968.64–66. With regard to Ares as the god who is the essence of bronze, see Muellner 1976.82 on *Iliad* XX 102.

§9n2. Moreover, the **meliē** functions as the word for both "ash tree" (e.g., XVI 767) and "ash spear" (e.g., XVI 143). For a thorough discussion of the Homeric evidence, see Shannon 1975, esp. pp. 46–48 for his comments on *W&D* 143–155.

They were forbidding: they had great **bíē** and overpowering hands growing
out of their shoulders, with firm foundations for limbs.[3]
Their implements were bronze, their houses were bronze, and they did their
work with bronze. There was no iron.
And they were wiped out when they killed each other,
and went nameless to the dank house of chill Hades.[4]
Terrible as they were, black Death still took them, and they left the bright
light of the Sun.

Hesiod *W&D* 146-155

§10. As the comparative studies of Francis Vian have shown,[1] this
blood-crazed behavior of the Bronze Men is like that of a runaway
Männerbund on the fringes of civilized society.[2] The Bronze Men are
in the same mold as various other bands of impious warriors in
Greek myth—most notably the Spartoi and the Phlegyai.[3] We may
note in particular that the Phlegyai are also characterized by **húbris**
(Φλεγύων . . . ὑβριστάων: *H.Apollo* 278),[4] while the Spartoi are traditionally depicted as bearing the sign of the spear as a birthmark
(Aristotle *Poetics* 1454b22).[5]

§11. Besides such remote figures as these Spartoi and Phlegyai, we
can find a much more immediate manifestation of the heroic type
represented by the Bronze Men. As we have seen in Chapter 7,
Achilles himself is associated—however remotely—with the theme of
plundering Delphi, as if he were of the same mold as the wanton

§9n3. Verses 148-149 are bracketed in Solmsen's edition on the grounds that their
phraseology recurs in the Hesiodic description of the Hundred-Handers at *Th.*
147-153, 649, 670-673. But the textual repetitions are well motivated by the thematic
parallelisms. See also Vian 1968.61-63 on the close thematic parallelisms between the
Bronze Generation and the general category of earth-born Giants.

§9n4. The Bronze Men are **nónumnoi** 'nameless' in that their deeds cannot be
glorified by poetry; so also the Achaeans would be **nónumnoi** if they were to be
destroyed at Troy without having succeeded in capturing the city (XII 70, XIII 227,
XIV 70). This is not to say that the deeds of the Bronze Men are not a fitting subject
for poetry—only that the treatment of their deeds in poetry will not win them any glory
(cf. §20 below). For the inherited poetic theme that the hero's name depends on being
glorified by poetry, see Schmitt 1967.90-93.

§10n1. See especially Vian 1968 (with further bibliography), following Vernant 1966
[= 1960].

§10n2. In this respect, their association with Ares is significant. As Nilsson (I
517-519) points out, by classical times this god has many myths but noticeably few
cults. Without cult, the figure of Ares is liable to be an outsider from the standpoint of
the **pólis**. Cf. also Vian 1968.55.

§10n3. On whom see Vian, pp. 59-61.

§10n4. See also Ch.7§5n3 on **phleguân = hubrízein**.

§10n5. Cf. Vernant 1966 [= 1960] 34.

Phlegyai.[1] Then too, Achilles himself has his epic moments of wanton slaughter, where the diction of even the *Iliad* presents its prime hero on the very fringes of savagery. More than that, we have seen in Chapters 3 and 4 that Achilles himself is the champion of **bíē** in the Homeric tradition.[2] Now as we begin to see in the *Works and Days* that **bíē** is also the mark of the Bronze Generation (*W&D* 148), we may be ready to infer that this Hesiodic classification of mankind suits the dark and latent side of the Homeric hero.[3] What may carry conviction is yet another striking convergence in detail between the figures of Achilles and the Bronze Men.

§12. We have already seen that bronze and ash wood are emblematic of the Third Generation (*W&D* 143–151) and that the spear of Homeric diction consists of the same elements: a tip of bronze and a shaft of ash wood. We must now observe further that the bronze-tipped ash spear of Achilles in particular is the only piece of the hero's armor that was not made by the divine smith Hephaistos (see XVII 194–197, XVIII 82–85). Rather, the spear of Achilles was inherited from his father, to whom it had been given by Cheiron the Centaur:

Πηλιάδα μελίην τὴν πατρὶ φίλῳ πόρε Χείρων
Πηλίου ἐκ κορυφῆς, φόνον ἔμμεναι ἡρώεσσιν

the Pelian <u>ash-spear</u>, which Cheiron had given to his **phílos** father,
from the heights of Mount Pelion, <u>to be death for heroes</u>

XVI 143–144

In fact, Achilles is described as the only hero who could wield this magnificent spear (XVI 140–142), which is also the only piece of the hero's armor that Patroklos did not take with him when he fatally replaced Achilles (XVI 139–141) and which is therefore the only piece not to be despoiled and then actually worn by the killer of Patroklos, Hektor. As Richard Shannon points out, the spear of Achilles is a theme that reaffirms the hero's connection with his mortal father, just as the rest of his armor connects him with his immortal mother.[1] What is more, as Shannon's whole monograph

§11n1. Ch.7§6.
§11n2. Ch.3§§5–8, Ch.4§5, Ch.7§22.
§11n3. See also Ch.7§17 and n4 for a correlation of *Iliad* I 177/V 891, where Achilles/Ares is reproached by Agamemnon/Zeus for being a lover of strife and war—precisely the characteristics of the Bronze Men!
§12n1. Shannon 1975.31. In fact, Hephaistos made not only the armor that Thetis gives to Achilles in *Iliad* XVIII but also the armor that has to be replaced when Hektor

shows convincingly, the **melíē** 'ash spear' of Achilles is a word that is "restricted in the *Iliad* to describing the individual weapon of a specific character in particular contexts."[2] In sum, the diction of the entire *Iliad* makes the bronze-tipped ash spear an emblem of Achilles just as surely as the birthmark of a spear characterizes the wanton Spartoi, or as bronze and ash wood characterize the equally wanton Bronze Men.[3]

§13. Having seen how the Third Generation corresponds to the recessive dark side of the Homeric hero, we are ready to examine whether the Fourth Generation corresponds to the dominant illustrious side, worthy of glorification by epic poetry.[n] In the process, we will also have to examine the more basic question: to what extent may we look at Generation IV as the positive side of Generation III?

§14. The Hesiodic description of those in the Fourth Generation overtly names them as the heroes who fought at Thebes and at Troy (*W&D* 159–165). Even the diction corresponds to that of Homeric Epos: the expression ἀνδρῶν ἡρώων θεῖον γένος 'the divine generation of **hḗrōes**' (*W&D* 159) features the conventional Homeric word for "hero": **hḗrōs/hḗrōes** (*Iliad* I 4, etc.). In the entire *Works and Days*, the word **hḗrōs/hḗrōes** is in fact restricted to the Fourth Generation (*W&D* 159, 172).

§15. Conversely, the next epithet applied to the Fourth Generation, **hēmítheoi** 'half-gods' (*W&D* 160), is restricted in the entire *Iliad* and *Odyssey* to one attestation, XII 23. The immediate context is one of those rare moments when the narrative of the *Iliad* distances itself from the epic action of the moment long enough to take in the wider view of the entire *Iliad*—and then the even wider view of the entire Trojan War. As the time frame expands, the perspective shifts from the heroic past to the here-and-now of the Homeric audience. The whole shift is occasioned by the topic of the wall that the Achaeans had built.[1] After a description of how the wall had functioned up to this point in the narrative (XII 3–9), we hear

strips Patroklos; this earlier set of arms was inherited by Achilles from his father, who had received it from the gods in honor of his marrying Thetis (see again XVII 194–197, XVIII 82–85; cf. also *Cypria fr.* 3 Allen).

§12n2. Shannon, p. 93.

§12n3. Compare the picture of Achilles as a boy, armed with nothing but a spear, in Pindar *N*.3.43–47 as discussed at Ch.20§8.

§13n. Contrast §9n4.

§15n1. Aside from what I intend to say here, see West 1969 for an interesting discussion of the Achaean Wall and the relation of this theme to the *Iliad* as a whole.

that it will no longer exist after a while (XII 9). Then comes a recounting of all the epic action that is yet to happen before the wall is destroyed: at this point in the narrative, Hektor is still alive (XII 10), Achilles still has his **mênis** (XII 10), and the Troy of Priam is not yet destroyed (XII 11). With the mention of the last theme, we are transported beyond the time frame of the *Iliad* into a brief account of Troy's destruction (XII 12–16)—after which Apollo and Poseidon let loose the rivers of the Troad in order to sweep away all traces of the Achaean Wall (XII 17–33, especially 26–32).[2]

§16. It is almost as if all the "props" that mark an Achaean expedition against Troy are to be obliterated once the expedition is over and the attention of epic switches to other places, other stories.[1] Among these "props" destined for obliteration, we get the following description of the remains lying on the riverbanks:

> ὅθι πολλὰ βοάγρια καὶ τρυφάλειαι
> κάππεσον ἐν κονίῃσι καὶ ἡμιθέων γένος ἀνδρῶν

where many cowhide-shields and helmets
fell in the dust—as also a generation of **hēmítheoi**[2]

XII 22–23

I have taken all this time in elaborating on the single Homeric attestation of **hēmítheoi** in order to show how closely the diction of archaic hexameter poetry responds to variant traditional perspectives on heroes. Whereas **hérōes** is the appropriate word in epic, **hēmítheoi** is more appropriate to a style of expression that looks beyond epic.[3]

§15n2. Even the diction that frames the naming of these rivers (XII 19–23) is parallel in style to the Hesiodic catalogue of rivers (*Th.* 337–345), those of the Troad included (*Th.* 340–345); cf. West 1966.259–260.

§16n1. Note in particular that the area by the Hellespont is explicitly smoothed over by the flooding rivers (XII 30–32). I suspect that this volunteered detail is consciously offered as a variant of the tradition that tells how the Achaeans had made a funeral mound for the dead Achilles by the Hellespont (xxiv 80–84). There is then an ironic fulfillment of the dire threat made by the river Xanthos/Skamandros to bury Achilles under a mound of silt (XXI 316–323), as if the funeral mound of Achilles were to be in the end simply a natural formation adorning the landscape of the Troad. I draw attention to the irony that the River calls this mound the **sêma** 'tomb' of Achilles (XXI 322), from which the Achaeans will not even be able to recover the hero's bones (XXI 320–321).

§16n2. This passage marks the only Homeric attestation of not just **hēmítheoi** but also **boágria** 'cowhide shields'. (Note too the use of the word **génos** with **hēmítheoi**!) Besides *W&D* 160, the word **hēmítheoi** occurs also at Hesiod *fr.* 204.100MW; the context (lines 95–103) is that Zeus plans the Trojan War in order that mortals may die and thus be separated from the immortal gods. Note the word **éris** 'strife' at line 96 and compare the opening of the *Cypria* as discussed at Ch.7§16.

§16n3. Note the context of the collocation γένος ἀνδρῶν ἡμιθέων 'generation of

§17. In sum, I propose that the diction of the *Works and Days* represents the Fourth Generation of Mankind in a manner that is both appropriate to the heroes of epic tradition (consider **hērōes** at *W&D* 159) and at the same time removed from the epic perspectives of the heroic age (consider **hēmítheoi** at *W&D* 160). It follows that we are now faced with an important question about the theme reflected by the diction. In specifically identifying the men of the Fourth Generation as those heroes who had fought at Thebes and at Troy, the *Works and Days* is doubtless making reference to actual epic traditions, and we have yet to ask what these may be.

§18. Let us look first at the Theban War. Actually, we may have to choose between two separate epic traditions about two separate Theban Wars: the *Seven against Thebes*, otherwise known as the *Thebais*, and the *Epigonoi*. Through the medium of Athenian trag-edy—specifically through the *Seven against Thebes* by Aeschylus—we at least know indirectly the main themes inherited by the first of these two epic traditions, although there is very little that survives directly from either (see *Thebais/Epigonoi* at pp. 112–114/115–116 Allen). Even aside from the Aeschylean play, however, the *Iliad* itself gives us valuable glimpses of themes from the traditions of both the *Thebais* and the *Epigonoi*.[n] In fact, the references in *Iliad* IV–V reveal an interesting contrast between heroic types as represented by two distinct epic traditions.

§19. As we join the action in *Iliad* IV, we find Agamemnon goading Diomedes into battle with taunting words of **neîkos** 'blame' ($\nu\epsilon\acute{\iota}$-$\kappa\epsilon\sigma\sigma\epsilon\nu$: IV 368).[1] The king's taunt takes the form of an episodic

---

men who were **hēmítheoi**' at Homeric *Hymn* 31.18–19 (cf. also Homeric *Hymn* 32.18–19). On the basis of the diction, I would infer that such compositions as Homeric *Hymn* 31 (and 32) are not preludes to an epic composition like the *Iliad*. Cf. Koller 1956, esp. p. 180. In Plato *Hippias Maior* 285d, stories about the "generations of heroes" ($\pi\epsilon\rho\grave{\iota}\ \tau\hat{\omega}\nu\ \gamma\epsilon\nu\hat{\omega}\nu \ldots \tau\hat{\omega}\nu\ \tau\epsilon\ \mathring{\eta}\rho\acute{\omega}\omega\nu\ \kappa\alpha\grave{\iota}\ \tau\hat{\omega}\nu\ \mathring{\alpha}\nu\theta\rho\acute{\omega}\pi\omega\nu$) are treated as a genre parallel to stories about colonizations ($\ldots \kappa\alpha\grave{\iota}\ \tau\hat{\omega}\nu\ \kappa\alpha\tauo\iota\kappa\acute{\iota}\sigma\epsilon\omega\nu,\ \mathring{\omega}\varsigma\ \tau\grave{o}\ \mathring{\alpha}\rho\chi\alpha\hat{\iota}o\nu\ \mathring{\epsilon}\kappa\tau\acute{\iota}\sigma\theta\eta\sigma\alpha\nu\ \alpha\mathring{\iota}\ \pi\acute{o}\lambda\epsilon\iota\varsigma$); see Schmid 1947.xiii. On the local orientation of **ktísis** ('colonization') poetry and its suitability for the subject of hero cults, see Ch.7§28n3. Note also the context of **hēmítheoi** at Alcaeus *fr.* 42.13LP ($\alpha\mathring{\iota}\mu\iota\theta\acute{\epsilon}\omega\nu$) and at Simonides *fr.* 523.3P; "the best of the **hēmítheoi**" in the first passage is Achilles himself, while the second passage is from a **thrênos**, on which see further at §§31–32, Ch.10§§1–5. Finally, note the application of **hēmítheoi** at Bacchylides 9.10 and 13.155 respectively to the Seven against Thebes and the Achaeans who fought Hektor at Troy.

§18n. We have to speak in terms of *traditions* rather than *compositions*. See Wehrli 1972 [= 1957] 65–66n27 for speculations over whether there was more than one extant composition known as the *Thebais* in the classical period.

§19n1. For the social context of **neîkos**, see Ch.12.

narrative about the heroic exploits of Tydeus in one of his skirmishes with the Thebans (IV 370–400).[2] Since Tydeus was of course not only the father of Diomedes but also one of the Seven against Thebes, the narrative has a special application as a taunt for Diomedes, since he in turn was one of the Epigonoi. Even more important, the conclusion of Agamemnon's taunt is that Diomedes is inferior, **khéreia** (accusative), to his father in battle (IV 400), and we note that we have seen a variant of the same word used in contrasting the Generations of Mankind (**kheiróteron** 'inferior': *W&D* 127).

§20. Diomedes responds to the taunt of Agamemnon by showing an eagerness to prove himself in battle (IV 401–402, 412–418), but his comrade Sthenelos cannot resist a rejoinder to Agamemnon. As we examine his words, we must keep in mind that Sthenelos was also one of the Epigonoi, while his father Kapaneus was also one of the Seven against Thebes:

'Ατρεΐδη, μὴ ψεύδε᾽ ἐπιστάμενος σάφα εἰπεῖν·
ἡμεῖς τοι πατέρων μέγ᾽ ἀμείνονες εὐχόμεθ᾽ εἶναι·
ἡμεῖς καὶ Θήβης ἕδος εἵλομεν ἑπταπύλοιο,
παυρότερον λαὸν ἀγαγόνθ᾽ ὑπὸ τεῖχος ἄρειον,
πειθόμενοι τεράεσσι θεῶν καὶ Ζηνὸς ἀρωγῇ·
κεῖνοι δὲ σφετέρῃσιν ἀτασθαλίῃσιν ὄλοντο.
τῷ μή μοι πατέρας ποθ᾽ ὁμοίῃ ἔνθεο τιμῇ

Son of Atreus! Don't warp your talk when you know how to speak clearly!
We boast to be much better than our fathers.
We even captured the foundations of seven-gated Thebes,
having mustered a smaller army against a stronger fortress,
and having heeded the signs of the gods and the help of Zeus.
But *they* perished, by their own wantonness.
So do not bestow on our fathers a **tīmḗ** that is like ours.

IV 404–410

Although Diomedes is socially compelled to answer Agamemnon's taunt with action rather than words,[1] the very theme of the taunt

---

§19n2. Cf. also V 793–813. As yet another instance of narrated heroic exploits that serve as taunts in the format of **neîkos**, we will examine in Chapter 15 the duel of Achilles and Aeneas, at *Iliad* XX. For an interesting parallel in Old Irish narrative, consider the *Tale of MacDathó's Pig*; a translation is conveniently available in Cross and Slover 1936.199–207.

§20n1. Note that Agamemnon's taunt accuses Diomedes of being worse in deeds *but better in words* than his father (IV 400). The situation is altogether different, however, when it comes to Athena's taunt at V 793–813: her challenge is both mental and physical. Appropriately, the immediate response of Diomedes is not action but clever words (V 815–824), which in turn are justified by his later heroic action.

leads to his vindication. If indeed action weighs more heavily than words—which is after all the ideological basis for the taunt itself— then surely the Epigonoi are better than the Seven against Thebes, since the sons captured Thebes and thus succeeded where their fathers had failed.[2] Thus the whole interchange that began with the taunt of Agamemnon amounts in the end to an affirmation that the Epigonoi were indeed superior to the Seven against Thebes.[3]

§21. Again, we are reminded of the Hesiodic Myth of the Five Generations. Since Generation IV is not only "more just" but also "better" (**áreion**: *W&D* 158) than Generation III, we may ask whether there is a traditional parallel in the theme that makes the Epigonoi superior to the Seven against Thebes. Here too, after all, we see a contrast of actual generations. Moreover, the fathers of the Epigonoi are said to have died because of their "wantonness," **atasthalíeisin** (IV 409), and we must recognize that the word **atásthalo-** 'wanton' and its derivatives are conventionally associated in Homeric diction with acts denoted by the word **húbris** and its derivatives (XI 695, XIII 633–634, iii 207, xvii 588, etc.); the adjective **atásthalo-** even serves as an epithet of the noun **húbris** (xvi 86, xxiv 352). So too in Hesiodic diction: in fact, it is the same epithet **atásthalo-** 'wanton' that marks the **húbris** of Generation II (*W&D* 134), which is parallel to the **húbris** of Generation III (*W&D* 146).

§22. As we look about for an instance illustrating the "wanton" (**atásthalo-**) nature of the Seven against Thebes, we come upon a particularly grisly and negative theme—one that also happens to contrast sharply with a positive theme that reflects on the nature of the Epigonoi. We begin by considering the positive theme. There is a poetic tradition, as we learn from *Skolion* 894P, that both Diomedes and Achilles were immortalized on the Isles of the Blessed.[1] In the case of Diomedes, we see from the Pindaric allusion at *Nemean* 10.7

§20n2. Even the *Catalogue* of the *Iliad* takes into account the destruction of Thebes by the Epigonoi (II 505). The failure of the original Seven to destroy Thebes qualifies them as **nónumnoi** 'nameless'. The point is not that we do not know their names (we do) but that epic cannot give them a good name, as it were: see §9n4.

§20n3. There is also the clear implication that the host assembled by the Epigonoi against Thebes was superior to the host of Agamemnon at Troy, in that the Epigonoi had fewer men arrayed against a stronger defense, as Sthenelos says (IV 407). The immediate foils here are the Seven against Thebes, but the negative contrast extends to the host assembled by Agamemnon, a king who is traditionally described as having far more men than what the Trojan defense could muster (cf. II 119–130, XIII 737–739, XV 405–407).

§22n1. See further at Ch.10§1.

that it was Athena who brought about his immortalization. The scholia to this passage reveal the corresponding negative theme.[2] Athena was about to confer immortality upon Tydeus, father of Diomedes, as he lay dying from wounds inflicted in his duel with the Theban hero Melanippos, who had also been mortally wounded. What stopped the goddess from fulfilling her initial design was her sheer disgust at what she saw: Tydeus was eating the brains of Melanippos.[3] Here, then, is the grisly deed that deprived Tydeus of an immortality that could have been his—but was passed on to his son Diomedes. Again we may compare the Hesiodic Myth of Generations, and how the men of Generation III are assigned to Hades (*W&D* 153) while those of Generation IV are eligible for the Isles of the Blessed (*W&D* 164–173).[4] For all these reasons, I conclude that the war against Thebes at *W&D* 162–163 is the war of the Epigonoi.[5]

§23. Having first looked at the Theban War, let us now turn to the Trojan War. The compressed Hesiodic retelling of the fate in store for the Achaean heroes who fought at Troy (*W&D* 167–173) resembles the plot of the *Aithiopis* more than that of the *Iliad*, in that the heroes who fell are said to be transported after death into a state of immortality on the Isles of the Blessed (*W&D* 171).[1] In the *Aithiopis*, both the main hero and the main heroic opponent—Achilles and Memnon respectively—are similarly transported after death into a state of immortality by their respective divine patronesses, Thetis and Eos (Proclus p. 106.14–15 and 6–7 Allen). By contrast, the plot of the *Iliad* ends on the theme of death for both the main hero and the main heroic opponent; the death of Hektor, which is the theme that ultimately closes the composition, explicitly requires the ensuing

§22n2. See Pindar scholia, vol. 3, pp. 167–168 Drachmann; see also the scholia (ABT) to *Iliad* V 126 (Pherecydes *FGrH* 3.97).

§22n3. For the thematic associations of this act with the ideologies of cult, see Delcourt 1966; cf. also Vian 1963.204 and 1968.65. In *W&D* 146–147, the Bronze Generation is described as not eating grain (see §9), and the scholia *ad loc.* interpret this detail as an allusion to cannibalism.

§22n4. As I read *W&D* 158–168, my understanding is that the heroes of the Theban as well as the Trojan War are eligible. On the problem of line 166, see West 1978.192; as my discussion will show, however, I do not agree with his reasoning ("Epic is constantly telling us that they went to Hades").

§22n5. The object of the war, "the sheep of Oedipus" (*W&D* 163), is a theme that applies not only to Eteokles and Polyneikes but also to their descendants. For sheep as an emblem of kingship, see the interesting, though diffuse, article of Orgogozo 1949. See also Ch.7§16n3.

§23n1. Whether all or only some of the heroes are meant depends on the authenticity of *W&D* 166 (cf. §22n4).

death of Achilles (XXII 359–360), and there is no overt prediction of impending immortality for either Achilles or Hektor anywhere in the *Iliad* (or in the *Odyssey*).[2]

§24. This dichotomy in how the Achilles story ends has led to the commonplace inference that the *Iliad*, being apparently an older composition than the *Aithiopis*, somehow represents an older set of beliefs according to which the Achilles figure fails to achieve immortality after death.[n] The two underlying assumptions are (1) that the Achilles *figure* ends at the same point where a given Achilles *story* ends and (2) that Hades had always represented an *eschatological* rather than a *transitional* state. Neither assumption carries conviction.

§25. Let us begin to look beyond these assumptions by quickly examining a parallel to the Iliadic finale of Achilles, in an epic composition known as the *Oikhalias Halosis* ('Capture of Oikhalia'),[1] transmitted by a rhapsodic organization at Samos known as the Kreophyleioi.[2] Thanks to Walter Burkert's meticulous survey of the attested documentation about this lost epic,[3] we know that there were several features in the plot structure of the *Oikhalias Halosis* that paralleled the specific conventions of the *Iliad*. (The parallelisms between this epic composed in the tradition of the Kreophyleioi of Samos and those composed in the tradition of the Homeridai of Chios[4] had even led to a myth that has the founding father Kreophylos being "given" the *Oikhalias Halosis* by Homer himself, who had left Chios to visit him in Samos and had then wanted to reward the host's cordial treatment of his guest.)[5] We find perhaps the most striking parallel between the *Iliad* and this particular Herakles epic in the emphasis on the theme of mortality. As we see from the retelling in Apollodorus 2.7.7, Herakles at the end of the *Oikhalias Halosis* arranges for the funeral of those who fought on his side,[6] much as

§23n2. For an instance of a latent prediction, see Ch.10§50.

§24n. For perhaps the most forceful presentation of this notion, see Rohde I 84–90.

§25n1. *Oikhalias Halosis* pp. 144–147 Allen.

§25n2. Cf. Neanthes *FGrH* 84.29, Aristotle *fr.* 611.10 Rose, and the other sources assembled by Burkert 1972b.76–80, esp. p. 77n15.

§25n3. Burkert 1972b, esp. pp. 82–85.

§25n4. On whom see the scholia to Pindar *N*.2.1 (Hippostratus *FGrH* 568.5) and Harpocration s.v. **Homēridai** (Acusilaus *FGrH* 2.2, Hellanicus *FGrH* 4.20). Cf. Dihle 1970.115 and Burkert 1972b.79.

§25n5. See especially Callimachus *Epigram* 6 Pfeiffer, and Burkert's commentary (1972b.76–77). See also Plato *Republic* 600b, as well as the truncated accounts in *Certamen* p. 237.322–323 Allen and Proclus p. 100.11–13 Allen.

§25n6. Burkert 1972b.84.

Achilles makes possible the funeral of Hektor at the end of the *Iliad*. Thus the *Oikhalias Halosis* ends on a note of death and lamentation, and Burkert infers that such an ending foreshadows the impending death of Herakles himself.[7] In fact we know from the Hesiodic tradition that the inherited story of Herakles and Iole, the central theme of the *Oikhalias Halosis*, *presupposes* his subsequent suffering and death on Mount Oeta (Hesiod *fr*. 25.20–25 and *fr*. 229MW)[8]—a traditional theme that is pictured again for us many years later by Sophocles in his *Women of Trachis*.[9] And yet we also know that the inherited theme of the hero's death and descent to Hades (Hesiod *fr*. 25.20–25MW) in turn presupposes his subsequent accession to Olympus and immortality (Hesiod *fr*. 25.26–33MW).[10] Note the transition from death and Hades to Olympus and immortalization:

καὶ] θάνε καί ῥ᾽ ᾽Αΐδ[αο πολύστονον ἵκε]το δῶμα.
νῦν δ᾽ ἤδη θεός ἐστι, κακῶν δ᾽ ἐξήλυθε πάντων,
ζώει δ᾽ ἐνθά περ ἄλλοι ᾽Ολύμπια δώματ᾽ ἔχοντες
ἀθάνατος καὶ ἄγηρος, ἔχων καλλ[ίσ]φυρον ῞Ηβην

And he died and went to the mournful house of Hades.
But now he is already a god, and he has emerged from all the evils,
and he lives where the others who have their abodes on Olympus live also;
he is immortal and unaging, having as wife Hebe with the beautiful ankles.[11]

Hesiod fr. 25.25–28MW

As Burkert points out, the theme of immortality in store for the hero is simply left outside the framework of the *Oikhalias Halosis*, by virtue of its epic ending.[12] In this respect, then, the composition bears a Homeric mark.[13]

§26. Accordingly, we should not be surprised to find an adherence to the same sort of Homeric touch in the genuinely Homeric *Odyssey*, where we indeed see Achilles languishing in Hades (xi 467–540, xxiv

§25n7. Burkert ibid.

§25n8. Burkert ibid. For the cult of Herakles on Mount Oeta, see Nilsson 1951 [= 1922].

§25n9. For the indebtedness of the dramatist to the *Oikhalias Halosis* in particular and to non-Homeric Epos in general, see the bibliography assembled by Burkert 1972b.80n27.

§25n10. See also Hesiod *fr*. 229MW and *Th*. 950–955.

§25n11. The sequence of events in Hesiod *fr*. 25.20–33MW (first Hades at 20–25 and then Olympus at 26–33) was confusing to scholars of the Hellenistic period and thereafter; witness the obelizing of lines 26–33 in *Pap.Oxy*. 2075. And yet consider *Odyssey* xi 601–627 and the discussion at §26n. Cf. also Roloff 1970.93.

§25n12. Burkert 1972b.83–84.

§25n13. Ibid.

15–18).[n] If the *Odyssey* is to complement the *Iliad*, Achilles must not yet be seen on the Isles of the Blessed.

§27. Beyond the *Iliad* and *Odyssey*, Achilles is regularly featured as having won immortality after death through the intervention of his divine mother Thetis; in this glorious state, he abides on the mythical island of Leuke (*Aithiopis*/Proclus p. 106.12–15 Allen),[1] which is an individualized variation on his other traditional abodes in the after-life—either the Isles of the Blessed (*Skolion* 894P, Pindar *O*.2.68–80) or Elysium itself (Ibycus 291P, Simonides 558P).[2]

§28. The formal description of these diverse mythical places in the diction of archaic poetry presents a remarkably unified vision. We begin our survey of the relevant passages with the Homeric account of the Plain of Elysium (**Ēlúsion pedíon**: iv 563), situated at the Edges of Earth (**peírata gaíēs**: iv 563),[1] where Menelaos will be "sent" by the gods because he is consort of Helen (iv 564–569). Life here is described as "most easy" for humans ($\rho\eta\ddot{\iota}\sigma\tau\eta$: iv 565), and there is no bad weather (iv 566), but instead the earth-encircling River Okeanos makes the Wind Zephyros blow so as to reanimate mortals (iv 567–568).[2] Let us straightway juxtapose this picture with

§26n. Similarly, the *Odyssey* presents a stop-motion picture of Herakles in Hades (xi 601–627). But the vision is hardly eschatological: Herakles is at that very moment on Olympus with the immortal gods (xi 602–604). What we see in the narrative is truly a "vision" (**eídōlon**: xi 602), appropriate for other phases in other tellings of the story. See further at Ch.10§48.

§27n1. The island is envisioned well beyond the Hellespont, in the Black Sea (see Alcaeus *fr*. 354LP and Pindar *N*.4.49); this orientation can be correlated with the penetration of Hellenic enterprises into that area (especially on the part of Miletos) and with the establishment of cult centers honoring Achilles in actual locales physically suitable for the description of **Leukḗ** 'White Rock'. For a survey of the places bearing that name in the Black Sea region, see Rohde II 371–373n2; for the thematic associations of the name **Leukḗ**, see Rohde ibid. and Diehl 1953; also Nagy 1973.137–148. For an illuminating article on the Iliadic evidence for the Hellenic penetration of the Black Sea, see Drews 1976, esp. pp. 20–22.

§27n2. See also Plato *Symposium* 179e, 180b; Apollonius of Rhodes *Argonautica* 4.811–816; Apollodorus *Epitome* 5.5. For an eloquent discussion of the thematic convergences that link Leuke, the Isles of the Blessed, and Elysium, see Rohde II 365–378, esp. pp. 369–370n2. He calls Leuke the "Sonderelysion" of Achilles (Rohde II 371).

§28n1. For the themes associated with the **peírata gaíēs** 'extremities of Earth', see in general Bergren 1975; for a correlation with the earth-encircling cosmic river Okeanos, see Nagy 1973.148–154.

§28n2. The verb **anapsúkhein** 'reanimate' (iv 568) implies, I propose, that death had somehow preceded the ultimate state of immortality. See further at Ch.10§28. After all, the prophecy at iv 561–562 says to Menelaos not that he will not die but that he will not die in Argos. In general, the experience of death seems to be a latent

the Hesiodic description of the Isles of the Blessed, the abode of such heroes as those who fell at Troy and were then given immortal life by divine agency (*W&D* 167–168). These Isles of the Blessed are also situated at the Edges of Earth (**peírata gaíēs**: *W&D* 168), where the earth-encircling Okeanos flows (*W&D* 171); here too life is easy (*W&D* 170) and the weather is so good that the Earth bears crops three times yearly (*W&D* 172–173).

§29. As we now look even more closely at this Hesiodic passage describing the heroes who inhabit the Isles of the Blessed (*W&D* 167–173), we discover a remarkable mirroring of both theme and diction between these representatives of Generation IV and those of Generation I:

I: ὥστε θεοὶ δ' ἔζωον ἀκηδέα θυμὸν ἔχοντες

They lived like gods, having a **thūmós** without cares.

W&D 112

IV: καὶ τοὶ μὲν ναίουσιν ἀκηδέα θυμὸν ἔχοντες

And they live having a **thūmós** without cares.

W&D 170

I: καρπὸν δ' ἔφερε ζείδωρος ἄρουρα
αὐτομάτη πολλόν τε καὶ ἄφθονον

And the grain-giving Earth bore crops
by itself—a great and generous supply.

W&D 117–118

IV: τοῖσιν μελιηδέα καρπὸν
τρὶς ἔτεος θάλλοντα φέρει ζείδωρος ἄρουρα

---

element in myths telling of abductions into a state of immortality: see Ch.10§§26–28. In its other attestations, **anapsúkhein** overtly means not "bring back to life" but simply "bring back to vigor" (see V 795, XIII 84, Hesiod *W&D* 608); this semantic restriction, however, is due to specialization of contexts. Compare the behavior of **psūkhḗ** in epic diction. Both swooning and dying can be conveyed by the theme of *losing one's psūkhḗ*, as at V 696 and XVI 856 respectively; in the case of a swoon as at V 696, revival is conveyed by the theme of *regaining one's breath*: note ἀμπνύνθη at V 697 (here it is the wind Boreas that restores the hero's breath: V 697–698). The actual word **psūkhḗ**, however, is not even used in contexts of reviving from a swoon—let alone reviving from death. Yet the **psūkhḗ** that is lost in the process of swooning is surely the same **psūkhḗ** that is regained in the process of reviving from the swoon. For the reading ἀμπνύνθη at V 697 and XIV 436 (instead of ἐμπνύνθη), see Schnaufer 1970.199n540. My interpretation, however, differs from his. Finally, consider the collocation of **psūkhaí** (subject) and **psúkhontai** (verb) in the gold leaf of Hipponion (Zuntz 1976.133, line 4); note too the mention of **psūkhròn húdōr** (ibid., line 7), flowing from the spring of **Mnāmosúnā** (ibid., lines 6 and 12). I propose to examine more closely the contexts of these words in another project.

And for them the grain-giving Earth bears delicious crops
that come into bloom three times a year.

W&D 172–173

I: οἱ μὲν ἐπὶ Κρόνου ἦσαν, ὅτ᾽ οὐρανῷ ἐμβασίλευεν

And they were in the time of Kronos, when he was king in the sky.

W&D 111

IV: τοῖσιν Κρόνος ἐμβασιλεύει

And Kronos is king for them.

W&D 169n

§30. The form of this ring composition is the reflex of a theme: that the progression of mankind has come full circle from Generation IV back to the Golden Age of Generation I. From these convergences in diction and theme, I infer that the ring-composed Hesiodic Myth of the Five Generations of Mankind operates in a *cycle* from Generation I to II to III to IV back to I, by way of the quintessential V of the here-and-now.[1] In line with this reasoning, I am ready to reinterpret the following verses:

μηκέτ᾽ ἔπειτ᾽ ὤφελλον ἐγὼ πέμπτοισι μετεῖναι
ἀνδράσιν, ἀλλ᾽ ἢ πρόσθε θανεῖν ἢ ἔπειτα γενέσθαι

If only I no longer lived in the Fifth Generation,
but had either died before it or been born after it!

Hesiod W&D 174–175

The poet's wish to have died before the Fifth Generation would place him in the Fourth, while his alternative wish to be born after the Fifth would place him ahead into the First. Either way, he would reach the Golden Age. His longing is for the Golden Age *as a permanent state*: he is seeking release from the *cycle* of human existence, which is diachronically represented in the sequence of I to II to III to IV back to I and synchronically represented in the quintessential V.[2]

§29n. W&D 169 has been renumbered as 173a and bracketed along with 173b–e in West's edition (1978.194–195). Even if 173b–e are indeed interpolated, it does not follow that the same goes for 169=173a. The instability of this line in the textual tradition may actually be due to a misunderstanding of the Kronos theme, which I interpret to be cyclic.

§30n1. In Celtic and Indic lore, the number 5 following the sequence 1–2–3–4 is a symbol of integration and centrality (see Rees and Rees 1961.118–204). I suspect that this symbolism is cognate with the traditions underlying the Hesiodic Myth of the Five Generations.

§30n2. The theme of being released after death from the cycle of man's existence is directly attested in the Thurian gold leaf A1 (Zuntz 1971.301 line 5), where the persona of the dead man declares:

§31. The theme of a cycle that leads to the permanency of a Golden Age is attested in the traditional poetic diction of Pindar. Significantly, one attestation comes from a specific type of lamentation, a **thrênos**:[1]

οἷσι δὲ Φερσεφόνα ποινὰν παλαιοῦ πένθεος
δέξεται, ἐς τὸν ὕπερθεν ἅλιον κείνων ἐνάτῳ ἔτεϊ
ἀνδιδοῖ ψυχὰς πάλιν, ἐκ τᾶν βασιλῆες ἀγαυοὶ
καὶ σθένει κραιπνοὶ σοφίᾳ τε μέγιστοι
ἄνδρες αὔξοντ'· ἐς δὲ τὸν λοιπὸν χρόνον ἥροες ἁ-
γνοὶ πρὸς ἀνθρώπων καλέονται

On whose behalf Persephone will receive compensation for a **pénthos** of long
standing,
the **psūkhaí** of these she sends back up, on the ninth year, to the sunlight
above,
and from these [**psūkhaí**] will grow illustrious kings,
vigorous in strength and very great in wisdom.
And for the rest of time they shall be called holy heroes.

Pindar fr. 133SM[2]

κύκλου δ' ἐξέπταν βαρυπενθέος ἀργαλέοιο.
I rushed out of the woeful **kúklos** of heavy **pénthos** [grief].

Whether we translate **kúklos** abstractly as "circle" or concretely as "wheel," it clearly applies here to the human condition (Zuntz, pp. 320–322). Note that the Pythagorean word for "reincarnation" is **anakúklōsis** (p. 99.30DK; cf. Zuntz, p. 336). For another instance where **kúklos** designates the cyclic nature of man's existence, cf. Herodotus 1.207.2: if Cyrus recognizes that he is a mortal rather than an immortal, says Croesus, then he should accept the teaching "that there is a **kúklos** of human affairs" (ἐκεῖνο πρῶτον μάθε ὡς κύκλος τῶν ἀνθρωπηΐων ἐστὶ πρηγμάτων). On a synchronic level, the immediate sense here is "wheel of fortune," but the ultimate context is still the predicament of mortality. Note that the persona of the dead man in the Thurian gold leaf A1 declares that he has become, after death, part of the **ólbion génos** 'blessed breed' of immortals (Zuntz, p. 301, line 3; cf. also gold leaves A2 and A3) and that he will henceforth be addressed as **ólbie kaì makaristé** 'holy and blessed' (line 8). Cf. **ólbioi hḗrōes** 'blessed heroes' (*W&D* 172), describing the immortalized fourth **génos** ('generation,' breed') of mankind, who abide ἐν μακάρων νήσοισι 'on the Isles of the Blessed [**mákares**]' (*W&D* 171). For more on the Thurian gold leaves, see Ch.10§20n5.

§31n1. For the inherited connections of the **thrênos** as a genre with the obsolescent institution of ancestor worship even in the classical period, see Ch.6§28: the cult of heroes in the **pólis** evolved at least partly from the worship of ancestors in the **génos** 'clan'. Note that Simonides *fr.* 523P, which tells how the **hēmítheoi** (line 2) are destined not to have a **bíos** 'lifespan' that is **áphthitos** 'unfailing' (line 3), is an excerpt from a **thrênos** (Stobaeus 4.34.14). From the standpoint of the comparative method, the themes of the **thrênos** include elements archaic enough to be of Indo-European pedigree (see Vian 1963.118).

§31n2. The passage is quoted by Plato *Meno* 81b to illustrate a traditional ideology preserved in social circles that he describes as well-versed in sacral lore. For a

The title **héroes hagnoí** 'holy heroes' at line 5 recalls the words **ólbioi héroes** 'blessed heroes' (*W&D* 172), describing the immortalized Fourth Generation. Moreover, the title **basilées** 'kings' at line 3 recalls the honor appropriate to the Golden Generation, which is called the **géras basiléïon** 'honorific portion of kings' (W&D 126).[3] In Pindar's *Olympian* 2, a composition that adopts the thematic apparatus of the **thrênos** apparently because of this genre's ad hoc appropriateness to the special circumstances of the performance and audience,[4] we see further elaboration on the traditional vision of the Golden Age:

O.2.70–71: The place is the Isles of the Blessed, with the Tower of Kronos as landmark. Compare the reign of Kronos in the Golden Age, *W&D* 111, and on the Isles of the Blessed, *W&D* 169.

O.2.70–72: The winds blow from the Okeanos. Compare the gusts of Zephyros blowing from the Okeanos bordering Elysium, iv 567–568; compare too the Okeanos bordering the Isles of the Blessed, *W&D* 171.

O.2.72–74: The plant life is golden.[5] Compare the golden essence of the First Generation, *W&D* 109–110.

O.2.75–77: Rhadamanthys is there, rendering justice. Compare his presence in Elysium, iv 564.

---

correlation of the ideology in this **thrênos** with the ideology of the Thurian gold leaves, cf. Zuntz 1971.313. I draw special attention to the words **poiná** 'compensation' and **pénthos** 'grief' in the Pindaric fragment. The function of the latter word as a formal mark of lamentation has already been examined in detail (Ch.6); we have also seen it characterize the **kúklos** of life in the Thurian gold leaf A1: βαρυπενθέος 'of heavy **pénthos**' (see §30n2). As for the former word, it figures prominently in the Thurian gold leaves A2 and A3 (Zuntz, pp. 303 and 305, line 4):

ποινὰν δ' ἀνταπέτεισ' ἔργων ἔνεκ' οὔτι δικαίων

and I paid compensation for unjust deeds [deeds without **díkē**]

We recall the absence and presence of **díkē** in Generations II/III and I/IV respectively (see §7).

§31n3. Cf. §4n5. In the Pharsalian gold leaf B1 (Zuntz, p. 359, line 11), the dead man is given the following promise for the afterlife:

καὶ τότ' ἔπειτ' ἄ[λλοισι μεθ'] ἡρώεσσιν ἀνάξει[ς

and then you will be king along with the other **héroes**

§31n4. See Finley 1955.59: "nominally an *epinikion*, it [Olympian 2] is in fact a consolatory poem and a meditation on death." See also Bollack 1963 and Sinos 1975.136. Note that the **thrênos** itself as a genre is not restricted to the actual occasion of a funeral (Proclus *Chrestomathy* p. 247.16 ff. Westphal); see also Nilsson 1951 [= 1911] 98.

§31n5. The same theme recurs in a genuine **thrênos** by Pindar, *fr.* 129.5SM, where the description again concerns the Isles of the Blessed; cf. Sinos 1975.134–138.

O.2.78–80: Achilles is among those heroes who abide on the Isles of the Blessed. Compare the transportation of heroes who fell at Troy to the Isles of the Blessed, *W&D* 167–173.

§32. The envisioning of Achilles on the Isles of the Blessed formalizes the promise of an afterlife—a consolatory theme that is apparently intrinsic to the genre of the **thrênos**. In the *Aithiopis*, moreover, the **thrênoi** sung by the Muses over the dead Achilles himself lead immediately to his being transported into the actual state of immortality by his divine mother (Proclus p. 106.13–15 Allen).[n] Thus the epic narrative here fulfills on the level of content the promise that the genre of the **thrênos** offers on the level of form. In the *Odyssey*, by contrast, no such self-fulfillment can come from the mention of the **thrênoi** sung by the Muses over the dead Achilles (**thréneon**: xxiv 61). It is Agamemnon who is telling of these **thrênoi**, and he is speaking to Achilles—who along with Agamemnon is at this very moment languishing in Hades!

§33. As we come back to the Hesiodic passage describing the Fourth Generation of Mankind (*W&D* 156–173), we can reaffirm that the heroes of the Trojan War in this representation belong to a narrative type that fits Achilles as he appears in the *Aithiopis*, not the Achilles of the *Iliad* and *Odyssey*. But we can also expand the comparison by considering the end in store for the Third Generation of Mankind. After these bloodthirsty warriors die, they are relegated specifically to Hades (*W&D* 152–155), which is in direct contrast with the Isles of the Blessed, the ultimate destination of the Fourth Generation. In this particular respect, then, the blood-thirsty warriors of the Third Generation resemble the Achilles of the *Iliad* and *Odyssey*, who is likewise destined for Hades. In other respects as well, we have seen resemblances: the wanton behavior of the Third Generation corresponds to the dark and recessive dimension of the prime Homeric hero, just as their very emblems of bronze and ash wood correspond to the spear of Achilles. As we have seen, that spear is the only mortal aspect of this hero's otherwise immortal apparatus.[1] I must add that our calling the armor of Achilles

---

§32n. In the Proclus summary of the *Aithiopis*, the distinction between the **thrênoi** of the Muses and the **góoi** of Thetis and the Nereids is blurred (Thetis, with the Muses, θρηνεῖ τὸν παῖδα 'mourns his son': Proclus p. 106.13–14 Allen). We may infer, however, that the actual narrative of the *Aithiopis* did maintain this distinction: cf. *Odyssey* xxiv 58–61 and the comments at Ch.6§§23–24.

§33n1. §12 above.

"immortal" is not a case of forcing an interpretation. The epithet **ámbrota** 'immortal' is actually applied to the **teúkhea** 'armor' of Achilles, as at XVII 194, 202.[2]

§34. Of course, the *Iliad* is hardly primitive on account of its delving into the mortal aspect of Achilles. If anything, the Iliadic emphasis on mortality is a mark of sophistication, which we can appreciate only after we take another look at traditional representations of immortality.

§33n2. For the limited time that Hektor is to be immune from death (see XVII 198–208), Zeus seals him in the armor of Achilles (XVII 209–212). Hektor had been able to kill Patroklos and despoil the armor of Achilles specifically because Apollo had first stripped away this armor in his attack on Patroklos (XVI 787–804). By the time that Hektor delivers the mortal blow, Patroklos has been denuded of the armor (XVI 815). See Thieme 1968 [= 1952] 120–121. When Hektor in turn wears this armor, he will be immune to everything except the ash spear of Achilles, with which he is mortally wounded (see XXII 319–330). Ironically, the immortal apparatus of Achilles can thus be penetrated only by an emblem of mortality (see further at §12 above).

10 | Poetic Visions of Immortality for the Hero

§1. Upon having their lifespan cut short by death, heroes receive as consolation the promise of immortality, but this state of immortality after death is located at the extremes of our universe, far removed from the realities of the here-and-now. We in this life have to keep reminding ourselves that the hero who died is still capable of pleasure, that he can still enjoy such real things as convivial feasts in the pleasant company of other youths like him. It is in this sort of spirit that the *Banquet Song for Harmodios* is composed, honoring the young man who had achieved the status of being worshiped as a hero by the Athenians for having died a tyrant killer:[1]

φίλταθ᾽ ᾽Αρμόδι᾽, οὔ τί που τέθνηκας,
νήσοις δ᾽ ἐν μακάρων σέ φασιν εἶναι,
ἵνα περ ποδώκης ᾽Αχιλεύς
Τυδείδην τέ φασι τὸν ἐσθλὸν Διομήδεα

Harmodios, most **phílos**! Surely you are not at all dead,
but they say that you are on the Isles of the Blessed,
the same place where swift-footed Achilles is,
and they say that the worthy Diomedes,[2] son of Tydeus, is there too.

Skolion 894P

The perfect tense of the verb οὐ ... τέθνηκας 'you are not dead' leaves room for the reality of the hero's death: it is not that he did not die, but that he is not dead now. The fact of death, even for the hero, is painfully real and preoccupying. Consider this excerpt from a **thrênos** by Simonides:[3]

§1n1. On the incorporation of Harmodios into the institutions of Athenian cult and myth, see Taylor 1975. On που τέθνηκας: Roloff 1970.124 and 122n26.

§1n2. For the epithet **esthlós** 'worthy, good' describing Diomedes on the Isles of the Blessed, see §3n2; also Ch.9§4n3.

§1n3. Previous references to this **thrênos**: Ch.9§16n3, §31n1. Kegel 1962.47 argues

οὐδὲ γὰρ οἳ πρότερόν ποτ' ἐπέλοντο
θεῶν δ' ἐξ ἀνάκτων ἐγένονθ' υἷες ἡμίθεοι,
ἄπονον οὐδ' ἄφθιτον οὐδ' ἀκίνδυνον βίον
ἐς γῆρας ἐξίκοντο τελέσαντες

Not even those who were before, once upon a time,
and who were born **hēmítheoi** as sons of the lord-gods,
not even they reached old age by bringing to a close a lifespan that is without
toil, that is **áphthitos** [unfailing], that is without danger.

Simonides fr. 523P

Not even heroes, then, have a **bíos** 'lifespan' that is **áphthitos** 'unfailing'; they too have to die before the immortality that is promised by the **thrênoi** comes true.[4]

§2. Even in the *Aithiopis*, the immortality reached by Achilles is not an immediate but a remote state: after death, the hero is permanently removed from the here-and-now of the Achaeans who mourn him. For them, the immediacy of Achilles after death has to take the form of a funeral (*Aithiopis*/Proclus p. 106.12–16 Allen), which includes not only such things as the singing of **thrênoi** over his body (ibid. 12–13) but also—even after Achilles has already been transported to his immortal state—the actual building of a funeral mound and the holding of funeral games in his honor (ibid. 15–16). I conclude, then, that even in the *Aithiopis* the immortality of Achilles is predicated on his death, which is the occasion for the **thrênoi** sung by the Muses as a consolation for his death. In the *Iliad*, the theme of immortality is similarly predicated on the death of Achilles, but here the focus of consolation is not on the hero's afterlife, but rather, on the eternal survival of the epic that glorifies him.

§3. As we now proceed to examine the diction in which this theme is expressed, we must keep in mind the words in the **thrênos** of Simonides (523P): even the heroes themselves fail to have a **bíos** 'lifespan' that is **áphthitos** 'unfailing'. In the *Iliad*, Achilles himself says that he will have no **kléos** if he leaves Troy and goes home to live on into old age (IX 414–416)—but that he will indeed have a **kléos** that is **áphthiton** 'unfailing' (IX 413) if he stays to fight at Troy

---

that ἄφθιτον at line 3 makes no sense and should therefore be considered corrupt; I offer the following discussion (§§1–18) as a counterargument.

§1n4. In the case of Ino, she apparently dies and then gets a **bíotos** 'lifespan' that is **áphthitos**: see Pindar *O*.2.29, as discussed at §41n2. On the affinities of Pindar's *Olympian* 2 with the poetic form of the **thrênos**, see again Ch.9§31.

and dies young.[1] The same theme of the eternity achieved by the hero *within epic* recurs in Pindar's *Isthmian* 8, and again it is expressed with the same root **phthi-** as in **áphthito-**; he will have a **kléos** that is everlasting (cf. xxiv 93–94):

τὸν μὲν οὐδὲ θανόντ᾽ ἀοιδαί τι λίπον
ἀλλά οἱ παρά τε πυρὰν τάφον θ᾽ ʿΕλικώνιαι παρθένοι
στάν, ἐπὶ θρῆνόν τε πολύφαμον ἔχεαν.
ἔδοξ᾽ ἄρα καὶ ἀθανάτοις,
ἐσθλόν γε φῶτα καὶ φθίμενον ὕμνοις θεᾶν διδόμεν

But when he [Achilles] died, the songs did not leave him,
but the Heliconian Maidens [Muses] stood by his funeral pyre and his funeral mound,
and they poured forth a **thrênos** that is very renowned.
And so the gods decided
to hand over the worthy man, dead as he was [**phthímenos**], to the songs of the goddesses [Muses].[2]

Pindar I.8.62–66

The key word of the moment, **phthí-menos**, which I translate here in the conventional mode as "dead," is formed from a root that also carries with it the inherited metaphorical force of vegetal imagery: **phthi-** inherits the meaning "wilt," as in **karpoû phthísin** 'wilting of the crops' (Pindar *Paean* 9.14).[3] Through the comparative method, we can recover kindred vegetal imagery in another derivative of the root, the epithet **á-phthi-ton** as it applies to the **kléos** of Achilles at IX 413.[4]

§4. As in the *Iliad*, the contrast in this Pindaric passage concerns the mortality of Achilles and the immortality conferred by the songs

§3n1. Ch.2§3.

§3n2. For the epithet **esthlós** 'worthy, good' describing Achilles here, cf. §1n2; also Ch.9§4n3. The collocation of **esthlós** and **phthímenos** as epithets of Achilles should be compared with the collocation of **esthlón** and **áphthiton** as epithets of the **kléos** of Achilles, at *Iliad* IX 415 and 413 respectively. Compare also the repeated use of **esthlós** at *Odyssey* viii 582 and 585, describing the hypothetical relative or comrade who perished at Troy (the word for "perished" at viii 581 is actually **apéphthito**!). The context for these occurrences is suggestive: Alkinoos is asking Odysseus why he wept over the epic song of Demodokos (viii 577–578), and his weeping is called an **ákhos** at viii 541. For the contrast of lamentation and Epos in this passage, see Ch.6§§8–9.

§3n3. Cf. also **phthinókarpos** 'having fruits that wilt' at Pindar *P*.4.265.

§3n4. See §§5–15 and Nagy 1974.231–255; also Schmitt 1967.61–69. Note that **áphthito-** in Homeric diction regularly refers to things made by Hephaistos (scholia V to XIV 238), and that the armor of Achilles is all made by Hephaistos—except for the hero's spear (see Ch.9§12).

of the Muses. More specifically, Pindar's words are also implying that the epic of Achilles amounts to an eternal outflow of the **thrênos** performed for Achilles by the Muses themselves. In this light, let us now consider again the Homeric evidence. In the *Odyssey*, the description of the funeral that the Achaeans hold for Achilles includes such details as the **thrênos** of the Muses (xxiv 60–61) and ends with the retrospective thought that "in this way" (ὣς: xxiv 93) the hero kept his fame even after death and that he will have a **kléos** that is everlasting (xxiv 93–94). We get more evidence from the *Iliad* in the form of a correlation between theme and form. The forms are the actual names of **Akhil(l)eús** (from *Akhí-lāu̯os 'having a grieving **lāós**') and **Patrokléēs** ('having the **kléos** of the ancestors'). As I have argued,[1] the figure of **Patro-kléēs** is in the *Iliad* the thematic key to the **kléos áphthiton** of Achilles, while **Akhi-l(l)eús** is commensurately the key to the collective **ákhos** 'grief' that the Achaeans have for Patroklos on the occasion of his funeral. Since this **ákhos** takes the social form of lamentations even within the epic of the *Iliad*,[2] we can say that the theme we found in Pindar's *Isthmian* 8 is already active in the Homeric tradition; here too, lamentation extends into epic.

§5. Up to now, I have been stressing the remoteness inherent in the concept of immortality after death, as we find it pictured in the formal discourse of the **thrênos** and then transposed into the narrative traditions of epic. In contrast to the remoteness of this immortality stands the stark immediacy of death, conveyed forcefully within the same medium of the **thrênos** and beyond. We are again reminded of the excerpt from the **thrênos** of Simonides, which says that even the **bíos** 'lifespan' of the heroes themselves fails to be **áphthitos** (523P). The latent vegetal imagery in this theme—that the life of man "wilts" like a plant—brings us now to yet another important contrast in the poetic representations of immortality and death. Traditional Hellenic poetry makes the opposition immortality/ death not only remote/immediate but also artificial/natural. To put it another way: death and immortality are presented in terms of nature and culture respectively.[n]

§4n1. Ch.6§§22–23; see also Sinos 1975.99–125.
§4n2. Ch.6§23.
§5n. For the validity of the distinction *nature/culture* from the vantage point of anthropology, see Redfield 1975.

§6. In *Iliad* VI, Diomedes is about to attack Glaukos, but first he asks his opponent whether he is a god, not wishing at this time to fight an immortal (VI 119–143; see the words for "mortal"/"immortal" at 123, 142/128, 140 respectively). In response, Glaukos begins by saying:

Τυδείδη μεγάθυμε, τίη γενεὴν ἐρεείνεις;
οἵη περ φύλλων γενεή, τοίη δὲ καὶ ἀνδρῶν.
φύλλα τὰ μέν τ' ἄνεμος χαμάδις χέει, ἄλλα δέ θ' ὕλη
τηλεθόωσα φύει, ἔαρος δ' ἐπιγίγνεται ὥρη.
ὣς ἀνδρῶν γενεὴ ἡ μὲν φύει ἡ δ' ἀπολήγει

Son of Tydeus, you with the great **thūmós**! Why do you ask about my **geneé**
  [lineage, line of birth]?[1]
The **geneé** of men is like the **geneé** of leaves.
Some leaves are shed on the earth by the wind,
while others are grown by the greening forest
—and the season of spring is at hand.
So also the **geneé** of men: one grows, another wilts.[2]

VI 145–149

Here the life and death of mortals are being overtly compared to a natural process, the growing and wilting of leaves on trees.[3] In another such Homeric display of vegetal imagery, in this case spoken by the god Apollo himself as he talks about the human condition, this *natural* aspect of death is expressed specifically with the root **phthi-**:

        εἰ δὴ σοί γε βροτῶν ἕνεκα πτολεμίξω
δειλῶν, οἳ φύλλοισιν ἐοικότες ἄλλοτε μέν τε
ζαφλεγέες τελέθουσιν, ἀρούρης καρπὸν ἔδοντες,
ἄλλοτε δὲ φθινύθουσιν ἀκήριοι

... if I should fight you on account of mortals,
the wretches, who are like leaves. At given times,
they come to their fullness, bursting forth in radiance,[4] eating the crops of

§6n1. For the distinction made in Homeric diction between **geneé** 'long-range lineage, complete ancestry' and **génos** 'immediate ancestry', see Muellner 1976.77.

§6n2. The response continues until the conclusion at VI 211: "It is from this **geneé** and bloodline that I boast to be." Note the intervening use of **génos** at VI 209, in collocation with **patéres** in the sense of "ancestors" (πατέρων: on which see Ch.6§12).

§6n3. The same theme recurs in Mimnermus *fr.* 2W; also in Hesiod *fr.* 204.124 ff. MW, where the correlation seems to apply specifically to the life and death of heroes who died in the Trojan War (discussion at Ch.11§14).

§6n4. The form **za-phlegé-es** 'very radiant' (XXI 465) is interesting. Consider its relation to **Phlegú-ās**, as discussed at Ch.7§5. Cf. Vian 1960.219.

the Earth,
while at other times they wilt [phthi-núthousin], victims of fate.

XXI 463–466

§7. Let us straightway contrast the immortalized heroes on the Isles of the Blessed, whose abode flourishes with *golden* plant life (Pindar *O*.2.72–74; *Thrênos fr.* 129.5SM). Also, let us contrast the First Generation of Mankind, whose very essence is gold (*W&D* 109). The immortality of the Golden Age is specifically correlated with the *suspension of a vegetal cycle*: in the Golden Age (*W&D* 117–118) as on the Isles of the Blessed (*W&D* 172–173), the earth bears crops *without interruption*. The description of Elysium supplements this picture: in the state of immortality, there is simply *no winter*, nor any bad weather at all (iv 566–568).

§8. In these images, we seé gold as a general symbol for the artificial continuum of immortality, in opposition to the natural cycle of life and death as symbolized by the flourishing and wilting of leaves on trees, where the theme of wilting is conventionally denoted with derivatives of the root **phthi-**. As we now set about to look for specific words that express this cultural negation of the vegetal cycle, we come back again to the negative epithet **áphthito-**. Let us begin with the **skêptron** 'scepter' of Agamemnon (I 245–246), by which Achilles takes his mighty oath (I 234–244), and which is specifically described as "gold-studded" (χρυσείοις ἥλοισι πεπαρμένον: I 246) and "golden" (χρυσέου: II 268). This **skêptron**, by which Agamemnon holds sway in Argos (II 108) and which an Achaean chieftain is bound by custom to hold in moments of solemn interchange (I 237–239, II 185–187), also qualifies specifically as **áphthiton aieí** 'imperishable forever' (II 46, 186). It was made by the ultimate craftsman, Hephaistos (II 101), whose divine handicraft may be conventionally designated as both golden and **áphthito-** (e.g., XIV 238–239).[1] Significantly, this everlasting artifact of a **skêptron** provides the basis for the Oath of Achilles in form as well as in function:

ἀλλ' ἔκ τοι ἐρέω καὶ ἐπὶ μέγαν ὅρκον ὀμοῦμαι·
ναὶ μὰ τόδε σκῆπτρον, τὸ μὲν οὔ ποτε φύλλα καὶ ὄζους
φύσει, ἐπεὶ δὴ πρῶτα τομὴν ἐν ὄρεσσι λέλοιπεν,
οὐδ' ἀναθηλήσει· περὶ γάρ ῥά ἑ χαλκὸς ἔλεψε

§8n1. Otherwise, the handicraft of Hephaistos is brazen and **áphthito-**, as at XVIII 369–371. The scholia (V) to XIV 238 claim that anything made by Hephaistos qualifies as **áphthito-** in Homeric diction. Compare the application of **ámbroto-** 'immortal' to the **teúkhea** 'armor' of Achilles at XVII 194, 202, as discussed at Ch.9§33 and n2.

φύλλα τε καὶ φλοιόν. νῦν αὖτέ μιν υἷες ᾿Αχαιῶν
ἐν παλάμῃς φορέουσι δικασπόλοι

But I will say to you and swear a great oath:
I swear by this **skêptron**, which will no longer ever grow leaves and shoots,
ever since it has left its place where it was cut down on the mountaintops—
and it will never bloom again, for Bronze has trimmed its leaves and bark.
But now the sons of the Achaeans hold it in their hands as they carry out
díkai.

I 233–237

Achilles is here swearing not only by the **skêptron** but also in terms
of what the **skêptron** is—a thing of nature that has been transformed
into a thing of culture.[2] The Oath of Achilles is meant to be just as
permanent and irreversible as the process of turning a shaft of living
wood into a social artifact.[3] And just as the **skêptron** is imperishable
'**áphthiton**', so also the Oath of Achilles is eternally valid, in that
Agamemnon and the Achaeans will permanently regret not having
given the hero of the *Iliad* his due **tīmế** (I 240–244).

§9. For another Homeric instance featuring **áphthito-** as an epithet
suitable for situations where the natural cycle of flourishing and
wilting is negated, let us consider the Island of the Cyclopes. In
Odyssey ix 116–141, this island and the mainland facing it are
described in a manner that would suit the ideal Hellenic colony and
its ideal **peraíā** respectively,[1] if it were not for two special circumstances: the mainland is inhabited by Cyclopes, who are devoid of
civilization (ix 106–115), while the island itself is populated by no
one at all—neither by humans nor even by Cyclopes, since they
cannot navigate (ix 123–125). At the very mention of navigation,
there now follows a "what-if" narrative about the idealized place that
the Island would become *if it were colonized* (ix 126–129).[2] If only
there were ships (ix 126–127), and these ships reached the Island,
there would be commerce (ix 127–129), and then there would also
be agriculture, yielding limitless crops (ix 130–135). What is more,
the grapevines produced by this ideal never-never land would be
áphthitoi 'unfailing' (ix 133). Thus if culture rather than nature

§8n2. Cf. Watkins 1975.22–23.
§8n3. On the cult of Agamemnon's **skêptron** at Khaironeia, where its local name is
the **dóru** 'wood, shaft', see Pausanias 9.40.11–12. Discussion by Nagy 1974.242–
243n16; see now also Watkins 1975.22–23.
§9n1. For the interrelation of island (**nêsos**) and mainland (**peraíā**) in archaic
patterns of colonization, see Jeffery 1976.50–59 in general and pp. 50–51 in particular.
§9n2. Cf. Kirk 1970.165 *en passant*.

prevailed on the Island of the Cyclopes, then its local wine would bear the mark of immortality. Again we see the epithet **áphthito-** denoting permanence in terms of *culture* imposed on *nature*.

§10. In fact, the epithet **áphthito-** functions as a mark of not only culture but even cult itself. In the Homeric *Hymn to Demeter*, the infant Demophon is destined by the goddess to have a **tīmḗ** 'cult' that is **áphthitos** (*H.Dem.* 261, 263), and this boon is contrasted directly with the certainty that he is *not* to avoid death (*H.Dem.* 262).[1] As Demophon's substitute mother, Demeter had actually been preparing him for a life that is never to be interrupted by death (*H.Dem.* 242, 261–262), but the inadvertence of the infant's real mother had brought that plan to naught (*H.Dem.* 243–258). Still, Demophon is destined by the goddess to achieve immortality on the level of cult, so that her preparation of the infant was not in vain. We in fact catch a glimpse of the child's destiny as a hero of cult in the following description of how the goddess had been preparing him to be immortal:

ἔτρεφεν ἐν μεγάροις· ὁ δ᾽ ἀέξετο δαίμονι ἶσος
οὔτ᾽ οὖν σῖτον ἔδων, οὐ θησάμενος

. . .

χρίεσκ᾽ ἀμβροσίῃ ὡς εἰ θεοῦ ἐκγεγαῶτα,
ἡδὺ καταπνείουσα καὶ ἐν κόλποισιν ἔχουσα[2]
νύκτας δὲ κρύπτεσκε πυρὸς μένει ἠΰτε δαλὸν
λάθρα φίλων γονέων· τοῖς δὲ μέγα θαῦμ᾽ ἐτέτυκτο
ὡς προθαλὴς τελέθεσκε, θεοῖσι δὲ ἄντα ἐῴκει

She nurtured him in the palace, and he grew up like a **daímōn**,
not eating food, not sucking from the breast

. . .

She used to anoint him with ambrosia, as if he had been born of the goddess,[3]
and she would breathe down her sweet breath on him as she held him at her bosom.
At nights she would conceal him within the **ménos** of fire,[4] as if he were a

§10n1. On *H.Dem.* 263, I prefer the direct sort of interpretation as offered by Richardson 1974.245, which does *not* presuppose any textual conflation involving verses 260–263.

§10n2. On the internal rhyme here, possibly connoting the magic of incantation, see Richardson, p. 239.

§10n3. I interpret θεοῦ here as 'of the goddess' rather than 'of a god'. For a parallel treatment of the infant god Apollo, see *H.Apollo* 123–125.

§10n4. Consider the infant's name, **Dēmophóōn** 'shining for the **dêmos**', also attested as ΔΕΜΟΦΑΟΝ = **Dēmopháōn** (Kretschmer 1894.142 no. 126) and even as

smoldering log,[5]
and his parents were kept unaware. But they marveled
at how full in bloom he came to be, and to look at him was like looking at
the gods.

H.Dem. 235–236, 237–241

The underscored phrase at verse 235, meaning "and he grew up like
a **daímōn**," contains a word that we have in fact already seen in the
specific function of designating heroes on the level of cult (Hesiod
W&D 122, *Th.* 991).[6]

§11. This same underscored phrase, as Sinos points out,[1] has an
important formal parallel in the *Iliad*:[2]

ὤ μοι ἐγὼ δειλή, ὤ μοι δυσαριστοτόκεια,
ἥ τ᾽ ἐπεὶ ἄρ τέκον υἱὸν ἀμύμονά τε κρατερόν τε,
ἔξοχον ἡρώων· ὁ δ᾽ ἀνέδραμεν ἔρνεϊ ἶσος·
τὸν μὲν ἐγὼ θρέψασα, φυτὸν ὡς γουνῷ ἀλωῆς,
νηυσὶν ἐπιπροέηκα κορωνίσιν Ἴλιον εἴσω
Τρωσὶ μαχησόμενον· τὸν δ᾽ οὐχ ὑποδέξομαι αὖτις
οἴκαδε νοστήσαντα δόμον Πηλήιον εἴσω.

Ah me, the wretch! Ah me, the mother—so sad it is—of the very best.
I gave birth to a faultless and strong son,
the very best of heroes.[3] And he shot up like a seedling.[4]

ΔΗΜΟΦΑΓΩΝ = **Dēmopháu̯ōn** (Priscian *Institutiones Grammaticae* 1.22, 6.69). For the
parallel forms **Pháōn** and **Phaéthōn**, see Nagy 1973.148. On the semantics of **dêmos**,
see Ch.8§11n6.

§10n5. On the thematic associations inherent in **dālós** 'smoldering log', see Detienne
1973b [= 1970] 298–299, who adduces the relevant myths about Meleager and the
dālós; cf. also *Odyssey* v 488.

§10n6. This same phrase ὁ δ᾽ ἀέξετο δαίμονι ἶσος 'and he grew up like a **daímōn**' at
H.Dem. 235 has a formal parallel at *H.Dem.* 300, describing the temple of the goddess
herself: ὁ δ᾽ ἀέξετο δαίμονος αἴσῃ 'and it [the temple] grew up by the **aîsa**
[dispensation] of the **daímōn**'. The **daímōn** here is surely Demeter. For the application
of the word **daímōn** to god and hero alike, see Ch.9§6; also Ch.7§15n1, §21n1.

§11n1. Sinos 1975.28–36.

§11n2. Verses 56–60 are also at XVIII 437–441.

§11n3. The phrasing ἥ τ᾽ . . . ἔξοχον ἡρώων at 55–56 serves to elaborate on the
compound epithet **dusaristotókeia** at 54, with the culminating theme conveyed by the
epithet **éxokhos hērṓōn** 'the very best of heroes'. (The element **dus-** 'bad, sad' of the
compound **dus-aristo-tókeia** is metalinguistic, in that it motivates the application of the
epithet **-aristo-tókeia** 'mother of the very best' in the context of **ó moi . . . ó moi**, the
language of lamentation.) Compare too the epithet **éxokhos hērṓōn** 'the very best of
heroes' with the phraseology at Alcaeus 42.13LP.

§11n4. For an instance where **anatrékhō** 'shoot up' applies directly to the growth of
a plant, see Herodotus 8.55, where the perfect participle of this verb (ἀναδεδρα-
μηκότα) describes the new shoot that grew from the stump of Athena's olive tree after

I nurtured him[5] like a shoot in the choicest spot of the orchard,[6]
only to send him off on curved ships to fight at Troy. And I will never be
welcoming him back home as returning warrior, back to the House of
Peleus.

XVIII 54–60

The context of these words is an actual lamentation (**góos**: XVIII 51),
sung by the mother of Achilles himself over the death of her son[7]—a
death that is presupposed by the narrative from the very moment that
the death of the hero's surrogate Patroklos is announced to him.[8]

§12. It appears, then, that the mortality of a cult figure like
Demophon is a theme that calls for the same sort of vegetal imagery
as is appropriate to the mortality of Achilles. The examples can be
multiplied: like the hero of the *Iliad*, who is likened to a young shoot
with words like **phutón** (XVIII 57, 438) and **érnos** (XVIII 56,437),[1]
the hero of the *Hymn to Demeter* is directly called a **néon thálos**
'young sprout' (*H.Dem.* 66, 187).[2] Moreover, we have seen that this
theme of mortality common to Demophon and Achilles is replete

---

the burning of Athens by the invading Persians; significantly, the tree was in the
precinct of the local hero Erekhtheus. See Sinos 1975.28–29.

§11n5. Note that the underscored phrases at XVIII 56 and *H.Dem.* 235, describing
the growth of Achilles and Demophon respectively, are both directly connected with
the theme of *nurturing goddesses*. On the relationship of the nurturing goddess,
Kourotróphos, with the **koûros** on the level of cult and with the **éphēbos** on the level
of society in general, see Sinos 1975.29–30 and Clader 1976.75–77; also Vidal-Naquet
1968.947–949 and Detienne 1973b.302, esp. n7. The word **koûros** 'male youth' is the
Ionic reflex of *kóryos, which in Attic yields **kóros** 'shoot [of a plant]'; see Merkelbach
1971. For **Kourotróphos** as a distinct cult figure in Attica, to whom the **éphēboi** made
sacrifice (*IG* II[2] 1039), see Quinn 1971.153. In Harpocration s.v. **Kourotróphos**, we
read that the custom of sacrificing to Kourotrophos was "founded" by the Athenian
hero Erekhtheus: he was the first to sacrifice to her, in gratitude to Gaia 'Earth' for
having given him birth. In the Athenian myth of Erekhtheus, there eventually
prevailed a distinction between one goddess (Athena) who nurtures the hero and
another goddess (Earth) who gives him birth; see *Iliad* II 547–551. The relationship of
Kourotrophos to Erekhtheus hints at a stage where Athena is not yet distinct from
Mother Earth. For more on the subject of Kourotrophos, see Hadzisteliou Price 1978.

§11n6. Besides the application of **phutòn hós** 'like a shoot' to Achilles at XVIII 57
(and 438), this simile is applied to no one else in the *Iliad* or *Odyssey*.

§11n7. See Reiner 1938.12–13, who also adduces an interesting parallel from
Euripides *Suppliants* 918–924.

§11n8. See Ch.6§24.

§12n1. Note too the comparison of the dead Euphorbos to an **érnos** 'sprout' cut off
from an olive tree, at XVII 52–58.

§12n2. Compare XXII 87: here the mother of Hektor addresses him as **phílon thálos**
in the context of conjuring up a future scene where Hektor will be laid out on the
funeral couch and his mother will be mourning him.

with the same sort of imagery that we find specifically in the genre of lamentation (consider again the **góos** of Thetis, XVIII 54–60).[3]

§13. In this light, let us reconsider the epithet **áphthito-**. We have already seen that it conveys the *cultural* negation of a *natural* process, the growing and the wilting of plants, and also, by extension, the life and the death of mortals. Now we must examine how this epithet conveys the theme of immortality in its application to Demophon and Achilles as heroes of cult and epic respectively. As compensation for the death that he cannot escape, Demophon gets a **tīmḗ** that is **áphthitos** (*H.Dem.* 261, 263); likewise, Achilles gets a **kléos** that is **áphthiton** (IX 413). Thus both heroes are destined for immortality in the form of a *cultural* institution that is predicated on the *natural* process of death. For Demophon, this predication is direct but implicit: by getting **tīmḗ** he is incorporated into hero cult, a general institution that is implicitly built around the basic principle that the hero must die.[1] For the Achilles of our *Iliad*, this same predication is explicit but indirect: by getting **kléos** he is incorporated into epic, which is presented *by epic itself* as an eternal extension of the lamentation sung by the Muses over the hero's death (xxiv 60–61, 93–94).[2] Thus the specific institution of lamentation, which is an aspect of hero-cult and which is implicit in the very name of Achilles, leads to the **kléos** of epic. For both heroes, the key to immortality is the permanence of the cultural institutions into which they are incorporated—cult for Demophon, epic for the Achilles of our *Iliad*. Both manifestations of both institutions qualify as **áphthito-**.

§14. For the Achilles of our *Iliad*, the **kléos áphthiton** of epic (IX 413) offers not only an apparatus of heroic immortality but also a paradox about the human condition of the hero. Achilles himself says that the way for him to achieve this **kléos áphthiton** is to die at Troy

§12n3. We should also note the ritual laments for Adonis in the Athenian festival known as the **Adṓnia**. From Plutarch's account (*Alcibiades* 18.5), we see that lamentation was but one aspect of an overall "funeral" for Adonis (see Alexiou 1974.217n2, who surveys the references to the **Adṓnia** in comedy). For the significance of the vegetal imagery surrounding the Adonis figure, especially the theme of *premature growth and death*, see Detienne 1972; cf. also Sinos 1975.9–37.

§13n1. Cf. Ch.6§27.

§13n2. See §§2–4. Of course, the inherited semantic range of the word **kléos** itself covers not just Epos in particular but praise poetry in general. Praise is in fact an integral element of lamentation; see Reiner 1938.23n1 and p. 63n3 on XXII 303–305. In the latter passage, Hektor recognizes that he will die but hopes that he will thereby get **kléos** if indeed he has acted heroically (line 304); then "those in the future" will also hear about him (line 305).

(IX 412–413), and that the way to lose **kléos** is to live life as a mortal, at home in **Phthíē** (IX 413–416). The overt Iliadic contrast of **kléos áphthiton** with the negation of **kléos** in the context of **Phthíē** is remarkable in view of the element **phthi-** contained by the place name. From the wording of *Iliad* IX 412–416, we are led to suspect that this element **phthi-** is either a genuine formant of **Phthíē** or is at least perceived as such in the process of Homeric composition. We see the actual correlation of the intransitive verb **phthi-** (middle endings) 'perish' with **Phthíē** at XIX 328–330, where Achilles is wishing that he alone had died at Troy and that his surrogate Patroklos had lived to come home. Again, coming home to **Phthíē** (XIX 330) is overtly contrasted with dying '**phthísesthai**' at Troy (XIX 329).[1] If indeed the name for the homeland of Achilles is motivated by the theme of vegetal death as conveyed by the root **phthi-**, then the traditional epithet reserved for the place is all the more remarkable: **Phthíē** is **bōtiáneira** 'nourisher of men' (I 155). The combination seems to produce a *coincidentia oppositorum*,[2] in that the place name conveys the death of plants while its epithet conveys the life of plants—as it sustains the life of mortals. The element **bōti-** in this compound **bōti-áneira** stems from the verb system of **bóskō** 'nourish', a word that specifically denotes the sustenance, *by vegetation*, of grazing animals, as at xiv 102, and of men, as at xi 365. In the latter instance, the object of the verb **bóskei** 'nourishes' is **anthrṓpous** 'men', and the subject is actually **gaîa** 'Earth'.[3] Thus the life and death of mortal men is based on the life and death of the plants that are grown for their nourishment: this is the message of the epithet **bōtiáneira** in its application to the homeland of Achilles. **Phthíē** is the hero's local Earth, offering him the natural cycle of life and death as an alternative to his permanent existence within the cultural medium of epic.

§15. In the Homeric *Hymn to Demeter*, the foil for the permanence of cult as a cultural institution is also expressed by way of vegetal imagery: this time the image that we are considering is not the prolonged life but the prolonged death of plants, as denoted by the

---

§14n1. Note also the ring composition in the placement of **phthi-** at XIX 322 (**apophthiménoio puthoímēn** /) and XIX 337 (**apophthiménoio púthētai** /), denoting respectively the hypothetical deaths of father and son, Peleus and Achilles.

§14n2. For the term, see Eliade 1963.419–429; see also §§43–44.

§14n3. Note the application of the same epithet **bōtiáneira** 'nourisher of men' to **khthṓn** 'Earth' at *H.Apollo* 363 and *H.Aphr.* 265.

root **phthi-**. In contrast with the application of **áphthito-** to the **tīmḗ** of Demophon, let us consider the wording of the myth that tells how the permanence of all cult was endangered when the goddess Demeter prolonged indefinitely the failure of plant life:

ἐπεὶ μέγα μήδεται ἔργον,
φθῖσαι φῦλ' ἀμενηνὰ χαμαιγενέων ἀνθρώπων
σπέρμ' ὑπὸ γῆς κρύπτουσα, καταφθινύθουσα δὲ τιμὰς
ἀθανάτων

For she [Demeter] is performing[1] a mighty deed,
to destroy [**phthî-sai**] the tribes of earth-born men, causing them to be without **ménos**,
by hiding the Seed underground—and she is destroying [**kata-phthi-núthousa**] the **tīmaí** of the immortal gods.

H.Dem. 351–354

First, we are shown what the prolonged death of vegetation does to mortals, and we start with the adjective **amenēná** 'without **ménos**' at verse 352, derived from the noun **ménos** 'power.'[2] This epithet is proleptic, in that it anticipates what Demeter does to mortals by virtue of taking away the sustenance of vegetation: she thereby takes away their **ménos**, and this action is here equated with the action of **phthîsai** at verse 352, meaning "destroy" or, from the metaphorical standpoint of human life as plant life, "cause [plants] to fail."[3] In Homeric diction, the intransitive uses of the same verb **phthi-** can designate the failing of wine supplies (ix 163) and of food supplies (xii 329); when the food supplies fail, **katéphthito**, the **ménea** of men who eat them fail also (iv 363). Second, we are shown what the prolonged death of vegetation does to the immortal gods: again, the action of Demeter is designated with the verb **phthi-** (**kataphthinú-thousa**, verse 353), but here the image of plant failure applies not to the gods directly but to their **tīmaí** 'cults' instead. The impact of prolonged plant failure on cult is explicit:

καί νύ κε πάμπαν ὄλεσσε γένος μερόπων ἀνθρώπων
λιμοῦ ὑπ' ἀργαλέης, γεράων τ' ἐρικυδέα τιμὴν
καὶ θυσιῶν ἤμερσεν Ὀλύμπια δώματ' ἔχοντας

§15n1. On the mental and supernatural aspects of the verb **médomai**: Nagy 1974.265–278.
§15n2. On the cosmic aspects of **ménos** and its Vedic cognate *mánas-*: Nagy 1974.268–269.
§15n3. Cf. §3.

She [Demeter] would have completely destroyed the **génos** of **méropes** men
with the painful famine, and she would have taken away from the gods who
 live in their Olympian abode
the **tīmḗ** of honorific portions and sacrifices.[4]

H.Dem. 310–312

We see, then, that the indefinite perpetuation of vegetal death as
expressed by **phthi-** is a natural image of cosmic disorder; it functions
as a foil for the cultural image of cosmic order, as represented by the
indefinite perpetuation of vegetal life and as expressed by **áphthito-**.
We also see now more clearly the suitability of this epithet **áphthito-**
for the function of defining not only cult in particular but also the
eternal cosmic apparatus of the immortal gods in general.[5]

§16. The cosmic order of the Olympians is of course not only
permanent but also *sacred*, and in fact both these qualities are
conveyed by the same epithet **áphthito-**.[1] As we see from the
Hesiodic tradition, nothing is more sacred or binding for the
Olympians than taking an oath in the name of the Styx (*Th.*
793–805), and the river's waters in this particular context are
specifically called **áphthito-** (Στυγὸς ἄφθιτον ὕδωρ: *Th.* 805). If a god
breaks such an oath, he has to endure the worst of punishments (*Th.*
793–805), which include the temporary withdrawal of divine sustenance, nectar and ambrosia (*Th.* 796–797).[2] The children of the Styx,
Krátos and **Bíē** (*Th.* 385), uphold the cosmic régime of Zeus (*Th.*
385–403), and in this context the river herself is called **áphthito-**
(Στὺξ ἄφθιτος: *Th.* 389, 397). In the Homeric tradition as well (the
Hymns included), to swear by the Styx is for any god the most
sacrosanct of actions (XV 37–38, v 185–186, *H.Apollo* 85–86). When
the goddess Demeter thus takes her oath in the name of the Styx
(*H.Dem.* 259), what she swears is that the infant Demophon would

§15n4. On the word **géras** 'honorific portion': Ch.7§19n3.

§15n5. The Indic cognate of Greek **áphthito-** is *ákṣita-* 'unfailing', and the semantic
range of this epithet reveals interesting parallels with that of its Greek counterpart. In
the *Rig-Veda*, the epithet *ákṣita-* applies to the unfailing flow of the cosmic powers
inherent in water, fire, light, milk, semen, urine, and *soma*-sap; for a survey of the
nouns that correspond to these elements and attract the epithet *ákṣita-*, see Nagy
1974.231–240.

§16n1. In the hymns of the *Rig-Veda*, by virtue of its being a sacrosanct medium,
the elements described as *ákṣita-* are uniformly sacred; see again Nagy 1974.231–240.

§16n2. One consequence of being deprived of nectar and ambrosia is that the
punished god *loses his breath*: he lies "breathless" (**anápneustos**: *Th.* 797), enveloped
in a "bad sleep" (**kakòn ... kôma**: *Th.* 798). On the supernatural connotations of
kôma 'sleep', see West 1966.375.

have had a life uninterrupted by death (*H.Dem.* 260–261) and a **tīmḗ** that is **áphthitos** (*H.Dem.* 261). Demeter then says that the inadvertence of the infant's real mother has negated the first part of the Oath (*H.Dem.* 262), but the second part remains valid: Demophon will still have a **tīmḗ** that is **áphthitos** (*H.Dem.* 263). We now see that the epithet **áphthito-** in this context conveys not only the permanence of Demophon's cult, but also its intrinsic sacredness, as conferred by the essence of Demeter's Oath.[3]

§17. So also Achilles swears by the **skêptron** of King Agamemnon (I 234–239), affirming both that the Achaeans will one day yearn for him and that Agamemnon will then regret not having given "the best of the Achaeans" his due **tīmḗ** (I 240–244). Here we must keep in mind that the **skêptron** itself is **áphthiton** (II 46, 186). Accordingly, the Oath of Achilles is not only permanent in its validity but also sacred. Moreover, the wish that the mother of Achilles conveys from the hero to Zeus is phrased from the standpoint of the Oath: let the Achaeans be hard pressed without the might of Achilles, and let their king regret not having given the hero his due **tīmḗ** (I 409–412). It is this wish that Thetis presents to Zeus (I 503–510), with special emphasis on the **tīmḗ** of Achilles (I 505, 507, 508, 510*bis*), and it is this wish that Zeus ratifies irrevocably (I 524–530). In this way, the Oath of Achilles is translated into the Will of Zeus, which, as we have seen, is the self-proclaimed plot of our *Iliad*.[n] The oath is sacred because it is founded on the **skêptron**, which is **áphthiton**; now we see that the epic validating the **tīmḗ** of Achilles is also sacred, for the very reason that it is founded on this Oath. Accordingly, the epithet **áphthito-** as it applies to the **kléos** of Achilles (IX 413) conveys not only the permanence of the hero's epic but also its intrinsic sacredness as conferred by the essence of the hero's Oath.

§18. The traditional application of **áphthito-** to both the cult of Demophon and the epic of Achilles serves as a key to what is for us a missing theme in the archaic story of Achilles. In the case of Demophon, we have seen how the hero gets a **tīmḗ** that is **áphthitos** because the goddess swears by the Styx, which is itself **áphthitos**. We have yet to follow through, however, on what such a combination of

---

§16n3. Cf. also the application of **áphthito-** to **sébas** 'object of reverence' at *Iliou Persis fr.* 1.1 Allen, referring to the Palladium of Troy, which its founder Dardanos is instructed by the Oracle to "revere" (**sébein**: *fr.* 1.2 Allen) by guarding it and by instituting sacrifices and songs/dances for its cult (ibid.).

§17n. Ch.5§25n2.

Stúx and **áphthitos** implies: *that the waters of the Styx are an elixir of life.*[1] The lore about the cosmic stream Styx applies commensurately to the actual stream Styx in Arcadia,[2] and in fact the belief prevails to this day that whoever drinks of that stream's waters *under the right conditions* may gain immortality.[3] The point is that there survives for us a story telling how Thetis had immersed the infant Achilles into the waters of the Styx, in an unsuccessful attempt to exempt him from death (Statius *Achilleid* 1.269; Servius *ad* Virgil *Aeneid* 6.57; etc.). This failure of Thetis must be compared with the failure of Demeter in her attempt to make Demophon immortal. It would indeed be conventional for scholars to consider the story of Achilles in the Styx as a parallel to that of Demophon in the fire, if it were not for the fact that there is no attestation of such an Achilles story in archaic poetry.[4] This obstacle may now perhaps be overcome with the indirect testimony of the epithet **áphthito-**: for both Demophon and Achilles, this word marks a compensatory form of immortality, and the Stygian authority of this deathlessness is overt in the case of Demophon. In the case of Achilles, we may say that the authority of the **skêptron** is a worthy variation on the authority of the **Stúx**, in that both **skêptron** and **Stúx** are intrinsically **áphthito-**. From the standpoint of diction, either could ratify the **kléos** of Achilles as **áphthiton**.

§19. As our lengthy survey of the word **áphthito-** in Homeric and Hesiodic diction comes to an end, we conclude that this epithet can denote the permanent and sacred order of the Olympians,[n] into which the hero is incorporated after death through such cultural media as epic in particular and cult in general.

§20. It remains to ask a more important question: whether the theme of the hero immortalized in cult is compatible with the poetic visions of the hero immortalized by being transported to Elysium, to the Isles of the Blessed, or even to Olympus itself. Rohde, for one, thought that the concept of heroes being transported into a remote state of immortality is purely poetic and thus alien to the religious concept of heroes being venerated in cult.[1] From the actual evidence

§18n1. See Richardson 1974.245.

§18n2. In Herodotus 6.74, we see that swearing by the Styx is a most sacred act for the Arcadians; see Frazer 1898 IV 253–254 *ad* Pausanias 8.18.4.

§18n3. For documentation, see West 1966.377–378.

§18n4. On the stories of Achilles in the fire, see Richardson 1974.237–238.

§19n. See again §15.

§20n1. Rohde I 68–110. His assumption has generally been followed; cf. Dihle 1970.18–20.

of cult, however, we see that the two concepts are not at all treated as if they were at odds with each other.[2] In fact, the forms **Elúsion** 'Elysium' and **Makárōn nêsoi** 'Isles of the Blessed' are appropriate as names for actual cult sites. The proper noun **Elúsion** coincides with the common noun **en-elúsion**, meaning 'place made sacred by virtue of being struck by the thunderbolt' (Polemon *fr.* 5 Tresp); correspondingly, the adjective **en-elúsios** means 'made sacred by virtue of being struck by the thunderbolt' (Aeschylus *fr.* 17N = *fr.* 263M).[3] The form **Elúsion** itself is glossed in the Alexandrian lexicographical tradition (Hesychius) as κεκεραυνωμένον χωρίον ἢ πεδίον 'a place or field that has been struck by the thunderbolt', with this added remark: καλεῖται δὲ καὶ ἐνηλύσια 'and it is also called **enelúsia**'. As for **Makárōn nêsos**, there is a tradition that the name was actually applied to the old acropolis of Thebes, the Kadmeion; specifically, the name designated the sacred precinct where Semele, the mother of Dionysos, had been struck dead by the thunderbolt of Zeus (Parmenides *ap.* Suda and *ap.* Photius, s.v. **Makárōn nêsos**; Tzetzes *ad* Lycophron 1194, 1204).[4] We are immediately reminded of the poetic tradition that tells how Semele became immortalized as a direct result of dying from the thunderbolt of Zeus (see Pindar *O.2.25*, in conjunction with Hesiod *Th.* 942).[5]

§21. We are in fact now ready to examine the general evidence of poetic traditions, in order to test whether the medium of poetry distinguishes this concept of heroes (or heroines) being transported into a state of immortality from the concept of their being venerated in cult. As with the evidence of cult itself, we will find that poetic diction reveals no contradiction between these two concepts.

§22. Actually, there are poetic themes that tell of a hero's actual veneration in cult, and these themes are even combined with those

§20n2. As Walter Burkert points out to me (*per litteras* 6/16/1977), there is a clear archaic example where the cult of a hero at his tomb coexists with the myth of his immortalization, in the report on Hyakinthos by Pausanias 3.19.4.

§20n3. See Burkert 1961.209; in the Aeschylus fragment, the form **enelúsios** applies to Kapaneus, who was struck by the thunderbolt of Zeus. For the semantic relationship of **enelúsios/enelúsion**, compare **hierós/hierón** 'sacred'/'sacred place'. Note that the body of the thunderstruck Kapaneus is described as **hieró-** in Euripides *Suppliants* 935.

§20n4. See Burkert 1961.212n2; cf. Vian 1963.123.

§20n5. See also Diodorus Siculus 5.52, Charax *FGrH* 103.14, etc. In the Pindaric account (*O.2.25*), her abode of immortality is Olympus itself. Cf. the immortalization of Herakles on Olympus, as discussed at §41n1. Cf. also the testimony of the Thurian gold leaves at A1.4, A2.5, A3.5 (Zuntz 1971.301–305), where the *persona* of the dead man declares in each instance that his immortalization was preceded by death from the thunderbolt.

that tell of his translation into immortality. Such combinations in fact form an integral picture of the heroic afterlife, as in the Hesiodic version of the Phaethon myth:[1]

αὐτάρ τοι Κεφάλῳ φιτύσατο φαίδιμον υἱόν,
ἴφθιμον Φαέθοντα, θεοῖς ἐπιείκελον ἄνδρα.
τόν ῥα νέον τέρεν ἄνθος ἔχοντ᾽ ἐρικυδέος ἥβης
παῖδ᾽ ἀταλὰ φρονέοντα φιλομμειδὴς Ἀφροδίτη
ὦρτ᾽ ἀνερειψαμένη, καί μιν ζαθέοις ἐνὶ νηοῖς
νηοπόλον μύχιον ποιήσατο, δαίμονα δῖον

And she [Eos] <u>sprouted</u> for Kephalos an illustrious son,
sturdy Phaethon, a man who looked like the gods.
When he was young and still had the tender <u>bloom</u> of glorious adolescence,
Aphrodite **philommeidḗs**[2] rushed up and snatched him away as he was thinking playful thoughts.
And she made him an underground temple attendant, a **dîos daímōn**, in her holy temple.

Hesiod Th. 986–991

Phaethon in the afterlife is overtly presented as a **daímōn** of cult (*Th.* 991) who functions within an undisturbed corner plot, **mukhós**, of Aphrodite's precinct (hence **múkhios** at *Th.* 991)[3] as the goddess's **nēopólos** 'temple attendant' (again *Th.* 991). The designation of Phaethon as **daímōn** also conveys the immortal aspect of the hero in his afterlife, since it puts him in the same category as the Golden Generation, who are themselves explicitly **daímones** (*W&D* 122).[4] As for the mortal aspect of Phaethon, we may observe the vegetal imagery surrounding his birth and adolescence. When he is about to be snatched away forever, he bears the **ánthos** 'bloom' of adolescence (*Th.* 988). Earlier, the verb that denotes his very birth from Eos is **phītúsato** (*Th.* 986): the Dawn Goddess "sprouted" him as if he were some plant. We see here in the *Theogony* the only application

---

§22n1. For the parallelism between the names **Phaéthōn/Pháōn** and **Dēmopháōn**, see §10n4.

§22n2. For more on this epithet, see Boedeker 1974.20, 23–26, 32–35.

§22n3. On the nature of the **mukhós**, see Rohde I 135n1 (cf. also Nagy 1973.171). I disagree, however, with Rohde's specific assumption that Phaethon's abduction does not involve death. See also n4.

§22n4. We may note that even those in the Golden Generation are subject to death, although this death is more like sleep (Hesiod *W&D* 116). The point is that death does not disqualify them from becoming **daímones** in cult. As such, they are immortalized and merit the title of **athánatoi** 'immortals' (*W&D* 250, 253). For a cogent set of arguments that the wording of *W&D* 249–255 applies to the same **daímones** as at *W&D* 122–126, see Vernant 1966 [= 1960] 29.

of **phītúein** 'sprout' to the act of reproduction, which is elsewhere conventionally denoted by **tíktein** and **geínasthai**.[5] The most immediate parallel is the birth of the Athenian hero Erekhtheus, who was directly sprouted by Earth herself:

ὅν ποτ᾽ ᾽Αθήνη
θρέψε Διὸς θυγάτηρ, τέκε δὲ ζείδωρος ἄρουρα,
κὰδ δ᾽ ἐν ᾽Αθήνης εἷσεν, ἑῷ ἐν πίονι νηῷ.
ἔνθα δέ μιν ταύροισι καὶ ἀρνειοῖς ἱλάονται
κοῦροι ᾽Αθηναίων περιτελλομένων ἐνιαυτῶν

Athena the daughter of Zeus once upon a time
nurtured him, but grain-giving earth gave him birth,[6]
and she [Athena] established him in Athens, in her own rich temple,
and there it is that the **koûroi** of the Athenians supplicate him,
every year when the time comes, with bulls and lambs.

II 547–551

As with Phaethon, the immortal aspect of the hero Erekhtheus is conveyed by his permanent installation within the sacred precinct of a goddess.[7]

§23. We have yet to examine the actual process of Phaethon's translation into heroic immortality.[1] The key word is the participle **anereipsaménē** (*Th.* 990), describing Aphrodite at the moment that she snatches Phaethon away to be with her forever. The word recurs in the finite form **anēreípsanto** (XX 234), describing the gods as they abduct Ganymedes to be the cup bearer of Zeus for all time to come. In the next verse, we hear the motive for the divine action:

κάλλεος εἵνεκα οἷο, ἵν᾽ ἀθανάτοισι μετείη

on account of his beauty, so that he might be among the Immortals.

XX 235

The Homeric *Hymn to Aphrodite* elaborates on the same myth: it was Zeus himself who abducted Ganymedes (*H.Aphr.* 202–203). Here too, the motive is presented as the same:

§22n5. West 1966.427.
§22n6. For the division of motherly functions, giving birth and nurturing, between Earth and Athena, see §11n5. On the eventual distinction between **Erekhtheús** and **Erikhthónios** in Athenian mythology, see Burkert 1972.176, 211.
§22n7. Cf. Nock 1972 [= 1930] 237 for other examples of goddess/hero symbiosis within a sacred precinct.
§23n1. In the discussion that follows, I have incorporated and revised parts of my earlier work on the subject of Phaethon (Nagy 1973.148–172).

ὃν διὰ κάλλος, ἵν' ἀθανάτοισι μετείη

on account of his beauty, so that he might be among the Immortals.

H.Aphr. 203

In this retelling as well as in all the others, Ganymedes becomes the cup bearer of Zeus; *and as such he abides in the gods' royal palace at Olympus* (*H.Aphr.* 204–206). By virtue of gaining Olympian status, he is in fact described as an Immortal himself:

ἀθάνατος καὶ ἀγήρως ἴσα θεοῖσιν

immortal and unaging, just as the gods are.[2]

H.Aphr. 214

As cup bearer and boy-love of Zeus, Ganymedes also qualifies as a **daímōn**:

παιδοφιλεῖν δέ τι τερπνόν, ἐπεί ποτε καὶ Γανυμήδους
ἤρατο καὶ Κρονίδης ἀθανάτων βασιλεύς,
ἁρπάξας δ' ἐς Ὄλυμπον ἀνήγαγε καί μιν ἔθηκεν
δαίμονα, παιδείης ἄνθος ἔχοντ' ἐρατόν

Loving a boy is a pleasant thing. For even the Son of Kronos,
king of the Immortals, loved Ganymedes.
He abducted him, took him up to Olympus,[3] and made him
a **daímōn**, having the lovely bloom of boyhood.

Theognis 1345–1348

The parallelisms between this Theognidean passage about Ganymedes and the Hesiodic passage about Phaethon (*Th.* 986–991) are remarkable not just because of the convergences in detail (both heroes are described as **daímōn**, both have the **ánthos** 'bloom' of youth, etc.). An even more remarkable fact about these parallelisms is that the processes of *preservation on Olympus* and *preservation in cult* function as equivalent poetic themes.

§24. The parallelisms between the myth of Ganymedes and that of Phaethon lead to our discovery of further details about the process of heroic preservation. When the gods abducted '**anēreípsanto**' the young Ganymedes (XX 234), the specific instrument of the divine action was a gust of wind, an **áella**:

§23n2. These words are the "correct" formula for immortalization; when the words are "incorrect," as in the myth of Eos and Tithonos, then the immortalization is ruined by the failure of preservation. See §30 below.

§23n3. For the mystical meaning of **anágō** as 'bring back to the light from the dead', see Nagy 1973.175.

... ὅππη οἱ φίλον υἱὸν ἀνήρπασε θέσπις ἄελλα

... to whatever place the wondrous **áella** abducted him

H.Aphr. 208

Actually, in every other Homeric attestation of **anēreípsanto** besides XX 234, the notion "gusts of wind" serves as subject of the verb.[1] When Penelope mourns the unknown fate of her absent son Telemachus, she says:

νῦν αὖ παῖδ᾽ ἀγαπητὸν ἀνηρείψαντο θύελλαι

But now the **thúellai** have abducted my beloved son.

iv 727

When Telemachus mourns the unknown fate of his absent father Odysseus, he says:[2]

νῦν δέ μιν ἀκλειῶς ἅρπυιαι ἀνηρείψαντο

But now the **hárpuiai** have abducted him, without **kléos**.

i 241

§25. The meaning of **thúella** 'gust of wind' is certain (see the collocation of **thúella** with **anémoio** 'of wind' at VI 346, etc.). As for **hárpuia**, a word that is also personified as "Harpy" (*Th.* 267),[1] the same meaning "gust of wind" is apparent from the only remaining Homeric attestation of the verb **anēreípsanto** 'abducted'. After Penelope wishes that Artemis smite her dead and take her **thūmós** immediately, we hear her make an alternative wish:

ἢ ἔπειτά μ᾽ ἀναρπάξασα θύελλα
οἴχοιτο προφέρουσα κατ᾽ ἠερόεντα κέλευθα,
ἐν προχοῇς δὲ βάλοι ἀψορρόου Ὠκεανοῖο

or later, may a **thúella** abduct me;
may it go off and take me away along misty ways,
and plunge me into the streams of Okeanos, which flows in a circle.

xx 63–65

As precedent for being abducted by a gust of wind and cast down into the Okeanos, her words evoke the story about the daughters of Pandareos:

---

§24n1. For what follows, see also Nagy 1973.156–161.

§24n2. The identical verse recurs when Eumaios mourns the unknown fate of his absent master Odysseus (xiv 371).

§25n1. Note that one of the **Hárpuiai** 'Harpies' is **Aellō** (Hesiod *Th.* 267), a name derived from **áella**.

ὡς δ' ὅτε Πανδαρέου κούρας ἀνέλοντο θύελλαι·

as when the **thúellai** took away the daughters of Pandareos

xx 66

This mention of abduction is followed by a description of how the Pandareids were preserved by the Olympian goddesses (xx 67–72). The preservation of the girls is then interrupted by death, at the very moment that Aphrodite is arranging for them to be married (xx 73–74). Death comes in the form of abduction:

τόφρα δὲ τὰς κούρας ἅρπυιαι ἀνηρείψαντο

then the **hárpuiai** abducted the girls[2]

xx 77

§26. Our survey has by now covered all the Homeric/Hesiodic attestations of **anēreípsanto/anereipsaménē**, and we can reach several conclusions. Most important of all, we see that the divine abduction of mortals by gusts of wind (**thúellai** or **hárpuiai**) entails not only preservation but also sex and death.[n] Of these last two experiences, we will leave the first in abeyance until we confront the second.

§27. In the imagery of passages featuring the forms **anēreípsanto/ anereipsaménē**, you experience death when the abducting winds plunge you into the earth-encircling river Okeanos. So we have seen from Penelope's death wish (xx 63–65). As we see further from Homeric diction, especially at xxiv 1–14, the Okeanos is one of the prime mythical boundaries that serve to delimit light from darkness, life from death, wakefulness from sleep, consciousness from uncon-

§25n2. I regret my earlier view (Nagy 1973.158–159, 167–168) that xx 66 and xx 77 represent two stages of action. If instead they represent the same action, then we can understand xx 61–81 as operating on the principle of ring composition. Penelope wishes an immediate death caused by the shafts of Artemis (xx 61–63) or a delayed death caused by the abducting winds (xx 63–65); xx 66 introduces as precedent the abduction of the Pandareids; an elaboration of the story follows at xx 67–76, climaxed by xx 77, which recaps xx 66. Then xx 79 returns to Penelope's wish for a delayed death, and xx 80 recaps her alternative wish for an immediate death. The force of ἢ ἔπειτα 'or later' in expressing a delayed death at xx 63 is that the winds would snatch Penelope away later, *just before her marriage to one of the suitors*. There is in that case a neat parallelism with the story of the Pandareids, who were abducted just before their own arranged marriage (see xx 73–74). I would therefore stand by my view (Nagy 1973.159n64) that the context of ἢ ἔπειτα 'or later' at xx 63 helps explain the epithet **metakhróniai** 'delayed' as applied to the **Hárpuiai** at Hesiod *Th.* 269.

§26n. Of course, this death may be more like sleep, of the sort that overcomes the Golden Generation (*W&D* 116); see §22n4.

sciousness.[1] The River Okeanos marks the cosmic extremities beyond Earth and Seas (cf. XIV 301–302). The Sun himself, Helios, plunges into it every sunset (VIII 485) and emerges from it every sunrise (VII 421–423, xix 433–434). As the Sun thus rises at Dawn from the Okeanos, he stirs the **árourai** 'fertile lands' (VII 421, xix 433),[2] and we are reminded by this action that the noun **ároura** itself traditionally attracts such epithets of fertility as **zeídōros** 'grain-giving' (II 548, VIII 486, etc.).[3] Since plunging into the Okeanos overtly conveys death (xx 63–65), it follows that the notion of emerging from it conveys regeneration. For the Sun, we infer that regeneration through Okeanos is cosmic, bringing with it the fertility of Earth itself; in fact, Okeanos qualifies not only as **theôn génesin** 'genesis of gods' (XIV 201, 302) but even as **génesis pántessi** 'genesis for all things' (XIV 246).

§28. In this light, it becomes significant that the Okeanos is also a traditional landmark both for the Isles of the Blessed (*W&D* 171) and for Elysium itself (iv 567–568). What is more, the Okeanos in the context of Elysium has the specific function of reanimating mortals:[1]

ἀλλ' αἰεὶ Ζεφύροιο λιγὺ πνείοντος ἀήτας
'Ωκεανὸς ἀνίησιν ἀναψύχειν ἀνθρώπους

but the Okeanos sends up the gusts of shrill-blowing Zephyros
at all times, so as to reanimate men[2]

iv 567–568

On the basis, then, of incidental references to the Sun and its movements in epic diction, we can detect a solar model of death and regeneration—both through the Okeanos. Moreover, we see that this solar model applies to the general theme of the hero's return from death. As we now look for specific instances of this theme, we turn to the myths about the personification of sunrise, Eos. In doing so we

§27n1. For a defense of this formulation, see Nagy 1973.149–153. The root *nes-, which Frame (1978) defines as 'return to life and light', denotes the act of crossing these boundaries: from darkness to light, from death to life, from sleep to wakefulness.

§27n2. The verb is **proséballen**; cf. the use of **éballen** at *Odyssey* v 479; for the notion of fertilization implied by such verbs of "striking," consider the comparative evidence of Rig-Vedic diction, as discussed by Watkins 1971.347.

§27n3. Besides giving life directly to crops (cf. also the epithet **pūrophóroio** 'wheat-bearing', as at XII 314), the **ároura** gives life indirectly to men, who eat the crops (as at VI 142 and XXI 465; cf. §6). At II 548, the **Ároura** gives life directly to man, by giving birth to Erekhtheus (cf. §22).

§28n1. See Ch.9§28n2.

§28n2. On the corresponding negative function of Zephyros: §41n4.

also confront a third theme in the myths of abduction: having already noted death and preservation, we are ready to reckon with a theme of sex.

§29. There is an archaic tradition that features the Dawn Goddess Eos herself abducting young male mortals, and her motive is in part sexual.[n] In the *Odyssey*, the immortal nymph Kalypso cites the abduction of Orion by Eos as a precedent for her mating with Odysseus (v 121–124). Similarly, Aphrodite herself cites both the abduction of Ganymedes by Zeus *and the abduction of Tithonos by Eos* as precedents for her mating with Anchises (*H.Aphr.* 202–238). As for the abduction of Phaethon, again by Aphrodite, the precedent is built into the young hero's genealogy: his father Kephalos had been abducted by his mother Eos (*Th.* 986; Euripides *Hippolytus* 455).

§30. As with the myth of Aphrodite and Phaethon, the myths of Eos too are marked by the design of making the hero immortal. Thus when Eos abducts Kleitos, her motive is described in these words:

κάλλεος εἵνεκα οἷο, ἵν᾽ ἀθανάτοισι μετείη

on account of his beauty, <u>so that he might be among the Immortals</u>

xv 251

The very same words, as we have seen, mark the immortalization of Ganymedes after his abduction by Zeus (XX 235; cf. *H.Aphr.* 203).[1] The divine motive for abduction by Eos is thus both preservative and sexual.[2]

§31. In order to see at a closer range the operation of a solar model in the myths of divine abduction, let us return to the Hesiodic myth of Phaethon (*Th.* 986–991).[n] The form of his name in Homeric

§29n. For an illuminating internal and comparative reconstruction of this theme, see Boedeker 1974.

§30n1. See §23.

§30n2. We may note an interesting elaboration in the myth of Eos and Tithonos, which makes a distinction between preservation and immortalization (*H.Aphr.* 218–238). Tithonos is immortalized and lives by the banks of Okeanos (*H.Aphr.* 225–227), but his **hḗbē** 'adolescence' is not made permanent (*H.Aphr.* 220–227); consequently, his preservation is corroded by old age (*H.Aphr.* 228–238). This failure is formalized by a lapse in the wording of the request made by Eos to Zeus for the preservation of Tithonos, at *H.Aphr.* 221 (also 240). We see the "correct" wording for the concept of preservation at *H.Aphr.* 214 (cf. v 136, vii 257, etc.), while the "incorrectness" of the wording by Eos is motivated at *H.Aphr.* 223–224. Since **hḗbē** 'adolescence' (*H.Aphr.* 224) is the key to the "correct" formulation of the request for immortalization, it is significant that the immortalization of Herakles is formalized by his being married to **Hḗbē** incarnate: see Hesiod *fr.* 25.28MW, as discussed at Ch.9§25.

§31n. See §22.

diction serves as an actual epithet of **Hélios** the Sun (as at XI 735). What is more, his mother is **Eós** the Dawn (*Th.* 986), while the goddess who abducted him embodies regeneration itself, Aphrodite (*Th.* 988–991).

§32. On the level of celestial dynamics, these associations imply the theme of a setting sun mating with the goddess of regeneration so that the rising sun may be reborn. Let us pursue this scheme—so far hypothetical only—one step further: if the setting sun is the same as the rising sun, then the goddess of regeneration may be viewed as both mate and mother. Such an ambivalent relationship actually survives in the hymns of the *Rig-Veda*, where the goddess of solar regeneration, *Uṣas-* 'Dawn', is the wife or bride of the sun god *Sūrya-* (*RV* 1.115.2, 7.75.5, etc.) as well as his mother (*RV* 7.63.3, 7.78.3). In the latter instance, the incestuous implications are attenuated by putting *Uṣas-* into the plural, representing a succession of dawns. Similarly, *Uṣas-* in the plural can designate the wives of *Sūrya-* (4.5.13). Yet even if each succeeding dawn is wife of the preceding dawn's son, the husband and son are always one and the same *Sūrya-*, and the basic theme of incest remains.

§33. There is more than one reason for comparing these Indic traditions about *Sūrya-* 'Sun' and *Uṣas-* 'Dawn' to such Greek traditions as we see in the myth of Phaethon. First and most obvious, the actual forms *Sūrya-* and *Uṣas-* are cognate with **Hélios** 'Sun' and **Eós** 'Dawn'.[1] Second, there are instances in Homeric diction where the relationship of the forms **Eós** and **Phaéthōn** is directly parallel to the relationship of Rig-Vedic *Uṣas-* and *Sūrya-*. Besides being an epithet of **Hélios** (XI 735, etc.), the form **Phaéthōn** also functions as a name for one of the two horses of **Eós**:

Λάμπον καὶ Φαέθονθ' οἵ τ' Ἠῶ πῶλοι ἄγουσι

<u>**Lámpos**</u> and <u>**Phaéthōn**</u>, who are the <u>horses</u> that pull **Eós**

xxiii 246

We may note that **Lámpos**, the name of her other horse, is also associated with the notion of brightness. The Rig-Vedic parallel here is that *Sūrya-* the sun god is called the "bright horse," *śvetám ...* *áśvam*, of the Dawn Goddess *Uṣas-* (*RV* 7.77.3; cf. 7.78.4). There is also, within Homeric diction itself, an internal analogue to the combination of **Phaéthōn** and **Lámpos** at xxiii 246. The names for the daughters of **Hélios** the sun god are **Phaéthousa** and **Lampetiē** (xii

§33n1. See Schmitt 1967.169–175.

132), which are feminine equivalents of **Phaéthōn** and **Lámpos**.[2] The Rig-Vedic parallel here is that the name for the daughter of *Sūrya-* the sun god is *Sūryā* (*RV* 1.116.17), a feminine equivalent of the masculine name. The comparative evidence of this contextual nexus suggests that the Horses of the Dawn at xxiii 246 had once been metaphorical aspects of the Sun. As in the *Rig-Veda*, the Sun could have been called the bright horse of the Dawn—by such names as **Phaéthōn** or **Lámpos**. Once the metaphor is suspended, then the notion "Horse of the Dawn" becomes reorganized: if the Dawn has a horse, she will actually have not one but two for a chariot team, and the two kindred solar aspects **Phaéthōn** 'bright' and **Lámpos** 'bright' will do nicely as names for two distinct horses. Yet the surviving function of **Phaéthousa** and **Lampetíē** as daughters of Helios serves as testimony for the eroded personal connotations of the names **Phaéthōn** and **Lámpos**. By contrast, the metaphor is maintained in the *Rig-Veda*, where *Sūrya-* the sun god is both bridegroom and horse of the dawn goddess *Uṣas-*. There is even a special word that conveys both functions of *Sūrya-*, namely *márya-* (*RV* 1.115.2, 7.76.3). In fact, the metaphorical equation of horse and bridegroom is built into various rituals of Indic society, such as that of initiation, and a key to this equation is the same word *márya-* and its Iranian cognate.[3]

§34. Significantly, there is a corresponding Greek attestation of such a metaphorical equation, in the context of a wedding song:

'Υμὴν 'Υμήν·
τὰν Διὸς οὐρανίαν ἀείδομεν,
τὰν ἐρώτων πότνιαν, τὰν παρθένοις
γαμήλιον 'Αφροδίταν.
πότνια, σοὶ τάδ' ἐγὼ νυμφεῖ' ἀείδω,
Κύπρι θεῶν καλλίστα,
τῷ τε νεόζυγι σῷ
πώλῳ τὸν ἐν αἰθέρι κρύπτεις,
σῶν γάμων γένναν

Hymen, Hymen!
We sing the celestial daughter of Zeus,
the Mistress of Love, the one who gets maidens united in matrimony,
  Aphrodite.
My Lady, I sing this wedding song to you,

§33n2. On the morphology of **Lampetíē**, see Nagy 1973.164n72; also Frame 1978.135–137 on Indic *Nā́satyā.*
§33n3. On the meaning and contexts of *márya-*: Wikander 1938.22–30, 81–85, esp. 84.

O Kypris, most beautiful of gods!
—and also to your newly yoked
pôlos [horse], the one you hide in the aether,
the offspring of your wedding.

Euripides Phaethon 227–235D

The **pôlos** 'horse' of Aphrodite is Hymen himself,[1] and we note that
the same word at xxiii 246 designates the horses of Eos, Phaethon
and Lampos. We also note that Hymen's epithet νεόζυγι 'newly
yoked' (line 233) marks him as Aphrodite's bridegroom (compare
the diction in Aeschylus *Persians* 541–542; Euripides *Medea* 804–805;
also *fr.* 821N). As for the appositive σῶν γάμων γένναν 'offspring of
your wedding' (line 235), it conveys that Hymen is also Aphrodite's
son. We must at the same time appreciate that this entire wedding
song to Aphrodite and Hymen is being sung in honor of **Phaéthōn**,
and that his bride-to-be is in all probability a daughter of the Sun.[2]
Finally, we note that Aphrodite here functions as τὰν Διὸς οὐρανίαν
'the celestial daughter of Zeus' (line 228). This characterization now
brings us to a third important reason for comparing the Indic
traditions about *Sūrya-* 'Sun' and *Uṣas-* 'Dawn' with the Greek
traditions about **Phaéthōn** and **Éós**.

§35. The epithets of *Uṣas-* 'Dawn' in the *Rig-Veda* prominently
include *divá(s) duhitár-* and *duhitár- divás* 'Daughter of Sky'—exact
formal cognates of the Homeric epithets **Diòs thugátēr** and **thugátēr
Diós** 'Daughter of Zeus'.[1] In the surviving traditions of Greek
poetry, however, this epithet is assigned not to Eos herself but to
Aphrodite and other goddesses.[2] When these goddesses qualify as
Diòs thugátēr/thugátēr Diós, they fulfill the inherited functions of
Eos herself,[3] and nowhere is this more apparent than in the story of
Aphrodite and Anchises. We have already seen that when Aphrodite
seduces the young hero, she herself cites the abduction of Tithonos
by Eos as precedent (*H.Aphr.* 218–238). Now we may add that
throughout this seduction episode, Aphrodite is actually called **Diòs
thugátēr** (*H.Aphr.* 81, 107, 191).

§34n1. See Diggle 1970.148–160.
§34n2. See Diggle, pp. 158–160. For an interpretation of the Phaethon myth as
preserved in the drama of Euripides, which is distinct from the Phaethon myth as
preserved in the Hesiodic tradition, see Nagy 1973.147–156.
§35n1. Schmitt 1967.169–175.
§35n2. Besides Aphrodite (III 374, etc.), we find Artemis (xx 61), Athena (IV 128,
etc.), Persephone (xi 217), Helen (iv 227), etc.
§35n3. See Boedeker 1974 for a discussion from the comparative viewpoint.

§36. The replacement of Eos as **Diòs thugátēr/thugátēr Diós** by Aphrodite and other goddesses leads to a fragmentation of her original functions. From the comparative evidence of the *Rig-Veda*, we might have expected Eos to be both the mother and the consort of a solar figure like Phaethon. Instead, the Hesiodic tradition assigns Aphrodite as consort of Phaethon, while Eos is only his mother (*Th.* 986–991). We may infer that the originally fused functions of mating with the consort and being reborn from the mother were split and divided between Aphrodite and Eos respectively. However, such a split leaves Phaethon as son of Eos simply by birth rather than by rebirth.

§37. For another instance of fragmentation in the functions of Eos, let us consider what happens to the originally fused functions of abduction, death, and preservation in the myth of Orion at v 121–124: here Eos abducts and preserves the young hero Orion, but then he is killed by Artemis. I infer that the function of causing the death of Orion has been reassigned from Eos to Artemis.[1] In this same function of causing death, Artemis actually qualifies as **thúgater Diós** (vocative) in Penelope's death wish (xx 61).[2] Eos, on the other hand, retains the function of abducting and preserving Orion. Accordingly, the Orion myth is marked by the sequence *abduction/preservation followed by death*; this pattern is the inverse of *abduction/death followed by preservation*—the sequence that marks the myth of Phaethon.[3]

§38. In contrast to the solar myth of Phaethon, the inverse sequence that marks the myth of Orion results in a scheme that is astral. We may note that the figure of Orion is in fact already an astral image in Homeric diction (v 274, XVIII 488), and that the relation of Orion's celestial movements to the Dawn is the inverse of the Sun's movements. Like the Sun, the constellation Orion rises from the Okeanos and sets in it (v 275, XVIII 489). Unlike the Sun, it rises and sets at night, not in daytime. In the summer, at threshing time, Orion starts rising before Dawn (*W&D* 598–599). In the

§37n1. I disagree with Delcourt 1966.148, who suggests that the verses about the death of Orion are interpolated.

§37n2. Even Persephone, goddess of the dead, qualifies as **Diòs thugátēr** (xi 217).

§37n3. For still another variation on a theme, consider the myth of the Pandareids (xx 66–78): here the sequence is *preservation followed by abduction/death*. Note that the Olympian goddesses who preserve the girls all qualify as **Diòs thugátēr/thugátēr Diós**: Aphrodite, Artemis, and Athena. The only exception is Hera, wife of Zeus. The word **hárpuiai** denoting the winds that abduct the girls (xx 77) is apparently suitable for such a negative situation, where abduction/death follows a period of preservation. Such a situation seems connected with the epithet **metakhróniai** 'delayed', describing the **Hárpuiai** 'Harpies' at Hesiod *Th.* 269. See §25n2.

winter, at ploughing time, Orion starts setting before Dawn (*W&D* 615–616). In summer days, the light of Dawn catches up with the rising Orion, and he can be her consort in the daytime.[n] In winter days, the light of Dawn arrives too late to keep Orion from setting into the Okeanos.

§39. One related star which does not set, however, is the **Árktos** 'Bear':

οἴη δ' ἄμμορός ἐστι λοετρῶν 'Ωκεανοῖο

She alone has no share in the baths of Okeanos.

v 275 = XVIII 489

Since the theme of plunging into the Okeanos conveys the process of death (see again xx 63–65), it follows that the exemption of Arktos from ever having to set into the Okeanos conveys her immortality. The Arktos "stalks Orion," **Ōríōna dokeúei** (v 274 = XVIII 488), and the verb **dokeúei** 'stalks' implies doom. In Homeric diction, it applies when marksmen or beasts take aim at their victims (XIII 545, XVI 313, VIII 340).[1] In the lore reported by Pausanias (8.35.6–7), the name **Árktos** applies also to Kallisto as mother of Arkas and hence progenitrix of the Arkades 'Arcadians'; she is represented as being turned into a bear and being killed by Artemis. The heroine **Kallistố** herself is the ritual antagonist of Artemis **Kallístē**, whose sanctuary is located on the "Mound of Kallisto" (Pausanias 8.35.8).[2] On the basis of such traditions, featuring an intimate nexus between Artemis and the concept of **Árktos**, we are encouraged to infer an actual identification in the astral scheme: an immortal Arktos stalks a mortal Orion at v 273–275 and XVIII 487–489, and the image implicitly retells the myth of Artemis killing Orion, explicit at v 121–124. As Odysseus is floating along on his nocturnal sea voyage, he contemplates this image of Arktos stalking Orion in the sky above (v 271–275), which Kalypso had marked out for him to fix the direction in which his raft is to sail (v 276–277). Since Kalypso

§38n. Formally, **Ōríōn** (**Ōaríōn**) seems to be connected with **óar** 'wife', **óaros** 'companionship, keeping company', etc.

§39n1. XIII 545: Antilokhos catches Thoön off guard and deals him a mortal blow. XVI 313: similarly, Phyleides kills Amphiklos. VIII 340: Hektor is compared to a hunting dog stalking a boar or lion. Cf. also Detienne/Vernant 1974.21n15.

§39n2. See Sale 1965 for a conscientious discussion of the sources and for a critical survey of previous studies on Artemis/Kallisto. I especially agree with Sale's distinguishing between goddess and heroine, although I find his treatment of the separate figures overly restrictive, partly because he offers no systematic coordination of the attested mythological variants.

herself had compared her seduction of Odysseus with the abduction of Orion by Eos (v 121), the connected theme of Orion's death from the shafts of Artemis (v 122-124) makes the image of Arktos stalking Orion at v 271-275 an ominous sign indeed for Odysseus. He is being guided away from the Island of Kalypso by a celestial sign that points to the fate awaiting him if he had stayed behind as bedmate of the immortal goddess.

§40. Such is the power of a myth that results ultimately from the fragmentation of the functions once encompassed by one figure, the pre-Olympian goddess Eos. It is through this figure that we can better appreciate the traditional nature not only of myths concerned with the immortalization of the hero but also of sundry other myths concerned with how this process can go wrong.

§41. Of course, it scarcely needs saying that we have so far managed to cover merely one type of myth concerning the immortalization of the hero. Besides this type, which centers on the theme of abduction by winds, there are doubtless other major types with other themes, other details. Here is my tentative list, surely incomplete, of alternative ways for the hero to achieve immortality:

- being struck by the thunderbolt of Zeus[1]
- plunging from a white rock into the deep waters below[2]
- being suddenly engulfed by the Earth.[3]

§41n1. This type has been at least partially treated in the preceding discussion, since the concept of **Ēlúsion** seems to be directly connected with it (cf. §20). From the standpoint of poetic diction, one of the clearest examples is the fate of Semele in Pindar *O*.2.25 (to be read in conjunction with Hesiod *Th*. 942). From the standpoint of poetic theme, the foremost example of immortalization by the thunderbolt is the fate of Herakles: as the hero is smitten by Zeus, he is elevated to Olympus as an immortal god; unfortunately, our best source for this theme is prosaic (Diodorus Siculus 4.38.4-4.39.1); see also Rohde I 320-322. Another important example on the level of theme is the myth of Phaethon as preserved in Euripides *Phaethon* (fragments edited by Diggle). In the traditions of this myth, Phaethon is struck dead by the thunderbolt of Zeus (for an extended discussion, see Nagy 1973.148-156; for the implication of Phaethon's rebirth through the river **Ēridanós**, see ibid., p. 161). Finally, note that there is a myth that tells of Erekhtheus as another hero who was struck dead by the thunderbolt of Zeus (Hyginus 46).

§41n2. See Nagy 1973.141-148, 172-173, esp. p. 145n31 on Ino Leukothea. Myth has it that Ino plunged into the deep from atop the white rock formations known as the **Skirōnídes Pétrai** (Pausanias 1.44.7-8). On her transformation from mortal to immortal, see *Odyssey* v 333-335. As an immortal, she is said to have a **bíotos** 'life' that is **áphthito-** 'unfailing' in Pindar *O*.2.29; note the parallelism at *O*.2.25-26, telling of Semele's immortalization after death from the thunderbolt of Zeus. For an interesting anecdote about the custom of singing **thrênoi** for Leukothea, see Xenophanes A 13DK (*ap.* Aristotle *Rhetoric* 1400b5).

§41n3. The discussion by Rohde I 111-145 is irreplaceable. We may wish to modify,

Ideally, we could embark on a detailed survey of these additional types, but it will suffice for us now to draw inferences from the model featuring abduction by Eos or by the divine figures that replaced her functions. Even in the case of this model, however, I dare make no claim that we have seen the whole picture. Every additional attestation would serve to enhance and even alter our perception of Eos and how she confers immortality on the hero.[4]

§42. This much, in any case, can be said with some confidence: the functions of Eos that prevail in the Greek myths have been by and large restricted to beneficent ones, in that we find her consistently promoting the immortality of the hero. The functions associated with her inherited epithet, on the other hand, remain ambivalent. We have already noted that this epithet, **Diòs thugátēr/thugátēr Diós**,[1] along with its thematic associations, has been reassigned to other goddesses, who are thereby endowed with maleficent as well as beneficent functions. The clearest example of the maleficent aspect in Homeric diction is the passage where Penelope prays to Artemis for death, invoking her in this context as **thúgater Diós** (xx 61). As for

---

however, his conclusion that there is no death involved in the process of being engulfed by the Earth. If, for example, we examine the attestations for the engulfment of Amphiaraos (Rohde I 114n1), we find that the emphasis on his being alive has to do more with his status in the here-and-now of cult than with his status at the moment of his engulfment. If we can agree that death is part of the process of engulfment, then Rohde's difficulties (I 114–115n2) with *Odyssey* xv 247 and 253 are eliminated: in these passages Amphiaraos is overtly said to have died. As for Rohde's idea that a cult name like **Zeùs Amphiáräos** implies that Amphiaraos is a "faded god" (I 125n2), there are other explanations available. Such combinations may imply that the name Amphiaraos is motivated primarily by the theme of ritual antagonism between god and hero. Cf. Chapter 8.

§41n4. In the storm that finally destroys all the remaining comrades of Odysseus (xii 403–426), the **thúella** of Zephyros (xii 409; cf. also **thúōn** at 408, 426) is directly coordinated with Zeus and the thunderbolt that he hurls at the hapless ship (xii 415–417). The storm itself was initiated by Zeus (xii 405), and it brings about a loss of **nóstos** 'safe homecoming' for the comrades (xii 419). The coordination of the **thúella** of Zephyros with the thunderbolt of Zeus in this narrative about the antithesis of immortalization serves to remind us of a local cult in Arcadia (Pausanias 8.29.1), where the following triad is worshipped: **Astrapaí**, **Thúellai**, and **Brontaí**. Note that the first and third are the personifications of lightning and thunder respectively. These traditional combinations suggest that the theme of death/immortalization by the thunderbolt of Zeus may not always have been distinct from the theme of death/immortalization by **thúellai** of wind. (There is also an interesting collocation of **thúellai** with **pūròs** . . . **olooîo** 'of baneful fire' at xii 68.)

§42n1. For the sake of convenience, I will henceforth arbitrarily refer to the nominative of this epithet by using only one word order: **Diòs thugátēr**.

the beneficent aspect, there are many examples available, and most of them are suited—no surprise—to the particular requirements of epic narrative. For instance, Athena qualifies as **Diòs thugátēr** (IV 128) when she rescues Menelaos from certain death on the battlefield (IV 127–130); in this context, she is specifically compared to a mother fostering her child (IV 130–131). This function of the **Diòs thugátēr** as a motherly goddess who preserves the hero from mortal harm is typical on the level of epic narrative.[2] On a more fundamental level, however, this function of the **Diòs thugátēr** entails not only the temporary preservation of the hero in epic action but also his permanent preservation in the afterlife. There is actually an important attestation of this basic function in epic action. Even more important, the goddess in question is not some derivative **Diòs thugátēr** but Eos herself. The only surviving attestation of her taking a direct part in epic action is the *Aithiopis*, where she translates her dead son Memnon into a state of immortality (Proclus p. 106.6–7 Allen).[3]

§43. The heroic figure Memnon, even within epic action, is ideally suited for this theme of immortalization, since tradition makes him not only son of Eos but also king of the Aithiopes (Hesiod *Th.* 985). The kingdom of the Aithiopes is situated on the banks of the Okeanos, and the Olympian gods themselves habitually go all the way to the Okeanos in order to receive sacrifice from them (I 423–424, XXIII 205–207, i 22–26).[n] And just as the world-encircling Okeanos flows in the extreme East and the extreme West, so also the kingdom of the Aithiopes is situated in the two extremities:

Αἰθίοπας, τοὶ διχθὰ δεδαίαται, ἔσχατοι ἀνδρῶν
οἱ μὲν δυσομένου Ὑπερίονος, οἱ δ' ἀνιόντος

§42n2. Other examples: Athena/Odysseus (xiii 359), Aphrodite/Paris (III 374), Aphrodite/Aeneas (V 312).

§42n3. The deeply traditional nature of the Memnon/Eos myth can be verified not only from the comparative standpoint of its Indo-European heritage. The internal evidence of iconographical representations confirms that the Memnon/Eos myth is a basic and pervasive tradition among the Hellenes: see Lung 1912, Clark and Coulsen 1978. It is in fact so much more pervasive than the parallel Sarpedon/Apollo myth of *Iliad* XVI that Clark and Coulsen consider the Iliadic story of Sarpedon's death to be modeled on that of Memnon's death. I would maintain, however, that the two stories are simply multiforms. To prove that there are artistic inadequacies in the Sarpedon/Apollo multiform that do not exist in the Memnon/Eos multiform is not to prove that one was modeled on the other.

§43n. The gods' participation in the sacrifices of the Aithiopes is conventionally pictured as a communal feast: Ch.11§9.

the Aithiopes, who are divided in two, the most remote of men:
some where Hyperion [Helios] sets, others where he rises

i 23–24

§44. This instance of *coincidentia oppositorum*,[1] where identity consists of two opposites, has an interesting parallel involving Okeanos and Eos directly. Again we are about to see how two opposite places can add up to the same place. To begin, from the overall plot of the Odyssey, we know that Odysseus is wandering in the realms of the extreme West when he comes upon the island of Aiaia (x 135). It is from Aiaia, island of Circe, that Odysseus is sent on his way to the underworld by traveling beyond the sea until he and his men reach the cosmic river Okeanos (xi 21–22).[2] Later, on the way back from the underworld, the ship of Odysseus has to leave the Okeanos before returning to Aiaia, which is now described as situated not in the extreme West but in the extreme East.[3] In fact, Aiaia now turns out to be the abode of Eos and sunrise:

αὐτὰρ ἐπεὶ ποταμοῖο λίπεν ῥόον Ὠκεανοῖο
νηῦς, ἀπὸ δ' ἵκετο κῦμα θαλάσσης εὐρυπόροιο
νῆσόν τ' Αἰαίην, ὅθι τ' Ἠοῦς ἠριγενείης
οἰκία καὶ χοροί εἰσι καὶ ἀντολαὶ Ἠελίοιο . . .

But when the ship left the stream of the river Okeanos,
and reached the waves of the sea with its wide-flung paths,
and then the Island Aiaia—and there are the abode and the dancing places
of early-born Eos, and the sunrises of Helios . . .

xii 1–4

In short, the Okeanos in the extreme East is a key to the emergence of Odysseus from his sojourn in the world of the dead—a sojourn that began when he reached the Okeanos in the extreme West.

§45. By being king of the realms along the banks of the Okeanos in the extreme East and West, the figure of Memnon is implicitly associated with a whole set of themes that center on the immortalization of the hero. We are reminded that Elysium itself is situated on the banks of the Okeanos, from which the wind Zephyros blows to reanimate mortals (iv 567–568). So too are the Isles of the Blessed (*W&D* 171), where heroes who fought and died in the Trojan War

§44n1. See also §14.
§44n2. See also Frame 1978.48–50, whose discussion takes into account the thematic intrusion of a northerly direction into the narrative.
§44n3. Cf. Rohde I 75n2.

were translated through the ultimate agency of Zeus (*W&D* 168). We see the same agency at work in the *Aithiopis*, when Eos herself asks the permission of Zeus that she may give immortality to her fallen son Memnon (Proclus p. 106.6–7 Allen).[1] The *Aithiopis* also has an important parallel to the action of Eos: the immortal Thetis translates her own son Achilles from a state of death into a state of immortality on the Island of Leuke (Proclus p. 106.14–15). To my mind, it is useless to argue, on the basis of such parallels, that the immortalization of Achilles was modeled on the immortalization of Memnon.[2] All that matters is that both are traditional themes that fit the essence of the hero in cult, and that both also fit the general pattern of the afterlife in store for the Fourth Generation of Mankind (*W&D* 167–173).

§46. Having returned to the Hesiodic Myth of the Five Generations of Mankind, we may conclude this chapter with the same theme that inaugurated the previous one. By now we see that the process of immortalization that comes after Generation IV is an essential link with the idyllic state of Generation I. Thus the picture of the hero in epic, as seen in Generations III/IV, can revert to the picture of the hero in cult, as seen in Generations I/II.[n] Even the most stylized hero of epic may get his due in cult, and in that spirit I close with two examples.

§47. For the first example, I choose a bit of lore from the Hellespont. As Pausanias surveys the paintings of Polygnotus in the Knidian Lesche at Delphi, his attention is suddenly riveted on a detail as he describes the picture of Memnon. On the hero's cloak are images of birds:

Μεμνονίδες ταῖς ὄρνισίν ἐστιν ὄνομα, κατὰ δὲ ἔτος οἱ Ἑλλησπόντιοί φασιν αὐτὰς ἐν εἰρημέναις ἡμέραις ἰέναι τε ἐπὶ τοῦ Μέμνονος τὸν τάφον, καὶ ὁπόσον τοῦ μνήματος δένδρων ἐστὶν ἢ πόας ψιλόν, τοῦτο καὶ σαίρουσιν αἱ ὄρνιθες καὶ ὑγροῖς τοῖς πτεροῖς τοῦ Αἰσήπου τῷ ὕδατι ῥαίνουσι.

And **Memnonídes** is the name of the birds. The people of the Hellespont say that every year on certain days these birds go to Memnon's grave, and where

---

§45n1. In Quintus of Smyrna II 550 ff., the agents of Eos are the winds Zephyros and Boreas, who snatch Memnon's body away (**anēreipsanto**: QS II 563). Memnon is even designated as their brother (QS II 555). The tradition that Zephyros and Boreas are the sons of Eos is also attested in Hesiod *Th.* 378–379. See Kakridis 1949.81–82.

§45n2. *Pace* Dihle 1970.18–20.

§46n. See Ch.9§§2–6.

the grave is bare of trees or grass the birds sweep through it and sprinkle it with their wings, which are wet with the water of the Aisepos.[1]

Pausanias 10.31.6

From this information, however fragmentary it may be, we discover that even a hero who has been translated into a remote state of immortality is traditionally eligible to have not only a cult but even a grave or funeral mound.[2]

§48. Of course, myths about the immortalization of a hero imply that his *body* has been regenerated, as we see from the application of the word **autós** 'himself' to the immortalized Herakles who abides on Olympus (xi 602). In Homeric diction, **autós** designates the hero's *body* after death (as at I 4), in comparison to his **psūkhḗ**, which travels to Hades (as at I 3).[1] Accordingly, the hero's remains cannot be pictured as being in his grave *once he is immortalized*, and there seems at first glance to be a conflict here with the requirements of cult, the original basis for which is the belief that the hero's bones are buried in his grave.[2] Unlike others, however, I see no conflict *so long as the promise of immortalization aims not at the here-and-now but rather at a fulfillment in the hero's future*. If this condition holds, then the ultimate aspect of the afterlife, from the standpoint of both cult and myth, turns out to be not Hades but rather Elysium, the Isles of the Blessed, and all the other variations on the theme of immortalization. Hades, on the other hand, would be the transitional aspect of the afterlife, when the **psūkhḗ** is separated from the body. Then, in a place like Elysium, body and **psūkhḗ** can be reintegrated when the Zephyros blows from the Okeanos to *reanimate* men—the word for which is **anapsū́khein** (iv 568).[3]

§49. In fact, the traditional emphasis on the hero's bones in cult represents a formal commitment to the promise of immortalization. The discipline of anthropology can help us here, with its vast reservoir of experience about parallel social institutions, taken from actual field work. On the basis of innumerable typological parallels as

---

§47n1. The translation is essentially that of Frazer 1898 I 546; see also his commentary V 387. Besides this passage from Pausanias, see also Dionysius *Ixeuticon* 1.8 and the comments of Vian 1959.28–29.

§47n2. See also §20n2.

§48n1. See Büchner 1937.116. I cannot agree with Schnaufer 1970.103–107, who argues that xi 602 is an interpolation. See also Ch.9§26n.

§48n2. See Rohde I 159–166.

§48n3. See Ch.9§28n2.

surveyed by Karl Meuli and his followers,[1] we now know that the function of bones in Hellenic cult and myth is to symbolize the ultimate regeneration not only of sacrificial animals but also of mortal men themselves. One of the prime models for this process of regeneration by way of dismembered bones is the god Dionysos himself (Diodorus Siculus 3.62.6;[2] Philodemus *De pietate*, pp. 34–38 Henrichs).[3] It is beyond my scope to offer even the briefest survey here of the themes and the sources,[4] but I must still mention an important application of the Dionysiac model to the immortalization of Achilles himself.[5] This particular application can bring us to my second example showing how an immortalized hero, no matter how stylized he may have become in the medium of epic, may still be envisioned in a context that pertains to the medium of cult.

§50. From Stesichorus *fr.* 234P, we know of a tradition that Dionysos had given a golden amphora, made by Hephaistos, to the goddess Thetis, in compensation for her having preserved him after he fled from Lykourgos by plunging into the sea (cf. VI 130–140). It is into this same golden amphora that the bones of Achilles were placed, together with those of his surrogate Patroklos, on the occasion of his funeral (xxiv 72–76; cf. XXIII 91–92).[1] From what we know about the symbolic function of bones in general and about regeneration in particular, we may see in this formal token the promise of an ultimate immortality in store for the hero of the *Iliad*.[2]

§49n1. See especially Meuli 1946, Uhsadel-Gülke 1972, Burkert 1972.

§49n2. = *Orphicorum Fragmenta* 301 Kern.

§49n3. For a brief survey of attestations: Uhsadel-Gülke 1972.40–41. Besides the 1975 article of Henrichs, I call attention to his forthcoming edition of Philodemus *De pietate*.

§49n4. For an illuminating synthesis: Detienne 1977.

§49n5. See Uhsadel-Gülke 1972.41–42.

§50n1. See Uhsadel-Gülke ibid.

§50n2. In this connection, it may be well to recall the traditions that picture an immortalized hero in the form of a solar horse, as discussed at §§33–34. Such traditions may underlie the figure of **Xánthos**, the immortal horse of Achilles (XVI 149–154). It is this Xanthos who pointedly tells Achilles that the hero's death cannot be prevented—any more than the death of Patroklos (XIX 408–417). And this affirmation of the hero's mortality is immediately preceded in the narrative by a simile comparing Achilles to Helios the Sun (XIX 398)! After the immortal horse has finished telling the mortal hero of his future death, the **Erīnúes** prevent him from speaking further (XIX 418). Perhaps the *Iliad* has here taken one segment from the cycle of heroic immortalization and stylized it with an ending imposed to suit the dimensions of the Epos. Perhaps also the figure of Xanthos conjured up a vision of Achilles beyond the narrative that ends with his death. Born on the banks of the Okeanos from the union of the Wind **Zéphuros** with an abducting gust described as a **Hárpuia** (XVI 150),

Xanthos seems a model of solar regeneration into immortality (on which see again §§23-36). We may note that heroes who have been immortalized attract the epithet **xanthós** 'blond': e.g., Rhadamanthys in Elysium (iv 564) and Ganymedes in Olympus (*H.Aphr.* 202). Menelaos is the hero who attracts this epithet by far the most frequently in the *Iliad* (III 284, IV 183, etc.) and the *Odyssey* (iii 257, 326, etc.)—and he is the only Homeric hero who is overtly said to have been immortalized (iv 561–569). Significantly, Achilles himself has hair that is **xanthó-** (I 197, XXIII 141). (In Homeric diction, Demeter is the only deity who is **xanthḗ** [V 500], and as **Dēmḗtēr Erīnús** in Arcadian cult she is actually said to have the form of a horse [Pausanias 8.25.4 ff.]. The thematic association of **Erīnús**/horse may be relevant to XIX 418, where the **Erīnúes** prevent Xanthos from speaking to Achilles of anything beyond the mention of his death.)

Part III
Praise, Blame, and the Hero

11 | On Strife and the Human Condition

§1. We have by now seen that Memnon's realm, the land of the Aithiopes, has landmarks that are parallel to those of the Golden Age and the Isles of the Blessed. By virtue of this parallelism, the land of the Aithiopes in fact affords an ideal setting for the immortality in store for Memnon after he dies the hero's death.[n] In the overall myth of the Aithiopes, however, Memnon's final immortalization is not the only theme that serves as a contrast with the here-and-now of the human condition. The land of the Aithiopes is also the setting for another such contrasting theme: the communion of gods and men. This theme in turn will be a key to our understanding the social functions of praise and blame.

§2. The Olympian gods have a custom of traveling all the way to the ends of the Earth, to the banks of the Okeanos, for the purpose of feasting with the native Aithiopes (I 423–424, XXIII 205–207, i 22–26). In the *spatial* perspective, these Aithiopes are the **éskhatoi andrôn** (i 23), the most remote humans in the universe.[n] Moreover, the gods had once also feasted with the earliest humans—those most remote in the *temporal* perspective of mythopoeic thinking. The following story, designed as an ideal that contrasts with the human condition, emerges from two separate types of Hesiodic narrative.

§3. We begin with Hesiod *fr.* 1MW, the first part of a catalogue that accounts for heroes born of female mortals and male immortals. As such, it complements Hesiod *Th.* 965–1020, a catalogue that accounts for heroes born of female immortals and male mortals.[1] In

§1n. Memnon's immortalization is actually unique, to the extent that the realm in which he lived before his death as a hero is also appropriate as the setting for his afterlife. For Memnon, the afterlife is by implication a homecoming. In the diction of archaic Greek poetry, the appropriate words for this theme are those containing the root *nes-; see Frame 1978.

§2n. See Ch.10§43.

§3n1. In fact, the text of our *Theogony* ends with the same two verses (*Th.*

both catalogues, the heroes born from the mating of mortals and immortals qualify as "children who look like the gods" (*Th.* 1020 and *fr.* 1.5 Merkelbach 1968.128–129).[2] Moreover, the catalogue of Hesiod *fr.* 1 presents its mortal mothers as parallel to such mortal fathers as we see in the catalogue of *Th.* 965–1020. The mortal males and females are formally correlated as ἀνέρες ἠδὲ γυναῖκες 'men and women' at *fr.* 1.9, corresponding to the ἀνδράσιν 'men' of *Th.* 967 and the γυναικῶν 'women' of *Th.* 1021 = *fr.* 1.1 respectively.[3] These men and women are distinguished from mortals in the here-and-now not only by virtue of having mated with the gods but also by virtue of having feasted with them:

ξυναὶ γὰρ τότε δαῖτες ἔσαν, ξυνοὶ δὲ θόωκοι
ἀθανάτοις τε θεοῖσι καταθνητοῖς τ' ἀνθρώποις

For at that time they had feasts [<u>**daís**</u> plural] together and they sat together, the immortal gods and the mortal men.

Hesiod fr. 1.6–7MW

The adverb τότε 'at that time' (verse 6) makes explicit the temporal remoteness of this state of affairs.

§4. There are further details about these primeval mortals: some lived for a long time (οἱ μὲν δηρὸν ... : *fr.* 1.11), while others died suddenly (τοὺς δ' εἶθ[αρ] ... : *fr.*1.12).[1] This description is parallel to that of the Golden and Silver Generations in the *Works and Days*.[2] There members of the Silver Generation are set off from the Golden in that they died soon after reaching adolescence (*W&D* 132–133).[3] Whereas the Golden Generation "lived like gods" (ὥστε θεοὶ δ'

1021–1022) that begin Hesiod *fr.* 1 (1–2). For a helpful discussion of the complementary relationship between *fr.* 1 and the *Theogony* as we have it, see Merkelbach 1968.

§3n2. Among these heroes are Memnon (*Th.* 984) and Achilles (*Th.* 1007).

§3n3. This correlation *within* the text of *fr.* 1 leads me to disagree with Merkelbach's suggestion (1968.132–133) that Hesiod *Th.* 965–1020 is a passage that had been inserted between *Th.* 964 and *Th.* 1021 (= *fr.* 1.1MW) after the verses of *fr.* 1MW had already been composed. The ἀνέρες of ἀνέρες ἠδὲ γυναῖκες at *fr.* 1.9 presupposes the contents of *Th.* 965–1020.

§4n1. The text is fragmentary beyond the words quoted, but the sense seems clear; see Merkelbach's collection of restorations (1968). I should add that the antithesis οἱ μὲν δηρὸν ... τοὺς δ' εἶθ[αρ] 'some for a long time ... others suddenly ... ' (Hesiod *fr.* 1.11–12) is set up with the phrase οὐδ' ἄρα ἰσαίωνες ... 'they [were] not with equal spans of life ... ' (Hesiod *fr.* 1.8).

§4n2. Cf. Merkelbach 1968.126, who notes a parallelism with the Golden Age. There is no mention, however, of the antithesis discussed at n1 above.

§4n3. On the prodigiously long lifespan of the Golden Generation, cf. Hesiod *fr.* 356MW.

ἔζωον: *W&D* 112), the men of the Silver Generation lost their heritage of a godlike existence. The reason given is that they refused to perform the proper sacrifices to the gods (*W&D* 136–137). As we have already seen,[4] their refusal is also defined in the same narrative tradition as their failure to give the proper **tīmaí** to the gods (*W&D* 138–139). Unfortunately for us, the parallel narrative of Hesiod *fr.* 1 (and beyond) is not complete enough to reveal explicitly how its mortals of yore came to lose their heritage of a godlike existence. There is an important clue, however, in a detail that we have already noted: these mortals used to have 'feasts' = **daís** [plural] with the gods (Hesiod *fr.* 1.6–7). Furthermore, this detail meshes with the story of Prometheus as it is told in the *Theogony*.

§5. Prometheus provokes Zeus in particular and the gods in general by tricking them into accepting as their portion the bones of a slaughtered ox and by reserving the edible meat for humanity (Hesiod *Th.* 536–557).[1] All this is presented as happening "at a time when the gods and mortal men *were having a definitive settlement*":[2]

... ὅτ' <u>ἐκρίνοντο</u> θεοὶ θνητοί τ' ἄνθρωποι

Hesiod Th. 535

The preceding passage implies a combination that is explicit in the following parallel:[3]

αὐτὰρ ἐπεί ῥα πόνον μάκαρες θεοὶ ἐξετέλεσσαν
Τιτήνεσσι δὲ <u>τιμάων κρίναντο</u> βίηφι ...

But when the blessed gods completed their effort
and <u>had a definitive settlement of</u> **tīmaí**, by way of **bíē** [might], with the
    Titans ...

Hesiod Th. 881–882

The key word here is **tīmaí**, the 'honors' of cult that the Olympian gods obtain by defeating the Titans, who are rival gods (**theoí**, as at *Th.* 630, 648, etc.).[4] The primary result of their definitive settlement is *a permanent separation*, with the Olympians remaining in the sky (*Th.* 820) while the Titans are cast down and imprisoned forever

---

§4n4. Ch.9§§2–3.

§5n1. The wording that denotes the division of meat by Prometheus is **dassámenos** (*Th.* 537) and **diedássao moírās** (*Th.* 544). The verb here is **daíomai** 'divide, apportion, allot', the derivative of which is **daís** 'feast'; see Ch.7§14.

§5n2. For the translation, cf. West 1966.317.

§5n3. The significance of this parallel was pointed out by Rudhardt 1970.6.

§5n4. For the notion of **tīmḗ** as the 'honor' conferred by cult, see Ch.7§1n2, §19nn1 and 3; Ch.9§3.

underneath the earth (see especially *Th.* 729–733). Similarly, there is a definitive settlement of **tīmaí** between the gods and men when Prometheus apportions the inedibles and edibles between them. Again, the primary result is *a permanent separation*, in that mankind is relegated to the human condition—a theme central to the entire Prometheus story (*Th.* 521–616).[5]

§6. We can now see an overall parallelism with the story of the Silver Generation (*W&D* 127–142). There the setting is a sacrifice (*W&D* 136–137), and the mortals fail to give **tīmaí** to the gods (*W&D* 138–139). What results is the negation of their godlike existence (*W&D* 132–133). As for the story of Prometheus, the setting here is a feast (see especially *Th.* 537, 544),[1] which becomes from that time onward the basis of all sacrifice to the gods (*Th.* 556–557). Prometheus as the agent of mortals cheats the gods out of the edible portions (*Th.* 538–541), and this settlement (implicitly, of **tīmaí**: *Th.* 535) leads indirectly to the evils of the human condition (*Th.* 570–616).[2]

§7. The Aithiopes, then, exist in a condition that serves as a foil for the condition of ordinary mortals. For the Aithiopes, having feasts with the gods is not just a privilege: it is a sign that they are not subject to being separated permanently from the gods. Again, we recall that the landmarks of their abode are parallel to those of the Golden Age and the Isles of the Blessed.[1] By contrast, the mortals of the here-and-now have sacrifices to the gods, not feasts with them. Moreover, we have seen that the story of Prometheus in the *Theogony* derives this continuous institution of making sacrifice from the single event of a feast shared by gods and men. Of course, this feast is not the same thing as a first sacrifice. Granted, it constitutes the definitive settlement whereby the mortals and immortals get the edible meat and the inedible bones respectively. Nevertheless, this feast is only the basis of sacrifice, whereas the act of sacrifice itself entails more. Men are to have at their disposal the distribution of edible portions not only for themselves *but also for the gods*. Every city-state has its own traditions for determining what portions of the

----

§5n5. For an illuminating commentary: Vernant 1974.177–194 (cf. also Vernant 1977).

§6n1. For the key words in these verses, see §5n1.

§6n2. For the parallelism of *Th.* 570–616 with the myth of Pandora (*W&D* 53–105), see Vernant 1974.192–194.

§7n1. See §1.

edible meat—*in addition to the bones and fat*—are assigned to the gods.[2] In return, the gods have at their disposal the function of alleviating in their manifold ways the manifold evils of the human condition. Of course, the gods may even grant the ultimate alleviation, immortality after death; the inedible bones that are at their disposal are in fact the very emblem of life after death.[3]

§8. There is, then, a fundamental difference between feasting with the gods and sacrificing to them. The Hesiodic story about the Silver Generation actually anticipates the human condition of these figures by describing them as men who owe sacrifice to the gods (*W&D* 135–137). Nevertheless, the nature of their offense against the gods is parallel to the offense of Prometheus. In both instances, the afflictions of the human condition are brought about by the withholding of **tīmaí** from the gods. In the context of a single event, a feast, Prometheus as the agent of humanity withholds **tīmaí** from the gods;[1] in the context of a continuous institution, sacrifice, men keep restoring **tīmaí** to them. When the Silver Generation refuses to sacrifice, the offense is the same as the primordial offense of Prometheus: the withholding of **tīmaí** from the gods.[2]

§9. In this connection, we must reexamine the evidence of diction: the vocabulary of archaic hexameter poetry does not distinguish between the feasting of men and gods together on the one hand and the sacrificing of men to gods on the other. Both the feasting and the

§7n2. See Puttkammer 1912.35. This fact has been generally overlooked until the appearance of an important article by Gill (1974), who documents the practice of depositing choice portions of meat on a given god's **trápeza**, 'table', which coexists with the practice of burning the other portions (notably the bones and fat) on the god's altar. In view of the general absence in Homeric poetry of references to setting aside choice cuts of meat for the god who receives sacrifice, Gill and others infer that the practice of depositing meat on a **trápeza** was originally distinct from the practice of burning meat on an altar. I would argue, however, that the Homeric silence on this aspect of sacrifice is for different reasons: Homeric Epos is Panhellenic, and as such it will tend to avoid any references to localized aspects of any Hellenic institution (cf. Intro. §14). To repeat: the choice of meat portions deposited on the god's **trápeza** actually varied from **pólis** to **pólis** (Gill, p. 125; cf. also Ch.7§19n3 above). Such localized variation would make this aspect of sacrifice unsuitable for Homeric presentation. One exception to the Homeric silence on the deposition of meat seems to be *Odyssey* xiv 418–438 (Gill, p. 134); even here, the description is so stylized that it is difficult to imagine what, if any, regional characteristics may be revealed. On the **trápeza** of the Sun in the land of the Aithiopes (Herodotus 3.17–26), see Vernant 1972.

§7n3. See Ch.10§49.

§8n1. See §§5–6.

§8n2. See §4.

sacrificing qualify as a **daís**. For example, Zeus calls the portions sacrificed to him on the altar his **daís** (IV 48, XXIV 69). The very event of a sacrifice may in fact be called simply **daís** (iii 33), without such qualifiers as **theoû** 'of the god' (as at iii 420, where **daís** refers to the same event as at iii 33).[1] Conversely, when the gods come to feast with the Aithiopes, their mutual **daís** (as at I 424, i 26) has the trappings of a sacrifice: **hekatómbai** 'hecatombs' (XXIII 206; cf. i 25) and **hīrá** 'sacred rites' (XXIII 207).[2] This ambivalence in the meaning of **daís** is of course due directly to the derivation of the noun from the verb **daíomai** 'divide, apportion, allot'.[3] A **daís**, then, is a 'division' not only of meat portions (a feast) but also of the **tīmaí** that go with them (a sacrifice).

§10. We are now ready to consider the wording that designates the primordial offense of Prometheus. In the process of cheating the gods out of **tīmaí** that correspond to meat portions, Prometheus caused **éris** 'strife' and made Zeus angry. This theme of **éris** introduces the entire story about the deceit of Prometheus—a story that begins with the following explanation for the anger of Zeus:

οὕνεκ' ἐρίζετο βουλὰς ὑπερμενέϊ Κρονίωνι

because he [Prometheus] <u>had a conflict of wills</u> with the mighty son of Kronos.[n]

Hesiod Th. 534

§11. Here at *Th.* 534, both the verb ἐρίζετο 'had **éris** [strife, conflict]' and the noun βουλάς [**boulé** = 'will, design, plan'] designate essential themes in the story. For a better understanding, we must compare the beginning of the *Cypria*, where the Trojan War is motivated by the **boulé** 'Will' of Zeus (*fr.* 1.7 Allen), who wants to depopulate Earth (*fr.* 1.1–7); significantly, the entire war is in fact designated as **éris** 'strife' (*fr.* 1.5).

§12. Moreover, the beginning of the *Cypria* tells how the war actually began with the appearance of **Éris** 'Strife' personified (Proclus summary p. 102.14 Allen). She came to a feast shared by gods and men, the Wedding of Peleus and Thetis (*Cypria*/Proclus p. 102.14–15), and there she caused a **neîkos** 'quarrel, fight' (p.102.15)

§9n1. See Ch.7§14.
§9n2. Cf. also Ch.7§16n1.
§9n3. See again Ch.7§14.
§10n. On the omission of Prometheus' name at the start of this narrative: West 1966.317.

involving the goddesses Hera, Athena, and Aphrodite (p. 102.15–16). The **éris** 'strife' and **neîkos** 'quarrel' then extend to the human dimension, as Paris is asked to judge which of the three goddesses is supreme (p. 102.16–17). Paris of course chooses Aphrodite and wins Helen, whose abduction causes the Trojan War; it too is directly called **éris** in the *Cypria* (*fr.* 1.5 Allen). Helen's own words in the *Iliad* itself motivate the Trojan War in this way: εἴνεκ' ἐμῆς ἔριδος 'on account of **éris** over me' (III 100). So also when the doomed Hektor is about to be killed by Achilles, he calls the abduction of Helen νείκεος ἀρχή 'the beginning of the **neîkos**' (XXII 116).[n]

§13. So far, we have merely noted a parallelism in theme and diction between the entire story of the Trojan War on the one hand and, on the other, a single-verse introduction to the story of Prometheus (Hesiod *Th.* 534). In the latter instance, the **éris** 'strife' between Zeus and Prometheus concerns their respective **boulaí** 'wills, designs' affecting humanity. In the former instance, we have seen that the **boulé** 'Will' of Zeus is that men should have **éris** 'strife' and **neîkos** 'quarreling', which is to result in the depopulation of Earth in the form of the Trojan War. Now we are ready to observe Hesiod *fr.* 204.95–123MW, a text that presents an actual convergence between the main themes in the overall story of the Trojan War and those in the story of Prometheus.

§14. At line 95 of Hesiod *fr.* 204MW, there is a compressed mention of a traditional theme that we find developed throughout the *Iliad*: the division of the Olympian gods into pro-Achaean and pro-Trojan factions during the Trojan War.[1] At line 96, we are told the ultimate source of this division: ἐξ ἔριδος 'ever since the **éris**'. The reference here is to the strife in the traditional story about the Judgment of Paris; then at lines 96–123, there follows a fragmentary passage that tells about the Will of Zeus and how it had caused the Trojan War.[2] This theme is more comprehensive here than at *Cypria fr.* 1 Allen, where the Will of Zeus entails the deaths of heroes in the

§12n. Note the epithet of Helen in the anonymous lyric fragment 1014 Page: **poluneikḗs**. Note too the usage of ἀρχή: whereas the theme of Helen is νείκεος ἀρχή 'the beginning of the **neîkos**', the theme of Achilles is πήματος ἀρχή 'the beginning of the **pêma** [pain]' (viii 81; cf. Ch.4§6 and §7n1).

§14n1. Cf. Stiewe 1963.5.

§14n2. Cf. Stiewe, pp. 4–6. I should add that there is no need to assume that the text of Hesiod *fr.* 204MW is based on one or several other *texts*; it is enough to say that the text is based on various *traditions* that occur also in the *Cypria* and in the *Iliad*.

Trojan War.[3] The gaps in the text leave many important questions without answers, but one additional detail is clear: besides entailing the death of heroes in the Trojan War (see especially lines 118-119),[4] the Will of Zeus also entails *the permanent separation of gods and men.* The crucial lines read as follows:

ἀλλ' οἳ μ[ὲ]ν μάκ[α]ρες κ[. . . . . . .]ν ὡς τὸ πάρος περ
χωρὶς ἀπ' ἀν[θ]ρώπων [βίοτον κα]ὶ ἤθε' ἔχωσιν

but so that the blessed gods . . . , as before,
may have their way of life and their accustomed places apart from men

Hesiod *fr.* 204.102-103MW

This detail shows that the **éris** willed by Zeus causes not only the Trojan War in particular but the human condition in general.[5]

§15. Returning to the expression ἐρίζετο βουλάς 'had a conflict [**éris**] of wills [**boulaí**]' at Hesiod *Th.* 534, we now see that the story of Prometheus here is a mythological variant of the story of Troy as told in Hesiod *fr.* 204MW, in that both stories are designed to explain the human condition in terms of **éris** 'strife, conflict'. In the story of the Trojan War, the **boulé** 'will' of Zeus causes **éris** for the gods and then for men, who had feasted with the gods. In the story of Prometheus, there is a primordial **éris** between the **boulé** of Zeus and the **boulé** of the deceitful Titan acting on behalf of men, men who had feasted with the gods. In both stories, **éris** disrupts the communication of men with gods, bringing about the human condition.

§16. Having observed the fundamental nature of **éris** 'strife' in these mythological visions of mankind's essence, we are ready to consider the social implications of the word itself. Our starting point will be another key word, **neîkos** 'quarrel, fight'. In the story about the Judgment of Paris, we have seen that the personified figure **Éris** had brought about a **neîkos** involving the goddesses Hera, Athena, and Aphrodite, and that Paris is then asked to judge which of the

§14n3. The Will of Zeus at the beginning of the *Cypria* is in turn more comprehensive than at the beginning of the *Iliad* (I 1-7), where it entails the deaths of heroes only in that portion of the Trojan War which begins with the **mênis** 'anger' of Achilles. See Ch.5§25 (esp. n2), Ch.7§17, Ch.10§17.

§14n4. Note the close parallelism in diction between *Iliad* I 3-4 and these lines 118-119 of Hesiod *fr.* 204MW.

§14n5. Note the extended metaphor at Hesiod *fr.* 204.123 ff.MW, which immediately follows the passage about the Will of Zeus: men die much as leaves fall from trees. On this theme of mortality, see Ch.10§6.

three is supreme (*Cypria*/Proclus p. 102.14–19).[1] From the Iliadic allusion to the story, we now see that Paris in effect rejected Hera and Athena by virtue of choosing Aphrodite and further that this rejection is presented as a **neîkos** against these two goddesses:

ὃς νείκεσσε θεάς, ὅτε οἱ μέσσαυλον ἵκοντο,
τὴν δ' ᾔνησ' ἥ οἱ πόρε μαχλοσύνην ἀλεγεινήν

[Paris] who blamed [made **neîkos** against] the goddesses [Hera and Athena],
    when they came to his courtyard,
but he praised her [Aphrodite] who gave him the baneful pleasure of sex.

XXIV 29–30

My task now is to show that the verb **neikéō** (which I translate as 'blame', from the noun **neîkos**)[2] and the verb **ainéō** ('praise', from the noun **aînos**)[3] reflect two antithetical social functions expressed in two formal modes of discourse.

§16n1. See §12.
§16n2. The translation "blame," like all other translations, is only partially adequate. In his suggestive discussion of the verb **neikéō/neikeíō**, Adkins (1960.59n17) weighs such translations as "upbraid" and "chide," finally deciding on "abuse" in order to emphasize that "in a society which does not distinguish between moral error and mistake, it is impossible to distinguish mockery, abuse, and rebuke. There is only one situation: unpleasant words directed at a man who has *in fact* fallen short of the expectations of society."
§16n3. I postpone any definition of **aînos** until later.

12 | Poetry of Praise, Poetry of Blame

§1. As we see from Georges Dumézil's comparative study *Servius et la Fortune*, Indo-European society operated on the principle of counterbalancing praise and blame, primarily through the medium of poetry.[1] This state of affairs is most overtly preserved in the evidence of Indic and Old Irish,[2] but we must now also include Greek. Thanks to the brilliant synthesis of Marcel Detienne, we are in a position to see the opposition of praise and blame as a fundamental principle in the archaic Greek community.[3]

§2. It is convenient to start by looking at such conservative Dorian societies as that of Sparta. The clearest evidence comes from Plutarch's *Lycurgus*: in Sparta, the law was based on two fundamental principles, namely **épainos** 'praise' and **psógos** 'blame'.[1] The social function of this antithesis can be seen from the objects of praise and blame respectively: **kalôn épainos** 'praise of the noble' compared to **aiskhrôn psógos** 'blame of the base' (Plutarch *Lycurgus* 8.3–4, 25.3; also 14.5, 26.6). Furthermore, the prime medium of praise and blame was poetry (14.5, 26.6).[2]

§3. In the traditional Dorian praise poetry of Pindar and Bacchylides, we find the most striking and most appealing sort of confirmation about the poetic function of praise and blame. Not only is praise poetry programmatically called **épainos** or **aînos** (verb **epainéō** or **ainéō**) by the praise poetry itself but its opposite is specified as **psógos** (verb **pségō**),[1] as in the following words of Pindar:

§1n1. Dumézil 1943; updated in Dumézil 1969.
§1n2. For a convenient collection and correlation of facts, with bibliography, see Caerwyn Williams 1972 and Ward 1973. Cf. also Watkins 1976.
§1n3. Detienne 1973.18–27.
§2n1. For details, see Detienne 1973.19.
§2n2. See also Detienne, pp. 18–20.
§3n1. For a survey of passages, see Detienne 1973.21. For the programmatic character of **aînos/épainos** and **ainéō/epainéō** as designating the poetic medium of

ξεῖνός εἰμι· σκοτεινὸν ἀπέχων ψόγον,
ὕδατος ὥτε ῥοὰς φίλον ἐς ἄνδρ' ἄγων
κλέος ἐτήτυμον αἰνέσω

I am a guest-stranger. Keeping away dark blame [psógos]
and bringing genuine kléos, like streams of water, to a man who is phílos,
I will praise [verb ainéō] him.

Pindar N.7.61–63

In other words, the actual antithesis between aînos/épainos and psógos is in itself a poetic tradition. Besides the programmatic words aînos/épainos and ainéō/epainéō, there are other elements in the diction of praise poetry that serve to designate its own function, the most important of which is kléos (as in the passage quoted, Pindar N.7.62).[2] The traditional diction of the praise poetry composed by Pindar and Bacchylides also has inherited, besides psógos, several other words that serve to mark blame as a foil for praise:[3]

éris 'strife'	ἔριδα	Pi.N.4.93
vs. ainéō 'praise'	αἰνέων	"
neîkos 'quarrel, fight'	νείκει	Pi.N.8.25
~ erízō 'have éris'	ἐρίζει	.22
~ phthoneroí 'those who have phthónos'	φθονεροῖσιν	.21
~ óneidos 'blame, reproach'[4]	ὄνειδος	.33
óneidos	"	"
vs. ainéō 'praise'	αἰνέων αἰνητά	.39
vs. kléos 'glory'	κλέος	.36
mômos 'blame, reproach'	μῶμος	Ba.13.202
vs. ainéō 'praise'[5]	αἰνείτω	.201

---

praise, I cite in particular Pindar O.6.12 and Bacchylides 5.16; see also the discussion of praise poetry by Bundy 1962.35.

§3n2. See Maehler 1963.85. As we have seen, the word kléos within the genre of epic denotes the glory conferred upon the hero by epic; see Ch.1§2. Note too the word etétumon 'true, genuine' applied to kléos here in Pindar N.7.63; the significance of this epithet will be discussed at Ch.14§12n3.

§3n3. The list I give here is of course incomplete. Moreover, the traditional diction of epic poetry has inherited its corresponding set of words indicating blame, as the discussion that follows will reveal (see esp. Ch.14§14). Of course, I do not mean to suggest that all the words in this list intrinsically indicate the concept of blame. In the case of a word like phthónos, for example, I will argue only that it indicates blame when it is being contrasted explicitly or implicitly with praise.

§3n4. On the Pindaric passage in which all these words occur, see Köhnken 1971.24–34.

§3n5. Cf. a parallel contrast of mômos and (ep)ainéō 'praise' in Theognis 169

phthónos 'envy, greed'	φθόνος	Ba.13.200
~ mômos	μῶμος	.202
vs. ainéō	αἰνείτω	.201
phthónos	φθόνος	Pi.*P*.1.85
~ mômos	μῶμος	.82
phthónos	φθόνον	Ba.5.188
vs. ainéō[6]	αἰνεῖν	"

I draw special attention to the first two entries in the list, **éris** and **neîkos**. In Homeric and Hesiodic poetry, we have seen that these words are appropriate for motivating the Trojan War in particular and the human condition in general. Now we see in the diction of praise poetry that **éris** and **neîkos** also can have a far more specific function: designating the opposite of praise poetry.

§4. Of course, blame is inimical to praise in praise poetry only if it is the blame of the noble, since the conceit of praise poetry is that it praises the noble only, not the base. For an illustration, let us isolate the word **phthónos** 'envy, greed' and examine its use as a foil for praise poetry within such poetry. In Bacchylides 5.188 and 13.199–201, we have just seen **phthónos** being directly contrasted with **ainéō** 'praise' (αἰνεῖν and αἰνείτω respectively).[1] He who *praises* (εὖ λέγειν 'speak well': Ba.3.67) is described as ὅστις μὴ φθόνῳ πιαίνεται 'one who does not fatten himself on **phthónos**' (Ba.3.67–68).[2] I draw attention to this combination in view of the following expression in Pindaric praise poetry:

ψογερὸν Ἀρχίλοχον βαρυλόγοις ἔχθεσιν
πιαινόμενον . . .

Archilochus, having **psógos**, fattening himself on heavy-worded hatreds . . .

Pindar *P*.2.55–56.

We see here a programmatic description of blame poetry (witness the epithet **psogerós** 'having **psógos**') as the opposite of praise poetry, in the specific context of rejecting blame within a poem of praise:

ἐμὲ δὲ χρεὼν
φεύγειν δάκος ἀδινὸν κακαγοριᾶν . . .

(μωμεύμενος and αἰνεῖ), 875–876 (μωμήσαιτο and ἐπαινήσαι), and 1079–1080 (μωμήσομαι and αἰνήσω); also in Alcman 1.43–44P (μωμῆσθαι and ἐπαινῆν).

§3n6. Cf. ἀφθόνητος αἶνος 'praise [**aînos**] without **phthónos**' at Pindar *O*.11.7.

§4n1. The concept of **mômos** 'blame, reproach' is associated with the **phthonéontes** 'those who have **phthónos**' in Pindar *O*.6.74.

§4n2. Cf. also Köhnken 1971.34–36.

but I must avoid
the relentless bite of speaking ill . . .

Pindar P.2.52–53

§5. Where the language of blame is unjustified, it is specifically correlated with imagery that dwells on the devouring of meat. As we have just observed, blaming is made parallel to biting; also, the blamer is said to fatten himself on **phthónos** or on the hatreds of **psógos**. As we look for further development of this imagery, we come upon the following passage:[1]

> ὄψον δὲ λόγοι φθονεροῖσιν,
> ἅπτεται δ᾽ ἐσλῶν ἀεί, χειρόνεσσι δ᾽ οὐκ ἐρίζει.
> κεῖνος καὶ Τελαμῶνος δάψεν υἱόν,
> φασγάνῳ ἀμφικυλίσαις.
> ἦ τιν᾽ ἄγλωσσον μέν, ἦτορ δ᾽ ἄλκιμον, λάθα κατέχει
> ἐν λυγρῷ νείκει· μέγιστον δ᾽ αἰόλῳ ψεύ-
> δει γέρας ἀντέταται

Words are a morsel for those who have **phthónos**.[2]
He [one who has **phthónos**][3] grabs at the noble rather than have **éris** with the inferior.
That one [Odysseus][4] even devoured the son of Telamon [Ajax], skewering him on the sword.[5]
One who is unversed in speech but stout at heart is held down by Neglect[6] on the occasion of a baneful **neîkos**.
And the biggest honorific portion is handed over to intricate Deceit.

Pindar N.8.21–25

At line 21, we see that **phthónos** is the food of the blamer only in a figurative sense: the language of **phthónos** is his means for getting a

---

§5n1. Cf. Köhnken 1971.30–32.

§5n2. I.e., the language of **phthónos** is like eating.

§5n3. My translation veers from the generally accepted interpretation, according to which the subject of ἅπτεται and ἐρίζει at line 22 is to be supplied as φθόνος, implied by φθονεροῖσιν at line 21 (for bibliography, see Köhnken 1971.30n38 and 33n57). The reasons for my interpretation will emerge from the discussion that follows. I should point out, however, that the main thesis of this discussion, that **phthónos** entails the "devouring" of a good hero, will not depend on whether or not my interpretation here is accepted.

§5n4. In line with my interpretation (n3), I posit that the thematic development is from the general to the specific: from "one who has **phthónos**" to "Odysseus."

§5n5. I.e., Odysseus caused Ajax to kill himself with his own sword. Cf. Pindar *I*.4.37, where the subject of ταμών 'cutting' is Ajax himself.

§5n6. Nonremembrance is the opposite of being remembered *by poetry*; on this traditional theme, see Detienne 1973.21–27. Cf. also Ch.1§3 above.

meal, not the meal itself.[7] But then, we also see at lines 22–23 of Pindar's praise poem a ghastly extension of the same theme: not only does the man of **phthónos** get a meal, but the meal may actually turn out to be his victim! The verb **háptomai** at line 22 (ἅπτεται) connotes not only 'grab at food', as at *Odyssey* iv 60 and x 379, but even 'grab at a victim with the teeth', as at *Iliad* VIII 339, where the subject of the verb is **kúōn** 'dog'. Similarly with δάψεν 'devoured' at line 23 of Pindar's poem: in Homeric diction, the same verb **dáptō** can be applied in contexts where corpses are 'devoured' by dogs rather than by the fire of cremation (XXIII 183; cf. XXII 339). So also with **piaínō** 'fatten' in the expression φθόνῳ πιαίνεται 'fattens himself on **phthónos**' at Bacchylides 3.68 and βαρυλόγοις ἔχθεσιν / πιαινόμενον 'fattening himself on heavy-worded hatreds' at Pindar *P.*2.55–56: in Homeric diction, dogs devour specifically the fat of uncremated corpses (VIII 379–380, XI 818, XIII 831–832).[8] In effect, then, the language of praise poetry presents the language of unjustified blame as parallel to the eating of heroes' corpses by dogs.

§6. Significantly, the language of epic itself quotes the language of blame within the framework of narrating quarrels,[1] and a prominent word of insult within such direct quotations is **kúōn** 'dog' and its derivatives.[2] For example, Achilles insults Agamemnon by calling him **kunôpa** 'having the looks of a dog' (I 159) and **kunòs ómmat' ékhōn** 'having the eyes of a dog' (I 225)[3] in the context of their quarrel, which is designated by **éris** and its derivative **erízō** (I 6, 8, 177, 210, 277, 319; II 376), as well as by **neîkos** (II 376).[4] The actual words of blame spoken by Achilles to Agamemnon are designated as **óneidos** 'blame, reproach' by the victim himself (ὀνείδεα: I 291; cf. I 211).[5] Similarly, in Pindar's praise poem, the quarrel between Ajax and Odysseus qualifies as an **éris** (ἐρίζει: *N.*8.22) and as a **neîkos** (νείκει: *N.*8.25). In addition, the unjustified blame of Ajax by Odysseus qualifies as **óneidos** (ὄνειδος: *N.*8.33). But here the praise poem itself insults Odysseus—not by calling him **kúōn** 'dog' but

§5n7. We see a clear instance of this theme in *Odyssey* xviii 1–19, on which see further at §9.

§5n8. At Pindar *N.*9.23, the verb **piaínō** is applied in a context where the corpses of the Seven against Thebes "fatten" the smoke of cremation; at line 24, the funeral pyres "feasted on" (**daísanto**) the heroes. (Only Amphiaraos is exempt: lines 24–26.)

§6n1. Cf. Ch.3§3n.

§6n2. See Faust 1970; also Faust 1969.109–125.

§6n3. Cf. IX 373.

§6n4. Cf. Ch.7§17.

§6n5. From the standpoint of Agamemnon, the blame is of course unjustified.

rather by describing his actions as those of a dog feeding on human flesh. Whereas the righteous indignation of Achilles is formalized in his words of justified blame against Agamemnon,[6] the corresponding indignation of Ajax is taken up by the praise poem itself. But the words of justified blame in Pindar's *Nemean* 8 are intended not so much against Odysseus but against the unjustified blame in the quarrel that led to the besting of the heroic Ajax by his deceitful adversary.

§7. After concluding its retrospective on the quarrel between Ajax and Odysseus, Pindar's praise poem has this to say about the language of blame:

> ἐχθρὰ δ' ἄρα πάρφασις ἦν καὶ πάλαι,
> αἱμύλων μύθων ὁμόφοι-
> τος, δολοφραδής, κακοποιὸν ὄνειδος

Hateful misrepresentation has existed for a long time,
companion of wily words, deviser of deceit,
maleficent **óneidos**.

Pindar N.8.32–33

These words serve as a foil for the words that later conclude Pindar's *Nemean* 8, where praise poetry itself gets the ultimate praise:[1]

> ἦν γε μὰν ἐπικώμιος ὕμνος
> δὴ πάλαι καὶ πρὶν γενέσθαι
> τὰν Ἀδράστου τάν τε Καδμείων ἔριν

The encomium[2] has existed for a long time
—even before the **éris** between Adrastos and the Thebans ever happened.[3]

Pindar N.8.50–51

§6n6. Significantly, Achilles himself is not called a **kúon** 'dog' (or any of its variants) by any of his adversaries in the *Iliad* (see the survey by Faust 1970.10–19, column D). When Achilles is blamed for his savagery, the *primary* image is that of a lion (see Ch.7§22), not a dog; this observation may serve as a supplement to the interesting discussion by Faust 1970.24. I concede that the verb **hélkō**, which denotes the dragging of Hektor's body by Achilles (XXII 401, XXIV 52; cf. XXIV 21), also denotes the dragging of corpses by dogs (see especially XXII 335–336). Nevertheless, the verb that denotes the dragging of victims by lions is **hélkō** (XI 239, XVIII 581).

§7n1. Cf. Köhnken 1971.34–35; also Carey 1976.37.

§7n2. For the function of the praise poem as a "song [**húmnos**] of the **kômos**" (adjective **epikómios**; or **enkómios**, as at Pindar *N.*1.7, *O.*2.47, etc.), see §20.

§7n3. On the function of the Nemean Games as a ritual extension of "the **éris** between Adrastos and the Thebans," cf. Köhnken 1971.35. On the theme of the strife between Eteokles and Polyneikes, see Ch.14§12n3. The strife is caused by the curse of Oedipus, to whom his sons had given the wrong **moîra** of meat (see Ch.7§16n3); by doing so, Eteokles and Polyneikes were in effect making **óneidos** against their father (**oneideíontes**: *Thebais fr.* 3.2 Allen).

Thus praise poetry recognizes its own deeply traditional nature by describing itself as a primordial institution. The ideal opposite of **óneidos** (*N*.8.34) is presented as **kléos** (*N*.8.36), which the righteous man wishes to leave behind for his children when he dies (*N*.8. 36–37). In the same connection, the praise poem presents the function of the righteous man as the function of the praise poet himself:

αἰνέων αἰνητά, μομφὰν δ' ἐπισπείρων ἀλιτροῖς

praising what is to be praised, sowing blame upon what is unrighteous[4]

Pindar *N*.8.39

§8. We may round out our survey of the word **phthónos** 'envy, greed' as a foil for praise poetry by considering a particularly suggestive occurrence at the beginning of *Odyssey* xviii. Here we see the beggar Iros making **neîkos** against Odysseus (νεικείων: xviii 9), who is himself disguised as a beggar; in his quoted **neîkos** (xviii 10–13), Iros commands Odysseus to get out of his way, threatening that the present **éris** between the two of them (ἔρις: xviii 13) may escalate from verbal to physical violence (cf. xviii 38–39).[1] The disguised master of the household refuses to budge from the doorway, answering Iros with these words:

δαιμόνι', οὔτε τί σε ῥέζω κακὸν οὔτ' ἀγορεύω,
οὔτε τινὰ φθονέω δόμεναι καὶ πόλλ' ἀνελόντα.
οὐδὸς δ' ἀμφοτέρους ὅδε χείσεται, οὐδέ τί σε χρὴ
ἀλλοτρίων φθονέειν· δοκέεις δέ μοι εἶναι ἀλήτης
ὥς περ ἐγών, ὄλβον δὲ θεοὶ μέλλουσιν ὀπάζειν

You **daimónios**![2] I am harming you by neither deed nor word.
And I do not begrudge [I have no **phthónos**] that someone should be a
    giver, after having been a taker in great quantities.
But this threshold will accommodate both of us, and you should not
have **phthónos** about the property of others. You seem to be a beggar like
    me,
and it is the gods who are likely to grant **ólbos** [prosperity].

xviii 15–19

The collocation of **ólbos** and **phthónos** here is striking in view of a traditional theme found time and again in the actual words of praise

§7n4. For **momphá** as 'blame' cf. also the corresponding verb **mémphomai** as at Pindar *N*.1.24 (μεμφομένοις).

§8n1. Note that the verbal **éris/neîkos** at the Wedding of Peleus and Thetis escalates into the physical **éris/neîkos** of the Trojan War; see Ch.11§12. To put it another way: the words **éris/neîkos** apply not only to the language of blame but also to the action of physical combat.

§8n2. On the use of this vocative: Brunius-Nilsson 1955.

poetry: that **ólbos** comes from the gods to the righteous and that it attracts the **phthónos** of the unrighteous (see especially Pindar *N*.11.29). Ironically, the **ólbos** of Odysseus himself is now being threatened by the suitors, whose "messenger" Iros has so much **phthónos** as to hinder our hero from even entering his own household.[3] Without having to identify himself as the owner, however, Odysseus warns Iros not "to have **phthónos** about the property of others" (ἀλλοτρίων φθονέειν: xviii 18).

§9. Such excessive **phthónos** on the part of Iros is directly comparable to **phthónos** in its function as a traditional negative foil of praise poetry within praise poetry. As we have seen, gluttony is a prime characteristic of **phthónos** in the diction of praise poetry;[1] hence the saying "words are a morsel for those who have **phthónos**" (Pindar *N*.8.21).[2] In fact, we now see from the Homeric description of Iros that his **phthónos** is manifested in precisely this sort of gluttony; the key word is **márgos** 'gluttonous, wanton':

ἦλθε δ᾽ ἐπὶ πτωχὸς πανδήμιος, ὃς κατὰ ἄστυ
πτωχεύεσκ᾽ Ἰθάκης, μετὰ δ᾽ ἔπρεπε γαστέρι <u>μάργῃ</u>
ἀζηχὲς φαγέμεν καὶ πιέμεν· οὐδέ οἱ ἦν ἲς
οὐδὲ βίη, εἶδος δὲ μάλα μέγας ἦν ὁράασθαι

And there came a beggar,[3] belonging to all the district [**dêmos**],
who used to go begging throughout the town of Ithaca; he was renowned for
   his endless eating and drinking with his **márgē** belly.
And he had no **ís** [force], nor **bíē** [might], but in appearance he was big to
   look at.[4]

xviii 1–4

§8n3. Iros is said to get his name for being messenger of the suitors (xviii 6–7); thus the function of Îros is presented as parallel to that of Îris, messenger of the Olympian gods in the *Iliad*. I see no internal evidence that would justify our dismissing this theme as a haphazard contrivance based on the formal parallelism of Îros and Îris. Indeed, Iros may well have functioned as the figure who quotes actual messages of the suitors in more expanded versions of the story.

§9n1. §§4–5.

§9n2. See §5.

§9n3. As Calvert Watkins points out to me, the syntax in the beginning of this narrative is strikingly parallel to the syntax in what is thought to be the beginning of the comic poem known as the *Margites* (*fr.* 1W). Note that the subject of the introductory sentence in xviii 1 is **ptōkhós** 'beggar', whereas the corresponding subject in the *Margites* (*fr.* 1.1W) is **aoidós** 'singer, poet'.

§9n4. Appearances are deceiving, however. The action of the narrative will reveal that Iros indeed has no **ís** or **bíē** (on the use of **bíē** as synonym of **ís**: Ch.5§37), since he is bested by his "rival" Odysseus when their **éris** 'strife' escalates from verbal to physical combat (on which see §8n1). Accordingly, those who witness the combat call him **Á-īros** (xviii 73), which may be reconstructed as *ṇ-u̯îros and glossed etymolog-

In the language of praise poetry, the same word **márgos** characterizes those whose words are inimical to the institution of praise:

ἐπί τοι
Ἀκράγαντι τανύσαις
αὐδάσομαι ἐνόρκιον λόγον ἀλαθεῖ νόῳ
τεκεῖν μή τιν' ἑκατόν γε ἐτέων πόλιν
    φίλοις ἄνδρα μᾶλλον
εὐεργέταν πραπίσιν ἀφθονέστερόν τε χέρα
Θήρωνος. ἀλλ' αἶνον ἐπέβα κόρος
οὐ δίκᾳ συναντόμενος ἀλλὰ μάργων ὑπ' ἀνδρῶν,
τὸ λαλαγῆσαι θέλον
    κρυφὸν τιθέμεν ἐσλῶν καλοῖς
ἔργοις.

Aiming my arrow at Akragas,
I will proclaim under oath, with unerring intent,
that no city in these last hundred years has produced
a man more beneficent in disposition to **phíloi**
and more ungrudging [from **á-phthonos** = having no **phthónos**] in hand
than Theron. But satiety[5] attacks praise [**aînos**].
It [satiety] is accompanied not by justice but by **márgoi** men.
It is idle talk, which wishes to put concealment upon the fine deeds of the
worthy.

Pindar O.2.90–98

In short, a man who is **márgos** is a man who has the mouth of **Éris** personified:

Ἔριδός ποτε μάργον ἔχων στόμα

... having the **márgon** mouth of **Éris**

Ibycus fr. 311 a P

§10. From the evidence of such traditional wording, I propose that the story of Iros in effect ridicules the stereotype of an unrighteous

---

ically as "he who has no force = *u̯ís." This form serves as a comic correction for what now emerges as the ironically misapplied meaning of **Îros** as *u̯îros "he who has force = *u̯ís." Thus the form **Îros** seems to be a play on an unattested Greek word *u̯îros, cognate with Latin *uir* 'man', etc. My reasoning here is based on the article of Bader 1976. I must add, however, that Bader's presentation does not account for the primary connection of **Îros** with **Îris** in the narrative (on which see §8n3). The apparent connection of **Îros** with *u̯îros 'he who has *u̯ís' has to be considered secondary from the standpoint of the narrative (see again xviii 6–7). Still, the name **Îris** itself may well be derived from the same root *u̯ī- as in **ís**: see Ch.20§9n6.

§9n5. For **kóros** 'satiety', cf. also Pindar *O*.1.55–57: the sin of Tantalos is called his **kóros** in that he could not "digest" (**katapépsai**) his vast **ólbos** 'prosperity'.

blame poet. Like the unrighteous blamers who are righteously blamed by praise poetry, Iros has **éris** 'strife' with a good man (xviii 13, 38–39) and makes **neîkos** 'quarreling' against him (xviii 9). Like the blamers, he is **márgos** 'gluttonous' (cf. xviii 2) and has **phthónos** 'greed' for the **ólbos** 'prosperity' that the good man gets from the gods (cf. xviii 17–19).[1] Moreover, we have seen that the good man who is praised by a praise poem must be a paragon of generosity (hence **á-phthonos** 'without **phthónos**', as in Pindar *O*.2.94). Now we also see that Odysseus himself is generous even with the provocative Iros (οὐ ... φθονέω 'I have no **phthónos**': xviii 16). In fact, this theme of generosity turns out to be crucial for our understanding of the Iros story, as we are about to see from the comparative evidence of ancient Irish tales. One of the most interesting Irish parallels comes from the *Second Battle of Mag Tured*: it is a story about the Dagdae, a prodigiously generous heroic figure, and Cridenbél, a prodigiously greedy blame poet.[2] Cridenbél was so gluttonous that his mouth grew out from his chest, not from his face. This poet made it his habit to demand from the Dagdae, under the threat of blame, the three best portions of each of the hero's meals. *Noblesse oblige*, and the Dagdae's generosity would never allow him to refuse the blame poet's demands. As a result, he became ill from malnutrition. At this point, the Dagdae resorts to deceit: he conceals three gold pieces in the three portions demanded by Cridenbél, and the blame poet unwittingly gluts himself to death on gold—ironically an emblem of ultimate prosperity.

§11. Like the story of Iros in the *Odyssey*, this story from ancient Irish tradition ridicules the function of the blame poet in society. Such ridicule is of course intensified in the *Odyssey* by way of presenting Iros as a beggar. But the actual function of the beggar in society is in fact vitally serious in the overall narrative of the *Odyssey*, as we see from the figure that serves as a positive foil for the beggar Iros, namely Odysseus himself in beggar's disguise. Odysseus plans specifically to beg for his meals—and the word for "meal" here is **daís** (xvii 11, 19); moreover, he plans to beg from the suitors! A stranger in his own house, the disguised Odysseus is received properly by Telemachus, who gives him food and encourages him to beg from the suitors (xvii 336–352); Odysseus responds by praying that Zeus grant **ólbos** 'prosperity' to Telemachus (ὄλβιον εἶναι: xvii

§10n1. Cf. Theognis 581–582.

§10n2. See Stokes 1891.64–67 for text and translation. The translation is also conveniently available in Cross and Slover 1936.31–32.

354). Odysseus proceeds to beg from the suitors, but the chief suitor Antinoos raises objections to the beggar's presence (xvii 360–395). Telemachus rebukes Antinoos: "you want to eat much, instead of giving to the other man" (xvii 404). "I myself," says Telemachus, "have no **phthónos**" (οὔ τοι φθονέω: xvii 400). The climactic moment comes when Odysseus begs from the suitor Antinoos. He addresses him as **phílos** (xvii 415), says that the young man seems like the "best of the Achaeans" (xvii 415–416), and promises to make **kléos** for him in return for generosity (xvii 418). *Noblesse oblige*, but Antinoos refuses.[1] In fact, his refusal not only disqualifies Antinoos himself but also undermines the position of all the other suitors. There is no generosity, says Antinoos, in giving away things that are not one's own (xvii 449–452). By contrast, Odysseus shows the ultimate generosity when he tells the "messenger" of the suitors:

1. that he [Odysseus] feels no **phthónos** if one gives away things that are not one's own (xviii 16)
2. that he [Iros] is entitled to feel no **phthónos** about things that are not his own (xviii 17–18).[2]

The suitors merit their death—and Iros, his beating—not for eating the food of Odysseus but for actually denying it to him. Odysseus himself formally blames Antinoos for withholding abundant food that belongs to someone else (xvii 454–457), and his words of blame are called **óneidos** by Antinoos (ὀνείδεα: xvii 461).

§12. To make matters worse, Antinoos is so angered by these words of **óneidos** 'blame' that his violence is escalated from the verbal to the physical: he throws a footstool at Odysseus and injures him (xvii 462–463). Penelope decries this act as a moral outrage (xvii 499–504), in that she considers the beggar to be a **xénos** 'guest-stranger' in the house of Odysseus (Homeric **xeînos**: xvii 501). As we examine the implications of this word **xénos**, it is appropriate to cite here the formulation devised by Émile Benveniste:[n]

We must envisage the situation of a *xénos*, of a "guest," who is visiting a country where, as a stranger, he is deprived of all rights, of all protection, of all means of existence. He finds no welcome, no lodging and no guarantee

§11n1. See Ch.2§15.

§11n2. See §8. When Telemachus urges Antinoos to give food to the disguised Odysseus, the expression δός οἱ ἑλών 'take and give to him' at xvii 400 corresponds to δόμεναι καὶ πόλλ' ἀνελόντα 'take much and give' at xviii 16. In both verses, these expressions are in collocation with οὐ ... φθονέω 'I do not have **phthónos**', applying to Telemachus and Odysseus respectively.

§12n. Benveniste 1969 I 341 = 1973.278.

except in the house of the man with whom he is connected by *philótēs*. . . . The pact concluded in the name of *philótēs* makes the contracting parties *phíloi*: they are henceforth committed to a reciprocity of services which constitute "hospitality."

Anyone, then, who would consider even a mere beggar as his or her **xénos** displays the maximum of generosity, since a beggar stands to offer the minimum in reciprocal services. Thus Telemachus in effect reveals the nobility of his royal family by receiving Odysseus in beggar's disguise as a **xénos** (xvii 342–355; hence ξείνῳ/ξεῖνε at 345/350). Antinoos, by contrast, proves himself ignoble by his failure to act likewise, and his bad behavior is compounded when he addresses the injured Odysseus sarcastically as a **xénos** (ξεῖνε: xvii 478). Ironically, the father of Antinoos had been treated as a **xénos** by Odysseus himself (xvi 424–432); it is thus appropriate that Odysseus should address Antinoos as **phílos** at the very moment that he tests him by begging for food (xvii 415).

§13. Different **xénoi** have different capacities to reciprocate the generosity of their host, and the swineherd Eumaios perceives that the disguised Odysseus is much more than a mere beggar. In other words, the stranger's capacity to reciprocate is much higher than that of a mere beggar. Thus when Antinoos reproaches Eumaios for inviting "another beggar" to the house of Odysseus (xvii 375–379), the swineherd replies as follows:

'Αντίνο', οὐ μὲν καλὰ καὶ ἐσθλὸς ἐὼν ἀγορεύεις·
τίς γὰρ δὴ ξεῖνον καλεῖ ἄλλοθεν αὐτὸς ἐπελθὼν
ἄλλον γ', εἰ μὴ τῶν οἳ δημιοεργοὶ ἔασι,
μάντιν ἢ ἰητῆρα κακῶν ἢ τέκτονα δούρων,
ἢ καὶ θέσπιν ἀοιδόν, ὅ κεν τέρπῃσιν ἀείδων;
οὗτοι γὰρ κλητοί γε βροτῶν ἐπ' ἀπείρονα γαῖαν·
πτωχὸν δ' οὐκ ἄν τις καλέοι τρύξοντα ἓ αὐτόν

Antinoos! Though you are noble, you do not speak properly.
What man who is from somewhere else himself[1]
will invite yet another **xénos** [guest-stranger], unless he [the **xénos**] is one of
   those who are workers of the **dêmos**,[2]
such as a seer, or a healer of illnesses, or a carpenter who works on wood,

§13n1. E.g., the speaker himself! For the story, see xv 403–484.
§13n2. On the formation of **dēmiourgós**, see Bader 1965.133–141. The prime concept inherent in the word seems to be social mobility: a **dēmiourgós** is affiliated with the whole **dêmos** 'district', not with any one household. Note that Ithaca counts as one **dêmos** (see, e.g., i 103, xiv 126, etc.). For more on the semantics of **dêmos**, see Ch.19§3n5.

or even an inspired singer who can give delight with his singing?[3]
For such men are apt to be invited anywhere in the world.
But one would not invite a beggar; such a man would feed on his host.

xvii 381–387

For Antinoos, these words are meant to convey that Eumaios, being
a stranger himself, would not invite a low-ranking stranger, such as a
beggar; if the stranger is a beggar, then he did not invite him. For
Odysseus, these same words mean that Eumaios considers him a
high-ranking stranger, such as a seer, physician, carpenter, or poet; if
the stranger is one of these, then he did invite him. The sequence of
enumerating the four occupations is arranged in a crescendo of detail,
starting with a single word to designate the seer (μάντιν: xvii 384)
and ending with a whole verse to designate the poet (xvii 385). Thus
the formal presentation of alternatives implies that the stranger is
most likely to be a poet.

§14. Later on, Eumaios tells Penelope explicitly that the stranger
indeed has the powers of a poet:

οἷ᾽ ὅ γε μυθεῖται, θέλγοιτό κέ τοι φίλον ἦτορ.
. . .

ὡς δ᾽ ὅτ᾽ ἀοιδὸν ἀνὴρ ποτιδέρκεται, ὅς τε θεῶν ἒξ
ἀείδῃ δεδαὼς ἔπε᾽ ἱμερόεντα βροτοῖσι,
τοῦ δ᾽ ἄμοτον μεμάασιν ἀκουέμεν, ὁππότ᾽ ἀείδῃ·
ὡς ἐμὲ κεῖνος ἔθελγε παρήμενος ἐν μεγάροισι

The kind of things he tells about—it would put your heart in a trance. . . .
As when a man is looking at[1] a singer who has learned his words from the
    gods—and the words give pleasure to mortals,
who yearn to hear him without pause when he sings—
so also that one was putting a trance on me as he sat in my house.

xvii 514, 518–521

The disguised Odysseus merits such a compliment from Eumaios not
only when he tells the first-person odyssey of the Cretan adventurer,
at xiv 192–359,[2] but also later when he employs a particular form of
discourse in asking for an overnight cloak, at xiv 462–506. In these
verses, the disguised Odysseus is narrating to Eumaios and his

---

§13n3. On the parallelism of artisans and poets, which is presented here as a social
reality within the context of the **dêmos**, see also Ch.17§§10–13.

§14n1. For the visual implications of the verb **thélgō** 'put into a trance' (used here at
lines 514 and 521), see Householder/Nagy 1972.769–770.

§14n2. On which see Ch.7§26. Note that dinner time is the context for the
performance of this entertaining narrative (xiv 192–198).

friends a story about the Trojan War: it happened on a cold night, during an ambush, that a man was tricked out of his cloak by Odysseus himself, who gave it to his own friend and equal, the narrator![3] As Leonard Muellner points out, the telling of this story to Eumaios has a parallel purpose: to get a cloak for the disguised Odysseus.[4] "The story is—in more ways than one—proud talk that raises its speaker's prestige (and almost gives away his identity),[5] but in the *Odyssey* it receives a moral interpretation ... by which Odysseus obtains proper treatment as a guest in the form of ... a symbolic mantle."[6] Significantly, these words of Odysseus constitute a form of discourse that Eumaios himself compliments as an **aînos** (αἶνος: xiv 508). And it is this same word **aînos** that designates praise poetry within the traditional diction of epinician praise poetry!

§15. From the evidence of Homeric diction alone, the meaning of **aînos** may be analyzed further:[1]

In particular, *aînos* designates a discourse that aims at praising and honoring someone or something or at being ingratiating toward a person. Accidental or not, in Homer the word always defines a polite, edifying speech that is in direct or indirect connection with a gift or a prize. In *Il.* 23.795 *aînos* means "praise," as is made evident by the verb *kūdaínō* ("to give honor") of line 793. Achilles repays this *aînos* with a gift. In the same book, Nestor's speech—in which he recalls his past deeds and thanks Achilles for his generous gift—is termed an *aînos* (*Il.* 23.652). In both poems we find *polúainos* as an epithet for Odysseus: in at least one passage the word is connected with Odysseus's cunning (*Il.* 11.430), and in *Od.* 14.508-9 Odysseus's speech—termed *aînos*—is explicitly defined as a discourse that will not "miss a reward." In *Od.* 21.110 Telemachos turns to the suitors, who are ready to compete for Penelope's hand, and says rhetorically that she does not need any praise (*aînos*). Yet Telemachos has in fact praised Penelope and enhanced her unique qualities (106–9): he therefore increases the suitors' willingness to compete for the prize, i.e., for Penelope.

The **aînos** told by Odysseus to Eumaios is parallel to the epinician praise poetry of the classical period both in name and in details of

§14n3. See Muellner 1976.96.
§14n4. Muellner, p. 97.
§14n5. The key word is **eúkhomai** (εὐξάμενος 'saying proudly': xiv 463), on which see Muellner, pp. 96–97. Note also the use of **eúkhomai** 'I say proudly' (xiv 199) at the beginning of the first-person narrative about the Cretan adventurer.
§14n6. Muellner, p. 97.
§15n1. Pucci 1977.76. Cf. also Meuli 1975 [= 1954] 739–742 and 751–753.

convention. Consider, for example, the elaborate excuse that introduces the story of the cloak as told by Odysseus:

κέκλυθι νῦν, Εὔμαιε καὶ ἄλλοι πάντες ἑταῖροι,
εὐξάμενός τι ἔπος ἐρέω· οἶνος γὰρ ἀνώγει
ἠλεός, ὅς τ᾽ ἐφέηκε πολύφρονά περ μάλ᾽ ἀεῖσαι
καί θ᾽ ἁπαλὸν γελάσαι, καί τ᾽ ὀρχήσασθαι ἀνῆκε,
καί τι ἔπος προέηκεν ὅ πέρ τ᾽ ἄρρητον ἄμεινον.
ἀλλ᾽ ἐπεὶ οὖν τὸ πρῶτον ἀνέκραγον, οὐκ ἐπικεύσω

Listen to me now, Eumaios and all you other **hetaîroi** [companions]!
Speaking proudly,[2] I will tell you an **épos** [poetic utterance].[3] The wine,
    which sets me loose, is telling me to do so.
Wine impels even the thinking man to sing
and to laugh softly. And it urges him on to dance.
It even prompts an **épos**[3] that may be better left unsaid.
But now that I have shouted out loud, I will not suppress it.

xiv 462–467

In the epinician praise poetry of the classical period, we find similar formalistic excuses:

ἔα με· νικῶντί γε χάριν, εἴ τι πέραν ἀερθεὶς
ἀνέκραγον, οὐ τραχύς εἰμι καταθέμεν

Your indulgence, please! If I—to reciprocate the victor—
shouted something out loud as I soared too far up, I am not
unversed in bringing it back down.[4]

Pindar N.7.75–76

Moreover, the festive mood that calls for "singing, laughter, and dancing" (xiv 464–465) is reminiscent of the formal setting for the epinician praise poetry of Pindar and Bacchylides: a song-and-dance composition performed in an atmosphere of **euphrosúnā** 'mirth' (e.g, Pindar N.4.1).[5]

§16. In the **aînos** told by Odysseus, the actual disposition of the audience constitutes a theme that rounds out the composition; the

§15n2. See §14n5.

§15n3. On the use of **épos** to mean not just 'utterance, word(s)' but also 'poetic utterance' *as quoted by the poetry itself*, see Koller 1972, esp. p. 17 on Tyrtaeus *fr.* 4.2W. Cf. also Ch.15§7 on XX 203–205 and Ch.17§12 on Theognis 15–18.

§15n4. My translation emphasizes the up/down motion conveyed by ἀερθείς/ καταθέσθαι. I should add, however, that the combination of καταθέσθαι with χάριν conveys yet another theme, that of fulfilled reciprocity.

§15n5. On the programmatic connotations of **euphrosúnā** as 'victory revel' in epinician poetry, see Bundy 1962.2. In *H.Hermes* 481–482, the lyre is said to be a means of **eüphrosúnē** 'mirth' at the **kômos**; on the **kômos**, see §20.

story of the cloak is concluded with an appeal to the host's sense of
philótēs 'being a **philos**' (φιλότητι: xiv 505). In other words,
Eumaios the host should be **philos** to Odysseus the **xénos** 'guest-
stranger'. So also in the praise poetry of Pindar, the poet may conventionally present himself as the **xénos** of the patron, who is his
philos:

ξεῖνός εἰμι· σκοτεινὸν ἀπέχων ψόγον,
ὕδατος ὥτε ῥοὰς φίλον ἐς ἄνδρ' ἄγων
κλέος ἐτήτυμον αἰνέσω

I am a **xénos** [guest-stranger]. Keeping away dark <u>blame</u> [**psógos**]
and bringing genuine **kléos**, like streams of water, to a man who is **philos**,
I will <u>praise</u> [**ainéō**] him.

Pindar N.7.61–63

In light of these patterns in traditional diction, we may now see
another dimension in the words employed by the disguised Odysseus
in his attempt to beg from Antinoos. Speaking as a **xénos**, however
lowly, the beggar addresses the suitor as **philos** (xvii 415) and
promises him **kléos** in return for any largesse (xvii 418). Antinoos
refuses to give anything, and in return he gets **óneidos** 'blame' from
Odysseus (ὀνείδεα: xvii 461).[n] Generosity and its opposite deserve
praise and blame respectively from this poetlike figure.

§17. We have seen, then, from the evidence of Homeric diction
that the word **aînos** designates a mode of poetic discourse appropriate
for purposes that go far beyond simply praising a patron. Although
aînos becomes the primary word for designating praise poetry even
within such poetry, it is also appropriate for designating, more
broadly, "an allusive tale containing an ulterior purpose."[1] In the case
of the **aînos** at xiv 508,[2] we see how a tale about a cloak—with the
Trojan War as the setting—has won a temporary cloak for the teller
as a pledge of the host's disposition as **philos** to his guest. As we
compare the epinician praise poetry of Pindar and Bacchylides, which
is also traditionally designated by the word **aînos**, we find that the
poetic occasion is of course far more grandiose; nevertheless, the
poetic form is essentially parallel. Here too, the central element is the
deployment of tales taken from Myth—and the Trojan War serves

§16n. See again §11.
§17n1. For the wording of this definition, see Verdenius 1962.389, who actually cites
xiv 508.
§17n2. Verdenius (ibid.) also cites an interesting parallel use of the word **aînos** in
Sophocles *Philoktetes* 1380.

frequently as the setting;[3] these tales, moreover, are arranged to convey an ad hoc message of praise and edification to the victor and his family, who are accordingly obligated as **phíloi** to the poet. A derivative of **aînos** even conveys the moralizing tone so characteristic of epinician poetry: the compound **par-ainéō** 'advise, instruct' applies to the edifying instructions given by the Centaur, Cheiron, to the youthful Achilles and also by the poet himself to his young patron (Pindar *P*.6.23).[4] This derivative word **parainéō** also applies to the didactic function of the Hesiodic tradition in general, and the application is actually attested in the diction of epinician praise poetry:

Λάμπων δὲ μελέταν
ἔργοις ὀπάζων Ἡσιό-
δου μάλα τιμᾷ τοῦτ' ἔπος,
υἱοῖσί τε φράζων παραινεῖ,
ξυνὸν ἄστει κόσμον ἑῷ προσάγων·
καὶ ξένων εὐεργεσίαις ἀγαπᾶται

And Lampon [the patron, father of the victorious athlete],
who adds preparedness to action, honors this **épos** [poetic utterance] of
Hesiod.
He instructs [**par-ainéō**] his sons by telling it to them,
thus bringing communal embellishment to his city.
And he is loved for treating well his **xénoi**.

Pindar *I*.6.66–70.

Such a poetic utterance or **épos** ('Add preparedness to action!'), which serves as an instructive legacy for the sons of Lampon, is actually attested in the Hesiodic tradition:

μελέτη δέ τοι ἔργον ὀφέλλει

Preparedness aids action.

Hesiod *W&D* 412

§18. In the sense of 'an allusive tale containing an ulterior purpose',[1] the word **aînos** applies not only to the specific genre of praise poetry but also to the general narrative device of animal fables. In the poetry of Archilochus, for example, we find **aînos** designating the fable about the fox and the eagle (*fr.* 174.1W), as well as the fable

§17n3. For a sound discussion of the mythological paradigm and its function in Pindaric poetry, I cite Köhnken 1971.
§17n4. Surely the words that Phoinix intends for Achilles in *Iliad* IX, spoken in the presence of an audience of **phíloi** (IX 528), qualify for designation by the word **parainesis** (abstract noun derived from verb **parainéō**). See Maehler 1963.47.
§18n1. See again §17.

about the ape and the fox (*fr.* 185.1W). The word is likewise appropriate for designating the animal fables belonging to the tradition of
Aesop.[2] In order to understand the formal connection between fable
and praise poetry, we may now turn to the **aînos** about the hawk and
the nightingale in Hesiod *W&D* 203–212.[3] I call special attention to
the fable's introductory description of the intended audience:

νῦν δ᾽ αἶνον βασιλεῦσιν ἐρέω φρονέουσι καὶ αὐτοῖς

Now I will tell an **aînos** for kings, aware as they are.

Hesiod W&D 202

Using the language of Prague School linguistics,[4] we may say that the
code of this **aînos** has a *message* for kings—but only if they are
"aware" (**phronéontes**, at verse 202). Such a built-in ideology of
exclusiveness also pervades the form of **aînos** that we know as
epinician praise poetry. Consider the following programmatic declara-
tions about this genre of poetry by the poetry itself:

φρονέοντι συνετὰ γαρύω

I proclaim things that can be understood to the man who is aware
[**phronéōn**].

Bacchylides 3.85

§18n2. In Aristophanes *Birds* 651–653, the fable known as "The Fox and the Eagle"
is actually attributed not to Archilochus (cf. *fr.* 174W) but to Aesop (cf. *Fable* 1 Perry).
For more on the Aesopic **aînos** and its applications in Attic comedy, see Fraenkel 1920.
On the classification of the Aesopic fable as **aînos**, see Quintilian 5.11.19–21 (Aesop
Testimonium 98 Perry) and Aelius Theon *Progymnasmata* 3 (*Rhetores Graeci* II 72 ff.
Spengel; Aesop *Testimonium* 103 Perry). Aelius Theon (ibid.) also observes that the
designation **aînos** is appropriate because the fables of Aesop have the function of
paraínesis (on this word see §17, esp. n4). It seems significant in this connection that
the adopted son of Aesop is called **Aînos** in the *Life of Aesop* tradition (*Vita* W
103–110 Perry), and that Aesop aims at him what may surely be classified as a
paraínesis (*Vita* W 109–110). The story of Aesop and Ainos is apparently built on
themes derived from the traditional story of Achiqar and Nadan (on which see Perry
1952.5–10), but its arrangement of these themes seems to suit the meaning of the
word **aînos** in particular and the social function of the figure Aesop in general. After
the adopted son's treachery against his father has been foiled, Aesop gives a
"**paraínesis**" to **Aînos**, whereas Achiqar gives both a scourging and a speech of blame
to Nadan (see Perry 1952.9). In both versions, the son dies, but his death in the
version of the *Life of Aesop* tradition is idiosyncratic: Ainos is so "scourged"
(μαστιγωθείς) by the words of Aesop that he kills himself by jumping off a cliff (*Vita*
W 110). In *Vita* G 142, Aesop himself dies by jumping off a cliff—instead of being
pushed off by the Delphians as in *Vita* W 142. Finally, we may note that the king of
Babylon in the story of Aesop and Ainos is called **Lukoûrgos** (both *Vitae* G and W).
For more on the name **Lukoûrgos** (from **Lukó-orgos**), see Ch.13§7.

§18n3. On which see Puelma 1972 and Pucci 1977.61–62, 76.

§18n4. For the terms *code* and *message*, see Jakobson 1960.

... φωνάεντα συνετοῖσιν ...

... having a sound for those who can understand ...

Pindar *O.2.85*

... ἐπαινέοντι συνετοί

... those who can understand give praise

Pindar *P.5.107*

Praise poetry is "understandable" (**sunetá**) only for the man who is "aware" (**phronéōn**). Only "those who can understand" (the **sunetoí**) can deliver or hear the message of praise.[5] Epic also recognizes this ideology of praise poetry, but it finds expression only in terms of quotations presented before an audience of Achaeans. Consider these words addressed by Odysseus to Diomedes:

Τυδείδη, μήτ' ἄρ με μάλ' αἴνεε μήτε τι νείκει·
εἰδόσι γάρ τοι ταῦτα μετ' 'Αργείοις ἀγορεύεις

Son of Tydeus! Do not give me too much praise [**ainéō**, from **aînos**] nor too much blame [**neikéō**, from **neîkos**].
You are saying these things in the presence of Argives who know.[6]

X 249–250

§19. The **aînos**, then, is a code bearing one message to its intended audience; aside from those exclusive listeners "who can understand," it is apt to be misunderstood, garbled.[1] With this ideology in mind, we will find it easier to understand the semantics of other attested words derived from **aînos**. I cite in particular a by-form of **ainéō** 'praise', **ainízomai/ainíssomai**: this verb means either 'praise' (as in viii 487) or 'utter an oracular response' (as in Pindar *P.8.40*). It can even mean 'speak riddles' (as in Herodotus 5.56) — hence the derivative noun **aínigma** 'riddle' (as in Sophocles *Oedipus Rex* 393, 1525). We may also find it easier now to understand the

§18n5. For the parallel use of **sophós** 'well-versed' to express this ideology of exclusiveness in praise poetry, cf. Maehler 1963.93–95; cf. also Nisetich 1975. For a variation on this theme, where being **sophós** is the key to understanding the poet's cryptic message, see Theognis 681–682. Even here, the *intended* audience is the **agathoí** 'good'.

§18n6. For more on the context: Ch.2§9.

§19n1. As for the words of instruction spoken by Phoinix to Achilles in *Iliad* IX (see §17n4), the code seems to bear one message from the speaker and another message to the listener; see Ch.6§16. Note too the argument of Meuli (1975 [= 1954] 742–743n2) that the epithet **polúainos** of Odysseus (e.g., xii 184) means 'having many **aînoi** = fables'. I would rephrase: Odysseus is **polúainos** in that he can speak about many things *in code* (witness his "Cretan lies"). Compare the discussion of **polúphēmos** at Ch.1§4n1.

semantics of the verb from which the noun **aînos** is derived: the negative form is **an-aínomai** 'say no', and the unattested positive counterpart *aínomai must have meant something like 'say [in a special way]'.[2]

§20. What, then, is the bond of communication that determines who can and who cannot understand the exclusive message of praise poetry? It is, I submit, the same principle that we find in the Homeric ideology of **philótēs**—the ties that bind the **phíloi hetaîroi** together.[1] In the Homeric tradition, as Dale Sinos has demonstrated in detail, the dimensions of **philótēs** are determined by the social base of the Achaean **lāós**.[2] In the epinician praise poetry of the classical period, on the other hand, the social base for the community of **phíloi** is the **kômos** 'revel, celebration, celebrating group of singers/dancers'.[3] The **kômos** is not only the context for celebrating the victor with praise (cf. Pindar *N*.3.5, *I*.8.4, etc.).[4] It is also, in a larger sense, a formal affirmation of the **philótēs** that flourishes among **hetaîroi** 'comrades' in society. This social function of the **kômos** is evident even in the diction of epinician praise poetry, as the following examples show:

φιλοφροσύναις ... κῶμον ...

with the disposition of a **phílos** ... **kômos** ...

Pindar *O*.6.98

κωμάζοντι φίλοις ... σὺν ἑταίροις ...

having a **kômos** with the **phíloi hetaîroi** ...

Pindar *O*.9.4

παρ' ἀνδρὶ φίλῳ ... κωμάζοντι ...

in the presence of a man who is **phílos** ... having a **kômos** ...

Pindar *P*.4.1–2

§21. The recipient of praise is of course **phílos** both to his **hetaîroi** in the **kômos** and to the poet himself (as in Pindar *N*.7.61–63).[1] Moreover, the poet's function is reciprocal negatively as well as positively. Pindar's own words reveal that the traditional function of

§19n2. See Chantraine I 35–36.
§20n1. See Ch.6§§12–19.
§20n2. Sinos 1975.65–79.
§20n3. See also §15n5.
§20n4. Cf. also the verb **kōmázō**, as at Pindar *N*.9.1, *P*.9.89, etc., and the adjective **enkómios**, as at Pindar *N*.1.7, *O*.2.47, etc. (cf. §7n2).
§21n1. See again §16.

the poet is to be not only **phílos** to the **phílos** but also **ekhthrós** 'hateful, hostile' to the **ekhthrós**:

φίλον εἴη φιλεῖν·
ποτὶ δ' ἐχθρὸν ἅτ' ἐχθρὸς ἐὼν λύκοιο
δίκαν ὑποθεύσομαι,
ἀλλ' ἄλλοτε πατέων ὁδοῖς σκολιαῖς

Let it happen that I be **phílos** to [φιλεῖν] the **phílos**.
But I will be like an **ekhthrós** to the **ekhthrós**,[2] heading him off in the manner of a wolf,
making different steps at different times, in twisting directions.

Pindar *P.*2.83−85

We have here a complete picture of reciprocity between the poet on the one hand and the man who gets the poet's praise or blame on the other.[3] It is also important to observe that the foil for being **phílos**, being **ekhthrós**, is described in words that amount to a periphrasis of the notion inherent in the name **Luk-ámbēs**, which has been traditionally interpreted as 'having the steps of a wolf'.[4] Pindar's words apparently connote the stylized movements of a dance that represents the steps of a wolf. So too with the name **Luk-ámbēs**: the second half of this compound, like that of **í-ambos**, seems to indicate an actual dance step.[5]

§21n2. Note the striking parallelism of lines 83−84 with Archilochus *fr.* 23.14−15W. We now see that being **ekhthrós** equals 'to blame' just as being **phílos** equals 'to praise'. The adjective **ekhthrós** belongs to the same family as the noun **ékhthos**, which we have observed in the following Pindaric characterization: ψογερὸν 'Αρχίλοχον βαρυλόγοις ἔχθεσιν / παινόμενον 'Archilochus, having **psógos**, fattening himself on heavy-worded hatreds [**ékhthos** plural]' (*Pythian* 2.55−56). Discussion at §4. Note too the Pindaric characterization of blame poetry as, by its very origin, ἐχθρὰ ... πάρφασις 'misrepresentation that is hateful [has **ékhthos**]' (*Nemean* 8.32). Discussion at §7.

§21n3. Compare the reciprocity of **kléos** in Ibycus *fr.* 282P: at line 48 the word applies to the poet and at line 47 it applies to the patron. See Nagy 1974.250−251 and Watkins 1975.17; cf. also Watkins 1976. For a supplemented text of Ibycus *fr.* 282P, see now Page 1974 S 151−165.

§21n4. Pickard-Cambridge 1927.15: "wolf's gait." On the Indo-European motif of the wolf as a figure who is outside of society: Gernet 1936. I owe this reference to O. M. Davidson.

§21n5. On the formal connections between **Luk-ámbēs** and **í-ambos**: West 1974. 26−27.

13 | Iambos

§1. With the mention of **Lukámbēs**, we may now turn to the **íamboi** of Archilochus.[1] Of course, we are dealing here not so much with a metrical category but rather with a genre of composition:[2] "iambic metre got its name from being particularly characteristic of **íamboi**, not vice versa."[3] The word **í-ambos**, as K. J. Dover observes, seems to have referred originally to the type of occasion for which this genre was appropriate;[4] so also with the word **dithúr-ambos**.[5] The point is, **Luk-ámbēs** figures as a prime **ekhthrós** 'hateful one, enemy' of Archilochus.

§2. By virtue of being singled out, even within epinician praise poetry, as "a man of **psógos**" (ψογερὸν 'Αρχίλοχον: Pindar *P.*2.55), the figure of Archilochus surely qualifies as a master of blame poetry.[1] Thus the **íamboi** composed against Lykambes qualify the poet as an **ekhthrós** to his victim.[2] Yet even an **ekhthrós** may have to deliver his poetry in the context of a receptive audience—who would have to be, by contrast, **phíloi** to him. In fact, Aristotle specifically identifies the audience of Archilochus as his **phíloi**:

πρὸς γὰρ τοὺς συνήθεις καὶ φίλους ὁ θυμὸς αἴρεται μᾶλλον ἢ πρὸς τοὺς ἀγνῶτας, ὀλιγωρεῖσθαι νομίσας. διὸ καὶ 'Αρχίλοχος προσηκόντως τοῖς φίλοις ἐγκαλῶν διαλέγεται πρὸς τὸν θυμόν·

For the **thūmós**, when it feels neglected, is stirred more towards acquaintances and **phíloi** than towards those who are unknown. Accordingly, it is

§1n1. This chapter is a reworking of an earlier article (Nagy 1976).

§1n2. The word **íamboi** is an appropriate designation for the following meters of Archilochus: iambic trimeters (18–87W) and tetrameters (88–167W); also epodes (168–204W), including the Cologne Epode (see §4).

§1n3. West 1974.22; see Aristotle *Poetics* 1448b31. Of course, the generalization of a meter for one genre does not preclude the use of the same meter for other genres.

§1n4. Dover 1964.189; cf. West 1974.23 and Richardson 1974.213–217.

§1n5. See West 1974.23–25.

§2n1. See Ch.12§4.

§2n2. Again, Ch.12§4 and §21.

appropriate that Archilochus should address the following words to his **thūmós**, as he is reproaching his **phíloi**:

σὺ γὰρ δὴ παρὰ φίλων ἀπάγχεαι

For you [the **thūmós**] are being choked off from the **phíloi**.

Aristotle *Politics* 1328a1
quoting
Archilochus (*fr.*129W)

The audience of **phíloi** is also apparent in the Archilochean epode that begins as follows:

'Ερασμονίδη Χαρίλαε,
  χρῆμά τοι γελοῖον
ἐρέω, πολὺ φίλταθ' ἑταίρων,
  τέρψεαι δ' ἀκούων

Kharilaos, son of Erasmon!
I will tell you something laughable,
you <u>most **phílos**</u> of <u>**hetaîroi**</u>!
And you will get pleasure hearing it.

Archilochus *fr.* 168W

In this particular instance, the target of reproach may have been the **Kharí-lāos** figure himself, whose very name suggests the notion of "mirth for the **lāós**."[3] Nevertheless, Kharilaos remains the "most **phílos** of **hetaîroi**," presumably in the company of other **phíloi hetaîroi**.

§3. Even if one of the **phíloi hetaîroi** were to be singled out for attack, the poetry of blame would not have to go far enough to rupture the **philótēs**. In the fragment concerning Kharilaos, we may infer as much from the promise τέρψεαι δ' ἀκούων 'you will have pleasure hearing it' (Archilochus *fr.* 168.4W).[1] Furthermore, in another fragment from the same composition, we actually see a reaffirmation of **philótēs**:

φιλεῖν στυγνόν περ ἐόντα . . .

to be **phílos** to him even when he is hostile . . .

Archilochus *fr.* 171.1W

In societies where blame poetry was an inherited institution, there must have been clearly defined traditional limits for degrees of insult.

---

§2n3. See Ch.5§39.
§3n1. Again, Ch.5§39.

Consider the following description of the Spartan **sussítia** 'communal meals':[2]

αὐτοί τε παίζειν εἰθίζοντο καὶ σκώπτειν ἄνευ βωμολοχίας, καὶ σκωπτόμενοι μὴ δυσχεραίνειν· σφόδρα γὰρ ἐδόκει καὶ τοῦτο Λακωνικὸν εἶναι, σκώμματος ἀνέχεσθαι· μὴ φέροντα δ' ἐξῆν παραιτεῖσθαι, καὶ ὁ σκώπτων ἐπέπαυτο.

They had the custom of engaging in playful mockery, without **bōmolokhíā**.[3] And when they were mocked themselves, they would not take offense, because putting up with mockery was the Laconian way to behave. And whenever someone could not bear it [the mockery], it was possible for him to be excused, and the one who was mocking him would stop then and there.[4]

Plutarch Lycurgus 12.6

We may also compare the Homeric *Hymn to Hermes* (55–58), where playful ridicule at banquets is associated with the theme of "**philótēs** befitting **hetaîroi**" (ἐταιρείη φιλότητι: verse 58).[5] At *fr.* 295d in his edition of archaic **íamboi**, Martin West gives a catalogue of fragments where various specific "amici" [**phíloi**] may have been targets of reproach by Archilochus; perhaps it is significant that there is only one "inimicus" [**ekhthrós**] attested, **Lukámbēs** himself!

§4. As we look further at the figure of **Lukámbēs**, we must also consider more closely the poetic conventions of the **íambos**. Clearly, the primary function of the Archilochean Iambos was blame poetry, and the primary target of this poetry was Lykambes and his

§3n2. See also West 1974.16–17 on the playful insults and retorts in the poetry of Theognis (577–578 , 1115, 1123, 1211).

§3n3. The word **bōmolókhos** 'he who ambushes at the altar' and its derivatives refer to a particularly offensive sort of discourse; cf. Aristophanes *Frogs* 358, *Knights* 902, *Peace* 748, etc. The verb **bōmo-lokhéō** can mean "beg" (Pollux 3.111). In Pherecrates *fr.* 141 Kock, we see that a **bōmolókhos** is one who literally 'ambushes' the sacrificer at the altar by asking for meat under the threat of verbal abuse. For the theme of verbal strife at a sacrifice, compare the myth of Prometheus (Ch.11§§10, 15, etc.). For the semantics of **bōmo-lókhos**, compare perhaps **Arkhí-lokhos**.

§3n4. The word for 'mock, ridicule' here is **skóptō**, on which see further at Ch.16§10 and n7; also Ch.18§3 and n4.

§3n5. There are textual difficulties at the beginning of verse 58. I prefer the readings ὡς over ὅν and ἠρίζεσκον over ὠρίζεσκον. My interpretation: Zeus and Maia had **éris** in a spirit of **philótēs**. (From the standpoint of, say, an Alexandrian exegete, this concept would have seemed contradictory.) When young men at the banquet table engage in playful ridicule (**kertoméousin**: verse 56), they sing of the **éris** that once took place between Zeus and Maia (verses 57–58). According to this interpretation, the young men are in effect reenacting this primal **éris**. For more on the verb **kertoméō** in the sense of 'reproach, ridicule' as in verse 56, see Ch.14§§11 (n6), 14.

daughters. On this point, the testimony of the ancient world is unambiguous, and I need cite only the most familiar reference, Horace *Epist.* 1.19.23–25.[1] With the appearance of the Cologne Epode (*Pap.Colon.* 7511),[2] we now have, for the first time, an extensive text about this family, made so infamous by the invectives of Archilochus.[3] The rest of the direct textual evidence about Lykambes and the Lykambides is so deficient that we have the greatest difficulties in reconstructing the overall structure of any other Archilochean composition from any of the attested fragments and excerpts. Even so, the bits and pieces at our disposal have led us to certain expectations, and the Cologne Epode now leaves us perhaps surprised at the nature of its blame poetry. Instead of railing at the family of Lykambes directly, the poem places them inside a narrative. The immediate victim of the narrative is a daughter of Lykambes,[4] who herself is not addressed directly but in quotations within the narrative. Within the overall structure of this composition, direct address happens only in quotations from the daughter and from the narrator. These in turn are not only opened but also closed with expressions inherited for precisely the function of framing dialogue:

τοσαῦτ' ἐφώνει ...	line 6, after the quote
... τὴν δ' ἐγὼ ἀνταμει[βόμην]	line 6, before the quote
[τοσ]αῦτ' ἐφώνεον ...	line 28, before the quote

In this connection, I refer to Führer's monograph about the mechanics of direct quotation in "lyric" (in the sense of "non-epic"), with its ample documentation on the traditional nature of such framing expressions and on their strict interrelation with the quotations.[5]

§4n1. For details, see West 1974.22, 25–28.

§4n2. For a convenient introduction and the text itself, see Van Sickle 1975(b).

§4n3. The figure of Neoboule, daughter of Lykambes, is mentioned at line 16. Throughout the poem, she is treated as a negative point of contrast—a veritable foil—to the other girl, who in turn gets seduced in the narrative. The poem has this other girl unwittingly introduce the subject of Neoboule for verbal abuse, when she volunteers her as a fitting substitute for the desires of the seducer (lines 3 ff.). Since the girl refers to Neoboule as "a maiden in our house who ... " (lines 3–4), we may reasonably infer that she too, like Neoboule, is a daughter of Lykambes. Compare also *fr.* 38 and *fr.* 54W and the discussions by West 1974b.482 and Koenen 1974.499. I find myself in sympathy with the proposal that Dioscorides *Epigr.* 17 (*Anthologia Palatina* 7.351), a poem about the daughters of Lykambes, was at least partly "inspired" by the poem of *Pap.Colon.* 7511; see Koenen 1974.499, West 1974b.482 and 1975.218.

§4n4. See again n3.

§4n5. Führer 1967. Cf. Gentili 1965.382 and 1972.69n82.

§5. Moreover, the inherited mechanics of direct quotation in epic are structurally parallel to those of lyric, the Iambos included.[1] They are in fact stricter, in that overt quote frames for dialogues (type προσέφη, προσεφώνεε, etc.) and for speeches (type μετέφη, μετεφώνεε, etc.) are *de rigueur* in Epos.[2] Conversely, the quote frames in a genre like the Iambos are only optional—a point to which we will have to return presently. But the point now is simply that the quote frames are indeed present in the Cologne Epode, so that the dialogue between the *persona* of the seducer and that of Lykambes' daughter—as we see it in this particular example of the Iambos—meets the strictest formal requirements of epic quotation. The essential difference between Epos and Iambos here can be seen from the standpoint of narration: whereas the epic narrative that frames dialogues is in the third person, the framing narrative of the Cologne Epode is in the first person—which coincides with the *persona* of the seducer.

§6. Shall we say, then, that this *persona* is Archilochus, whose actions determined the narrative of this iambic composition? Or rather, shall we say that the function of the composition determined the narrative, which in turn determined the *persona* that acts and speaks within?[1] If we choose the second alternative, then the function of blame poetry is a cause; if we choose the first, then it is merely an effect. There are also other consequences that accompany our choice. The first alternative leads us to approach Archilochean poems as biographical documents, and we then find ourselves taking the same attitude as most of the ancient commentaries that have survived. The second alternative leads us to ask whether the details and essentials about the *persona* of the composer are to be derived from his role as composer of blame poetry. For example, those ancient commentators who took a biographical approach to Archilochean poetry were upset to read in the poet's own words that his mother was a slave-woman, called **Enīpó** (Critias *fr*. 88 B 44DK, Aelian *VH* 10.13; see Archilochus *fr*. 295W). And yet, this very detail reflects on the function of Archilochean poetry, in that **Enīpó** is derived from a word used in Epos to designate 'blame', **enīpé** (as at xx 266).[2]

§5n1. Führer 1967.1–4, 66–67. See now also Stoessl 1976.
§5n2. Cf. Nagy 1974.84–94.
§6n1. As Pietro Pucci points out (*per litteras* 1/10/1976), the term *persona* must be understood as "the role which is traditional for a poet to assume in a specific genre."
§6n2. On **Enīpó**, see Treu 1959.157 (following earlier proposals that the name is a

§7. In this connection, I return to the argument that even the prime target of Archilochean blame poetry, **Lukámbēs** himself, is a stock character whose name is connected with the very notion of **íambos**.[1] Moreover, if indeed one of the original contexts of the **í-ambos** was Dionysiac in nature,[2] we may compare West's collection of thematic evidence about **Luk-ámbēs** with the tradition that Dionysus was persecuted by **Lukó-orgos**, wielder of the **bouplḗx** 'cattle prod' (VI 130–140).[3] Be that as it may, the traditional form of iambic blame poetry—as we can see from the fragments of Hipponax and Semonides beside those of Archilochus—is replete with a great variety of stock situations and stock characters.[4]

§8. Further, K. J. Dover raises the possibility that the poet can even assume the *persona* of a stock figure like Charon the carpenter (Archilochus *fr.* 19W) or the father reproaching his daughter (Archilochus *fr.* 122W).[1] In these two cases, however, we may not have to go that far. Although lyric in general allows the occasional assumption by the composer of a *persona* that is overtly distinct from his own self (e.g., Alcaeus *fr.* 10LP),[2] the specific genre of Iambos may perhaps be more strict. At least, the Archilochean poems about Charon and about the father-to-daughter reproach are inconclusive, since their endings have not survived. They may both have ended with a quote frame even though they began without one. The effect may have been an amusing surprise.[3] The suppression of the quoting mechanism till the very end of the composition is a comic device well known to us from Horace *Epode* 2.[4]

---

personification misunderstood by Critias); see also Van Sickle 1975b.151, whose discussion supplements that of West 1974.28.

§7n1. Cf. Ch.12§21. See also West 1974.25–28. For a discussion of **Kharílāos** as a stock figure, see §2 and Ch.5§39. As for Lykambes' daughter **Neoboúlē**, I cite Van Sickle's observation that the name "suits the kind of girl who changes her marriage plans" (1975b.152).

§7n2. See West 1974.23–25. Another context, as Albert Henrichs points out to me, would have been the cult of Demeter. Consider the function of **Iámbē** in *H.Dem.* 192–205. For further discussion, see West, ibid. and Richardson 1974.213–217.

§7n3. Note that **Lukóorgos** "had **éris**" against Dionysos (ἔριζεν: VI 131); on **éris** see Ch.11§§10–16, Ch. 12§3. The **éris** of the god's persecutor is in this story punished by blindness (VI 139)—a theme that I propose to examine in detail elsewhere.

§7n4. See Dover 1964.205–212 and West 1974.28–33.

§8n1. Dover 1964.206–208.

§8n2. For a survey, see Führer 1967.5–7.

§8n3. See Führer 1967; cf. also the comments of M. Treu following the presentation of Dover, 1964.218–219.

§8n4. See Fraenkel 1957.60.

§9. The point remains, then, that Archilochean blame poetry against Lykambes and his daughters is a stylized poetic form, with strict formal regulation of narrative and of dialogue quoted within the narrative; also, that the personification of the composer and that of his targets is similarly stylized within the narrative and dialogue. As Aristotle says in the *Rhetoric* (1418b23–31), such personifications as in Archilochus *frr.* 19 and 122W (both of which he actually cites)[n] are an example of how the poet composed blame poetry: καὶ ὡς Ἀρχίλοχος ψέγει 'and as Archilochus reproaches [makes **psógos**]'. The evidence of the Cologne Epode serves as an invaluable confirmation for what we can also infer from the other fragments: the Archilochean **íamboi** against **Lukámbēs** and family, with their stylized themes and characters, are as universal in content as they are ad hoc.

§10. We are left with the more fundamental problem of examining the traditional function of this Hellenic form of blame poetry, the Iambos. Looking forward in time, beyond Archilochus, we see a medium kindred to Archilochean **íamboi** in the complex poetic form of the Athenian **kōmōidíā** 'comedy', which in turn must be compared with its less sophisticated counterparts in other city-states. I leave the details of exposition to Martin West and others,[1] confining myself here to stressing what Pickard-Cambridge had proved long ago—that the traditional notion of **kōmōidíā** was derived from **kômos** 'revel, celebration, celebrating group of singers/dancers'.[2] In the **kômos** we see the social origins of comedy, a medium of blame poetry that has the capacity of being applied on the universal or ad hoc level.[3] In other words, the blame poetry that we may find in **kōmōidíā** is by origin an extension of a social function that is associated with the **kômos**. This connection helps explain an aetiological story about sixth-century Naxos, as reported in Aristotle's *Constitution of the Naxians* (*fr.* 558 Rose, as directly quoted by Athenaeus 348b–c). On that island, which is hours away from Paros, the traditional home of Archilochus, a group of young men made a **kômos** to the house of an eminent citizen after a drinking party; they insulted him and his two marriageable daughters, and the ensuing

§9n. See §8.
§10n1. West 1974.33–39, with bibliography.
§10n2. Pickard-Cambridge 1927.225–253.
§10n3. Of course, comedy is more than blame poetry: it is a combination of artistic forms, including several types of poetry/song and dance.

riot led to the emergence of the tyrant Lygdamis.[4] We have here a theme where the **kômos** actually affects the social order, in a context that connotes blame poetry.

§11. Looking backwards in time beyond Archilochus, we see from the comparative evidence of other Indo-European civilizations that the blame poetry of the Archilochean Iambos has an inherited converse in the institution of praise poetry.[1] From the standpoint of their heritage, the **psógoi** 'reproaches' of an Archilochus are thematically the converse of the **épainoi** 'praises' of a Pindar. Actually, in Pindar's own words, praise and blame are two sides of the same thing:

... ὁ γὰρ ἐξ οἴκου ποτὶ μῶμον ἔπαινος κίρναται

... for praise [épainos] is by nature mixed with blame [mômos][2]

Pindar fr. 181SM

Even on the level of form, we may observe in general that the dactylo-epitrites of epinician praise poetry are comprised of metrical elements that are cognate with those used to build the epodes of Archilochean **íamboi**.[3] Most important of all, both blame and praise poetry have a common social context in the institution of the **kômos**. This convergence can be instantly and most dramatically illustrated by simply citing the formation of two words: **kōmōidíā** 'comedy'[4] and **enkómion** 'encomium'.[5]

§12. In the very language of epinician praise poetry, it is the "Dorian" **kômos** (as it is called in Pindar *P.8.20*) that serves as the context for celebrating the victor with **aînos** 'praise'.[1] Conversely, in the blame poetry of Archilochus, the same word **aînos** designates the use of animal fables (*frr.* 174.1, 185.1W),[2] the basic themes of which would have been appropriate for performance by a **khorós** 'song/dance group' comprised of "animals" in some formal analogue of **kōmōidíā**.[3]

§10n4. See West 1974.27–28.

§11n1. See Ch.12§§1–3.

§11n2. On **mômos** 'blame, reproach', cf. Ch.12§3.

§11n3. Cf. Nagy 1974.167–168, 173–174, 297–302.

§11n4. See §10.

§11n5. See Ch.12§7n2.

§12n1. See Ch.12§20.

§12n2. See Ch.12§18. Moreover, Archilochus *fr.* 174W is from a poem against Lykambes and family (172–181W).

§12n3. Cf. the theme of "wolf steps," as discussed at Ch.12§21. On the purely technical (as compared to theoretical) notion of **mímēsis** as 'performance' of

§13. In short, the **íamboi** of Archilochus against **Lukámbēs** and his daughters are a special case of blame poetry. The insults are against an **ekhthrós**, not a **phílos**. Nevertheless, they are in all likelihood framed for a general audience of receptive **phíloi**, whose social outlook may well have resembled that of the famous Naxian **kômos** mentioned by Aristotle. At least, the transmission of Archilochean poetry at Paros suggests that his blame poetry was not against the social outlook of the local state that helped preserve this poetry.[n] Whether we view the audience of Archilochus as the immediate **phíloi** or, teleologically, as the social order that helped preserve and propagate Archilochean **íamboi**, the point remains that such poetry is an affirmation of **philótēs** in the community. If indeed these **íamboi** are intended for the **phíloi** as audience, then a direct approach to Lykambes is poetically unnecessary. If the insults aimed at Lykambes are for the entertainment of the **phíloi**, then the device of a first-person narrative *about* Lykambes and his daughters is appropriate and effective.

§14. As a discourse that has the capacity of *telling about* its subjects without necessarily *speaking to* them, the blame poetry of Archilochus is farther from the praise poetry of Pindar and closer to the epic poetry of Homer. As a correlate to this distinction, we may note that the subjects of Archilochean blame seem to be stock characters,[1] whereas the immediate subjects of Pindaric praise are of course historical figures. Moreover, we have seen that there is a narrative frame for the direct speeches of blame in the poetry of Archilochus, which in this respect too is farther away from a Pindaric and closer to a Homeric model. In the poetry of Pindar, there is no narrative frame for the poet's direct speech of praise. On the other hand, the Cologne Papyrus has revealed that the direct speeches of Archilochean poetry can be framed within a first-person narrative. In this respect,

---

song/dance (in reenactment of myth), see Koller 1954.11. For parallels to the **aînoi** of Archilochus, cf. Stesichorus *fr.* 281P.

§13n. An essential factor, I submit, is the archaic cult of Archilochus at Paros (see Ch.18§1, esp. n1); this factor also accounts for the *Life of Archilochus* tradition, which I view as a development parallel to the transmission of the poetry itself (see Ch.18§4). In other words, I reject the notion that the *Life of Archilochus* tradition is merely the result of otiose exercises in fabricating stories on the basis of the attested poetic text. Cf. Brelich 1958.321-322 on the *Life of Hesiod* tradition, which follows traditional narrative patterns associated with cult heroes. In this connection, I will also adduce the *Life of Aesop* tradition (Ch.12§18n2 and Ch.16).

§14n1. See §§6-7; also Ch.12§21.

Archilochus is farther away from epic and closer to comedy. In terms of comedy, the equivalent of the first-person narrator would be a character interacting with other characters; most appropriately, this character would be assumed by the first actor, who was originally the poet himself.[2]

§14n2. The word **exárkhō**, used by Aristotle to designate the function of first actor (participle **exárkhōn**: *Poetics* 1449a11) is also found in Archilochus *fr.* 120 and *fr.* 121W designating the poet's leading off a choral performance (dithyramb and paean respectively). See Pickard-Cambridge 1927.123 and Lucas 1968.80–83.

14 | Epos, the Language of Blame, and the Worst of the Achaeans

§1. The resemblances in poetic form between the Archilochean Iambos and the Homeric Epos suggest that blame poetry may have evolved away from an old (and unattested) form corresponding to that of praise poetry (as still attested in Pindar and Bacchylides) into its newer form resembling comedy. The key here to formulating the evolution of blame poetry is the evolution of epic poetry itself into a superbly versatile medium equally capable of dialogue and narrative. In fact, Aristotle singles out Homeric Epos as an ideal medium of dialogue (*Poetics* 1448a20–24, 1460a7), with as much dramatic potential as he finds in Aristophanic comedy or Sophoclean tragedy (*Poetics* 1448a25–28).[n]

§2. Aristotle actually reconstructs a primordial form of blame poetry, which he designates as **psógoi**, and a coexisting proto-form of praise poetry, which he designates as **enkṓmia** or **húmnoi** (*Poetics* 1448b27). He traces the blame and praise poetry forward in time to the attested forms of Iambos and Epos respectively (**íamboi** vs. **hērōïká**: *Poetics* 1448b32–34), adding that comedy and tragedy respectively are the ultimate successors if not descendants of these poetic forms (1449a2–6). This formulation provides us with an attractive set of parallelisms. We see the direct address of blame and praise poetry becoming framed within the narratives of Iambos and Epos. We can also imagine that interchanges of direct address within the narrative can evolve into dialogue, which in turn corresponds to the dialogue of comedy and tragedy. Despite its advantages, however,

§1n. Cf. Plato *Republic* 392d–394d. From Plato *Ion* 535c, we see that a rhapsode of epic uses its dialogues to show off his full powers of dramatic performance (**mímēsis**); cf. also *Ion* 536a. Else (1965.69) summarizes: "The rhapsodes did not merely recite Homer, they acted him, and from this quasi-impersonation of Homeric characters it was only a step to full impersonation, from the rhapsode who momentarily spoke in the person of Achilles or Odysseus to the 'actor' who presented himself as Achilles or Odysseus."

253

Aristotle's formulation seems too restrictive, especially in its treatment of Epos as a direct descendant of praise poetry. We may expect, granted, that Epos can quote direct speeches of praise[1] just as Iambos can quote direct speeches of blame. But Epos is in fact more inclusive: we have already seen, for instance, that it also can quote direct speeches of blame—as in the context of narrating a quarrel.[2]

§3. Another difficulty with Aristotle's scheme is that his definition of primordial praise and blame poetry is itself overly restrictive. These poetic forms are said to have their beginnings when the **spoudaîoi** 'noble' praised the noble and the **phaûloi** 'base' blamed the base (*Poetics* 1448b24–27 in conjunction with 1448a1–2).[1] For Aristotle, **spoudaîoi** and **phaûloi** "indicate the two ends of the ordinary, aristocratically based, Greek scale of values".[2] In fact, he uses these same words at *Nicomachean Ethics* 1145b9 as synonyms for "praise-worthy" (**spoudaîos kaì epainetós**) and "blameworthy" (**phaûlos kaì psektós**).[3] From our own examination of what traditional praise poetry actually says about itself, however, we have already seen that *blaming the noble* and *praising the base* are also presented as poetic functions—which are of course themselves blamed as base by praise poetry, with its avowed functions of both *praising the noble* and *blaming the base*.[4] Moreover, the program of praise poetry entails not only that *the noble praise the noble* but also that *the noble blame the base*—a function omitted in Aristotle's formulation. In fact, we hear nothing from Aristotle about the **enkómia** of Pindar and Bacchylides—the evolution of which should surely be traced from the proto-**enkómia** that he himself has posited (see again *Poetics* 1448b27).

§4. It may well be by way of retrojecting his scheme of current poetic forms that Aristotle conceives of proto-**psógoi** as blame of the base *by the base only* and proto-**enkómia** as praise of the noble *by the noble only*. This restrictive formulation actually fits the Aristotelian view of attested comedy and tragedy respectively. There is an impor-

---

§2n1. A worthy example is the praise of Odysseus by Agamemnon at xxiv 192–202 (discussion at Ch.2§13). Compare also Semonides 7.30–31W, where the praise of a woman by a **xénos** 'guest-stranger' is quoted directly. The quotation itself is introduced with the word **epainései** 'will praise' (7.29).

§2n2. Above, Ch.12§6.

§3n1. See Lucas 1968.75 on 1448b25–26; also p. 63 on 1448a2.

§3n2. Lucas, p. 63.

§3n3. For a discussion of the words **epainéō** 'praise' and **pségō** 'blame', see again Ch.12§§2–3.

§3n4. See esp. Ch.12§4.

tant adjustment, however: for these attested poetic forms, the actual elements of blame and praise are left out of the formulation. Comedy is seen simply as a base medium representing the actions of the base and tragedy as a noble medium representing the actions of the noble (cf. especially *Poetics* 1449a32–39). By analogy, then, Aristotle sees proto-**psógoi** as a base medium representing the actions of the base *by way of blame*, and likewise proto-**enkómia** as a noble medium representing the actions of the noble *by way of praise* (see again *Poetics* 1448b24–27). There is a clear recognition here that blame and praise had been functional elements "at first" (**próton:** 1448b27), in the poetic forms of **psógoi** and **enkómia**. There also is a clear implication that they are no longer directly functional in comedy and tragedy. In fact, Aristotle explicitly says so in the case of comedy. He specifies that this poetic form has the dramatic function not of **psógos** 'blame' but simply of **tò geloîon** 'laughter' (*Poetics* 1448b37–38).

§5. Since laughter is recognized as the obvious function of comedy also in English usage, we may henceforth approximate Aristotle's **tò geloîon** with 'the comic element' as well as 'laughter' while we proceed to examine further the relationship of blame poetry with Iambos and comedy. Aristotle remarks that comedy represents the actions of the base because **tò geloîon** 'the comic element' is an aspect of **tò aiskhrón** 'baseness' (*Poetics* 1449a32–34) and further, that the laughter of comedy—**tò geloîon**—is intrinsic to **aîskhos** 'baseness', so long as it is not too painful or destructive (1449a34–37). If indeed the comic element is intrinsic to what is **aiskhró-** 'base' and **aîskhos** 'baseness', it is significant that the diction of Homeric Epos itself associates these same words with the overall concept of blame poetry. For example, **aîskhos** is used as a synonym of **óneidos** 'blame, reproach' at III 242.[1] Moreover, we see that Melantho **enénīpe** 'reproached' the disguised Odysseus **aiskhrôs** 'in a base manner', at xviii 321. Five verses later, the same action is restated: at xviii 326, she **enénīpe** 'reproached' Odysseus **oneideíois epéessi** 'with words of **óneidos**'.

§5n1. On the word **óneidos**, see Ch.12§§3, 7 (usage in praise poetry) and Ch.12§§6, 11 (usage in Epos). Also, **aîskhos** is used as a synonym of **lóbē** 'outrage, disgrace' at XIII 622, xviii 225, xix 373. Finally, note that Clytemnestra is said at xi 433 to have made **aîskhos** not only for herself but also for all womankind in the future by way of betraying Agamemnon. At xxiv 200, this same betrayal turns the very concept of Clytemnestra into a **stugerè** ... **aoidé** 'hateful song' that will survive into the future (xxiv 201) and will bring a bad name to all womankind (xxiv 201–202). We have here one of the clearest instances of blame as blame *poetry*. For more on xxiv 192–202, see Ch.2§13.

Finally, Hektor **neíkessen** 'reproached [made **neîkos** against]' Paris **aiskhroîs epéessi** 'with base words', at both III 38 and VI 325. The last example is particularly instructive: Hektor's words of blame against Paris are **aiskhrá** 'base' not because Hektor himself is base but because Paris is so. In other words, the subject of blame is base, and so too are the words that describe him, but the blamer himself can remain noble. Such a situation cannot be accommodated by Aristotle's scheme of blame poetry, where the blamer too would have to be base.[2] Moreover, Hektor's words of blame are hardly comic, any more than the words of Achilles when he blamed Agamemnon.[3] Here it is useful to consider again Aristotle's observation that laughter is intrinsic to **aîskhos** 'baseness' (*Poetics* 1449a32–37). We may now wish to restate: baseness has merely a *potential* for the comic element. Having noted that epic diction itself equates **aîskhos** 'baseness' with the substance of blame, we can now appreciate Aristotle's observation that **tò geloîon** 'laughter' rather than **psógos** 'blame' is the function of comedy (*Poetics* 1448b37–38). Again we may restate: blame poetry has a *potential* for the comic element, and comedy formalizes this element of blame poetry. But blame poetry itself is more inclusive and thus cannot be equated with comedy. Blame poetry can be serious as well as comic; it can condemn as well as ridicule.

§6. Still, the nonserious side of blame poetry is also formally indicated in Homeric diction, and the key word is **hepsiáomai** 'play, get amusement'.[1] The only Homeric attestation of the simplex verb occurs in a particularly suggestive context:

> ... ἐψιάασθαι
> μολπῇ καὶ φόρμιγγι· τὰ γάρ τ' ἀναθήματα δαιτός

> ... to get amusement
with singing and the lyre: for these are the things that go on at a feast [**daís**][2]
> xxi 429–430

---

§5n2. See again §3.

§5n3. See Ch.12§6. Consider also the **aoidé** 'song' of blame directed at Clytemnestra in particular and women in general (xxiv 199–202), as discussed at n1. This **aoidé** blaming Clytemnestra serves as a serious foil for the **aoidé** praising Penelope (xxiv 196–198). For the typology of praising/blaming the wives of others and one's own, cf. Semonides 7.112–113W, on which there is more at §7.

§6n1. For the semantics, see Chantraine II 394.

§6n2. Whereas the conventional 'amusement' denoted by this word is nonserious, the actual 'amusement' intended by Odysseus for the suitors is of course dead serious.

Whereas we see the simplex verb **hepsiáomai** reflecting the element of *poetry*, the compound **kath-epsiáomai** reflects a complementary element, that of *blame by way of ridicule*. We begin at xix 372, where the disloyal handmaidens **kathepsióōntai** 'ridicule' the disguised Odysseus. This action of the women is then designated in the next verse as a **lóbē** 'outrage, disgrace' and as **aískhea** 'acts of baseness [**aîskhos**]' (xix 373). In other words, *the ridicule committed by the women is an act of blame*.[3] As the blamers of Odysseus, the women are themselves counterblamed by being called **kúnes** 'dogs' at xix 372.[4] The equivalent of **kathepsióōntai** 'ridicule' at xix 372 is in turn **ephepsióonto** 'ridiculed' at xix 370, likewise designating the action of the disrespectful handmaidens. This other compound **eph-epsiáomai** now leads us to another attestation, in one of the most revealing Homeric passages on blame as a foil for praise:

ὃς μὲν ἀπηνὴς αὐτὸς ἔῃ καὶ ἀπηνέα εἰδῇ,
τῷ δὲ καταρῶνται πάντες βροτοὶ ἄλγε' ὀπίσσω
ζωῷ, ἀτὰρ τεθνεῶτί γ' ἐφεψιόωνται ἅπαντες.
ὃς δ' ἂν <u>ἀμύμων</u> αὐτὸς ἔῃ καὶ <u>ἀμύμονα</u> εἰδῇ,
τοῦ μέν τε <u>κλέος</u> εὐρὺ διὰ ξεῖνοι φορέουσι
πάντας ἐπ' ἀνθρώπους, πολλοί τέ μιν ἐσθλὸν ἔειπον

If a man is harsh himself and thinks harsh thoughts,
all men pray that pains should befall him hereafter
while he is alive. And when he is dead, all men **ephepsióōntai** [ridicule] him.
But if a man is <u>blameless</u>[5] himself and thinks <u>blameless</u> thoughts,[5]
the guest-strangers he has entertained carry his **kléos** far and wide
to all mankind, and many are they who call him **esthlós** [worthy].[6]

xix 329–334

§7. Of course, the nonserious aspect of blame poetry depends on personal noninvolvement. Blame may be a **khárma** 'thing of mirth' to others while at the same time being an **elenkheíē** 'disgrace' to the

---

§6n3. On **lóbē** and **aîskhos** as indicators of blame, see §5n1.

§6n4. On the traditional use of **kúōn** 'dog' and its derivatives in the language of blame: Ch.12§6.

§6n5. On the etymology of **amúmōn** 'blameless', see Chantraine I 79. The word is probably related to **mômos** 'blame, reproach' (on which see Ch.12§3). In Hesychius, the related noun **mûmar** is glossed as **aîskhos** and **psógos**; also, the verb **mūmarízei** is glossed as **geloiázei** 'jests'.

§6n6. Whereas the harsh man gets the ridicule of blame poetry, the blameless man gets the **kléos** of praise poetry. As such, the blameless man qualifies as **esthlós** 'worthy'. The collocation of **kléos** with this epithet **esthlós** is suggestive: see Ch.10§3n2.

one who is to experience it (as at **XXIII** 342).[1] As a particularly striking instance, let us consider these words warning about the ridicule of blame that every husband is meant to fear:

ἥτις δέ τοι μάλιστα σωφρονεῖν δοκεῖ,
αὕτη μέγιστα τυγχάνει λωβωμένη·
κεχηνότος γὰρ ἀνδρός, οἱ δὲ γείτονες
χαίρουσ᾽ ὁρῶντες καὶ τόν, ὡς ἁμαρτάνει.
τὴν ἥν δ᾽ ἕκαστος αἰνέσει μεμνημένος
γυναῖκα, τὴν δὲ τουτέρου μωμήσεται.
ἴσην δ᾽ ἔχοντες μοῖραν οὐ γιγνώσκομεν

And she [the wife] who seems to have the most even disposition
happens to be the very one who commits the greatest disgrace.[2]
Her husband has his mouth agape, and the neighbors make merry at seeing
   how he too has gone wrong.[3]
Every man will keep it in mind to praise his own wife
and will blame the wife of the other man.
And we do not recognize that we all have the same lot.

Semonides 7.108–114W

In such a situation, the ridicule of blame formalizes the disgrace of the involved and the laughter of the uninvolved.[4]

§8. Since Homeric Epos is of course serious in content (cf. Aristotle *Poetics* 1448b34–35), it is hardly suited to reflect the comic aspect of blame poetry. By contrast, the Iambos is ideal for this purpose; in fact, the poem of Archilochus that is addressed to **Kharí-lãos** 'whose **lãós**

§7n1. The words **élenkhos/elenkheíē** designate the shame and disgrace that result from blame (cf. XI 314). The derivative adjective **elenkhḗs** 'worthy of reproach' is specifically applied to the person who is being blamed (as at IV 242, where the quoted words of blame are introduced by **neikeíeske** 'made **neîkos**' at verse 241). Note too the use of **élenkhos** in Pindar *N.*8.21, introducing the theme of blame poetry at lines 21–25 (on which see Ch.12§5).

§7n2. For more on **lóbē** 'outrage, disgrace': §5n1.

§7n3. Cf. Hesiod *W&D* 701, warning men not to choose a bad wife—the source of **khármata** 'merriment' for the neighbors. Cf. also Theognis 1107–1108 = 1318a–b W, where one man's misfortunes are described as a **katákharma** 'thing of merriment' to one's **ekhthroí** 'enemies' and a **pónos** 'pain' to one's **phíloi** 'friends'. For more on the semantics of root *khar- as in **khaírō** and **kháris**, see Ch.5§39.

§7n4. At XXI 389–390, Zeus "laughed" (**egélasse**) in his heart with "mirth" (**gēthosúnēi**) when he saw the other Olympians confronting each other in **éris** (ἔριδι). Compare the epithet **kakókhartos** 'made happy by evil/misfortune' as applied to **Éris** personified in Hesiod *W&D* 28; compare also the image of **Éris** as she "made merry" (**khaîre**) over the fighting of the Achaeans and Trojans, at XI 73. For more on the theme of blame as grief for the one who is blamed and laughter for the ones who hear the blame, see §11n6 below.

has mirth' specifically promises **khrêma** ... **geloîon** 'a thing of laughter' (*fr.* 168.2W).[1] We may speculate that there might have been a quality of timelessness in such laughter if indeed the subjects of blame in the Iambos were stock characters.[2] Be that as it may, however, we may surmise from the attested evidence that Iambos was more concerned with laughter than with blame for the sake of blame. In this connection, we come back to Aristotle's useful formulation about comedy: its function is laughter, not blame (*Poetics* 1448b37–38).

§9. Although Homeric Epos is not intrinsically suited for the comic element, Aristotle does find an attested poetic form, *within the Homeric tradition*,[1] that has a function parallel to that of comedy. The form in question is represented by the Homeric *Margites*, which shares with comedy the prime function of **tò geloîon** (*Poetics* 1448b28–38).[2] From both Aristotle's brief account (ibid.) and the few fragments that have survived (most notably *fr.* 1W), we know that the *Margites* even combines the meters of both Epos and Iambos. It consists of dactylic hexameters interspersed with iambic trimeters. From the fragments and the overall testimonia (pp. 69–76 West 1972),[3] we also know that the contents of the *Margites* resemble those of the Iambos: both the story and its characters are base and ridiculous. Finally, we may note that the very name **Margī́tēs** is built from the adjective **márgos** 'gluttonous, wanton'—a word that serves to designate a base exponent of blame poetry.[4]

§10. In fact, the name **Margī́tēs** has a strikingly close formal parallel in **Thersī́tēs**, the name of a figure described in the *Iliad* itself as the most base of all the Achaeans who came to Troy. The actual word here for 'most base' is **aískhistos** (II 216), belonging to the family of the same noun **aîskhos** that conventionally designates the baseness of blame poetry. This man who is *the worst of the Achaeans*

§8n1. Cf. Ch.5§39.

§8n2. Cf. Ch.12§21, Ch.13§§2, 6, 7.

§9n1. I note again—as I have done throughout—that in matters of archaic Greek poetry our concern should be more with questions of poetic tradition than with questions of poetic authorship.

§9n2. Aristotle specifically attributes the *Margites* to "Homer" (ibid.). My own formulation is that the poem is within the Homeric tradition (n1). Aristotle's attribution is nevertheless valuable because it implies an affinity of the *Margites* with Homeric composition that cannot be matched by the Cycle, which Aristotle does not even attribute to "Homer" (*Poetics* 1459b1). For more on the *Margites* as archaic poetry in the Homeric tradition, see Forderer 1960.

§9n3. For an interesting supplement: West 1974.190.

§9n4. See Ch.12§9.

(cf. also II 248–249) is also described as **ékhthistos** 'most hateful' to Achilles and Odysseus specifically (II 220), who happen to be *the best of the Achaeans* in the *Iliad* and *Odyssey* respectively—and thereby the two preeminent figures of Panhellenic Epos.[1] In this respect also, the word **ékhthistos** is significant. It belongs to the family of the same noun **ékhthos** 'hatred' that conventionally designates the nature of blame poetry compared to that of praise poetry: "being **ekhthrós**" as against "being **phílos**."[2] Moreover, Thersites is said to be **ékhthistos** 'most hateful' in particular to Achilles and Odysseus (II 220) for the following reason:

> ... τὼ γὰρ <u>νεικείεσκε</u>

... because he <u>made **neîkos**</u> against these two

II 221

Thersites is the most inimical figure to the two prime characters of Homeric Epos *precisely because it is his function to blame them.* Epos is here actually presenting itself as parallel to praise poetry by being an institutional opposite of blame poetry. This passage, then, even supports Aristotle's formulation of Epos as a descendant of **enkṓmia** 'praise poetry' (*Poetics* 1448b24–38).[3] We should add the qualification, however, that Epos is more likely a partial and maybe even an indirect descendant.[4] Nevertheless, it implicitly recognizes its own affinity to praise poetry.

§11. The name of **Thersítēs** connotes blame poetry not only by way of its parallelism with the formation **Margîtēs**.[1] The boldness conveyed by the element **thersi-** is not the same as a warrior's **thérsos/thársos** 'boldness'.[2] Rather, it is akin to the **thérsos/thársos** 'boldness' of the blame poet. Consider the expression **thersi-epḕs phthónos** 'bold-worded envy' at Bacchylides 13.199, which serves as a foil for **aineítō** 'let him praise' at line 201.[3] Or again, we may note

§10n1. See Ch.2; cf. also Puelma 1972.105n74.

§10n2. See Ch.12§21n2.

§10n3. In this connection, we may note again the interesting expression used by the **rhapsōidoí** 'rhapsodes' to designate "recite Homer": **Hómēron epaineîn** (discussion at Ch.6§6n4). Moreover, the word **kléos** designates both praise poetry (Ch.12§3) and Epos (Ch.1§2).

§10n4. Cf. §2.

§11n1. On the forms, see Chantraine 1963.21.

§11n2. See Chantraine, p. 20, for attestations of historical figures in Thessaly named **Thersítās**, where indeed the naming must have been inspired by the concept of a warrior's **thérsos** (Aeolic for **thársos**).

§11n3. On this instance of **phthónos**, see also Ch.12§4.

that Antinoos calls Odysseus **tharsaléos** 'bold' (xvii 449) after hearing a speech directed at him by the would-be beggar, who is asking him for food (xvii 415–444). When the base suitor refuses, he is reproached by Odysseus (xvii 454–457), whose words are actually acknowledged as **óneidos** [plural] 'blame' by Antinoos.⁴ Finally, consider the collocation **Polutherseḯdē philokértome** at xxii 287, applied in derision to Ktesippos, another of the base suitors, at the moment of his death by the man who killed him, the loyal Philoitios. The **lóbē** 'outrage' of Ktesippos against the disguised Odysseus (xx 285)⁵ had been verbal as well as physical: while sarcastically advocating that the apparent beggar be treated as a **xénos** (xx 292–298), Ktesippos had thrown a foot of beef at him (xx 299–300). Having now avenged this insult, Philoitios ridicules the slain Ktesippos by calling him **Polu-therseḯdēs** and **philo-kértomos** (xxii 287) in the context of reproaching him specifically for improper speech at the time of his physical attack on Odysseus (xxii 287–289). The mock patronymic **Polu-therseḯdēs** 'son of Bold-in-many-ways' reinforces the epithet **philo-kértomos** 'lover of reproaches'.⁶ In sum, a man who had reproached Odysseus is now getting a taste of his own medicine.

§12. Similarly, Thersites in the *Iliad* gets blame for having given blame. He dares to reproach Agamemnon (II 225–242), and the narrative introduces his words with **neíkee** 'made **neîkos**' (II 224), then concludes them with **pháto neikeíōn** 'spoke making **neîkos**' (II

§11n4. See Ch.12§11. Compare also xviii 390, where the suitor Eurymakhos tells the disguised Odysseus that he has spoken **tharsaléōs** 'boldly'. The would-be beggar has just spoken words of counter-reproach to the suitor (xviii 366–386), who had reproached Odysseus for being a glutton (xviii 357–364). Note that Eurymakhos specifically reproaches Odysseus for having an insatiable **gastér** 'belly' (xviii 364), and that Odysseus refers to this in his counter-reproach when he speaks to Eurymakhos as one who is "reproaching my belly," **tḕn gastér' oneidízōn** (xviii 380). In this connection, we should observe the insulting of the poet by the Muses in Hesiod *Th.* 26: shepherds are **gastéres oîon** 'mere bellies'. For the appositive **kák' elénkhea** 'base objects of reproach' (again, *Th.* 26), see the brief discussion of **élenkhos** at §7n1; cf. §14. For a brilliant exercise in correlating *Th.* 26 with *Odyssey* xiv 124–125, see Svenbro 1976.50–59: the **gastér** is an emblem of the poet's readiness to adjust his themes in accordance with what his immediate audience wants to hear.

§11n5. For the implications of **lóbē**: §5n1.

§11n6. The word **kertomíai** 'reproaches' at xx 263 is equated with **thūmòs enīpês** 'spirit of blame' at xx 266. (For more on the noun **enīpé** 'blame, reproach' and the corresponding verb **enénīpe** 'blamed, reproached [aorist]', see §5 and Ch.13§6.) Note too the use of the verb **kertoméō** 'reproach' at xviii 350: the suitor Eurymakhos is **kertoméōn** 'reproaching' Odysseus, and his words of blame are said to cause **ákhos** 'grief' for Odysseus (xviii 348) and **gélōs** 'laughter' for the other suitors (xviii 350).

243). Thersites is in turn reproached by Odysseus himself (II 246–264), whose own words of blame are introduced with **ēnípape** 'reproached' (II 245)[1] and concluded with his actually beating Thersites (II 265–268). Significantly, this combined physical and verbal abuse of Thersites results in pain and tears for the victim (II 269) but laughter for the rest of the Achaeans (II 270).[2] Here again, we see a theme of reversal, since the function of Thersites himself was "to make **éris** against kings" (ἐριζέμεναι βασιλεῦσιν: II 214)[3] — in accordance not with the established order of things[4] but rather with *whatever he thought would make the Achaeans laugh* (II 214–215).

§13. We may note that the word here for 'laughable' is actually **geloîion** (II 215), corresponding to Aristotle's term for the function of comedy, **tò geloîon** (*Poetics* 1448b37, 1449a32–37). We may note also that Aristotle's concept of **aîskhos** 'baseness', to which the concept of **tò geloîon** 'laughter' is intrinsic (*Poetics* 1449a32–37), corresponds to the characterization of Thersites as the **aískhistos** 'most base' of all the Achaeans who came to Troy (II 216). I infer, then, that Homeric Epos can indeed reflect the comic aspect of blame poetry, but that it does so at the expense of the blame poet. In the Thersites episode of the *Iliad*, it is Epos that gets the last laugh on the blame poet, rather than the other way around. Not only the maltreatment of Thersites by Odysseus but even his physical description by the narrative makes him an object of ridicule. Epos dwells on his deformities in repulsive detail (II 217–219), thus compounding the laughter elicited by his baseness. He is **aískhistos** 'most base' not only for what he says and does (or for what is said and done to him

§12n1. On the family of **enīpḗ** 'blame, reproach' (with expressively reduplicated aorists **enénīpe** and **ēnípape**), see Chantraine II 349. Cf. §§5, 11(n6); also Ch.13§6.

§12n2. Cf. §§7 and 11(n6).

§12n3. Since the function of Thersites as blame poet is described as the making of **éris** against kings and since the **kléos** of praise poetry is traditionally described as **etḗtumon** 'true, genuine' (see Ch.12§3n2), we may compare the epic antithesis of **Eteo-kléēs** ('whose **kléos** is genuine') as king and **Polu-neíkēs** ('whose reproaches are many') as potential usurper. Cf. Reinhardt 1951.339 *en passant*; also Burkert 1972b.83. For more on the strife between Eteokles and Polyneikes, see Ch.7§16n3 and Ch.12§7n3. For more on **neîkos** 'quarrel, fight' as a word marking blame as a foil for praise, see above at Ch.12§3. Finally, compare the semantics of **Thersítēs** with the name given to the son of **Polu-neíkēs**, **Thérs-andros** (Pindar *O*.2.43). On the convention of naming heroes after the father's prime characteristic, see further at Ch.8§9n2.

§12n4. The expression **katà kósmon** 'according to the established order of things' (II 214) implies that blame poetry, when justified, has a positive social function. Cf. Ch.2§13n5.

by Odysseus!) but also for his very ugliness. And surely the base appearance of Thersites serves to mirror in form the content of his blame poetry. The content, in fact, is a striking illustration of what is called in Pindaric praise poetry **ekhthrà** ... **párphasis** 'hateful misrepresentation' (*N*.8.32)—the negative essence of blame poetry.[1] In the words that Thersites is quoted as saying, we actually find such a misrepresentation: the anger of Achilles, he says, is nonexistent, since such a superior hero would surely have killed Agamemnon if he had really been angry (II 241–242). Since the **mênis** 'anger' of Achilles is the self-proclaimed subject of the *Iliad* (I 1), these words of Thersites amount to an actual misrepresentation of epic traditions about Achilles.[2] As a blamer of the *Iliad*, Thersites is deservedly described at II 220 as **ékhthistos** 'most hateful' to the prime hero of our epic.

§14. From what we have seen up to now, the story of Thersites in the *Iliad* surely stands out as the one epic passage with by far the most overt representation of blame poetry. And we have yet to add the cumulative evidence from the overall diction in this passage, with its striking concentration of words indicating blame as a foil for Epos:[1]

éris 'strife'/Thersites makes **éris** against kings (ἐριζέμεναι βασιλεῦσιν: II 214, 247).

neîkos 'quarrel, fight'/Thersites makes **neîkos** against kings in general (νεικείειν: II 277) and Agamemnon in particular (νείκεε: II 224, 243); also against Achilles and Odysseus (νεικείεσκε: II 221), who are also kings (cf. I 331 and IX 346 respectively).

óneidos 'blame, reproach'/Thersites speaks "with words of **óneidos**" (ὀνειδείοις ἐπέεσσιν: II 277), equated with "making **neîkos**" against kings (νεικείειν: same verse), on which see the previous entry in our list. The plural of **óneidos** designates his words against kings in general and Agamemnon in particular (ὀνείδεα at II 251 and 222 respectively). He is "making **óneidos**" against Agamemnon (ὀνειδίζων: II 255).

kertoméō 'reproach [verb]'[2]/The participle (κερτομέων: II 256) is equated with the participle of **oneidízō** 'make óneidos' (ὀνειδίζων: II 255). The subject is Thersites. For the ridiculing aspect in the semantics of **kertoméō**, see §11n6.

§13n1. See Ch.12§7.
§13n2. Note too that Thersites here fails to use the word **mênis** for 'anger', resorting instead to the unmarked **khólos** (II 241). Cf. Ch.5§8n2.
§14n1. Compare this list with the original list at Ch.12§3, comprised of words indicating blame as a foil for praise poetry.
§14n2. Cf. also **kertomeîn** at Archilochus *fr.* 134W.

élenkhos 'reproach, disgrace'/Thersites reproaches all the Achaeans by addressing them with the plural of this neuter noun, described as **kaká** 'base' (κάκ' ἐλέγχεα: II 235).[3] For more on **élenkhos**, see §7, especially n1; also §11n4.

lōbētḗr 'man of **lṓbē** [outrage]'[4]/This epithet is applied to Thersites by Odysseus (II 275). For more on **lṓbē**, see §§5(n1), 6, 11.

aískhistos 'most base'/See again §§10, 13.

ékhthistos 'most hateful'/See again §10.

Finally, we may append a set of negative epithets applied to Thersites that serve to reproach not only the poetic form of his discourse but also its very style:

a-metro-epḗs 'whose words [**épos** plural] have no moderation' (II 212)
a-kritó-mūthos 'whose words [**mûthos** plural] cannot be sorted out' (II 246)
epes-bólos 'who throws his words [**épos** plural]' (II 275).[5]

§14n3. Cf. also the reproach of the poet by the Muses in Hesiod *Th*. 26: shepherds are **kák' elénkhea** 'base objects of reproach'; see §11n4. We may note that the Judgment of Paris took place in his **méssaulos** 'courtyard [for animals]' (XXIV 29), where he *blamed* Hera and Athena but *praised* Aphrodite (see Ch.11§16). On the pastoral background of the Paris figure: scholia (A) to *Iliad* III 325.

§14n4. Cf. also **lōbēt**[... at Archilochus *fr.* 54.9W (the same fragment also contains the name of Lykambes!).

§14n5. For the formation of this word, cf. the interesting collocation **épesin ... ēdè bolêisin** at xxiv 161, referring to the way in which the suitors had *reproached* Odysseus (**eníssomen**, same verse).

15 | The Best of the Achaeans Confronts an *Aeneid* Tradition

§1. Having finished with the diction surrounding the Thersites figure, we may now turn to another Iliadic passage, XX 246–256, which rivals the passage about Thersites in its wealth of information relating to the poetry of blame. For a proper understanding, however, we must begin with an Iliadic passage found earlier on in the action.

§2. In the heat of battle, the Trojan hero Deiphobos suddenly finds that he needs help from his ally Aeneas, and he goes to look for him:

> ... τὸν δ' ὕστατον εὗρεν ὁμίλου
> ἑσταότ'· αἰεὶ γὰρ Πριάμῳ ἐπεμήνιε δίῳ,
> οὕνεκ' ἄρ' ἐσθλὸν ἐόντα μετ' ἀνδράσιν οὔ τι τίεσκεν

And he found him standing hindmost in the battle,
for he had **mênis** [anger] always against brilliant Priam,
because he [Priam] did not <u>honor</u> him [Aeneas], <u>worthy</u> that he was among heroes.

XIII 459–461

There is a striking thematic parallelism here between Aeneas and Achilles, who likewise had withdrawn from battle because he had **mênis** against Agamemnon (I 1, etc.). The king had not given the hero **tīmế** 'honor'—even though Achilles is not just "worthy among heroes" but actually the "best of the Achaeans" (I 244, etc.).[1] These themes of **mênis**/withdrawal/**tīmế**/excellence are not only present in the *Iliad*; they are in fact central to it, permeating the composition in its monumental dimensions.[2] It is the expansion of these central themes in the *Iliad* that makes us so aware of their compression in the mention of Aeneas at XIII 459–461. Moreover, this Iliadic mention contains a unique attribution of **mênis** to Aeneas. With the

§2n1. Ch.2§§1–7.
§2n2. Ch.5§§7–8.

exception of XIII 460, the word **mênis** (and its derivatives) always applies to the reciprocal anger of Achilles as the individual warrior against Agamemnon as king of the collective Achaeans. This anger is the prime theme of the *Iliad*, and no other anger on the part of any other hero ever qualifies as **mênis** in the entire epic[3]—with the exception of XIII 460. Thus the microcosm of XIII 459–461 shares a distinctive pattern with the macrocosm of the *Iliad*. In short, the nature of the themes attributed to Aeneas in this passage suggests that they are central to another epic tradition—this one featuring Aeneas rather than Achilles as its prime hero.

§3. Let us reconsider the words describing the withdrawal of Aeneas:

τὸν δ' ὕστατον εὗρεν ὁμίλου
ἑσταότ'·

And he found him standing hindmost in the battle

XIII 459–460

This stance of the hero is in sharp contrast with his later involvement in the fighting:

Αἰνεία, τί σὺ τόσσον ὁμίλου πολλὸν ἐπελθὼν
ἔστης;

Aeneas! Why are you standing so far up front in the battle?[1]

XX 178–179

The speaker here is none other than Achilles himself, who has just been confronted in battle by this hero whose epic tradition is parallel in its themes to his own.[2] After this question alluding to the specific theme of a withdrawal by Aeneas, Achilles continues with another taunting question:

ἦ σέ γε θυμὸς ἐμοὶ μαχέσασθαι ἀνώγει
ἐλπόμενον Τρώεσσιν ἀνάξειν ἱπποδάμοισι
τιμῆς τῆς Πριάμου; ἀτὰρ εἴ κεν ἔμ' ἐξεναρίξῃς,
οὔ τοι τοὔνεκά γε Πρίαμος γέρας ἐν χερὶ θήσει·
εἰσὶν γάρ οἱ παῖδες, ὁ δ' ἔμπεδος οὐδ' ἀεσίφρων

Does your **thūmós** urge you to fight against me
because you hope to be king of the horse-taming Trojans,

§2n3. Ch.5§8n2.
§3n1. Cf. also XVII 342.
§3n2. As the two heroes confront each other in combat, they are described as **dúo ... ánéres éxokh' áristoi** 'two men who were by far the best' (XX 158).

which is the **tīmḗ** of Priam?[3] But even if you kill me,
Priam will not place the **géras** [honorific portion] in your hand on that
account.[4]
He has children,[5] and he is sound and not unstable.[6]

XX 179–183

There is a conflict going on here between Achilles and Aeneas as
warriors in battle and also between the epic traditions about each of
the two heroes. Moreover, the *Iliad* here is actually allowing part of
the Aeneas tradition to assert itself at the expense of the Achilles
tradition. We have just seen Achilles taunt Aeneas by predicting that
he will never replace Priam as king of Troy. And yet, the god
Poseidon himself then prophesies the exact opposite:

ἤδη γὰρ Πριάμου γενεὴν ἤχθηρε Κρονίων·
νῦν δὲ δὴ Αἰνείαο βίη Τρώεσσιν ἀνάξει
καὶ παίδων παῖδες, τοί κεν μετόπισθε γένωνται

For the son of Kronos has already abominated the line of Priam.
And presently the might of Aeneas will be king of the Trojans
and his children's children, who are to be born hereafter.

XX 306–308

This destiny prophesied by Poseidon is part of a poetic tradition
glorifying the Aeneadae, as we see from the independent evidence of
the Homeric *Hymn to Aphrodite*.[7] There we find Aphrodite making a
parallel prophecy to the father of Aeneas:

σοὶ δ' ἔσται φίλος υἱὸς ὃς ἐν Τρώεσσιν ἀνάξει
καὶ παῖδες παίδεσσι διαμπερὲς ἐκγεγάονται

§3n3. Compare the conflict between Aeneas and Priam over **tīmḗ** with the conflict
between Achilles and Agamemnon, as discussed at Ch.5§§7–8. Cf. Reinhardt 1961.453
and Fenik 1968.121–122.

§3n4. Compare the **géras** deprived from Achilles: discussion at Ch.7§19.

§3n5. An ironic understatement!

§3n6. The taunts of Achilles continue at XX 184–186: if Aeneas kills him, does he
expect that the Trojans will assign him a **témenos** 'precinct' of fertile land? Perhaps
this description is appropriate to the grove of a cult hero: see Ch.16§8n1 (cf. the notion
of **tīmḗ** for Aeneas from the **dêmos**, at XI 58; discussion at Ch.8§11n5).

§3n7. The valuable work of Heitsch 1965 on the *Hymn* and its relationship with the
Aeneas stories in the *Iliad* is for me marred by his persistent assumption that he is
dealing with interrelationships of texts rather than traditions. I also value the
interesting work of Dihle (1970.65 ff.) on the idiosyncratic diction of the Iliadic
passages about Aeneas. But for me his evidence shows not that the passages about
Aeneas are "non-oral" but that they reflect an Aeneas tradition that is significantly
different from the Achilles tradition of our *Iliad*. I have similar problems with the
admirable work of Lenz 1975, who offers a conscientious reassessment of the
interpretations found in Heitsch and Dihle.

You will have a **phílos** son who will be king of the Trojans,
and children will be born to his children, and so on forever.[8]

H.Aphr. 196-197

Moreover, Poseidon rescues Aeneas in the middle of his battle with
Achilles precisely because, as the god himself says, "it is destined"
(μόριμον: XX 302) that Aeneas must not die at this point. In this
way, the line of Aeneas will not die out, and he will have
descendants (XX 302-305)—as compared to the doomed line of
Priam (XX 306). At XX 336, Poseidon personally tells Aeneas that
his death at this point in the narrative would have been **hupèr
moîran** 'beyond destiny'. In effect, then, it would be untraditional for
the narrative to let Achilles kill Aeneas in *Iliad* XX, since there is a
poetic tradition that tells how Aeneas later became king of Troy;
accordingly, Poseidon intervenes in the narrative and keeps Aeneas
alive for further narratives about his future.[9]

§4. One of the most obvious traces of a variant epic tradition about
Aeneas in *Iliad* XX is this surprising rescue of a pro-Trojan hero by a
decidedly pro-Achaean god, Poseidon himself. This is not to say,
however, that the narrative about the rescue is out of joint with the
overall composition of the *Iliad*. True, we may have expected Apollo
rather than Poseidon to rescue Aeneas. And yet, if this pro-Trojan
god had attempted such a rescue, then the timing of the other gods'
respective interventions would have been thrown off, *as the narrative
itself says* (XX 138-141). In other words, the *Theomachia* would have
begun prematurely.[1] Whereas a rescue by Apollo would have been
simply a pro-Trojan act, the rescue by Poseidon puts the act *above*
taking sides; the figure of Aeneas thus transcends the war of the
Trojans and Achaeans.[2] In this sense, Aeneas is beyond the scope of
the Trojan War tradition in general, reflecting other themes and
perhaps even other concerns of other times. The favorable relationship of Poseidon with Aeneas may in fact reveal a special cult affinity

§3n8. The everlasting continuity predicted for the line of the Aeneadae is in
compensation for the mortality of their ancestor Anchises, father of Aeneas; see
Ch.7§1n5.

§3n9. For more on **hupèr moîran** as 'contrary to destiny' and **katà moîran** as
'according to destiny' (as at viii 496), where **moîra** is the 'destiny' inherited by the
traditional poetic narrative, see Ch.2§17 and Ch.5§25n2; cf. also Pestalozzi 1945.40.
Note too the traditional function of **Diòs boulé** 'the Will of Zeus' as the given plot of a
given epic narrative. Discussion at Ch.5§25n2 (with further references).

§4n1. See Scheibner 1939.6-7.

§4n2. Cf. Scheibner ibid.

between the god and a dynasty of Aeneadae;[3] during the times that the *Iliad* and the *Hymn to Aphrodite* traditions were separately evolving into their ultimate forms, the current importance of such a dynasty could be retrojected into the Heroic Age by such poetic devices as the prophecy to Aeneas that his descendants, not Priam's, will be the ones who are to hold sway in the Troad (*Iliad* XX 302–308, *H.Aphr.* 196–197).[4] I avoid saying, however, that the *Hymn to Aphrodite*—let alone the *Iliad*—was expressly composed for an audience of Aeneadae.[5] Even when we take into account the observation by Reinhardt that Aeneas is the only attested Iliadic hero who is mentioned as having descendants *in the present*,[6] it does not necessarily follow that such descendants are the key figures in the poet's audience, nor that the "poet of the *Iliad*" had made an ad hoc reference to the presence of this audience by virtue of narrating a self-fulfilling prophecy.[7] Rather, we see from the evidence of *Iliad* XX and the Homeric *Hymn to Aphrodite* that the perpetuity of the line of Aeneadae was itself a traditional poetic theme.[8] The *Iliad* does not invent something, even if it is historically true, just to please a given group. Of course, it can still please those in any given group by repeating something traditional about them.[9]

§5. Our *Iliad*, then, invalidates not only the prediction made by Achilles when he taunts Aeneas but also the actual combat between the two heroes. The divine intervention of Poseidon is a clear sign even to Achilles that Aeneas had not "boasted in vain" about his heroic identity (μὰψ αὕτως εὐχετάασθαι: XX 348).[n] Such an asser-

§4n3. Note XI 58, where it is said of Aeneas himself that "he got tīmḗ from the dêmos, like a god"; this characterization of the ancestor of the Aeneadae is appropriate to a cult hero (Ch.8§11nn5, 6).

§4n4. Cf. Jacoby 1961 [=1933] I 39–48, 51–53; also Donini 1967.

§4n5. So Scheibner 1939.133 on the *Hymn to Aphrodite.* I also distance myself from any of the theories featuring the "poet of the *Iliad*" at the court of the Aeneadae (cf. Jacoby, ibid.).

§4n6. Reinhardt 1961.451. I would note, however, that there are other Homeric passages that refer to the present: see Ch.9§§15–16.

§4n7. *Pace* Reinhardt ibid.

§4n8. Cf. Kullmann 1960.283n1.

§4n9. Besides *Iliad* XX 306–308 and *H.Aphr.* 196–197, there are attestations of still other prophecies addressed to the Aeneadae: see Acusilaus *FGrH* 2.39 and the commentary by Jacoby I 383.

§5n. The infinitive **eukhetáasthai** refers to the boast of Aeneas to Achilles at XX 206–209, as expressed by **eúkhomai** 'I boast' at XX 209 (recapped at XX 241). As Muellner points out (1976.93), "When a hero **eúkhetai** [boasts], he says the most significant facts he can about himself." From the diction of XX 206–209, Muellner (pp.

tion of the Aeneas tradition at the expense of the Achilles tradition can only go so far, however. The heroic momentum of Achilles in the *Iliad* may be temporarily stalled but never deflected. Within the *Iliad*, the tempo of events after the death of Patroklos preordains that Achilles will win in any duel with any challenger. Within a composition from some other tradition, however, the outcome of a duel involving Achilles may not be inevitable.

§6. Ironically, Achilles himself conjures up the presence of other traditions when he tries to intimidate Aeneas by *reminding* him[1] of an incident that happened when Achilles was capturing the cities of Lyrnessos and Pedasos (XX 187–198). As Achilles tells it, Aeneas was handily routed by him (ibid.).[2] Moreover, Aeneas himself had earlier told Apollo that he was indeed intimidated at the prospect of facing Achilles in combat; the reason for his fear, he says, is that he remembers how Achilles had routed him when the Achaean hero captured Lyrnessos and Pedasos (XX 89–98). But now a curious thing happens: as he is being reminded of the same incident by Achilles, Aeneas is suddenly no longer intimidated. He replies to Achilles:

Πηλείδη, μὴ δὴ ἐπέεσσί με νηπύτιον ὣς
ἔλπεο δειδίξεσθαι, ἐπεὶ σάφα οἶδα καὶ αὐτὸς
ἠμὲν κερτομίας ἠδ' αἴσυλα μυθήσασθαι

Son of Peleus! Do not hope to intimidate me with words [épos plural] as if I were some child.
For I myself know clearly how to tell
reproaches [kertomíai] and unseemly things.[3]

XX 200–202

Aeneas is saying that he too can narrate **kertomíai** and **aísula**— words that indicate the poetry of blame.[4] By implication, the words

---

76–77) can also show that Aeneas is using words that formally assign Achilles to a heroic stature lower than his own. On the etiquette-rules of such **eúkhomai** speeches, see Muellner, pp. 74–75n9.

§6n1. Note the expression **è ou mémnēi** 'do you not remember' at XX 188; for the poetic implications of **mimnḗskō** 'remind' and **mémnēmai** 'have in mind', see Ch.1§3n2 and Ch.6§§5–9.

§6n2. On the poetic traditions that told of the Capture of Lyrnessos and Pedasos: Ch.7§29.

§6n3. Note that **kertomíās ēd' aísula mūthḗsasthai** at XX 202 is equated with **oneídea mūthḗsasthai** 'tell reproaches [óneidos plural]' at XX 246, on which see further at §8.

§6n4. See n3. On **kertomíai**, see Ch.14§§11(n6) and 14. On **aísula** see Ch.19§6n6.

[**épos** plural] that Achilles had just narrated about the Capture of Lyrnessos and Pedasos—words that make Aeneas the object of blame—are not the only possible narration. It seems that Aeneas now has in mind other words [**épos** plural], words that Aeneas could in turn relate about Achilles—words that make Achilles the object of blame.

§7. The very word **épos** [plural] at XX 200 (also recapped at XX 256) indicates not just "words" in general but "poetic words" in particular,[1] as we can see from the lines that immediately follow XX 200–202:

ἴδμεν δ' ἀλλήλων γενεήν, ἴδμεν δὲ τοκῆας
πρόκλυτ' ἀκούοντες ἔπεα θνητῶν ἀνθρώπων·
ὄψει δ' οὔτ' ἄρ πω σὺ ἐμοὺς ἴδες οὔτ' ἄρ ἐγὼ σούς

We know each other's lineage, we know each other's parentage,
hearing the famed[2] words [**épos** plural] of mortal men.
But by sight you have never yet seen my parents, nor I yours.

XX 203–205

The words of Aeneas to Achilles here reveal the traditional conceit of the **aoidós** 'singer, poet', who *knows* nothing but *hears* the **kléos** 'fame' = 'that which is heard' from the Muses, who in turn *know* everything.[3] As the poet declares at the beginning of the *Catalogue*:

ὑμεῖς γὰρ θεαί ἐστε, πάρεστέ τε, ἴστε τε πάντα,
ἡμεῖς δὲ κλέος οἶον ἀκούομεν οὐδέ τι ἴδμεν

For you [the Muses] are goddesses; you are always present, and you know
   everything;
but we [poets] only hear the **kléos** and know nothing.[4]

II 485–486

When a poet starts his performance by asking his Muse to *tell* him the subject (cf. I 1, i 1), the composition is in fact being presented to his audience as something that he *hears* from the very custodians of

§7n1. See Ch.12§15n3. Compare also the use of **épos** in Theognis 16 and 18 as discussed at Ch.17§12.

§7n2. The epithet **pró-kluto-** 'famed', applied to **épos** [plural], is from the same root as **kléos** 'fame' = 'that which is *heard*' (on which see Ch.1§2).

§7n3. Again, Ch.1§2. As for the theme of *hearing* instead of *seeing*, compare the theme of the blind poet (Ch.1§§3–4) and the story of the poet who was taken beyond the field of vision (Ch.2§13n5).

§7n4. Compare the **íste** ... **ídmen** in II 485–486 and the **ídmen** ... **ídmen** in XX 203 (recapped by **ísāsi** at XX 214) with the **ídmen** ... **ídmen** of the Muses in Hesiod *Th.* 27–28 and the **ídmen** ... **ídmen** of the Sirens in *Odyssey* xii 189–191.

all stages of reality. The poet's inherited conceit, then, is that he has access to both the content and the actual form of what his eyewitnesses, the Muses, speak as they describe the realities of remote generations. I should emphasize that this conceit is linked with the poet's inherited role as an individual performer, and that "only in performance can the formula exist and have clear definition."[5] The formulas are the selfsame words spoken by the Muses themselves: they are recordings of the Muses who were always present when anything happened. In fact, the frame in which these formulas are contained, the dactylic hexameter, was traditionally called **épos** by the poetry itself.[6] Since the dactylic hexameter, as well as all verses, has an inherited tendency to be syntactically self-contained,[7] the **épos** is truly an epic utterance, an epic sentence, from the standpoint of the Muses or of any character quoted by the Muses. The word introducing Homeric quotations is in fact regularly **épos**. There are even some subtle grammatical distinctions, in traditions of phraseology, between the **épos** the Muses quote and the **épos** they simply narrate.[8] In a medium that carries with it such inherited conceits about accuracy and even reality, we can easily imagine generations after generations of audiences conditioned to expect from the performer the most extreme degrees of fixity in content, fixity in form. In sum, the words of Aeneas to Achilles imply that they both have complete poetic access to each other's heroic lineage and, by extension, to each other's heroic essence.[9]

§8. It remains to be seen what sort of **épos** [plural] Aeneas had threatened to relate about Achilles at XX 200–202. The key is the **épos** [plural] related by Achilles about Aeneas—words that made the Trojan ally an object of blame. As we have already observed, these words [**épos** plural] of Achilles concerned the Capture of Lyrnessos and Pedasos. Significantly, this story comes from an epic tradition that is different from that of the *Iliad*. Whereas the Homeric *Iliad* is Panhellenic in scope, the *Capture of Lyrnessos and Pedasos* tradition is decidedly local. Its orientation is that of **ktísis** poetry, which is

§7n5. Lord 1960.33.

§7n6. See Koller 1972; cf. also Ch.17§12(n4).

§7n7. Cf. Nagy 1974.143–145.

§7n8. Cf. Kelly 1974 on the different patterns of correption in quoted speeches compared to plain narrative.

§7n9. For lineage as essence in the etiquette of **eúkhomai**, see again Muellner 1976.74–77.

distinguished by its adaptability to the ever-shifting character of whatever local community it happens to glorify.[1] From place to place, the heroic themes of **ktísis** poetry can be expected to shift in accordance with local lore and ideology.[2] It may even be that different local traditions could present the same incident to the disadvantage of different heroes—so that different heroes would become the object of blame. In fact, the words of Aeneas himself allude to precisely this factor of local variation in theme:

ἔστι γὰρ ἀμφοτέροισιν <u>ὀνείδεα</u> μυθήσασθαι
πολλὰ μάλ', οὐδ' ἂν νηῦς ἑκατόζυγος ἄχθος ἄροιτο.
στρεπτὴ δὲ γλῶσσ' ἐστὶ βροτῶν, πολέες δ' ἔνι μῦθοι
παντοῖοι, ἐπέων δὲ πολὺς νομὸς ἔνθα καὶ ἔνθα.
ὁπποῖόν κ' εἴπησθα <u>ἔπος</u>, τοῖόν κ' <u>ἐπακούσαις</u>.
ἀλλὰ τίη <u>ἔριδας</u> καὶ <u>νείκεα</u> νῶϊν ἀνάγκη
<u>νεικεῖν</u> ἀλλήλοισιν ἐναντίον, ὥς τε γυναῖκας,
αἵ τε χολωσάμεναι <u>ἔριδος</u> πέρι θυμοβόροιο
<u>νεικεῦσ'</u> ἀλλήλῃσι μέσην ἐς ἄγυιαν ἰοῦσαι,
πόλλ' ἐτεά τε καὶ οὐκί· χόλος δέ τε καὶ τὰ κελεύει.
ἀλκῆς δ' οὔ μ' ἐπέεσσιν ἀποτρέψεις μεμαῶτα . . .

It is possible for the two of us to tell each other very many <u>reproaches</u>
[<u>óneidos</u> plural],[3]
and not even a hundred-benched ship could bear their burden.
But the tongue of men is twisted, bearing many stories
of all kinds. And there is a manifold range of **épos** [plural] from place to place.[4]
The sort of **épos** you say is just the thing that <u>you will hear told</u> about yourself.[5]
But why must there be <u>éris</u> and <u>neîkos</u> [plural][6] for the two of us
to <u>make neîkos</u> against each other, like women[7]
who are angry in a **thūmós**-devouring <u>éris</u>
and who <u>make neîkos</u> against each other in the middle of the assembly,

§8n1. See Ch.7§§29–30.
§8n2. Ibid.
§8n3. On the word **óneidos** as an indicator of blame poetry, see Ch.12§§3 and 7 (usage in praise poetry) and §§6 and 11 (usage in Epos).
§8n4. On **nomós** in the metaphorical sense of a pastoral "range": Pohlenz 1965 [= 1948] 337.
§8n5. On the semantics of **epi-** in **epakoúsais**, cf. Ch.6§6n4.
§8n6. On the words **éris** and **neîkos** as indicators of blame poetry, see Ch.12§§3, 6, etc.
§8n7. Richardson (1974.215) provides a list of festivals and cults where **aiskhrologíā** was restricted to women. On **aiskhrologíā** as 'ritual jesting', see Richardson, pp. 213–217. On **tò aiskhrón** 'baseness' as a formal mark of blame poetry, see Ch.14§§4–5.

saying many <u>true things</u> and many false.[8] Anger urges them on.
But I am eager for battle and you will not deflect me from my strength with
épos [plural] ...

XX 246–256

At verse 250, Aeneas is in effect saying that he could recount **épos**
[plural] about Achilles as an object of blame, and that his narration
would be the exact opposite of the **épos** [plural] Achilles had
recounted about him. Instead of any further talk, however, the
Trojan ally is now determined to start fighting (XX 244–245, 256 ff.).
The ensuing narrative of the duel between Aeneas and Achilles may
even reveal some details from a variant local tradition in which the
hero of our *Iliad* was actually injured by his opponent. At XX 291,
the action of the duel is interrupted by Poseidon at the very moment
when Aeneas has the initiative: he is about to throw a huge rock at
Achilles (XX 285–287). On the basis of parallels in other narratives
about duels where one hero throws a rock at another, we should
expect Aeneas to win the encounter.[9] But then the thematic
requirements of the *Iliad* take over: *even if* Aeneas had succeeded in
hitting Achilles with the rock (XX 288), the hero's shield or helmet
would surely have withstood the blow (XX 289), and then Achilles
would surely have killed Aeneas (XX 290)!

§9. To sum up: the war of words between Aeneas and Achilles
reveals the presence of an independent *Aeneid* tradition within the
Iliad. Moreover, it reveals Aeneas himself as a master of poetic skills
in the language of praise and blame. On the one hand, he has the
power to tell stories about Achilles that make him the object of
blame. On the other, he actually tells the full story of his own
genealogy—an exercise in heroic self-affirmation that amounts to the
ultimate praise of the hero by the hero.[1] In view of these characteristics of Aeneas, we may consider the etymology of his name. As
Karl Meister has argued,[2] Homeric **Aineíās** is the Ionic reflex of

§8n8. From the standpoint of praise poetry, the words of the blame poet are
conventionally false (cf. Pindar *N*.8.21–25 and 32–33); discussion at Ch.12§§5–7. By
contrast, the **kléos** conferred by the praise poet is *true* (cf. Pindar *N*.7.63); discussion
at Ch.12§3(n2), Ch.14§12(n3). The theme that blame can actually be *true* reflects an
earlier time when the concept of a blame poet was not yet distinct from that of a praise
poet: see Ch.16§10n6.

§8n9. See Merkelbach 1948.307–308; also Heitsch 1965.66–71, esp. p. 67. I do not
agree, however, with their inferences about textual interpolation.

§9n1. Cf. again Muellner 1976.74–77.

§9n2. Meister 1921.156–157; cf. Perpillou 1973.186.

*Aináās (by way of *Ainéās), derivative of a noun that survives as aínē. As a formal parallel, Meister cites Homeric **Augeíās** (XI 701), the Ionic reflex of *Augáās (by way of *Augéās), derivative of a noun that survives as augé. Now this word aínē (as in Herodotus 3.74, 8.112) is a by-form of aînos, the semantic range of which has revealed a bivalence of praise and blame.[3] There is a parallel bivalence in the figure of Aeneas.

§9n3. Ch.12§§18-19, Ch.13§12.

Part IV
Beyond Epic

Part 1.

16 | The Death of a Poet

§1. In the story of Thersites, we have seen that the details told about him consistently reflect his function as poet of blame.[n] As it happens, even the story of his death reflects this function. From the epic tradition of the *Aithiopis*, we learn that Thersites was killed by Achilles himself; the reason given for the killing is that the hero had been "reproached and blamed" by Thersites (λοιδορηθείς ... καὶ ὀνειδισθείς: Proclus summary p. 105.25–26 Allen). Specifically, Thersites had alleged that Achilles loved Penthesileia (*Aithiopis*/Proclus p.105.26–27). The killing is followed by dissension among the Achaeans, and Achilles has to atone for his deed: he sails off to Lesbos, sacrifices to Apollo and his divine family, and is ritually purified by Odysseus (*Aithiopis*/Proclus pp. 105.27–106.1).

§2. In these details from the *Aithiopis*, the figure of Thersites is parallel to that of a **pharmakós** 'scapegoat'.[1] We turn to an **aítion** 'cause'[2] motivating a ritual that entails the expulsion of **pharmakoí** at the Thargelia, an Ionian festival in honor of Apollo. According to Istros (*FGrH* 344.50, *ap.* Harpocration, s.v.), this ritual is a set of reenactments or **apomīmḗmata**.[3] In particular, the ritual reenacts the

§1n. Ch.14§§10–14.

§2n1. Cf. Usener 1912/1913 [= 1897] 244; also Wiechers 1961.44n2.

§2n2. To be more precise: I use **aítion** in the sense of "a myth that *traditionally* motivates an institution, such as a ritual." I stress "traditionally" because the myth may be a tradition *parallel to* the ritual, not *derivative from* it. Unless we have evidence otherwise, we cannot assume in any particular instance that an aetiological myth was an *untraditional* fabrication intended simply to explain a given ritual. The factor of *motivating*—as distinct from *explaining*—is itself a traditional function in religion, parallel to the traditional function of ritual. It is only when the traditions of religion become obsolescent that rituals may become so obscure as to invite explanations of a purely literary nature. For a particularly illuminating discussion of a specific **aítion** as a traditional complement to a specific ritual, I cite Brelich 1969.229–311.

§2n3. On **mímēsis** as 'reenactment', in song and dance, of themes in myth, see Ch.13§12n3.

279

killing of one **Pharmakós**, personified, by Achilles and his men; he was stoned to death on the grounds that he stole sacred **phiálai** 'bowls' belonging to Apollo (Istros, ibid.). Whereas this ritual of **pharmakoí** has the function of purifying the community (Istros, ibid.),[4] the myth of the primordial **pharmakós** has the opposite function, in that his death had been the original cause of impurity and pestilence. We see this theme in another attested **aítion** that likewise motivates the ritual. According to Helladios (*ap.* Photius *Bibliotheca* 279, p. 534a3–4 Bekker), a ritual of **pharmakoí** was instituted at Athens for the purpose of purifying the city, which had been afflicted by a pestilence resulting from the unjustified death of Androgeos the Cretan. In effect, then, the primordial death of the primordial **pharmakós** on the level of myth causes a potentially permanent impurity, which in turn calls for permanent purification by way of year-to-year reenactment on the level of ritual.[5] There is too little evidence for us to know for sure whether such reenactments could once have taken the form of real executions or whether the ritual deaths of **pharmakoí** were normally stylized in song and dance, as the word **apomīmémata** indicates (Istros, ibid.). For now, it is more important to observe two modes of killing the **pharmakós** on the idealized level of myth: death either by stoning (Istros, ibid.) or by being thrown off a cliff (Ammonius 142 Valckenaer).[6] Returning to the story from the *Aithiopis* (in the abbreviated form that survives in the Proclus summary), we may speculate as to whether Thersites too had been stoned to death by Achilles and his men, as was **Pharmakós**. In this case, however, the medium of epic collapses the distinction between the perspectives of myth and ritual: the same figure who caused the impurity—Achilles himself—is also given the chance to be purified for his action.[7]

§3. Such details about the death of a **pharmakós** are strikingly parallel to the details about the death of Aesop at Delphi, as we find them in the *Life of Aesop* tradition (*Vitae* G+W Perry; also papyrus fragments of *Vitae*: *Pap.Oxy.* 1800 and *Pap.Soc.Ital.* 1094).[1] Aesop too

§2n4. For further testimonia on purification by way of **pharmakoí**, see Wiechers 1961.34n9.

§2n5. For more on this sort of logic in the linking of myth and ritual, cf. the discussion of the Bouphonia by Wiechers 1961.37–42.

§2n6. For further references, see Wiechers 1961.34nn7, 8.

§2n7. For a similar collapsing of myth/ritual distinctions, see Sinos 1975.131–143 on the funeral of Patroklos as instituted by Achilles.

§3n1. For the fragments, see in general Aesop *Testimonia* 20–32 Perry. As for the

is killed on the grounds that he stole a sacred **phiálē** 'bowl' of Apollo (*Vitae* G+W 127). The Delphians had deliberately hidden the bowl amidst Aesop's belongings as he was about to leave Delphi, so that they might accuse him of stealing it (ibid.). Like some primordial **pharmakós**, Aesop is unjustly accused and executed by the Delphians, who either stone him to death (*Pap.Soc.Ital.* 1094, p. 165 Callimachus I ed. Pfeiffer) or throw him off a cliff (ibid. and *Vita* W 142).[2] As in an **aítion** about **pharmakoí**, the Delphians are then afflicted by a pestilence resulting from the unjustified death of Aesop (*Vitae* G+W 142).

§4. I omit here several other details that can be adduced about the death of Aesop as parallel to the death of a **pharmakós**.[1] I also postpone our considering how it was that the Delphians purified themselves of the pestilence resulting from Aesop's death.[2] Our immediate concern is the similarity of Aesop not just with **pharmakoí** in general but also with Thersites in particular. We must now consider how it was that Aesop provoked the people of Delphi to kill him. Just as Thersites had incurred death by blaming Achilles, so also Aesop incurs his own death by blaming the Delphians (cf. Aristotle *Constitution of the Delphians fr.* 487 Rose). And the medium of his blame is the Aesopic fable, the formal word for which is **aînos**.[3]

§5. Since the **aînos** is by nature an ambiguous mode of discourse, its effect will be praise *or* blame on the basis of ad hoc application—whether explicit or even implicit.[1] A story like "The Travelers and the Driftwood," one of the fables that Aesop initially tells the Delphians in our attested *Life of Aesop* tradition (*Vitae* G+W 125),[2]

Life of Aesop as attested in *Vitae* G+W, Perry says (1936.1): "It is almost without parallel among the ancient Greek texts that have come down to us. For, although many popular traditions have survived concerning the doings and sayings of Homer, Hesiod, and the Seven Wise Men of Greece, yet these are either scattered and fragmentary or else, when embodied in continuous accounts such as the *Contest between Homer and Hesiod*, the *Lives* of Homer, or Plutarch's *Banquet of the Seven Sages*, have taken on something of the formal and learned character of the environment in which they were composed or through which, at any rate, they have been transmitted to us whatever their original character may have been."

§3n2. In *Pap.Oxy.* 1800, Aesop is stoned and *then* thrown off a cliff.

§4n1. For an exhaustive listing: Wiechers 1961.35–36.

§4n2. See §8 and n1.

§4n3. See Ch.12§18 and n2.

§5n1. Ch.12§§18–19, Ch.13§12, Ch.15§9.

§5n2. The story is also attested in the canonical corpus of Aesopic fables: *Fable* 177 Perry.

contains an *implicit* message of blame by virtue of the context set by the narrative. Aesop's explicit likening of the Delphians to driftwood, which looks from afar like a seaworthy ship as it floats towards travelers waiting on the shore (but turns out to be a piece of nothing as it comes closer into view) is actually redundant from the hindsight of all the other fables he is yet to tell—fables bearing similar implicit messages of blame against the Delphians. The blame is fulfilled through the development of the narrative, and the deployment of interlocking fables is intensified as the time of Aesop's execution draws near. Among the fables that he tells just before he dies are "The Frog and the Mouse" (*Vitae* G+W 133) and "The Dung Beetle and the Eagle" (G+W 134–139).[3] With each telling of each **aînos**, the narrative reinforces the ad hoc application of Aesop's words to the Delphians as objects of blame. Without its framing narrative, of course, the ad hoc moral of any given **aînos** could be lost.[4] It is highly significant, therefore, that the actual framing of an **aînos** like "The Dung Beetle and the Eagle" within a narrative about the death of Aesop *is itself traditional*. In the comedy of fifth-century Athens, there is an overt reference to this fable *as one that was told by Aesop when the Delphians accused him of stealing Apollo's bowl* (Aristophanes *Wasps* 1446–1448; cf. also *Peace* 129–132).[5] We have here the most compelling sort of evidence for drawing two conclusions:

1. In particular, the *Life of Aesop*—as it survives in *Vitae* G and W—preserves a traditional context for the telling of the Aesopic **aînos**.[6]

§5n3. The second story is also attested as Aesop *Fable* 3 Perry.

§5n4. When an **aînos** like "The Dung Beetle and the Eagle" is taken out of its narrative context, it can function simply as a nature story that explains why eagles and beetles breed in different seasons; there is a trace of this function at line 12 of Aesop *Fable* 3 Perry, side-by-side with the moral at lines 13–14. The moral, of course, functions as the message of the **aînos** in the context of the narrative, as made explicit in *Vitae* G+W 139. The moral attached to each **aînos** in the canonical collection of Aesopic fables serves as a compensation for the context that a framing narrative would supply.

§5n5. Again, the word for 'bowl' is **phiálē** (Aristophanes *Wasps* 1447): so also in the story of **Pharmakós** (§2) and in the *Life of Aesop* (§3).

§5n6. Cf. Wiechers 1961.11–13. It follows that the canonical collections of Aesopic fables, *presented without framing narratives*, entail the truncation (sometimes even distortion) of the **aînos** as a traditional genre. Granted, some of the themes found in **aînoi** may have an independent existence in other genres such as the nature story (cf. n4 and Wiechers, p.12n13). But the point still remains that the *Fables* as we find them in Perry's edition do not represent the **aînos** in its archaic traditional form.

2. In general, the **aînos** takes on its distinct message of praise or
   blame only within the context of the narrative that frames it, and
   the *Vitae* are a survival of such a narrative tradition.
   We may also observe again that the Archilochean Iambos is itself a
   medium where the words of blame can be framed within narrative.[7]
   Further, an **aînos** like "The Fox and the Eagle" (Archilochus *fr.*
   174W)[8] is actually framed within a poem of blame against Lykambes
   himself (Archilochus *frr.* 172–181W).[9]

§6. In the *Life of Aesop* tradition, the various fables that Aesop
tells the Delphians serve to blame them for various things. As an
example, I will single out again "The Travelers and the Driftwood,"
for the main purpose of emphasizing that the *Life of Aesop* is deeply
archaic in content if not in diction.[1] When Aesop narrates this fable,
he concludes from it that the Delphians are inferior to other Hellenes
and that their behavior is worthy of their ancestors (*Vitae* G+W
125). When the Delphians challenge him to say outright what he
means, Aesop answers: since the ancient custom is to make one-
tenth of a captured city—population and all—sacred to Apollo, and
since the Delphians are by ancestry sacred to Apollo, they are
therefore slaves of all the Hellenes (*Vitae* G+W 126). As Anton
Wiechers has argued in detail, these words of reproach actually reflect
the political situation of Delphi in the era of the First Sacred War (ca.
590 B.C.).[2] However, the sequence of events in the *Life of Aesop*
tradition reverses the sequence in history:[3] Aesop's reproach—
causing his death—is based on the situation immediately *after* the
First Sacred War, but his death—effected by his reproach—sets the
stage for the events immediately *before* it, namely, the undertaking
of a joint expedition against Delphi (*Vitae* G+W 142).[4] To put it

§5n7. See Ch.13§§4, 9, 13.

§5n8. The story is also attested as Aesop *Fable* 1 Perry; see Ch.12§18n2.

§5n9. See Ch.12§§18–19, Ch.13§12.

§6n1. Even in matters of language, however, we can detect archaic traces of Ionic
underneath the Koine that pervades the narrative. See Wiechers 1961.9n5 on the fable
about the girl without **nóos** 'sense', who is tricked into having sex with a man whom
she sees having sex with an **ónos** 'ass' (*Vitae* G+W 131). The point of the whole story
depends on a misunderstanding by way of metathesis: **ónos** instead of **nóos**, the Ionic
equivalent of **noûs**. The form **noûs**, which is what we read in the Koine of our attested
Vitae, conceals the play on words and in effect renders the story unintelligible.

§6n2. His argument has to be read in its entirety: see Wiechers, pp. 7–30.

§6n3. Cf. Wiechers, p. 27n45.

§6n4. The First Sacred War was actually directed against Cirrha/Crisa, which
controlled and in that sense defined the sacred center of Delphi. Before Delphi was

another way, the *Life of Aesop* tradition actually presents the death of Aesop as a *cause* of the First Sacred War, but the institutional reality that Aesop reproaches—namely, that the people of Delphi are sacred to Apollo—is a lasting *effect* of the First Sacred War.[5] From the standpoint of the myth, the death of Aesop is the *effect* of his reproaching the institutions of Delphi; from the standpoint of these institutions, on the other hand, his death is their indirect *cause*. It is this sort of "cause" that qualifies as an **aítion**.[6] Only here, the **aítion** of Aesop's death motivates not simply one institution, such as a ritual, but an entire conglomeration of institutions sacred to Apollo— the very essence of Delphi after the First Sacred War.

§7. We also have, in a fragment from the *Life of Aesop* tradition, an example of a specific description concerning one single Delphic institution, which happens to be a ritual. As before, we see this institution being reproached by Aesop. Here too, we see him killed by the people of Delphi as a result of his reproach. And again we may say that the death of Aesop is an **aítion**, implicitly motivating the particular ritual that he reproaches. The fragment first describes the ritual in question, then tells of Aesop's death. I present the text in its entirety:

ἔσ]τ]ιν δ' αἰτία τοια[ύτη] εἰρ[η]μένη·¹ ἐπὰν [εἰσέ]λθη τ[ις] τῷ θεῷ θυσιάσ[ων ο]ἱ Δελφ[ο]ὶ περ[ι]εστήκασι τὸν βωμ[ὸ]ν ὑφ' ἑαυτοῖς μαχαίρας κ[ο]μί- ζοντες, σφαγιασαμένου δὲ τοῦ ἱερέως² καὶ δείραντος τὸ ἱερεῖον καὶ τὰ σπλάγχνα περιεξελομένου, οἱ περιεστῶτες ἕκαστος ἣν ἂν ἰσχύσῃ μοῖραν ἀποτεμνόμενος ἄπεισιν, ὡς πολλάκις τὸν θυσιάσαντα αὐτὸν ἄμοιρ[ο]ν ἀπι[έ]ναι. τοῦτο οὖν Αἴ[σ]ωπ[ο]ς Δελφοὺς ὀνιδ[ί]ζων ἐπέσκωψεν, ἐφ' οἷς διοργισθέντες οἱ πολλοὶ λίθοις αὐτὸν βάλλοντες κατὰ κρημνοῦ ἔωσαν. μετ' οὐ πολὺ δὲ λοιμικὸν πάθος ἐπέσκηψε τῇ πόλει, χρηστηριαζομένοις δ' αὐτοῖς

---

reconstituted as distinct from the defeated Cirrha/Crisa, however, the First Sacred War could be envisaged as an expedition against Delphi. See Wiechers, p. 27. On Cirrha/Crisa: Giovannini 1969.19–20.

§6n5. Before the First Sacred War, Delphi was a sacred center controlled by the **pólis** Cirrha/Crisa; after it, the defeated Cirrha/Crisa ceases to exist as a **pólis**. Its fertile territory and its population are now sacred to Apollo, since Delphi now controls Cirrha/Crisa. In that sense, the **pólis** is now controlled by the sacred center. See Wiechers, p. 24, for testimonia indicating that the territory of Cirrha/Crisa became **hieró**- 'sacred' to Apollo; his discussion should be supplemented, however, with Benveniste's observations on the semantics of **hieró**- (1969 II 192–196).

§6n6. On our use of the word **aítion**, see again §2n2.

§7n1. The lines that precede this sentence unfortunately are lost.

§7n2. Hunt corrects from ἱερείου: Perry 1952.221.

ὁ θεὸς ἀνεῖλεν³ οὐ πρότερον [λή]ξ]ειν τὴν νόσ[ον μέ]χρις [ἂν Α]ἴσωπον
ἐξι[λάσκωντ]αι. οἱ δὲ περιτει[χίσ]αντες τὸν τόπον [ἐν ᾧ κ]ατέπεσεν βωμό[ν
θ' ἱ]δ[ρυσά]μενοι λυτήρ[ι]ο[ν]⁴ τῆς νόσου, ὡς ἥρῳ θ[υσίας] προ[σ]ήνεγκαν.

The cause is said to be this:⁵ When someone goes in for the purpose of
initiating sacrifice to the god, the Delphians stand around the altar carrying
concealed daggers [**mákhairai**]. And after the priest has slaughtered and
flayed the sacrificial victim and after he has apportioned the innards, those
who have been standing around cut off whatever **moîra** [portion] of meat
each of them is able to cut off and then depart, with the result that the one
who initiated the sacrifice oftentimes departs without having a **moîra** himself.
Now Aesop <u>reproached</u> and <u>ridiculed</u> the Delphians for this, which made the
people angry. They stoned him and pushed him off a cliff. Not much later, a
pestilence fell upon the city, and when they consulted the Oracle, the god
revealed that the disease would not cease until they propitiated Aesop. So
they built a wall around the place where he fell, set up an altar as an antidote
to the disease, and sacrificed to him as a hero.

Pap.Oxy. 1800 *fr.* 2 ii 32–63
= Aesop *Testimonia* 25 Perry

§8. Explicitly, the death of Aesop is motivating a specific institution, the hero cult of Aesop at Delphi. There is a striking parallel in
Vitae G+W 142. As in *Pap.Oxy.* 1800, we see that a pestilence falls
upon Delphi after Aesop's death (G+W), that the Oracle tells the
Delphians to propitiate the dead Aesop (G+W), that the Delphians
accordingly build a shrine and set up a **stélē** for Aesop (W).¹ But the

§7n3. Maas corrects from ἀπεῖπεν, as noted by Wiechers 1961.23 but not by Perry
(ibid.).
§7n4. Reading by Perry (ibid.).
§7n5. See n1. The sense of the missing sentence that precedes would have been
something to the effect that Aesop had a hero cult at Delphi. As Albert Henrichs
points out to me, **aitíā** 'cause' is a word used by mythographers and scholiasts as an
equivalent of **aítion** 'cause' (as defined at §2n2 and as applied at §6); cf. the scholia to
the Αἴτια of Callimachus!
§8n1. Instituting a hero cult for Aesop as purification for his death is parallel to
instituting a ritual of **pharmakoí**. For the parallelisms between the death of Aesop and
the death of a proto-**pharmakós**, see §3. There are also traces in *Vitae* G+W of a
variant tradition, of Samian origin, concerning the hero cult of Aesop. The people of
Samos voted **tīmaí** for Aesop (G+W 100); one version says that they assigned a
témenos 'precinct' to him (W 100), while the other adds that this precinct came to be
called the **Aisópeion** (G 100). At this point, while he is being honored by the Samians,
Aesop himself neglects to honor Apollo (G 100); for the significance of this neglect,
see Ch.17§1. (Note too the parallelism with Hesiod *W&D* 138–139 compared to 142:
the Silver Generation get **tīmaí** from us mortals although they themselves failed to
give **tīmaí** to the gods. Discussion at Ch.9§§1–3.) From another detail in the narrative
about Aesop in Samos, we can even infer that the Samians may have believed that

same passage in *Vitae* G+W 142 presents a complex **aítion**. Aesop's death motivates not only his cult as hero but also, as we have already seen, the undertaking of a joint expedition against Delphi. The death of Aesop is thus motivating the First Sacred War and the institutional reality resulting from it, namely, that all Delphi is sacred to Apollo.[2] As we have also seen,[3] the death of Aesop in *Vitae* G+W 142 is thereby an **aítion** or 'cause' that implicitly motivates the very institutions that he reproaches—from the standpoint of these institutions. From the standpoint of the myth, however, Aesop's death is the explicit *effect* of his reproaching these institutions. So also with *Pap. Oxy.* 1800: from the standpoint of its myth, Aesop's death is the explicit *effect* of his reproaching the ritual described. From the combined standpoints of myth and ritual, however, we may conclude by way of the comparative evidence in *Vitae* G+W 142 that the myth of Aesop's death is an **aítion** or 'cause' that implicitly motivates this very ritual.

§9. Actually, we have already seen a parallelism between this ritual concerning the distribution of meat, exactly as we find it described in *Pap. Oxy.* 1800, and the myth concerning the death of Pyrrhos as we find it described in Pindar's *Paean* 6 and *Nemean* 7.[1] In fact, the parallelism in theme between ritual and myth is so close here that we also have considered the possibility that the death of Pyrrhos is an **aítion** that had once explicitly motivated the ritual described in *Pap. Oxy.* 1800.[2]

§10. Following through on this hypothesis, we may tentatively formulate a twofold pattern wherein the deaths of Pyrrhos/Aesop are the explicit/implicit motivations for the Delphic ritual that dramatizes strife over cuts of sacrificial meat. The pattern can be extended much further. Whereas Pyrrhos is killed because he reacts to strife over meat by resorting to *physical* violence (Pindar *Paean* 6.117–120 and

---

Aesop was actually buried on their island. When Aesop tells the Samians the story of "The Wolves and the Sheep" (= *Fable* 153 Perry), he gives this as the reason: "so that you may engrave it on my **mnêma** [memorial] after my death" (*Vita G* 96). This narrative device of a self-fulfilling prophecy implies that the *Life of Aesop* tradition had once been suitable for an inscription in a precinct of Aesop as cult hero. (Compare the *Life of Archilochus* tradition on the Mnesiepes Inscription in the precinct of Archilochus, the **Arkhilókheion**, at Paros; discussion at Ch.18§§3–5.) For traces of Samian traditions about Aesop, see also Aristotle *Constitution of the Samians fr.* 573 Rose.

§8n2. See §6 and n5.
§8n3. Above, §6.
§9n1. Ch.7§§10–12.
§9n2. This is a modified restatement of the hypothesis offered at Ch.7§12.

N.7.40–43),[1] Aesop is killed because he reacts to the institution of this strife with *verbal* violence: he makes **óneidos** against the Delphians (*Pap.Oxy.* 1800: ὀνιδίζων).[2] While the hero cult of Pyrrhos is based on his death as a *warrior*, the hero cult of Aesop is based on *his* death as a *poet*. I say "poet" rather than "blame poet" because the word **aînos**, applicable to Aesop's fables of blame for the Delphians, also designates praise poetry itself.[3] In fact, Aesop's blaming the Delphic procedure of meat cutting fits the self-avowed function of the praise poet, who blames what is base while praising what is noble. Significantly, one of the main traditional targets for the praise poet to blame is **phthónos** 'greed'.[4] Moreover, we have seen that the **phthónos** blamed by praise poetry is primarily manifested in the imagery of greedily devouring meat.[5] Accordingly, Aesop's blaming the ritualized strife and greed inherent in the Delphic distribution of meat represents an archetypal function of praise poetry.[6] On the other hand, Aesop's blame takes the specific form of

§10n1. Note the use of **dēriázomai** 'fight', derivative of the noun **dêris** 'fight', in Pindar *Paean* 6.119. Another derivative, **dēríomai**, applies twice to the fight between Achilles and Odysseus "at a **daís** of the gods" (viii 76, 78), as we have observed in Ch.7§13. Significantly, this fight between Achilles and Odysseus is called a **neîkos** (viii 75), on which see Ch.7§17 as also the discussion of **éris/neîkos** at Ch.11§16 and Ch.12§§3, 6, etc. See also Hesiod *W&D* 27–41, a particularly explicit passage about **Éris** (line 28) and **neîkos** (the word occurs in this passage four times!); at line 33, **dêris** is equated with **neîkos** [plural]. Note too that the Strife Scene of Pyrrhos concerns his **tīmaí** (Pindar *Paean* 6.118), which are formalized as portions of meat; compare the primal **éris** between Prometheus and Zeus, again concerning **tīmaí** formalized as cuts of meat (above, Ch.11§§5–10).

§10n2. While the words **éris/neîkos** apply not only to the language of blame but also to the action of physical combat (Ch.12§8n1), the semantic range of the word **óneidos** and its derivatives seems to be restricted to the verbal dimension (cf. the discussion of **óneidos** as the opposite of **kléos**, at Ch.12§7; cf. also Ch.12§§6, 11). Note that Aesop's blame was provoked when the Delphians specifically "gave no **tīmḗ** to him" (οὐδὲν ... ἐτίμησαν: *Vita* W 124).

§10n3. See §5; also Ch.12§§18–19, Ch.13§12.

§10n4. See Ch.12§§4–6.

§10n5. See especially Ch.12§5.

§10n6. The blaming of anything *by* praise poetry is programmatically justified as a positive social function. See esp. Ch.12§4, Ch.14§3. So also on the two occasions that Hektor justifiably blames Paris (on which see Ch.14§5): both times the words of blame are introduced by νείκεσσεν 'made **neîkos**' (III 38, VI 325), and both times Paris acknowledges the justness of the blame by saying ἐπεί με κατ' αἶσαν ἐνείκεσας οὐδ' ὑπὲρ αἶσαν 'since you made neîkos against me according to **aîsa**, not beyond **aîsa**' (III 59, VI 333). Note that the word **aîsa** can designate not only the ordained way that things are to be—that is, 'fate'—but also 'cut of meat' (see Ch.7§21n1). Proper and improper blame are presented in imagery that connotes the proper and improper apportioning of meat. For another allusion to blame as a positive social function, see Ch.14§12n4.

ridicule (*Pap.Oxy.* 1800: ἐπέσκωψεν), which in turn is a characteristic of blame poetry.[7] I conclude, then, that the themes surrounding the Aesop figure go back to a time when the concept of a blame poet was not yet distinct from that of a praise poet—that is, to a time when the poet blamed or praised in accordance with what he saw was bad or good. The semantic range of the very word **aînos** reveals a parallel bivalence of blame and praise.[8]

§10n7. See esp. Ch.14§§7 and 13. On the word **skóptō** 'ridicule' (ἐπέσκωψεν), see Ch.13§3 and n4; also Ch.18§3 and n4. Since the greed blamed by Aesop is ritualized (Ch.7§11), it may well be that Aesop's act of blaming is itself an **aítion** that motivates ritualized blaming in the form of ridicule. Note too the ridiculing of the Delphians' greed in comedy—e.g., Aristophanes *fr.* 684 Kock, Anon. *fr.* 460 Kock.

§10n8. See again §5; also Ch.12§§18–19, Ch.13§12.

17 | On the Antagonism of God and Hero

§1. Aside from the direct testimony of *Pap.Oxy.* 1800 and Aesop *Vitae* G+W 142 about a hero cult of Aesop, there is important indirect evidence for his actual function as cult hero. Again we turn to the parallelism between the deaths of Aesop and Pyrrhos. In the myth of Pyrrhos, the theme of his antagonism with Apollo is fundamental to his essence as cult hero of Delphi.[1] Now we see a parallel pattern of antagonism in the *Life of Aesop* tradition. At the moment that the Delphians plot the death of Aesop, Apollo is described as having **mênis** 'anger' against him ($\mu\eta\nu\iota\sigma\nu\tau\sigma\varsigma$: *Vita* G 127).[2] There is a crucial supplementary detail in the Goleniščev Papyrus, where the god is described as actively helping the Delphians bring about Aesop's death (*Pap.Gol.*: $\sigma\upsilon\nu\epsilon\rho\gamma\sigma\hat{\upsilon}\nu\tau\sigma\varsigma$).[3] Apollo's anger is motivated by an incident in Samos: Aesop had sacrificed to the Muses and set up a shrine for them, neglecting to place Apollo in the center (*Vita* G 100, 127; *Pap.Gol.*).[4] The pattern of antipathy between Aesop and Apollo is in fact complemented by a pattern of sympathy between him and the Muses. In the course of *Vita* G, there is mention of the Muses no fewer than twenty-five times, often in the context of Aesop's swearing by them.[5] It was the Muses who had

§1n1. See Ch.7 in general and Ch.7§4 in particular.

§1n2. Here as well as throughout the *Life of Aesop*, the involvement of Apollo as Aesop's antagonist has been eliminated in the "W" branch of the story's transmission. For evidence that this adjustment is secondary and amounts to a distortion, see Wiechers 1961.11n9.

§1n3. For the pertinent passage in this fragment, see Perry 1952.11. For the entire text of the Goleniščev Papyrus, see Perry 1936.58–67.

§1n4. Instead, the central place is assigned to Mnemosyne, mother of the Muses (*Vita* G 100). This incident in the *Life of Aesop* tradition is linked by the narrative itself with Aesop's ultimate position as cult hero: see Ch.16§8 and n1.

§1n5. Conversely, there is not a single mention of the Muses in *Vita* W; see n2 and cf. Perry 1952.11.

originally given Aesop his power of verbal skills (*Vita* G 7).[6] Before he dies, it is at a sanctuary of the Muses that Aesop takes refuge (*Vita* G 134), imploring the Delphians in the name of Zeus **Xénios** not to despise the smallness of the sanctuary (*Vita* G 139)—as the eagle had once despised the smallness of the dung beetle (*Vita* G 135).[7] The implicit but obvious foil here for the smallness of the Muses' sanctuary is the overwhelming greatness of Apollo's sanctuary at Delphi. In this connection, we may observe that Aesop never mentions Apollo by name in *Vita* G: instead, he refers to the god either as the **prostátēs** 'leader' of the Muses (G 33, 142) or simply as 'he who is greater than the Muses' (G 33). The latter designation meshes neatly with the implicit theme that the Muses' sanctuary is small in comparison to Apollo's.

§2. Significantly, the two contexts of these references by Aesop to Apollo are by no means marginal to the central themes of Aesop's death. In the first instance, Aesop is telling a humorous fable about Apollo's powers of prophecy, and the humor is at the god's expense (*Vita* G 33);[1] in effect, Aesop is here implicitly provoking Apollo's anger. In the second instance, Aesop is by now at the actual moment of his death and is calling upon Apollo to be a witness of his unjust execution by the Delphians (*Vita* G 142). It seems a matter of ostentatious indirectness that Aesop is presented as referring to Apollo at these very moments by way of tabu periphrasis. Moreover, the timing as well as the meaning of Aesop's reference to Apollo as "leader of the Muses" and as "he who is greater than the Muses" amount to a clear acknowledgment by the narrative *that Aesop's essence as poet is defined not only by the Muses but also by their leader, Apollo himself.*[2]

§1n6. The role of Isis as leader of the Muses (*Vita* G 6) is an innovation made possible by (1) an Egyptian phase in the transmission of the Aesop story and (2) the Egyptian religious trend of associating the cult of Isis with the cult of the Muses (on which see the evidence adduced by Perry, p.2n8, esp. Plutarch *De Iside* 352b).

§1n7. The message of "The Dung-Beetle and the Eagle," as built into the narrative of *Vita* G 135 and as formally enunciated in the moral that concludes Aesop *Fable* 3 Perry, is that one should not despise the small, since no one is so negligible as to be incapable of revenge. For more on this fable, see Ch.16§5. Note that Aesop appeals to the ultimate protector of guest-strangers, Zeus **Xénios**, in acknowledging the smallness of the Muses' sanctuary; compare the appeal made by Odysseus, in his disguise as a lowly beggar, to the same moral code of the **xénos** 'guest-stranger' (Ch.12§16). See in general Ch.12§§12–16 on the ideology of the poet as **xénos**.

§2n1. See Perry 1962.299–300 on the probability that this fable was in the collection of Demetrius of Phaleron.

§2n2. I disagree here with Wiechers 1961.14n21, who thinks that Aesop's peri-

§3. In fact, the traditional diction of archaic Greek poetry makes it explicit that the essence of the poet is defined by the Muses *and* Apollo:

ἐκ γάρ τοι Μουσέων καὶ ἐκηβόλου Ἀπόλλωνος
ἄνδρες <u>ἀοιδοὶ</u> ἔασιν ἐπὶ χθόνα καὶ κιθαρισταί

For it is from the Muses and from far-shooting Apollo
that there are <u>poets</u> on earth, and lyre players too.[1]

Hesiod *Th.* 94–95[2]

Moreover, Apollo is traditionally the leader of the Muses from the standpoint of ritual poetry, as we see from the following spondaic fragment concerning libations:

σπένδωμεν ταῖς Μνάμας παισὶν Μούσαις
καὶ τῷ Μουσάρχῳ Λατοῦς υἱεῖ[3]

Let us pour libations to the Muses, children of **Mnămă** [Memory]
and to the **Moúsarkhos** [Leader of the Muses], the son of Leto.

fr.adesp. 941 Page

Besides the title **Moúsarkhos**, Apollo also qualifies as **Mouseîos** (*IG* 7.1.36: Megara) and **Mousagétēs** 'Leader of the Muses' (*IG* 12.5.893: Tenos).[4] Still, in view of this evidence, an important question arises:

---

phrastic references to Apollo in *Vita* G 142 are an innovation, not an archaism. Also, I think that the story of Aesop's encounter with Isis and the Muses at *Vita* G 6–7 is the reflex of an older version in which Apollo functioned as the leader of the Muses. The replacement of Apollo by the polymorphous Egyptian goddess Isis would have been facilitated if the references to Apollo had been periphrastic even in this older version. From the Egyptian standpoint, Isis could then be substituted easily as "leader of the Muses" or as "she who is greater than the Muses" (cf. §1n6). Still, the question remains: if indeed the older version presents Apollo and the Muses as givers of speech and speech skills respectively to Aesop, why is Apollo in this case beneficent, rather than maleficent? See Ch.18§2.

§3n1. Whereas **aoidoí** 'poets' ('singers') are traditionally pictured as accompanying themselves on the lyre (as at *Odyssey* viii 67–69), they are here mentioned *along with* "lyre players" (**kitharistaí**). This doublet of singers and lyre players reflects not the fragmentation of the poet's traditional function but rather the ensemble of song as embodied by the Muses and Apollo combined: the former sing while the latter plays the lyre, as at *Iliad* I 603–604. In this passage, the ensemble of the Muses and Apollo is described in a manner more appropriate to a specific *picture* than to a general *event*; cf. *H.Apollo* 186–206. By "picture" I mean a traditional mode of iconographic representation.

§3n2. The same verses recur in *Homeric Hymn* 25.2–3. On the integrity of this hymn as a piece of traditional poetry, see Koller 1956.178–179 (*pace* West 1966.186: "a senseless bit of patchwork").

§3n3. Page (1962) supplies τῷ in front of Λατοῦς.

§3n4. Cf. Plato *Laws* 653d; Strabo 468; Pausanias 5.18.4, 8.32.2, 10.19.4. Cf. also *Iliad* I 603–604 and *H.Hermes* 450–452.

why is it, then, that the archaic poet as a rule invokes the Muses *without* Apollo at the beginning of his composition (*Iliad* I 1, *Odyssey* i 1, *W&D* 1, etc.)? We will arrive at an answer, I submit, by looking further at the context of the same Hesiodic passage that explicitly derives the essence of the poet from the Muses *and* Apollo (*Th.* 94–95): the **aoidós** 'poet' is now specifically called Μουσάων θεράπων 'the **therápōn** of the Muses' (*Th.* 100). Before we can interpret this expression, however, an excursus on the word **therápōn** is in order.

§4. As Nadia Van Brock can show,[1] **therápōn** had actually meant something like 'ritual substitute' at the time it was borrowed into Greek from Anatolia, probably in the second millennium B.C. Compare Hittite *tarpašša-/tarpan(alli)-* 'ritual substitute', corresponding formally to Greek **théraps/therápōn**. To paraphrase Van Brock, the Hittite word designates an entity's *alter ego* ("un autre soi-même"), a projection upon whom the impurities of this entity may be transferred.[2] She goes on to cite a Greek reflex of these semantics in the Iliadic application of **therápōn** to Patroklos,[3] the one Achaean who is by far the most **phílos** to Achilles[4]—and who is killed wearing the very armor of Achilles.[5] Without any such comparative evidence, without even having to consider the word **therápōn**, Cedric Whitman has independently reached a parallel conclusion: that Patroklos functions as the epic surrogate of Achilles.[6] Granted, the prevailing applications of the word **therápōn** in ancient Greek poetry are semantically secondary: 'warrior's companion' (as typically at IV 227, VIII 104, XIII 246, etc.) or simply 'attendant' (XI 843, XIX 143, xviii 424, etc.). But we can see from the contexts where Patroklos is **therápōn** of Achilles (XVI 165, 244, 653; XVII 164, 271, 388) that the force of the word goes far beyond the dimensions of 'warrior's companion'. As Dale Sinos has convincingly argued,[7] Patroklos qualifies as **therápōn** of Achilles *only so long as he stays within his limits as the recessive equivalent of the dominant hero*.[8] In the words of Achilles himself, Patroklos and he are equivalent warriors, *so long as*

§4n1. Van Brock 1959.
§4n2. Van Brock, p. 119; cf. also Lowenstam 1975.
§4n3. Van Brock, pp. 125–126.
§4n4. Ch.6§§12–21.
§4n5. Cf. Householder/Nagy 1972.774–776.
§4n6. Whitman 1958.199–203.
§4n7. Sinos 1975.46–52.
§4n8. Cf. Ch.2§8 (and Ch.6).

Patroklos stays by his side; once he is on his own, however, the identity of Patroklos as warrior is in question:

τῷ κῦδος ἅμα πρόες, εὐρύοπα Ζεῦ,
θάρσυνον δέ οἱ ἦτορ ἐνὶ φρεσίν, ὅφρα καὶ Ἕκτωρ
εἴσεται ἦ ῥα καὶ οἷος ἐπίστηται πολεμίζειν
ἡμέτερος θεράπων, ἦ οἱ τότε χεῖρες ἄαπτοι
μαίνονθ', ὁππότ' ἐγώ περ ἴω μετὰ μῶλον Ἄρηος

Far-seeing Zeus! Let the glory of victory go forth with him.
Make him breathe courage from inside, so that Hektor too
will find out whether our **therápōn** knows how to fight in battle alone,
or whether his hands rage invincible only those times
when I myself enter the struggle of Ares.[9]

XVI 241-245

By its very outcome, the fatal impersonation of Achilles by Patroklos reveals that the **therápōn** is no longer the equivalent of Achilles *once he leaves his side* and goes beyond the limits Achilles had set for him (XVI 87–96).[10] Since even the epithet assigned to the **therápontes** of Achilles is **ankhémakhoi** 'those who fight nearby' (XVI 272, XVII 165),[11] we may infer that Patroklos has ceased to be **therápōn** of Achilles at the moment of his death. As we shall now see, he has become the **therápōn** of someone else.

§5. When Patroklos has his fatal confrontation with Apollo, he is described as **daímoni îsos** 'equal to a **daímōn**' (XVI 786), and we have observed that this epithet is traditionally appropriate for marking the climactic moment of god-hero antagonism in epic narrative.[1] In the Death Scene of Patroklos, this climactic moment is also the context of a more specific epithet: he is described as **thoôi atálantos Árēï** 'equal to swift Ares' (XVI 784). There was one other time when Patroklos was equated with Ares: back in *Iliad* XI, when he first became involved in his fatal impersonation of Achilles. There we find Patroklos leaving the tent of Achilles and coming out of seclusion; he is described at that very moment as **îsos Árēï** 'equal to Ares' (XI

---

§4n9. Whitman (1958.200) quotes the same passage, adding: "When Achilles prays to Zeus for Patroclus' safety, he seems to ask, indirectly, whether his friend can play his role adequately or not."

§4n10. Note especially what Achilles tells him at XVI 89: do not be eager to fight ἄνευθεν ἐμεῖο 'apart from me'. Dan Petegorsky draws my attention to a parallel: Pindar *O.* 9.76–79.

§4n11. See Sinos, pp. 46, 61(n6).

§5n1. Ch.8§§3–4.

604). In the very same verse, the narrative itself takes note that the application of this epithet marks Patroklos for death:

ἔκμολεν ἶσος Ἄρηϊ, κακοῦ δ᾽ ἄρα οἱ πέλεν ἀρχή

He came out, equal to Ares, and that was the beginning of his doom.[2]

XI 604

We recall that the designation 'equal to Ares' is particularly appropriate in the *Iliad* to the two other heroes who wear the armor of Achilles—the two main antagonists who are thereby cast in the same mold of warrior:[3]

Achilles	ἶσος Ἄρηϊ	XX 46
	ἶσος Ἐνυαλίῳ[4]	XXII 132
Hektor	ἶσος Ἄρηϊ	XI 295, XIII 802
	ἀτάλαντος Ἄρηϊ	VIII 215, XVII 72.

In fact, when Hektor puts on the armor of Achilles which he had despoiled from the body of Patroklos,[5] he is sealed in this armor by Zeus (XVII 209–210) and then, quite literally, "Ares entered him" (δῦ δέ μιν Ἄρης: XVII 210). Here we see Ares not so much as an Olympian ally of the Trojans but as the divine embodiment of murderous war. The same notion is inherent in such Homeric adjectives as **Arēḯphatos** (XIX 31, etc.) and **Arēïktámenos** (XXII 72), both meaning 'killed by Ares' = 'killed in war'. No matter who the immediate killer may be in any given narrative of mortal combat, the ultimate killer is Ares as god of war. For example, the Achaean Idomeneus kills the Trojan Alkathoos[6] in mortal combat (XIII 424–444), *with the direct help of the god Poseidon* (XIII 434–435); nevertheless, Ares is designated as the god who actually takes the hero's life (XIII 444).[7] So also with the death of Patroklos: although

§5n2. See Nagy 1974.230–231. Cf. Whitman 1958.200: "Then he is 'like Ares'; but here the poet is looking forward consciously to the *Patrocleia*, as is shown by the remark, 'this was the beginning of his woe' [XI 604]." Cf. also Whitman, pp. 114, 194.

§5n3. Cf. Ch.2§8. When Hektor sets out to fight in the armor of Achilles, he is specifically described as looking just like him (XVII 213–214).

§5n4. On the equivalence of Ares and Enyalios, see Nagy 1974.136.

§5n5. The manner in which Patroklos is denuded of Achilles' armor is highly significant: see Ch.9§33n2.

§5n6. The semantics of **-thoos** in **Alkă-thoos** seems relevant to the passage: Ch.20§10. On **alkă-**, see Ch.5§31n5. On the parallelisms between the death of Patroklos and the death of Alkathoos, see Fenik 1968.132–133.

§5n7. For another striking example, consider the description of the tapestry woven by Helen depicting the **áethloi** 'struggles' endured by Trojans and Achaeans alike *at the*

it is Hektor who kills him, *with the direct help of the god Apollo*, Patroklos is the ultimate victim of the war god, Ares. In his fatal moment of god-hero antagonism, the **therápōn** of Achilles is overtly equated with Ares, who is the ultimate motivation for his dying as a warrior of epic. Accordingly, *Patroklos is identified no longer with Achilles but rather with Ares himself.* In that sense, he is now the **therápōn** of Ares! And the most important evidence for this assertion has yet to be adduced: as an aggregate of warriors, the Achaeans [Danaans] are specifically addressed as θεράποντες "Αρηος '**therápontes** of Ares' (II 110, VI 67, XV 733, XIX 78). As a generic warrior, the hero of epic qualifies as a **therápōn** of Ares.[8]

§6. This formulation needs further refinement, for besides the dimension of myth as stylized in epic, we must also consider the dimension of ritual. As a generic warrior, the hero of epic is a **therápōn** of Ares *precisely because he must experience death.* The requirement of the hero's death, however, is dictated not so much by the narrative traditions of epic but by the ritual traditions of cult. Death is fundamental to the essence of the hero in cult, as we have already had occasion to observe.[1] This much said, we may finally return to the designation of the poet as Μουσάων θεράπων '**therápōn** of the Muses' in Hesiod *Th.* 100, and, in this same context, to the explicit derivation of the poet's essence from the Muses *and* Apollo (*Th.* 94–95).[2] We see from this testimony the emergence of a parallel pattern: whereas the generic warrior is the '**therápōn** of Ares', the generic poet is the '**therápōn** of the Muses'. Furthermore, the parallelism in itself indicates that the poet, as '**therápōn** of the Muses', is thereby worthy of being a cult hero.

---

hands of Ares (III 125–128). For the connotations of poetic theme ("The Ordeals of the Trojans and Achaeans") in the image of weaving here, see Clader 1976.6–9.

§5n8. Note also the epithet **ózos Árēos** (ten times in *Iliad*), where **ózos** is not the same word as the one meaning 'branch' but rather a reflex of a compound: o-'together' + *-**sd-os** 'seated'; see Chantraine III 777. The hero Leonteus, described as **îsos Árēi** (XII 130), also qualifies as **ózos Árēos** (II 745, XII 188, XXIII 841). In the Alexandrian lexicographical tradition, **ózos** and **therápōn** were apparently considered synonyms (cf. Hesychius s.v. ὀζεία· θεραπεία). The semantics of **ózos** are suggestive of the relationship between god and hero in cult. Compare the description of Erikhthonios as a hero who gets a share of the sacrifices offered to Athena in her temple: *Epigrammata* 1046.89–90 Kaibel (on which see Nock 1972 [= 1930] 237). For more on Erikhthonios/Erekhtheus, see Nagy 1973.170–171. On the convergences and divergences of the Erikhthonios and Erekhtheus figures, see Burkert 1972.176, 211.

§6n1. Ch.10.

§6n2. Above, §3.

§7. We find supporting evidence in the *Life of Hesiod* tradition (see especially Aristotle *Constitution of the Orchomenians fr.* 565 Rose). Its themes, especially the theme of Hesiod's death, correspond to the typical mythology surrounding the cult of a typical epichoric hero. For a convincing exposition, I simply refer to the discussion of Hesiod as cult hero by Angelo Brelich—a discussion framed by countless other examples of typical mythology surrounding local heroes.[1] I will content myself here by citing his conclusion: the figure of Hesiod in the *Life of Hesiod* tradition fits perfectly the characteristic morphology of the cult hero.[2]

§8. Significantly, even the figure of Hesiod as presented by Hesiodic poetry itself fits this same pattern of the cult hero; Brelich cites in particular such details as the poetic contest entered by Hesiod at the Funeral Games of Amphidamas (*W&D* 654–659).[1] It follows, then, *that the Hesiodic compositions determine the identity of their composer.* This inference may strike us at first as an absurdity—until we reconsider the implications of the simple fact that Hesiodic poetry is not idiosyncratic but deeply traditional in both form and content.[2] The ambition of a poem like the *Theogony* is to present the traditions that reveal the very essence of the universe, and to do so with a Panhellenic "audience" in mind.[3] To enact such a vast program, the composer must surely be presented as the ultimate poet and sage who has all of tradition under his control.

§9. This ambition even motivates the generic function of the poet's name at *Th.* 22: **Hēsíodos** 'he who emits the Voice'.[1] Compare also the generic function of the name **Hómēros** 'he who fits [the Song] together',[2] to be interpreted in conjunction with the patterns charac-

§7n1. Brelich 1958.321–322. The most convincing aspect of Brelich's book is the sheer accumulation of evidence for parallel patterns; it is well worth reading in its entirety.

§7n2. Brelich, p. 322: "Così il poeta rientra perfettamente nella morfologia caratteristica dell' eroe."

§8n1. Brelich, p. 321. Note that Hesiod's divine patronage is local: the Muses of Helicon (*W&D* 658–659) as distinct from the Muses of Olympus/Pieria as invoked in the proem (*W&D* 1). In the *Theogony* too, we see that Hesiod's essence as poet is defined by the Muses of Helicon (*Th.* 22–34).

§8n2. Cf. Ch.5§§4, 18–19.

§8n3. Note the transformation of the Muses from Heliconian (*Th.* 1) to Olympian (*Th.* 25, 52, etc.), once they have defined Hesiod's essence as poet *at Helicon* (*Th.* 22–34). For the correlation of Olympus and Panhellenic ideology, see Intro. §14.

§9n1. The root *$\ast\vartheta$yod- of *$\ast$Hēsí-yodos recurs as *$\ast\vartheta$yd- in **audé** 'voice' and **audáō** 'speak': Chantraine I 137–138, II 417. At *Th.* 31, **audé** designates the poetry with which the Muses themselves inspire **Hēsíodos**.

§9n2. I agree with Durante 1976.194–197 (cf. Welcker 1835.128) that **Hóm-ēros** is a

teristic of a cult hero as we find them in the *Life of Homer* tradition.[3] In fact, the themes inherent in both names **Hēsí-odos** and **Hóm-ēros** recur in the actual diction of the proem to the Hesiodic *Theogony* itself, and the context for these themes is the actual description of the Muses and their poetic function:

περικαλλέα ὄσσαν ἱεῖσαι	'emitting a beautiful voice'	*Th.* 10
ἄμβροτον ὄσσαν ἱεῖσαι	'emitting an immortal voice'	*Th.* 43
ἐρατὴν ... ὄσσαν ἱεῖσαι	'emitting a lovely voice'	*Th.* 65
ἐπήρατον ὄσσαν ἱεῖσαι	'emitting a lovely voice'	*Th.* 67[4]
So also 'Ησί-οδος	'he who emits the voice'[5]	
ἀρτιέπειαι	'having words [**épos** plural] fitted together'	*Th.* 29
φωνῇ ὁμηρεῦσαι	'fitting [the song] together with their voice'[6]	*Th.* 39
So also "Ομ-ηρος	'he who fits [the song] together'	

In short, the names **Hēsíodos** and **Hómēros** identify the poet's function with that of the Muses themselves.[7] Thus the poet's very name indicates that he is '**therápōn** of the Muses' (*Th.* 100), in that the word **therápōn** identifies god with hero through death. And by being a **therápōn**, the generic poet assumes the ritual dimensions of a cult hero.

Supplement: The Name of Homer

§10. More needs to be said about the name of Homer, since its meaning seems to reveal a particularly archaic view of the poet and his function. For the interpretation of **Hóm-ēros** as 'he who fits [the song] together', built from the verb root *ar- as in **ar-ar-ískō** 'fit,

---

compound built from the Indo-European elements *som- 'together' and *ə₂r- 'fit, join' (as in Greek **ar-ar-ískō** 'fit, join'). My interpretation of the semantics, however, is different (see §§10–13; so too is my reconstruction of the earliest Greek form: *homo-ar-os, becoming *hom-āros.

§9n3. On these patterns, see the brief remarks of Brelich 1958.320–321.

§9n4. For a defense of this line, see West 1966.178–179 (I fail to agree, however, with his objections to the line on esthetic grounds).

§9n5. In Pindar *O*.6.61–62, the oracular response of Apollo is called **artiepḕs / patríā óssa** 'the ancestral voice having words [**épos** plural] fitted together'; for more on **óssa**, see Ch.7§25n1.

§9n6. West (1966.170) translates "with voices in tune," helpfully adducing *H.Apollo* 164 for comparison.

§9n7. And, latently, with that of Apollo. Cf. n5.

join', we may compare the following use of the same verb, as an intransitive perfect:

οὕτω σφιν καλὴ συνάρηρεν ἀοιδή

So beautifully is their song fitted together.[1]

H.Apollo 164

Moreover, I adduce the semantics of the Indo-European root *tek(s)-, which like *ar- means 'fit, join'. From the comparative evidence assembled by Rüdiger Schmitt,[2] we see that *tek(s)- was traditionally used to indicate the activity of a carpenter in general (compare the semantics of *joiner*, an older English word for "carpenter") and of a chariot-carpenter in particular. In addition, Schmitt adduces comparative evidence to show that *tek(s)- was also used to indicate, by metaphor, the activity of a poet: much as a chariot-carpenter fits together his chariot, so also the poet fits together his poem/song.[3] This comparison is actually attested as an overt simile in the most archaic body of Indic poetry:

imā́ṃ te vā́caṃ vasūyánta āyávo
rátham ná dhírah̥ svápā atakṣiṣuḥ

The sons of Āyu, wishing for good things, have fitted together [root *takṣ*-, from *tek(s)-] this utterance,[4]
just as the skilled artisan (fits together) a chariot.

Rig-Veda 1.130.6ab

It is, then, an Indo-European poetic tradition that the poet may compare his activity with that of artisans like carpenters.[5] Moreover, we see from *Odyssey* xvii 381–387 that poets are in fact the social equals of artisans—carpenters included.[6]

§11. In this light, we may now turn to the internal Greek evidence of *ar-, which parallels the comparative evidence on *tek(s)-. In the Linear B texts (e.g., Knossos tablets Sg 1811, So 0437, etc.), the word for "chariot-wheel" is *a-mo* = **hármo**, by etymology an abstract noun ("fitting") derived from the verb root *ar- as in **ar-ar-ískō** 'fit,

§10n1. Cf. West 1966.170.
§10n2. Schmitt 1967.296–298.
§10n3. Ibid.
§10n4. The *vā́k* 'utterance' here is the sacral hymn itself; see Muellner 1976.128.
§10n5. On the comparative evidence for the likening with weavers, see Schmitt, pp. 298–301. For an attestation of this comparison in the semantics of the word **rhapsōidós** 'he who stitches the song together', see Durante 1976.177–179.
§10n6. For the text of this passage from the *Odyssey*, with discussion, see Ch.12§13.

join'.[1] Note too the Homeric name at V 59–60: **Harmonídēs** 'son of **Hármōn**' (root *ar-), the patronymic of one **Téktōn** 'Carpenter' (root *tek[s]-).[2]

§12. The technical sense of **Harmonídēs** is parallel to that of **harmoníē** 'joint [in woodwork]' (e.g., v 248),[1] but the latter form also has the social sense of "accord" (e.g., XXII 255)—as well as a musical sense roughly corresponding to our notion of "harmony" (e.g., Sophocles *fr.* 244 Pearson).[2] Both the musical and the social aspects of the word are incorporated in the figure **Harmoníē**, bride of Kadmos (Hesiod *Th.* 937, 975),[3] at whose wedding the Muses themselves sang a song inaugurating the social order of Thebes—a song quoted by Theognis (verses 17–18W) in the context of his invoking the Muses and thus inaugurating his own poetry (verses 15–16W):

Μοῦσαι καὶ Χάριτες, κοῦραι Διός, αἵ ποτε Κάδμου
ἐς γάμον ἐλθοῦσαι καλὸν ἀείσατ' ἔπος·
"ὅττι καλὸν φίλον ἐστί, τὸ δ' οὐ καλὸν οὐ φίλον ἐστί"·
τοῦτ' ἔπος ἀθανάτων ἦλθε διὰ στομάτων

Muses and Kharites, daughters of Zeus! You were the ones
who once came to the wedding of Kadmos, and you sang this beautiful **épos:**[4]
"What is beautiful is **phílon**, what is not beautiful is not **phílon**."[5]
This is the **épos**[6] that came through their immortal mouths.

Theognis 15–18W

§11n1. See Chantraine I 110–111.

§11n2. The noun **téktōn** occasionally designates 'artisan' in general, not necessarily 'carpenter', but the context of V 60–63 clearly indicates carpentry. For more on **téktōn**, see §12n1.

§12n1. The woodwork here is described as the kind done by one well-versed in **tektosúnai** 'carpentry' (v 250).

§12n2. On which see Nagy 1974.45.

§12n3. Note that **Harmoníē** is daughter of Ares (*Th.* 937). For the theory that the name **Árēs** itself is derived from *ar- 'fit, join', see Sinos 1975.52–54 and 71–72, who argues that Ares is the obsolete embodiment of the principles joining together the members of society in general and of warrior-society in particular.

§12n4. On the use of **épos** to mean not just 'utterance' but also 'poetic utterance' *as quoted by the poetry itself*: Ch.12§15n3 and Ch.15§7.

§12n5. Neuter **phílon** indicates the institutional and sentimental bonds that join society together (cf. Ch.6§13). Since beauty is **phílon**, the social cohesion of Thebes is implicitly embodied in the esthetics of the Muses' song, which in turn sets the cohesion of the poetry composed by Theognis. The concept of **Harmoníē** is appropriate to both the social and the artistic cohesion.

§12n6. Note that the quoted utterance of the Muses is called an **épos** both before and after the quotation. This framing effect may itself suggest **Harmoníē**.

§13. I conclude, then, that the root *ar- in **Hómēros** traditionally denotes the activity of a poet as well as that of a carpenter, and this semantic bivalence corresponds neatly with the Indo-European tradition of comparing music/poetry with carpentry, by way of the root *tek(s)-.[1] This tradition is proudly recaptured in the words of Pindar extolling the themes of Homer:[2]

Νέστορα καὶ Λύκιον Σαρπηδόν᾽, ἀνθρώπων φάτις,
ἐξ ἐπέων κελαδεννῶν, <u>τέκτονες</u> οἶα σοφοὶ
ἄρμοσαν, γινώσκομεν

We know of Nestor and Lycian Sarpedon—subjects for men to talk about—
from famed words [**épos** plural]
such as skilled <u>carpenters</u> <u>fitted together</u>.[3]

Pindar P.3.112-114

§13n1. The Latin and Greek words *ars* and **tékhnē** are formed from verb roots that are no longer attested in the respective languages: Latin no longer has the verb *ar- from which the noun *ars* (*ar-ti-) is derived, while Greek no longer has the verb *tek(s)- from which the noun **tékhnē** (*téks-nā) is derived. But Latin does have the verb *texō* ('build, join' in the older Latin, 'weave' in the later), and Greek does have the verb **ar-ar-ískō** ('fit, join'). Note that Homeric diction actually combines the verb **ar-ar-ískō** with **téktōn** 'artisan' as subject: **érare téktōn** (IV 110, XXIII 712; in the latter passage, the artisan is actually a carpenter). This word **téktōn** is by origin an agent noun derived from the verb *tek(s)- 'fit, join'.

§13n2. For further discussion, see Schmitt 1967.297.

§13n3. The verb **harmózō** 'fit together' is derived from the noun *hármo, by origin an abstract noun ("fitting") which came to have a concrete designation ("chariot wheel") and which is in turn derived from the verb *ar- as in **ar-ar-ískō** ('join, fit'); see §11. The phonology of **harmózō** (from *hármo as distinct from standard classical **hárma**, meaning 'chariot') suggests that the word was inherited from the élite social strata of the second millennium B.C. See Risch 1966, esp. p. 157.

18 | On the Stories of a Poet's Life

§1. In the preceding chapters, I have argued that the generic warrior/poet, as **therápōn** of Ares/Muses, is implicitly worthy of becoming a cult hero after death. This in fact is the explicit message, I now submit, of the famous poetic declaration made by the one attested figure who boasts of being both warrior and poet:

εἰμὶ δ' ἐγὼ θεράπων μὲν 'Ενυαλίοιο ἄνακτος
καὶ Μουσέων ἐρατὸν δῶρον ἐπιστάμενος

I am a **therápōn** of Lord Enyalios [Ares],
and of the Muses, well-versed in their lovely gift.

Archilochus *fr.* 1W

The poet's own words imply that Archilochus deserves a hero cult as both warrior and poet. And a hero cult is what he actually has on his native island of Paros, from archaic times onward, as we know both from the literary testimonia and from the evidence of archaeology.[1] Moreover, the *Life of Archilochus* tradition motivates the death of the poet as also being the death of a warrior.[2] He is killed in combat by a figure whose eponym is **Kórax** 'Raven'.[3] Apollo is angry at Korax, who approaches his sanctuary at Delphi,[4] and he orders him to depart:

Μουσάων θεράποντα κατέκτανες· ἔξιθι νηοῦ

You killed the **therápōn** of the Muses. Get out of the Sanctuary!

Oracle 4 Parke/Wormell[5]

§1n1. See Kontoleon 1964, esp. p. 46, and Treu 1959.250; see now also Kontoleon 1965, esp. pp. 413–418, on the discovery at Paros of an archaic iconographical representation of Archilochus as cult hero.

§1n2. The references that follow are conveniently assembled by Treu, pp. 122–124.

§1n3. Plutarch *De sera numinis vindicta* 560e. See also the references at nn5, 6.

§1n4. I infer that Korax does so for the purpose of purification, on account of a pestilence or the like.

§1n5. From Galen *Protreptikos* 23, to be read in conjunction with Dio Chrysostomus 33.12.

Korax protests that Archilochus had been killed *as a warrior*, not as a poet,[6] but Apollo again declares that Korax has killed the **therápōn** of the Muses.[7] After further entreaties, Korax is finally granted an oracular directive: he must go "to the House of the **Téttīx** [Cicada],"[8] where he must propitiate the **psūkhḗ** of Archilochus.[9] We may detect a deeper significance in the names and themes of this story by considering the traditions of the Aesopic **aînos**. In the fables of Aesop, the **kórax** 'raven' is conventionally presented as the bird of Apollo (*Fable* 323 Perry), endowed with powers of prophecy (*Fables* 125, 236); he is also a harbinger of death (*Fable* 162).[10] The **téttīges** 'cicadas', on the other hand, are creatures of the Muses (*Fable* 470).[11] As we turn back to the *Life of Archilochus* tradition, we may infer that the figures of **Kórax** and **Téttīx** are parallel to Apollo and the Muses respectively. More specifically, the parallelism of Apollo and **Kórax** implies that Apollo is maleficent as well as beneficent towards the poet.

§2. Similarly in the *Life of Aesop* tradition, Apollo is in fact both maleficent and beneficent to Aesop. We have already examined the maleficent aspect: Apollo is angry at Aesop for his neglect of the god at a sacrifice, and he actively helps the Delphians to bring about Aesop's death.[1] Now we see that there is also a beneficent aspect of Apollo's involvement in the killing of Aesop. Surely the pestilence that descends upon the Delphians after Aesop's death is ordained by Apollo himself, and it is his Oracle that commands the Delphians to propitiate Aesop by worshiping him as a cult hero (*Pap.Oxy.* 1800, *Vitae* G+W 142; cf. Aristotle *Constitution of the Delphians fr.* 487). This beneficent aspect of Apollo helps account for the final gesture of Aesop, when he calls upon Apollo as "leader of the Muses" to be witness of his unjust execution by the Delphians (*Vita* G 142). I propose, then, that the traditional themes of antagonism between god and hero do not preclude a beneficent aspect on the god's part. There

§1n6. Heraclides Ponticus *Perì politeiôn* 8 (cf. Aristotle *fr.* 611.25 Rose).

§1n7. Dio Chrysostomus (n5) ibid.

§1n8. Plutarch (n3) ibid.: ἐπὶ τὴν τοῦ τέττιγγος οἴκησιν.

§1n9. Plutarch (n3) ibid.; the author also supplies an interpretation of the oracular response, suggesting why the "House of the **Téttīx**" should be Tainaros.

§1n10. In this fable, the **kórax** of death turns out to be the cover of the **lárnax** in which the overprotective mother is sheltering her child.

§1n11. This fable is transmitted by Plato *Phaedrus* 259b–c. From Archilochus *fr.* 223W, we know that the poet called himself a **téttīx** in the context of composing blame poetry against those who harmed him.

§2n1. Above, Ch.17§1.

is in fact solid evidence that the ambivalence of a god in being both maleficent and beneficent towards a hero is so archaic as to have a heritage in the Indo-European traditions of epic narrative: it comes from the comparative studies of Georges Dumézil in linking the Old Norse hero *Starkaðr* and the Indic hero *Śiśupāla* with the Greek hero **Hēraklḗēs**.[2] Aided by Dumézil's findings, we now know that the suckling of **Hēraklḗēs** by **Hḗrā** after his birth (Diodorus Siculus 4.9.6) and the adoption of Herakles by Hera after his death (Diodorus 4.39.2–3) are themes of beneficence that complement the prevalent themes of her maleficence towards this **hḗrōs** 'hero',[3] and that together these themes of beneficence/maleficence constitute the traditional epic theme embodied in the very name of **Hēraklḗēs** 'he who has the **kléos** of **Hḗrā**'.[4]

§3. Whereas Apollo's relationship to Archilochus and to Aesop in the *Lives* is ambivalent, that of the Muses is not; rather, it appears to be one-sidedly beneficent. Having already seen the evidence in the *Life of Aesop* tradition,[1] we turn to another story from the *Life of Archilochus*—this time as preserved in section E₁ col.II of the Parian Mnesiepes Inscription.[2] According to this story,[3] Archilochus received his verbal powers of poetry from the Muses, who appeared to him in disguise as he was on his way to sell a cow (E₁ col.II 23–29). Archilochus thinks that they are rustic women leaving the fields and heading for the city; he draws near and "ridicules" them (lines 29–30: σκώπτειν),[4] but the Muses respond with playful laughter (lines 30–31). They then induce Archilochus to trade them his cow for a lyre; once the transaction is made, they disappear (lines 32–35). He falls into a swoon, and when he awakens he is aware that the Muses have just given him the gift of poetry (lines 36–38).

§2n2. Dumézil 1971.13–132; to be fully appreciated, the argument must be read in its entirety.

§2n3. For the semantic relationship of **Hḗrā** and **hḗrōs**, see the important article of Pötscher 1961; cf. also Householder/Nagy 1972.770–771.

§2n4. See Dumézil, p. 120, to be supplemented by Pötscher 1961 and 1971; cf. also Davidson 1980.

§3n1. Above, Ch.17§1.

§3n2. Conveniently available in Treu 1959.40–45. Although the inscription is of a relatively late date (ca. third century B.C.), its contents are archaic in theme: see Maehler 1963.49n2, with bibliography and brief polemics.

§3n3. There is an archaic iconographical attestation of the same story (or of a close parallel) on a Boston pyxis from Eretria, dated ca. 460 B.C. (no. 37 tab. 15 Caskey/Beazley); see Kontoleon 1964.47–50.

§3n4. On the verb **skṓptō** 'ridicule', see Ch.13§3 and n4; also Ch.16§10 and n7.

§4. The rest of this story about Archilochus is beyond our immediate interest, except for what it says about the future. An oracle from Apollo himself at Delphi prophesies to the father of Archilochus that his son will have immortality and fame:

ἀ]θάνατός σοι παῖς καὶ ἀοίδιμος, ὦ Τελεσίκλεις,
ἔσται ἐν ἀνθρώποισιν

Your son, O Telesikles, will be immortal among men,
a subject of song . . . [1]

E₁ col.II 50–51[2]

We see here an important dovetailing of the story with the self-avowed function of the entire Mnesiepes Inscription, which is to motivate the hero cult of Archilochus at Paros. First, the inscription formally restates an oracular command by Apollo to **Mnesiépēs**, with specific directives about the cult of Archilochus and other attendant ritual practices (E₁ col.II 1–15). Then it briefly tells how the Parians complied with the Oracle's directives, instituting the cult in a sacred precinct called the **Arkhilókheion** (E₁ col.II 16–19). Finally, it tells the Life of Archilochus (E₁ col.II 20 ff.), in which context we find the story of the poet and the Muses (E₁ col.II 23 ff.). In other words, the Mnesiepes Inscription is itself the clearest evidence for arguing that the *Life of Archilochus* tradition is deeply rooted in the realia of cult. Moreover, the poetry of Archilochus *and its transmission* also are rooted in cult, as we have seen from the poet's traditional concept of himself as "**therápōn** of the Muses" (Archilochus *fr.* 1W).[3] I conclude, then, that the *Life of Archilochus* tradition is not only derived from the poetic tradition of Archilochus but also parallel to it.[4]

§4n1. For more on **aoídimos** 'subject of song', cf. VI 358 and *H.Apollo* 299; note the orientation of both passages toward the audiences of the future.

§4n2. The rest of the oracle (lines 51–52) links up with the continuation of the story (E₁ col.II 53 ff.).

§4n3. As an indication that the transmission of Archilochean poetry was rooted in the cult of Archilochus, I cite not only the function of the Mnesiepes Inscription but also the meaning of the name **Mnēsiépēs** 'he who remembers the words [épos plural]'. As the figure to whom Apollo ordains the cult of Archilochus in the **Arkhilókheion**, Mnesiepes bears a name that seems to correspond to his own function. The semantics of his name integrate Mnesiepes into the mythology surrounding the foundation of the **Arkhilókheion**. Compare also the mythology surrounding the **Aisópeion** at Samos, as discussed in Ch.16§8n1.

§4n4. Cf. Ch.17§§7–8 on the *Life of Hesiod* tradition. In the case of a typical local hero who is not a poet, his life story is simply a function of his cult. In the case of the poet-hero, on the other hand, his life story is a function of his cult *and of the poetry ascribed to him*. I would reconstruct, then, an archaic poet's life story as a *Vita* tradition

§5. This conclusion can be dismissed only if the Mnesiepes Inscription can be discredited as untraditional in its contents. For this to be so, one would have to argue that the commissioning of the inscription, dated as it is to the third century B.C., is coeval with the information that it contains about the oracular directives, about the cult itself, and about the *Life of Archilochus*. But we have in fact already seen direct evidence that the commissioning of the Mnesiepes Inscription is predated by reports about the cult of Archilochus (cf. Alcidamas *ap.* Aristotle *Rhetoric* 1398b11),[1] as also by the story about Archilochus and the Muses.[2] We may now add an interesting piece of indirect evidence from the ideology of the oracular directive about cult procedures in the sacred precinct (E_1 col.II 1–15): the cult of the main gods in the **Arkhilókheion** is the first element to be formulated (lines 3–6, 10–12), whereas the cult of the hero himself is the last (lines 14–15). Significantly, the listing of the main gods is headed by the Muses and Apollo **Mousagétēs** 'Leader of the Muses' (lines 3–4). Such a grouping of Apollo and the Muses is clearly archaic.[3] Also, this grouping presents a relationship between Archilochus and Apollo/Muses on the level of cult that corresponds on the level of myth to the identity of Archilochus as poet: **therápōn** of the Muses.

§6. In fact, I am now in a position to offer an overall interpretation of the epithet Μουσάων θεράπων '**therápōn** of the Muses' (Hesiod *Th.* 100, Archilochus *fr.* 1W). I propose that the designation "Muses" here *includes Apollo as leader of the Muses*. Whereas the Muses are one-sidedly beneficent toward the poet, Apollo is ambivalently beneficent and maleficent.[1] It is Apollo who causes the impurity of a poet's death, thereby also causing eternal purification through the hero cult of this poet. If indeed Apollo is latent in the

---

originally controlled both by the ideologies of his cult and by the contents of his poems. With the passing of the archaic period, however, the factor of cult recedes, and the genre of the poet's *Vita* becomes totally dependent on the poems themselves. Without the control of the religious ideologies conveyed by the cult, the narrative patterns of the *Vita* become subject to arbitrary interpretations based on the contents of the poetry. On the other hand, if indeed the traditional narrative patterns of the *Vita* are historically rooted in the institution of hero cults, the characters in the *Vita* traditions will assume the roles of heroes even when they are historical figures. Consider the *Life of Pindar* tradition as discussed at Ch.7§9n1.

§5n1. See Treu 1959.250.

§5n2. See §3n3.

§5n3. See Ch.17§3.

§6n1. I must allow, however, that the Muses may not always be one-sided in every variant.

designation "**therápōn** of the Muses," his maleficent stance toward the poet is thereby also latent. In this line of reasoning, I can also offer an explanation for why the archaic poet invokes the Muses without mentioning Apollo:[2] in this manner, he invokes the one-sidedly beneficent aspect of his divine patronage.

§7. Throughout our discussion of the poet as antagonist of his patron deities, we have had numerous occasions to see information taken from the *Lives* of the poets and used as evidence. I have tried to defend the validity of such information on a detailed case-to-case basis, but the ultimate defense rests on the cumulative evidence of the patterns that have by now emerged from our collection of the details. Admittedly, the *Lives* are extremely difficult source material, requiring the greatest caution. It is unfortunate that they are generally attested in versions that are late or fragmentary—or both. Worse still, we seldom have historical controls. Worst of all, the *Lives* have no strict literary form, and they are in the course of their transmission most vulnerable to distortion at the hands of transmitting scholars of the ancient world who supplement and modify, sometimes on the basis of the poet's attested poetry.[n] To use the *Lives*, one must be selective and critical, since the ultimate evidence is not so much in the *text* but in the *tradition* underneath. This much said, I now offer a brief reassessment of my conclusions about the *Lives*.

§8. We begin with the findings of Brelich about the *Life of Hesiod* tradition: the themes here fit the mythology surrounding a typical cult hero.[1] From such findings, I infer that the purpose of this and other *Life* traditions is to motivate not so much the poet's poetry but the poet's hero cult. This purpose is actually overt in the *Life of Archilochus* tradition as presented in the Mnesiepes Inscription, which serves explicitly to motivate the poet's hero cult.[2] The inscription also specifies that the primary gods worshiped within the frame of this hero cult are the Muses—and Apollo as their leader.[3] This symbiotic connection of Muses/Apollo with Archilochus in cult is matched by an antagonistic connection in myth: the *Life of Archilochus* tradition implies that Apollo is ambivalently beneficent/maleficent towards the poet, whereas the Muses are one-sidedly beneficent.[4] Such an

§6n2. See Ch.17§3.
§7n. Cf. Slater 1971, esp. p. 150, and Lefkowitz 1976. But cf. also §4n4 above.
§8n1. Ch.17§7.
§8n2. §4.
§8n3. §5.
§8n4. §§1, 3.

antagonistic relationship in myth is overtly attested in the *Life of Aesop* tradition: Apollo abets the poet's death and then makes him a cult hero.[5] Aesop's very essence as poet is defined both by the beneficent Muses and by the beneficent/maleficent Apollo as their leader.[6] These relationships of god and poet correspond to the relationships of god and hero: antagonism in myth, symbiosis in cult.[7]

§9. We continue our reassessment by summarizing the evidence of epic diction, which amplifies our understanding of the antagonistic relationship between god and hero. At the moment of his death, the hero of epic in effect loses his identity to the god who takes his life; as such, the hero qualifies as the god's **therápōn**.[1] A "**therápōn** of Ares," then, is a hero who forfeits his identification with his **phílos** or **phíloi** and becomes "equal to Ares" at the moment of his death.[2] On the surface, of course, the hero's death is motivated by the inherited conventions of epic narrative; underneath the surface, however, it is motivated by the requirements of ritual ideology. As the semantic prehistory of the word indicates, the **therápōn** has a distinctly religious function. By losing his identification with a person or group and by identifying himself with a god who takes his life in the process, the hero effects a purification *by transferring impurity*.[3]

§10. Keeping in mind this religious dimension of purification inherent in the word **therápōn**, we turn from the hero as warrior to the hero as poet. From the evidence of ancient poetic diction, we know that the generic poet is "**therápōn** of the Muses" just as the generic warrior is "**therápōn** of Ares."[1] From the evidence of the *Lives*, on the other hand, we know that the poet becomes a hero because he forfeits his life and identity to Apollo, the leader of the Muses. The evidence is perhaps clearest in the *Life of Aesop* tradition, where Apollo ordains first the death and then the hero cult of Aesop.[2] In such a hero cult, god and hero are to be institutionalized as the respectively dominant and recessive members of an eternal symbiotic relationship. The clearest evidence for this sort of institutionalization is to be found in the actual cult of Apollo/Muses

§8n5. §2; also Ch.16§8n1, Ch.17§1.
§8n6. Ibid.
§8n7. See again Ch.7.
§9n1. Ch.17§5.
§9n2. Ibid.
§9n3. Ch.17§4.
§10n1. Ch.17§6.
§10n2. §2.

and Archilochus at Paros, as actually documented by the Mnesiepes Inscription.[3] Finally, we see from the *Life of Aesop* tradition that the poet's death results in purification. The immediate result from the death itself is impurity, but the ultimate result is eternal purification by way of propitiating the hero in cult—as ordained by Apollo himself.[4] Moreover, the mode of Aesop's death is itself a purification, in that he dies like a **pharmakós** 'scapegoat'.[5] His very appearance indicates a transfer of impurities upon himself: Aesop is notoriously ugly and misshapen (*Vitae* G+W 1), much like that other image of a **pharmakós**, Thersites (II 217–219).[6]

§10n3. §§4, 5.

§10n4. Ch.16§8. This formulation helps account for the semantics of **ágos** 'pollution'/'expiation' and **enagízein** 'perform sacrifice in the cult of a hero' as distinct from **thúein** 'perform sacrifice in the cult of a god'. For a discussion of the formal and semantic connection between **ágos** and **enagízein**, see Chantraine/Masson 1954. Nock (1944) has reservations about the god/hero distinction in **thúein/enagízein**, on the grounds that **thúein** is also attested in the context of sacrificing to heroes. Even so, I maintain that the god/hero distinction remains valid so long as **enagízein** is not attested in the context of sacrificing to the celestial gods. Thus, **thúein/enagízein** would be the *unmarked/marked* members of the opposition. For the terms *unmarked/marked*, see Jakobson 1971.136: "The general meaning of a marked category states the presence of a certain (whether positive or negative) property A; the general meaning of the corresponding unmarked category states nothing about the presence of A, and is used chiefly, *but not exclusively*, to indicate the absence of A" (italics mine). In the case of **thúein/enagízein**, "property A" is the factor of a hero (or of a chthonic god—where I intend "chthonic" in the sense of "noncelestial").

§10n5. Ch.16§3.

§10n6. Note the use of **kátharma** 'purification, refuse of purification' in the sense of 'outcast' when it is applied to Aesop as a term of insult by the other characters in the *Life* tradition (e.g., *Vitae* G+W 31); cf. Wiechers 1961.35.

19 | More on Strife and the Human Condition

§1. The deaths of Aesop and Thersites result directly from their engaging in blame,[1] and the result of their deaths is purification.[2] It follows, then, that their engaging in blame is itself an ultimately purifying act. Thus even in the ideology of myth, blame and the ridicule that it can bring have a potentially positive social function.[3] Moreover, among the things that Aesop actually blamed was the negative social function of blame itself, formalized *in ritual* as strife over cuts of sacrificial meat (*Pap.Oxy.* 1800).[4] The same negative social function is formalized in classical praise poetry as **éris** 'strife, conflict' (Pindar *N*.4.93), a negative foil of praise poetry itself.[5] A parallel negative foil is **phthónos** 'envy, greed', conventionally visualized by praise poetry as a bestially gluttonous appetite for meat (Bacchylides 3.67–68, Pindar *N*.8.21–25).[6] The negative social function of blame is also formalized *in myth* as the primal **éris** between Prometheus and Zeus (Hesiod *Th.* 534) — a conflict over cuts of meat that is the very cause of the human condition (*Th.* 535–616).[7] Alternatively, it is formalized as the personified **Éris** at the Judgment of Paris, the cause of the Trojan War in particular (*Cypria*/Proclus p. 102.14–19 Allen) and of the human condition in general (Hesiod *fr.* 204MW).[8] At the Judgment of Paris, **Éris** overtly takes the form of blame: as our *Iliad* tells it, Paris had engaged in blaming Hera and Athena, while praising Aphrodite (XXIV 29–30).[9]

§1n1. Ch.16§4.
§1n2. Ch.16§§1–2, Ch.18§10.
§1n3. On the acknowledgment of this social function in the ideology of epic, cf. Ch.14§12 and n4.
§1n4. For the text, see again Ch.16§7.
§1n5. Ch.12§3.
§1n6. Ch.12§§4–5 and §§6–11.
§1n7. Ch.11§15.
§1n8. Ch.11§14.
§1n9. Ch.11§16.

§2. If there is a *positive* social function assigned by myth to the institution of blame, there might also be a parallel assignment to the Hellenic concept of **éris** 'strife, conflict', a word we have seen so far as formalizing only the *negative* social function of blame. The social ambivalence of **Éris** is in fact a prime theme of the *Works and Days*:

οὐκ ἄρα μοῦνον ἔην Ἐρίδων γένος, ἀλλ' ἐπὶ γαῖαν
εἰσὶ δύω· τὴν μέν κεν ἐπαινήσειε νοήσας,
ἡ δ' ἐπιμωμητή· διὰ δ' ἄνδιχα θυμὸν ἔχουσιν.
ἡ μὲν γὰρ πόλεμόν τε κακὸν καὶ δῆριν ὀφέλλει,
σχετλίη· οὔ τις τήν γε φιλεῖ βροτός, ἀλλ' ὑπ' ἀνάγκης
ἀθανάτων βουλῇσιν Ἔριν τιμῶσι βαρεῖαν.
τὴν δ' ἑτέρην προτέρην μὲν ἐγείνατο Νὺξ ἐρεβεννή,
θῆκε δέ μιν Κρονίδης ὑψίζυγος, αἰθέρι ναίων,
γαίης τ' ἐν ῥίζῃσι καὶ ἀνδράσι πολλὸν ἀμείνω·
ἥ τε καὶ ἀπάλαμόν περ ὅμως ἐπὶ ἔργον ἔγειρεν.
εἰς ἕτερον γάρ τίς τε ἰδὼν ἔργοιο χατίζων
πλούσιον, ὃς σπεύδει μὲν ἀρώμεναι ἠδὲ φυτεύειν
οἶκόν τ' εὖ θέσθαι· ζηλοῖ δέ τε γείτονα γείτων
εἰς ἄφενος σπεύδοντ'· ἀγαθὴ δ' Ἔρις ἥδε βροτοῖσιν.
καὶ κεραμεὺς κεραμεῖ κοτέει καὶ τέκτονι τέκτων,
καὶ πτωχὸς πτωχῷ φθονέει καὶ ἀοιδὸς ἀοιδῷ

There was not just one **Éris** born, but there are two
on earth. When a man recognizes one, he should <u>praise</u> it.
The other one is <u>worthy of blame</u>. The two have split dispositions.
One brings about the evil of war and fighting.[1]
It is wretched. No man loves it, but, by necessity,
in accord with the Will of the Immortals, men give **tīmḗ** to this burdensome
Éris.[2]
The other one was the elder-born from dark Night.
The son of Kronos, who sits on high and abides in the aether,
placed it in the very roots of Earth. And this one is far better for men.
This one incites even the resourceless man to work—
as one man who is out of work looks at another
who is rich and busy with ploughing, planting,
and maintaining his household properly. Neighbor envies neighbor,
striving for wealth. This **Éris** is good for men.
And the potter is angry with the potter, and the artisan with the artisan.[3]

§2n1. For more on **dêris** 'fighting', see Ch.16§10n1.

§2n2. For the correlation of **Éris** and the **Diòs boulḗ** 'Will of Zeus', see Ch.11§§10–15.

§2n3. The "anger" of potter against potter and artisan against artisan is equivalent to **phthónos**, as we see from the parallelisms in the next verse. On the inherited

And the beggar has **phthónos** [envy] for the beggar, and the poet for the poet.[4]

Hesiod W&D 11-26

We see here the "good" Éris in her positive social function as the principle of competition, that fundamental aspect of most Hellenic institutions—including poetry itself.[5] In this connection, it is important to keep in mind that even the performance of such sublime poetic compositions as Pindar's *Paean* 6 took place in the framework of a competition. This song that tells about the **éris** of the gods (*Paean* 6.50, 87) in the awesome setting of Delphi's Panhellenic **theoxénia** is actually being performed, in the song's own words, at an **agón** 'place of contest' (ἀγῶνα: *Paean* 6.60).[6] In sum, one can praise and blame the good and the evil Éris, as the *Works and Days* tells us, but these very activities of praising and blaming are subsumed in the principle of competition itself—that elder and hence more primordial kind of Éris.

§3. Evil or good, **éris** functions as a prime definition of the human condition. It comes as no surprise, then, that **éris** is the overt catalyst for many of the major poems of Hellenic civilization. We have already seen that **éris** or **neîkos** precipitates not only the *Cypria* in particular but also in general the entire mass of epic material framed by the Trojan War.[1] Moreover, the *Iliad* itself begins with the **éris/neîkos** between Achilles and Agamemnon.[2] When Achilles tells

---

parallelism of the **téktōn** 'carpenter' as artisan *par excellence* with the **aoidós** 'poet', see Ch.17§§10-13. On the poet as **dēmiourgós**, see xvii 381-387 as discussed at Ch.12§13 and nn2, 3.

§2n4. On the convention of presenting the **xénos** 'guest-stranger' on a social scale that ranges from *beggar* all the way to *poet*, see Ch.12§§13-16.

§2n5. Cf. Pucci 1977.31-32, 130-135.

§2n6. The **agón** is also the traditional context of such archaic poetic forms as the Homeric Hymns—and we can see this from the use of the word **agón** at *HH* 6.19-20. See also the Hesiodic and Homeric references to poetic contests at *W&D* 654-659 and II 594-600, and the commentary by Maehler 1963.16. In fact, the name of the competitive poet **Thámuris** at II 595 seems to be the embodiment of the social context for poetic competition. In the Alexandrian lexicographical tradition and elsewhere, we see that **thámuris** means 'assembly'; see Durante 1976.202 for documentation and commentary. Moreover, the word **agón** itself denotes 'assembly' (from **ágō**; cf. Chantraine I 17); the semantic extension 'place of contest' reveals that the holding of contests was a basic social function of such an 'assembly'. Compare the semantics of *samaryá-* 'poetic contest' in the *Rig-Veda*, as discussed by Durante, pp. 198-201. I disagree, however, with Durante's equating the meaning of *samaryá-* with that of **Hómēros**: see Ch.17§9n2.

§3n1. Ch.11§12; also Ch.7§16.

§3n2. Above, Ch.7§17.

Agamemnon that the Achaeans will long remember their mutual **éris** (XIX 63-64), his words apply—far beyond the Achaeans of their time—to the future generations of Hellenic listeners who will ask to hear the story of the *Iliad*.[3] The grand Strife Scene between Agamemnon and Achilles is even recapitulated on the Shield of Achilles, in that microcosmic stop-motion picture of litigation between a defendant who offers compensation and a plaintiff who refuses it (XVIII 497-508).[4] Like its major counterpart, this minor Strife Scene is also a **neîkos** (νεῖκος/ἐνείκεον: XVIII 497/498). But here the quarrel is a formal litigation, with claims and counterclaims expressed in correct legal language.[5] And the objective of the whole procedure is **díkē** 'justice' (δίκαζον/δίκην: XVIII 506/508). This quarrel is in fact strikingly similar to the one between Perses and Hesiod himself, where the objective is again **díkē** (δίκης/δίκην ... δικάσσαι: W&D 36/39) and where the quarrel itself is a **neîkos** (νεῖκος at W&D 35; cf. also νείκε'/νεικέων/νείκεα at W&D 29/30/33).[6]

§4. The **neîkos** of Perses and Hesiod is in fact a formal context for engaging in blame as a positive social function, as we see from the corresponding quarrel of Agamemnon and Achilles. Here the words spoken by the aggrieved warrior against the king of his **phíloi** are taken from the language of blame-poetry.[1] Achilles insults Agamemnon by calling him such names as **kunôpa** 'having the looks of a dog' (I 159) and **kunòs ómmat' ékhōn** 'having the eyes of a dog' (I 225)—epithets that typify a bestial degree of gluttony.[2] When blame is justified, the application of **kúōn** 'dog' and its derivatives is a quint-

§3n3. For the poetic self-references associated with the theme of *remembering* and *not forgetting* a story of grief, see Ch.6§§4 ff.

§3n4. Ch.6§20.

§3n5. See Muellner 1976.100-106 on the legal use of **eúkheto** 'claimed' at XVIII 499, for which he finds a striking parallel in the use of *e-u-ke-to* = **eúkhetoi** 'claims' in the Linear B texts (Pylos tablets Ep 704 and Eb 297). Muellner (p. 104) also notes the collocation of *e-u-ke-to* with *da-mo* = **dâmos** (Ep 704), corresponding to the collocation of **eúkheto** with **dêmos** in the Homeric passage at hand (XVIII lines 499 and 500 respectively). For Linear B **dâmos** as 'an administrative entity endowed with a juridical function', see Lejeune 1965.12.

§3n6. Cf. Vernant 1977. Note especially the expression **diakrīnómetha neîkos** 'let us settle our quarrel' at W&D 35. The compound verb **diakrínomai** here must be compared to the simple **krínomai** 'have a definitive settlement' as used in Hesiod *Th.* 535 and 882, where the settlements lead to the permanent separation of gods/men and gods/Titans respectively. Discussion at Ch.11§5. Cf. also the semantics of the passive formation **kríthen** 'they separated from each other' in Pindar *P.*4.168.

§4n1. Ch.12§6.

§4n2. Ch.12§5.

essentially appropriate insult.[3] With other insults as well, Achilles attacks Agamemnon by picturing him as the ultimate glutton: most notably, he calls him **dēmobóros basileús** 'a king who is the devourer of the **dêmos**' (I 231).[4] Agamemnon is here branded as a king so greedy that he consumes his own community.[5] This insult is immediately pertinent to the **neîkos** of Perses and Hesiod, where the adjudicating **basilêes** 'kings' are themselves called **dōrophágoi** 'devourers of gifts' on account of their lack of **díkē** 'justice' (*W&D* 38–39 and 263–264; cf. 220–221). The figure of Hesiod is engaged in making justified blame, expressed in language appropriate to blame-poetry, just as Achilles had done in his quarrel with Agamemnon. Here too we see blame-poetry in its positive social function. Moreover, this blaming of unjust kings whose injustice promotes the **neîkos** of Perses and Hesiod is in sharp contrast with the praising of the just kings in Hesiod *Th.* 80–93. A king who makes settlements with **díkē** (*Th.* 85–86) is described as one who can stop "even a great **neîkos**" (καὶ μέγα νεῖκος: *Th.* 87). Such just kings are **ekhéphrones** 'aware' (*Th.* 88) precisely because they heed what the Muses say (*Th.* 80 ff.) — through the intermediacy of the poets.[6] Thus only those kings who are **phronéontes** 'aware' can understand the message of Hesiod the poet, as he tells them the **aînos** of the hawk and the nightingale:

νῦν δ᾽ αἶνον βασιλεῦσιν ἐρέω φρονέουσι καὶ αὐτοῖς

Now I will tell an **aînos** for kings, aware [**phronéontes**] as they are.[7]

Hesiod *W&D* 202

In sum, the **neîkos** of Perses and Hesiod is a context for blaming the unjust king; it is a **neîkos** that can be stopped only by the just king.

§4n3. Consider again Ch.12§§5-6.

§4n4. For the semantics of **dêmos** in this context of **neîkos**, see §3n5. Since there is a traditional interplay in Homeric diction between **dêmos** 'district, community' and **dēmós** 'fat' (Nagler 1974.5–9), we may note that **dēmobóros** can also be understood as 'devourer of fat'. On the traditional theme that tells of dogs devouring the **dēmós** 'fat' of corpses (VIII 379–380, XI 818, XIII 831–832), see Ch.12§5. If this interpretation is valid, then Agamemnon is being described by Achilles with an epithet that befits a corpse-devouring dog.

§4n5. Note that Thersites himself blames Agamemnon for his greed (II 225–238). At II 236–237, he even says that the Achaeans should forsake Agamemnon, leaving him behind "to digest his **géras** [plural; = honorific portions]" all to himself (γέρα πεσσέμεν: II 237). For **géras** 'honorific portion' in the sense of 'cut of meat', see Ch.7§19. On the greed of Agamemnon, consider also **philokteanótate** 'preeminent lover of possessions' (I 122), an epithet applied to him again by Achilles.

§4n6. Cf. Puelma 1972.97–98.

§4n7. See Ch.12§18.

The blaming itself is justified so long as the injustice remains—which is **húbris** as opposed to **díkē** (*W&D* 213–285).³ In this sense, the **neîkos** of Perses and Hesiod has the positive social function of precipitating the *Works and Days*. Moreover, this very **neîkos** motivates the major theme that has served as our point of departure—the Hesiodic portrait of **Éris** as a prime determinant of the human condition (*W&D* 11–26).⁹

§5. The human condition is not only defined by **éris**; it is even caused by it. On the level of myth, this **éris** is formalized as one primordial Strife Scene that takes place at one primordial **daís** 'feast' shared by gods and men.¹ There are various multiforms of this feast, such as the one attended by Prometheus (Hesiod *Th.* 535 ff.) or the one celebrating the Wedding of Peleus and Thetis (Hesiod *fr.* 204.95 ff.; *Cypria*/Proclus p. 102.13 ff. Allen; Pindar *Paean* 6.50 ff.). But, aside from such variables, there is also an essential constant: by disrupting the **daís**, the **éris** of the Strife Scene disrupts the communion of gods and men, thereby bringing to an end the golden existence of mankind.² Since **éris** is inevitable and since it also can be formalized as blame,³ the institution of blame in general and blame poetry in particular is itself conceived as one of life's necessary evils.

§6. Ironically, the **aînos** as a traditional form of blame is not only an institution of **éris** but also an eternal reminder of what had been disrupted by **éris** at a primal Strife Scene, namely, the golden existence of mankind. The standard setting for the narrative of the **aînos** is the Golden Age itself. In the proem to the versified fables of Babrius, where the poet cites the prosaic retellings of the Aesopic tradition as his immediate source (lines 14–16),¹ we read that the Golden Age was a time when:

1. animals had the same **phōné** 'power of speech' as men (lines 5–12)
2. men and gods were one community (**hetaireíē**: line 13).

In other words, there had been in the Golden Age a communion of animals and men and of men and gods. In the fables of Aesop, we find animals actually communicating with men as well as one another

§4n8. For more on **díkē** and **húbris**: Ch.9§7 and n2.
§4n9. See again §2.
§5n1. Ch.11§15.
§5n2. Ch.11§§1–14.
§5n3. §1; also Ch.11§16.
§6n1. This is not to say, of course, that the original Aesopic tradition of **aînoi** was not poetry.

through the power of speech,[2] and there are instances where the fable is actually introduced with an explicit statement to that effect:[3]

καθ' ὃν καιρὸν ἦν ὁμόφωνα τὰ ζῷα τοῖς ἀνθρώποις ...

At the time when animals had the same **phōnḗ** as men have ...

Life of Aesop G 99, introducing
"The Poor Man Catching Insects"
= *Fable* 387 Perry

καθ' ὃν καιρὸν ἦν ὁμόφωνα τὰ ζῷα ...

At the time when animals had the same **phōnḗ** ...

Life of Aesop W 97,[4] introducing
"The Wolves and the Sheep"
= *Fable* 153 Perry

Ironically too, Aesop himself had no **phōnḗ** 'power of speech' before he received the gift of verbal skills from the Muses (*Life of Aesop* G 7).[5] In the beginning, he had been like an animal, doubly removed from the Golden Age. By having no **phōnḗ**, he had been excluded from the community of both gods and men. We see as a permanent reminder of his primal state the simple fact that Aesop actually remains a theriomorphic figure throughout his *Life*.[6] In the end,

§6n2. For an example of verbal communication between animals and men, see Aesop *Fable* 465 Perry.

§6n3. Cf. also Callimachus *Iambus* 2 = *fr.* 192 Pfeiffer.

§6n4. Also at G 97, where the introductory phrasing is exactly as at G 99.

§6n5. In the attested version (G 7), Isis gives Aesop the power of speech itself (**phōnḗ**) while the Muses give him the power of speech skills. I believe that earlier versions had Apollo in place of Isis: see Ch.17§1n6, §2n2; Ch.18§2. Note too that the epiphany of the Muses to Aesop is in the setting of an elaborately lush garden, where the **téttīx** 'cicada' sings (G 6). For more on the **téttīx**, see Ch.18§1.

§6n6. There is a collection of epithets applied to Aesop, many of them having to do with the various grotesque forms of various animals, at the very beginning of the *Life* narrative (*Vitae* G+W 1), on which see Wiechers 1961.31–32. Throughout the narrative, in fact, the other characters keep insulting Aesop by way of appellations like **kunoképhalon** 'dog-head' (G 11, 30; W 31). The association of Aesop with the figure of a dog is especially interesting in view of the traditional use of **kúōn** 'dog' and its derivatives in the language of blame; see in particular Ch.12§6 on *Iliad* I 159 and 225, where Achilles insults Agamemnon by calling him **kunôpa** 'having the looks of a dog' and **kunòs ómmat' ékhōn** 'having the eyes of a dog'. In fact, the name of Aesop himself may be a semantic parallel: **Aís-ōpos** may mean 'having the looks of baseness', if the element **ais-** can be connected with **ais-kh-** as in the word **aîskhos** 'baseness' and its family (on the semantics of which see Ch.14§13). The element **ais-** also may be connected with the adjective **aís-ulo-** 'unseemly'. Note that the speaking of **aísula** 'unseemly things' is equated with **kertomíai** 'reproaches' at *Iliad* XX 202 and 433. On the semantics of **kertoméō** 'reproach' and its family, see Ch.14§§11(n6) and 14. Questions of etymology aside, however, the strong association of Aesop with the figure

however, after having died for blaming a ritualized Strife Scene (*Pap.Oxy.* 1800), Aesop wins immortality (Plato Comicus *fr.* 68 Kock).[7] It was in fact immortality that the animals had demanded from Zeus in their own Strife Scene, which had plummeted them from their own golden existence (Callimachus *Iambus* 2 = *fr.* 192 Pfeiffer).[8] In the end, Aesop transcends the condition of both animals and men. The gaps that are bridged in his **aînoi** between animals and men and gods are bridged in the course of his *Life*.

---

of a dog seems to be connected with the function of the Aesopic **aînos** as blame poetry. We observe the message of Aesop's fable about "The Wolves and the Sheep" (*Fable* 97 Perry), as conveyed by the context of its retelling in *Vitae* G+W 97: just as the dogs' barking protects the sheep from the wolves, so also the fable of Aesop protects the Samians from Croesus. In connection with the Samian phase of Aesop's *Life* (on which see also Ch.16§8n1), I should note in passing a curious passage in *Vita* G 87, featuring a barrage of insulting appellations as spoken by the Samians against Aesop (the last one of which is "a dog in a wicker basket"!). The categories of these appellations are well worth careful study, since they may match some stock characters in the Aesopic fables (though their language is certainly far more picturesque than that of the rhetorical retellings in the Aesopic corpus that has come down to us).

§6n7. For a collection of other testimonia on the immortalization of Aesop, see Perry 1952.226; cf. Wiechers 1961.41.

§6n8. The contents of this Callimachean fragment can be supplemented by two paraphrases of its substance: (1) a papyrus from Tebtynis [see Maas 1934] and (2) Philo of Alexandria *De confusione linguarum* 6–8. See Perry 1962.312–313. Significantly, this same Callimachean passage telling of the animals' loss of immortality also alludes to Aesop's death at Delphi (*fr.* 192.15–17 Pfeiffer).

20 | Achilles beyond the *Iliad*

§1. Having just seen how the **neîkos** 'quarrel' between Hesiod and Perses (*W&D* 35) serves as the context for a grand definition of **díkē** by way of its opposition to **húbris**,[1] we return one last time to the **neîkos** between Odysseus and Achilles (*Odyssey* viii 75) in the first song of Demodokos (viii 72–82). This quarrel too serves as a context for defining one theme, the **mêtis** 'artifice' of Odysseus, by opposing it to another theme, the **bíē** 'might' of Achilles.[2] But here it is not simply a matter of choosing between negative and positive, as with **húbris** and **díkē**. True, the **mêtis** of Odysseus is vindicated as the heroic resource that will lead to the ultimate capture of Troy. But the **bíē** of Achilles is also vindicated by the events of traditional epic narrative, in that the Achaeans survived to capture Troy *only because they had been rescued earlier by Patroklos/Achilles from the onslaught of Hektor.*[3] The **kléos** of Achilles as the best of the Achaeans in the *Iliad* is achieved because the Achaeans are doomed without his **bíē**. For his own **kléos** as best of the Achaeans in the *Odyssey*,[4] even Odysseus will need to have **bíē** against the suitors. When they fail in their attempts to string the bow of Odysseus, the suitors themselves must recognize the hero's superiority in **bíē**:

πολλὸν δὲ βίης ἐπιδευέες ἦσαν

and they were by far inferior in **bíē**

xxi 185

ἀλλ' εἰ δὴ τοσσόνδε βίης ἐπιδευέες εἰμὲν
ἀντιθέου Ὀδυσῆος

§1n1. Ch.19§§3–4.
§1n2. Ch.3§§1–8.
§1n3. Ibid.
§1n4. Ch.2§§12–18.

317

but if indeed we are so inferior in **bíē** to godlike Odysseus

xxi 253–254

In Penelope's own conditional words, the disguised Odysseus would have to use his **bíē** in order to string the bow (xxi 314–315) *and thereby win her as wife* (xxi 316). Odysseus is of course not only about to string the bow, thus fulfilling the condition set down by Penelope. He will also kill the suitors with it.

§2. We may proceed, then, with the understanding that **bíē** is a key to the **kléos** of Achilles/Odysseus in the *Iliad/Odyssey*. Now we are about to see that it is also a key element in epic traditions about other prominent heroes. In the case of Herakles, for example, the theme of **bíē** is actually embodied in the hero's identity, since he is conventionally named not only as **Hēra-kléēs** but also as **bíē** + adjective of **Hēraklēes**:[1]

nominative	βίη ῾Ηρακληείη	XI 690; Hes.*Th.* 289, 982, *fr.* 35.1(MW)
genitive	βίης ῾Ηρακληείης	II 666; Hes.*Th.* 332; *fr.* 33(a)25, 30
dative	βίη ῾Ηρακληείη	II 658, XV 640; Hes.*Th.* 315, *fr.* 25.18, 165.9
accusative	βίην ῾Ηρακληείην	V 638, XIX 98, xi 601; Hes.*Th.* 943, *fr.* 33(a)23

The fact that a full declension of this periphrastic naming construct **bíē** + adjective of **Hēraklēes** is attested in the diction of archaic hexameter poetry is itself striking evidence, on the level of form, that the Herakles figure and **bíē** are traditionally linked on the level of theme.[2] Since the very name **Hēra-kléēs** 'he who has the **kléos** of Hera' embodies the theme of glory *through epic*,[3] the traditional combination of **bíē** with **kléos** in the periphrastic naming construct **bíē** + adjective of **Hēra-kléēs** is a formal indication that **bíē** is a traditional epic theme. In fact, other heroic names built with **kléos** are also found in the same naming construct:

---

§2n1. For a survey of other such periphrastic naming constructs: Schmitt 1967.109–111. On **ís** as a synonym of **bíē**: Ch.5§37 and Ch.12§9n4.

§2n2. There is also an attestation of **bíē** + genitive of **Hēra-kléēs** at XVIII 117; also at Hesiod *fr.* 1.22MW. Periphrases combining a noun with the genitive of a name are less archaic than those combining a noun with the adjective of a name: Schmitt, p. 110n670. In this light, the preponderance of **bíē** + adjective of **Hēra-kléēs** over **bíē** + genitive of **Hēra-kléēs** is itself significant.

§2n3. Ch.18§2.

bíē + adjective of **Eteo-kléēs** (-́klos)[4] = Ἐτεοκληείη   IV 386
bíē + adjective of **Iphi-kléēs** (-́klos)[5] = Ἰφικληείη   xi 290, 296
Cf.
bíē + genitive of **Patro-kléēs** (-́klos)[6] = Πατρόκλοιο   XVII 187, XXII 323

§3. The heroic resource of **bíē**, then, has a distinctly positive aspect as a key to the hero's **kléos**. Nevertheless, it has a disquieting negative aspect as well. For our first example, let us turn again to the *Odyssey*. Whereas Odysseus uses **bíē** to kill the suitors, the overall behavior of the suitors themselves in the course of the *Odyssey* is also characterized as **bíē** (e.g., xxiii 31). Moreover, the **bíē** of the suitors in the House of Odysseus is equated with **húbris** (xv 329, xvii 565). This noun **húbris** characterizes not only the outrageous behavior of the suitors (xvi 86, xxiv 352) but also that of the blood-crazed warriors belonging to Generation III of mankind (Hesiod *W&D* 146).[1] In fact, the **húbris** of Generation III is correlated with their **bíē** (*W&D* 148).[2] Furthermore, the **húbris** that characterizes the blood-crazed warriors of Generation III is in direct opposition to the **díkē** of the noble Generation IV warriors (*W&D* 158).[3] We come back, then, to our point of departure, the negative/positive opposition of **húbris/díkē** as dramatized by the **neîkos** of Perses and Hesiod (*W&D* 35). We now see that **bíē** itself has a negative aspect, an element of **húbris**. In this way, **bíē** can even be contrasted directly with **díkē**:

καί νυ δίκης ἐπάκουε, βίης δ' ἐπιλήθεο πάμπαν

Listen to **díkē**! Forget **bíē** entirely!

W&D 275

§4. The ambivalence of **bíē** is also reflected by the *Iliad*. Only here it is not a matter of assigning good and bad **bíē** to good and bad characters respectively. Rather, the good/bad ambivalence of **bíē** is

§2n4. On the semantics of this name: Ch.7§16n3, Ch.12§7n3, Ch.14§12n3.

§2n5. The element **īphi-** is the instrumental of **ís**, a synonym of **bíē** (cf. n1). For a similar pleonasm in a naming construct, consider Hesiod *Th.* 332: **ís** + genitive of **bíē** + adjective of **Hēra-kléēs** (ἴς ... βίης Ἡρακληείης).

§2n6. This construct is less archaic not only because of the genitive (n2) but also because the compound name **Patro-kléēs** is truncated to **Pátroklos** in these combinations (Πατρόκλοιο βίην); see Ch.6§12 and n1.

§3n1. Ch.9§21.

§3n2. Ch.9§9.

§3n3. Ch.9§§7, 21.

built into one character, Achilles himself. The good aspect has already been mentioned: without the **bíē** of Achilles, no **mētis** can rescue the Achaeans from Hektor's onslaught.[1] As for the bad aspect, it is manifested throughout the rampage of Achilles as he finally enters his war in the *Iliad*. He does more, much more, than simply kill Hektor. A veritable slaughter is to precede Hektor's death, only to be followed by mutilation and human sacrifice.[2] Apollo says it all when he compares Achilles to a ravenous lion who lunges for his **daís** 'portion', yielding to his own savage **bíē** (XXIV 41–43).[3] The words of Apollo describing the hero's disposition correspond to the words used by Achilles himself as he expresses his own brutal urge to devour the vanquished Hektor (XXII 346–347).[4] Such ghastly aspects of **bíē** lead us to wonder what words the man of **mētis** may possibly have used against the man of **bíē** during their **neîkos** 'quarrel', which actually took place at a **daís** 'feast' (viii 76). One thing is certain: when Odysseus for a single moment despairs of his **mētis**, the reaction of his men is to be overwhelmed by thoughts about **bíē**. Let us observe first the hero's words of despair:

ὦ φίλοι, οὐ γὰρ ἴδμεν ὅπῃ ζόφος οὐδ' ὅπῃ ἠώς,
οὐδ' ὅπῃ ἠέλιος φαεσίμβροτος εἶσ' ὑπὸ γαῖαν
οὐδ' ὅπῃ ἀννεῖται· ἀλλὰ <u>φραζώμεθα</u> θᾶσσον
εἴ τις ἔτ' ἔσται <u>μῆτις</u>· ἐγὼ δ' οὐκ οἴομαι εἶναι.

Dear friends! I speak because we know neither where the western darkness is
    nor the dawn,
neither where the sun that shines upon mortals sets below the earth
nor where it rises,[5] but let us hasten to <u>think</u>[6]
whether there is any **mētis** any longer. I myself think there is none.

x 190–193

Then the reaction of his men:

ὡς ἐφάμην, τοῖσιν δὲ κατεκλάσθη φίλον ἦτορ
μνησαμένοις ἔργων Λαιστρυγόνος 'Αντιφάταο
Κύκλωπός τε <u>βίης</u> μεγαλήτορος, ἀνδροφάγοιο.

§4n1. Again, Ch.3§§1–8.
§4n2. On these themes see Segal 1971 and Redfield 1975.
§4n3. Ch.7§22.
§4n4. Ibid. Note that the contrast of **bíē** and **díkē** in Hesiod *W&D* 275 is illustrated with the behavior of beasts: since they do not have **díkē** (*W&D* 278), they devour each other (*W&D* 276–278).
§4n5. On the theme of orientation as it relates to **mētis**: §27.
§4n6. On **phrázomai** as the verb of **mētis**: Ch.3§5n4, §7n2.

κλαῖον δὲ λιγέως, θαλερὸν κατὰ δάκρυ χέοντες·
ἀλλ᾽ οὐ γάρ τις πρῆξις ἐγίγνετο μυρομένοισιν.

So I spoke. And their heart was broken
as they remembered the deeds of Antiphates the Laestrygonian
and the **bíē** of the great-hearted Cyclops, the man eater.[7]
And they wept loud and shrill, letting many a tear fall.
But crying did not get them anywhere.

x 198-202

In the absence of **mêtis**, disorienting thoughts of **bíē** are stirred up in the mind. And the nightmarish vision of the man-eating Cyclops in the *Odyssey* is marked by the same **bíē** that marks the epic vision of a rampaging Achilles in the *Iliad*. Significantly, it is only here in the *Odyssey* that the Cyclops is ever called "great-hearted" (μεγαλήτορος: x 200)—an epithet generically applied to the warriors of the Trojan War.[8]

§5. The theme of **bíē** is not only ambivalent in its positive and negative aspects, it is also elemental. Most prominently, the power of the winds is designated by **bíē** (βίας ἀνέμων: XVI 213, XXIII 713) or by its synonym **ís** (ἲς ἀνέμου/ἀνέμοιο: XV 383/XVII 739, etc.).[1] Also, the power of fire is called the "**bíē** of Hephaistos" (Ἡφαίστοιο βίηφι: XXI 367),[2] and this appellation applies at the very moment when the power of fire is defeating the power of water. The latter is manifested in the river god Xanthos, who in turn is called the "**ís** of the river" (ἲς ποτάμοιο: XXI 356).[3] Before Hephaistos, Achilles himself had confronted the river god, but Xanthos says that the hero's **bíē** will not suffice against a god (οὐ ... βίην χραισμησέμεν: XXI 316). What strikes us in particular here is that the narrative is

§4n7. Like the Cyclops, Antiphates too is a cannibal: x 116, 124. Ironically, Odysseus had defeated the Cyclops by way of **mêtis** (ix 414, 422). Note also the word play of **mé tis** 'no one' in εἰ ... μή τίς σε βιάζεται 'if no one uses **bíē** against you' at ix 410 (cf. also ix 405, 406): **mé tis** conjures up **mêtis**!

§4n8. Besides the application of **megalḗtor**- 'great-hearted' to a wide range of warriors in both the *Iliad* and the *Odyssey*, we may note in particular the combination of this epithet with **Phlégues** at XIII 302 and with the **thūmós** of Achilles as at IX 629 (on which see Ch.7§22). It is this same **thūmós** that tempts the hero to eat Hektor raw (XXII 346-347).

§5n1. Also in Hesiod *W&D* 518.

§5n2. Also in *H.Hermes* 115.

§5n3. Note also Ξάνθοιο ... μένος 'the **ménos** of Xanthos' at XXI 383. The noun **ménos**, which like **bíē** and **ís** is used to designate the power of heroes as well as to name heroes in periphrastic constructs, also designates the power of the rivers (XII 18), of the winds (xix 440), of fire (VI 182), of the sun itself (XXIII 190). See Nagy 1974.268-269.

presenting the **bíē** of Achilles as parallel to the **bíē** of fire itself. The god of water even says it about Achilles:

μέμονεν δ' ὅ γε ἶσα θεοῖσι

He is in a rage, equal to the rage of the gods.[4]

XXI 315

§6. The ultimate cosmic **bíē** is that of Zeus himself as he readies himself for battle with the Titans:

οὐδ' ἄρ' ἔτι Ζεὺς ἴσχεν ἐὸν μένος, ἀλλά νυ τοῦ γε
εἶθαρ μὲν μένεος πλῆντο φρένες, ἐκ δέ τε πᾶσαν
φαῖνε βίην

Zeus did not any longer restrain his **ménos** [might], but straightway his breathing was filled with **ménos**[1] and he showed forth all his **bíē**.[2]

Hesiod *Th.* 687–689

What follows these verses is an elaborate description of an ultimate thunderstorm (*Th.* 689–712) marked by thunder and lightning (*Th.* 689–692, 699, 707–708) that brings *fire* (*Th.* 692–700) and is conducted by *winds* (*Th.* 706–709).[3] The Cyclopes themselves, who had actually made thunder and lightning for Zeus (*Th.* 139–141), are characterized by their **bíē** (*Th.* 146). And here we see at least one interesting point of convergence between the Cyclopes of the *Theogony* and those of the *Odyssey*, who in turn are described as "better in **bíē**" than the Phaeacians (βίηφι ... φέρτεροι: vi 6). We should also recall the **bíē** of the man-eating Cyclops Polyphemus (x 200).[4] The main point remains, however, that the cosmic aspect of **bíē** as manifested in the thunderstorm of Zeus is parallel in epic diction to the heroic aspect of **bíē** as manifested in the martial rage of

---

§5n4. The verb **mémonen** 'is in a rage' is from the same root *men- that yields **mênis**, a word applied in the *Iliad* to the anger of gods *and* to the anger of Achilles—exclusively among heroes (Ch.5§8n2). Note that **ménos** can designate 'rage, anger' as well as 'might, power' (ibid.).

§6n1. On **ménos** as 'might, power' and as 'rage, anger': §5nn3,4.

§6n2. Overall as well, the war between the Titans and the Olympians is settled "by **bíē**" (βίηφι: *Th.* 882). In fact, the cosmic régime of Zeus and his Olympians is maintained by **Krátos** and **Bíē** personified (*Th.* 385–401). On the other hand, Zeus had originally achieved his cosmic supremacy by using both **bíē** 'might' and **tékhnai** 'artifice' (*Th.* 496) against his father Kronos.

§6n3. Cf. the thunderstorm of Zeus at xii 403–426. I draw special attention to the **thúella** 'gust' of wind at xii 409; elsewhere, **thúellai** are described as conduits of fire (xii 68). Discussion at Ch.10§41n4.

§6n4. §4.

Achilles. The slaughter of the Trojans by Achilles is directly compared to the burning of a city (XXI 520–525) as effected by the **mênis** 'anger' of the gods (XXI 523). The anger of the gods in general and of Zeus in particular is of course manifested directly in the fire and wind of a thunderstorm inflicted by Zeus, as we have already seen in Hesiod *Th.* 687–712.[5] Moreover, cosmic fire marks the reentry of Achilles in battle: Athena brings about a **phlóx** 'flame' that burns over the hero's head (XVIII 206), and the Trojans are terrified at the sight of this **akámaton pûr** 'inexhaustible fire' (XVIII 225). We may compare the **phlóx** of Zeus during his thunderstorm against the Titans (Hesiod *Th.* 692, 697), and in addition, the **phlóx** and the **akámaton pûr** of Hephaistos as the fire god stands in for Achilles by combating the element of water itself (XXI 333/349 and 341 respectively). Again I note that the **phlégma** 'conflagration' of Hephaistos is conducted by the **thúella** 'gust' of the West and South Winds (XXI 334–337),[6] just as the thunderbolt of Zeus is conducted by **ánemoi** 'winds' *(Th.* 706–709).

§7. The cosmic and heroic aspects of **bíē** combined bring us now to a striking parallel in Indo-Iranian religion and epic. The parallelism is to be found in the Indo-Iranian storm god *Vāyu*: his very name means "Wind," and he had once functioned as a god of the Männerbund or warrior society.[1] The parallelism is also to be found in the Indic hero *Bhīma*, one of the main figures in the epic *Mahābhārata*. Begotten of a mortal woman Kuntī by the war god Vāyu himself, Bhīma is the very embodiment of *balam* 'physical might', who is destined to be "the best among the strong" (*MBh.* 1.114.8–10).[2] He is, for that matter, not only strong but fast as well, running "with the speed of wind" (e.g., *MBh.* 1.136.19). He is also decidedly brutal—a quality that occasionally earns the solemn blame of his older brother Yudhiṣṭhira (*MBh.* 9.58.15 ff.). In one episode (*MBh.* 3.153), he goes on a rampage of violence (again blamed by

---

§6n5. Cf. again the thunderstorm at xii 403–426; in this case, the collective anger of the gods (cf. xii 349) is initiated by Helios (xii 348–349, 376, 377–383) and executed by Zeus (xii 387–388). On occasion, water rather than fire is the predominant manifestation of a thunderstorm inflicted by Zeus: cf. XVI 383–393.

§6n6. Cf. n3.

§7n1. For a basic work on the Indo-Iranian figure *Vāyu*: Wikander 1941. On the Indo-Iranian forms of Männerbund: Wikander 1938; for the broader standpoint of the Indo-European peoples in general: Dumézil 1969b.

§7n2. Cf. Dumézil 1968.63–64. My citations from the *Mahābhārata* follow the numbering of the critical (Poona) edition.

Yudhiṣṭhira) that is actually inaugurated by a violent windstorm. Bhīma has a younger brother Arjuna, begotten of Kuntī by the war god Indra. This hero is the embodiment not only of *balam* 'physical might' as applied to enemies but also of beneficence as applied to friends (*MBh.* 1.114.23). In this connection, we must note the important discussions of Stig Wikander and Georges Dumézil, who have convincingly shown that the relationship of the five brothers Yudhiṣṭhira, Bhīma & Arjuna, Nakula & Sahadeva, collectively known as the Pāṇḍava-s, reflects an ideology so archaic that it is Indo-European in origin.[3] What is of more immediate concern, however, is the specific relationship of the heroes Bhīma and Arjuna, which reflects an ideology that is no longer apparent in the relationship of the gods who fathered them, Vāyu and Indra respectively. By the time that the *Mahābhārata* was taking on its present shape, Vāyu had long been obsolescent, while Indra had long ago evolved from a god of war into a far more complex and versatile figure.[4] The contrast between Bhīma and Arjuna in epic, however, remains unaffected—or at least less affected—by the trends of Indic religion. For my own purposes, I note in particular the following details of contrast from among a more extensive list of details assembled by Dumézil:[5]

- Bhīma is defiant of military institutions; Arjuna is respectful
- Bhīma is a solitary combatant; Arjuna fights in the army
- Bhīma tends to fight without armor; Arjuna is equipped with a spectacular array of weaponry.

§8. Each of these thematic contrasts between the two Indic figures evokes a striking parallel within the single figure of Achilles. There is on one hand the Hellenic hero's defiance of military institutions, taking the specific form of his challenge to Agamemnon in *Iliad* I as well as his rejection of the Embassy in *Iliad* IX. On the other hand, his treatment of Priam in *Iliad* XXIV reflects a stance of ultimate military etiquette. Or again, there is his solitary disposition as manifested in his refusal to aid the **phíloi** despite the entreaties of the Embassy. Only after the death of Patroklos, who is to him more **phílos** than anyone else, is Achilles finally reintegrated with the rest of his **phíloi**.[1] Before his reintegration into the Männerbund of his

§7n3. Wikander 1947, Dumézil 1968 part I.

§7n4. There are still traces of an archaic relationship between Vāyu and Indra in the oldest body of Indic literature: see *Rig-Veda* 1.139.1–2, 2.41.1–3, and the commentary by Dumézil, p. 51 (cf. also his p. 58n2).

§7n5. Dumézil, pp. 63–65.

§8n1. Ch.6§§12–22.

phíloi,[2] Achilles is pictured spending his time together with Patroklos in their mutual isolation, as we hear from the retrospective words spoken by the apparition of Patroklos himself:

οὐ μὲν γὰρ ζωοί γε φίλων ἀπάνευθεν ἑταίρων
βουλὰς ἑζόμενοι βουλεύσομεν

No longer shall you and I, alive, be planning our plans
as we sit far away from the **phíloi** companions [**hetaîroi**].[3]

XXIII 77–78

Achilles had even expressed the wish that he and Patroklos should be the only Achaeans to survive for the grand event of capturing Troy:

αἲ γάρ, Ζεῦ τε πάτερ καὶ ᾿Αθηναίη καὶ ῎Απολλον,
μήτε τις οὖν Τρώων θάνατον φύγοι, ὅσσοι ἔασι,
μήτε τις ᾿Αργείων, νῶϊν δ᾿ ἐκδῦμεν ὄλεθρον,
ὄφρ᾿ οἶοι Τροίης ἱερὰ κρήδεμνα λύωμεν

Father Zeus, Athena, and Apollo! If only
not one of all the Trojans could escape destruction,
nor a single one of the Argives, while you and I emerge from the slaughter,
so that we two alone may break Troy's sacred coronal.

XVI 97–100

Finally, we come to the third contrast. Achilles, like Arjuna, has the most splendid armor, and the lengthy description of his shield in *Iliad* XVIII (468–608) even entails a distinct narrative form. The tradition that tells of his armor is in fact so strong that the *Iliad* itself reckons with not one but two occasions when Achilles was given a set of armor made by Hephaistos himself (the later occasion at XVIII 468–613, the earlier at XVII 194–197 and XVIII 82–85).[4] As for the image of an Achilles without armor, I find an interesting attestation in Pindar *N*.3.43–66, a rare survival from the poetic traditions that had told about the boyhood deeds of Achilles.[5] Here we see the

§8n2. On the **phíloi** as a Männerbund: Ch.5§27.
§8n3. Compare the wording that describes the isolation of the Cyclops at ix 188–189.
§8n4. Ch.9§§12(n1),33(n2).
§8n5. In the poet's own words: λεγόμενον δὲ τοῦτο προτέρων / ἔπος ἔχω 'I have this **épos** as spoken of those that came before' (Pindar *N*.3.52–53). To defend my translation "of" (instead of "by"), I cite the discussion by Schmitt 1967.93–95. (I admit, however, that my interpretation may be undermined by an apparent parallel in Pindar *P*.3.80; thanks to Mark Griffith.) Compare also the introduction to a tale about another hunter, Meleager, at IX 524–525 (Ch.6§12). The stories about the boyhood of Achilles may be compared with parallel traditions as attested in the Irish evidence; I cite the *Boyhood Deeds of CúChulainn* and the *Boyhood Deeds of Finn*, with translations conveniently available in Cross and Slover 1936.137–152, 360–369. Cf. J. Nagy 1978.

young hero killing lions and boars while armed with nothing but a spear (lines 46–47);[6] in motion he is *as fast as the winds* (ἴσα τ' ἀνέμοις: line 45), and his speed is such that he even outruns deer, hunting them down without the aid of hunting dogs or traps (lines 51–52).[7]

§9. Mention of Achilles' wondrous speed brings us back to the theme of **bíē** as manifested by wind. The hero's speed is reflected even by the epithet system that adorns him in epic diction. Achilles is in fact the only hero in the *Iliad* who is called **podárkēs** 'relying on his feet' (over 20x),[1] **pódas ōkús** 'swift with his feet' (over 30x), and **podṓkēs** 'swift-footed' (over 20x).[2] Moreover, his windlike speed is a direct function of his **bíē**, as we see from the words directed at Hektor by Athena in disguise:

ἠθεῖ', ἦ μάλα δή σε βιάζεται ὠκὺς Ἀχιλλεύς,
ἄστυ πέρι Πριάμοιο ποσὶν ταχέεσσι διώκων

Dear brother, indeed <u>swift</u> Achilles <u>uses</u> **bíē** <u>against</u> you,
as he chases you <u>with swift feet</u>[3] around the city of Priam.

XXII 229–230

In other heroic traditions as well, **bíē** is manifested in the speed of wind. An ideal example is **Íphiklos**, who is also called **bíē** + adjective of **Íphi-kléēs** (as at xi 290, 296: βίη Ἰφικληείη).[4] This

---

§8n6. It is tempting to identify this spear with the **melíē** that Achilles inherited from his father Peleus (Ch.9§12). From Pindar's words we also hear that Peleus himself, when he was still in his prime, had captured Iolkos "alone, without an army" (μόνος ἄνευ στρατιᾶς: N.3.34).

§8n7. On the theme of the hunter in general: Vidal-Naquet 1968(b). On the manner in which Achilles eats his game: Ch.7§22n5. Even within the span of this boyhood narrative, the theme of eventually taming the savage disposition of Achilles is replayed: the Centaur Cheiron is responsible for the upbringing of the young hero, and as such he is described as "augmenting his **thūmós** [of Achilles] in all things that are fitting" (ἐν ἀρμένοισι πᾶσι θυμὸν αὔξων: Pindar N.3.58). On the savage **thūmós** of Achilles as replayed in the *Iliad*, see Ch.7§22 (compare Bhīma, who himself commits cannibalism: *Mahābhārata* 8.61.5 ff., anticipated at 2.61.44–46). Cheiron, by contrast, is "the Centaur who has the most **díkē**" (δικαιότατος Κενταύρων: XI 832).

§9n1. On the meaning: Chantraine I 109–110.

§9n2. There is one exception, in the *Doloneia*, where Dolon is called **podṓkēs** (X 316). I do not count the instances in the plural, where **podōkes** is a conventional epithet for swift horses (e.g., II 764) and for their charioteers (XXIII 262).

§9n3. Cf. XXI 564, XXII 173. It is also "with swift feet" that Achilles routs Aeneas from Mount Ida (XX 189) and confronts the god Apollo himself (XXII 8). Cf. also XXI 265, where Achilles is described as **podárkēs** as he stands up against the river god Xanthos and matches "**bíē** against **bíē**" (ἐναντίβιον: XXI 266).

§9n4. §2.

hero's identity, which is the very embodiment of **bíē** *and* its synonym **ís**,[5] is determined predominantly by his windlike speed. He is pictured in Hesiod *fr.* 62MW (quoted by Eustathius 323.42) as racing through a field of grain with such speed that his feet barely touch the tips of the grain stalks. His epithet is **podōkēs** 'swift footed', and he is said to have races with the winds themselves (scholia *ad* xi 326 and *Pap.Soc.Ital.* 1173.78–81). He even has a son called **Podárkēs** 'relying on his feet ' (Hesiod *fr.* 199.5MW).[6]

§10. The verb **théō** 'run, speed', as we see it applied to the speeding **Íphiklos** (θέεν: Hesiod *fr.* 62.1MW), also applies to speeding ships (I 483, ii 429, etc.) and to speeding horses (X 437, XIX 415, XX 227, 229).[1] In the case of horses, we may be more specific: their speed is by convention compared directly to the speed of wind, by way of the verb **théō**. At X 437, the horses of Rhesos are "like the winds in speed [θείειν]." At XIX 415, Xanthos, the wondrous horse of Achilles, says that they, the hero's horse team, could run [θέοιμεν] as fast as the gust of Zephyros the West Wind, described as the fastest of all. Despite their speed, however, Achilles is fated to die "by **ís** [ἶφι], at the hands of a god and a man" (XIX 417). Finally, at XX 227, the wondrous horses fathered by Boreas the North Wind are described as so swift that their feet barely touch the tips of the grain stalks as they race [θέον] across fields of grain. Also, at XX 229, their feet barely touch the tips of the waves as they race [θέεσκον] across the surface of the sea. Needless to say, the parallel with the speeding Iphiklos (Hesiod *fr.* 62MW) is striking. I lay such emphasis on the associations of the verb **théō** in Homeric diction because I see an interesting semantic complement in the associations of the adjective derived from **théō**, **thoós** 'swift'. As an epithet, **thoós** applies to Ares the war god himself (V 430, VIII 215, etc.) as well as to occasional

§9n5. §2n1.

§9n6. In view of such pervasive associations between the themes of windspeed and **ís/bíē** in epic diction, I am inclined to reconsider the standard etymology offered for **íris**: root *ui̯- 'bend' (e.g., Chantraine II 468–469). Instead, I propose the root *ui̯- as in **ís** 'force, might', and I defend this alternative by adducing the traditional epithet system of Iris, which consistently dwells on the theme of windspeed: **podénemos** 'having feet of wind' (exclusive to her, in *Iliad* 10x), **pódas ōkéa** 'swift with her feet' (exclusive to her, in *Iliad* 9x), **aellópos** 'having feet of wind' (exclusive to her, in *Iliad* 3x). The **îris** is a 'rainbow' at XVII 547 insomuch as it functions as a **téras** 'foreboding sign' *either of war* (XVII 548) *or of a storm* (XVII 549)—precisely the two themes associated with **ís**!

§10n1. Achilles is compared to such a speeding horse at XXII 21–24 (θέῃσι at 23). When Achilles is chasing Hektor, the verb **théō** applies to both (θέον: XXII 161).

warriors (V 571, XV 585, etc.). Moreover, the epithet **Arēḯthoos** 'swift with Ares' applies in the plural to **aizēoí**, an obscure noun designating *warriors* at VIII 298/XV 315 and *hunters* at XX 167. We are reminded of the Indo-Iranian war god *Vāyu*, whose very name means "Wind"; also of the warrior *Bhīma*, son of Vāyu, who runs with the speed of wind.[2] In the associations of Greek **théō** and **thoós**, we find close parallels to these Indo-Iranian themes: the semantic range of the two words combined conveys a fusion of the elemental and martial functions.[3]

§11. The form **Arēḯthoos** recurs as the name of an Arcadian hero in a particularly interesting narrative tradition preserved by the *Iliad*. The context is set as Nestor is reproaching the Achaeans (νείκεσσ' 'made **neîkos**': VII 161) because not one of them has yet taken up Hektor's challenge issued to whoever is "best of the Achaeans" (VII 50). The old man wishes that he were young again (VII 132–133), as he was at the time of his youthful exploits during a war between the Pylians and the Arcadians (VII 133–156). The tale of his exploits is concluded with a reiteration by Nestor of his wish that he were as young as he had been at that time:

εἴθ᾽ ὡς ἡβώοιμι, βίη δέ μοι ἔμπεδος εἴη

If only I were that young! If only my **bíē** had remained as it was!

VII 157

The narrative framed by Nestor's wish, which took place in those former days when he still had his full **bíē**, concerns a duel between Nestor and a gigantic Arcadian hero—a duel that the old man is now contrasting with the present prospect of a duel between Hektor and whoever is "best of the Achaeans." The Arcadian hero was **Ereuthalíōn**, wearing the armor of **Arēḯthoos**:

τοῖσι δ᾽ Ἐρευθαλίων πρόμος ἵστατο, ἰσόθεος φώς,
τεύχε᾽ ἔχων ὤμοισιν Ἀρηϊθόοιο ἄνακτος,
δίου Ἀρηϊθόου, τὸν ἐπίκλησιν <u>κορυνήτην</u>

§10n2. §7.

§10n3. In this connection, we should note that the feminine plural of **thoós** serves as the ubiquitous epithet for the ships of the Achaeans (I 12, 371, etc.), which of course have a distinctly martial function in the *Iliad*. We recall that the Battle of the Ships was a **loigós** 'devastation' for the Achaeans, who were to be rescued from Hektor's onslaught by Achilles/Patroklos (Ch.5§§10–12). What bears emphasizing is that the Achaeans were rescued *because their ships were rescued from Hektor's fire* (cf. XVI 80–82; further discussion at §§15–20). In this sense, Achilles (/Patroklos) is savior of the Achaeans by being the guardian of their ships (discussion at §20).

ἄνδρες κίκλησκον καλλίζωνοί τε γυναῖκες,
140 οὕνεκ' ἄρ' οὐ τόξοισι μαχέσκετο δουρί τε μακρῷ,
ἀλλὰ σιδηρείῃ <u>κορύνῃ</u> ῥήγνυσκε φάλαγγας.
τὸν Λυκόοργος ἔπεφνε δόλῳ, οὔ τι κράτεΐ γε,
στεινωπῷ ἐν ὁδῷ, ὅθ' ἄρ' οὐ <u>κορύνη</u> οἱ ὄλεθρον
χραῖσμε σιδηρείη· πρὶν γὰρ Λυκόοργος ὑποφθὰς
145 δουρὶ μέσον περόνησεν, ὁ δ' ὕπτιος οὔδει ἐρείσθη·
<u>τεύχεα δ' ἐξενάριξε, τά οἱ πόρε χάλκεος Ἄρης.</u>
καὶ τὰ μὲν αὐτὸς ἔπειτα φόρει μετὰ μῶλον Ἄρηος·
αὐτὰρ ἐπεὶ Λυκόοργος ἐνὶ μεγάροισιν ἐγήρα,
δῶκε δ' Ἐρευθαλίωνι φίλῳ θεράποντι φορῆναι·
150 τοῦ ὅ γε τεύχε' ἔχων <u>προκαλίζετο πάντας ἀρίστους.</u>
οἱ δὲ μάλ' ἐτρόμεον καὶ ἐδείδισαν, οὐδέ τις ἔτλη·
ἀλλ' ἐμὲ θυμὸς ἀνῆκε πολυτλήμων πολεμίζειν
θάρσεϊ ᾧ· γενεῇ δὲ νεώτατος ἔσκον ἁπάντων·
καὶ μαχόμην οἱ ἐγώ, δῶκεν δέ μοι εὖχος Ἀθήνη.
155 τὸν δὴ μήκιστον καὶ <u>κάρτιστον</u> κτάνον ἄνδρα·
πολλὸς γάρ τις ἔκειτο παρήορος ἔνθα καὶ ἔνθα.

Their champion stood forth, **Ereuthalíōn**, a man godlike,
wearing upon his shoulders the armor of King **Arēíthoos**,
Arēíthoos the brilliant, named the <u>Club Bearer</u>[1]
by the men and fair-girdled women of that time,
140 because he fought not with bow and arrows, nor with a long spear,
but with a <u>club</u> coated with iron he smashed the army ranks.
Lukóorgos killed him—with a stratagem, not with **krátos**—[2]
in a narrow pass, where the iron <u>club</u> could not ward off
his destruction, since **Lukóorgos** anticipated him
145 by pinning him through the middle with his spear, and he fell down
backwards to the ground.
And he stripped off <u>the armor that brazen Ares had given him</u>.
And from then on he wore the armor himself whenever he went <u>to the</u>
mōlos [struggle] of Ares.

§11n1. Here the poetry itself is actually referring to an epithet as an epithet; then it follows up by explaining why the epithet is appropriate. The same epithet **korunḗtēs** 'club-bearer' is applied to Areithoos at VII 9; if we had only the latter attestation, we would never know that the epithet is directly pertinent to the story of this hero.

§11n2. The **krátos** 'superior power' of a warrior takes the form of **bíē** 'might': Ch.5§37. In other words, a warrior may have **bíē** and still lose without the **krátos** that only Zeus and the Olympians can grant. In this case, Areithoos implicitly has **bíē** but has failed to get **krátos** from the gods. On the other hand, Lykoorgos wins by using *stratagem* rather than the *might* of **bíē**. Still, he wins without **krátos**, which is properly a requisite of **bíē**. (Even the cosmic regime of the Olympians is actually maintained by the combination of **Krátos** and **Bíē** personified: Hesiod *Th.* 385–401.) The implicit **bíē** of Areithoos is in direct contrast with the stratagem of Lykoorgos.

But when **Lukóorgos** was growing old in his halls,
he gave it to **Ereuthalíōn** to wear, his **philos therápōn**.
150 So, wearing his armor [of Areithoos], he [Ereuthalion] <u>was challenging</u>
   <u>all the best</u> to fight him.
But they were all afraid and trembling: no one undertook to do it.
I was the only one, driven to fight by my **thūmós** which was ready to
   undertake much,
with all its boldness, even though I was the youngest of them all.
I fought him, and Athena gave me fame.[3]
155 For I killed the biggest and the <u>best</u> man:[4]
he sprawled in his great bulk from here to here.[5]

VII 136–156

Within the limits of my present inquiry, I cannot do justice to the
many details of this fascinating narrative, and I content myself by
citing only those points that are immediately pertinent. Surely the key
point is that **Areíthoos** is an ideal exponent of **bíē**, by virtue of both
his name and his primary attribute, the club. The themes of war and
swiftness inherent in the name **Areíthoos** remind us of the warrior
Bhīma, who runs "with the speed of wind" (e.g., *Mahābhārata*
1.136.19). So also with the theme of the club: Bhīma has the epic
reputation, well-known to other warriors, of wielding clubs (e.g.,
MBh. 1.123.40, 4.32.16, 9.57.43).[6] Aside from the comparative
evidence, there is also the internal evidence provided by the context:
Areíthoos was actually killed as an exponent of **bíē**, which is to be
contrasted with the *stratagem* of the man who killed him, **Lukóorgos**.[7]
Furthermore, we may suspect that the Arcadian hero who inherited
the armor of **Areíthoos** is also by implication a man of **bíē**, since
Nestor's whole narrative here is intended as an illustration of the old
man's **bíē** in the days when he was young.

§12. Let us pursue, then, the idea that **Ereuthalíōn** is a man of **bíē**.
From local Arcadian traditions, we learn that the young Nestor gave
form to his joy over defeating **Ereuthalíōn** by doing a dance without
taking off his armor (Ariaithos of Tegea *FGrH* 316.7). As Francis Vian

§11n3. On **eûkhos** as 'fame': Muellner 1976.110–112.
§11n4. That is, "the man with the most **krátos**" (κάρτιστον).
§11n5. Surely the phrasing here calls for an accompanying gesture by the performer.
§11n6. On the context of *MBh.* 4.32.16, see Dumézil 1968.90,92; cf. also his p. 63.
In one episode (*MBh.* 3.157.68), Bhīma's club is compared to Indra's bolt, *released with
the speed of wind.*
§11n7. For further traces of Areithoos and Lykoorgos in Arcadian lore, see
Pausanias 8.4.10, 8.11.4.

points out,[1] the dance as it is described corresponds to the formal war dance called the **purríkhē**.[2] In fact, what Nestor did corresponds to the basic definition of the **purríkhē** as we find it in Hesychius (s.v. πυρριχίζειν): τὴν ἐνόπλιον ὄρχησιν καὶ σύντονον πυρρίχην ἔλεγον 'the word for energetic dancing in armor was **purríkhē**'.[3] This word is actually derived from **purrhós** 'fiery red', which in turn is derived from **pûr** 'fire'.[4] Vian accordingly links the semantics of **purríkhē** with the name **Ereuthalíōn**, which must mean something like "red" (cf. verb **ereúthō** 'be red').[5] What could be more appropriate, he asks, than a "red dance" celebrating a "red warrior"?[6] We may go considerably further than this formulation. The fact is that **pûr** 'fire' is a prime manifestation of **bíē**, on the cosmic level and on the heroic as well.[7] Moreover, the figures of myth who are especially noted for their **bíē** are frequently called by names denoting fire—we are immediately reminded of **Púrrhos** himself, as also of the wanton society of warriors known as the **Phlegúai**.[8] The element **phleg-** of **Phlegúai** is actually the same root as in **phlóx** 'flame', a word that marks the **bíē** of Achilles in the *Iliad*.[9] The point is, the concept of **purríkhē** is appropriate to the name **Púrrhos** as well as to the adjective **purrhós**. In fact, there are traditions that derive the name of the dance from the name of the hero. In Archilochus *fr.* 304W, for example, the **purríkhē** gets its name because **Púrrhos** danced it for joy over his defeat of Eurypylos.[10] In another tradition used by Lucian (*De*

§12n1. Vian 1952.242–243.

§12n2. For collections of testimonia on the **purríkhē** and related dances: Latte 1913.27–63 and Prudhommeau 1965.300–312; also Vian, pp. 249–250. One thing that emerges from Vian's documentation is the association of the **purríkhē** with the **kômos**; the institution of the **kômos**, as we have seen, is in turn a partial heir to the ideologies of the **lāós** (Ch.12§§20–21).

§12n3. Cf. also Hephaestion 213.10 Consbruch. On poetry that can be sung to the accompaniment of the **purríkhē**: Severyns 1938 II 176.

§12n4. Chantraine III 959–960.

§12n5. Vian, p. 242; on the formal relationship of **Ereuthalíōn** and **ereúthō**: Chantraine II 369.

§12n6. Vian, p. 242. Cf. Latte 1913.27–29, who argues that the "red dance" is motivated by the red garb traditionally worn by warriors in war (cf. Aristotle *fr.* 542 Rose on the martial **phoinikís** 'red cape' of the Lacedaemonians).

§12n7. §§5–6.

§12n8. Ch.7§5, Ch.9§10.

§12n9. Above, §6.

§12n10. Preserved in Hesychius s.v. πυρριχίζειν, in the same article that commenced with the basic definition of the word. For further testimonia relating to Archilochus *fr.* 304, see the scholia to Pindar *P.*2.127, the scholia (T) to *Iliad* XVI 617 (= Eustathius 1078.23), and *Etymologicum Magnum* 699.1. Cf. Latte, p. 30.

saltatione 9), **Púrrhos** not only "invented" the **purrhíkhē** but also captured Troy through the power of this dance.[11] It also bears emphasizing that the dance themes of the **purrhíkhē** seem to be connected with fires at specific occasions, such as the cremation of Patroklos[12] or the holocaust of Troy itself.[13] In sum, the name of the warrior **Ereuthalíōn** is not motivated by the theme of Nestor's "red dance," nor for that matter is the **purrhíkhē** motivated by the name of **Púrrhos**. Rather, the names of such heroes as **Ereuthalíōn** and **Púrrhos** are motivated by the theme of martial **bíē** as manifested in the element of fire—and the same goes for the dance **purrhíkhē**. We may even say that the **purrhíkhē** is a dramatization of **bíē** itself. There is in fact an Arcadian festival called the **Móleia**, which dramatizes a duel between **Ereuthalíōn** and **Lukóorgos** (scholia *ad* Apollonius of Rhodes *Argonautica* 1.164).[14] In Panhellenic Epos, **môlos Áreōs** is combat, 'the struggle of Ares' (as at VII 147; also at II 401, etc.). In local ritual, the **Móleia** is a reenactment of such combat. And again, the reenactment amounts to a dramatization of martial **bíē**.[15]

§12n11. Cf. also Eustathius 1697.1–6 *ad Odyssey* xi 505 and the scholia (B) to Hephaestion 299.1 Consbruch, where we hear that the **purrhíkhē** originated when **Púrrhos** leapt out of the Trojan Horse. On the alternative tradition that Achilles "invented" the **purrhíkhē**: Aristotle *fr*. 519 Rose. On the **Trōïkòn pédēma** 'Trojan Leap' as a dance form that apparently served to signal the Capture of Troy, see the scholia to Euripides *Andromache* 1139 and to Lycophron 245–246: as Achilles leapt off his ship, he hit the ground with such **bíā** 'force' that he caused a spring to gush forth, which was named **Trōïkòn pédēma** (cf. Antimachus *fr*. 84 Wyss). On the **Trōïkòn pédēma** of Pyrrhos himself at the hour of his death at Delphi, see Euripides *Andromache* 1139–1140. In the same context (verse 1135), the offensive and defensive maneuvers of **Púrrhos** are actually designated as **purrhíkhai**. On the offensive and defensive motions of the **purrhíkhē**: Plato *Laws* 815a. As Borthwick 1967 argues cogently, the death dance of Pyrrhos at Delphi reenacts his own **Trōïkòn pédēma** when he captured Troy. Cf. Pindar *Paean* 6.114–115, where Pyrrhos is described as ἐ[πι/εν]θορόντα 'leaping upon' the very altar of Priam in order to kill the old king.

§12n12. Aristotle *fr*. 519 Rose (see Ch.6§30n3).

§12n13. See again n11.

§12n14. Since we have only one source for this information, we cannot know for sure whether we are dealing here with a mistake, in that the duel in the *Iliad* is between Areithoos and Lykoorgos. On the other hand, we may be dealing with a genuine variant. Discussion by Vian, pp. 242–243n8. In either case, the essential thing is the ritualization itself.

§12n15. I would expect the reenactment of the **môlos** 'struggle' to take primarily the form of a dance, with a **mímēsis** of the maneuvers taken by Lykoorgos against the hero of **bíē**. Compare the epic narrative of these maneuvers at VII 142–145 with the dancelike description of a wolf's movements in Pindar *P*.2.83–85. Discussion at Ch.12§21. In terms of "drama," the fate of Ereuthalion/Areithoos is of course "tragic"; as for the **môlos** 'struggle' between Odysseus and **Îros** at *Odyssey* xviii 233, the fate of the loser, this mock hero of **bíē**, is of course "comic." On **Îros** and the theme of **bíē** ridiculed: Ch.12§9n4.

§13. Now that we have surveyed the heroic attributes of wind and fire as conveyed by the themes of **Areïthoos** and **Ereuthalíōn** respectively, we are brought back to our central point of interest, the figure of Achilles, whose **bíē** happens to incorporate both of these elemental attributes. So far, the most direct Iliadic example of a traditional parallel between the martial rage of the hero and the thunderstorm of Zeus has been XXI 520–525, where the slaughter of the Trojans by Achilles is being directly compared to the burning of a city by divine agency.[1] But the overt description of divine power as manifested in fire and wind combined is actually to be found elsewhere, as in the Hesiodic description of the ultimate thunderstorm effected by Zeus against the Titans (*Th.* 687–712).[2] Moreover, an overt description of the *hero's* power as manifested in fire and wind is also to be found elsewhere. So far, the most striking instance has been the intervention of Hephaistos on the side of Achilles, where the **phlégma** 'conflagration' of the fire god is being conducted by Zephyros the West Wind and Notos the South Wind (XXI 334–337).[3] Now we may add the scene where Achilles prays to Boreas the North Wind and Zephyros the West Wind to conduct the fires that will cremate Patroklos (XXIII 194–198); without the winds, the funeral pyre will not burn (XXIII 192). As the winds blow, they literally "throw flame," and the word for flame is again **phlóx** (φλόγ' ἔβαλλον: XXIII 217).[4]

§14. In the Cremation Scene, the epiphany of the winds Boreas and Zephyros takes the form of a violent storm (XXIII 212–215), described as happening over the **póntos** 'sea' (XXIII 214).[1] This image, as I will attempt to show in the next several pages, relates directly to the figure of Achilles. We begin with a simile. When the Achaeans and their king Agamemnon are afflicted by **pénthos** 'grief' and **ákhos** 'grief' at IX 3 and 9 respectively, their affliction is directly compared to a violent storm brought about by the winds Boreas and Zephyros (IX 4–7); again, the storm is described as happening over the **póntos** 'sea' (IX 4). The **ákhos/pénthos** of the Achaeans and the corresponding **krátos** of the Trojans are of course brought about ultimately by the Will of Zeus, which takes the form of Hektor's

§13n1. §5.
§13n2. Again, §6.
§13n3. Again, §6.
§13n4. Cf. §6.
§14n1. The winds then move inland, approaching the pyre of Patroklos (XXIII 215–216). When their work is done, they take their leave the same way as when they arrived—over the **póntos** (XXIII 230).

onslaught.[2] In the same scene where Diomedes acknowledges that Zeus has given the **krátos** to the Trojans and not to the Achaeans (XI 317–319),[3] Hektor is actually being compared to a violently blowing wind that stirs up the **póntos** (XI 297–298). The expression ὑπεραέι ἶσος ἀέλλῃ 'equal to a violently blowing wind' at XI 297 follows a parallel simile applied to Hektor at XI 295: βροτολοιγῷ ἶσος Ἄρηϊ 'equal to Ares, the **loigós** [devastation] of mankind'.[4]

§15. But the immediate **loigós** 'devastation' afflicting the Achaeans in the *Iliad* is of course not the winds of the **póntos** that threaten to destroy their ships, but the fire of Hektor.[1] Significantly, even this fire threatens specifically *to destroy the ships of the Achaeans*, and this theme is central to the *Iliad*. The Will of Zeus, to give **krátos** to the Trojans until the Achaeans give Achilles his proper **tīmḗ** 'honor' (I 509–510), is of course what Achilles himself prays for in his **mênis** 'anger'. The hero's prayer in fact specifically entails that the Trojans should prevail *until they reach the ships of the Achaeans* (I 408–412, 559, II 3–5, XVIII 74–77). In this light, let us consider the first indication of the **álgea** 'pains' that the **mênis** of Achilles inflicted on the Achaeans through the Will of Zeus (I 1–5). It happens when the Achaeans first begin to be losers in the absence of Achilles: as Zeus is weighing the fates of the two sides, the Trojans are found to be on the winning and the Achaeans on the losing side (VIII 66–74). Zeus signals the decision with thunder and a **sélas** 'flash' of lightning hurled towards the Achaeans, who are panic stricken (VIII 75–77). As Cedric Whitman remarks, "The lightning flash which dismays the Achaeans is a direct reflex of Achilles' retirement. The action of the god and the inaction of the hero are essentially one."[2] Until now, the most successful Achaean in battle has been Diomedes, and Zeus hurls at him a special thunderbolt with a terrifying **phlóx** 'flame' (VIII 133–135), forcing the hero to retreat and giving him **ákhos** 'grief' (VIII 147). The thunderings of Zeus are a **sêma** 'signal' of victory for the Trojans (VIII 170–171), and Hektor straightway recognizes that the Will of Zeus entails the **kûdos** 'glory' of victory for the Trojans and **pêma** 'pain' for the Achaeans (VIII 175–176; recalled at XII 235–236, 255–256).

§14n2. Ch.5§25.
§14n3. Again, Ch.5§25.
§14n4. On the parallelism of Ares and the winds: §10.
§15n1. Ch.5§§10–12.
§15n2. Whitman 1958.133–134.

§16. Now we are ready to examine how the Will of Zeus is translated into the fire of Hektor's onslaught against the Achaean ships.
Once Zeus sends the flash of his thunderstroke, "lightning carries the
day; fire is on the Trojan side, and burns threateningly in the form of
watchfires which at the end of Book VIII dot the plain, and burn
throughout the succeeding night."[1] By the beginning of Book IX and
thereafter, the threat of fire from the Trojan side is consistently
formalized in one theme: *Hektor will burn the ships of the Achaeans*:
IX 76-77, 241-242, 347, 435-436, 602, 653
XI 666-667
XII 198, 441
XIII 628-629
XV 417, 420, 597-598, 600, 702, 718-725, 743-744.[2]
In fact, Hektor already realizes his function as threatening fire against
the Achaeans' ships when Zeus signals victory for the Trojans by way
of his thunderstroke (VIII 170-171), and the hero actually says then
and there to his fellow Trojans:

ἀλλ' ὅτε κεν δὴ νηυσὶν ἔπι γλαφυρῇσι γένωμαι,
μνημοσύνη τις ἔπειτα πυρὸς δηΐοιο γενέσθω,
ὡς πυρὶ νῆας ἐνιπρήσω, κτείνω δὲ καὶ αὐτοὺς
Ἀργείους παρὰ νηυσὶν ἀτυζομένους ὑπὸ καπνοῦ

But when I get to the hollow ships,
let there be some memory in the future[3] of the burning fire,
how I will set the ships on fire and kill
the Argives right by their ships, confounded as they will be by the smoke.

VIII 180-183

When the fire of Hektor finally reaches the Achaean ships, the
Muses are specially invoked for the telling of this vital event (XVI
112-113).[4] Zeus himself has been waiting to see the **sélas** 'flash' of
the first ship to be set on fire (XV 599-600), which is to be the
signal that his Will has been fulfilled, that the **kûdos** 'glory' of victory
has been taken away from the Achaeans and awarded to the Trojans
(XV 592-599). The **sélas** 'flash' that marks the final enactment of
Zeus' Will must be compared with the **sélas** 'flash' of his thunderstroke at VIII 76, which had signaled the beginning of the reverses

§16n1. Whitman, p. 135.
§16n2. Cf. Whitman, ibid.
§16n3. This expression indicates a *poetic* recording of an epic event for audiences of
the future: Ch.1§3n2.
§16n4. Again, Ch.1§3n2.

suffered by the Achaeans.[5] Once the fire of Hektor reaches the ships of the Achaeans, the Will of Zeus is complete: the narrative makes it explicit that Zeus will now shift the **kûdos** 'glory' of victory from the Trojans to the Achaeans (XV 601–602). Even this reversal is expressed in terms of "driving the Trojans away from the ships" (ibid.).

§17. Once the Will of Zeus is complete, the prayer of Achilles in his **mênis** is thereby fulfilled. The hero's prayer, as we have seen, has the same limit as the Will of Zeus: the Trojans should prevail *until they reach the ships of the Achaeans* (I 408–412, 559, II 3–5, XVIII 74–77). Thus when Achilles himself sees the fire of Hektor reaching the ships of the Achaeans at XVI 127, he sees in effect the ultimate fulfillment of his **mênis**. For Zeus, the **sélas** 'flash' of Hektor's fire at XV 600 signals the termination of the Trojan onslaught, which was inaugurated by the **sélas** of his own thunderstroke at VIII 76. For Achilles, the same fire at XVI 122–124, called **phlóx** 'flame' at 123, signals the end of his wish that the Trojans should reach the ships of the Achaeans and the beginning of his concern that their ships should be saved from the fire of Hektor (XVI 127–128). The hero now calls upon his substitute, Patroklos, to avert the fiery threat that his own **mênis** had originally brought about:

ἀλλὰ καὶ ὥς, Πάτροκλε, νεῶν ἀπὸ λοιγὸν ἀμύνων
ἔμπεσ' ἐπικρατέως, μὴ δὴ πυρὸς αἰθομένοιο
νῆας ἐνιπρήσωσι, φίλον δ' ἀπὸ νόστον ἕλωνται

Even so, Patroklos, ward off the **loigós** [devastation] from the ships
and attack with **krátos**, lest they [the Trojans] burn
the ships with blazing fire and take away a safe homecoming [**nóstos**].[1]

XVI 80–82

Patroklos is a savior of the Achaeans by virtue of temporarily averting *from their ships* the fire of the Trojans:

ἐκ νηῶν δ' ἔλασεν κατὰ δ' ἔσβεσεν αἰθόμενον πῦρ

He drove them [the Trojans] from the ships, and he quenched the blazing fire.

XVI 293

ὡς Δαναοὶ νηῶν μὲν ἀπωσάμενοι δήϊον πῦρ

Thus the Danaans, having averted from the ships the burning fire ...

XVI 301

§16n5. §15.
§17n1. Cf. Ch.5§12

Appropriately, Hektor is called φλογὶ εἴκελος ʽΗφαίστοιο 'like the **phlóx** [flame] of Hephaistos' (XVII 88) in the very action where he has killed Patroklos;[2] the word **phlóx** in this expression again implies the thunderstroke of Zeus.[3]

§18. To sum up, the **krátos** of the Trojans is signaled by the *fire* of Zeus in a thunderstorm, which is expressed with the same diction that expresses the *fire* of Hektor's onslaught against the ships of the Achaeans. On the other hand, the **krátos** of the Trojans is also signaled by the *wind* of Zeus in a thunderstorm. What is **krátos** for the Trojans is **pénthos/ákhos** for the Achaeans at IX 3/9, which in turn is compared by way of simile to violent winds raging over the **póntos** 'sea' at IX 4–7.[1] In the same scene where Diomedes acknowledges that Zeus has given the **krátos** to the Trojans (XI 317–319), Hektor is likened to a violent wind raging over the **póntos** (XI 297–298).[2] Just like Hektor's fire, these winds signaling **krátos** are expressed with the same diction that expresses the overall image of a thunderstorm brought by Zeus. As further illustration, I add the following simile describing the Trojans on the offensive:

οἱ δ᾽ ἴσαν ἀργαλέων ἀνέμων ἀτάλαντοι ἀέλλῃ,
ἥ ῥά θ᾽ ὑπὸ βροντῆς πατρὸς Διὸς εἶσι πέδονδε,
θεσπεσίῳ δ᾽ ὁμάδῳ ἁλὶ μίσγεται, ἐν δέ τε πολλὰ
κύματα παφλάζοντα πολυφλοίσβοιο θαλάσσης,
κυρτὰ φαληριόωντα, πρὸ μέν τ᾽ ἄλλ᾽, αὐτὰρ ἐπ᾽ ἄλλα.

And they came, like a gust of the racking winds,
which under the thunderstroke of Father Zeus drives downward
and with gigantic clamor hits the sea, and the many
boiling waves along the length of the roaring sea
bend and whiten to foam in ranks, one upon the other.

XIII 795–799

§19. Since the traditional imagery that marks Hektor's onslaught as the ultimate bane of the Achaeans is appropriate to either the fire or the wind of a thunderstorm, Hektor is presented as a hero who is either "like fire" or "like wind" in Homeric diction. But there is an obvious difference in the Iliadic treatment of these two images. Whereas the threat of fire to the Achaean ships is both figurative and real, the threat of wind is only figurative, conveyed by similes. For

§17n2. He is also φλογὶ εἴκελον 'like a flame' at XIII 688.
§17n3. §6.
§18n1. §14; also Ch.5§25.
§18n2. Ibid.

the *Iliad*, Hektor's fire is real, even though it is expressed with imagery that suits the celestial fire of thundering Zeus; the threat of the god's winds, however, is real only as a general condition that can be expected to affect the Achaeans as a seafaring society. Still, the point remains that the most direct threat to the Achaeans, on land as well as sea, is the destruction of their ships—expressed in images most appropriate to a thunderstorm of Zeus. On the land, Achilles had it in his power both to bring the ships to the brink of fiery destruction by way of his **mênis** and then to rescue them from the fire by way of his surrogate Patroklos. On the sea, we may then ask, does Achilles have a power over winds that matches this power that he has over fire when he is on the land?

§20. Since the *Iliad* treats the onslaught of the Trojans as wind *only by way of simile*, we should expect the same mode of expression for any Iliadic treatment of the theme for which we are searching: how Achilles has the power to rescue the Achaean ships from the winds. I submit that I have found this theme in the simile deployed at the very moment Achilles has just put on the new armor made by Hephaistos. As the hero takes hold of his magnificent shield, it gives off a **sélas** 'flash' described as follows:

> τοῦ δ' ἀπάνευθε σέλας γένετ' ἠΰτε μήνης.
> ὡς δ' ὅτ' ἄν ἐκ πόντοιο σέλας ναύτῃσι φανήῃ
> καιομένοιο πυρός, τό τε καίεται ὑψόθ' ὄρεσφι
> σταθμῷ ἐν οἰοπόλῳ· τοὺς δ' οὐκ ἐθέλοντας ἄελλαι
> πόντον ἐπ' ἰχθυόεντα φίλων ἀπάνευθε φέρουσιν·
> ὡς ἀπ' Ἀχιλλῆος σάκεος σέλας αἰθέρ' ἵκανε
> καλοῦ δαιδαλέου

From it [the shield] there was a **sélas** [flash] from far away, as from the moon,
or as when from out of the **póntos** [sea] a **sélas** [flash] appears to sailors,
a flash of blazing fire, and it blazes up above in the mountains,
at a solitary station, while they [the sailors] are being carried along against their will by winds
over the fishy **póntos**, far away from their **phíloi**.
So also the **sélas** from the beautiful and well-wrought shield of Achilles shot up into the aether.

XIX 374–380

Previously, we have seen the **sélas** 'flash' of fire as a signal of destruction for the Achaean ships (VIII 76, XV 600);[1] here, on the

§20n1. §§15, 16.

other hand, it is a signal of salvation from the winds. The winds threaten the isolation of the sailors from their **phíloi**, while the fire promises reintegration with them. Yet, ironically, the fire of reintegration is itself isolated and remote, much as the hero who is himself signaled by its flame.[2] The fire at the solitary station overlooking the **póntos** shoots up into the ethereal realms (XIX 379), and the transcendence of this earthly fire marking Achilles is matched by a multiple comparison with celestial fire: the light from the hero's shield is compared both to this earthly fire and to the light of the moon as well. Moreover, the light from his helmet is then likened to that of a star (XIX 381–383). And finally, the sight of Achilles fully armed is compared to the sun itself (XIX 397–398). At this moment, of course, Achilles is about to enter his war in the *Iliad*. Not only in simile but in reality as well, Achilles is emerging as savior of the Achaeans.

§21. For the moment, however, let us restrict our vision to the inner world of the simile, where the fire that is compared to Achilles is pictured as rescuing sailors from the winds that blow over the **póntos** 'sea'. I draw attention in particular to the word **póntos**, which serves as the setting for the dangerous winds in our simile. We have in fact already seen **póntos** as the setting for the winds that are compared to Hektor's onslaught, which in turn is endangering specifically the Achaean ships (IX 4–7, XI 297–298).[1] The theme of danger is actually inherent in **póntos**. From a comparative study of words that are cognate with **póntos** in other Indo-European languages, most notably Indic *pánthāḥ* 'path' and Latin *pōns* 'bridge', Émile Benveniste found that the basic meaning of the word is 'crossing, transition', with an underlying implication that the actual act of *crossing* is at the same time marked by *danger*.[2] The semantic aspect of crossing is inherent in the place name **Hellés-pontos** 'Crossing of **Héllē**',[3] a compound recalling the myth that told how **Phríxos** and **Héllē** crossed the Hellespont by riding on the Ram with the Golden Fleece. The aspect of danger is likewise inherent in the myth itself. During their crossing, Helle drowns, while Phrixos is

§20n2. Just as the fire is ἀπάνευθε 'far away' at XIX 374 and the sailors are φίλων ἀπάνευθε 'far away from their **phíloi**' at XIX 378, so also Achilles and Patroklos are described as φίλων ἀπάνευθεν ἑταίρων 'far away from their **philoi** companions [**hetaîroi**]' at XXIII 77; discussion at §8.

§21n1. §§14, 18.

§21n2. Benveniste 1966 [= 1954] 296–298.

§21n3. Benveniste, p. 298.

saved (cf. Apollodorus 1.9.1).[4] The contrasting themes of danger and salvation here are reflected formally in the words of Pindar: Phrixos was "rescued out of the **póntos**" by way of the Golden Fleece (ἐκ πόντου σαώθη: *P*.4.161). Even the epithet system of **póntos** in epic diction reflects the word's dangerous aspect. Let us consider the qualifier **ikhthuóeis** 'fishy, fish-swarming' as applied to **póntos** at XIX 378 (also IX 4!)[5] and to **Hellέspontos** at IX 360. The application of this epithet is motivated not so much by a fanciful striving for picturesque visualizations of the sea, but rather by the sinister implication of dangers lurking beneath a traveling ship. As we survey the collocations of **póntos** with the plain noun for "fish," **ikhthús**, the ghastly themes of danger become overt:

ἦ τόν γ᾽ ἐν πόντῳ φάγον ἰχθύες ...

... or the fish devoured him in the **póntos**

xiv 135

ἠέ που ἐν πόντῳ φάγον ἰχθύες ...

... or perhaps the fish devoured him in the **póntos**[6]

xxiv 291

§22. We come back to the image of a fire on high that flashes salvation for sailors bedeviled by violent winds as they make their way over the **póntos** (XIX 374–380). It remains to ask whether there are any other instances, besides the simile of XIX 374–380, where the figure of Achilles is directly associated with such an image. The answer is yes, with an added detail that is not without interest. *The flash of salvation for sailors may emanate from the tomb of Achilles himself, situated on a headland overlooking the Hellespont:*

ἀμφ᾽ αὐτοῖσι δ᾽ ἔπειτα μέγαν καὶ ἀμύμονα τύμβον
χεύαμεν Ἀργείων ἱερὸς στρατὸς αἰχμητάων
ἀκτῇ ἔπι προὐχούσῃ, ἐπὶ πλατεῖ Ἑλλησπόντῳ,
ὥς κεν τηλεφανὴς ἐκ ποντόφιν ἀνδράσιν εἴη
τοῖς οἳ νῦν γεγάασι καὶ οἳ μετόπισθεν ἔσονται

Over their bodies [of Achilles and Patroklos] we the sacred army of Argive
  spearmen piled up a huge and perfect tomb,
on a jutting headland, by the wide **Hellέspontos**,

§21n4. On the name **Phríxos**, see Radermacher 1943.312. I would also adduce VII 63–64, describing the **phríx** 'shudder' brought down on the **póntos** by Zephyros the West Wind as it begins to blow violently, "and the **póntos** becomes black from it [the **phríx**]."
§21n5. On the context of IX 4, see again §§14, 18.
§21n6. Cf. Householder/Nagy 1972.768.

so that it may be <u>bright from afar</u> for men coming from the **póntos**
both those who are now and those who will be in the future.

xxiv 80–84

The preoccupation with future generations who will sail the Hellespont is also apparent in the words of Achilles himself, as he lays
down instructions for the building of his tomb:

τύμβον δ᾽ οὐ μάλα πολλὸν ἐγὼ πονέεσθαι ἄνωγα,
ἀλλ᾽ ἐπιεικέα τοῖον· ἔπειτα δὲ καὶ τὸν Ἀχαιοὶ
εὐρύν θ᾽ ὑψηλόν τε τιθήμεναι, οἵ κεν ἐμεῖο
δεύτεροι ἐν νήεσσι πολυκλήϊσι λίπησθε

And I bid you to build a tomb,[1] not a very big one,
only a beautiful one. Later [when Achilles dies and is enshrined with
    Patroklos], you Achaeans
will make it wide and tall—you who will be left behind me in your many-
benched ships.

XXIII 245–248

The Achaeans of the future who survive Achilles are "Achaeans in
ships." The tomb of Achilles maintains its impact on future generations even in the warped vision of Hektor, who fancies himself as the
man who will kill the one who is "best of the Achaeans":[2]

τὸν δὲ νέκυν ἐπὶ νῆας ἐϋσσέλμους ἀποδώσω,
ὄφρα ἑ ταρχύσωσι κάρη κομόωντες Ἀχαιοί,
σῆμά τε οἱ χεύωσιν ἐπὶ πλατεῖ Ἑλλησπόντῳ.
καί ποτέ τις εἴπῃσι καὶ ὀψιγόνων ἀνθρώπων,
νηῒ πολυκληῒδι πλέων ἐπὶ οἴνοπα <u>πόντον</u>·
'ἀνδρὸς μὲν τόδε σῆμα πάλαι κατατεθνηῶτος,
ὅν ποτ᾽ ἀριστεύοντα κατέκτανε φαίδιμος Ἕκτωρ.'
ὥς ποτέ τις ἐρέει· τὸ δ᾽ ἐμὸν κλέος οὔ ποτ᾽ ὀλεῖται.

And I will return his corpse to where the well-benched ships are,
so that the long-haired Achaeans may give him a proper funeral
and pile up a tomb for him by the wide **Helléspontos**.
And some day someone from a future generation will say
as he is sailing on a many-benched ship over the wine-dark **póntos**:
"This is the tomb of a man who died a long time ago.
He was performing his **aristeíā** when illustrious Hektor killed him."
That is what someone will say, and my **kléos** shall never perish.

VII 84–91

§22n1. The **túmbos** 'tomb', also called **sêma** 'marker' at XXIII 257, is to be located
ἐπ᾽ ἀκτῆς 'on a headland': XXIII 125. Note the parallel with xxiv 82: ἀκτῇ ἔπι
προὐχούσῃ 'on a jutting headland'.
§22n2. Ch.2§3.

Having long ago considered the irony of Hektor's words,[3] we are concerned now only with the vision of Achilles' tomb. The insistent references, here and in the other passages, to a future time beyond the narrative—a time when men will still contemplate the hero's tomb—reveal Achilles as not so much a hero of epic but rather a hero of cult. The future of the narrative is the here-and-now of the Homeric audience, and to them the tomb of Achilles is a matter of religion, reflecting this era's marked preoccupation with hero cults.[4] We recall *Iliad* XII 2–33, that other isolated instance where the perspective of the narrative switches from the heroic past to the here-and-now of the Homeric audience.[5] There too, the Achaean warriors who fell at Troy are suddenly perceived not as heroes of epic, **hḗrōes**, but as heroes of cult, **hēmítheoi** (XII 23).[6]

§23. With his tomb overlooking the Hellespont, Achilles manifests the religious aspects of his essence as hero even within the epic framework of the *Iliad* and *Odyssey*. His cosmic affinity with fire and with the winds that blow violently over the **póntos** is appropriate to his being the Hero of the Hellespont, whose tomb flashes a light from afar to sailors who pass through it (xxiv 83)[1]—and we may compare again the light that is their very salvation from the violent winds of the **póntos** (XIX 375–378).[2] Achilles is needed because the danger is there—not only in the semantics of **póntos** but also in the reality of the **Hellḗspontos**. The sailing conditions that prevail at the Hellespont have always been most difficult, and I merely cite the following report from our own time:[3]

It is probably not too much to say that on three days out of four during the sailing season what a landsman would describe as a tearing north-easter is blowing during a good part of the day right down the channel.

But this is not all. A ship has not only this headwind on its sails to fight with; it has the opposing current under its keel, at least whenever it is in mid channel. The surplus of the enormous masses of fresh water poured into the

§22n3. Ibid.

§22n4. Ch.6§§28–30. The narrative of the *Iliad* leaves it open, however, whether the Tomb of Achilles is man-made or a natural formation: Ch.9§16n1.

§22n5. Ch.9§§15–16.

§22n6. Ibid. Whereas Thetis calls Achilles ἔξοχον ἡρώων 'best of **hḗrōes**' in the diction of Panhellenic Epos (XVIII 56), he is called 'best of **hemítheoi**' in the diction of the local lyric of Lesbos (Alcaeus 42.13LP: αἰμιθέων [...], where the word for 'best' is lost in a lacuna).

§23n1. §22.

§23n2. §20.

§23n3. Leaf 1912.358–359.

Black Sea over the evaporation from its surface is enough to cause a stream; and when this is reinforced by the wind, it becomes a very serious matter for a sailing ship.

§24. The Hellespont, then, is a focal point for the heroic essence of Achilles: Homeric poetry presents his tomb as overlooking its dangerous waters, the setting for violent storms expressed by the same imagery that expresses the hero's cosmic affinity with fire and wind. Moreover, epic diction presents this fire and wind as primarily endangering the ships of the Achaeans, which are conventionally described as being beached on the Hellespont (XV 233, XVII 432, XVIII 150, XXIII 2). In other words, the Hellespont is also a focal point for the heroic essence of all the Achaeans who came to fight at Troy. Moreover, Troy itself and the Hellespont are presented in epic diction as parallel markers of the place where the Trojan War took place (XII 30, XXIV 346). It is by sailing down the Ἑλλήσποντον ... ἰχθυόεντα 'fish-swarming Hellespont' that Achilles could have left Troy and come back home safely to Phthia (IX 359–363).[1] In fact, from the standpoint of a Homeric audience in the eighth or seventh centuries B.C., the site of the Trojan War is significant not so much because of Troy itself but because of the Hellespont, passage to the Black Sea.[2] And the prime affinity of Achilles with the Hellespont and the realms to which it leads will survive for centuries, well beyond the classical period. From inscriptions found in the Black Sea area, we know that Achilles still presides over the **póntos** even as late as the second/third centuries A.D.: he is in fact still worshiped as the **Pontárkhēs** 'Ruler of the **Póntos**'.[3]

§25. The cosmic affinity of Achilles with the **póntos** in general and with the **Hellḗspontos** in particular is of course inherited from his mother **Thḗtis**. We are reminded of the initial Iliadic scene where the solitary figure of a weeping Achilles is pictured gazing out toward the **póntos** (I 350),[1] actually praying to the divine Thetis (I 351–356). The

§24n1. The theme that Achilles would reach home "on the third day" (IX 363) may be connected with the controversial expression τριταῖον ἄνεμον in Pindar *N*.7.17, which has been variously explained as "third-day's wind" or "third wind." For an introduction to the controversy: Lloyd-Jones 1973.130.

§24n2. On the penetration of the Black Sea in the eighth/seventh centuries B.C.: Drews 1976.

§24n3. For documentation, see Fontenrose 1960.256n37, who also points out that Farnell's 1921 book on Greek hero cults fails to take this epithet into account, even at p. 409n69. For more on Achilles as **Pontárkhēs**: Pfister 1909.536–537 and Diehl 1953.

§25n1. Of course the **póntos** here is the **Hellḗspontos**.

goddess then makes an epiphany that is characteristic of a true Nereid, emerging from the sea like a cloud of mist (I 357–359). Of course, Thetis was actually born in the **póntos** (Hesiod *Th.* 241/244), the granddaughter of **Póntos** incarnate (*Th.* 233). In Pindar's *Isthmian* 8, a poem that tells how she would have given birth to a son greater than his father if Zeus or Poseidon had mated with her (lines 31–35), she is actually called ποντίαν θεόν 'goddess of the **póntos**' (line 34). To avoid the danger that the essence of Thetis poses to the cosmic order, the gods get her married off to the mortal Peleus (lines 35–40).[2] And the son that issues from this marriage of Peleus and Thetis grows up to fulfill a function that is latent in the very word **póntos**:

γεφύρωσέ τ' Ἀτρεῖδαι-
σι νόστον

... and he [Achilles] <u>bridged</u> a safe homecoming for the sons of Atreus.

Pindar *I.8.51*

In other words: by dint of his exploits at Troy (*I.8.51–55*), Achilles made it possible for the leaders of the Achaeans to traverse the sea and go back home. The semantics of "bridge" here correspond to the semantics of Latin *pōns*, cognate of Greek **póntos**.[3]

§26. The cosmic powers of Thetis over the **póntos** are evident from local traditions connected with her actual cult. Perhaps the most striking example is in Herodotus 7.188–192, the account of a shipwreck suffered by the Persian fleet off the coast of Magnesia. The precise location of the shipwreck was an **akté** 'headland' called **Sēpiás** (after **sēpíā** 'sepia, cuttlefish')—given that name, says Herodotus, because local tradition had it that Thetis was abducted by Peleus at this spot (192). Moreover, the storm that wrecked the ships of the Persians took the form of a violent wind that the local Hellenic population called the **Hellēspontíēs** (188). We are reminded that the tomb of Achilles was on an **akté** 'headland' at the **Helléspontos** (xxiv 82)![n] After the storm has raged for three days, the Magi of the Persians sing incantations to the wind and *sacrifice to Thetis*, having been informed by the natives of the lore connecting the name **Sēpiás** with her and the other Nereids (Herodotus 7.191).

§25n2. Cf. *Iliad* XVIII 429–434.
§25n3. On Latin *pōns* and Greek **póntos**, see again Benveniste 1966 [= 1954] 296–298.
§26n. Cf. also §22n1.

§27. The place **Sēpiás** is connected with Thetis not only because Peleus abducted her from there. In a story that was probably incorporated in the epic *Cypria*, the polymorphous Thetis actually assumes the shape of a **sēpíā** 'sepia, cuttlefish' at the very moment when Peleus mates with her (scholia *ad* Lycophron 2.175, 178).[1] This identification is most significant in view of the sepia's function as animal of **mêtis** in Greek lore (e.g., σηπίη δολόμητις in Oppian *Halieutica* 2.120).[2] As Marcel Detienne and Jean-Pierre Vernant have argued most convincingly, Thetis herself is a figure of **mêtis**.[3] To go into this topic now would be to stray far beyond my line of inquiry, which has been confined mainly to the **bíē** of Achilles and its cosmic affinities. Suffice it to say that the **mêtis** of Thetis also relates to the **póntos**. It is a key to the fundamentals of navigation, as embodied in the orienting principles of **Póros** 'charted path [over the sea]' and **Tékmōr** 'goal', which are opposed to the disorienting principle of **Skótos** 'darkness'. These personifications of opposing themes stem from the local cosmogonic traditions of Laconia as preserved in the poetry of Alcman, *fr.* 2P. From this same fragment, we also know that the opposing figures of **Póros/Tékmōr** vs. **Skótos** are presented as fundamental cosmic principles that are transcended by one all-encompassing figure, who is none other than the goddess Thetis![4] I will simply refer to Detienne and Vernant for a discussion of the rich mythology surrounding these related themes of navigation, orientation, and cosmogony,[5] confining myself here to one point: in local traditions such as the Laconian, Thetis figures as a primordial goddess with the most fundamental cosmic powers, and her primacy is reflected by the utmost reverence that is her due in cult (consider the Laconian practices mentioned by Pausanias 3.14.4).[6]

§27n1. Detienne/Vernant 1974.159(n129).

§27n2. For a wealth of further documentation: Detienne/Vernant, pp. 160–164.

§27n3. Detienne/Vernant, pp. 127–164; their argument is well worth reading in its entirety.

§27n4. For a detailed treatment: West 1963, 1967; Detienne/Vernant, pp. 134–138.

§27n5. Detienne/Vernant, pp. 127–164. Cf. also Penwill 1974; much as I admire this article, I disagree with its interpretation of **Póros** and with its separating of Thetis from *thétis 'creation'.

§27n6. Divine figures with local traits that resist Panhellenic systematization tend to be non-Olympian, no matter how important they may be in the local traditions; cf. Rohde I 39–40n1. So also with Thetis in the Panhellenic Epos of Homeric poetry: she is distinctly non-Olympian and is treated as *socially* inferior to the Olympians (cf. XX 105–107, XXIV 90–91). But her cosmic powers are clearly recognized (I 396–406, XVIII 429–434). Cf. Nagy 1974.277–278; also West 1963, 1967 (esp. p. 3).

§28. My point is that Thetis must by nature also transcend the concept of Achilles, a son who is after all a mere "demigod," **hēmítheos**. Her power over the **póntos** entails the principle of **mêtis**, whereas his power has affinities only with the **bíē** of wind and fire.[n] And yet, the heroic irony is that Achilles as son of Thetis could actually be more powerful than Zeus himself, *if only he had been fathered by the god instead of a mortal* (Pindar *I*.8.31–35). We have indeed seen that the **mênis** of Achilles creates effects that are parallel to those created by the **bíē** of Zeus in a thunderstorm, and that these effects are actually validated by the Will of Zeus. In this sense, Zeus himself is validating the divine potential of the mortal Achilles. Moreover, the theme of the hero's divine potential is actually conjured up by the manner in which the Will of Zeus goes into effect in the *Iliad*. The wind- and firelike devastation from the **mênis** of Achilles is willed by Zeus because Thetis asks for it (I 407–412, 503–510). Moreover, the validation of the hero's essence in the *Iliad* is in return for what Thetis had done for Zeus, when she rescued him from imprisonment by his fellow Olympians (I 396–406). Here we see a vital link with the theme of the hero's divine potential. Thetis rescued Zeus by summoning **Briáreōs** the Hundred-Hander, who then frightened the Olympian rebels away from ever endangering Zeus again (I 401–406). In this context, the Hundred-Hander is specifically described as βίην οὗ πατρὸς ἀμείνων 'better in **bíē** than his father' (I 404). The theme is strikingly parallel to what would have been if Zeus or Poseidon had mated with Thetis.

§29. The figure of **Briáreōs**, also called **Aigaíōn** (I 404), is a sort of nightmarish variant of Achilles himself. In the Hesiodic tradition, **Briáreōs/Obriáreōs**[1] is likewise one of the Hundred-Handers (Hesiod *Th.* 147–153). These figures are equal to the Titans themselves in **bíē** (*Th.* 677–678), and they use their **bíē** to defeat the Titans (*Th.* 649–650), thus ensuring the **krátos** of Zeus (*Th.* 662).[2] Their action in defeating the Titans (*Th.* 674–686, 713–719) is in fact a correlate of the victorious action taken by Zeus himself with the **bíē** of a cosmic thunderstorm (*Th.* 687–712).[3] In other traditions, **Aigaíōn** is

§28n. Similarly with the fire god Hephaistos: his fire entails not only **bíē** as at XXI 367 but also **mêtis** as at XXI 355, where the god is called **polúmētis** 'whose **mêtis** is manifold'.

§29n1. On the name: West 1966.210.

§29n2. On the theme that **Krátos** and **Bíē** maintain the cosmic régime of Zeus, see *Th.* 385–401 (cf. §11n2).

§29n3. To put it another way, in defeating the Titans the **bíē** of the Hundred-

likewise a figure who fights against the Titans (*Titanomachy fr.* 2 p. 110 Allen); moreover, he lives in the sea and was actually fathered by **Póntos** (ibid.). On the other hand, still another tradition has **Briáreōs** fathered by Poseidon himself (scholia *ad Iliad* I 404).[4] These variant figures **Briáreōs** and **Aigaíōn**,[5] synthesized as one figure in *Iliad* I 403–404, conjure up the Iliadic theme of Achilles. He too is an exponent of **bíē**; he too has strong affinities with the **póntos**. Here is a hero who would have been better than Poseidon—better than Zeus himself—if either had fathered him. Just as the divine essence of Zeus was validated by the **bíē** of **Briáreōs/Aigaíōn**, so also the god will now validate in return the heroic essence of Achilles in the *Iliad*. The **bíē** of the Hundred-Hander is an antecedent for the **bíē** that will mark Achilles. The hero cannot be the best of the gods, but he will be the best of heroes. And in the poetry that all Hellenes must recognize, he will be the best of the Achaeans.

Handers and the **bíē** of Zeus are two variants of one theme that are combined in the narrative of the *Theogony*. For more on the **bíē** of Zeus: §6 (esp. n2).

§29n4. There seems to be a concession to this variant in *Th.* 817–819; cf. West, p. 210.

§29n5. Solinus 11.6 says that Briareos had a cult at Karystos and Aigaion, at Khalkis.

Appendix | On the Forms *krataió-* and *Akhaió-*

§1. Our point of departure is the verse-final form **krataiís/Krátaiin** in *Odyssey* xi 597/xii 124.[1] The conventional explanation, that we have here an **id**-stem feminine built from the adjective **krataió-**, is plagued with difficulties on the formal and functional levels.[2] I cite in particular the verse-final **ā**-stem feminine **krataié**.[3] Where an **id**-stem feminine adjective is formed from an **o**-stem adjective, we do not expect the parallel inheritance of an **ā**-stem feminine. The clearest example of this restriction is Homeric feminine **thoûris** (never *thoúrē*) compared to masculine/neuter **thoûr-os/-on**.[4] Even in the two most obvious archaic instances where the **id**-stem becomes a substantive, the corresponding **o**-stem adjective retains a two-gender system. Thus: **hēmerís** 'cultivated vine' compared to **hémer-os/-on** 'tame' and **nukterís** 'bat' compared to **núkter-os/-on** 'nocturnal'.[5] In fact, the author of an exhaustive monograph on the family of **id**-stems in Greek allows the inclusion of **krataiís** into this family only on condition that it be considered anomalous: in the face of the attested verse-final feminine **krataié**, he treats **krataiís** as a likely case of "Augenblicksbildung."[6] What with such difficulties in explaining **krataiís** as an **id**-stem, I offer an alternative morphological explanation, however tentative, that is in accord with the contextual interpretation of *Odyssey* xi 597/xii 124. I propose that in both

§1n1. See Ch.5§36.
§1n2. See Chantraine II 579 and Risch 1974.144.
§1n3. See Ch.5§30.
§1n4. For a survey of **id**-stem feminines built from **o**-stem adjectives: Meier 1975.46–47.
§1n5. See Kastner 1967.100, who infers that the **i**-stems have here precluded the building of **ā**-stems. In compounds, of course, the preclusion of feminine **ā**-stems by **i**-stems is a general rule: e.g., **haplo-ís** and **hapló-os/-on** (see Meier, pp. 47–50).
§1n6. Meier, p. 47.

attestations, **krataiis** is a *bahuvrīhi* adjective originally shaped *krataiu̯is 'whose force has **krátos**'.[7]

§2. The immediate problem with this explanation is the short i in the reconstructed compound element *u̯i-.[1] The radical form *u̯ī- 'force' survives in Homeric diction as a simplex noun with long ī: nominative **ís** (XI 668, etc.), accusative **în**' (three attestations, all prevocalic: hence probably **în**),[2] instrumental **î-phi** (I 38, etc.). There is also a cognate noun in Latin, again with long ī: nominative *uīs*, ablative *uī*, and plural nominative/accusative *uīrēs*. The question, then, is whether *u̯i- can be the variant of *u̯ī- in the posited formation of a *bahuvrīhi* compound *kratai-u̯is.[3] There seems to be comparative evidence from Indic, where nouns ending with radical or even suffixal *ī* (nominative singular -*īs*) have variants with *ĭ* (nominative singular -*ĭs*) in the second element of *bahuvrīhi* compounds.[4] As for Greek, nouns other than **ís** that end with radical ī are practically nonexistent.[5] On the other hand, nouns ending with suffixal ī (nominative singular -**īs**) are well attested, although the ī is regularly extended by -**d**- or -**n**- when followed by a vowel in the ending. Hence the genitive of **knēm-ís** is **knēm-îdos**, not *knēm-íos; likewise, the genitive of **akt-ís** is **akt-înos**, not *akt-íos. In this category too, however, there are definite traces of ĭ coexisting with ī. Consider **knǎmĭdes** (Alcaeus *fr.* 357.5LP), **stamĭnessi** (*Odyssey* v 252), **klǎĭdes** (Pindar *P.*9.39; compare **klâîdas** at *P.*8.4), etc.[6]

§3. I pursue the hypothesis further by positing besides *kratai-u̯i- an extended feminine *bahuvrīhi* formation with suffix *-i̯ǎ-/-i̯ǎ́-, of the

§1n7. See again Ch.5§36.

§2n1. For the moment, it is necessary to posit a short i simply in order to account for the accentuation of **Krátaiin** at xii 124; on which see Wackernagel 1953 [= 1914] 1167–1168 and Meier 1975.47n110.

§2n2. Chantraine II 469.

§2n3. See also the arguments of Bader 1976 for the coexistence of radical *u̯ĭ- and *u̯ī- (from *u̯i-ə₂-), which she posits to explain *u̯ĭ-ro- (as in Latin *uir*, Tocharian A *wir*, Irish *fer*, Old English *wer*, etc.) compared to *u̯ī-ro- (as in Indic *vīra*-, Lithuanian *výras*, etc.). Note that the Italic languages seem to attest both *u̯ĭ-ro- (Latin *uir*) and *u̯ī-ro- (Umbrian *ueiro/uiro*; Volscian *couehriu* from *ko-u̯īriōd); see Bader, pp. 207–208.

§2n4. See Wackernagel 1905.98–99 and 1930.187; compare also the radical element *bhū*- which may be either -*bhū*- or -*bhŭ*- as the second element of *bahuvrīhi* compounds.

§2n5. In Schwyzer's list (I 570–571), we find only two other sure examples: **kís** and **lís**, neither of which has a definite Indo-European pedigree.

§2n6. See Schwyzer I 465. Consider also nominative singular **órnīs** (IX 323, XII 218) and **órnĭs** (XXIV 219). But here the original stem may have been -ĭ-: cf. **órneon** from *órnei̯on.

type **kūdi-áneira** (from *kūdi-áner-jǎ).[1] Such a formation may be the actual ancestor of the attested Homeric feminine **krataié**, under the following two conditions:

1. the suffix *-́jǎ-/-jǎ- was leveled to *-jā́-
2. an original combination *-u̯i-je_{ə2}- survived as *-u̯jā́-.

In the case of the second condition, we may note that there are solid parallels for the loss of *ə without trace in the second member of compound formations. Consider Greek **neo-gn-ó-** (from *-gnə-ó-), Indic *á-bhv-a-* (from *-bhu̯ə-o-), etc.[2] As for the first condition, there is a clear Homeric example of *-jā́- leveled from *-́jǎ-/-jā́-: the feminine **hetaírē** 'companion' results from the leveling of *hétairǎ/ hetaírēs/etc. (from *hétarjǎ/hetarjâs/etc.).[3] Accordingly, I offer the reconstruction *krataiu̯jā́ for Homeric **krataié**.

§4. The example of Homeric **hetaírē** is instructive in other respects as well. Like **krataié** (9x, *Iliad* only), it occurs only in verse-final position (**hetaírē** IX 2, **hetaírēn** xvii 271).[1] Whereas the feminine **hetaírē** is rare, the corresponding masculine **hetaîro-** 'companion' is common, with more than 250 Homeric occurrences. Moreover, about one-sixth of these are in verse-medial rather than verse-final position. Similarly, masculine **krataió-** occurs in verse-medial (XI 119) as well as in verse-final position (XIII 345, xv 242, xviii 382).[2] The masculine/feminine distribution of **hetaîros/hetaírē** in Homeric diction is significant for the present argument because the masculine **hetaîros** is actually built from the feminine **hetaírē** (which in turn was built from another masculine form, **hétaros**).[3] In fact, the leveling of feminine *hétarjǎ/hetarjâs/etc. to **hetaírē/hetaírēs**/etc. can be attributed directly to the pressure of the new masculine type **hetaîros** upon the old feminine type that had given it shape: **hetaîr-os** requires a new feminine adjunct with stem in -ā́-, so that **hetaír-ē** displaces *hétairǎ. Thus we may even argue that verse-final **hetaírē** and verse-final **krataié** both conceal an earlier *hétairǎ and *krátaiǎ respectively.[4]

§3n1. For the cognate type of compound feminine in Indic: Wackernagel/Debrunner 1954.388–390.

§3n2. See Kuryłowicz 1968.213. Cf. also Indic feminine *-bhv-ī-* besides *-bhū-* in compounds (Wackernagel 1930.197 and Wackernagel/Debrunner 1954.387–388).

§3n3. Risch 1974.167; also Chantraine II 380–381.

§4n1. Also verse-final **hetaírē** at *H.Herm.* 31, 478.

§4n2. Also in verse-medial position at *H.Herm.* 265, 377.

§4n3. Risch 1974.167; Chantraine II 380–381.

§4n4. There is also an interesting comparison to be made on the level of semantics: whereas **krataié** functions exclusively as the epithet of **Moîra** 'fate' in Homeric diction, **hetaírē** at IX 2 is applied to **Phûza**, a supernatural personification of **phûza** 'routing of

§5. As a parallel for the accent of **krataió-**, we may cite the unique Homeric instance of masculine **Trōioús** 'of Trōs' (XXIII 291: metrically shaped $--$; epithet of **híppous** 'horses'), apparently built from the feminine visible in **Trōiaí** 'Trojan' (see especially XVI 393: metrically shaped $--$; epithet of **híppoi** 'horses').[1] We may contrast the oxytone accentuation of this secondary masculine **Trōioús** with the barytone of primary masculine **Trốioi** 'of Trōs' (V 222, VIII 106, XXIII 378: metrically shaped $-\smile\smile$; epithet of **híppoi** 'horses'). The accentuation of disyllabic feminine **Trōiaí** 'Trojan' and its declension shows clearly that this word was originally built with a stem in *-ʲ̆ă-/ -ʲắ-,[2] as I have also argued in the case of **krataié**.

§6. My provisional reconstruction of **krataiá** from *krataiu̯i̯ắ- leads to a parallel explanation of **Akhaiá-**: after loss of laryngeals, I posit *Akhaiu̯i̯ắ (from *u̯i̯ə-i̯eə₂-). Like **hetaîro-**, **krataió-**, and **Trōió-**, the masculine **Akhaió-** would be a secondary formation built from an older feminine. The distribution of **Akhaió-** in Homeric diction is also similar to that of **hetaîro-**: the vast majority of the masculine forms occur in verse-final position, but a distinct minority are verse-medial (again, roughly one-sixth). The two forms even share a distinctive epithet: besides verse-final **eüknémīdes Akhaioí** 'Achaeans with fair greaves' (36x in *Iliad* and *Odyssey*), we find verse-final **eüknémīdes hetaîroi** 'companions with fair greaves' (5x in *Odyssey*). Likewise, the distribution of Homeric **Akhaiá-** is similar to that of **hetaírā-**: it is extremely rare and occurs only in verse-final position: **eüplokámīdes Akhaiaí** 'Achaean women with fair curls' at ii 119, xix 542. Compare **Trōiaí eüplókamoi** 'Trojan women with fair curls' at VI 380, 385.[n]

§7. If indeed *Akhaiu̯i̯ắ- is basic to a secondary masculine *Akhai-u̯i̯ó-, the latter's function as an ethnic noun could in turn motivate such feminine derivatives as *Akhaiu̯íd- 'Achaean' and *Akhaiu̯íā.[1] Compare Homeric **Dardaníd-** (XVIII 122, etc.) and **Dardaníē** (XX

the enemy'. **Phûza** is the **hetaírē** of **Phóbos**, personification of **phóbos** 'turning and running out of fear'. The immediate context is that the Trojans are routing the Achaeans (IX 1–2), who are afflicted by **pénthos** (IX 3).

§5n1. Wackernagel 1953 [= 1914] 1176.

§5n2. Ibid.

§6n. The form **eüplokámīdes** (+ **Akhaiaí**) need not be an ad hoc feminine created on the model of **eüknémīdes** (+ **Akhaioí**), *pace* Risch 1974.144 and Meier 1975.65. Even if it were so, however, it does not follow that the entire combination of **eüplokámīdes** + **Akhaiaí** was created on the model of **eüknémīdes** + **Akhaioí**. The two combinations function as a set containing traditional variants, and the possibility remains that the older noun may have attracted the newer epithet.

§7n1. Presumably *-u̯i̯id- and *-u̯i̯ā- yield *-u̯id- and *-u̯íā-.

216), motivated by the ethnic noun **Dárdano-** (II 701, etc.).[2] The reconstruction *Akhaiu̯íd- would account for the Homeric feminine **Akhaiḯd-** (I 254, etc.); as for *Akhaiu̯íā-, we may find it in the Linear B texts as *a-ka-wi-ja-de*, if indeed this spelling may be interpreted as *Akhaiu̯íān-de 'to Achaea'.[3] We also find it as **Akhaiḯē** in Herodotus 5.61 (epithet of Demeter!) and as **Akhaiḯēs** in Semonides 23.1W.[4]

§8. I have perhaps taken up too much time in pursuing what must remain merely a formal possibility: that **krataió-** and **Akhaió-** are compounds built with *u̯í-. The main justification for raising this possibility remains the thematic evidence of **krátos**, **ákhos**, **ís**, and other forms related to them. I admit, however, that the purely formal evidence could still take us in many other possible directions.[n] For the time being, I will simply close with a few comments on some formal difficulties that remain.

- From the evidence of Linear B texts, we see that **palaió-** 'not new' is probably a thematization of **pálai** 'near in past time' (see Chadwick 1976). Perhaps **krataió-** is likewise from *kratai plus -o-? But **kratai-** is not attested as an adverb like **pálai**. Or perhaps **krataió-** is *krata plus -i̯ó- (cf. adverb **kárta**)? But how to explain the accent of -i̯ó-?

- A reconstruction like *Akhaiu̯i̯oí may perhaps not account properly for the Latin borrowing *Achīuī*; of course, the latter form may be simply the reflex of **Akhaioí**, with the *u* serving as hiatus breaker. Compare Latin *Argīuī* from **Argeîoi** (the Greek has no u̯ before -oi); this Latin borrowing is attested early (e.g., Plautus), and I see no reason to insist on an analogical insertion of *u* by way of *Achīuī*.

- Another problem is that the reconstruction *Akhaiu̯i̯ó- would fail to account for *Akhaiu̯ó-; this form, however, is not attested to my knowledge in Greek, unless we read the Cypriote spelling *ti-mo-wa-na-ko-to/ sa-ka-i-wo-se* (Masson 1961 no. 405.1) as *Timo-u̯anaktos Akhaiu̯os. This reading is vitiated, however, by the necessary assumption that word division has been neglected between the patronymic (genitive) and the hypothetical ethnic

§7n2. For this type of derivation: Meier 1975.26–29.

§7n3. See Ch.5§35. For an attempt at establishing a regional distinction in the prehistoric usage of **Akhaiḯd-** and **Akhaiḯā-**, see Aitchison 1964.

§7n4. West reads **Akhā́ḯēs**, which represents an apparent phonological development from **Akhaiḯēs**: Schmidt 1968.8n24.

§8n. Alan Nussbaum and Jochem Schindler have kindly offered me their advice on the available evidence. They are of course not to be held accountable for the views I have expressed.

(nominative). In fact, word divisions are faithfully observed in attested Cypriote spelling (word-final -*s* spelled -*se*). Also, there is an actual word divider between *ti-mo-wa-na-ko-to* and *sa-ka-i-wo-se*. Discussion in Masson 1961.69. Besides, etymologically genuine ɥo can be spelled *o* in Cypriote (Thumb/Scherer 1959.160), and we may therefore expect the reverse as well (*ɥo* for o).

• If indeed **Akhaió**- was never *Akhaiɥó-, then an argument could be made for its morphological parallelism with **krataió**- even without positing compound formations.

Bibliography

Adkins, A.W.H. 1960. *Merit and Responsibility: A Study in Greek Values.* Oxford.

———. 1969. "Threatening, Abusing, and Feeling Angry in the Homeric Poems." *Journal of Hellenic Studies* 89:7–21.

Aitchison, J. M. 1964. "The Achaean Homeland: ΑΧΑΙϜΙΑ or ΑΧΑΙϜΙΣ?" *Glotta* 42:19–28.

Alexiou, M. 1974. *The Ritual Lament in Greek Tradition.* Cambridge.

Allen, T. W., ed. 1912. *Homeri Opera* V (Hymns, Cycle, fragments, etc.). Oxford.

Arbois de Jubainville, H. d'. 1899. *Cours de littérature celtique.* VI. *La civilisation des Celtes et celle de l'épopée homérique.* Paris.

Austin, C., ed. 1973. *Comicorum Graecorum Fragmenta in Papyris Reperta.* Berlin.

Austin, N. 1975. *Archery at the Dark of the Moon: Poetic Problems in Homer's Odyssey.* Berkeley and Los Angeles.

Bader, F. 1965. *Les composés grecs du type de* ΔΗΜΙΟΥΡΓΟΣ. Paris.

———. 1976. "Un nom indo-européen de l'homme chez Homère." *Revue de Philologie* 50:206–212.

Bassett, S. E. 1933. "Achilles' Treatment of Hector's Body." *Transactions of the American Philological Association* 64:41–65.

———. 1938. *The Poetry of Homer.* Berkeley.

Bechtel, F. 1917. *Die historischen Personennamen des Griechischen bis zur Kaiserzeit.* Halle.

Benveniste, E. 1945. "La doctrine médicale des Indo-Européens." *Revue de l'Histoire des Religions* 130:5–12.

———. 1948. *Noms d'agent et noms d'action en indo-européen.* Paris.

———. 1954. "Problèmes sémantiques de la reconstruction." *Word* 10: 251–264. Reprinted (1966) 289–307.

———. 1966. *Problèmes de linguistique générale.* Paris.

———. 1969. *Le vocabulaire des institutions indo-européennes.* I. *Economie, parenté, société.* II. *Pouvoir, droit, religion.* Paris. = *Indo-European Language and Society.* Translated by E. Palmer. London and Coral Gables, Florida, 1973.

Bergren, A. L. 1975. *The Etymology and Usage of* ΠΕΙΡΑP *in Early Greek Poetry: A Study of the Interrelationships of Metrics, Linguistics, and Poetics. American Classical Studies* 2 (American Philological Association). New York.

Berthiaume, G. 1976. "Viandes grecques: Le statut social et religieux du cuisinier-sacrificateur (ΜΑΓΕΙΡΟΣ) en Grèce ancienne." Thesis, Université de Paris VIII (Vincennes).

Bethe, E. 1927. *Homer: Dichtung und Sage.* III. *Die Sage vom Troischen Kriege.* Leipzig.

Boedeker, D. D. 1974. *Aphrodite's Entry into Greek Epic.* Leiden.

Bollack, J. 1963. "L'or des rois: Le mythe de la Deuxième Olympique." *Revue de Philologie* 37:234–254.

Borecký, B. 1965. *Survivals of Some Tribal Ideas in Classical Greek.* Prague.

Borthwick, E. K. 1967. "Trojan Leap and Pyrrhic Dance in Euripides' *Andromache* 1129–41." *Journal of Hellenic Studies* 87:18–23.

Brelich, A. 1958. *Gli eroi greci.* Rome.

———. 1969. *Paides e Parthenoi.* I. *Incunabula Graeca* 36. Rome.

Broccia, G. 1967. *La forma poetica dell'*Iliade *e la genesi dell'epos omerico.* Messina.

Brunius-Nilsson, E. 1955. ΔΑΙΜΟΝΙΕ: *An Inquiry into a Mode of Apostrophe in Old Greek Literature.* Uppsala.

Büchner,W. 1937. "Probleme der homerischen Nekyia." *Hermes* 72:104–122.

Bundy, E. L. 1962. "Studia Pindarica I/II. The Eleventh Olympian Ode/The First Isthmian Ode." *University of California Publications in Classical Philology* 18:1–34/35–92.

Burkert, W. 1961. "Elysion." *Glotta* 39:208–213.

———. 1966. "Greek Tragedy and Sacrificial Ritual." *Greek Roman and Byzantine Studies* 7:87–121.

———. 1966b. *Gnomon* 38:436–440. Review of Delcourt 1965.

———. 1972. *Homo Necans: Interpretationen altgriechischer Opferriten und Mythen.* Berlin

———. 1972b. "Die Leistung eines Kreophylos: Kreophyleer, Homeriden und die archaische Herakleepik." *Museum Helveticum* 29:74–85.

———. 1975. "Apellai und Apollon." *Rheinisches Museum* 118:1–21.

———. 1977. *Griechische Religion der archaischen und klassischen Epoche.* Stuttgart.

Caerwyn Williams, J. E. 1972. *The Court Poet in Mediaeval Ireland. Proceedings of the British Academy* 57. Oxford.

Caland, W. 1893. "Beiträge zur kenntnis des Avesta: Adjectiva auf -*ra* in der composition." *Zeitschrift für vergleichende Sprachforschung* 32:592.

Calhoun, G. M. 1937. "Homer's Gods: Prolegomena." *Transactions of the American Philological Association* 68:11–25.

———. 1939. "Homer's Gods: Myth and Märchen." *American Journal of Philology* 60:1–28.

———. 1941. "The Divine Entourage in Homer." *American Journal of Philology* 61:257–277.

———. 1962. "Polity and Society: The Homeric Picture." In *A Companion to Homer*, edited by A.J.B. Wace and F. Stubbings, pp. 431–452. London.

Carey, C. 1976. "Pindar's Eighth Nemean." *Proceedings of the Cambridge Philological Society* 22:26–41.

Caskey, L. D., and Beazley, J. D. 1931–1963. *Attic Vase Paintings in the Museum of Fine Arts, Boston* I–III. London.

Chadwick, J. 1976. "The Etymology of Greek ΠΑΛΑΙ." *Glotta* 54:62–67.

———, and Baumbach, L. 1963. "The Mycenaean Greek Vocabulary." *Glotta* 41:157–306.

Chantraine, P. 1963. "A propos de Thersite." *Antiquité Classique* 32:18–27.

———. 1968, 1970, 1975, 1977. *Dictionnaire étymologique de la langue grecque* I, II, III, IV–1. Paris.

Chantraine, P., and Masson, O. 1954. "Sur quelques termes du vocabulaire religieux des Grecs: La valeur du mot ΑΓΟΣ et de ses dérivés." In *Festschrift A. Debrunner*, pp. 85–107. Berne.

Chirassi Colombo, I. 1977. "Heros Achilleus—Theos Apollon." In Gentili and Paioni, pp. 231–269.

Clader, L. L. 1976. *Helen: The Evolution from Divine to Heroic in Greek Epic Tradition.* Leiden.

Clark, M. E., and Coulsen, W.D.E. 1978. "Memnon and Sarpedon." *Museum Helveticum* 35:65–73.

Clay, J. S. 1976. "The Beginning of the *Odyssey*." *American Journal of Philology* 97:313–326.

Coldstream, J. N. 1976. "Hero-Cults in the Age of Homer." *Journal of Hellenic Studies* 96:8–17.

Consbruch, M., ed. 1906. *Hephaistionis Enchiridion.* Leipzig.

Considine, P. 1966. "Some Homeric Terms for Anger." *Acta Classica* 9:15–25.

Cook, J. M. 1973. *The Troad: An Archaeological and Topographical Study.* Oxford.

Cross, T. P., and Slover, C. H. 1936. *Ancient Irish Tales.* New York. Reissued, with revised bibliography by C. W. Dunn. Dublin, 1969.

Damon, P. 1974. "The Cults of the Epic Heroes and the Evidence of Epic Poetry." In *Center for Hermeneutical Studies in Hellenistic and Modern Culture, Colloquy* 9, edited by W. Wuellner. Berkeley.

Davidson, O. M. 1980. "Indo-European Dimensions of Herakles in *Iliad* 19.95–133." *Arethusa* 13.197–202.

Delcourt, M. 1965. *Pyrrhos et Pyrrha: Recherches sur les valeurs du feu dans les légendes helléniques. Bibliothèque de la Faculté de Philosophie et Lettres de l'Université de Liège* 174. Paris.

———. 1966. "Tydée et Mélanippe." *Studi e Materiali di Storia delle Religioni* 37:139–188.

Deneken, F. 1881. *De Theoxeniis*. Berlin.

Detienne, M. 1963. *La notion de* ΔΑΙΜΩΝ *dans le pythagorisme ancien: De la pensée religieuse à la pensée philosophique*. Bibliothèque de la Faculté de Philosophie et Lettres de l'Université de Liège 165. Paris.

―――. 1968. "La phalange: Problèmes et controverses." In Vernant 1968, pp. 119–142.

―――. 1970. "L'olivier: Un mythe politico-religieux." *Revue de l'Histoire des Religions* 178:5–23. For a reworking, see *id.* 1973b.

―――. 1971. "Orphée au miel." *Quaderni Urbinati di Cultura Classica* 12:7–23. For a reworking, see *id.* 1973c.

―――. 1972. *Les jardins d'Adonis: La mythologie des aromates en Grèce*. Paris. = *The Gardens of Adonis*. Translated by J. Lloyd. Hassocks and Sussex, 1977.

―――. 1973. *Les maîtres de vérité dans la Grèce archaïque*. 2nd ed. Paris.

―――. 1973b. "L'olivier: Un mythe politico-religieux." In *Problèmes de la Terre en Grèce ancienne*, edited by M. I. Finley, pp. 293–306. Paris.

―――. 1973c. "Le mythe: Orphée au miel." In *Faire de l'histoire*, edited by J. le Goff and P. Nora, pp. 56–75. Paris.

―――. 1975. "Les Grecs ne sont pas comme les autres." *Critique* 332:3–24.

―――. 1977. *Dionysos mis à mort*. Paris.

―――. 1977b. "La viande et le sacrifice en Grèce ancienne." *La Recherche* 8:152–160.

Detienne, M., and Vernant, J. P. 1974. *Les ruses de l'intelligence: La* ΜΗΤΙΣ *des Grecs*. Paris.

DGE = E. Schwyzer, ed. 1923. *Dialectorum Graecarum exempla epigraphica potiora*. Leipzig.

Diano, C. 1968. "La poetica dei Feaci." In *Saggezza e poetiche degli antichi*, pp. 185–214. Venice.

Diehl, E. 1953. "Pontarches." *Pauly-Wissowa Realencyclopädie* 22:1–18.

Diggle, J. 1970. *Euripides:* Phaethon. Edited, with prolegomena and commentary. Cambridge.

Dihle, A. 1970. *Homer-Probleme*. Opladen.

DK = H. Diels and W. Kranz, eds. 1954. *Die Fragmente der Vorsokratiker*. 6th ed. Berlin.

Donini, G. 1967. "Osservazioni sui rapporti tra alcuni passi dell'*Iliade* riguardanti Enea." *Rivista di Filologia e di Istruzione Classica* 95:389–396.

Dover, K. J. 1964. "The Poetry of Archilochos." In *Archiloque* (*Fondation Hardt Entretiens* 10), pp. 183–222. Geneva.

Drachmann, A. B., ed. 1903, 1910. *Pindarus: Scholia Vetera*. Leipzig.

Drews, R. 1976. "The Earliest Greek Settlements on the Black Sea." *Journal of Hellenic Studies* 96:18–31.

Duban, J. 1975. "Epic Prooemium: A Study in the Design and Purpose of Hesiod's *Theogony*." Ph.D. dissertation, The Johns Hopkins University.

Dumézil, G. 1943. *Servius et la Fortune: Essai sur la fonction sociale de louange et de blâme et sur les éléments indo-européens du* cens *romain.* Paris.

———. 1968. *Mythe et épopée.* I. *L'idéologie des trois fonctions dans les épopées des peuples indo-européens.* Paris.

———. 1969. *Idées romaines.* Paris.

———. 1969b. *Heur et malheur du guerrier.* Paris.

———. 1971. *Mythe et épopée.* II. *Types épiques indo-européens: Un héros, un sorcier, un roi.* Paris.

Dunbar, H., ed. *A Complete Concordance to the* Odyssey *of Homer.* Oxford. Revised ed. by B. Marzullo. Hildesheim, 1962.

Durand, J. L. 1977. "Le corps du délit." *Communications* 26:46–61.

Durante, M. 1971, 1976. *Sulla preistoria della tradizione poetica greca.* I. *Continuità della tradizione poetica dall'età micenea ai primi documenti.* II. *Risultanze della comparazione indoeuropea. Incunabula Graeca* 50/64. Rome.

Dyer, R. R. 1969. "The Evidence for Apolline Purification Rituals." *Journal of Hellenic Studies* 89:38–56.

Ebeling, H., ed. 1880–1885. *Lexicon Homericum.* Leipzig.

Edmunds, S. 1976. "Homeric ΝΗΠΙΟΣ." Ph.D. dissertation, Harvard University.

Edwards, G. P. 1971. *The Language of Hesiod in Its Traditional Context.* Oxford.

Edwards, M. W. 1966. "Some Features of Homeric Craftsmanship." *Transactions of the American Philological Association* 97:115–179.

Ehrlich, H. 1912. *Untersuchungen über die Natur der griechischen Betonung.* Berlin.

Eliade, M. 1963. *Patterns in Comparative Religion.* Translated by R. Sheed from *Traité d'histoire des religions.* Cleveland and New York.

Else, G. F. 1965. *The Origin and Early Form of Greek Tragedy.* Cambridge, Mass.

Erbse, H., ed. 1969–1977. *Scholia Graeca in Homeri* Iliadem. Berlin.

Farnell, L. R. 1896–1909. *The Cults of the Greek States* I–V. Oxford.

———. 1921. *Greek Hero Cults and Ideas of Immortality.* Oxford.

Faust, M. 1969. "Metaphorische Schimpfwörter." *Indogermanische Forschungen* 74:54–125.

———. 1970. "Die künstlerische Verwendung von ΚΥΩΝ 'Hund' in den homerischen Epen." *Glotta* 48:8–31.

Fenik, B. 1964. Iliad *X and the* Rhesus: *The Myth.* Brussels.

———. 1968. *Typical Battle Scenes in the* Iliad: *Studies in the Narrative Techniques of Homeric Battle Descriptions. Hermes Einzelschriften* 21. Wiesbaden.

Festugière, J. 1959. "Deux notes sur le *de Iside* de Plutarque." In *Comptes Rendus de l'Académie des Inscriptions et Belles-Lettres*, pp. 316–319. Paris. Reprinted in his *Etudes de religion grecque et hellénistique*, pp. 170–177. Paris.

FGrH = Jacoby 1923–1958.

Finley, J. H. 1951. "The Date of *Paean* 6 and *Nemean* 7." *Harvard Studies in Classical Philology* 60:61–80.

———. 1955. *Pindar and Aeschylus.* Cambridge, Mass.

———. 1978. *Homer's* Odyssey. Cambridge, Mass.

Finnegan, R. 1977. *Oral Poetry: Its Nature, Significance, and Social Context.* Cambridge.

Fontenrose, J. 1960. "The Cult and Myth of Pyrros at Delphi." *University of California Publications in Classical Archaeology* 4:191–266.

Forderer, M. 1960. *Zum homerischen Margites.* Amsterdam.

Forssman, B. 1966. *Untersuchungen zur Sprache Pindars.* Wiesbaden.

Fraenkel, E. 1920. "Zur Form der AINOI." *Rheinisches Museum* 73:366–370. Reprinted in his *Kleine Schriften* I, pp. 235–239. Rome, 1964.

———. 1957. *Horace.* Oxford.

Fränkel, H. 1962. *Dichtung und Philosophie der frühen Griechentums.* 2nd ed. Munich.

Frame, D. 1971. "The Origins of Greek NOYΣ." Ph.D. dissertation, Harvard University.

———. 1978. *The Myth of Return in Early Greek Epic.* New Haven.

Frazer, J. G., ed. 1898. *Pausanias's Description of Greece* I–VI. London.

———, ed. 1921. *Apollodorus* I–II. London and Cambridge, Mass.

Friedrich, P., and Redfield, J. M. 1978. "Speech as a Personality Symbol: The Case of Achilles." *Language* 54:263–288.

Friis Johansen, K. 1967. *The* Iliad *in Early Greek Art.* Copenhagen.

Frisk, H. 1960–1970. *Griechisches etymologisches Wörterbuch.* Heidelberg.

Frontisi-Ducroux, F. 1975. *Dédale.* Paris.

———. 1976. "Homère et le temps retrouvé." *Critique* 348:538–548.

Führer, R. 1967. *Formproblem-Untersuchungen zu den Reden in der frühgriechischen Lyrik. Zetemata* 44. Munich.

Gelzer, T. 1969. "Zur Versreihe der *Heroes* aus der alten Komödie." *Zeitschrift für Papyrologie und Epigraphik* 4:123–133.

Gentili, B. 1965. "Aspetti del rapporto poeta, committente, uditorio nella lirica corale greca." *Studi Urbinati* 39:70–88.

———. 1969. "L'interpretazione dei lirici greci arcaici nella dimensione del nostro tempo. Sincronia e diacronia nello studio di una cultura orale." *Quaderni Urbinati di Cultura Classica* 8:7–21.

———. 1972. "Lirica greca arcaica e tardo arcaica." In *Introduzione allo studio della Cultura Classica,* pp. 57–105. Milan.

———, and Paioni, G., eds. 1977. *Il mito greco: Atti del Convegno Internazionale* (Urbino 7–12 May 1973). Rome.

Gernet, L. 1917. *Recherches sur le développement de la pensée juridique et morale en Grèce.* Paris.

———. 1928. "Frairies antiques." *Revue des Etudes Grecques* 41:313–359. Reprinted (1968):23–61.

———. 1936. "Dolon le loup." *Mélanges F. Cumont. Annuaire de l'Institut de Philologie et d'Histoire Orientales et Slaves* 4:189–208. Reprinted (1968): 54–171.

———. 1948/1949. "Droit et prédroit en Grèce ancienne." *L'Année Sociologique* [no vol.]:21–119. Reprinted (1968):175–260.

———. 1968. *Anthropologie de la Grèce antique.* Paris.

Gill, D. 1974. "Trapezomata: A Neglected Aspect of Greek Sacrifice." *Harvard Theological Review* 67:117–137.

Giovannini, A. 1969. *Etude historique sur les origines du Catalogue des Vaisseaux.* Berne.

Girard, P. 1902. "Comment a dû se former l'*Iliade*." *Revue des Etudes Grecques* 15:229–287.

Glotz, G. 1904. *La solidarité de la famille dans le droit criminel en Grèce.* Paris.

Goldschmidt, V. 1950. "Theologia." *Revue des Etudes Grecques* 63:20–42.

Griffin, J. 1977. "The Epic Cycle and the Uniqueness of Homer." *Journal of Hellenic Studies* 97:39–53.

———. 1978. "The Divine Audience and the Religion of the *Iliad*." *Classical Quarterly* 28:1–22.

Hack, R. K. 1929. "Homer and the Cult of Heroes." *Transactions of the American Philological Association* 60:57–74.

———. 1940. "Homer's Transformation of History." *Classical Journal* 35: 471–481.

Hadzisteliou Price, T. 1978. *Kourotrophos: Cults and Representations of the Greek Nursing Deities.* Leiden.

Harrison, E. L. 1971. "Odysseus and Demodocus: Homer, *Odyssey* viii 492 f." *Hermes* 99:378–379.

Heitsch, E. 1965. *Aphroditehymnus, Aeneas und Homer. Hypomnemata* 15. Göttingen.

Henrichs, A. 1975. "Philodems *De Pietate* als mythographische Quelle." *Cronache Ercolanesi* 5:5–38.

Heubeck, A. 1969. "Gedanken zu griech. ΛΑΟΣ." In *Studi V. Pisani* II, pp. 535–544. Brescia.

———. 1974. *Die homerische Frage.* Darmstadt.

Höfler, O. 1934. *Kultische Geheimbünde der Germanen.* Frankfurt.

Householder, F. W., and Nagy, G. 1972. "Greek." In *Current Trends in Linguistics* IX, edited by T. A. Sebeok, pp. 735–816. The Hague.

Howald, E. 1946. *Der Dichter der* Ilias. Zürich.

Jacoby, F. 1933. "Homerisches I." *Hermes* 68:1–50. Reprinted in his *Kleine Schriften* I, pp. 1–53. Berlin, 1961.

———, ed. 1923–1958. *Die Fragmente der griechischen Historiker.* Berlin and Leiden.

Jakobson, R. 1960. "Linguistics and Poetics." In *Style in Language*, edited by T. A. Sebeok, pp. 350–377. Cambridge, Mass.

————. 1971. *Selected Writings* II. *Word and Language*. The Hague and Paris.

Jeanmaire, H. 1939. *Couroi et Courètes: Essai sur l'éducation spartiate et sur les rites d'adolescence dans l'antiquité hellénique*. Lille.

Jeffery, L. H. 1976. *Archaic Greece: The City-States c. 700–500 B.C.* New York.

Kahn, L. 1978. *Hermès passe ou les ambiguïtés de la communication*. Paris.

Kaibel, G., ed. 1878. *Epigrammata Graeca*. Berlin.

Kakridis, J. T. 1949. *Homeric Researches*. Lund.

Kastner, W. 1967. *Die griechischen Adjektive zweier Endungen auf -ΟΣ.* Heidelberg.

Kegel, W.J.H.F. 1962. *Simonides*. Groningen.

Kelly, S. T. 1974. "Homeric Correption and the Metrical Distinctions between Speeches and Narrative." Ph.D. dissertation, Harvard University.

Kern, O., ed. 1922. *Orphicorum Fragmenta*. Berlin.

Kinkel, G., ed. 1877. *Epicorum Graecorum Fragmenta*. Leipzig.

Kirk, G. S. 1962. *The Songs of Homer*. Cambridge.

————. 1968. "War and the Warrior in the Homeric Poems." In Vernant 1968, pp. 93–117.

————. 1970. *Myth: Its Meaning and Functions in Ancient and Other Cultures*. Berkeley and Los Angeles. For an interesting review, see Detienne 1975.

Koch, H. J. 1976. "ΑΙΠΥΣ ΟΛΕΘΡΟΣ and the Etymology of ΟΛΛΥΜΙ." *Glotta* 54:216–222.

Kock, T., ed. 1880–1888. *Comicorum Atticorum Fragmenta*. Leipzig.

Köhnken, A. 1971. *Die Funktion des Mythos bei Pindar. Interpretationen zu sechs Pindargedichten*. Berlin.

————. 1975. "Die Rolle des Phoinix und die Duale im I der *Ilias*." *Glotta* 53:25–36.

————. 1978. "Noch einmal Phoinix und die Duale." *Glotta* 56:5–14.

Koenen, L. 1974. "Ein wiedergefundenes Archilochos-Gedicht?" *Poetica* 6:499–508.

Koller, H. 1954. *Die Mimesis in der Antike*. Berne.

————. 1956. "Das kitharodische Prooimion: Eine formgeschichtliche Untersuchung." *Philologus* 100:159–206.

————. 1972. "Epos." *Glotta* 50:16–24.

Kontoleon, N. M. 1964. "Archilochos und Paros." In *Archiloque* (*Fondation Hardt Entretiens* 10), pp. 39–73. Geneva.

————. 1965. "'Αρχαϊκὴ ζῳφόρος ἐκ Πάρου." In *Charisterion A. K. Orlandos* I, pp. 348–418. Athens.

Koonce, D. 1962. "Formal Lamentation for the Dead in Greek Tragedy." Ph.D. dissertation, University of Pennsylvania.

Kretschmer, P., ed. 1894. *Die griechischen Vaseninschriften*. Gütersloh.

————. 1921. "Ares." *Glotta* 11:195–198.

Kullmann, W. 1956. *Das Wirken der Götter in der* Ilias. *Untersuchungen zur Frage der Entstehung des homerischen "Götterapparats."* Berlin.

———. 1960. *Die Quellen der* Ilias. *Hermes Einzelschriften* 14. Wiesbaden.

Kuryłowicz, J. 1968. *Indogermanische Grammatik.* II. *Akzent-Ablaut.* Heidelberg.

Latacz, J. 1966. *Zum Wortfeld "Freude" in der Sprache Homers.* Heidelberg.

Latte, K. 1913. *De saltationibus Graecorum.* Giessen.

Lattimore, R. 1951. *The* Iliad *of Homer.* Translation, with introduction. Chicago.

———. 1965. *The* Odyssey *of Homer.* Translation, with introduction. New York.

Leaf, W. 1912. *Troy: A Study in Homeric Geography.* London.

———. 1923. *Strabo on the Troad: Book xiii, Cap. i.* Cambridge.

Lee, D.J.N. 1961. "Homeric KHP and Others." *Glotta* 39:191–207.

Lefkowitz, M. 1976. "Fictions in Literary Biography: The New Poem and the Archilochus Legend." *Arethusa* 9:181–189.

———. 1977. "Pindar's *Pythian* 8." *Classical Journal* 72:209–221.

Lehrs, K. 1882. *De Aristarchi Studiis Homericis.* 3rd ed. Leipzig.

Lejeune, M. 1960. "Prêtres et prêtresses dans les documents mycéniens." In *Hommages à Georges Dumézil* (*Collection Latomus* 45), pp. 129–139. Brussels.

———. 1965. "Le ΔΑΜΟΣ dans la société mycénienne." *Revue des Etudes Grecques* 78:1–22.

———. 1968. "La civilisation mycénienne et la guerre." In Vernant 1968, pp. 31–51.

Lenz, L. H. 1975. *Der homerische Aphroditehymnus und die Aristie des Aineias in der* Ilias. Bonn.

Lesky, A. 1961. *Göttliche und menschliche Motivation im homerischen Epos.* Heidelberg.

———. 1967. *Homeros. Sonderausgaben der Paulyschen Realencyclopädie der classischen Altertumswissenschaft.* Stuttgart.

Leutsch, E. L. von, and Schneidewin, F. G., eds. 1839–1851. *Corpus Paroemiographorum Graecorum.* Göttingen.

Lloyd-Jones, H. 1973. "Modern Interpretation of Pindar: The Second *Pythian* and Seventh *Nemean* Odes." *Journal of Hellenic Studies* 93:109–137.

Loraux, N. 1977. "La 'belle mort' spartiate." *Ktema* 2:105–120.

Lord, A. B. 1960. *The Singer of Tales.* Cambridge, Mass.

———. 1968. "Homer as Oral Poet." *Harvard Studies in Classical Philology* 72:1–46.

———. 1970. "Tradition and the Oral Poet: Homer, Huso, and Avdo Medjedović." *Problemi Attuali di Scienze e di Cultura* 139. *Atti del Convegno Internazionale sul Tema: La poesia epica e la sua formazione. Accademia dei Lincei,* pp. 13–28. Rome. (Pp. 29–30 contain a reply to D. M. Lang on the question of historicity.)

———. 1974. "Perspectives on Recent Work on Oral Literature." *Forum for Modern Language Studies* 10:187–210.

Lord, M. L. 1967. "Withdrawal and Return: An Epic Story Pattern in the Homeric *Hymn to Demeter* and in the Homeric Poems." *Classical Journal* 62:241–248.

Lowenstam, S. 1975. "The Typological Death of Patroklos." Ph.D. dissertation, Harvard University.

LP = E. Lobel and D. Page, eds. 1955. *Poetarum Lesbiorum Fragmenta*. Oxford.

Lucas, D. W. 1968. *Aristotle*: Poetics. Text, with prolegomena and commentary. Oxford.

Luce, J. V. 1978. "The *Polis* in Homer and Hesiod." *Proceedings of the Royal Irish Academy* (Section C) 78:1–15.

Lung, G. E. 1912. *Memnon: Archäologische Studien zur Aithiopis*. Bonn.

Maas, P. 1934. *Gnomon* 10:436–439. Review of M. Norsa and G. Vitelli, eds., ΔΙΗΓΗΣΕΙΣ *di poemi di Callimaco in un papiro di Tebtynis* (Florence, 1934).

Maehler, H. 1963. *Die Auffassung des Dichterberufs im frühen Griechentum bis zur Zeit Pindars*. Hypomnemata 3. Göttingen.

Marg, W. 1956. "Das erste Lied des Demodokos." In *Navicula Chiloniensis: Festschrift für F. Jacoby*, pp. 16–29. Leiden.

Masson, O., ed. 1961. *Les inscriptions chypriotes syllabiques*. Paris.

Mathews, G. 1976. "The Expression ΥΠΕΡ ΜΟΙΡΑΝ in Homer." A.B. dissertation, Harvard University.

Meier, M. 1975. -ΙΔ-: *Zur Geschichte eines griechischen Nominalsuffixes. Ergänzungshefte zur Zeitschrift für vergleichende Sprachforschung* 23. Göttingen.

———. 1976. "ΕΧΩ und seine Bedeutung im Frühgriechischen." *Museum Helveticum* 33:180–181.

Meillet, A. 1923. *Les origines indo-européennes des mètres grecs*. Paris.

———. 1925. *La méthode comparative en linguistique historique*. Paris.

Meister, K. 1921. *Die homerische Kunstsprache*. Leipzig.

Merkelbach, R. 1948. "Zum Υ der *Ilias*." *Philologus* 97:303–311.

———. 1967. "Die Heroen als Geber des Guten und Bösen." *Zeitschrift für Papyrologie und Epigraphik* 1:97–99.

———. 1968. "Das Prooemium des hesiodeischen Katalogs." *Zeitschrift für Papyrologie und Epigraphik* 3:126–133.

———. 1971. "ΚΟΡΟΣ." *Zeitschrift für Papyrologie und Epigraphik* 8:80.

Meuli, K. 1946. "Griechische Opferbräuche." In *Phyllobolia für P. Von der Mühll*, pp. 185–288. Basel. Reprinted (1975) II 906–1021.

———. 1954. "Herkunft und Wesen der Fabel." *Schweizerisches Archiv für Volkskunde* 50:65–88. Reprinted (1975) II 731–756.

———. 1968. *Der griechische Agon* (publication of his 1926 *Habilitationsschrift*, edited by R. Merkelbach). Cologne.

———. 1975. *Gesammelte Schriften* I–II. Edited by T. Gelzer. Basel and Stuttgart.

Miller, A. 1977. "The Homeric Hymn to Apollo." Ph.D. dissertation, Berkeley.

Minton, W. W., ed. 1976. *Concordance to the Hesiodic Corpus.* Leiden.

Mondi, R. J. 1978. "The Function and Social Position of the ΚΗΡΥΞ in Early Greece." Ph.D. dissertation, Harvard University.

Monro, D. B., ed. 1901. *Odyssey*, Books 13–24. Oxford.

Motto, A. L., and Clark, J. R. 1969. "ΙΣΗ ΔΑΙΣ: The Honor of Achilles." *Arethusa* 2:109–125.

Müller, M. 1966. *Athene als göttliche Helferin in der* Odyssee: *Untersuchungen zur Form der epischen Aristie.* Heidelberg.

Muellner, L. 1976. *The Meaning of Homeric* ΕΥΧΟΜΑΙ *through its Formulas.* Innsbruck.

MW = R. Merkelbach and M. L. West, eds. 1967. *Fragmenta Hesiodea.* Oxford.

N = A. Nauck, ed. 1889. *Tragicorum Graecorum Fragmenta.* 2nd ed. Leipzig.

Nagler, M. 1967. "Towards a Generative View of the Oral Formula." *Transactions of the American Philological Association.* 98:269–311.

———. 1974. *Spontaneity and Tradition: A Study in the Oral Art of Homer.* Berkeley and Los Angeles.

Nagy, G. 1973. "Phaethon, Sappho's Phaon, and the White Rock of Leukas." *Harvard Studies in Classical Philology* 77:137–177.

———. 1974. *Comparative Studies in Greek and Indic Meter.* Cambridge, Mass.

———. 1976. "Iambos: Typologies of Invective and Praise." *Arethusa* 9:191–205. Rewritten here as Ch.13.

———. 1976b. "Formula and Meter." In *Oral Literature and the Formula*, edited by B. A. Stolz and R. S. Shannon, pp. 239–260. Ann Arbor.

———. 1976c. "The Name of Achilles: Etymology and Epic." In *Studies in Greek, Italic, and Indo-European Linguistics Offered to L. R. Palmer*, edited by A. M. Davies and W. Meid, pp. 209–237. Innsbruck. Rewritten here as Ch.5 and Ch.6.

Nagy, J. 1978. "The Boyhood Deeds of Finn in the Fenian Tradition." Ph.D. dissertation, Harvard University.

Nilsson, M. P. 1906. *Griechische Feste.* Leipzig.

———. 1911. "Der Ursprung der Tragödie." *Neue Jahrbücher für das klassische Altertum* 27:609–696. Reprinted (1951):61–145.

———. 1922. "Der Flammentod des Herakles auf dem Oite." *Archiv für Religionswissenschaft* 21:310–316. Reprinted (1951):348–354.

———. 1951, 1952, 1960. *Opuscula Selecta* I, II, III. Lund.

———. 1967, 1961. *Geschichte der griechischen Religion.* I 3rd ed., II 2nd ed. Munich. Abbreviated as "Nilsson I–II."

Nisetich, F. J. 1975. "*Olympian* 1.8–11: An Epinician Metaphor." *Harvard Studies in Classical Philology* 79:55–68.

Nock, A. D. 1930. "ΣΥΝΝΑΟΣ ΘΕΟΣ." *Harvard Studies in Classical Philology* 41:1–62. Reprinted (1972):202–251.

————. 1944. "The Cult of Heroes." *Harvard Theological Review* 37:141–174. Reprinted (1972) 575–602.

————. 1972. *Essays on Religion and the Ancient World* I–II. Edited by Z. Stewart. Oxford.

Norden, E. 1922. *Die germanische Urgeschichte in Tacitus* Germania. Leipzig.

Notopoulos, J. A. 1964. "Studies in Early Greek Oral Poetry." *Harvard Studies in Classical Philology* 68:1–77.

Nussbaum, A. J. 1976. "Caland's 'Law' and the Caland System." Ph.D. dissertation, Harvard University.

Orgogozo, J. J. 1949. "L'Hermès des Achéens." *Revue de l'Histoire des Religions* 136:10–30, 139–179.

P = D. Page, ed. 1962. *Poetae Melici Graeci.* Oxford.

Packard, D., and Meyers, T. 1974. *A Bibliography of Homeric Scholarship.* Malibu.

Page, D. 1955. *The Homeric* Odyssey. Oxford.

————. 1959. *History and the Homeric* Iliad. Berkeley and Los Angeles.

————, ed. 1974. *Supplementum Lyricis Graecis.* Oxford.

Pagliaro, A. 1956. *Nuovi saggi di critica semantica.* Messina and Florence.

————. 1961. *Altri saggi di critica semantica.* 2nd ed. Messina and Florence.

————. 1970. "Origini liriche e formazione agonale dell'epica greca." *Problemi Attuali di Scienze e di Cultura* 139. *Atti del Convegno Internazionale sul Tema: La poesia epica e la sua formazione.* Accademia dei Lincei, pp. 31–58. Rome.

Palmer, L. R. 1955. *Achaeans and Indo-Europeans.* Oxford.

————. 1963. *The Interpretation of Mycenaean Greek Texts.* Oxford.

Parke, H. W., and Wormell, D.E.W. 1956. *The Delphic Oracle* I–II. Oxford.

Parry, A., ed. 1971. *The Making of Homeric Verse: The Collected Papers of Milman Parry.* Oxford.

Parry, M. 1930. "Studies in the Epic Technique of Oral Verse-Making. I: Homer and Homeric Style." *Harvard Studies in Classical Philology* 41: 73–147. Reprinted (1971) 266–324.

Pavese, C. 1967. "La lingua della poesia corale come lingua d'una tradizione poetica settentrionale." *Glotta* 45:164–185.

————. 1972. *Tradizioni e generi poetici della Grecia arcaica.* Rome.

Pearson, A. C., ed. 1917. *The Fragments of Sophocles* I–III. Cambridge.

Penwill, J. 1974. "Alkman's Cosmology." *Apeiron* 8:13–39.

Perpillou, J. L. 1973. *Les substantifs grecs en* -ΕΥΣ. Paris.

Perry, B. E. 1936. "Studies in the Text History of the Life and Fables of Aesop." *American Philological Association Monographs* 7. Haverford.

————, ed. 1952. *Aesopica* I. Urbana.

————. 1962. "Demetrius of Phalerum and the Aesopic Fables." *Transactions of the American Philological Association* 93:287–346.

Pestalozzi, H. 1945. *Die* Achilleis *als Quelle der* Ilias. Erlenbach and Zürich.

Petegorsky, D. 1975. "Demeter and the Black Robe of Grief." Unpublished.

Pfeiffer, R., ed. 1949, 1953. *Callimachus* I–II. Oxford.

Pfister, F. 1909. *Der Reliquienkult im Altertum* I–II. Giessen.

———. 1948. "Studien zum homerischen Epos." *Würzburger Jahrbücher für die Altertumswissenschaft* 3:137–162.

Pickard-Cambridge, A. W. 1927. *Dithyramb, Tragedy, and Comedy*. Oxford. For the sake of "history of ideas," I deliberately avoid citing the 1962 version as revised by T.B.L. Webster.

Pötscher, W. 1961. "Hera und Heros." *Rheinisches Museum* 104:302–355.

———. 1971. "Der Name des Herakles." *Emerita* 39:169–184.

Pohlenz, M. 1948. "Nomos." *Philologus* 97:135–142. Reprinted in his *Kleine Schriften* II, edited by H. Dörrie, pp. 333–340. Hildesheim, 1965.

Prendergast, G. L., ed. 1875. *A Complete Concordance to the* Iliad *of Homer*. London. Revised ed. by B. Marzullo. Hildesheim, 1962.

Prudhommeau, G. 1965. *La danse grecque antique*. Paris.

Przyluski, J. 1940. "Les confréries de loups-garous dans les sociétés indo-européennes." *Revue de l'Histoire des Religions* 121:128–145.

Pucci, P. 1977. *Hesiod and the Language of Poetry*. Baltimore.

Puelma, M. 1972. "Sänger und König: Zum Verständnis von Hesiods Tierfabel." *Museum Helveticum* 29:86–109.

Puhvel, J. 1976. *Oral literature and the Formula*, edited by B. A. Stolz and R. S. Shannon, pp. 261–263. Ann Arbor. (Response to Nagy 1976b.)

Puttkammer, F. 1912. "Quo modo Graeci victimarum carnes distribuerint." Dissertation, Königsberg.

Quinn, G. M. 1971. "The Sacrificial Calendar of the Marathonian Tetrapolis." Ph.D. dissertation, Harvard University.

Radermacher, L. 1943. *Mythos und Sage bei den Griechen*. Brünn, Munich, Vienna.

Radloff, W. 1885. *Proben der Volksliteratur der nördlichen türkischen Stämme*. V. *Der Dialekt der Kara-Kirgisen*. St. Petersburg.

Radt, S. L. 1958. *Pindars zweiter und sechster Paian: Text, Scholien und Kommentar*. Amsterdam.

———, ed. 1977. *Tragicorum Graecorum Fragmenta*. IV. *Sophocles*. Göttingen.

Redfield, J. M. 1973. "The Making of the *Odyssey*." In *Parnassus Revisited*, edited by A. C. Yu, pp. 141–154. Chicago.

———. 1975. *Nature and Culture in the* Iliad*: The Tragedy of Hector*. Chicago.

Rees, A., and Rees, B. 1961. *Celtic Heritage: Ancient Tradition in Ireland and Wales*. London.

Reiner, E. 1938. *Die rituelle Totenklage der Griechen*. *Tübinger Beiträge zur Altertumswissenschaft* 30. Tübingen.

Reinhardt, K. 1951. "Tradition und Geist im homerischen Epos." *Studium Generale* 4:334–339.

————. 1956. "Zum homerischen Aphroditehymnus." In *Festschrift B. Snell*, edited by H. Erbse, pp. 1–14. Hamburg.

————. 1960. *Tradition und Geist: Gesammelte Essays zur Dichtung*. Edited by C. Becker. Göttingen.

————. 1961. *Die Ilias und ihr Dichter*. Edited by U. Hölscher. Göttingen.

Richardson, N. J. 1974. *The Homeric Hymn to Demeter*. Edited, with prolegomena and commentary. Oxford.

Risch, E. 1966. "Les différences dialectales dans le mycénien." In *Proceedings of the Cambridge Colloquium on Mycenaean Studies*, edited by L. R. Palmer and J. Chadwick, pp. 150–157. Cambridge.

————. 1974. *Wortbildung der homerischen Sprache*. 2nd ed. Berlin.

Robertson, D. S. 1940. "The Food of Achilles." *Classical Review* 54:177–180.

Rohde, E. 1898. *Psyche: Seelencult und Unsterblichkeitsglaube der Griechen* I/II. 2nd ed. Freiburg i.B. Translated by W. B. Hillis. New York, 1925. Abbreviated as "Rohde I–II."

Rohlfs, G. 1964. *Lexicon Graecanicum Italiae Inferioris: Etymologisches Wörterbuch der unteritalienischen Gräzität*. 2nd ed. Tübingen.

Roloff, D. 1970. *Gottähnlichkeit, Vergöttlichung und Erhöhung zu seligem Leben: Untersuchungen zur Herkunft der platonischen Angleichung an Gott*. Berlin.

Rose, V., ed. 1886. *Aristoteles: Fragmenta*. Leipzig.

Rosner, J. A. 1976. "The Speech of Phoenix: *Iliad* 9.434–605." *Phoenix* 30:314–327.

Rossi, L. E. 1978. "I poemi omerici come testimonianza di poesia orale." In *Storia e civiltà dei Greci* I, edited by R. Bianchi Bandinelli, pp. 73–147. Milan.

Rudhardt, J. 1970. "Les mythes grecs relatifs à l'instauration du sacrifice." *Museum Helveticum* 27:1–15.

Rüter, K. 1969. *Odysseeinterpretationen: Untersuchungen zum ersten Buch und zur Phaiakis*. Edited by K. Matthiessen. *Hypomnemata* 19. Göttingen.

Ruijgh, C. J. 1967. *Etudes sur le grammaire et le vocabulaire du grec mycénien*. Amsterdam.

Russo, J. 1974. "The Inner Man in Archilochus and the *Odyssey*." *Greek Roman and Byzantine Studies* 15:139–152.

Rusten, J. S. 1977. "*Wasps* 1360–1369: Philokleon's ΤΩΘΑΣΜΟΣ." *Harvard Studies in Classical Philology* 81:157–161.

Sacks, R. 1975. "Old Norse *moðsefa tjǫld* and Greek ΔΕΛΤΟΙΣ ΦΡΕΝΩΝ." In *Indo-European Studies* II, edited by C. Watkins, pp. 454–486. Cambridge, Mass.

————. 1978. "ΥΠΟ ΚΕΥΘΕΣΙ ΓΑΙΗΣ: Two Studies of the Art of the Phrase in Homer." Ph.D. dissertation, Harvard University.

Sale, W. 1965. "Callisto and the Virginity of Artemis." *Rheinisches Museum* 108:11–35.

Scheibner, G. 1939. *Der Aufbau des 20. und 21. Buches der* Ilias. Borna and Leipzig.

Schmid, B. 1947. *Studien zu griechischen Ktisissagen.* Freiburg.

Schmidt, V. 1968. *Sprachliche Untersuchungen zu Herondas.* Berlin.

Schmitt, R. 1967. *Dichtung und Dichtersprache in indogermanischer Zeit.* Wiesbaden.

———, ed. 1968. *Indogermanische Dichtersprache.* Darmstadt.

Schnaufer, A. 1970. *Frühgriechischer Totenglaube: Untersuchungen zum Totenglauben der mykenischen und homerischen Zeit. Spudasmata* 20. Hildesheim.

Schoeck, G. 1961. Ilias *und* Aithiopis: *Kyklische Motive in homerischer Brechung.* Zürich.

Schroeter, R. 1960. *Die Aristie als Grundform epischer Dichtung und der Freiermord der Odyssee.* Marburg.

Schwyzer, E. 1939. *Griechische Grammatik* I. Munich.

———, and Debrunner, A. 1950. *Griechische Grammatik* II. Munich.

Scodel, R. 1977. "Apollo's Perfidy: *Iliad* Ω 59–63." *Harvard Studies in Classical Philology* 81:55–57.

Segal, C. 1968. "The Embassy and the Duals of *Iliad* 9:182–98." *Greek Roman and Byzantine Studies* 9:101–114.

———. 1971. *The Theme of the Mutilation of the Corpse in the* Iliad. Leiden.

———. 1971b. "Nestor and the Honor of Achilles." *Studi Micenei ed Egeo-Anatolici* 13:90–105.

Seidensticker, B. 1978. "Archilochus and Odysseus." *Greek Roman and Byzantine Studies* 19:5–22. Presents evidence showing that the *persona* of Archilochus is a function of Archilochean poetry and that it is parallel to the *persona* of Odysseus in the *Odyssey.*

Severyns, A. 1938, 1953, 1963. *Recherches sur la Chréstomathie de Proclos* I–II, III, IV. Liège.

Shannon, R. S. 1975. *The Arms of Achilles and Homeric Compositional Technique.* Leiden.

SIG = *Sylloge Inscriptionum Graecarum* I–IV. Edited by W. Dittenberger. 3rd ed. Leipzig, 1915–1923.

Sinos, D. 1975. "The Entry of Achilles into Greek Epic." Ph.D. dissertation, The Johns Hopkins University.

Slater, W. J. 1971. "Pindar's House." *Greek Roman and Byzantine Studies* 12:141–152.

SM = Snell and Maehler, eds. of Pindar (1971/1975) and Bacchylides (1970).

Snell, B., and Maehler, H., eds. 1970. *Bacchylidis carmina cum fragmentis.* Leipzig.

———, eds. 1971, 1975. *Pindari carmina cum fragmentis.* Leipzig.

Snodgrass, A. M. 1971. *The Dark Age of Greece: An Archaeological Survey of the Eleventh to the Eighth Centuries.* Edinburgh.

Sokolowski, F., ed. 1955. *Lois sacrées de l'Asie Mineure.* Paris.

———, ed. 1969. *Lois sacrées des cités grecques.* Paris.

Solmsen, F., Merkelbach, R., and West, M. L., eds. 1970. *Hesiodi Theogonia, Opera et Dies, Scutum, Fragmenta Selecta.* Oxford.

Spengel, L., ed. 1853, 1856. *Rhetores Graeci* I–II. Leipzig.

Steiner, G. 1964. "Die *Aḫḫijawa*-Frage heute." *Saeculum* 15:365–392.

Stengel, P. 1910. *Opfergebräuche der Griechen.* Leipzig.

———. 1920. *Die griechischen Kultusaltertümer.* 3rd ed. Munich.

Stiewe, K. 1962, 1963. "Die Entstehungszeit der hesiodischen Frauen-kataloge." *Philologus* 106:291–299, 107:1–29.

Stoessl, F. 1976. "Das Liebesgedicht des Archilochos (P.Colon. 7511), seine literarische Form und sein Zeugnis über Leben und Sitten im Paros des 7. Jh. a.C." *Rheinisches Museum* 119:242–266.

Stokes, W. 1891. "The Second Battle of Moytura." *Revue Celtique* 12:52–130.

Strömberg, R. 1940. *Griechische Pflanzennamen.* Göteborg.

Suárez de la Torre, E. 1977. "Observaciones acerca del ΛΑΓΕΤΑΣ pin-dárico." *Cuadérnos de Filología Clásica* 13:269–280.

Svenbro, J. 1976. *La Parole et le Marbre: Aux origines de la poétique grecque.* Lund.

Taylor, M. W. 1975. "The Tyrant-Slayers: The Heroic Ideal in Fifth-Century B.C. Athenian Art and Politics." Ph.D. dissertation, Harvard University.

Thieme, P. 1952. *Studien zur indogermanischen Wortkunde und Religionsgeschichte. Berichte über die Verhandlungen der Sächsischen Akademie der Wissenschaften zu Leipzig, Philologisch-historische Klasse.* Berlin. Chapters I–III reprinted in Schmitt 1968:102–153.

———. 1971. *Kleine Schriften* I–II. Wiesbaden.

Thornton, A. 1978. "Once Again, the Duals in Book 9 of the *Iliad.*" *Glotta* 56:1–4.

Thumb, A., and Scherer, A. 1959. *Handbuch der griechischen Dialekte* II. 2nd ed. Heidelberg.

Toepffer, J. 1888. "Thargeliengebräuche." *Rheinisches Museum* 43:142–145.

Tresp, A., ed. 1914. *Die Fragmente der griechischen Kultschriftsteller.* Giessen.

Treu, M. 1959. *Archilochus.* Munich.

Uhsadel-Gülke, C. 1972. *Knochen und Kessel.* Meisenheim am Glan.

Usener, H. 1875. "Italische Mythen." *Rheinisches Museum* 30:182–229. Reprinted (1913) IV 93–143.

———. 1897. "Der Stoff des griechischen Epos." *Sitzungsberichte der kaiserlichen Akademie der Wissenschaften in Wien (Philosophisch-historische Klasse)* 137:1–63. Reprinted (1913) IV 199–259.

———. 1904. "Heilige Handlung III: Ilions Fall." *Archiv für Religionswissenschaft* 7:313–339. Reprinted (1913) IV 447–467.

———. 1912, 1913. *Kleine Schriften* I–IV. Stuttgart.

Valckenaer, L. K., ed. 1822. *Ammonius.* Leipzig.

Van Brock, N. 1959. "Substitution rituelle." *Revue Hittite et Asianique* 65:117–146.

van der Valk, M. 1958. "On Apollodori *Bibliotheca.*" *Revue des Etudes Grecques* 71:100–168.

Van Sickle, J. 1975. "Archilochus: A New Fragment of an Epode." *Classical Journal* 71:1–15.

———. 1975b. "The New Erotic Fragment of Archilochus." *Quaderni Urbinati di Cultura Classica* 20:65–98.

Verdenius, W. J. 1962. "ΑΙΝΟΣ." *Mnemosyne* 15:389.

Vermeule, E.D.T. 1974. *Götterkult. Archaeologia Homerica* III–5. Göttingen.

———. 1979. *Aspects of Death in Early Greek Art and Poetry.* Berkeley and Los Angeles.

Vernant, J.-P. 1959. "Aspects mythiques de la mémoire en Grèce." *Journal de Psychologie* 56:1–29. Incorporated in Vernant 1966.

———. 1960. "Le mythe hésiodique des races: Essai d'analyse structurale." *Revue de l'Histoire des Religions* 157:21–54. Incorporated in Vernant 1966.

———. 1966. *Mythe et pensée chez les Grecs: Etudes de psychologie historique.* 2nd ed. Paris.

———. 1966b. "Le mythe hésiodique des races: Sur un essai de mise au point." *Revue de Philologie* 40:247–276.

———, ed. 1968. *Problèmes de la guerre en Grèce ancienne.* Paris and The Hague.

———. 1972. "Les troupeaux du Soleil et la Table du Soleil." *Revue des Etudes Grecques* 85:xiv–xvii.

———. 1974. "Le mythe prométhéen chez Hésiode." *Mythe et société en Grèce ancienne,* pp. 177–194. Paris.

———. 1977. "Sacrifice et alimentation humaine à propos du Prométhée d'Hésiode." *Accademia Nazionale dei Lincei. Annali della Scuola Normale Superiore. Classe di Lettere e Filosofia,* pp. 905–940.

Vian, F. 1952. *La guerre des Géants: Le mythe avant l'époque hellénistique.* Paris.

———. 1959. *Recherches sur les Posthomerica de Quintus de Smyrne.* Paris.

———. 1960. "La triade des rois d'Orchomène: Etéoclès, Phlégyas, Minyas." In *Hommages à Georges Dumézil (Collection Latomus* 45), pp. 215–224. Brussels.

———. 1963. *Les origines de Thèbes: Cadmos et les Spartes.* Paris.

———. 1968. "La fonction guerrière dans la mythologie grecque." In Vernant 1968, pp. 53–68.

———. 1970. *Gnomon* 42:53–58. Review of Dumézil 1968.

Vidal-Naquet, P. 1968. "Le chasseur noir et l'origine de l'éphébie athénienne." *Annales: Economies, Sociétés, Civilisations* [no vol.], pp. 947–964.

———. 1968b. "The Black Hunter and the Origin of the Athenian Ephebia." *Proceedings of the Cambridge Philological Society* 14:49–64.

———. 1970. "Valeurs religieuses et mythiques de la terre et du sacrifice dans l'*Odyssée.*" *Annales: Economies, Sociétés, Civilisations* [no vol.], pp. 1278–1297.

Von der Mühll, P. 1954. "Zur Frage, wie sich die *Kyprien* zur *Odyssee* verhalten." In *Festschrift R. Tschudi*, pp. 1–5. Wiesbaden.

W = M. L. West, ed. 1971/1972. *Iambi et Elegi Graeci.* Oxford.

Wackernagel, J. 1914. "Akzentstudien III. Zum homerischen Akzent." *Nachrichten der Gesellschaft der Wissenschaften zu Göttingen* [no vol.], pp. 97–130. Reprinted (1953) 1154–1187.

————. 1895, 1905, 1930. *Altindische Grammatik* I, II–1, III. Göttingen.

————. 1943. "Indogermanische Dichtersprache." *Philologus* 95:1–19. Reprinted (1953) 186–204 and in Schmitt 1968:83–101.

————. 1953. *Kleine Schriften* I–II. Göttingen.

(————,) and Debrunner, A. 1954. *Altindische Grammatik* II–2. Göttingen.

Wade-Gery, H. T. 1952. *The Poet of the* Iliad. Cambridge.

Ward, D. 1973. "On the Poets and Poetry of the Indo-Europeans." *Journal of Indo-European Studies* 1:127–144.

Watkins, C. 1971. "Studies in Indo-European Legal Language, Institutions, and Mythology." In *Indo-European and Indo-Europeans*, edited by G. Cardona, H. M. Hoenigswald, and A. Senn, pp. 321–354. Philadelphia.

————. 1975. "La famille indo-européenne de grec ΟΡΧΙΣ: Linguistique, poétique et mythologie." *Bulletin de la Société de Linguistique de Paris* 70:11–26.

————. 1976. "The Etymology of Irish *dúan.*" *Celtica* 11:270–277.

————. 1976b. "A Hittite-Celtic Etymology." *Ériu* 27:116–122.

————. 1977. "A propos de ΜΗΝΙΣ." *Bulletin de la Société de Linguistique de Paris* 72:187–209.

Wehrli, F. 1957. "Oidipus." *Museum Helveticum* 14:108–117. Reprinted (1972) 60–71.

————. 1972. *Theoria und Humanitas.* Zürich.

Welcker, F. G. 1835. *Der epische Cyclus.* Bonn.

West, M. L. 1961. "Hesiodea III." *Classical Quarterly* 11:142–145.

————. 1963. "Three Presocratic Cosmologies. I: Alcman." *Classical Quarterly* 13:154–156.

————. 1966. *Hesiod:* Theogony. Edited, with prolegomena and commentary. Oxford.

————. 1967. "Alcman and Pythagoras." *Classical Quarterly* 17:1–15.

————. 1969. "The Achaean Wall." *Classical Review* 19:255–260.

————. 1973. "Greek Poetry, 2000–700 B.C." *Classical Quarterly* 23:179–192.

————. 1974. *Studies in Greek Elegy and Iambus.* Berlin.

————. 1974b. "Ein wiedergefundenes Archilochos-Gedicht?" *Poetica* 6:481–485.

————. 1975. "Archilochus Ludens: Epilogue of the Other Editor." *Zeitschrift für Papyrologie und Epigraphik* 16:217–219.

————. 1978. *Hesiod:* Works and Days. Edited, with prolegomena and commentary. Oxford.

Westermann, A., ed. 1843. ΜΥΘΟΓΡΑΦΟΙ: *Scriptores Poeticae Historiae Graeci*. Braunschweig.

———, ed. 1845. ΒΙΟΓΡΑΦΟΙ: *Vitarum Scriptores Graeci Minores*. Braunschweig.

Westphal, R., ed. 1866. *Scriptores Metrici Graeci* I (including Proclus *Chrestomathia*). Leipzig.

Whitman, C. 1958. *Homer and the Heroic Tradition*. Cambridge, Mass.

Wiechers, A. 1961. *Aesop in Delphi*. Meisenheim am Glan.

Wikander, S. 1938. *Der arische Männerbund: Studien zur indo-iranischen Sprach- und Religionsgeschichte*. Lund.

———. 1941. *Vayu: Texte und Untersuchungen zur indoiranischen Religionsgeschichte* I. Uppsala.

Wyss, B., ed. 1936. *Antimachi Colophonii Reliquiae*. Berlin.

Yoshida, A. 1964. "La structure de l'illustration du bouclier d'Achille." *Revue Belge de Philologie et d'Histoire* 42:5–15.

Zuntz, G. 1971. *Persephone: Three Essays on Religion and Thought in Magna Graecia*. Oxford.

———. 1976. "Die Goldlamelle von Hipponion." *Wiener Studien* 89: 129–151.

Index of Sources

Acusilaus, 165, 269
Aelian, 247
Aelius Theon, 239
Aeschylus: *Eumenides*, 125; *fr.*, 190; *Persians*, 200; *Seven against Thebes*, 161
Aesop: *Fables 1*, 239, 283; *3*, 282, 290; *97*, 316; *125*, 302; *153*, 286, 315; *177*, 281–83; *236*, 302; *387*, 315; *465*, 315; *470*, 302. See also *Life of Aesop*
Aithiopis: an epic poem from the Cycle, 7–8; evidence from, 164–65, 167, 172, 175, 205, 207, 279
Alcaeus, 161, 167, 182, 248, 342, 350
Alcidamas, 305
Alcman, 114, 224, 345
Ammonius, 280
Anacreon, 91
Anon., *com. fr.*, 288
Anthologia Palatina, 111, 246
Antimachus, 332
Apollodorus, 137, 165, 167, 340
Apollonius of Rhodes, 167; scholia to, 332
Archilochus: *fr. 1*, 301, 304–5; *fr. 19*, 248–49; *fr. 23*, 242; *fr. 38*, 246; *fr. 54*, 246, 264; *frs. 120–21*, 252; *fr. 122*, 248–49; *fr. 129*, 244; *fr. 134*, 263; *fr. 168*, 91–92, 244, 259; *fr. 171*, 244; *fr. 174*, 238, 250, 283; *fr. 185*, 239, 250; *fr. 223*, 302; *fr. 295*, 245, 247; *fr. 304*, 331. See also *Life of Archilochus*; *Pap. Colon.* 7511 ("Cologne Epode").
Ariaithos of Tegea, 330
Aristophanes: *Birds*, 239; *fr.*, 288; *Frogs*, 245; *Heroes*, 153; *Knights*, 245; *Peace*, 245, 282; *Wasps*, 282
Aristotle: *fr. 487*, 281, 302; *fr. 519*, 117, 332; *fr. 542*, 331; *fr. 558*, 249; *fr. 565*, 296; *fr. 573*, 286; *fr. 611*, 165, 302;

Nichomachean Ethics, 254; *Poetics*, 157, 243, 252, 253–56, 258–60, 262; *Politics*, 244; *Rhetoric*, 131, 203, 249, 305
Asclepiades, 121, 124
Athenaeus, 124, 249

Babrius, 314
Bacchylides: *3*, 224, 226, 239, 309; *5*, 223–24; *9*, 161; *13*, 161, 223–24, 260
Banquet Song for Harmodios, 163, 167, 174
Boyhood Deeds of CúChulainn, 325
Boyhood Deeds of Finn, 325
Bricriu's Feast, 133

Callimachus, 124, 126, 165, 281, 285, 315–16
Certamen, 165
Charax, 190
Corpus Paroemiographorum Graecorum, 126
Critias, 247
Cycle, epic: list of poems of, 7–8
Cypria: an epic poem from the Cycle, 7–8; evidence from, 23, 42–43, 62, 119, 130–31, 138, 140, 159, 218–21, 309, 311, 314, 345

Delphic Oracle 4, 301
DGE (*Dialectorum Graecarum exempla epigraphica potiora*), 125
Dio Chrysostomus, 301–2
Diodorus Siculus, 190, 203, 209, 303
Dionysius, *Ixeuticon*, 208
Dioscorides, *Epigr.*, 246

Ephorus, 122
Epigonoi, 161
Epigrammata, 295

Where fewer than ten passages are cited from one source, only the name/title is listed.
Page numbers refer to text and/or footnotes.

375

Index of Names

Adkins, A.W.H., 221
Aitchison, J. M., 353
Alexiou, M., 80, 111–13, 115–16, 184
Arbois de Jubainville, H. d', 133
Austin, N., 5

Bader, F., 230, 233, 350
Bassett, S. E., 18, 102
Baumbach, L., 87–88
Bechtel, F., 70, 86–88
Benveniste, E., 64, 72, 81, 83, 86, 91,
    103, 114, 132, 155, 232–33, 284, 339,
    344
Bergren, A. L., 167
Bethe, E., 140, 150
Boedecker, D. D., 191, 197, 200
Bollack, J., 171
Borecký, B., 129
Borthwick, E. K., 332
Brelich, A., 114–15, 251, 279, 296–97
Brunius-Nilsson, E., 228
Büchner, W., 208
Bundy, E. L., 223, 236
Burkert, W., 9, 74, 117, 119, 121, 125–
    26, 143, 165–66, 190, 192, 209, 262,
    295

Caerwyn Williams, J. E., 222
Caland, W., 70, 86–87
Calhoun, G. M., 24, 127
Carey, C., 227
Chadwick, J., 87–88, 353
Chantraine, P., 18, 69, 73, 85, 88, 129,
    134–35, 146–47, 149, 241, 256–57,
    260, 262, 295–96, 299, 308, 311, 326–
    27, 331, 349–51
Chirassi Colombo, I., 143
Clader, L. L., 84, 146, 183, 295
Clark, J. R., 127–28, 132
Clark, M. E., 205

Coldstream, J. N., 115
Considine, P., 73
Cook, J. M., 140
Coulsen, W.D.E., 205
Cross, T. P. (with C. H. Slover), 133,
    162, 231, 325

Davidson, O. M., 48, 242, 303
Debrunner, A., 56, 351
Delcourt, M., 119, 121–22, 126, 164, 201
Deneken, F., 124
Detienne, M., 17, 46, 98, 122, 145, 149,
    154, 182–84, 202, 222, 225, 345
Diehl, E., 167, 343
Diggle, J., 200, 203
Dihle, A., 21, 165, 189, 207, 267
Donini, G., 269
Dover, K. J., 243, 248
Drews, R., 167, 343
Duban, J., 96
Dumézil, G., 15, 83, 222, 303, 323–24,
    330
Durante, M., 18, 71, 296–98, 311

Edmunds, S., 146
Edwards, G. P., 42, 71
Eliade, M., 185
Else, G. F., 253

Farnell, L. R., 114–15, 343
Faust, M., 226–27
Fenik, B., 23, 34–35, 71, 267, 294
Festugière, J., 84–85
Finley, J. H., 123, 171
Finnegan, R., 15
Fontenrose, J., 119–21, 123, 343
Forderer, M., 259
Fraenkel, E., 239, 248
Fränkel, H., 40

Page numbers refer to text and/or footnotes.

Index of Key Words and Themes

Underlining indicates pages where the meaning of a word is discussed. Some difficult words, like **thūmós**, have been left unglossed. Page numbers refer to text and/or footnotes. Bracketed pages indicate related concepts if not actual index entries.

386